Evaluating
Gun Policy

Evaluating Gun Policy

Effects on Crime and Violence

Jens Ludwig
Philip J. Cook
editors

BROOKINGS INSTITUTION PRESS
Washington, D.C.

Copyright © 2003
THE BROOKINGS INSTITUTION
1775 Massachusetts Avenue, N.W.
Washington, D.C. 20036
www.brookings.edu

Library of Congress Cataloging-in-Publication data

Evaluating gun policy: effects on crime and violence / Jens Ludwig and
Philip J. Cook, editors.
    p.   cm.
Includes bibliographical references and index.
  ISBN 0-8157-5312-8 (cloth : alk. paper)—
  ISBN 0-8157-5311-X (pbk. : alk. paper)
    1. Gun control—United States. 2. Violent crimes—United States.
I. Ludwig, Jens. II. Cook, Philip J., 1946–

HV7436 .E9 2003
364.15'0973—dc21   2002014696

9 8 7 6 5 4 3 2 1

The paper used in this publication meets minimum requirements of the
American National Standard for Information Sciences—Permanence of Paper
for Printed Library Materials: ANSI Z39.48-1992.

Typeset in Adobe Garamond

Composition by Circle Graphics
Columbia, Md.

Printed by R. R. Donnelley
Harrisonburg, Virginia

Contents

Foreword

This book is going to press soon after a horrifying but emblematic moment for the nation and particularly for the citizens of the greater Washington, D.C., area, where most of us at Brookings live. A pair of snipers, armed with a sophisticated rifle, murdered ten people, seemingly at random. The episode has refocused our attention on the issue of gun control—and reawakened the passions of a debate, as old as the nation itself, over the constitutional right to bear arms.

During the 1930s President Franklin Delano Roosevelt signed two national firearm laws into effect. Since then only a handful of substantive new gun laws have been enacted at the federal level. Some activity on the problem of gun violence is currently visible on the national stage, including the Bush administration's Project Safe Neighborhoods law-enforcement program and a congressional proposal for additional regulation of gun shows. But both major political parties have remained largely silent on the issue in the midterm elections of 2002.

The real action on gun policy in the United States is at the state and local levels. In California, state legislators have proposed a tax on firearm ammunition. Recent legislative and court battles about gun carrying have been fought in Alaska, Michigan, Minnesota, Missouri, Ohio, and Utah. Law enforcement officials in Boston are working to disrupt illegal gun running, while police in New York City are offering $100 to anyone who voluntarily turns in a handgun. More than thirty municipalities across the country have filed lawsuits against the gun industry concerning how guns are manufactured or distributed. In response, more than twenty states have passed laws shielding the industry from such litigation. And one of the nation's most prominent local firearm laws, the District of Columbia's ban on handguns, has recently been challenged in court on Second Amendment grounds. These policy debates will be resolved in part on the basis of legal and political arguments, as well as the value judgments of politicians, judges, jurors, and voters. But facts should also count.

The contributors to this book provide new insights about the consequences of different gun policy options for the public's health and safety, applying dispassionate policy analysis to contentious policy questions. The editors, Jens Ludwig and Philip J. Cook, have assembled an outstanding group of experts from several disciplines, including economics, public policy, criminology, law, medicine, and public health. The results of their careful analyses do not conform neatly to any particular ideological position in the gun debate but do begin to distinguish promising from less promising steps in the effort to reduce lethal violence.

Ludwig, an associate professor of public policy at Georgetown University, was the Andrew W. Mellon Fellow in Economic Studies at Brookings when the papers included in this volume were first presented at a Brookings Center on Urban and Metropolitan Policy conference in January 2002. Cook is the ITT/ Terry Sanford Professor of Public Policy at Duke University. He is a member of the National Academies' Institute of Medicine and a fellow of the American Society of Criminology. They previously collaborated on *Gun Violence: The Real Costs,* published by Oxford University Press in 2000.

Brookings received financial support for the conference and the volume from the Annie E. Casey Foundation, the Smith Richardson Foundation, the U.S. Department of Justice's National Institute of Justice, and the National Consortium on Violence Research. In addition, the Joyce Foundation provided support for dissemination of the book's findings.

STROBE TALBOTT
President

Washington, D.C.
January 2003

ACKNOWLEDGMENTS

The editors wish to thank their collaborators Bruce Katz, Amy Liu, Jennifer Vey, Jennifer Bradley, Jamaine Tinker, and Saundra Honeysett in the Brookings Center on Urban and Metropolitan Policy, and Janet Walker, Theresa Walker, and Susan Woollen in the Brookings Press for their assistance with the book's production. Inge Lockwood proofread the book, and Enid Zafran prepared the index. William T. Dickens deserves special thanks for the idea that led to this book.

PHILIP J. COOK
JENS LUDWIG

1 | *Pragmatic Gun Policy*

There is no lack of opinions on policies to regulate gun commerce, possession, and use, with most policy proposals engendering intense controversy. For example, should most adults be allowed to carry a concealed gun? Some assert that a gun-carrying public will serve as an extension of the police in deterring crime, while others believe more guns on the street will inevitably lead to more shootings. Another example: Should people who keep guns at home be required to store them safely? Advocates point to the risk that unlocked guns pose to children, while opponents assert that the more important concern is preserving householders' immediate access to a gun in the event of an intruder. More generally, some advocates insist that "an armed society is a polite society," while others insist that widespread private armament only serves to fill the morgues with homicide and suicide victims.

The clash in opinion results in divergent policy approaches across jurisdictions. More than twenty years ago, Washington, D.C., and Chicago responded to the crime problems in their cities by banning handguns. Kennesaw, Georgia, however, enacted an ordinance that *required* every home to contain a gun. And while the New York City Police Department made it a priority during the 1990s to keep guns off the street, a majority of states now let almost any adult obtain a permit to legally carry a concealed handgun in public. Differing beliefs are also reflected in private behavior. About 36 percent of American households own a gun, while the rest tend to be uncomfortable with guns or see little or no reason

1

to have one. For many of those who do keep a gun, the paramount reason is self-protection—one member of the Second Amendment Sisters argued that without a gun, "You might as well be wearing a T-shirt that says 'I'm unarmed, please don't hurt me.' "[1] But a more common belief, especially among women, is that guns are hazardous.

Differences in opinion flourish partly because of the lack of sound evidence that might help cut through conflicting assertions. Improving the quality of evidence on what works in reducing gun violence requires sound research by scholars who maintain an open mind on the relevant issues.

Our inspiration, then, is the pragmatic belief that there is an important role for dispassionate analysis of the evidence. As philosopher William James argued in 1904, "a pragmatist turns away—from bad *a priori* reasons, from fixed principles . . . [and from] dogma, artificiality, and the pretence of finality in truth"—and turns "towards facts." Pragmatism, James noted, "does not stand for any special results. It is a method only . . . an attitude of orientation."[2] Applied to gun policy this approach is a potential challenge to both pro- and anti-gun-control dogmas, both of which may incorporate flawed assertions about matters that are ultimately factual. Of course we would not go so far as to assert that facts trump values, and in particular the value of freedom from unwarranted government intrusion into private lives. Policymakers, voters, and the courts must in the end decide the appropriate trade-off between safety, on the one hand, and public expenditure and imposition, on the other. But good evidence, rather than preconceived notions, should be the basis for assessing the consequences of available policy options.

The research presented here is of course not the first to examine the consequences of gun possession and policies regarding gun commerce and use. But we believe that these articles deserve consideration as exceptionally thorough, open, careful, and technically sound. The comments of the discussants add further balance and perspective.

The results of this research do not conform neatly to the claims of any one political position. For example, those who oppose gun control often advocate the alternative of tougher law enforcement, an approach that gets mixed support in what follows: policing against illegal gun carrying appears to reduce gun violence, but the threat of longer prison terms for "felons in possession," as in Richmond's Project Exile, does not stand up as well to empirical test. Several of the contributions challenge flawed conclusions that have been offered by other researchers: Expanded gun carrying does *not* save lives. Widespread ownership

1. Phil Garber, "Gun Control Advocates Lock Horns with Handgun Users; Smart Gun Technology Is Latest Issue." *Morris (NJ) News Bee,* March 5, 2002.
2. James (1904).

does *not* deter home-intrusion burglaries. The dramatic policy experiments in Australia and Britain to reduce gun ownership clearly did *not* result in an up-surge of violence but also may not have done much to further widen the homi-cide gap between these countries and the United States. A chapter on suicide provides support for both those who warn that the positive correlation between gun ownership and suicide may be partly spurious (reflecting the influence of one or more factors that influence both suicide and gun-ownership rates) *and* those who believe that widespread gun ownership does nonetheless increase the suicide rate. Another chapter provides an encouraging positive finding, offering evidence that restricting gun ownership by people with histories of domestic violence, as required by recent federal law (currently under constitutional chal-lenge in the federal courts), may be somewhat effective, despite problems with the relevant criminal-record data. America's problem with gun violence is not hopeless, although progress may require a flexible approach that focuses on proven measures—regardless of their ideological flavor.

Guns and Violence

Compared with other developed nations, the United States is unique in its high rates of both gun ownership and murder.[3] Although widespread gun ownership does not have much effect on the overall crime rate, gun use does make crimi-nal violence more lethal and has a unique capacity to terrorize the public. But that is not the whole story. Guns also provide recreational benefits and some-times are used virtuously in fending off or forestalling criminal attacks.

Gun Ownership

America has at least 200 million firearms in private circulation, enough for every adult to have one.[4] But only one-quarter of all adults own a gun, the great majority of them men. Most people who have guns own many: three-quarters of all guns are owned by those who own four or more guns, amounting to just 10 percent of adults.

Around 65 million of America's 200 million privately held firearms are hand-guns, which are more likely than long guns to be kept for defense against crime.[5] In the 1970s one-third of new guns were handguns (pistols or revolvers), a

---

3. Zimring and Hawkins (1997).
4. Cook and Ludwig (1996).
5. Cook and Ludwig (1996).

figure that grew to nearly half by the early 1990s and then fell back to around 40 percent.[6] Despite the long-term increase in the relative importance of handgun sales, a mere 20 percent of gun-owning individuals have only handguns; 44 percent have both handguns and long guns, reflecting the fact that most people who have acquired guns for self-protection are also hunters and target shooters. Less than half of gun owners say that their primary motivation for having a gun is self-protection against crime.

Given the importance of hunting and sport shooting it is not surprising that gun ownership is concentrated in rural areas and small towns, and among middle-aged, middle-income households.[7] These attributes are associated with relatively low involvement in criminal violence, and it is reasonable to suppose that most guns are in the hands of people who are unlikely to misuse them. Some support for this view comes from the fact that most of the people arrested for gun homicides, unlike most gun owners, have prior criminal records.[8]

Most of the guns in circulation were obtained by their owners directly from a federally licensed firearm dealer (FFL). However, the 30 to 40 percent of all gun transfers that do not involve licensed dealers, the so-called secondary market,[9] account for most guns used in crime.[10] Despite the prominence of gun shows in current policy debates, the best available evidence suggests that such shows account for only a small share of all secondary market sales.[11] Another important source of crime guns is theft—more than 500,000 guns are stolen each year.[12]

Gun Use

Including homicide, suicide, and accident, 28,874 Americans died by gunfire in 1999, a mortality rate of 10.6 deaths per 100,000 people.[13] This figure is down substantially from 1990 (14.9 per 100,000) but is still much higher than

6. ATF (2000a).

7. Cook and Ludwig (1996).

8. Don Kates and Daniel Polsby note that around three-quarters of those arrested for murder in urban counties have prior adult criminal histories; some additional unknown fraction presumably have juvenile criminal records that are sealed in most states; Kates and Polsby (2000). By comparison they note that around 15 percent of the general population has a criminal record of any kind. A national survey of gun owners in 1994 suggests that around a third have ever been arrested for a non-traffic offense, although the proportion of these arrests that result in a criminal record is not known; Cook and Ludwig (1996).

9. Cook, Molliconi, and Cole (1995)

10. See Wright and Rossi (1994); Beck and Gilliard (1993); Sheley and Wright (1995); Cook and Braga (2001).

11. Cook and Ludwig (1996).

12. Cook and Ludwig (1996).

13. NCHS (2001, p. 10).

what was observed in the United States in, say, 1950.[14] Intentional violence is the major exception to the secular decline in deaths from injury during the past fifty years.[15]

Guns are not the only consumer products that are involved in large numbers of deaths; more Americans die in motor vehicle crashes each year than by gunshot injuries. But, as one local district attorney notes, "Gun violence is what makes people afraid to go to the corner store at night."[16] The threat of being shot causes private citizens and public institutions to undertake a variety of costly measures to reduce this risk, and all of us must live with the anxiety caused by the lingering chance that we or a loved one could be shot. All told, gun violence imposes costs on our society on the order of $100 billion a year, most of which is accounted for by criminal assault.[17] While more Americans die each year by gun suicide than homicide, suicide seems more of a private concern than a public risk. The number of fatal gun accidents is an order of magnitude lower than for homicides or suicides.

Even though everyone shares in the costs of gun violence, the shooters and victims are not a representative slice of the population. The gun-homicide-victimization rate in 1996 for Hispanic men, 18 to 29 years old, was seven times the rate for non-Hispanic white men of the same age; the gun homicide rate for black men, 18 to 29 years old, was 133 per 100,000, twenty-five times the rate for white males in that age group.[18] There seems to be considerable overlap between the populations of potential offenders and victims: the large majority of both groups have prior criminal records.[19] The demographics of gun suicide look somewhat different: while suicides and homicides occur disproportionately to those with low incomes or educational attainment, gun suicides are more common among whites than blacks and among the old than among young or middle-aged adults.[20] Men are vastly overrepresented in all categories.

Instrumentality

Since both guns and homicides are unusually common in the United States compared with their prevalence in other developed nations, it is natural to won-

14. Cook and Ludwig (2000).

15. Cook and Ludwig (2000).

16. J. M. Kalil, "A New Approach: Prosecutors Take Aim at Gun Crimes." *Las Vegas Review-Journal,* March 9, 2002, p. 1B.

17. Cook and Ludwig (2000).

18. Cook and Ludwig (2000).

19. See Kennedy, Piehl, and Braga (1996); McGonigal and others (1993); Schwab and others (1999); Kates and Polsby (2000).

20. Cook and Ludwig (2000).

der whether the two are linked. In the 1950s and 1960s criminologists generally ignored the issue of weapon choice as a determinant of homicide, preferring to focus on more "fundamental" issues. One exception was Marvin Wolfgang,[21] although he argued that the gun itself had little effect on the outcome of a violent encounter—a judgment that he later retracted.[22]

In a seminal article, Franklin Zimring provided systematic evidence that the weapon type matters independent of motivation.[23] Zimring drew on crime data from Chicago to show that case-fatality rates in gun attacks are a multiple of those in knife attacks, despite the fact that the circumstances are generally similar. Many criminal assailants were inebriated at the time and thus unlikely to be acting in a calculating fashion, and few attackers administered more than one or two wounds to the victim—even in fatal cases. Similarly, robberies are far more likely to result in the victim's death if a gun is involved, even though gun robbers are less likely to attack their victim than those armed with another weapon.[24] Inflicting a fatal wound with a gun requires less effort, determination, involvement, or strength than with other common weapons.

A gun also provides a quick and reliable exit for suicidal people. But in suicide, unlike assault, there are other highly lethal means available to anyone who takes the time to plan, including hanging and jumping from a high building or bridge. Nonetheless there is some evidence that gun access does affect suicide rates.[25]

Self-Defense and Deterrence

The same features of guns that make them valuable to criminals may also make guns useful in self-defense. Just how often guns are used in defense against criminal attack has been hotly debated and remains unclear. Estimates from the National Crime Victimization Survey, a large government-sponsored in-person survey that is generally considered the most reliable source of information on predatory crime, suggests that guns are used in defense against criminal predation around 100,000 times a year.[26] In contrast are the results of several smaller one-time telephone surveys, which provide a basis for asserting that there are millions of defensive gun uses per year.[27]

21. Wolfgang (1958).
22. Wolfgang (1995).
23. Zimring (1968).
24. See Cook (1976, 1980, 1987).
25. Miller and Hemenway (1999); Brent (2001); Miller and Hemenway (2001).
26. Cook, Ludwig, and Hemenway (1997).
27. Kleck and Gertz (1995).

Whatever the actual number of defensive gun uses, the mere threat of encountering an armed victim may exert a deterrent effect on the behavior of criminals. A growing body of research within criminology and economics supports the notion that some criminals are sensitive to the threat of punishment.[28] It is therefore not surprising that the threat of armed victim response may also figure in a criminal's decision: around 40 percent of prisoners in one survey indicated that they had decided against committing a crime at least once because they feared that the potential victim was carrying a gun.[29]

Given that guns may be used for both good and ill, the goal of gun policy in the United States has been to reduce the flow of guns to the highest-risk groups while preserving access for most people. Whether the current system achieves the proper balance between preserving access and preventing misuse remains the subject of considerable debate.

Policy Response

Federal law affords most people access to most types of guns; the law is permissive but with delineated exceptions, specifying certain categories of people that are prohibited from possession, and certain categories of guns that are banned or tightly regulated. Federal law also establishes a licensing system for gun dealers and regulates transactions and record keeping by these dealers. States and localities may supplement federal regulations on firearms commerce and use. In some cases state laws supplement the federal restrictions regarding "who" and "what" is prohibited or impose additional requirements on transactions. Almost all states regulate gun carrying more closely than guns in the home and also specify penalties for misuse. Federal regulations on gun commerce are intended to help insulate states with more stringent regulations from those with lax regulation.

Gun Design

Efforts to regulate gun design began in earnest with the National Firearms Act of 1934 (NFA), which required the registration of machine guns and sawed-off shotguns and imposed a confiscatory tax on transactions involving these weapons. The goal of the NFA was to strictly regulate a class of weapons that is of particular value to criminals but has little value for hunting or other sporting uses. Ex-

28. See Nagin (1998); Levitt (2001).
29. Wright and Rossi (1994).

isting regulations of gun design are also targeted at the other end of the weapons market: the Gun Control Act of 1968 banned the importation of cheap, easily concealed handguns ("Saturday night specials"), and some states have banned such handguns altogether.[30] A federal ban on sale of new military-style "assault" weapons and large-capacity magazines was enacted in 1994.[31]

Recent design proposals have focused on reducing gun accidents by adding new safety features to handguns, including mechanisms to indicate whether the weapon is loaded.[32] Because firearms are exempt from regulation by the Consumer Product Safety Commission (CPSC), new legislation would be required for the federal government to mandate design changes, although Massachusetts is now regulating the design of guns sold in that state on the same basis as other consumer products. The potential effect of such regulation on the overall number of gunshot injuries is likely to be relatively small since most gun injuries are inflicted intentionally. But for other products it is common for the CPSC to negotiate or impose costly design requirements on products that are associated with only a few dozen injuries per year.[33]

More sweeping proposals to change the design of firearms call for "personalized guns," which prevent the weapon from being fired by someone other than the owner by means of a lock that is controlled by a standard key, a magnetic ring worn by the shooter, or more advanced biometric methods. Each of these personalization schemes would help prevent accidental discharges or suicides by unauthorized users and could make the guns inoperable if they were stolen. Technologies such as fingerprint recognition that required specialized equipment to transfer the weapon from one person to another would have the additional effect of facilitating regulation of voluntary exchanges in the secondary market.[34]

Interestingly, personalized guns have come under attack from both the left and the right. The National Rifle Association (NRA) opposes any requirement that new guns be personalized, arguing that any such device would be unreliable, that owners might be induced by a false sense of confidence to store the gun unsafely, and that the requirement would make guns more expensive.[35] Some pro-control groups oppose personalized guns in part because the technology does nothing about existing guns and may increase the number of guns in circula-

---

30. Webster, Vernick, and Hepburn (2002).
31. Koper and Roth (2001).
32. See Vernick and Teret (2000); Vernick and others (1999).
33. Tengs and Wallace (2000).
34. Cook and Leitzel (2002).
35. NRA (2002); see also Leonardatos, Blackman, and Kopel (2001).

tion.[36] In any event, the federal government is continuing to invest in developing new safety devices of this sort.

Gun Transactions

In most parts of the United States almost anyone can legally buy a handgun or long gun, except for those prohibited from acquiring firearms by the Gun Control Act (GCA) of 1968: minors; adults under indictment or having any prior felony conviction or (due to a 1996 amendment) misdemeanor conviction for domestic violence; illegal aliens; those confined by court order because of mental illness; and a few other categories. These basic restrictions enjoy almost unanimous support in debates about gun policy. More controversial is what government should do to keep guns away from people in these high-risk categories.

The GCA stipulates that licensed dealers must require buyers to show identification and complete a form attesting that they are eligible to obtain a firearm. A number of states stipulated additional requirements for a legal sale of a handgun, including a requirement of a criminal-record check on potential buyers. In 1994 background checks in handgun sales by dealers became mandatory in all states as a result of the federal Brady Handgun Violence Prevention Act, a requirement that was extended to long gun sales in 1998.

The requirements for gun sales by people who are not licensed dealers—defined by the 1968 GCA as anyone who is not "engaged in the business of selling firearms at wholesale or retail . . . engaged in the business of repairing firearms or of making or fitting special barrels, stocks, or trigger mechanisms to firearms," or a pawnbroker—are more lax: nondealers are prohibited from *knowingly* selling a gun to someone banned from possession but are not required to determine the buyer's eligibility or follow other paperwork reporting requirements. The exemption of sales by nondealers from most existing federal regulations is, of course, a huge loophole in the federal regulatory system.

States or localities may go beyond the federal regulations on gun transactions. Washington, D.C., Chicago, and a handful of other cities have banned handguns, while Massachusetts, New York City, and some other jurisdictions have highly restrictive regulations that stop short of a ban. Other states have imposed licensing and registration systems to help law enforcement solve crimes and help regulate secondary market transfers. For example, in Illinois all gun owners are required to obtain a Firearm Owners Identification (FOID) card. Gun owners are required to report thefts to the police and are only allowed to resell their guns to those with a FOID. An owner whose weapon turns up at a crime scene

36. Violence Policy Center (2002).

is at risk for being visited by the police and held legally liable if the gun was trans-ferred inappropriately to an ineligible buyer. The Illinois system thus provides gun owners with an incentive to verify a buyer's eligibility status and to resist re-quests to serve as a straw purchaser for friends and family who are ineligible.

Most states, however, have chosen not to expand federal regulations on gun transactions or possession and have pre-empted localities from doing so. States with lax controls serve as an attractive source for gun traffickers who seek to sup-ply the black markets in tight-control states. The 1968 GCA was intended to insulate states from one another by prohibiting interstate transfers of handguns or long guns except to licensed gun dealers. Before 1994, however, trafficking of this sort had been an important source of guns to criminals in tight-control states; the Brady requirements appear to have reduced this type of interstate "arbitrage."[37]

Gun Carrying

While keeping a gun in the home is in most states regarded as a private matter, taking guns out into public spaces is viewed as a public concern. As a result gov-ernment regulations of gun carrying have traditionally been more restrictive than those regarding gun acquisitions: all but one state (Vermont) require peo-ple to obtain a special permit to legally carry a concealed gun, or the state bans the practice entirely.

In recent years a growing number of states have liberalized the requirements to obtain a concealed gun-carrying permit. These new laws limit or even elimi-nate the discretion about whether to issue permits invested in local law enforce-ment authorities, who in many areas were often reluctant to grant such permits. As Jon S. Vernick and Lisa Hepburn note in chapter 9, more than thirty states currently have permissive concealed-carry laws on the books. A number of other states are currently considering following suit.

Justification for any of the regulations regarding gun design, acquisition, and carrying rests in part on beliefs about their consequences. One fundamental as-sumption crucial to a variety of regulations concerns whether reducing the num-ber of guns in private hands would lead to more or less violence and crime.

The Prevalence of Gun Ownership

If guns are more lethal than other means of violence, then keeping guns away from those at high risk of criminal activity may save lives. The number of guns

37. See Cook and Braga (2001); Webster, Vernick and Hepburn (2001).

in circulation is then of direct policy interest, since more guns in private hands may increase availability to violent criminals through theft or voluntary transfers in secondary markets. Of course an increase in the prevalence of guns could also serve as a deterrent to robbery, assault, and burglary. On balance, the available empirical evidence supports the conclusion that the net effect of guns on the volume of crime is strongly positive, in the case of homicide, and more-or-less neutral with respect to other common crimes. There is also some evidence that gun availability is associated with increased suicide rates.

Gun Availability and Violent Crime

Perhaps the question of primary interest to individual citizens is whether guns make the owners and members of their household more or less safe. One type of evidence in support of the claim that guns increase the risk of homicide victimization comes from comparing gun ownership rates of homicide victims with those of neighbors who share similar sociodemographic characteristics.[38] While this case-control evidence is suggestive, it is not entirely persuasive. One problem in interpreting it is the possibility that the decision to keep a gun is confounded in some way with the risk of criminal victimization. Statistical controls for such observable qualities as age, sex, alcohol and drug use, and prior criminal record help alleviate this concern but do not resolve it entirely.

A deeper concern with case-control studies is that they ignore the possibility that individual gun ownership affects other people in the community. These external effects could be salutary if widespread gun ownership deters criminals, or negative if widespread ownership facilitates diversion to criminal use through theft and secondary sales. Hence it is important to assess the effects of overall rates of gun ownership within a community.

One way to learn about the effects of community gun prevalence on crime is to compare crime rates at a point in time across jurisdictions that have different rates of gun ownership. However, there are no administrative data on gun-ownership rates, so small-area estimates must be based on some proxy. The best generally available proxy for gun prevalence is the fraction of suicides involving a firearm, which is highly correlated with survey-based measures of gun ownership rates in cross-section data (at both the state and county level) and also tracks movements over time at the regional level.[39] That proxy reveals

38. Kellermann and others (1993).
39. Azrael, Cook, and Miller (2001).

a strong positive relationship across counties between gun prevalence and the homicide rate.[40]

The fundamental problem with cross-sectional studies is that gun-rich jurisdictions like Mississippi are systematically different in various ways from jurisdictions with relatively few guns, such as Massachusetts. The usual approach for addressing this "apples and oranges" problem has been to statistically control for the handful of local characteristics that are readily available in standard data sources, such as population density, poverty, and the age and racial composition of the population. But these variables never explain very much of the cross-sectional variation in crime rates, suggesting that the list of control variables is inadequate to the task.[41] Also unclear is whether widespread gun ownership is the cause or effect of an area's crime problem, since high crime rates may induce residents to buy guns for self-protection. These same concerns are arguably even more severe with cross-sectional comparisons across countries.

Some of the problems with cross-section studies can be overcome by using panel data—repeated cross-sections of city, county, or state data measured at multiple points in time—to compare *changes* in gun ownership with *changes* in crime. Compared with Massachusetts, the state of Mississippi may have much higher homicide rates year after year for reasons that cannot be fully explained by standard sociodemographic or other variables. But by comparing changes across areas we implicitly control for any unmeasured differences across areas that are relatively fixed over time, such as a "Southern culture of violence."[42] The reverse causation problem, in which crime may be both cause and effect of gun ownership, can be at least partially addressed within this "fixed effects" frame-

---

40. Cook and Ludwig (2002); Miller, Azrael and Hemenway (2002d). Kleck and Patterson (1993) use a similar proxy with city-level data and find no statistically significant cross-section relationship between gun ownership rates and homicide or other crime rates. However, rather than relying on a simple cross-section regression-adjusted comparison of crime rates across areas with different rates of gun ownership, they attempt to isolate variation in gun ownership rates that will be arguably unrelated to the unmeasured determinants of local crime rates. Their choice of "instrumental variable" to explain variation in gun prevalence—per capita rates of hunting licenses and subscriptions to gun magazines—are, as we argue in chapter 3 in the present volume, likely to be biased in the direction of overstating the net deterrent effect of guns on crime. It should also be noted that Lott (2000) reports that homicide rates are inversely related to gun prevalence across states; however, his measure of gun ownership seems problematic. He makes use of voter-exit surveys for 1988 and 1996, which among other problems suggest that gun ownership greatly increased during this period—in fact, there was little change in ownership rates. Kleck (1997, pp. 98–99).

41. Glaeser, Sacerdote, and Scheinkman (1996).

42. See Butterfield (1996); Loftin and others (1991).

work by relating changes in gun ownership *this* year with changes in crime rates *next* year.

The best available evidence on the relationship between gun prevalence and crime comes from a recent paper by Mark Duggan, which reports that more guns lead to more homicides.[43] Duggan's measure of local gun ownership rates—gun magazine subscriptions per capita—is highly correlated with survey-based estimates of gun ownership.[44] He finds that a 10 percent increase in gun prevalence in one year increases a county or state's homicide rate the next year by around 2 percent but has little effect on other types of crime. This result accords with the belief that while guns do not contribute much to the overall volume of crime, they do make it more lethal.[45]

Gun Availability and Suicide

Do guns also increase the lethality or frequency of suicide attempts? There is surprisingly little reliable evidence on this point. Case-control studies have typically either compared gun ownership rates of suicide victims with other people in the community or compared suicide rates between those who do and do not own guns.[46] These comparisons, however, suffer the same general problem found with similar studies of homicide: people who choose to obtain guns are likely to be systematically different from those who do not and in fact may purchase guns with suicide in mind. Similarly, simple cross-sectional comparisons of suicide rates in high- versus low-gun ownership areas at a point in time are likely to confound the effects of gun prevalence with those of hard-to-measure attributes of the local population that are related to the propensity to both acquire guns and contemplate suicide.[47]

Mark Duggan's analysis in chapter 2 presents important new evidence on the relationship between guns and suicide. He argues that if access to guns causes some people to attempt suicide who otherwise would have used other means, or perhaps would not have attempted suicide at all, one would expect local gun prevalence to be positively related with gun suicide rates and have a negative (or at least null) relationship with nongun suicides. However, Duggan finds that, at least for young and middle-aged people, gun prevalence is positively related

43. Duggan (2001).
44. Azrael, Cook, and Miller (2001).
45. Zimring and Hawkins (1997).
46. Wintemute and others (1999); Cummings and others (1997); Kellermann and others (1992); Brent and others (1991).
47. For a review of this literature, see Miller and Hemenway (1999).

to both gun *and* nongun suicides.[48] Because there is no obvious reason why gun availability should increase nongun suicides (other than perhaps the possibility of suicide clusters), these findings suggest that the propensity to attempt suicide might be higher in gun-rich areas for reasons unrelated to gun availability. Put differently, at least part of the relationship between guns and suicide that has been identified in earlier research may occur because of something other than the causal effect of guns.[49]

Although previous studies may overstate the relationship between guns and suicide, Duggan's analysis still finds that guns may exert some causal effect on the lethality of suicide attempts. His strategy for identifying the causal effect of guns on suicide rests on the fact that men are far more likely than women to own guns and to use a gun in a suicide attempt.[50] If guns increase the lethality of suicide attempts, then states with a relatively high gun-ownership rate should also have a higher ratio of male to female suicides compared with states with fewer guns. Duggan finds that increased gun prevalence increases the ratio of male to female suicides, confirmatory evidence that gun availability has a direct effect on the suicide rate.

Policy Experiments

An alternative approach for learning about the effects of gun availability on public health and safety is to examine the effects of policy changes that influence overall gun ownership rates. The effects of these policy experiments are, of course, of direct interest in their own right as well.

One widely cited policy change is Washington, D.C.'s 1976 ban on handgun acquisitions. By the late 1980s the notion that Washington's handgun ban had achieved anything useful seemed hard to believe, given common references to the

48. This result is contradicted by other recent studies. Using the fraction of suicides that involve a firearm as their proxy for gun prevalence, Miller, Azrael, and Hemenway (2002a, b, c, d) find that gun prevalence is negatively associated with nongun suicide across states. It is not obvious which proxy provides more reliable results in this context. As Duggan notes in chapter 2, the fact that the nongun suicide rate is a component of the denominator (overall suicide) may impart a negative bias to the estimated coefficient. But Duggan's estimated coefficient on his proxy measure will also be biased owing to measurement error. Without further study the direction of that bias remains unknown (since the measurement error is likely to be correlated with state characteristics) but may be substantial. In any event, there is a positive estimated effect of gun prevalence on overall suicide using either of the two proxies.

49. Other recent ecological studies account for such factors as divorce, education, unemployment, urbanicity, alcohol consumption, and even lifetime major depression and serious suicidal thoughts, and still find a strong association between gun prevalence and completed suicide. Birckmayer and Hemenway (2001); Hemenway and Miller (2002); Miller, Azrael, and Hemenway (2002a, b, c, d). Of course even these detailed measures may not fully account for difficult-to-measure individual attributes that vary across areas and affect both the propensity to attempt suicide and gun ownership.

50. Cook and Ludwig (1996, 2000); Kleck (1997).

city as the "homicide capital of the world." Nevertheless the available data do suggest that homicides and suicides declined by around 25 percent around the time of the District's handgun ban, led by reductions in homicides and suicides with guns.[51]

Still controversial is the question of how much of this decline can be attributed to the handgun ban rather than other factors. In an influential article published in the *New England Journal of Medicine,* criminologist Colin Loftin and his colleagues showed that homicides and suicides declined in Washington and by more than in the city's Maryland and Virginia suburbs.[52] A challenge to the use of affluent suburbs as a control group for the city led to additional research using Baltimore data.[53] Like D.C., Baltimore also experienced a decline in firearm homicides around 1976. But unlike Washington, Baltimore experienced a reduction in nongun as well as gun homicides, suggesting some general change in Baltimore around this time that was not specific to guns. Further, Baltimore did not experience a decline in gun suicides.[54] Conclusions about the effects of big-city handgun bans would be stronger if the evidence for Washington were replicated for Chicago, which implemented a similar law in 1982. However to date there has not yet been a systematic study of Chicago's experience.

Gun "buy-back" programs may seem to offer another opportunity to learn more about the effects of gun prevalence on crime. In practice American buy-back programs have had little effect on prevalence because they are brief and voluntary and leave open the possibility of owners buying new guns to replace those they turn in. Further, the sellers in these buyback programs have been shown to be people at low risk for criminal offending, and the guns that are turned in are often broken or quite different from those that are used in crime.[55]

An interesting example of a large-scale combined gun ban and buy-back program comes from Australia, which in 1996–97 banned self-loading rifles and shotguns, and during a postban grace period offered to buy them back from the citizenry at "fair value." The consequences of this intervention are examined in chapter 4 by Peter Reuter and Jenny Mouzos. The context in which this ban was imposed differs in important ways from the United States. Handguns were already strictly regulated, and rates of gun ownership and use in crime were much lower than here. In particular, while guns are used in two-thirds of all homicides

51. Loftin and others (1991).
52. Loftin and others (1991).
53. Britt, Kleck, and Burdua (1996).
54. McDowall, Loftin, and Wiersema (1996).
55. Callahan and others (1994); Rosenfeld (1996); Romero and others (1998). Gun buy-back programs also face conceptual challenges. For example, if the trade-in price is set too low, no one will participate. But a sufficiently high price can increase overall gun ownership by reducing the cost to owners of upgrading to newer weapons. Mullin (2001).

in the United States, less than a quarter of Australian homicides are committed with a firearm.

Reuter and Mouzos report that Australia's policy resulted in the destruction of a large percentage of prohibited long guns, reducing the nation's overall stock of guns by as much as 20 percent. The average homicide rate has been lower in the years following the initiation of the ban (1997–2001) than during the five years before, and the proportion of homicides with guns has continued a secular decline since the ban. Given the very small numbers involved (about fifty gun homicides a year) it is difficult to reach any firm conclusions about the effects of the ban. The trends are compatible with a conclusion that the ban and buyback saved lives, but that conclusion cannot be offered with great confidence. But there is absolutely no evidence that the Australian policy innovations had a perverse effect, as has sometimes been claimed.[56]

Even when clear-cut conclusions emerge from the evaluation of a particular policy innovation, generalizing to other jurisdictions or circumstances must be done with care. The problems of extrapolating from the Australian experience with a ban and buyback to the United States are perhaps obvious. Extrapolating from the experience with a handgun ban in Washington may be somewhat easier, especially if it were to another large city bordering on a state with lax controls on gun transactions. But the Washington experience provides little guide to predicting the consequences of a *nationwide* ban on handguns, given notable differences in scale, initial prevalence, and enforcement problems. Still, a close look at dramatic policy changes provides potentially generalizable evidence on basic causal processes, such as the effect on crime and violence of a reduction in gun availability, however that is achieved.

Gun Availability and Residential Burglary

Survey evidence indicates that residences are more likely to be occupied during a burglary attempt in Britain, where relatively few homes have guns, than in the United States. Based on that observation and others, commentators have asserted that one of the benefits of widespread gun ownership is to deter burglars from breaking into occupied dwellings.[57] But no systematic analysis of this claim has ever been performed.

In chapter 3 we move beyond crude international comparisons and examine how burglary patterns within the United States relate to the prevalence of gun ownership. We use both National Crime Victimization Survey data on residen-

56. John R. Lott, "Gun Control Misfires in Europe." *Wall Street Journal,* April 30, 2002, p. A16.
57. Kleck (1997); Kopel (2001).

tial burglary and the FBI's *Uniform Crime Reports* panel data on burglaries reported to the police. Using a variety of statistical methods to deal with the problems of confounding variables and reverse causation, we conclude that an increase in gun prevalence has no effect on the likelihood that a residential burglary involves an occupied dwelling (a "hot" burglary), while it appears to have, if anything, a positive effect on the overall rate of residential burglary. Our tentative explanation for that surprising conclusion is that guns are valuable loot and that gun-rich communities are especially profitable to burglars.

In his comment, discussant David Kopel raises the reasonable concern that limitations of the available data prevent us from including the smallest counties in our analysis. But accounting for rural counties does not affect our central conclusion, since we obtain similar findings from our analysis of state-level data. Both Kopel and discussant Bruce Sacerdote echo our own concern that variation across states in "rurality"—what we use to isolate variation across counties and states in gun prevalence that is not contaminated by the reverse-causation problem—is likely to impart some bias to our estimates. But, as we note in the Appendix to chapter 3, this bias is likely to *overstate* any deterrent effects of guns on burglary. So we are reasonably confident that more guns do not lead to fewer burglaries, hot or otherwise.

More Guns, More Crime

As a whole, this research suggests that within the generally gun-rich context of the United States, higher gun prevalence is associated with more homicides and suicides, and possibly even more residential burglaries, while having little effect on other types of crime. Of course in the social sciences anything short of a true randomized experiment must inevitably leave some room for doubt about the causal interpretation of such findings, since whatever causes people and jurisdictions to have different rates of gun ownership may also affect their experiences with crime and violence. Policy changes, such as the ban on handguns in Washington, D.C., and on semiautomatic rifles in Australia, provide something closer to experimental evidence, though problems remain of finding a suitable control group and of generalizing to other times and places.

Gun Acquisitions

In practice most firearm regulation in the United States is not intended to have much effect on the overall prevalence of guns but rather to reduce criminal and reckless use of guns by banning possession by certain groups, such as youths and felons. Fortunately an effective program to deny guns to those likely to misuse them does not require a house-to-house search; it would be enough to regulate transactions effectively. The reason is that criminal misuse usually follows rather quickly after gun acquisition. In other words, the millions of current gun possessors will account for little of the violent crime five years from now. A reasonable goal, then, is to increase the effective price of guns to the high-risk segment of the market.[58]

A critical review of this literature suggests mixed results on the effectiveness of targeted regulations of gun acquisition. The most important federal firearm law since 1968, the Brady Act, has not had a discernible effect on gun homicide, perhaps because it has been undercut by the largely unregulated secondary market. However, as Elizabeth Richardson Vigdor and James Mercy show in chapter 5, regulations to ban possession by domestic batterers seem to have been somewhat effective.

Gun Markets

To some people the notion of trying to keep guns away from a small subset of the population with 200 million guns already in circulation seems hopeless. But targeted regulation in an environment of widespread availability is not always futile, as suggested by the analogy to minimum drinking age laws. Many readers, particularly parents and those who were once teenagers themselves, may be surprised that minimum drinking age laws have any effect given the widespread use of alcohol among American adolescents. Yet there is consensus among scholars that these laws, while routinely violated by a majority of older teens, are nonetheless effective; the quasi-experimental evidence of numerous changes in state minimum-age laws during the 1970s and 1980s provide evidence that this partial prohibition lowers alcohol abuse, traffic accidents, and crime.[59]

Whether restrictions on gun acquisitions are or could be similarly effective is not clear, although the prospect is somewhat less daunting when we recognize that the stock of guns in America probably matters less than the flow. Most of our country's guns are in the hands of relatively low-risk people and are likely to remain there (theft notwithstanding) for many years. Most gun crimes are committed by a small group of criminally active people whose criminal "careers" are

---

58. In response to the question "Is there any gun control NRA supports?," the National Rifle Association's Institute for Legislative Action answers on its web page: "Yes. NRA supports 'gun control' that is designed to prohibit felons from buying and possessing firearms as long as those laws do not also infringe on the rights of law-abiding citizens." NRA (2002). The term "effective price" was coined by Mark Moore in 1973.

59. Cook and Moore (2001).

typically fairly short. Regulation might be effective if it makes it harder for each new cohort of criminally active young people to acquire guns, particularly the new guns that they seem to favor.[60]

Since the secondary market is the proximate source for the vast majority of crime guns, one obvious intervention point is the movement of guns from the primary to secondary markets. High-volume traffickers play some role in moving guns across markets, as demonstrated by Bureau of Alcohol, Tobacco, and Firearms (ATF) investigation files and crime-gun trace data.[61] Other "traffickers" may simply be girlfriends or relatives who engage in one or two straw purchases to provide guns to someone with a disqualifying criminal record.

Some licensed gun dealers are willing accomplices to gun trafficking or straw purchases, or are selling to criminals off the books.[62] One ATF investigation of the relatively small subset of dealers who account for the original retail sale of most crime guns submitted for tracing found that 75 percent were in violation of at least one federal regulation. Although most of these were for minor violations, 20 percent of dealers in this sample were recommended for license revocation.[63]

Regardless of the actual frequency of dealer malfeasance, the ability of ATF to monitor dealers under the current regulatory system is limited. As a practical matter there are so many retail licensees—currently about 80,000—that ATF can only inspect a few percent of them in any one year.[64] Even when ATF investigators determine that a dealer is in serious violation of the law it can be very difficult to take effective action, thanks in part to federal legislation (the McClure-Volkmer Act, or Firearm Owners Protection Act of 1986), which limits regulatory actions and establishes a near-impossible evidentiary requirement for successful prosecution.[65]

If regulation could reduce the flow of guns from primary to secondary market, standard economic analysis suggests that the resulting decline in supply would increase the price of guns in secondary markets. Diverting high-risk buyers from the primary to the secondary market (by, for example, improving background checks) would further increase prices in the secondary market by increasing demand.[66] Whether these price increases translate into decreased gun misuse depends on how sensitive teens and criminally inclined adults are to the price of guns.

---

60. Cook and Braga (2001).
61. Cook and Braga (2001).
62. Wachtel (1998).
63. ATF (2000b).
64. ATF (2000a).
65. Cook and Ludwig (2002); Butterfield (2001).
66. Cook and Leitzel (1996).

Surprisingly little is known about the sensitivity of high-risk groups to gun prices, although scattered survey evidence suggests that criminals are not entirely immune to the financial and other costs of getting guns. In one survey of incarcerated adults, 21 percent of those who chose not to use a gun to commit their crimes said that the trouble of getting a gun played a "very" or "somewhat" important role in their decision; 17 percent cited the financial cost.[67] In a survey of incarcerated teens in North Carolina, one said that "When [people] are short of money, they have no choice but to sell [their guns]," while another remarked that he had "traded a .22 for a Super Nintendo and some other guns for a VCR and for my waterbed. I got other stuff for my room, like a phone with lights and a copy [fax] machine for a twenty-gauge."[68] With higher prices we would expect cash-strapped youths to be less inclined to buy a gun and more inclined to sell whatever guns come their way. Further, higher prices would provide an incentive for those who do have a gun to exercise greater caution against theft and confiscation by law enforcement, by, for example, leaving it at home.

The goal of gun control is thus to increase the effective price of guns to that segment of the market that is at highest risk for misuse, while doing little to the price facing most other people. Unless eligible buyers are substantially more price sensitive than are teens and convicted felons, the result should be a decline in gun ownership among prohibited buyers with little effect on overall gun prevalence. What the system achieves in practice is of course an empirical matter.

The Brady Act

One sign of the 1968 GCA's effectiveness comes from the fact that surveys of prisoners from the 1980s show that only around one-fifth obtained their guns directly from a licensed gun dealer, even though dealers in most states were not required to conduct background checks to verify the buyer's eligibility.[69] The GCA's restrictions were strengthened in 1993 with the Brady Handgun Violence Prevention Act, which required gun dealers in states without background-check requirements to begin to conduct such checks on prospective buyers. Hundreds of thousands of potential buyers have been denied handguns as a result of Brady-mandated background checks, leading many to conclude that the Brady Act has had a substantial effect on crime and suicide.[70]

More direct evidence on the Brady Act's effects on public safety comes from comparing mortality trends in the thirty-two states that were required to abide

---

67. Wright and Rossi (1994, pp. 128–29).
68. Cook, Molliconi, and Cole (1995).
69. Wright and Rossi (1994).
70. Manson and Gilliard (1997).

by Brady's background check and waiting period requirements with the eighteen states (plus the District of Columbia) that already had sufficiently stringent policies in place, and as a result were exempt from the Brady provisions. Our own analysis published in the *Journal of the American Medical Association* reveals no detectable difference in homicide trends between the "Brady" (treatment) and "non-Brady" (control) states among people 25 and older.[71] Our focus on *adult* mortality rates is motivated by the different trajectories that juvenile homicides follow in treatment and control states even before the Brady law went into effect. As a result, any differences in juvenile homicide trends following implementation of the Brady Act cannot be confidently attributed to the effects of the law itself. Excluding juvenile victims is not particularly problematic, since most of them were shot by those who would have been too young to be directly affected by the Brady background check requirement.[72]

Our methodological point is that in evaluating discrete policy interventions, one check on the validity of the "control" group is whether it follows a trajectory similar to the "treatment" group *before* the intervention. If not, then the resulting estimates of the treatment effect may well be biased.[73] This type of objective test provides the basis for a rejoinder to the common complaint that statistics can be used to "say anything" and argue either side of an issue.

The *Brady* case provides an illustration. Although our analysis finds no statistically significant effect of the Brady Act on homicides or other violent crime, John Lott asserts that *Brady* increased the number of rapes and perhaps assaults as well.[74] The contradiction results from the fact that Lott's evidence comes from comparing crime rates in treatment and control states following Brady's implementation for people of *all* ages, including juvenile as well as adult perpetrators. Since juvenile crime trends in the Brady treatment and control states diverge even before Brady goes into effect, Lott's analysis is likely to confound the effects of the Brady Act with those of whatever unmeasured factors cause juvenile trends to differ across the two groups of states during the pre-Brady period.

A distinct concern in evaluating the effects of the Brady Act is that the new law may have reduced gun running from the treatment to control states, in which case comparing the two groups of states might understate the overall effects of the law. In a nutshell, the concern is that the "control" states were in fact affected by the intervention. Some support for this concern comes from ATF trace data in Chicago showing that the fraction of crime guns in the city that could be traced

71. Ludwig and Cook (2000).
72. Cook and Laub (1998).
73. See Bassi (1984); Heckman and Hotz (1989); Black and Nagin (1998); Ludwig (2000); Smith and Todd (forthcoming).
74. Lott (2000, pp. 90, 200).

to the *Brady* treatment states declined dramatically following implementation of the Brady law.[75] However, the proportion of homicides in Chicago committed with guns did not change over this period, despite the substantial changes in gun-trafficking patterns. One explanation is that traffickers can adapt easily to changes in the larger environment. If correct, that suggests that any bias introduced into comparisons of *Brady* treatment and control states owing to changes in across-state gun running is minor.

Of course the Brady Act may affect outcomes other than crime. Comparing trends in treatment and control states suggests that Brady may have reduced gun suicide rates among those 55 and older, who commit suicide at higher rates than younger people, and that the waiting period requirement of the law may have been responsible. However these gains were at least partially offset by an increase in nongun suicides, so whether the waiting periods reduced overall suicides among this age group is unclear.[76]

Gun Possession by Violent Misdemeanants

State or federal initiatives occasionally move the boundary between who is and is not eligible to purchase a firearm. Two recent federal examples include the 1994 ban on gun possession essentially by people under a restraining order for domestic violence, and the 1996 Lautenberg Amendment that extended that ban to anyone convicted of a domestic-violence misdemeanor.[77] Although neither act has been evaluated directly, encouraging evidence for the effects of these laws comes from study of similar state-level laws.

California's experience has been of particular interest because it is a large state and an early mover in this area. The state's 1991 law prohibits handgun purchases by people convicted of any violent misdemeanor, not just those for domestic violence, and has been subject to evaluation by Garen Wintemute and his colleagues.[78] Their analysis compares the likelihood of arrest during the three years following a handgun purchase attempt for two groups of people with misdemeanor convictions: The treatment group—those who attempted to purchase their guns in 1991 and were denied because of the new law; and the control group—those who succeeded in purchasing a handgun in 1989 and 1990, be-

---

75. Cook and Braga (2001).

76. Ludwig and Cook (2000).

77. We say "essentially" because, as Elizabeth Richardson Vigdor and James Mercy note in their chapter, only restraining orders issued as a result of a hearing in which the individual had a chance to participate invoke the gun prohibition.

78. Wintemute and others (2001).

fore the law was in effect. California data on criminal histories demonstrate that those in the control group were one-third more likely to have been arrested during the three years following their purchase attempt than was the treatment group that was denied guns.

Although of considerable interest, the proper interpretation of Wintemute's findings remains unclear for two reasons. First, the number of people with disqualifying records who attempted to purchase guns in 1991 (1,099) is greater than the combined numbers for 1989 and 1990 together (877). This surprising surge in the number of violent misdemeanants who tried to purchase handguns after the ban went into effect (perhaps resulting from misinformation about the date the ban was to be imposed) raises the possibility that the 1991 applicants were not really comparable in criminal propensity to the earlier applicants. In fact the criminal records of the treatment and control groups were somewhat different even before the purchase attempts. Although Wintemute's analysis controls for measured differences in demographics and prior criminal records, we cannot rule out the possibility of unmeasured compositional changes. Second, the analysis may confound the effects of California's law with the effects of overall crime trends within the state, since the treatment and control groups were observed in different years in a time when crime rates were changing. The direction of bias from any unmeasured "period effects" is difficult to determine.[79]

In chapter 5, Elizabeth Richardson Vigdor and James Mercy provide new evidence on the effects of state laws that prohibit gun ownership to those with histories of domestic violence. Vigdor and Mercy find that laws that prevent those who are subject to a restraining order from owning or purchasing a handgun reduce rates of homicides of intimate partners, while there are no clear effects for prohibitions directed against those people with prior misdemeanor convictions for domestic violence. Presumably the difference in the effects of the two laws is because of some combination of the inability of available data systems to identify all those with records of domestic violence, the close timing between state and federal laws that keep guns from those convicted of domestic violence misdemeanors, and the fact that there may be more people subject to restraining orders than with prior convictions for domestic-violence misdemeanors.

---

79. Predicting the direction of bias is complicated in part because individuals are only tracked up until they experience their first arrest or three years have elapsed since they tried to purchase a handgun, whichever comes first. If everyone were followed for the full three years, the control group would be tracked for the period 1989–93 and the treatment group for 1991–94. In California UCR property crimes declined gradually starting in 1989, while the overall rate of violent crimes was increasing until its peak in 1992, and then began to decline thereafter (*www.disastercenter.com/crime/cacrime.htm*, [March 6, 2002]).

The results for the restraining-order laws are also more likely to reflect causal policy effects than those for domestic-violence misdemeanors. Prohibitions on those people with restraining orders are consistently related to intimate partner homicides and unrelated to other crimes that should less clearly be affected by gun regulations; the reverse is true for the domestic-violence laws. The data also suggest that states with restraining-order prohibitions experience rates of intimate partner homicides similar to those observed in other areas before these gun laws go into effect, at least up to one year before passage. While discussants John Laub, Garen Wintemute, and Brian Jacob are concerned that the estimated effects are biased because of covariation of these prohibitions with other unmeasured factors, the general similarity in trends across states before the restraining-order laws go into effect and the lack of relationship with other non-domestic crimes makes us somewhat more confident that Vigdor and Mercy have isolated the effects of this legislation. Improved enforcement of these laws, another concern of Laub and Wintemute, would almost surely improve the effectiveness of such policies in preventing intimate partner homicides.

Concluding Thoughts

What do these results imply for the prospects of regulating gun acquisitions? Evidence that the Brady Act did not have the substantial effect on crime that proponents had hoped suggests a limited potential for regulations seeking to deny dangerous people access to the primary market while leaving the secondary market unregulated. If mild, inexpensive regulations save even just a few lives, however, they may be justified. That principle applies to the case of banning gun possession by domestic batterers, where there appears to be a small but discernible effect. More information about how high-risk groups respond to changes in the effective price of guns, as well as about how gun markets operate, would have substantial value in refining evaluations of regulations and determining why some regulations appear to be effective in saving lives while others seem less so.

The uneven evidence on the effectiveness of gun-control measures stands in seeming contrast to the relatively strong evidence that gun availability has a positive effect on homicide rates. There are several possible explanations, including that most gun-control measures have not affected gun availability to dangerous people very much in practice—certainly not as much as would a substantial reduction in the prevalence of gun ownership. As pointed out by Franklin Zimring in chapter 11, modest interventions produce, at best, modest results. Although he encourages advocates to aim higher, rather than squander political effort on trivial gains, even modest results may be enough to justify an intervention if the costs are sufficiently low.

Gun Carrying

Whether or not it is possible to sustain effective discrimination in the gun markets between the minority who are banned from acquisition and the majority who are entitled, criminal misuse will not be eliminated. Some observers argue that a gun policy should focus on reducing misuse directly rather than on forestalling misuse by regulating acquisition. Indeed, in most states the criminal law specifies a harsher sentence if a gun is used in a violent crime than a less lethal weapon. One step back from gun use in crime is illegal carrying, and policies to deter carrying by dangerous people may be an efficient strategy for reducing misuse. As Lawrence Sherman notes, "To the extent that homicide frequently occurs spontaneously among young men in public places, it is the *carrying* of firearms, rather than their ownership, that is the immediate proximate cause of criminal injury."[80] James Q. Wilson extends the argument: "Our goal should not be the disarming of law-abiding citizens. It should be to reduce the number of people who carry guns unlawfully, especially in places—on streets, in taverns—where the mere presence of a gun can increase the hazards we all face."[81] Others, impressed by the potential value of an armed public in deterring street crime, have successfully advocated for relaxing restrictions on carrying by adults who can pass a criminal-record check.

Policing Against Illegal Guns

The most straightforward way to keep people from carrying guns illegally is to arrest them when they do so. The widespread belief in the effectiveness of police patrols against illegal gun carrying is motivated in large part by findings from the Kansas City Gun Experiment, in which patrol resources were added in one high-crime neighborhood to search pedestrians and motorists for guns. Analysis by Lawrence Sherman and his colleagues suggests that gun seizures increased by 65 percent in the target neighborhood during the program, while gun crime declined by 49 percent. In contrast there was little change over this period in either outcome in a comparison neighborhood several miles away.[82]

Despite the apparent promise of the Kansas City Gun Experiment, it is important to recognize that this program was not an "experiment" in the true sense of the term. There were just two neighborhoods involved, and they experienced

80. Sherman (2000, p. 1193).
81. James Q. Wilson, "Just Take Away Their Guns." *New York Times Magazine,* March 20, 1994, sec. 6, p. 47.
82. Sherman, Shaw, and Rogan (1995); Sherman and Rogan (1995).

different levels and trends in firearm offenses even before the policing program was put into place.[83] As we have argued, that difference should make for caution in drawing inferences from differences in crime rates after the program was put into place. While policymakers in New York City and elsewhere have implemented police patrols against illegal guns, more convincing evidence on the effects of this strategy is lacking.

This void is addressed in chapter 6, in which Jacqueline Cohen and Jens Ludwig provide new evidence on the effects of such policing programs in Pittsburgh. Their evaluation strategy seeks to isolate the causal effect of the police program by exploiting the fact that gun-oriented patrol was implemented in some parts of the city but not others, and that in the targeted areas the extra patrols were focused on just four evenings each week (Wednesday through Saturday). Their main finding is that during the targeted nights of the week, the target neighborhoods experienced much larger declines in gunshot injuries and citizen reports of shots fired compared with the experience in control areas.

The innovation of this evaluation is to provide evidence that at least for gunshot injuries the control neighborhoods in Pittsburgh provide a reasonable estimate for what *would have* happened in the treatment areas had the program not been enacted—the necessary condition for determining the intervention's effect. First, the authors show that following the launch of the program there was little difference in injury or shots-fired trends between treatment and control neighborhoods on days in which the new antigun patrols were *not* scheduled (Sunday through Tuesday). Second, the treatment and control neighborhoods have similar trends in gunshot injuries *before* the policing program was implemented. However the treatment and control neighborhoods did have significantly different experiences with reports of shots fired even before the program was in effect, so we should be more confident in the results for gunshot injuries than shots fired.

This evaluation supplements existing evidence that police programs targeted against illegal gun carrying may reduce gun violence. Given the substantial costs of gun violence to society—on the order of $1 million per gunshot injury—these policing programs easily generate benefits to society in excess of their operational costs.[84] Of course aggressive police patrols may generate other costs, impinging on civil liberties and straining police-community relations. In Pittsburgh, at least, the police appear to have been mindful of these concerns, and quite restrained.

83. Sherman, Shaw, and Rogan (1995).
84. Cook and Ludwig (2000); Ludwig and Cook (2001).

Enhanced Punishment

Another approach to deterring illegal gun carrying is to enhance the threatened severity of punishment for those who are caught. In the 1970s this approach was used with apparent success in Massachusetts, which enacted the Bartley-Fox Amendment mandating a one-year prison sentence for unlicensed gun carrying. The new law prohibited plea bargaining and was widely advertised; the law was subsequently evaluated in several careful studies, which agreed that it caused a substantial drop in the homicide rate and in gun use in street crime.[85]

In recent years the most highly touted example of this approach is in Richmond, Virginia's Project Exile, which diverted convicted felons arrested for gun possession from state courts into the federal system where penalties are more severe. The Bush administration has taken Exile nationwide as one model for the new Project Safe Neighborhoods initiative. Advocates for Project Exile often point to the 40 percent reduction in gun homicides in Richmond between 1997 and 1998 as evidence.[86] But skeptics point out that homicides actually increased during the last ten months of 1997 following Exile's launch in February, and that the homicide rate during 1997 as a whole was around 40 percent higher than in 1996.

In chapter 7 Steven Raphael and Jens Ludwig provide the first rigorous evaluation of Project Exile. They note that previous claims about Exile's success rest on simple before-and-after comparisons for the city of Richmond, and even those are problematic given the short-term increase in homicide. Without a control group, there remains the obvious question of what Richmond's crime trajectory would have been in the absence of this "Project": after all, crime rates were declining dramatically across the country during the 1990s.[87]

Raphael and Ludwig's analysis offers no evidence that Project Exile effected a reduction in homicides or other types of crime in Richmond. They show that Richmond's crime trajectory (even removing 1997 data from the picture) in the late 1990s is not notably better than other cities that had experienced similarly volatile homicide rates since 1980. This null finding is robust to a variety of methodological adjustments, including a check for omitted variables bias that uses juveniles (who are generally exempt from the federal felon-in-possession charges that make up the bulk of Exile prosecutions) as an additional within-city control group.

85. Pierce and Bowers (1981); Cook (1991).

86. See, for example, Elaine Shannon, "Have Gun? Will Travel," *Time Magazine,* August 16, 1999, p. 154; and "Remarks by the President on Project Safe Neighborhood," White House, Office of the Press Secretary, May 14, 2001.

87. Blumstein and Wallman (2000).

In their comments the discussants note that expectations of large impacts were probably unrealistic from the start; Steven Levitt notes that Exile engendered a fairly modest objective increase in the threat of punishment, while Peter Greenwood suggests that the program did not focus sufficiently on the most dangerous group of offenders. But the failure of Richmond's Project Exile to live up to the inflated expectations of some proponents does not rule out the possibility that the program is worthwhile. Given the substantial costs that gun violence impose on society, even modest effects of the size suggested by Steven Levitt in his discussion—which would be too small to be detected by the analysis in chapter 7—might be large enough to justify the program. Our bottom line is that policymakers searching for ways to reduce gun violence should not necessarily eliminate Project Exile from their portfolio but should recognize that the program is not the miraculous intervention that has been claimed and is not a substitute for other efforts to address the problem.

Permissive Gun-Carrying Laws

While many big city police departments devote substantial resources to keeping guns off the street, during the past several decades state governments across the country have made it easier for people to carry guns legally in public. More than thirty states have now enacted permissive gun-carrying laws, and a number of others such as Missouri, Minnesota, Ohio, and Wisconsin are considering such laws.[88] These laws are not necessarily in conflict with police patrols against illegal gun carrying, since there is not much overlap in the population characteristics of those who apply for permits to carry and those who are targeted in police patrols.

Proponents of permissive gun-carrying laws hope that the increased likelihood of encountering an armed victim will deter criminals, a possibility that receives some support from prisoner surveys: 80 percent in one survey agreed with the statement that "a smart criminal always tries to find out if his potential victim is armed."[89] But the same data also raise the possibility that an increase in gun carrying could prompt an arms race: two-thirds of prisoners incarcerated for gun offenses reported that the chance of running into an armed victim was very or somewhat important in their own choice to use a gun. Currently criminals use guns in only around one-quarter of robberies and one of every twenty assaults.[90] If increased gun carrying among potential victims causes criminals to carry guns more often themselves, or become quicker to use guns to avert armed self-defense, the end result could be that street crime becomes more lethal.

88. Dvorak (2002).
89. Wright and Rossi (1994).
90. Rennison (2001).

Economist John Lott has argued that the deterrent effects of permissive gun-carrying laws dominate: "Of all the methods studied so far by economists, the carrying of concealed handguns appears to be the most cost-effective method for reducing crime."[91] A previous evaluation of permissive concealed-carry laws focused on how crime rates changed within jurisdictions that enacted such measures.[92] But, as with Project Exile, having a valid control group is important in making a credible assessment of program effects. Lott and fellow economist David Mustard improved on earlier research by comparing crime changes in states that enact concealed-carry laws with changes in other jurisdictions.[93] Lott has now performed this analysis in several ways, reaching differing conclusions about the effect on property crime, but always finding that adopting permissive gun-carrying laws reduced homicide rates.[94]

In chapter 8 economist John Donohue argues that while Lott's analysis improves on previous research on this topic, in the end Lott's findings cannot support the conclusion that permissive concealed-carry laws reduce crime. Donohue shows that Lott's estimates are sensitive to the correction of several coding errors and to reasonable changes in the model specification. More important, Donohue's reanalysis of the Lott data shows that states that eventually passed permissive concealed-carry laws had systematically different crime trends from the other states even before these gun-carry laws went into effect—violating what we have argued is a minimum necessary condition for deriving unbiased estimates of policy impacts. The violation of this condition implies that the estimated treatment effect may occur because of whatever unmeasured factors caused crime trends to diverge before the laws are enacted.

In his comment, David Mustard notes that his work with John Lott addresses this apparent omitted-variables problem in several ways. In our own judgment none of these approaches is entirely persuasive.[95] The puzzling pattern of results for robberies and property crimes in this literature is one manifestation of this issue; another is Donohue's findings that right-to-carry laws in the 1980s seemed

91. Lott (2000, p. 20).
92. McDowall, Loftin, and Wiersema (1995).
93. Lott and Mustard (1997).
94. Cook and others (2002); Lott (2000, pp. 90, 100).
95. For example, the instrumental variables (two-stage least squares) estimates presented by John Lott and David Mustard yield implausibly large estimates for the effects of right-to-carry laws on crime; see Donohue's chapter as well as Ludwig (1998, 2000). Using nonlinear state-specific trends may yield evidence for right-to-carry laws when separate trends are included for the pre- and postlaw periods, but not when each state's crime trend over the entire sample period as a whole is modeled using a linear and quadratic term. See Black and Nagin (1998). Because crime rates follow the same types of cyclical patterns as do many economic indicators and these right-to-carry laws are adopted during periods of increasing crime, isolating their causal effects is difficult. That the postlaw crime levels are below the prelaw levels does not rule out the influence of other factors that drive these crime cycles over time.

to reduce crime, while those adopted in the 1990s appear to have the opposite effect.[96] Willard Manning notes in his comment that few of the estimates reported in this literature may be statistically significant anyway once one correctly calculates standard errors and the relevant statistical tests.

Whether the net effect of permissive gun-carry laws is to increase or reduce the burden of crime, there is good reason to believe that it is not large. One recent study found that in twelve of the sixteen concealed-carry states studied, fewer than 2 percent of adults had obtained permits to carry concealed handguns.[97] The actual change in gun-carrying prevalence will be smaller than the number of permits issued would suggest because many of those who obtain permits were already carrying guns in public.[98] Moreover, the change in gun carrying seems concentrated in rural and suburban areas where crime rates are already relatively low, among people who are at relatively low risk of victimization–white, middle-aged, middle-class males.[99] The available data about permit holders also imply that they are at fairly low risk of misusing guns, consistent with the relatively low arrest rates observed to date for permit holders.[100] In sum, right-to-carry laws are likely to induce only modest changes in the incentives facing criminals to go armed themselves or to avoid potentially armed victims.

Summary

The available results on the effects of permissive gun-carrying regulation are mixed. While there is no evidence at this point to suggest that states should repeal the laws that are already in effect, there is also no reliable evidence that en-

96. In his commentary David Mustard argues that the net effect of right-to-carry laws on a county or state's robbery rate is ambiguous because not all robberies occur in public places, and right-to-carry laws may cause some criminals to substitute from robbing people in public places to committing such crimes in private areas instead. But the proportion of criminal events that occur in public areas is higher for robbery than for murder, rape, and other violent crimes. Why we should see substitution from public to private areas suppressing the right-to-carry effect on robbery more than for other violent crimes is unclear.

Mustard argues that compared with right-to-carry laws enacted in the 1980s, the laws adopted in the 1990s involved higher fees, more stringent training requirements, and more restrictions on where those with permits can legally carry their firearms. Although this argument offers some hypotheses about why the crime-reducing effect of the laws adopted in the 1990s might be more muted compared with those enacted in the 1980s, it cannot explain why Donohue finds that right-to-carry laws adopted in the 1990s seem to increase crime. A more likely explanation in our view for the conflicting results between the laws of the 1980s and 1990s is that both sets of estimates are driven by confounding factors that are not captured by the regression model.

97. Hill (1997).

98. Robuck-Mangum (1997).

99. Hill (1997).

100. Lott (2000).

acting these laws will save lives or reduce street crime. States that enact such laws in the expectation of launching an effective deterrent to crime are likely to be disappointed.

However, strategies to reduce gun carrying by youths and felons deserve consideration. Among the strategies that have made it onto the current policy "menu," directed police patrol is promising, while the threat of more severe punishment seems less reliably effective.

Finally, we take note of an important new twist on the least controversial approach to reducing gun violence: threatening punishment for criminal misuse of guns. The Boston Gun Project's Operation Ceasefire was developed in 1995 in response to the epidemic of lethal gang violence. One of its innovations was to reach out directly, with an explicit and personalized message that gun violence would be met with severe sanctions, to members of targeted gangs. Then the threat was backed up.[101] The hope was to shift gang norms about gun use. Following the adoption of this strategy in Boston in May 1996, youth homicides fell dramatically and stayed down thereafter. One influential evaluation concluded that this drop was the direct result of the intervention, although that conclusion has not gone uncontested.[102]

Future Research

The research discussed in this book provides some guidance for a pragmatic approach to gun policy. The use of empirical evidence in place of dogmatic assertion does have a major drawback, which must be obvious by now: the conclusions are usually hedged by uncertainty. Indeed, some of the more confident conclusions offered, as in the case of the Project Exile evaluation, have the effect of challenging received opinion (that the evidence claimed in support of Project Exile's success does not stand up to close scrutiny) without providing a firm alternative answer. This problem is by no means unique to gun policy.[103] Good empirical research does not necessarily yield definitive results but should serve as an important check on other means by which policymakers form opinions and choose among the available options.

101. Braga and others (2001).
102. Braga and others (2001); Fagan (2002).
103. Take the case of welfare reform. Robert Moffitt observes that "making recommendations for reauthorization is difficult not only for the obvious reason that the goals of the next round of welfare reform are unclear, but also because the evidential base to support specific policy recommendations is weak. Despite the great volume of data analysis conducted on welfare reform since 1996, a careful review of what has been done reveals, unfortunately, that there is very little strong research evidence on many of the key reforms." Moffitt (2001).

Two of the contributions in this book are concerned with the basic ingredients for policy research—a database on state gun laws and the ongoing development of a violent-death reporting system. First, in chapter 9 Jon S. Vernick and Lisa M. Hepburn provide a meticulous description of laws affecting firearm manufacture, sale, possession, and use since 1970, listed by individual state, with the dates of implementation. This is an important research tool that will facilitate the work of future researchers who seek to take advantage of the experience generated by the laboratory of state policymaking. As an interesting by-product, this work provides a basis for assessing an old "chestnut" of anticontrol rhetoric, that there are more than 20,000 gun-control laws on the books in the United States. The earliest use of this figure that Vernick and Hepburn could identify was in testimony by Congressman John D. Dingell in 1965, though no basis for the figure was provided. Yet it has been repeated thousands of times since then, usually coupled with the assertion that no additional legislation is needed when we have so much already—as if laws were some sort of homogeneous commodity, like eggs. In any event, the authors conclude that there are about 300 state laws, and that few local laws are of much importance, especially since some forty states now preempt localities from legislating in this area.

In chapter 10, Deborah Azrael, Catherine Barber, David Hemenway, and Matthew Miller discuss the type of data system that would improve our ability to understand gun violence and evaluate the injury-related outcomes of policies. They point out that currently available data systems lack the detail and consistency needed to support a sensitive evaluation of such measures as a ban on a particular type of weapon or a requirement that guns be stored safely. Indeed, the fact that no such "surveillance" system is currently in operation may strike many as surprising, given the magnitude of the problem.[104] The authors are leaders in the effort, described in this chapter, to develop a workable system, and can take much of the credit for the Centers for Disease Control's recent initiation of a pilot effort. As discussants Alfred Blumstein and David McDowall note, taking such a system to scale will raise a number of challenges in securing complete, consistent data from law enforcement, public health, and medical officials across the country. But if all goes well, the National Violent Death Reporting System might do for intentional injury what the Fatal Accident Reporting System has done for the analysis of highway accidents.

In conclusion, we offer this book in support of the view that the goal of a skilled and dispassionate analysis of the evidence is attainable, even in an area as

---

104. The National Rifle Association opposes a national injury data system on the grounds that "data collection, even if objectively conducted, would inevitably have biased results" because the data system would fail to capture information about defensive gun uses. This does not strike us as a compelling argument, since one desired outcome of a defensive gun use is often the avoidance of an injury.

contentious as firearm policy. For pragmatists who wish to reduce the social burden of gun violence, there is no acceptable alternative.

References

Bureau of Alcohol, Tobacco and Firearms (ATF). 2000a. *Commerce in Firearms in the United States.* U.S. Department of the Treasury.

———. 2000b. *ATF Regulatory Actions: Report to the Secretary on Firearms Initiatives.* U.S. Department of the Treasury.

Azrael, Deborah, Philip J. Cook, and Matthew Miller. 2001. *State and Local Prevalence of Firearms Ownership: Measurement, Structure, and Trends.* Working Paper 8570. Cambridge, Mass.: National Bureau of Economic Research.

Bassi, Laurie J. 1984. "Estimating the Effects of Training Programs with Non-Random Selection." *Review of Economics and Statistics* 66 (1): 36–43.

Beck, A., and D. K. Gilliard, 1993. *Survey of State Prison Inmates 1991.* U.S. Department of Justice.

Birckmayer, Jo, and David Hemenway. 2001. "Suicide and Gun Prevalence: Are Youth Disproportionately Affected?" *Suicide and Life Threatening Behavior* 31: 303–10.

Black, David, and Daniel S. Nagin. 1998. "Do 'Right-to-Carry' Laws Reduce Violent Crime?" *Journal of Legal Studies* 27: 209–19.

Blumstein, Alfred, and Joel Wallman. 2000. *The Crime Drop in America.* Cambridge University Press.

Braga, Anthony A., David M. Kennedy, Elin J. Waring, and Anne Morrison Piehl. 2001. "Problem-Oriented Policing, Deterrence, and Youth Violence: An Evaluation of Boston's Project Ceasefire." *Journal of Research in Crime and Delinquency* 38(3): 195–225.

Brent, David A. 2001. "Firearms and Suicide." *Annals of the New York Academy of Sciences* 932: 225–39.

Brent, D. A., Joshua A. Perper, Christopher J. Allman, Grace M. Moritz, Mary E. Wartella, and Janice P. Zelenak. 1991. "The Presence and Accessibility of Firearms in the Homes of Adolescent Suicides: A Case-Control Study." *Journal of the American Medical Association* 266 (21): 2989–95.

Britt, Chester L., Gary Kleck, and David J. Bordua. 1996. "A Reassessment of the D.C. Gun Law: Some Cautionary Notes on the Use of Interrupted Time Series Designs for Policy Assessment." *Law and Society Review* 30 (2): 361–80.

Butterfield, Fox. 1996. *All God's Children: The Bosket Family and the American Tradition of Violence.* Avon Books.

———. 2001. "The Federal Gun Laws: The First Obstacle to Enforcement." Conference on Guns, Crime and Punishment in America. University of Arizona College of Law, Tucson.

Callahan, Charles M., Frederick P. Rivara, and Thomas D. Koepsell. 1994. "Money for Guns: Evaluation of the Seattle Gun Buy-Back Program." *Public Health Reports* 109 (4): 472–77.

Cook, Philip J. 1976. "A Strategic Choice Analysis of Robbery." In *Sample Surveys of the Victims of Crimes,* edited by Wesley Skogan, 173–87. Ballinger.

———. 1980. "Reducing Injury and Death Rates in Robbery." *Policy Analysis* (Winter): 21–45.

————. 1987. "Robbery Violence." *Journal of Criminal Law and Criminology* 78: 357–76.

————. 1991. "The Technology of Personal Violence." In *Crime and Justice: An Annual Review of Research,* edited by Michael Tonry, 1–71. University of Chicago Press.

Cook, Philip J., and Anthony A. Braga. 2001. "Comprehensive Firearms Tracing: Strategic and Investigative Uses of New Data on Firearms Markets." *Arizona Law Review* 43 (2): 277–310.

Cook, Philip J., and John H. Laub. 1998. "The Unprecedented Epidemic of Youth Violence." In *Crime and Justice: An Annual Review of Research,* edited by Michael Tonry, 26–64. University of Chicago Press.

Cook, Philip J., and James A. Leitzel. 1996. " 'Perversity, Futility, Jeopardy': An Economic Analysis of the Attack on Gun Control." *Law and Contemporary Problems* 59 (1): 91–118.

————. 2002. " 'Smart' Guns: A Technological Fix for Regulating the Secondary Gun Market." *Contemporary Economic Problems* 20 (1): 38–49.

Cook, Philip J., and Jens Ludwig. 1996. *Guns in America: Results of a Comprehensive Survey of Gun Ownership and Use.* Washington: Police Foundation.

————. 2000. *Gun Violence: The Real Costs.* Oxford University Press.

————. 2002. "Firearms." In *Litigation as Regulation,* edited by W. Kip Viscusi, 67–105. Brookings.

Cook, Philip J., and Michael J. Moore. 2001. "Environment and Persistence in Youthful Drinking Patterns." In *Risky Behavior Among Youths: An Economic Analysis,* edited by Jonathan Gruber, 375–438. University of Chicago Press.

Cook, Philip J., Jens Ludwig, and David Hemenway. 1997. "The Gun Debate's New Mythical Number: *How* Many Defensive Uses Per Year?" *Journal of Policy Analysis and Management* 16 (3): 463–69.

Cook, Philip J., Mark H. Moore, and Anthony A. Braga. 2002. "Gun Control." In *Crime: Public Policies for Crime Control,* edited by James Q. Wilson and Joan Peterselia, 291–330. ICS Press.

Cook, Philip J., Stephanie Molliconi, and Thomas B. Cole. 1995. "Regulating Gun Markets." *Journal of Criminal Law and Criminology* 86 (1): 59–92.

Cummings, Peter, Thomas D. Koepsell, David C. Grossman, James Savarino, and Robert S. Thompson. 1997. "The Association between the Purchase of a Handgun and Homicide or Suicide." *American Journal of Public Health* 87 (6): 974–78.

Duggan, Mark. 2001. "More Guns, More Crime." *Journal of Political Economy* 109 (5): 1086–1114.

Dvorak, John A. 2002. "Concealed Weapons Laws Taking Hold." Knight-Ridder Newspapers (March 1).

Fagan, Jeffrey. 2002. "Policing Guns and Youth Violence." *The Future of Children* 12 (2): 133–51.

Glaeser, Edward L., Bruce Sacerdote, and Jose A. Scheinkman. 1996. "Crime and Social Interactions." *Quarterly Journal of Economics* 111 (2): 507–48.

Heckman, James J., and Joseph V. Hotz. 1989. "Choosing among Alternative Nonexperimental Methods for Estimating the Impact of Social Programs: The Case of Manpower Training." *Journal of the American Statistical Association* 84: 862–80.

Hemenway, David, and Matthew Miller. 2002. "The Association of Rates of Household Handgun Ownership, Lifetime Depression and Serious Suicidal Thoughts with Rates of Suicide Across U.S. Census Regions." Harvard Injury Control Research Center Discussion Paper, 2002-2. Harvard University.

Hill, Jeffrey M. 1997. "The Impact of Liberalized Concealed Weapons Statutes on Rates of Violent Crime." B.A. thesis. Duke University, Sanford Institute of Public Policy.

James, William. 1904. "What is Pragmatism?" Lecture delivered December 1904 (www. marxists.org/reference/subject/philosophy/works/us/james.htm).

Kates, Don B., and Daniel D. Polsby. 2000. "The Myth of the 'Virgin Killer': Law-Abiding Persons Who Kill in a Fit of Rage." Paper presented at the American Society of Criminology Annual Meetings, San Francisco.

Kellermann, Arthur L., Frederick P. Rivara, Grant Somes, Donald T. Reay, Jerry Francisco, Joyce Gillentine Banton, Janice Prodzinski, Corinne Fligner, and Bela B. Hackman. 1992. "Suicide in the Home in Relation to Gun Ownership." *New England Journal of Medicine* 327 (7): 467–72.

Kellermann, Arthur L., Frederick P. Rivara, Norman B. Rushforth, Joyce G. Banton, Donald T. Reay, Jerry T. Francisco, Ana B. Locci, Janice Prodzinski, Bela B. Hackman, and Grant Somes. 1993. "Gun Ownership as a Risk Factor for Homicide in the Home." *New England Journal of Medicine* 329: 1084–91.

Kennedy, David M., Anne M. Piehl, and Anthony A. Braga. 1996. "Youth Violence in Boston: Gun Markets, Serious Youth Offenders, and a Use-Reduction Strategy." *Law and Contemporary Problems* 59 (1): 147–83.

Kleck, Gary. 1997. *Targeting Guns: Firearms and Their Control.* Aldine de Gruyter.

Kleck, Gary, and Marc Gertz. 1995. "Armed Resistance to Crime: The Prevalence and Nature of Self-Defense with a Gun." *Journal of Criminal Law and Criminology* 86: 150–87.

Kleck, Gary, and E. Britt Patterson. 1993. "The Impact of Gun Control and Gun Ownership Levels on Violence Rates." *Journal of Quantitative Criminology* 9 (3): 249–87.

Kopel, David B. 2001. "Lawyers, Guns and Burglars." *Arizona Law Review* 43 (2): 345–68.

Koper, C., and J. Roth. 2001. "The Impact of the 1994 Federal Assault Weapon Ban on Gun Violence Outcomes: An Assessment of Multiple Outcome Measures and Some Lessons for Policy Evaluation." *Journal of Quantitative Criminology* 17 (1): 33–74.

Leonardatos, Cynthia, Paul H. Blackman, and David B. Kopel. 2001. "Smart Guns / Foolish Legislators: Finding the Right Public Safety Laws, and Avoiding the Wrong Ones." *Connecticut Law Review* 34 (1): 157–219.

Levitt, Steven D. 2001. "Deterrence." In *Crime: Public Policies for Crime Control,* edited by James Q. Wilson and Joan Petersilia, 435–50. Oakland: Institute for Contemporary Studies.

Loftin, Colin, David McDowall, Brian Wiersema, and Talbert J. Cottey. 1991. "Effects of Restrictive Licensing of Handguns on Homicide and Suicide in the District of Columbia." *New England Journal of Medicine* 325 (23): 1615–20.

Lott, John R. 2000. *More Guns, Less Crime, 2d ed.* University of Chicago Press.

Lott, John R., and David B. Mustard. 1997. "Crime, Deterrence, and Right-to-Carry Concealed Handguns." *Journal of Legal Studies* 16 (1): 1–68.

Ludwig, Jens. 1998. "Concealed Gun-Carrying Laws and Violent Crime: Evidence from State-Panel Data." *International Review of Law and Economics* 18: 239–54.

———. 2000. "Gun Self-Defense and Deterrence." In *Crime and Justice: A Review of Research, Volume 27,* edited by Michael Tonry, 363–417. University of Chicago Press.

Ludwig, Jens, and Philip J. Cook. 2000. "Homicide and Suicide Rates Associated with Implementation of the Brady Handgun Violence Prevention Act." *Journal of the American Medical Association* 284 (5): 585–91.

———. 2001. "The Benefits of Reducing Gun Violence: Evidence from Contingent-Valuation Data." *Journal of Risk and Uncertainty* 22 (3): 207–26.

Manson, D. A., and D. K. Gilliard. 1997. *Presale Handgun Checks, 1996: A National Estimate*. NCJ 165704. Bureau of Justice Statistics. U.S. Department of Justice.

McDowall, David, Colin Loftin, and Brian Wiersema. 1995. "Easing Concealed Firearms Laws: Effects on Homicide in Three States." *Journal of Criminal Law and Criminology* 86 (1): 193–206.

———. 1996. "Using Quasi-Experiments to Evaluate Firearm Laws: Comment on Britt et al.'s Reassessment of the D.C. Gun Law." *Law and Society Review* 30 (2): 381–91.

McGonigal, Michael D., John Cole, C. William Schwab, Donald R. Kauder, Michael F. Rotondo, and Peter B. Angood. 1993. "Urban Firearm Deaths: A Five-Year Perspective." *Journal of Trauma* 35 (4): 532–36.

Miller, Matthew, Deborah Azrael and David Hemenway. 2002a. (Forthcoming). "Household Firearm Ownership Levels and Suicide Across U.S. Regions and States, 1988–1997." *Epidemiology*.

———. 2002b. "Firearm Availability and Unintentional Firearm Deaths, Suicide and Homicide among 5–14 Year-Olds." *Journal of Trauma* 52 (February): 267–75.

———. 2002c. "Firearm Availability and Unintentional Firearm Deaths, Suicide, and Homicide among Women." *Journal of Urban Health* 79 (1): 26–38.

———. 2002d (Forthcoming). "Household Firearm Ownership Levels and Homicide Rates across U.S. Regions and States, 1988–1997." *American Journal of Public Health*.

Miller, Matthew, and David Hemenway. 1999. "The Relationship between Firearms and Suicide: A Review of the Literature." *Aggression and Violent Behavior* 4 (1): 59–75.

———. 2001. "Firearm Prevalence and the Risk of Suicide: A Review." *Harvard Health Policy Review* 2 (2): 29–37.

Moffitt, Robert. 2001. "A Return to Categorical Welfare." *Poverty Research News* 5 (6): 12–13.

Mullin, Wallace P. 2001. "Will Gun Buyback Programs Increase the Quantity of Guns?" *International Review of Law and Economics* 21 (1): 87–102.

Nagin, Daniel S. 1998. "Criminal Deterrence Research at the Outset of the Twenty-First Century." In *Crime and Justice: A Review of Research, Volume 23,* edited by Michael Tonry, 1–42. University of Chicago Press.

National Center for Health Statistics (NCHS). 2001. "Deaths: Final Data for 1999." *National Vital Statistics Report* 48 (9): 1–118.

National Rifle Association (NRA). 2002. "A Fact Sheet: SmartGuns." NRA Institute for Legislative Action.

Pierce, Glenn L., and William J. Bowers. 1981. "The Bartley-Fox Gun Law's Short-Term Impact on Crime in Boston." *Annals of the American Academy of Political and Social Science* 455: 120–37. Philadelphia.

Rennison, Callie Marie. 2001. *Criminal Victimization 2000: Changes 1999–2000 with Trends 1993–2000.* NCJ 187007. Bureau of Justice Statistics. U.S. Department of Justice.

Robuck-Mangum, Gail. 1997. "Concealed Weapon Permit Holders in North Carolina: A Descriptive Study of Handgun-Carrying Behaviors." Master's thesis. University of North Carolina at Chapel Hill, School of Public Health.

Romero, Michael P., Garen J. Wintemute and Jon S. Vernick. 1998. "Characteristics of a Gun Exchange Program, and an Assessment of Potential Benefits." *Injury Prevention* 4: 206–10.

Rosenfeld, Richard. 1996. "Crime Prevention or Community Mobilization? The Dilemma of the Gun Buy-Back Program." In *Under Fire: Gun Buy-Backs, Exchanges and Amnesty Programs,* edited by M. Plotkin, 1–28. Washington: Police Executive Research Forum.

Schwab, C. William, and others. 1999. "Urban Firearm Deaths: Trends Over a Decade." Working Paper. University of Pennsylvania School of Medicine.

Sheley, Joseph F., and James D. Wright. 1995. *In the Line of Fire: Youths, Guns and Violence in Urban America.* Aldine de Gruyter.

Sherman, Lawrence W. 2000. "Gun Carrying and Homicide Prevention." *Journal of the American Medical Association* 283 (9): 1193–95.

Sherman, Lawrence W., James W. Shaw, and Dennis P. Rogan. 1995. *The Kansas City Gun Experiment.* Research in Brief, NCJ 150855. Washington: National Institute of Justice.

Sherman, Lawrence W., and Dennis P. Rogan. 1995. "Effects of Gun Seizures on Gun Violence: 'Hot Spots' Patrol in Kansas City." *Justice Quarterly* 12 (4): 673–93.

Smith, Jeffrey, and Petra Todd. Forthcoming. "Does Matching Overcome Lalonde's Critique of Nonexperimental Estimators?" *Journal of Econometrics.*

Tengs, Tammy, and A. Wallace. 2000. "One Thousand Health-Related Quality-of-life Estimates." *Medical Care* 38 (6): 583–637.

Vernick, Jon S., and Stephen P. Teret. 2000. "A Public Health Approach to Regulating Firearms as Consumer Products." *University of Pennsylvania Law Review* 148 (4): 1193–2111.

Vernick, Jon S., Zachary F. Meisel, Stephen P. Teret, John S. Milne, and Stephen W. Hargarten. 1999. " 'I Didn't Know the Gun Was Loaded': An Examination of Two Safety Devices That Can Reduce the Risk of Unintentional Firearm Injuries." *Journal of Public Health Policy* 20 (4): 427–40.

Violence Policy Center. 2002. "The False Hope of the 'Smart Gun.' " (*www.vpc.org* [March 12]).

Wachtel, Julius. 1998. "Sources of Crime Guns in Los Angeles, California." *Policing* 21 (2): 220–39.

Webster, Daniel W., Jon S. Vernick, and Lisa M. Hepburn. 2001. "Relationship between Licensing, Registration, and Other Gun Sales Laws and the Source State of Crime Guns." *Injury Prevention* 7 (3): 184–89.

———. 2002. "Effects of Maryland's Law Banning 'Saturday Night Special' Handguns on Homicide." *American Journal of Epidemiology* 155 (5): 406–12.

Wintemute, Garen J., Carrie A. Parham, James Jay Beaumont, Mona Wright, and Christiana Drake. 1999. "Mortality among Recent Purchasers of Handguns." *New England Journal of Medicine* 341 (21): 1583–89.

Wintemute, Garen J., Mona A. Wright, Christiana M. Drake, and James J. Beaumont. 2001. "Subsequent Criminal Activity among Violent Misdemeanants Who Seek to Purchase Handguns." *Journal of the American Medical Association* 265 (8): 1019–26.

Wolfgang, Marvin E. 1958. *Patterns in Criminal Homicide.* Philadelphia. University of Pennsylvania.

———. 1995. "A Tribute to a View I Have Opposed." *Journal of Criminal Law and Criminology 86* (1): 188–92.

Wright, James D., and Peter H. Rossi. 1994. *Armed and Considered Dangerous: A Survey of Felons and Their Firearms (Expanded Edition).* Aldine de Gruyter.

Zimring, Franklin E. 1968. "Is Gun Control Likely to Reduce Violent Killings?" *University of Chicago Law Review* 35: 21–37.

Zimring, Franklin E., and Gordon Hawkins. 1997. *Crime Is Not the Problem: Lethal Violence in America.* Oxford University Press.

PART I

Gun Prevalence

MARK DUGGAN

2 | *Guns and Suicide*

In 1998 more than 30,000 American citizens took their own lives, making suicide the ninth leading cause of death in that year. Furthermore, it represented the third leading cause of death for the 10–14, 15–19, and 20–24 age groups, and the fourth leading cause of death for those 25–44 years old. Although the suicide rate has been declining during the past decade, the high rates of suicide that still exist in the United States represent an important social problem.

Nearly 60 percent of suicides are committed with a gun. Previous research suggests that individuals who use a firearm when attempting to commit suicide are more likely to be "successful."[1] If this is true, then gun availability may affect the overall suicide rate rather than simply the fraction of suicides in which a gun is used. Similar instrumentality effects have been persuasively documented for assaults and robberies, though if suicidal tendencies are persistent or if suicide-prone individuals simply substitute other equally effective methods when a gun is not available, they may have much less of an impact on the suicide rate.[2]

I am grateful to John Mullahy, Karen Norberg, and seminar participants at the Brookings Conference on Gun Violence for many helpful comments.

1. Clarke and Lester (1989); Card (1974).
2. Zimring (1968); Zimring (1972); Cook (1987). Newton and Zimring (1969) point out that other methods of attempting to commit suicide (that is, jumping from heights or drowning) are just as likely to result in an individual's death.

41

An alternative channel through which gun availability may affect the suicide rate is by increasing the number of attempts. Certain individuals may find suicide with a gun more appealing than alternative methods—perhaps because of the speed, the high probability of success, or because it is a culturally accepted method—and thus only attempt suicide when a gun is available.[3]

Determining whether availability affects the suicide rate through either of these channels presents a difficult identification problem. In the United States, rates of suicide at the state and local level are significantly positively related to the fraction of individuals who own a gun. But this could plausibly be driven by self-selection—individuals who own a gun or live in an area with relatively many gun owners may be more inclined than observably similar individuals in other places to attempt to take their own lives. To investigate the importance of each of these three forces—the instrumentality effect, the impact of firearm availability on the number of suicide attempts, and the relationship between suicidal tendencies and gun ownership—I take three primary approaches in my empirical analyses.

I begin by examining the relationship between state-level gun and nongun suicide rates and the average rate of gun ownership. If suicide rates are higher in places with more gun ownership simply because firearms are more likely than alternative methods to result in an individual's death, then one would expect to observe a positive relationship between gun ownership and gun suicides and negative relationship of gun ownership with nongun suicides. My findings demonstrate, however, that nongun suicide rates are not significantly lower in places with more gun ownership while gun suicide rates are, suggesting that the fraction of the population that attempts to commit suicide is higher in places with relatively many gun owners.

An alternative explanation is that availability influences the suicide rate by increasing the number of suicide attempts rather than simply the success probabilities. Perhaps use of a firearm differentially appeals to some individuals who would not otherwise try to take their own lives. If this were true, one would not necessarily detect a negative relationship between gun availability and the nongun suicide rate even though access to firearms was causing an increase in the number of suicides. However, my findings suggest that gun owners in high-ownership states are more likely than gun owners in low-ownership states to take their own lives. This suggests that suicidal tendencies are significantly higher in states with the highest rates of gun ownership and thus that a significant part of the state-level relationship between gun owner-

---

3. Boor (1981).

ship and suicide is driven by a correlation between firearm ownership and this other factor.

These results do not rule out the possibility that gun availability increases the number of suicides but instead strongly suggests that a significant part of the relationship is driven by a correlation between gun ownership and suicidal tendencies. To further explore whether the availability of a firearm has a causal effect, I exploit differences between men and women in the probability of using a gun to commit suicide. While almost 62 percent of males who commit suicide use a firearm, only 38 percent of their female counterparts do. If gun availability causes an increase in the suicide rate, then one would, under plausible assumptions, expect to find that the male suicide rate is more responsive to the rate of gun ownership than is the female suicide rate. To test this hypothesis, I explore whether the ratio of the male suicide rate to the female suicide rate is associated with the average rate of gun ownership. My finding that this ratio is significantly positively related to gun ownership suggests that instrumentality effects may partially explain the relationship between gun ownership and suicide, though I cannot rule out the alternative hypothesis that suicidal tendencies among men are more strongly related to gun ownership than they are for women.

In the final empirical section, I exploit two decades of annual state data to examine whether changes in gun ownership are significantly related to the overall suicide rate. During this period, the household prevalence of gun ownership has declined substantially, and the overall suicide rate has fallen to its lowest level in more than three decades. My findings suggest that the decline in gun ownership is not driving the recent reduction in the suicide rate, as states with the largest declines in gun ownership do not see significantly larger reductions in their suicide rates. The power of this empirical test is limited, however, as state-level rates of gun ownership have been stable, and the actual ownership rate is measured with error.[4]

Taken together, the results presented in this chapter suggest that much of the positive relationship between firearm ownership and suicide is driven by selection—individuals with above average suicidal tendencies are more likely to own a gun and to live in areas with relatively many gun owners. But because female suicide rates are less responsive to the rate of gun ownership than are male suicide rates, it does seem that instrumentality effects also play some role. And finally, while suicide rates have been declining in the United States in recent years, the reduction in the fraction of households who own a gun does not seem to be the force that is driving this decline.

4. Azrael, Cook, and Miller (2001).

Background

In 1980 the U.S. suicide rate stood at 11.8 per 100,000, with approximately 57 percent of cases involving a firearm. As shown in figure 2-1, during the next six years the suicide rate steadily increased, reaching a peak of more than 12.9 per 100,000 in 1986. During this time, the fraction of suicides in which a gun was used also increased slightly and continued to do so during the next several years until it rose above 61 percent in 1990 (figure 2-2). By 1998 both the suicide rate and the fraction in which a gun was used were below their 1980 levels.[5]

The likelihood that an individual will commit suicide varies substantially by gender and age. In 1998 a man was more than four times as likely as a woman to take his own life, with gender-specific suicide rates equaling 18.6 and 4.4 per 100,000, respectively.[6] Table 2-1 demonstrates that suicide rates are significantly lower among teenagers than among nonelderly adults but are especially high for those over the age of 75. Interestingly, this effect is entirely driven by elderly male suicides, as women 75 and up are less likely than nonelderly adult women to take their own lives.

From 1980 to 1998, suicide rates declined substantially for women but less so for men, as is shown in table 2-2.[7] During this period, the fraction of women who committed suicide in the year fell by more than 20 percent, while the corresponding fraction for males remained virtually unchanged. The decline was especially large for women between the ages of 20 and 34 and those aged 55–74, whose suicide rates fell by approximately one-third. Male suicide rates in these age categories also declined but by a much smaller percentage. Had it not been for changes in the age structure of the U.S. population, overall male suicide rates would have declined, and the 20 percent drop for women would have been even larger.

Perhaps the most disturbing trend that is apparent from this table is the increase in the suicide rate among teenagers. Specifically, the suicide rate among boys 10–14 years old almost doubled from 1980 to 1998 while the rate for girls in this age group more than tripled. Rates for "older teenagers" between the ages of 15 and 19 increased slightly over this period. Thus even though teenagers are

---

5. Gender, age, and state-specific suicide data were not available at the time of this writing for 1999 but aggregate U.S. data are.

6. Suicide rates also vary substantially by race. For example, in 1998 the suicide rate among African Americans was 5.7 per 100,000 versus 12.4 for whites. The fraction of suicides in which a gun is used does not vary much across races, with the 1998 values standing at 56 percent and 58 percent, respectively, for these two groups.

7. See Stevenson and Wolfers (2000) for an empirical examination of changes in divorce laws, which they argue led to a substantial decline in the suicide rate among women.

Figure 2-1. *U.S. Suicide Rate, 1980–99*

Suicides per 100,000

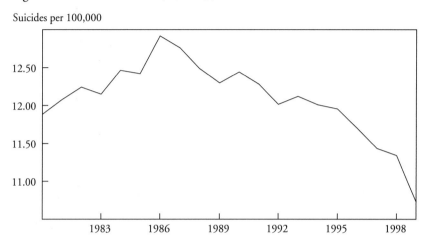

Figure 2-2. *Share of Suicides in Which Gun Was Used*

Percent

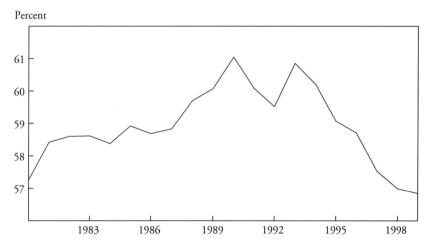

Table 2-1. *Suicide Rates, by Gender and Age, 1998*

Age	All	Males	Females	Male-female ratio
All ages	11.3	18.6	4.4	4.3
10–14	1.7	2.4	0.9	2.7
15–19	8.9	14.6	2.9	5.1
20–24	13.6	23.1	3.8	6.1
25–29	14.0	23.5	4.6	5.2
30–34	13.6	22.1	5.2	4.2
35–39	15.2	23.7	6.8	3.5
40–44	15.6	24.4	7.0	3.5
45–49	15.4	24.1	7.0	3.4
50–54	14.4	22.2	7.1	3.1
55–59	13.9	22.4	6.1	3.7
60–64	12.3	20.5	5.0	4.1
65–69	13.1	23.4	4.4	5.3
70–74	15.2	29.4	4.2	7.0
75+	20.2	45.5	5.2	8.8

Source: Suicide data are obtained from the National Center for Health Statistics (NCHS), and population data from the U.S. Bureau of the Census. Numbers in the table represent suicide rates per 100,000.

Table 2-2. *Changes in Male and Female Age-Specific Suicide Rates, 1980–98*

Age	Male suicide rate			Female suicide rate		
	1980	1998	Change (percent)	1980	1998	Change (percent)
All ages	18.7	18.6	−0	5.5	4.4	−20
10–14	1.2	2.4	+96	0.3	0.9	+204
15–19	13.8	14.6	+6	3.0	2.9	−4
20–24	26.8	23.1	−14	5.6	3.8	−32
25–29	26.8	23.5	−12	6.5	4.6	−30
30–34	23.2	22.1	−5	7.7	5.2	−32
35–39	23.0	23.7	+3	8.1	6.8	−16
40–44	22.0	24.4	+11	9.0	7.0	−22
45–49	21.9	24.1	+10	9.2	7.0	−24
50–54	23.9	22.2	−7	9.6	7.1	−26
55–59	25.0	22.4	−10	8.6	6.1	−29
60–64	24.0	20.5	−14	8.2	5.0	−39
65–69	28.1	23.4	−17	6.6	4.4	−34
70–74	33.5	29.4	−12	6.4	4.2	−35
75+	43.9	45.5	+4	5.5	5.2	−5

Source: Suicide data are obtained from the NCHS, and population data from the U.S. Bureau of the Census. Numbers in the table represent suicide rates per 100,000.

Table 2-3. *Cause of Death among 1998 Suicide Victims*
Percent

Method of suicide	Male	Female
Firearm	61.6	38.4
Drug, medicaments, or biologicals	6.4	26.1
Hanging, strangulation, or suffocation	19.2	16.8
Gases and vapors	5.4	6.7
All other	7.5	12.0
Total number of suicides in 1998	24,538	6,037

Source: Cause-of-death data are obtained from the NCHS website.

still much less likely than adults to commit suicide, the recent increases represent an important social problem.[8]

The way in which individuals kill themselves varies substantially by gender. Males who commit suicide are much more likely than their female counterparts to use a firearm, as is shown in table 2-3. Much of this difference is accounted for by a greater likelihood of suicide by drugs among women. As table 2-4 shows, the likelihood that male and female suicide victims do use a gun has remained fairly stable over the sample period, with the male fraction declining from 63.0 percent to 61.6 percent and the female share falling from 38.6 percent to 38.4 percent.

The relationship between age and method of suicide is somewhat similar for males and females. For both groups, middle-aged individuals who commit suicide are the least likely to use a gun, with teenagers being somewhat more likely than the average. Elderly males who commit suicide are much more likely to use a firearm than are the nonelderly, while no corresponding relationship is observed for elderly women relative to middle-aged women.

While the fraction of all suicides in which a gun is used has remained fairly stable from 1980 to 1998, there has been substantial variation within age groups during this same time period. This is especially true for males, as can be seen in table 2-4. Males under the age of 55 are now much less likely to use a firearm when committing suicide than they were in 1980, while males 55 and older are significantly more likely to use a firearm when taking their own lives. Interestingly, the fraction of older women who use a gun to commit suicide has also increased during the period of interest.

8. See Cutler, Glaeser, and Norberg (2001) for an explanation of the increase in the teenage suicide rate in the post–World War II period.

Table 2-4. *Fraction of Suicides by Firearm, by Gender and Age, 1980 and 1998*

Percent

	Males		Females	
Age	1980	1998	1980	1998
All ages	63.0	61.6	38.6	38.4
10–14	53.1	50.0	69.2	43.4
15–19	64.7	64.9	56.0	50.4
20–24	63.8	61.4	50.7	46.5
25–29	58.6	56.2	43.6	45.1
30–34	57.4	52.4	41.2	38.7
35–39	61.3	52.0	41.5	38.4
40–44	60.9	52.7	35.4	33.9
45–49	61.4	54.9	35.8	38.9
50–54	62.9	59.2	36.5	31.6
55–59	63.6	67.5	35.7	39.3
60–64	68.0	72.8	36.2	41.6
65–69	71.0	74.5	30.9	37.6
70–74	71.1	79.0	27.6	41.1
75+	66.2	78.9	16.2	31.2

Note: Figures represent the fraction of suicides in which a firearm is used (ICD9 codes 9550–9554).

Theoretical Framework

Isolating the causal effect of gun ownership presents a difficult identification problem. Individuals who choose to purchase a gun are likely to differ in unobservable ways from those who do not. A finding that suicide rates are significantly related to gun ownership may reflect a causal effect of gun ownership on suicide or instead simply a different propensity to commit suicide among gun owners. Suppose that the probability individual i commits suicide depends on his/her observable characteristics, gun ownership, and his/her unobserved tendency to commit suicide as specified in the following equation.

(1) $Prob(Suicide_i) = \alpha + \beta * X_i + \gamma * Gun_i + \lambda * Propensity_i + \varepsilon_i$

Here X_i represents a set of observable control variables, Gun_i equals one if the individual owns a gun and zero otherwise, and $Propensity_i$ is the unobserved tendency to commit suicide. The parameter of interest is γ, which represents the induced change in the probability of committing suicide after the acquisition of a firearm. Suppose that the propensity to commit suicide is correlated with gun ownership as follows:

(2) $$Propensity = \mu + \sigma \, p \, Gun_i + \zeta_i$$

If $Propensity_i$ is unobserved by the econometrician, then the coefficient estimate in equation 1 above will be biased if σ is nonzero. Combining equations 1 and 2 yields:

(3) $$Prob(Suicide_i) = (\alpha + \lambda\mu) + \beta * X_i + (\gamma + \lambda\sigma) * Gun_i + (\varepsilon_i + \lambda\zeta_i)$$

While one would like to know the value of the parameter γ, instead the coefficient estimate on Gun_i in equation 3 confounds the correlation between suicidal tendencies and gun ownership with the effect of gun ownership on suicide.

Absent an instrumental variable that provides plausibly exogenous variation in gun ownership, one can try to gauge the relative importance of causality (γ) versus selection ($\lambda\sigma$) by determining the empirical regularities that should be observed in the data in the limiting case with $\sigma = 0$. Suppose that the probability that an attempted suicide results in death is equal to γ_g if a gun is used and γ_o if an alternative method is chosen. Overall suicide rates will differ if γ_g is not equal to γ_o and if those who unsuccessfully attempt to commit suicide in the current period do not necessarily try again in the subsequent period (for example, suicidal impulses are, to some extent, temporary). In this limiting case, if $\gamma_g > \gamma_o$ and if owners are more likely to use a gun when trying to commit suicide, then one should observe higher rates of gun suicide and lower rates of nongun suicide in areas with more gun ownership.

Consider the case in which each individual will, with identical probability η, attempt to commit suicide in the current period. Aggregating across individuals, rates of gun and nongun suicide will be related to the fraction of individuals who own a gun as follows:

(4) $$GunSuicRate_j = \eta * \gamma_g * Gun_j$$

(5) $$NonGunSuicRate_j = \eta * \gamma_o * (1 - Gun_j)$$

If γ_g equals γ_o then suicide rates will be unrelated to gun ownership, and only the method will vary across geographic areas. If instead $\gamma_g > \gamma_o$ then overall suicide rates will be higher in places with more gun ownership:

(6) $$SuicideRate_j = \eta * ((\gamma_g - \gamma_o) * Gun_j + \gamma_o)$$

This setup assumes that individuals who are unsuccessful in a suicide attempt have the same probability η of attempting suicide in the next period as do those who did not attempt to commit suicide in the current period. Even if one relaxes this assumption, the positive relationship between gun ownership and suicide rates would remain as long as η was less than 1 for those who failed in a suicide attempt in the previous period.

The implication of this simple model is that, if the propensity to commit suicide is unrelated to gun ownership, rates of nongun suicide would be lower in places with more gun ownership, but overall suicide rates would be higher. The magnitude of the effect would be positively related to the difference in the two probabilities γ_g and γ_o and declining as the persistence of suicidal tendencies increased. If one observed that gun suicide rates were significantly greater in areas with more gun ownership, but that this was not partially offset by a lower rate of nongun suicides, then this would suggest that unobservable factors play an important role, though an alternative explanation would be that gun availability increases the number of suicide attempts.

A final way to assess the role that firearms play in determining the suicide rate is to examine the relationship between changes in the suicide rate and changes in gun ownership. Suppose that the propensity to commit suicide η varies across individuals but that the distribution of η does not vary within geographic areas over time. In this case, the overall suicide rate would increase following a rise in gun ownership if firearms increase the probability of suicide for the marginal gun owner. The elasticity of the suicide rate with respect to gun ownership would depend on the difference $(\gamma_g - \gamma_o)$, the suicide propensity for the marginal gun owner, and the persistence of suicidal motives. However, if the change in gun ownership is correlated with changes in suicidal tendencies then one must probe more carefully to determine whether the relationship is driven by gun ownership or this other factor.

To summarize, the theoretical framework presented here underscores the difficulty associated with estimating the effect of gun ownership on the suicide rate, even if one did have perfect data. Cross-sectional approaches can differentiate between different methods of suicide to test for a relationship between gun ownership and average suicidal tendencies. But this approach is not fully satisfactory because it does not pin down the relative importance of gun ownership and unobservable factors. Empirical analyses that exploit within-area variation in gun ownership must confront the possibility that the observed changes in gun ownership are driven by factors that are simultaneously affecting the suicide rate.

Thus while neither approach is ideal for identifying the effect of gun ownership on suicide, each one can shed some light on this issue. In the empirical work at the end of this chapter, I use both approaches to investigate whether gun ownership partially explains the cross-area and within-area variation in the suicide rate.

Previous Literature

A substantial body of previous work has examined the relationship between gun availability and suicide, with some arguing that firearms increase the suicide rate through an "instrumentality effect" while others assert that individuals simply use alternative methods when a gun is not available.[9] It seems plausible that, for many of the 18,000 individuals who commit suicide with a gun during a typical year in the United States, the alternative methods with similarly high "success" rates (that is, hanging or leaping) are less appealing. If this is true and if suicidal impulses are to some extent temporary, then gun availability could cause an increase in the suicide rate.

Studies of international data have shown, however, that gun availability is by no means the only determinant of the suicide rate. While the United States has much higher rates of gun ownership than most other industrialized countries, its suicide rate is much lower.[10] For example, during the 1980s, the U.S. suicide rate was approximately 12 per 100,000, while in Japan, West Germany, and France the corresponding rates stood at 20, 20, and 22, respectively.

One widely cited study finds that individuals who commit suicide in their own homes were more likely to own a gun than were observably similar individuals in the same neighborhood.[11] The authors conclude that gun ownership may increase the risk of suicide but are careful to point out that the victims may differ in unobservable ways from their matching controls with respect to their suicide propensities. While suggestive, it is therefore difficult to assign a causal interpretation to this set of findings.

Another prominent article compared suicide rates in Seattle and Vancouver, arguing that these two metropolitan areas in the Pacific Northwest are similar on most dimensions but are, as a result of government legislation, quite different in rates of gun ownership.[12] The authors' findings demonstrate that suicide victims in Seattle are much more likely to use a firearm, but that overall suicide rates are not significantly different between the two areas, suggesting that individuals hoping to take their own lives will substitute to other methods if a

---

9. Brent and others (1988); Rich and others (1990).
10. Kates (1990).
11. Kellerman and others (1992).
12. Sloan and others (1990).

gun is not available. The results do suggest that suicide rates for younger individuals (15–24 years old) are significantly greater in Seattle, though this is offset by a significantly lower suicide rate among older residents of Seattle. Of course no strong conclusions can be drawn from a cross-sectional study that compares just two local areas.

A related body of research examines the effect of changes in gun control legislation. One study compares the suicide rate in Washington, D.C., before and after the passage of a law that banned the purchase, sale, transfer, or possession of handguns by civilians.[13] The authors show that gun suicides occurring in the D.C. metro area declined by 23 percent following the passage of the law, and that nongun suicides declined by a statistically insignificant 9 percent. One result that is potentially problematic for this analysis is that gun suicides occurring in nearby Maryland and Virginia suburbs rose by a statistically significant 12 percent, suggesting that many of the suicides that were prevented in Washington, D.C., may have occurred in a neighboring area. Additionally, the finding that nongun suicides also declined suggests that the share of the D.C. population with suicidal tendencies was declining.

In a recent paper, Jens Ludwig and Philip Cook investigate the effect of the Brady Handgun Violence Prevention Act on state-level suicide rates.[14] This legislation required that federal firearm dealers conduct a background check and observe a five-day waiting period for individuals 21 and older who purchased a gun. The authors find that this legislation did not reduce the overall suicide rate, though it did appear to cause a reduction in the gun suicide rate among those 55 and older.[15] This finding suggests that suicidal impulses are, to some extent, temporary, as individuals who did not own a gun but tried to purchase one were apparently less likely to take their own lives once the five-day period had elapsed. This policy experiment presumably does not allow one to estimate the effect on suicide rates for those who already owned a gun but provides convincing evidence that restricting gun availability may reduce the suicide rate among older individuals. The fact that suicide victims in this age group are much more likely to use a gun (partially because a larger proportion are males) suggests that this "heterogeneous treatment effect" is plausible.

---

13. Loftin and others (1991). See McDowall, Loftin, and Wiersema (1996) for a follow-up analysis that uses similarly sized cities (rather than suburbs) such as Baltimore as a control group when estimating the effect of the law change. The potential for a "spillover effect" in this case is much lower, as most of these cities are located further away from Washington, D.C., than the suburbs used in the 1991 paper.

14. Ludwig and Cook (2000).

15. The authors find a partially offsetting positive effect on nongun suicides, so the estimated effect for the total suicide rate is negative but not statistically significant.

One final study that examines the relationship between gun ownership and suicide compares mortality among the 238,292 individuals who purchased a handgun in the state of California in 1991 with the rate for other observably similar individuals in the state.[16] The authors find that, in the week following the purchase, individuals were fifty-seven times more likely than other observably similar California residents to take their own lives, and that this group was several times more likely to commit suicide in the year following purchase. Interestingly, the study points out that most handgun purchasers in California were young, with just 3.5 percent of them over the age of 65. Given the result for the previous study, which suggested that older individuals were more affected by laws that influenced the ease of purchase, this age distribution is surprising. Additionally, one cannot know from this set of results whether the suicide rates among handgun purchasers would have been any different if guns were less available.

Taken together, the literature has demonstrated that gun owners in the United States are more likely to take their own lives but has reached different conclusions about whether the availability of a gun is partially responsible for this finding. Certain policies that have restricted access to firearms appear to lead to fewer suicides for particular groups but have relatively little effect on the overall suicide rate. The empirical analysis presented in the next section takes a different approach from the studies described here to gauge the relative importance of gun availability and suicide propensity in explaining the significantly greater suicide rate among gun owners.

Correlation or Causation?

The difficulties associated with investigating the causal effect of gun ownership on the suicide rate would be significant even if one did have complete data. Adding to the difficulty is that available data are far from perfect. The suicide data are actually quite good, as one can, for example, know from available data sets that 1,036 Illinois residents committed suicide in 1998, and that in 486 of these cases the decedent used a firearm. Unfortunately, one cannot obtain similarly reliable data on rates of gun ownership, so instead researchers have typically used proxy variables to estimate average rates of gun ownership by geographic area.[17]

---

16. Wintemute and others (1999).

17. Survey data do exist, though the sample sizes for most states are usually small, and the surveys are typically not designed to be representative at the state, county, or MSA level. For example, the General Social Survey polls approximately 1,500 individuals in a year about gun ownership, and thus the sample size for the average state is just 30. Furthermore, the survey is not designed to be representative at the state level, and concerns have been raised that some individuals do not tell the truth. The limitations of the survey data have prompted researchers to utilize proxy measures.

Table 2-5. *Gun Magazine Sales and Percentage of Suicides with Gun as Proxies for Gun Ownership*

	Log (FS/S)		Log (GSS ownership)			
	(1)	(2)	(3)	(4)	(5)	(6)
Log (G&A)	.632*	.101*	.975*		.354*	
	(.127)	(.018)	(.188)		(.114)	
Log (FS/S)				1.299*		.472*
				(.155)		(.239)
R²	.337	.959	.384	.748	.712	.708
Number of observations	51	969	45	45	488	488

Note: The dependent variable in the first two specifications is equal to the log of the fraction of suicides that are committed with a gun, while the variable in specifications 3 through 6 is equal to the log of the fraction of GSS respondents who own a gun. Survey data from 1980–98 are used, with average state data over this period used in (3) and (4) and annual state data in (5) and (6). Log (G&A) is equal to the log of the magazine sales rate. Regressions are weighted by state population in (1) and (2) and by number of survey respondents in (5) and (6). Robust standard errors are in parentheses.
*Significant at 1 percent level.

Measuring Gun Ownership

Two proxies have recently been proposed to estimate this elusive variable. One study uses sales rates for *Guns & Ammo,* one of the nation's largest gun magazines and the largest one that focuses primarily on handguns, to estimate annual rates of gun ownership at the state and the county level. Results from another recent paper suggest that the fraction of suicides in which a gun is used more reliably estimates differences across areas and the variation in geographic areas over time in the rate of gun ownership.[18]

The results presented in the first column of table 2-5 demonstrate that there is a significantly positive relationship between these two variables. The variable Log(G&A) in this first specification is equal to the log of each state's average magazine sales rate from 1980–98, while the variable Log(FS/S) is equal to the log of the fraction of suicides during that time period in which a gun is used. The coefficient estimate of 0.632 is precisely estimated and reveals that the variables are quite closely related. The second column demonstrates that this significantly positive relationship also holds up when one uses nineteen years of state-level data (1980–98) and state and year fixed effects. It therefore appears that these variables are capturing similar variation.

The next four columns compare the "fit" of each of these variables to survey data from the General Social Survey. These regressions utilize both aver-

18. Duggan (2001); Azrael, Cook, and Miller (2001).

age state- and annual state-level data and show that one cannot reject the hypothesis that there exists a one-for-one relationship between the estimated rate of gun ownership from the GSS and the gun magazine sales rate.[19] The observed relationship is slightly more than one-for-one using the fraction of suicides with a gun as a proxy.

Using annual state data in the last two specifications, both proxy variables are significantly related to the rate of gun ownership after controlling for state and year fixed effects. While the coefficient estimate for the Log(*FS/S*) variable is closer to one, the precision of the corresponding estimate for Log(*G&A*) is greater. Thus it appears that both variables are good proxies for the average rate of gun ownership.

In most of the empirical work that follows, however, I utilize the magazine sales rate as my estimate of the rate of gun ownership in a state. The reason for this is that, even if the gun suicide fraction is an excellent proxy for gun ownership, random fluctuations in it will lead to a mechanical relationship between the outcome variables of interest and the estimated rate of gun ownership.[20] Of course the Log(*G&A*) variable is by no means immune to measurement error problems. The sales rate of the gun magazine will depend not only on the rate of gun ownership but also on the propensity of both gun owners and those who do not own a gun to purchase this magazine as specified in the following equation:

$$(7) \qquad \frac{Magazines_j}{Population_j} = \mu_{gun,j} * \theta_j + \mu_{non,j} * \left(1 - \theta_j\right)$$

in which μ_{gun} and μ_{non} represent the probability that individuals in each group will purchase the magazine and θ_j equals the share of people who own a gun. Even if only gun owners buy the magazine ($\mu_{non} = 0$), variation in this proxy variable could be driven either by variation in gun ownership or in the propensity of gun owners to buy it. But the same is also true for the gun suicide fraction, which will depend on the rate of gun ownership and on the likelihood that the average gun owner commits suicide.[21]

Unlike variation in the gun suicide fraction, however, random variation in the magazine sales rate should not be mechanically related to the outcome variable

19. It is worth pointing out that the state-level data are not intended to be representative of each state's population. The fact that Cook, Moore, and Braga (2002) obtain similar results when using regional data suggests that the bias introduced is not too great, but it should be kept in mind when interpreting the results.

20. I discuss this issue in detail in the appendix to this chapter.

21. This measure will also depend on the probability that those who do not own a gun commit suicide and the probability that individuals in each group use a firearm when committing suicide.

of interest and is much more likely to be unrelated to the measurement error in the suicide rate. In most of the empirical analyses in the following paragraphs, I therefore use the magazine sales rate as the proxy for gun ownership.

The Cross-Sectional Relationship between Gun Ownership and Suicide

The number of suicides depends on the number of suicide attempts and on the average probability that each one of those attempts will result in the individual's death. Thus there are two channels through which gun availability could affect the suicide rate. First, if some individuals who try to take their lives choose a gun when it is available but an alternative method when no gun is present, then access to firearms could increase the suicide rate if the "success probability" for guns is relatively high. This mechanism has been referred to as the instrumentality effect in the literature that examines the relationship between gun ownership and crime.[22] The potential importance of instrumentality effects for suicide will be a decreasing function of the persistence of suicidal tendencies—if a person who survives a suicide attempt today will simply try again tomorrow then the steady state rate of suicides would be relatively unaffected by access to firearms.

The second channel through which gun prevalence could affect the suicide rate is by causing some individuals who would not otherwise have tried to take their own lives to do so. Myron Boor points out that the accepted method of suicide varies greatly across cultures and argues that the availability of this method influences the probability that an individual will attempt to take his or her own life.[23] Thus by influencing the success rate or the number of suicide attempts, gun ownership could plausibly be related to the overall suicide rate.

I begin the empirical analysis by exploring the relationship between overall suicide rates and rates of gun ownership at the state level.[24] The results summarized in table 2-6 utilize both of the proxy measures as explanatory variables in specifications of the following type:

$$(8) \qquad \text{Log}(SuicideRate_{ij}) = \alpha + \beta * \text{Log}(GunOwnRate_j) + \varepsilon_{ij}$$

22. Cook, Moore, and Braga (2002).
23. Boor (1981).
24. It would be preferable to estimate this set of regressions at the individual level. One could then differentiate between gun owners who kept their guns locked versus those that did not, and between nonowners who had friends or neighbors with access to a gun and those that did not. Absent this type of detailed data, I am unable to do this.

Table 2-6. *The Relationship between Gun Ownership and Suicide*

Age	Gun ownership measure	
	Log (G&A)	Log (FS/S)
All ages	.747	.690
	(.101)	(.104)
10–19	1.143	1.036
	(.132)	(.174)
20–29	.842	.688
	(.096)	(.124)
30–39	.755	.622
	(.084)	(.107)
40–49	.731	.732
	(.141)	(.125)
50–59	.591	.619
	(.151)	(.131)
60–69	.651	.730
	(.136)	(.110)
70–79	.715	.818
	(.185)	(.131)

Note: Dependent variable in the first row is equal to the log of the state suicide rate in 1996, the most recent year for which individual-level NCHS mortality data are available. Dependent variables in each subsequent row are equal to the age-specific suicide rate in the state. The first column of coefficient estimates utilize log (G&A) as the explanatory variable, while those in the second column use log (FS/S). Cell entries correspond to the estimates for each of these variables in specifications analogous to (13). Regressions are weighted by state population in the first row and by the number of state residents in the age group in the subsequent rows. Robust standard errors are in parentheses.

with j indexing states and i indexing age groups within each state.[25] The coefficients presented in the first row suggest that suicide rates are substantially higher in places with more gun ownership. The estimate of 0.747 on the Log(G&A) coefficient is virtually identical to the corresponding estimate of 0.690 for the Log(FS/S). The estimates presented in the next several rows utilize age-specific suicide rates as the dependent variables.[26] In virtually every case, the coefficient estimates are quite similar in magnitude. The estimates for the Log(G&A)

25. These regressions utilize data from 1996, the most recent year in which individual-level death data are available from the National Center for Health Statistics.

26. I am unable to get age-specific magazine sales rates and must therefore use the overall state sales rate. If, as seems likely, the sales rate does vary systematically by age group, then the coefficient estimates will provide a biased estimate of the relationship between gun availability for a particular age group and the suicide rate. The estimates obtained from using both state-level aggregate and age-specific Log(FS/S) measures are quite similar, suggesting that the absence of state-level, age-specific sales rates is not too problematic.

Table 2-7. *The Relationship between Gun Ownership and Gun versus Nongun Suicides*

Age	Log (suicide rate)	Log (gun suicide rate)	Log (nonsuicide rate)
All ages	.747	1.439	.044
	(.101)	(.207)	(.105)
10–19	1.143	1.598	.673
	(.132)	(.234)	(.174)
20–29	.842	1.471	.182
	(.096)	(.169)	(.119)
30–39	.755	1.595	.122
	(.084)	(.174)	(.133)
40–49	.731	1.410	.151
	(.141)	(.242)	(.144)
50–59	.591	1.294	−.197
	(.151)	(.244)	(.128)
60–69	.651	1.231	−.326
	(.136)	(.253)	(.191)
70–79	.715	1.516	−.593
	(.185)	(.365)	(.205)

Note: Dependent variables in each column are the state-level suicide rate, gun suicide rate, and nongun suicide rate in 1996. The first row is the overall state rate, while the subsequent rows use age-specific suicide rates. The entries in each cell represent the coefficient estimate for the log (*G&A*) variable in specifications analogous to (13). Regressions are weighted by state population in the first row and by the number of state residents in the age group in the subsequent rows. Robust standard errors are in parentheses.

coefficients are generally higher than the corresponding ones for Log(*FS/S*) for younger age groups, while the reverse is true for the older age groups. Perhaps surprisingly, both measures suggest that the relationship between rates of gun ownership and the frequency of suicide is strongest for teenagers.

The next set of regressions presented in table 2-7 divides suicides into those committed with a gun and ones in which an alternative method was used. If gun ownership was not related to suicidal tendencies and affected suicides only through the instrumentality channel described above, then one would expect to observe a positive relationship between gun ownership and gun suicides and a negative one between gun ownership and the nongun suicide rate. The first row of results suggests that instrumentality alone cannot explain the positive relationship between the suicide rate and gun ownership, as nongun suicide rates are not significantly lower in places with more firearms. In fact, for younger individuals the nongun suicide rate is found to be somewhat higher in states with greater gun ownership. One possible, but by no means the only, explanation for this relationship is that some teenagers may choose to imitate their peers. Thus gun availability could directly affect the suicide propensity of individuals with access to a gun and indirectly affect the probability for other individuals with no such access through a "contagion effect." The results for the three oldest age groups are consistent with the hypothesis that gun availability may lead to fewer nongun suicides, but overall suicide rates are not more strongly related to gun ownership for this group than for the younger age categories.

This first set of results suggests that the fraction of individuals with suicidal tendencies is larger in states with more gun ownership, as the relationship between the overall suicide rate and gun availability cannot simply be explained by substitution from nongun to gun suicide attempts. The fact that all of the coefficient estimates in the Log(GunSuicideRate) specifications are greater than one provides further support for this hypothesis. The intuition for this is straightforward and can be seen from the following equation that describes the average number of gun suicides within state j:

$$(9) \qquad \frac{GunSuicides_j}{Population_j} = \left(\frac{Gun\ Owners_j}{Population_j} \right) * \omega_j * P_{j,gun}$$

with ω_j equaling the fraction of the state's gun owners who try to commit suicide with a gun and $P_{j,gun}$ set equal to the probability that the attempt results in the individual's death. If ω_j and $P_{j,gun}$ were common across states, then one would expect to find a coefficient closer to 1.00 in the gun suicide regressions in table 2-7.[27] The fact that it is substantially greater suggests that ω_j is higher in places with more gun ownership. Thus both those who own and those who do not own a gun in states with high rates of firearm ownership appear to be more likely than their counterparts in low-ownership states to take their own lives.

While this set of results suggests that part of the relationship between gun ownership and the suicide rate is induced by cross-state differences in the propensity to commit suicide, it does not demonstrate whether instrumentality also partially explains it. One way to probe the likely importance of this effect is to exploit differences between men and women in the probability of using a gun in a suicide attempt. Women are significantly less likely than men to commit suicide and to use a gun when committing suicide. This latter difference is partially driven by the higher rates of gun ownership among men, though many

27. The coefficient estimate of 1.439 in the middle column of table 2-7 indicates that a 10 percent increase in the rate of gun ownership is associated with approximately a 14.4 percent increase in the gun suicide rate. It therefore appears that gun owners in a state with a 22 percent rate of ownership would be 4 percent (equals (1.144/.22)/(1.000/.20)) more likely than their counterparts in a state with a 20 percent rate to commit suicide.

women who do not themselves own a gun may still have access to one if other individuals in their households do.

The number of suicides that occur is the product of the number of attempts and the average success probability. This average probability can be expressed as depending on the fraction of households with one or more guns (Gun_j), the likelihood that a person with access to a gun uses it when trying to commit suicide (δ), the success probability for guns (P_g), and the success probability for the alternative method (P_d) as follows:

$$(10) \qquad P = Gun_j * \left(\delta P_g + \left(1 - \delta\right)P_d\right) + \left(1 - Gun_j\right) * P_d$$

If $P_g > P_d$ and if $\delta_f < \delta_m$ (women with access to a gun are less likely to use it if they attempt suicide), then this average success probability should increase more rapidly for men than for women in areas with relatively many guns.[28]

Using this framework, one can now test empirically for instrumentality effects by examining whether the ratio of the male to the female suicide rate is systematically related to the rate of gun ownership. If suicidal impulses are persistent (that is, a person who attempts today but does not succeed will continue trying) and if the number of females with suicidal tendencies is proportional to the number of males with suicidal tendencies, then one should detect no systematic relationship between the rate of gun ownership and the male/female suicide ratio.

The set of regressions summarized in table 2-8 suggests that there is a positive relationship between the rate of gun ownership and the male/female suicide ratio. The coefficient estimates in the first two columns of the first row reveal that suicide rates among males are more strongly related to the rate of gun ownership than are suicide rates among females. Specifically, a 10 percent increase in gun ownership is associated with a 7.9 percent increase in the male suicide rate but only a 5.2 percent increase in the female suicide rate.[29] This difference is statistically significant, as the coefficient estimate of 0.272 in the third specification shows. In every age category, the male suicide rate is more strongly related to the rate of gun ownership than is the female suicide rate, with an especially

28. In other words, if attempts with a gun are more likely to result in the individual's death, then $d(PM/PF)/dGun > 0$. This assumes that the number of attempts is not affected by the availability of a gun, that women are less likely to use a gun when committing suicide (either because they are less inclined to use a gun when one is available or because they have less access to firearms), and that the ratio of male to female suicide attempts in a state is not systematically related to the state-level rate of gun ownership.

29. See Lester and Murrell (1980) for a study that examines whether the effect of gun control laws on suicide rates differs by gender.

Table 2-8. *The Relationship between Gun Ownership and Gender-Specific Suicide Rates*

Age	Log (male suicide rate)	Log (female suicide rate)	Log (male-female ratio)
All ages	.785	.515	.272
	(.098)	(.131)	(.077)
10–19	1.206	.910	.300
	(.160)	(.152)	(.240)
20–29	.905	.459	.439
	(.106)	(.173)	(.182)
30–39	.759	.660	.100
	(.085)	(.111)	(.081)
40–49	.737	.562	.188
	(.131)	(.210)	(.142)
50–59	.583	.508	.082
	(.133)	(.248)	(.161)
60–69	.647	.480	.170
	(.168)	(.188)	(.237)
70–79	.822	−.143	.980
	(.178)	(.214)	(.138)

Note: Dependent variables in each column are the male suicide rate, the female suicide rate, and the ratio of the male to the female suicide rate in 1996. The first row contains data for all state residents, while the subsequent rows use age-specific suicide rates. The entries in each cell represent the coefficient estimate for the log (G&A) variable in specifications analogous to (13). Regressions in the first row are weighted by the state's gender-specific population in the first two columns and by the total population in the third column. The corresponding age-specific weights are used in the subsequent rows. Robust standard errors are in parentheses.

large difference for the youngest and oldest age groups. Thus while one can tell alternative stories to explain this pattern, this set of results is consistent with the hypothesis that instrumentality effects partially explain the high rates of suicide in states with relatively many gun owners.[30]

Taken together, the results presented in this section suggest that much of the observed relationship between rates of suicide and gun ownership at the state level is driven by differences in suicidal tendencies that are themselves correlated with gun ownership. The difference in the relationship for men and women suggests that instrumentality may also play a role, though one cannot rule out other plausible stories that could also explain this relationship. The empirical analysis

30. For example, if the ratio of men to women with suicidal tendencies is higher in places with more gun ownership, then one would, all else equal, observe a positive relationship even in the absence of an instrumentality effect.

in the next section investigates whether within state changes in gun ownership during the past two decades partially explain changes in the suicide rate that have occurred during this time period.

Do Changes in Gun Ownership Partially Explain Changes in the Suicide Rate?

During the past decade, the U.S. suicide rate has fallen substantially, from a peak of 12.9 per 100,000 in 1986 to just 11.3 per 100,000 in 1998. This decline has coincided with a downward trend in the rate of gun ownership. In this section, I investigate whether these two series are related by estimating specifications of the following type:

$$(11) \quad \Delta SuicideRate_{jt} = \alpha_1 + \beta_1 * \Delta GunOwnershipRate_{jt} + \mu_{1t} + \rho_{1j} + \varepsilon_{1jt}$$

$$(12) \quad \begin{aligned} \Delta GunSuicideRate_{jt} &= \alpha_2 + \beta_2 * \Delta GunOwnershipRate_{jt} \\ &+ \mu_{2t} + \rho_{2j} + \varepsilon_{2jt} \end{aligned}$$

$$(13) \quad \begin{aligned} \Delta NonGunSuicideRate_{jt} &= \alpha_3 + \beta_3 * \Delta GunOwnershipRate_{jt} \\ &+ \mu_{3t} + \rho_{3j} + \varepsilon_{3jt} \end{aligned}$$

There are two important limitations to this approach. First, even if one finds a significant estimate for the parameter β_1, it is possible that the very factors leading some individuals to purchase firearms are also causing them to commit more suicides, and thus β_1, β_2, and β_3 would not represent causal effects of gun ownership on suicide. Second, even if firearms do lead to more suicides than would otherwise occur, if state-level rates of gun ownership are quite stable, then one may fail to detect a relationship because the variation in measured gun ownership would be driven primarily by measurement error. While the former effect would lead to an upward bias in the estimate for β_1, the latter one would be likely to induce a downward one.[31]

Despite these limitations, this approach can provide some insight into the role (if any) that gun availability plays in determining the suicide rate by answering the question—did suicide decline more in the places with the largest

---

31. This specification only examines the relationship between current changes in gun ownership and current changes in the suicide rate. I estimated a similar set of specifications that included once and/or twice lagged changes in gun ownership. The findings from those regressions are similar to the ones reported here—past changes in gun ownership are not significantly related to current changes in the gun, nongun, or overall suicide rate.

Table 2-9. *The Relationship between Changes in Gun Ownership and Suicide: Proxy #1*

	Δ Log (suicide)		Δ Log (gun suicide)		Δ Log (nongun suicide)	
	(1)	(2)	(3)	(4)	(5)	(6)
Δ Log (G&A)	.033	.004	.072	.046	.007	−.029
	(.048)	(.051)	(.060)	(.064)	(.077)	(.081)
Year effects?	Yes	Yes	Yes	Yes	Yes	Yes
County effects?	No	Yes	No	Yes	No	Yes
Number of observations	918	918	918	918	918	918
R²	.063	.078	.076	.085	.038	.054

Note: The dependent variable in each specification is equal to the change in the log of the state-level suicide rate (total in 1 and 2, gun in 3 and 4, all other in 5 and 6). The explanatory variable is equal to the change in the log of the gun magazine sales rate. The number of observations is 918 in all regressions. Each specification includes year fixed effects, and (2), (4), and (6) have state-specific effects. Specifications are weighted by the state's population share in each year, and robust standard errors are in parentheses.

declines in gun ownership? The set of results presented in table 2-9 summarizes specifications similar to (11), (12), and (13) above and reveals that changes in the suicide rate are not significantly related to changes in estimated gun ownership. The estimate of .033 for β_1 in the first column suggests that a 10 percent increase in gun ownership is, on average, associated with just a 0.3 percent rise in the suicide rate. This variable is not precisely estimated, though, so one cannot reject the hypothesis that there is no relationship between changes in gun ownership and the suicide rate.[32] The estimates for β_2 in the third and fourth specifications are somewhat larger than the corresponding ones for β_3 in the last two columns of this table, though the difference is not statistically significant. This is consistent with the findings just presented, which suggested that increases in gun ownership are associated with increases in the fraction of suicides in which a gun is used.[33]

It is worth comparing these estimates to the corresponding ones obtained using the alternative proxy variable Log(*FS/S*). As was just mentioned, random

32. The magnitude of the estimate for β_1 is just one-seventh as large as the estimate for the analogous parameter in the homicide rate specification found in Duggan (2001). Given that the table 2-5 estimates suggest that a 10 percent increase in magazine sales is associated with just a 3.5 percent rise in gun ownership, a more accurate point estimate of the relationship between gun ownership and the suicide rate is closer to 0.1 (=.033/.35).

33. The analogous state fixed effect (rather than first difference) regressions—either with or without state-specific time trends—also indicate that the state-level gun suicide rate is more strongly related to the rate of gun ownership than is the nongun suicide rate.

Table 2-10. *The Relationship between Changes in Gun Ownership and Suicide: Proxy #2*

	Δ Log (suicide)		Δ Log (gun suicide)		Δ Log (nongun suicide)	
	(1)	*(2)*	*(3)*	*(4)*	*(5)*	*(6)*
Δ Log(*FS/S*)	−.128	−.125	.872	.875	−1.218	−1.215
	(.038)	(.039)	(.038)	(.039)	(.046)	(.047)
Year effects?	Yes	Yes	Yes	Yes	Yes	Yes
County effects?	No	Yes	No	Yes	No	Yes
Number of observations	918	918	918	918	918	918
R²	.075	.089	.415	.423	.463	.472

Note: The dependent variable in each specification is equal to the change in the log of the state-level suicide rate (total in 1 and 2, gun in 3 and 4, all other in 5 and 6). The explanatory variable is equal to the change in the log of the gun suicide fraction. The number of observations is 918 in all regressions. Each specification includes year fixed effects, and (2), (4), and (6) have state-specific effects. Specifications are weighted by the state's population share in each year, and robust standard errors are in parentheses.

fluctuations in the number of gun and nongun suicides will lead to a mechanical relationship between estimated gun ownership and each of the three suicide rates. This problem is likely to be especially severe if rates of gun ownership are quite stable within states over time, with the magnitude of the bias depending on the extent of random variation in both gun and nongun suicides. If, conditional on a particular rate of gun ownership, nongun suicides are much more variable than gun suicides, then one would observe a negative relationship between overall suicide rates and estimated gun ownership, as high realizations of nongun suicides would tend to be associated both with high rates of suicide and relatively low rates of gun ownership. The opposite would be true if instead gun suicides were more variable.

The set of results summarized in table 2-10 suggests that this proxy may not be the appropriate one for estimating the relationship between changes in gun ownership and changes in the suicide rate. Of particular concern is the precision of the estimates for β_2 and β_3, which have t-statistics of 26.5 and −22.4, respectively, in specifications 3 and 5. This precision suggests that the mechanical relationship implied in a first-differences version of equations 10 and 11 is dominating the estimation. The estimate of −.128 for β_1 suggests that changes in gun ownership are associated with significant *reductions* in the suicide rate.

One explanation is that nongun suicides may be more variable than gun suicides because the success probability with a gun is closer to one. Thus the total number of gun suicides would have a lower variance than the number of nongun suicides because both are a function of $P * (1 - P)$, which will be closer to zero as P rises above 50 percent and toward 100 percent. An alternative one is that gun ownership causes individuals to become less suicide prone. The fact that the measurement error effect seems so important in this set of regressions suggests that the previous proxy is preferable for this application, as the measurement error in that variable does not cause a mechanical relationship.

Taken together, the set of results presented in this section suggests that changes in gun ownership have not been a central factor in explaining the observed changes in the suicide rate during the past two decades. But one must stop short of the statement that firearms do not exert a causal effect, as the estimation is limited by the actual changes that have occurred. If gun purchase decisions by suicide-prone individuals are not changing substantially within states over time, then this estimation strategy will not reliably estimate the change in the probability of suicide induced by the acquisition of a firearm.

Conclusion

Individuals who own a gun are more likely to commit suicide than are other individuals. The results presented in this chapter demonstrate that much of the relationship between state-level gun ownership and suicide rates seems driven by a positive correlation between suicidal tendencies and gun ownership. The finding that the male-female suicide ratio is significantly greater in places with more gun ownership suggests that instrumentality effects may also partially explain this relationship, though one cannot rule out the hypothesis that gender-specific suicidal tendencies vary with the availability of guns. Finally, it appears that reductions in gun ownership have not been the driving force behind the fall in the suicide rate.

The ideal approach to estimating the causal effect of gun ownership on the suicide rate would be an experiment that randomly allocated gun ownership to households, giving firearms to those in a treatment group and then preventing those in the control group from obtaining access to guns. But because fewer than 12 in 100,000 individuals take their own lives in a year, the number of guns that would need to be randomly allocated to obtain a precise estimate of the causal effect would number in the millions.

A second-best approach to the problem would exploit a regulatory change that induced a substantial change in gun ownership and then identified the groups whose purchase decisions were affected by the policy. Although some previous studies have utilized this "natural experiment" strategy, few have identified the group whose gun ownership decisions were impacted. The existence of individual-level gun purchase and registration data in particular states would permit a detailed analysis of the effects of recent policies. Combining this information with comparably detailed information about suicide victims, one could estimate the "treatment effect" of gun ownership for the marginal owner whose behavior is most likely to change in response to government policies. This represents an important direction for future research.

Appendix: Value Fluctuations

Suppose that the mean number of suicides in jurisdiction j for its current level of gun ownership is equal to S_j but that the realized value fluctuates around this value according to $s_j = S_j + \varepsilon_{sj}$.[34] The corresponding realizations for gun and nongun suicides are g_j and n_j, respectively, and the fraction of individuals who own a gun is assumed to be equal to $G_j/(G_j + N_j)$. As the following pair of equations demonstrates, even if the rate of gun ownership does not vary across areas and thus all jurisdictions have the identical values for G_j and N_j, one will observe a significant relationship between gun ownership and each of the two types of suicide:

$$(A1) \quad \text{Log}\left(\frac{G_j + \varepsilon_{gj}}{Pop_j}\right) = \alpha_1 + \beta_1 * \text{Log}\left(\frac{G_j + \varepsilon_{gj}}{G_j + \varepsilon_{gj} + N_j + \varepsilon_{nj}}\right)$$

$$(A2) \quad \text{Log}\left(\frac{N_j + \varepsilon_{nj}}{Pop_j}\right) = \alpha_2 + \beta_2 * \text{Log}\left(\frac{G_j + \varepsilon_{gj}}{G_j + \varepsilon_{gj} + N_j + \varepsilon_{nj}}\right)$$

Above average realizations of ε_{gj} will lead to an increase in both the left- and right-hand side variables in (A1), while similar variation in ε_{nj} will cause a negative relationship between the two variables of interest in (A2). Even without any variation in gun ownership or in the true suicide rates G_j and N_j across geographic

---

34. This variation could simply be driven by random fluctuations in the number of individuals who try to commit suicide and in the uncertain "success" of each suicide attempt. Suppose that there are N individuals in a jurisdiction, a fraction θ of whom own a gun. If the probability that a gun owner will try to commit suicide is λ_{gun} and the corresponding probability for a non-gun owner is λ_{non}, then the total number of suicides will equal $\theta N \lambda_{gun} P_{gun} + (1-\theta) N \lambda_{non} P_{non}$, with P_{gun} and P_{non} equaling the probability that a suicide attempt of each type results in the individual's death. Even for a constant θ, the number of suicides that occur in each period will vary depending on how many individuals in each group try to commit suicide and the frequency with which these attempts result in the individual's death.

areas, one would find a positive relationship between gun ownership and gun suicide rates, and a negative relationship of gun ownership with nongun suicides. The magnitude of the coefficient estimates for β_1 and β_2 would then depend on the variance of ε_{gj} and ε_{nj}, as well as the covariance between these two error terms. This would also affect the estimate for β_3 in the following specification that explains the overall suicide rate:

(A3)
$$\text{Log}\left(\frac{G_j + \varepsilon_{gj} + N_j + \varepsilon_{nj}}{Pop_j}\right) = \alpha_3 + \beta_3$$
$$* \text{Log}\left(\frac{G_j + \varepsilon_{gj}}{G_j + \varepsilon_{gj} + N_j + \varepsilon_{nj}}\right)$$

If, for example, the variance of ε_{gj} were much greater than the corresponding one for ε_{nj}, one would find a positive relationship between the overall suicide rate and the estimated rate of gun ownership even in the absence of any variation in the true rate of gun ownership across areas.

Of course, actual rates of gun ownership do vary substantially across geographic areas. If the measurement error caused by random fluctuations in ε_{gj} and ε_{nj} is much smaller in magnitude than the variation in G_j and N_j, then the results from cross-sectional regressions similar to equations 9, 10, and 11 will provide more accurate estimates of the relationship between gun ownership (estimated by the fraction of suicides in which a gun was used) and the suicide rate. Thus one can investigate whether suicide rates are systematically different in places with more gun ownership using the gun suicide fraction as a proxy, recognizing that the mechanical relationship described above may lead to biased estimates of the parameters of interest.

It seems plausible, however, that within-area variation in gun ownership will be much smaller than this variation across geographic areas. As Deborah Azrael, Philip Cook, and Matthew Miller point out, "The geographic structure of gun ownership has been highly stable."[35] Thus even if the fraction of suicides in which a gun is used is an excellent proxy for the rate of gun ownership, the measurement error effect described above is likely to be important in a regression that investigates the relationship between changes in suicide rates and changes in gun ownership, as estimated by the fraction of suicides in which a gun is used.

---

35. Azrael, Cook, and Miller (2001).

COMMENT BY
John Mullahy

Mark Duggan has written a thought-provoking chapter on the relationship between guns and suicides. The central messages of the chapter—which now
likely define the line in the research sand—are that gun owners' suicidal propensities may be above average, and that instrumentality effects may be important.
In light of the disturbing increase in overall youth and in middle-aged-male
suicides—and the evidence that guns figure in roughly half these suicides—
there is a *prima facie* compelling case for understanding the causal structure
of the guns-suicides relationship so policymakers' efforts might be aimed in
useful directions.

Duggan confronts two formidable obstacles in his investigation of how gun
ownership influences suicides: there exist neither repositories of data on gun
ownership generally nor microdata on ownership and suicide outcomes specifically *(measurement)*; and unobserved propensities to commit suicide may also
influence gun ownership *(identification)*. The measurement obstacle is attacked
using the *Guns&Ammo* sales proxy for ownership, while the identification
obstacle is handled by utilizing panel data econometric methods. Subject to the
constraints imposed by the ownership (or perhaps more accurately, "command,"
"keeping and bearing," or "possession") proxies marshalled for this investigation, Duggan executes what I view as a laudably fair-minded interrogation
of the data.

In sorting out some of the potential policy implications of this line of research, an economic conceptualization of the suicide phenomenon might be
helpful and could go something like this. Individuals can "produce" suicides by
combining variable inputs (ammunition, lethal dosages of drugs, automobile
CO emissions, their own time and effort, and so on) and various forms of capital inputs (guns, rope, garages, and others). Specifically, one might imagine a
quantity "firepower capital," representing the lethality potential of the firearms
possessed by an individual. At time period t, individual i's firepower capital
(FC) can be thought to be determined by a standard economic model of investment and depreciation:

$$FC_t = A_t + (1 - \delta)FC_{t-1}$$

A_t represents net acquisitions (purchases, thefts by and against, and so on) by an
individual or in a state at time t, and δ represents the rate of depreciation of the

existing stock of firepower capital, the extent to which its lethality decays with age, which might be quite small. My reading is that a quantity akin to FC_t is what Duggan has in mind with his $G\&A$ proxy measure. It might be noted that it is not obvious a priori whether the $G\&A$ proxy is more highly correlated with the A_t component or the FC_{t-1} component of FC_t; to the extent that the former correlation is stronger, then Duggan's results may be speaking more specifically to acquisition-suicide relationships than to ownership-suicide relationships (more below).

This FC_t quantity may well be the conceptually appropriate one on which to focus in assessing how guns influence suicides. As such, the economic version of the main hypotheses Duggan tests would be that increases in the FC capital stock are, other things equal, influential on conditional probabilities like $Prob$(commit gun suicide$|X,FC$) or $Prob$(commit gun or nongun suicide$|X,FC$) whose structure economists would like to think of as grounded in some sort of ex ante optimizing behavior. Yet the inability to measure directly FC_t (ownership, possession, and so on) and, consequently, the inability to know how much of the variation in FC_t can be explained systematically by the $G\&A$ proxy make one less confident in Duggan's findings on how ownership influences suicides than one might like.

At least two complementary lines of future research are suggested by Duggan's paper. First, researchers might consider the merits of examining how acquisitions, rather than ownership/possession, influence suicides. Even if the stock of firepower capital may be the conceptually relevant quantity in an econometric model of suicides, there is a trade-off since acquisitions/sales may be more likely to be the target of many imaginable policy innovations (short of Second Amendment repeal). Second, although researchers do not have the luxury of accessing comprehensive subnational data on acquisitions (specifically) or ownership (generally), progress is still possible by advancing the research that relies on reduced-form estimation of models of gun-related violence outcomes. In this case, such models would relate state-level suicide rates to state-level acquisition-related policy instruments (for example, purchase permits) and state-level ownership-related policy instruments (for example, handgun registrations).

Of course, the research community should not lose sight of the ultimate goal: a robust econometric description of the causal relationships between suicides and ownership (or acquisitions) whose parameters would usefully serve to educate policymakers. For instance, if in some counterfactual policy world there would arise fewer acquisitions and/or reduced ownership and consequently fewer suicides, this would seem a very useful thing to know. Duggan's results provide an important and large step along this research path.

COMMENT BY
Karen Norberg

Does access to a gun make a difference in the risk of suicide? In this thoughtful chapter Mark Duggan finds that state-level proxies for gun ownership predict state suicide rates in the United States, but he concludes that the association may be a correlation without causation.

It is not obvious that access to firearms would increase the risk of suicide. Logically, there are three possibilities:

— Substitution: access to a gun might increase the likelihood of using a gun in the event of suicide, but if similarly acceptable and lethal substitutes are widely available, then the overall risk of suicide may be unaffected.

— Instrumentality: access to a gun might increase the overall risk of suicide by increasing the likelihood of suicide among persons who would not commit suicide if a firearm were not available.

— Confounding: The availability of firearms could be a marker for some other background factor that is associated with risk of suicide. This possibility seems to deserve more attention than it has received so far.

Duggan begins by comparing three possible proxies for firearm ownership: the ratio of gun to nongun suicides, the proportion of households subscribing to a gun magazine (*Guns & Ammo*), and the proportion of respondents reporting a gun in the household in the General Social Survey. Each of these measures has important limits. The GSS results are only available by region; magazine subscriptions only reflect the gun owners who read that particular magazine; and there may be a biased and "mechanical" association between the suicide rate, appearing as the dependent variable on the left-hand side of the equation, and the ratio of gun to nongun suicides, appearing as a measure of gun ownership on the right-hand side of the equation.

Using the *Guns&Ammo* proxy, Duggan examines the age- and sex-specific gun and nongun suicide rates for U.S. states from 1980 to 1998. He reports three key findings:

— Gun suicides and total suicides are higher in states and years with higher rates of gun ownership.

— More *Guns&Ammo* subscriptions predict more nongun suicides for the young but fewer nongun suicides for the old.

— More *Guns&Ammo* subscriptions predict more suicides for men than women.

It appears that there may be different links between guns and suicide for different persons. Specifically, Duggan's evidence suggests a substitution between gun and nongun suicides among older persons and a positive correlation between gun and nongun suicide among younger persons. Even if magazine subscriptions are an imperfect measure of firearm ownership, the positive association between *Guns&Ammo* and nongun suicide cannot be explained as an instrumental effect of firearms. It appears that high-firearm communities are different from other communities in ways that may increase the overall risk of suicide, especially for the young.

Duggan interprets the ratio of male to female suicides as evidence for an instrumentality effect, but differences in gun ownership, suicide rates, and the propensity to use a gun for suicide could all be due to gender differences in the propensity for aggression. If guns are more important to the social status of men than of women, then gun ownership may be more highly correlated with other male attributes in communities where gun ownership is common.

Firearms may have a direct effect on the risk of suicide for some people but not for others. Most clinicians view self-injury as a continuum from nonlethal to lethal intent. Parasuicidal persons would prefer to survive and to receive help; nonlethal self-injury is a costly and honest signal of distress, and part of the cost of the signal may be the risk of an unintentionally lethal outcome. The most lethally suicidal persons see no prospect for change. Most others can be thought of as gamblers: for various reasons, they place themselves in high-risk situations with some probability of positive outcomes (in which case they would prefer to live), and some probability of negative outcomes (in which case they may prefer to die).

Access to particular methods may influence the likelihood of suicide in three situations. First is the parasuicidal person, who would prefer to live. Such individuals may be most likely to hurt themselves if somewhat dangerous but nonlethal methods are easily available. Second is the acutely agitated and transiently suicidal person, who may "impulsively" commit suicide if a lethal method is available before the suicidal feeling subsides. The person with a gun in his hand, being chased by the police, falls into this category; so does the clinically depressed individual who has not yet received treatment; and so does the adolescent who has just totaled the family car. In this case, "impulsivity" becomes a relative term, describing the time course of a motivational state relative to the ease of access to a weapon. An intensely emotional state may often be required to use what we usually call violent methods: cutting oneself, jumping from a height, and gunshot. Last is the planned suicide. Many persons who are planning a "rational" suicide do so by establishing a specific mental script; the availability and acceptability of particular methods might influence the likelihood that the planned suicide will be carried out, and if the chosen method becomes unavailable, it may take a long time for a substitute plan to be developed. The overall effect of firearms on suicide would depend on the prevalence of each type of suicidal person in the population.

It is very likely that firearm owners are different from other persons, and it is possible that communities with high prevalence of firearms are different from other communities in ways that might increase the risk of suicide, regardless of individual access to a gun. Law-abiding gun owners may live in communities that place a high value on self-reliance and defense of honor; such values might make it harder to seek help in the face of distress. Other persons may carry guns because they are engaged in illegal or high-risk activities. Finally, gun owners may be more likely to live in rural areas that have experienced an exodus of money, jobs, population, social capital, and political influence, and social and economic changes in the family may have had different impacts on men, women, and children, and on the young and the old.

References

Azrael, Deborah, Philip Cook, and Matthew Miller. 2001. "State and Local Prevalence of Firearms Ownership Measurement, Structure, and Trends." Working Paper 8570. Cambridge, Mass.: National Bureau of Economic Research.

Boor, Myron. 1981. "Methods of Suicide and Implications for Suicide Prevention." *Journal of Clinical Psychology* 37 (1): 70–75.

Brent, David A., Joshua A. Perper, Charles E. Goldstein, David J. Kolko, Marjorie J. Allan, Christopher J. Allman, and Janice P. Zelenak. 1988. "Risk Factors for Adolescent Suicide." *Archives of General Psychiatry* 45: 581–88.

Card, J. J. 1974. "Lethality of Suicide Methods and Suicide Risk: Two Distinct Concepts." *Omega* 5: 37–45.

Clarke, Ronald, and David Lester. 1989. *Suicide: Closing the Exits.* Springer-Verlag.

Cook, Philip, Mark Moore, and Anthony Braga. 2002. "Gun Control," in *Crime,* edited by James Q. Wilson and Joan Peterselia, 291–329. ICS Press.

Cook, Philip. 1987. "Robbery Violence." *Journal of Criminal Law and Criminology* 70 (2): 357–76.

———. 1991. "The Technology of Personal Violence." In *Crime and Justice,* vol. 14, edited by Michael Tonry. University of Chicago Press.

Cutler, David, Edward Glaeser, and Karen Norberg. 2001. "Explaining the Rise in Youth Suicide." Working Paper 7713. Cambridge, Mass.: National Bureau of Economic Research.

Duggan, Mark. 2001. "More Guns, More Crime." *Journal of Political Economy* 109 (October): 1086–1114.

Kates, Donald B. 1990. *Guns, Murder, and the Constitution: A Realistic Assessment of Gun Control.* San Francisco: Pacific Research Institute.

Kellermann, Arthur, Frederick Rivara, Grant Somes, Donald Reay, Jerry Francisco, Joyce Gillentine Banton, Janice Prodzinski, Corinne Fligner, Bela Hackman. 1992. "Suicide in the Home in Relation to Gun Ownership." *New England Journal of Medicine* 327 (7): 467–72.

Lester, David, and Mary Murrell. 1980. "The Influence of Gun Control Laws on Suicidal Behavior." *American Journal of Psychiatry* 137 (January): 121–22.

Loftin, Colin, David McDowall, Brian Wiersema, and Talbert Cottey. 1991. "Effects of Restrictive Licensing of Handguns on Homicide and Suicide in the District of Columbia." *New England Journal of Medicine* 325 (23): 1615–20.

Ludwig, Jens, and Philip Cook. 2000. "Homicide and Suicide Rates Associated with Implementation of the Brady Handgun Violence Prevention Act." *Journal of the American Medical Association* 284 (5): 585–91.

McDowall, David, Colin Loftin, and Brian Wiersema. 1996. "Using Quasi-Experiments to Evaluate Firearm Laws: Comment on Britt et al.'s Reassessment of the D.C. Gun Law." *Law and Society Review* 30 (2): 381–91.

Newton, Greg, and Franklin Zimring. 1969. *Firearms and Violence in American Life.* Government Printing Office.

Rich, Charles, James Young, Richard Fowler, John Wagner, and Nancy Black. 1990. "Guns and Suicide: Possible Effects of Some Specific Legislation." *American Journal of Psychiatry* 147 (3): 342–46.

Sloan, John, Frederick Rivara, Donald Reay, James Ferris, M. Path, and Arthur Kellermann. 1990. "Firearm Regulations and Rates of Suicide: A Comparison of Two Metropolitan Areas." *New England Journal of Medicine* 322 (6): 369–73.

Stevenson, Betsey, and Justin Wolfers. 2000. " 'Til Death Do Us Part': Effects of Unilateral Divorce on Suicide, Domestic Violence, and Intimate Homicide." Stanford University. Mimeo.

Wintemute, Garen, Carrie Parham, James Beaumont, Mona Wright, and Christiana Drake. 1999. "Mortality among Recent Purchasers of Handguns." *New England Journal of Medicine* 341 (21): 1583–89.

Zimring, Franklin E. 1968. "Is Gun Control Likely to Reduce Violent Killings?" *University of Chicago Law Review* 35: 721–37.

———. 1972. "The Medium Is the Message: Firearm Calibre as a Determinant of Death from Assault." *Journal of Legal Studies* 1: 97–124.

PHILIP J. COOK
JENS LUDWIG

3 | *Guns and*
Burglary

Compared with other wealthy nations, the United States has a high rate of civilian firearms ownership, with 35–40 percent of all households possessing at least one gun.[1] The net effect of widespread gun ownership on the amount and costs of crime remains a contentious issue because guns have virtuous as well as vicious uses: the ready availability of guns may increase gun use by criminal assailants and thereby increase the lethality of assaults and robberies.[2] The widespread ownership of guns, however, may in-

This paper was supported in part by a grant from the Joyce Foundation. Thanks to Marjorie Cohen, Brian Deer, Zac Hudson, Sinead Keegan, Josh Pinkston, Justin Treloar, Eric Younger, and especially Bob Malme for excellent research assistance, to the Prince George's County Police Department, Stacy Dickert-Conlin, Mark Duggan, Pat Mayhew (and others at the British Crime Survey), Robert Moffitt and Steve Raphael for data, and to Ed Glaeser, David Kopel, Arik Levinson, Bruce Sacerdote and seminar participants at the National Bureau of Economic Research, University of Maryland, William and Mary, and the Brookings Conference on Gun Violence for helpful comments. The research in this paper was conducted while the authors were Census Bureau research associates at the Triangle Census Research Data Center. Research results and conclusions are those of the authors and do not necessarily indicate concurrence by the Bureau of the Census. This paper has been screened to ensure that no confidential data are revealed. We thank Alison Hagy and Michelle Danis for their guidance at the Center.

1. Smith (2000).
2. See Zimring (1968, 1972); Cook (1987, 1991); Zimring and Hawkins (1997); and Duggan (2001). Besides its effects on crime, gun ownership may impose other costs on society. It may increase the suicide rate (Miller and Hemenway [1999]; Ludwig and Cook [2000]; Cutler, Glaeser and Norberg [2001]; Wintemute and others [1999]; Mark Duggan, chapter 2 in this volume) and the rate of unintentional shootings (Miller, Azrael, and Hemenway [2001]). The relative frequency of different circumstances for shootings in residences has been documented in Kellermann and Reay (1986) and Lee and others (1991).

crease the likelihood that victims will be able to defend themselves against attack and even inflict injury on would-be assailants, which would tend to deter assaults and reduce the likelihood of victim losses in the event of assault.[3]

The balance between virtuous and vicious uses has traditionally favored keeping a gun at home over carrying one in public, with the latter subject to more stringent regulation. Guns in the home do not threaten the public at large in any direct way and may enhance the capacity for defending against intruders. Furthermore, armed households arguably provide a deterrent to residential burglary, particularly to "hot" burglaries of occupied dwellings; if burglars lack "inside" knowledge about which households are armed, this crime-control benefit is not limited to those homes that actually have guns ready at hand but extends to the entire community.[4] Thus there may be a positive externality to keeping a gun at home for self-defense.

Although the existence of a burglary-deterrent effect is asserted frequently and with great confidence by advocates, the empirical support for this assertion is weak.[5] The available evidence consists of anecdotes, interviews with burglars, casual comparisons with other countries, and the like. A more systematic exploration requires data on local rates of gun ownership and of residential burglary, and such data have only recently become available. In this chapter we exploit a new well-validated proxy for local gun-ownership prevalence—the proportion of suicides that involve firearms—together with newly available geo-coded data from the National Crime Victimization Survey, to produce the first systematic estimates of the net effects of gun prevalence on residential burglary patterns.

The importance of such empirical work stems in part from the fact that theoretical considerations do not provide much guidance in predicting the net effects of widespread gun ownership. Guns in the home may pose a threat to burglars but may also serve as an inducement, since guns are particularly valuable loot.[6] Other things equal, a gun-rich community provides more lucrative burglary opportunities than one in which guns are more sparse.[7] The net result

3. Kleck (1997); Lott (2000).
4. Kopel (2001).
5. For some recent assertions on the deterrent effect in the popular press, see, for example, Thomas Armstrong, "Will More Gun Control Just Do More Harm?" *San Diego Union-Tribune,* March 23, 2000, p. B13; Gordon Witkin, "Should You Own a Gun?" *USNews,* August 15, 1994, p. 24; Dan Rowe, "Expert Links Gun Control to High Rate of Break-Ins," *National Post* (Canada). December 19, 2001. Tucker (1996); Steyn (2000);
6. Cook, Molliconi, and Cole (1995).
7. Guns may also be useful inputs into the burglary production process and may be less costly for criminals to obtain in areas with high levels of gun ownership.

for burglary rates and "hot" burglary rates depends in part on the extent to which burglars can discriminate between occupied and unoccupied homes, and on how they assess the relevant risk-reward trade-off.

The new empirical results reported here provide no support for a net deterrent effect from widespread gun ownership. Indeed, our analysis concludes that residential burglary rates tend to increase with community gun prevalence, while the "hot" proportion of these burglaries is unaffected. The challenge to establishing a causal interpretation to these results comes from the possibility that gun ownership may be both cause and effect of local burglary patterns or that both variables may be driven by some unmeasured third factor. Although there is no entirely persuasive way to rule out such competing explanations, our findings are robust to a variety of empirical approaches.

Our main results come from cross-section regression analysis of National Crime Victimization Survey (NCVS) data augmented by a proxy measure of county-level gun prevalence. In this analysis we control for a long list of household- and county-level attributes. In one specification we also allow each state to have its own intercept, which controls for unmeasured state-level variables by focusing on within-state, across-county variation in gun ownership and burglary rates.

To deal with the potential problem of reverse causation, we replicate our analyses using a twenty-two-year panel of police-reported crime data obtained from the FBI's *Uniform Crime Reports* (UCR) finding that lagged gun-ownership rates are positively related to future burglary rates. However, lagged burglary rates appear to have a negligible effect on future gun prevalence, at least in the short run. Unfortunately the UCR data do not distinguish between burglaries to occupied versus unoccupied homes and thus cannot support a separate analysis of hot burglaries.

The issue of reverse causation is also addressed by use of "instrumental variables" (IV) estimates. The specific instrument employed in these estimates is the percentage of the state population living in rural areas in 1950, an indicator of rural tradition in the state to which gun ownership is closely tied. The resulting estimates are compatible with the ordinary-least-squares estimates in suggesting a nonnegative relationship between gun density and burglary rates.

Review of the Existing Evidence

The evidence typically cited in discussions of how gun prevalence affects residential burglary rates is of five types. First, data on the frequency of gun use by householders against intruders are cited to support the plausibility of the deterrence hypothesis. Second, interviews with burglars or former burglars provide more direct evidence on the deterrent effect and also on the inducement to burglary of guns in the home. Third, international comparisons are offered, usually comparing the percentage of residential burglaries that are "hot" in the United States with one or more other countries that have lower gun prevalence. Fourth, anecdotes (sometimes supported with data) are recounted about how burglary rates were affected by interventions intended to change household gun prevalence. Finally, there have been two systematic studies, including regression analyses of panel data, on the effect of gun prevalence on overall (residential plus nonresidential) burglary rates.[8]

Frequency of Gun Use in Self-Defense

The frequency with which guns are used in defense against burglary has been estimated from survey data from time to time. Unfortunately, the estimates differ by an order of magnitude, depending on how the survey is conducted and what questions are asked.

At the high end is a 1994 random-digit-dial telephone survey that generated an estimate of 503,000 instances in the preceding twelve months in which some member of the household retrieved a gun to fend off an intruder who was actually seen.[9] The survey was conducted by a private firm, DataStat, on behalf of the federal government. It completed 5,238 interviews, of which twenty-two respondents reported one or more uses of a gun in the event of an intruder; five of these accounted for nearly half of all the reported instances. Almost all of these reports (98.9 percent) indicated that the intruder had been scared off.

At the low end are estimates based on the National Crime Victimization Survey (NCVS), which is conducted every six months by the Census Bureau. The NCVS includes respondents from a sample of about 50,000 households, the members of which are usually interviewed in person; the design of this survey represents best practice in the area. Based on a special tabulation of NCVS data by the Bureau of Justice Statistics, Philip Cook estimated that there were an annual average of just 32,000 instances a year for the period 1979–87 in which a householder used a gun against someone who broke into the home or attempted to do so.[10]

---

8. Lott (2000); Duggan (2001).
9. Ikeda and others (1997).
10. Cook (1991, p. 56).

Is the "right" answer 32,000 or 503,000? There is no obvious way to reconcile these two estimates. The same puzzle has arisen in survey-based estimates of self-defense uses of guns in other circumstances, which also differ by an order of magnitude, and that discussion will not be reviewed here.[11] Suffice it to say that survey-based estimates for rare and normatively charged events such as gun self-defense are highly sensitive to survey method, and that we are inclined to place somewhat more faith in the NCVS results for reasons explained in our earlier work.[12]

Cook estimated that there were about 1.0 million burglaries each year of occupied residences during the period 1979–87.[13] The NCVS estimate then implies that in one in every thirty such burglaries was a gun used in self-defense. The DataStat estimate suggests that fully half of such burglaries resulted in self-defense with a gun. The credibility of the "deterrence" claim depends in part on which of these two estimates is closer to the truth.[14]

Interviews with Burglars

Evidence directly relevant for judging the "deterrence" and "inducement" hypotheses comes from surveys of felons. For example, in one 1982 convenience sample of 1,823 state prisoners, 35 percent of respondents "strongly agreed" and 39 percent "agreed" that "one reason burglars avoid houses when people are at home is that they fear being shot." Of the respondents who used a gun to commit the crime for which they were incarcerated, 50 percent reported that the possibility of encountering an armed victim was "very important" in their decision to employ a gun, while another 12 percent reported that this motivation was "somewhat important."[15]

At the same time guns are of considerable value to burglars, who typically prefer items that are easy to carry, easily concealed, and have high "pound for pound value."[16] As one St. Louis burglar reported, "A gun is money with a trigger."[17] Another respondent in the same study expressed a preference for working in neighborhoods with high proportions of white residents since households

11. Kleck and Gertz (1995); Smith (1997).
12. Cook, Ludwig, and Hemenway (1997).
13. Cook (1991).
14. A study of home-invasion burglaries (unwanted entry of a single-family home while one or more individuals were present in the home) in Atlanta based on 198 police reports during summer 1994 found that just 1.5 percent of victims used a gun in self-defense. Kellermann and others (1995).
15. Wright and Rossi (1994).
16. Shover (1991); Wright and Decker (1994).
17. Wright and Decker (1994).

in these areas are likely to have "the basics," including guns: "White people hunt a lot more so than blacks."[18]

Nearly half of the respondents to the prison survey mentioned above report that they have stolen a gun during their lifetimes; of this group, 70 percent usually steal guns to sell or trade rather than to keep for themselves.[19]

International Comparisons

Since the prevalence of household gun possession is much higher in the United States than in Canada, Britain, and other wealthy nations, one common test of the "deterrence" hypothesis has been to compare residential burglary rates and patterns across these nations. As it turns out, relevant data are hard to come by. The *Uniform Crime Reports* do not provide a basis for estimating the number of "hot" burglaries (burglaries of occupied residences), nor do the police-recorded data systems of other countries. Relevant survey-based estimates can be generated for the United States from the NCVS, but no other country has an annual crime survey of comparable quality.[20] There have been occasional crime surveys in other nations, which suggest that other countries tend to have a higher percentage of residential burglaries involving occupied dwellings than the United States. Table 3-1 (top panel) lists some of the relevant estimates that have been reported by Gary Kleck and David Kopel.[21]

One obvious problem with these comparisons is that the hot burglary rate for each country or city is measured at a different point in time. For two countries—the United States and Great Britain—survey measures of hot burglary rates are available for a common year, 1998. When we standardize for period effects in this way, the difference across the two countries in the hot burglary rate is reduced from the factor of 4 or 5 to 1 reported by Kleck and Kopel (top panel) to a factor of about 2 to 1 (bottom panel).

18. See Wright and Decker (1994, p. 90). On the other hand, a burglar interviewed by Rengert and Wasilchick (1985, p. 62) said that he shunned burglaries in neighborhoods in which the residents were of a different race because, "You'll get shot if you're caught there."

19. See Wright and Rossi (1994). The prevalence of gun theft in the Wright and Rossi convenience sample of prisoners is higher than in the nationally representative sample of prisoners interviewed as part of the 1991 Survey of Inmates of State Correctional Facilities, in which only 10 percent of respondents report ever having stolen a gun.

20. One attempt to generate internationally comparable survey-based results is the United Nations–sponsored International Crime Survey. This survey includes the United States, but it is far smaller and in other ways inferior to the NCVS. More to the point, it does not include items that would permit the estimate of a hot burglary rate.

21. Kleck (1997); Kopel (2001).

Table 3-1. *International Comparisons of Hot Burglary Rates*

Source	Country	Year	Hot burglary rate (percent)
Mayhew and others (1993)[a]	United Kingdom	1982–88	43
Block (1984)[a]	Netherlands	1977	48
Block (1984)[a]	United States	1976	9
Bureau of Justice Statistics (BJS) (1985)[b]	United States	1983	12
BJS (1999)	United States	1998	
Resident at home			20.5
Resident's location at time of burglary unspecified or unknown			28.3
Home Office (1999)	United Kingdom	1998	
Resident at home			46
Aware of burglary			25
Unaware of burglary			21
Adjusted U.K. hot burglary rate	United Kingdom	1998	
Upper bound			45
Lower bound			36

a. Cited in Kleck (1997).
b. Cited in Kopel (2001).

But comparability problems remain. The bottom panel of table 3-1 high-lights one difference. In 28 percent of American burglaries NCVS respondents did not know their whereabouts at the time of the burglary, a category that is not included in the British Crime Survey (BCS). Judging from the open-ended narratives provided by BCS burglary victims, a number of cases in which the re-spondent apparently did not know whether anyone was at home at the time of the burglary are classified as "respondent home, unaware of the burglary."[22] As seen in the last row of table 3-1, adjusting for this coding discrepancy between

22. Our best guess is that at least 7 percent and perhaps as many as 46 percent of the cases coded as "respondent home but unaware of burglary" in the BCS—and thus counted as "hot"—would be coded as "victim location unknown" in the NCVS and counted as "cold" burglaries. This inference stems from the fact that many of the respondents in this BCS category discover evidence of the burglary only after the fact, in the form of damage or other signs of forcible entry. Examples of such cases include the BCS respondent who reported that "there was evidence on the patio door that a tool had been used to try to open it; the marks were noticed in April, we don't know when they tried to break in," and another who

the BCS and NCVS lowers the hot burglary rate in the United Kingdom from 46 percent to between 36 percent and 45 percent.[23]

More important, even if we had comparable data there would remain the fact that a variety of potential explanations are plausible for an observed difference in the percentage of residential burglaries that involve occupied dwellings. For example, when burglars are arrested, the punishment is more certain and severe in the United States than in England and Wales (table 3-2). The difference in penalties provides an alternative explanation for why American burglars take extra care to avoid contact with victims. American and British households differ in several other ways that are also likely to affect the cost-benefit calculus facing burglars, including substantial differences in the proportion of households that have dogs or lack men. Without controlling for the other differences that may be important, attributing the disparity in hot burglary rates to one particular difference—gun prevalence—is entirely unpersuasive.

Case Studies

A variety of anecdotes have been offered in support of the deterrence hypothesis, but few have been well documented.[24] The case of Kennesaw, Georgia, which adopted an ordinance in 1982 requiring every household to keep a gun, has been prominent. There have been several published analyses of the burglary trend in Kennesaw around the time of the ordinance, with contradictory results.[25] In any event, this is not a good test of the deterrence hypothesis, since the ordinance was purely symbolic. Most homes in Kennesaw already had

reported that "someone came into my flat, probably while I was asleep after my dinner, and stole a metal case." Cases in which the respondent simply reports finding evidence of an attempted break-in, but does not elaborate on his or her uncertainty about when the crime occurred or where he or she was at the time, are far more common.

23. However, differences in survey methods or reporting across countries could also in principle mask even larger differences in hot burglary rates than those reported in table 3-1. The ratio of completed to attempted burglaries is far higher in the United States (3 or 4 to 1) than in the United Kingdom (nearly equal in most years). Perkins and others (1996); Home Office (1999). One possible explanation for the relative scarcity of burglary attempts in the American NCVS data is that Americans are less likely then the English to report burglary attempts to interviewers. In this case, the denominator for the NCVS-based "hot burglary" calculations are too low, which could lead us to either over- or understate the hot burglary rate in the United States, depending on what fraction of the unreported burglary attempts are to occupied homes.

24. Kopel (2001).

25. Kleck (1991, pp. 136–38); McDowall, Lizotte, and Wiersema (1991); Kleck (1998).

Table 3-2. *Socioeconomic and Other Differences between United States and United Kingdom, 1998*

	United States	United Kingdom
Average punishment for burglars, 1996[a]		
Convictions per 1,000 burglary arrests	10	6
Probability of custody given conviction (percent)	55	45
Average time served for those given custody (months)	15	7
Households headed by single female (percent)	29[b]	22[c]
People living in free-standing, single-family homes (percent)	63[d]	23[c]
People who own their own home (percent)	66[e]	69[c]
Households that contain children (percent)	34 (child is under 18)[b]	29 (youngest person under 15)[c]
Population nonwhite (percent)	17[b]	7[c]
Households that own dogs (percent)[f]	40	20

a. The U.K. figure is for England and Wales, courtesy of David Farrington. Probability of custody given conviction for England and Wales is for 1997, from *Criminal Statistics, England and Wales* (The Stationery Office, 1997). Other findings are from the British Crime Survey, Criminal Sentencing Statistics, Bureau of Justice Statistics, U.S. Department of Justice, 1998.

b. U.S. Bureau of the Census (1999).

c. Living in Britain 1998 (General Household Survey).

d. U.S. Bureau of the Census, American Housing Survey for the United States, 1999.

e. U.S. Bureau of the Census, Housing Vacancy Survey, Third Quarter 2001.

f. Figure for United Kingdom is for 2000 from Claritas Precision Marketing Solutions. Figure for United States is from American Pet Products Manufacturers Association, National Pet Owners Survey, 2001–02.

a gun before the ordinance, and it seems unlikely that the ordinance had an effect on prevalence since there was no penalty specified in the law for refusal to comply.

Regression Analysis of Panel Data

Two previous studies have examined the relationship between gun ownership and overall burglary rates within the United States. Both studies rely on UCR data that lump together residential and nonresidential burglary and do not allow hot burglaries to be identified separately. These studies yield conflicting results about the relationship between gun prevalence and burglary rates.

John Lott analyzes state-level UCR data for two years—1988 and 1996—and finds that after controlling for region and period effects as well as a variety of state covariates, a 1 percentage point increase in gun-ownership rates reduces burglary rates by 1.6 percentage points. One problem with this analysis is Lott's choice of data to measure state gun ownership rates. He employs two voter-exit surveys that, among other problems, are not comparable with each other, as suggested by the fact that the individual gun-ownership rate is 10 percentage points higher in the 1996 survey than the 1988 survey, 37 percent versus 27 percent.[26] In contrast, estimates from the General Social Survey, which has included items on guns since 1972 and is widely regarded as the best ongoing source of data on this topic, indicate that gun-ownership rates were actually declining slightly during this period.[27]

Mark Duggan uses a different measure for local gun prevalence—subscription rates to *Guns&Ammo Magazine*.[28] While Lott relies on state-level UCR data measured at just two points in time, Duggan uses annual county- and state-level UCR data for the period 1980–98, which enables him to control for county or state fixed effects as well as other covariates. Duggan's state-level analysis finds a positive and statistically significant relationship between changes in gun ownership rates and UCR burglary rates two years in the future, while the regression coefficient on the one-year lag of the change in gun prevalence is negligible.

Measuring Crime Rates and Gun Prevalence

Direct measures of burglary rates are available from two independent sources, the *Uniform Crime Reports* (UCR), which are tabulations of crime reported to and recorded by the police and then forwarded to the Federal Bureau of Investigation (FBI), and the National Crime Victimization Survey (NCVS). For measuring gun ownership rates at the local level we rely on a well-validated proxy measure, the proportion of suicides that involve firearms.

26. Lott (2000, p. 36).
27. Smith (2000).
28. Duggan (2001).

Uniform Crime Reports

The FBI's UCR system compiles records each year from law enforcement agencies across the country for crimes known to the police. While the UCR is the only source for measuring annual crime rates for subnational jurisdictions such as states or counties, these data have several problems. First, only a fraction of serious crimes are reported to the police, and the probability that victims do report crimes seems to be systematically related to factors such as socioeconomic status, urbanicity, and local police resources.[29] Second, some law enforcement agencies do not report complete crime information to the FBI in some years. The FBI attempts to fill in missing data by an imputation procedure, which of course introduces another sort of error. Third, the published data on UCR burglary rates lump together residential and nonresidential burglaries. Although local jurisdictions are supposed to report a breakdown of burglary counts by the type of victim (residential or nonresidential) and these data are available from the UCR in unpublished form, in practice the quality control on these data seems weaker than for the overall burglary counts. Nationwide, nonresidential burglaries make up one-third of the total reported in the UCR.[30]

The UCR data do not distinguish between burglaries of occupied and unoccupied buildings. In fact, some of the hot burglaries will not even be included in the UCR burglary count, since incidents are classified by the most serious of the crimes recorded by the police. If the police record that the perpetrator robbed the occupant after breaking into the dwelling, for example, then the entire incident is recorded as a robbery rather than a burglary.

Our calculations draw on UCR data for the period 1977 through 1998, measured at both the state and county levels. The advantage of using county-level data is that we are able to account for some sources of within-state heterogeneity. The disadvantage is that they appear to be far more sensitive to problems with the imputation methods used to correct for missing data, and information on the local-area sociodemographic characteristics that may be relevant in explaining burglary rates are less readily available at the county than state level.[31]

29. Laub (1981); Levitt (1998a).
30. FBI (1996, p. 39).
31. Maltz (1999).

National Crime Victimization Survey

Since 1973 the National Crime Victimization Survey (NCVS) has provided analysts with a rich source of information on certain household and personal
crimes. Conducted by the Census Bureau for the Bureau of Justice Statistics,
the NCVS collects victimization reports from residents drawn from a sample of
50,000 to 60,000 housing units. Households are selected to participate using a
multistage sampling procedure in which the probability of selection depends in
part on the size of the respondent's county as well as other factors; sampling
weights are provided with the NCVS to generate nationally representative estimates, which are used in all of the analysis that follows. Housing units selected
for the NCVS are interviewed initially in person and then reinterviewed six
more times at six-month intervals either in person or on the telephone. Surveys
are conducted with every household resident who is 12 years of age or older,
yielding a total of 90,000 to 100,000 survey responses. Response rates with the
NCVS are typically on the order of 95 percent.[32]

Our analysis relies on a special restricted-use version of the NCVS that identifies the county in which survey respondents reside. This geocoding enables us
to merge information from the NCVS with a measure of gun prevalence in the
respondent's county. Given the limited number of years for which geocoded
NCVS data are available, we pool these data and focus our attention on cross-
sectional analyses with the NCVS.[33]

Household Gun Prevalence

Since the United States does not maintain a registry of guns in private hands,
survey data are the primary means of generating national and regional estimates
for gun ownership rates and patterns. According to the 1999 General Social Survey, 36 percent of households own at least one firearm.[34] Unfortunately, neither
the General Social Survey nor any other provides reliable estimates for each of
the fifty states or for local jurisdictions. Hence exploring the effect of gun prevalence at the subregional level requires use of a proxy variable.

Recent research demonstrates that among the readily computed proxies that
have been used for this purpose, one has the greatest validity: the percentage of

32. Perkins and others (1996).
33. While geocoded NCVS data are now available through restricted-use Census data centers
for 1987 through 1998, our own analyses rely on data for the period 1994–98. Even with the full
1987–98 sample, however, there is unlikely to be enough overtime variation in gun ownership rates
to support a fixed-effects analysis, since (as we discuss) there is only modest overtime variation even
for the 1977–98 period.
34. Smith (2000, p. 52).

suicides committed with a gun. This proxy "outperforms" such measures as the percentage of homicides committed with a gun, the prevalence of membership in the National Rifle Association, or the subscription rates for gun-oriented magazines.[35] As an example, the cross-section correlation between this proxy and survey-based estimates available for twenty-one states (from the Behavioral Risk Factor Surveillance System) is .90; the corresponding correlation for the subscription rate to *Guns&Ammo* is .67, and to the NRA membership prevalence is .55.

Inspection of our proxy highlights the substantial variation in gun ownership across states within the United States. Since suicide is a fairly rare event, in our cross-sectional analyses we improve the reliability of our proxy measure by combining suicide data for the period 1987 through 1996. This measure ranges from close to 30 percent in Hawaii and Massachusetts to more than 75 percent in Louisiana, Alabama, and Mississippi. Although these examples highlight the substantial regional differences in gun ownership rates, there is also considerable intraregional variation.[36] For example, the proportion of suicides involving guns equaled 67 percent in Vermont but only 57 percent in nearby New Hampshire and 31 percent in Massachusetts. In Illinois, guns were involved in 47 percent of suicides, compared with 55 and 63 percent in Wisconsin and Indiana, respectively. There is also substantial within-state variation among counties, even when the sample is limited to the set of large counties (with populations of 100,000 or more) for which Vital Statistics reports separate county-level mortality information.[37]

Our ability to exploit standard panel-data techniques to control for confounding factors and reverse causation is limited somewhat by the fact that the cross-section structure of gun ownership is quite stable over time. For example, in our state panel data for 1977–98 fully 90 percent of the variation in gun ownership rates is cross sectional. But the inter-temporal variation is still sufficient to generate reliable results.

Gun Prevalence and Burglary Rates

Our empirical strategy is to explore the effect of gun prevalence on burglary rates and then turn to hot burglary. We begin by developing a simple model demon-

---

35. Azrael, Cook, and Miller (2001).
36. Cook and Ludwig (1996); Glaeser and Glendon (1998).
37. We also exclude from our analytic sample counties that have fewer than fifty suicides during the 1987–96 period, although this constraint excludes relatively few additional counties.

strating that the net effect of gun prevalence on residential burglary rates may be positive or negative, depending on the relative magnitude of the deterrence effect and what we are calling the "inducement" effect. We then estimate this relationship using data from the UCR and NCVS.

Model

The opposing effects of gun prevalence on residential burglary rates are highlighted by a simple model of the expected utility of a single burglary opportunity, as in equation 1. Let G represent the proportion of households in the community that possess guns, where P is the probability that the burglar encounters an armed household resident and is shot, D is the utility associated with being shot (which we assume is independent of wealth), and L is the expected loot associated with committing a successful burglary. To further simplify the model, we assume that the burglar is risk neutral with respect to wealth and is endowed with wealth W.

$$(1) \qquad E[U[G]] = P[G] \times D + (1 - P[G]) \times (L[G] + W)$$

The probability of being shot (P) is an upward-sloping function of G. The loot associated with successful burglaries (L) is a function of G with $L'>0$ because guns present an attractive target for theft.[38]

An increase in gun prevalence will increase the utility of this burglary prospect if the additional utility from increased loot outweighs the increased probability of suffering a loss in utility from being shot, as in (2). If burglars are able to determine which homes are occupied, reducing P for a given level of G, then the inducement effect becomes more important compared with the deterrent effect. In the extreme case in which burglars are always able to avoid occupied homes (that is, $P = 0$), more guns unambiguously increase the net gains to burglary.

$$(2) \qquad (1 - P)L' > P'(L + W - D)$$

This result can be translated into a corresponding prediction about the burglary rate on the assumption that one such prospect is available to each potential

---

38. Gun prices may also be relevant in two opposing respects. First, as Mark Kleiman has pointed out to us, black-market gun prices may be inversely related to G, which if true would weaken the argument that the expected loot increases with gun prevalence. By the same reasoning, it will be cheaper for burglars to arm themselves in cities with high gun prevalence, a fact that may be relevant to the extent that gun possession makes a burglar bolder. See Cook (1976, 1991) for a similar argument on robbery.

burglar during each period. (The only complication has to do with the logical possibility that a burglar who is shot will drop out in subsequent periods.) The model demonstrates the possibility that more guns will result in more or fewer burglaries. Empirical work may help resolve this ambiguity.

UCR Results

We begin our empirical exploration using data from the Uniform Crime Reports, which are available for each year since 1977 and form the basis of earlier analyses on the same topic by John Lott and Mark Duggan.[39] Standard panel-data techniques yield a positive estimated relationship between changes in gun prevalence and changes in burglary rates. In an effort to deal with the possibility of omitted-variables bias, a set of estimates utilizing an instrumental variable for gun prevalence is also presented, with qualitatively similar findings.

Panel Data Results. The baseline model is described in equation 3, which we estimate using state-level UCR data. The key outcome measure of interest, ΔB_{it}, equals the change in state i's burglary rate between period $t-1$ and t. The key explanatory variable of interest is the change in the state's gun index, ΔG_{it-1}, which is lagged one period to minimize the problem of reverse causation; this problem arises because burglary rates may be the cause as well as the effect of gun prevalence if the demand for guns is influenced by a concern for defending against intruders. To reduce the measurement error associated with the gun proxy, each observation in our panel corresponds to a state rather than a county, and to a three-year rather than the more usual single-year period.[40] Thus for the period 1977–98 each state contributes seven observations to the panel.[41] To control for possibly confounding factors the model conditions on a vector of state sociodemographic characteristics X_{it} including per capita income, racial composition, prisoners per capita, the poverty rate, and alcohol consumption.

$$(3) \qquad \Delta B_{it} = \beta_0 + \beta_1 \Delta G_{it-1} + \beta_2 \Delta X_{it} + \gamma_i + \delta_t + v_{it}$$

---

39. See Lott (2000) and Duggan (2001). Because of problems with the crime data reported by law enforcement authorities to the UCR system our analytic sample excludes observations from Illinois, 1993–98, Kansas, 1993–98, Kentucky, 1996–98, and New Hampshire, 1997. Maltz (1999).

40. As it turns out, estimating equation 3 using single-year observations for each state rather than three-year averages yields point estimates that are similar to those in table 3-4 but with larger standard errors.

41. The last observations in the series are for the four-year period 1995–98.

Since the outcome variable is measured in change rather than level form, the time-invariant inter-state structure of burglary rates drops out. The model also includes state fixed effects (γ_i) to control for unmeasured factors that may change over time and drive state-specific *trends* in burglary rates, and period effects (δ_t) to adjust for nationwide changes over time in burglary trends. Because a given change in gun prevalence may have a larger effect on burglary rates in areas in which those rates are high, we also estimate a constant-proportional-effect version of equation 3 that uses the natural logarithm of the burglary rate as the outcome measure. To further control for time-varying unmeasured state attributes that may bias our findings, we reestimate equation 3 in a variety of alternative forms, including models that condition on lagged changes in burglary rates, state-specific linear trends, and region-period interactions, as well as a version that controls for serial correlation by allowing the error structure in (3) to follow an autoregressive process that is unique to each state. The UCR-based results are consistent in demonstrating that gun prevalence has a positive association with burglary. Table 3-3 summarizes the results for the coefficient and standard-error estimates on the gun-prevalence variable in our models. (Since the additional covariates generally have the expected effect we do not focus on them in our discussion; the full set of coefficient estimates for the "base" model is relegated to the appendix, table 3A-1).

The base model includes state and year fixed effects and several covariates. The estimated coefficients (reported in the first line of table 3-4) are positive and statistically significant in both the linear and semilog specifications and imply an elasticity of burglary with respect to the gun-prevalence proxy on the order of +0.67. The elasticity of burglaries with respect to gun ownership is slightly lower (around +0.4 or +0.5) because the proxy measure, while linearly related to gun prevalence over the relevant range, is not proportional.[42] For simplicity, and to facilitate comparisons with previous research, we focus on the elasticity of the burglary rate with respect to our gun proxy measure.

These findings are fairly robust to changes in how the model is estimated. Subsequent lines of table 3-3 report the results of conditioning on the lagged value of the dependent variable, including linear state-specific trends or region-period

42. See Azrael, Cook, and Miller (2001). The average burglary rate for the 1977–98 period was 1,276 per 100,000, while the average value for our gun prevalence proxy equaled fifty-eight, and the average gun ownership rate in the United States equaled around 40 percent. The discrepancy in elasticity estimates occurs because the gun proxy increases one-for-one with actual household gun ownership rates, while the national average for the former is far higher than for the latter (58 versus 40 percent). Thus a forty-point increase in the proportion of suicides that involve guns represents around a 70 percent increase with respect to our gun proxy but a 100 percent increase in actual household gun ownership rates.

Table 3-3. *Effects of Gun Prevalence on Burglary Rates*

Model	Dependent variable UCR burglary rate	Log UCR burglary rate
Base model	14.62*	0.0115*
	(6.78)	(0.0045)
Use log gun prevalence in base model	609**	0.4898*
	(331)	(0.2306)
Condition on lagged dependent variable in base model	9.67*	0.0076*
	(4.75)	(0.0033)
Add linear state-specific trends in base model	11.11	0.0090
	(7.84)	(0.0053)
Add region-year interactions to base model	9.00	0.0075**
	(6.46)	(0.0044)
Correct for serial correlation in error term	16.96*	0.0115*
	(3.81)	(0.0025)

Note: Table shows repeated thirty-six-month cross-sections; UCR state-level data, 1977–98, coefficients on lagged gun-prevalence variable in specified model, and robust standard errors in parentheses. Base model also includes state and year fixed effects, as well as controls for state unemployment rate, median per capita income, alcohol consumption per capita, percent poor, and percent black. State population used as weights. The correction for serial correlation allows the intertemporal correlation in the error structure to be state specific. County-level model controls for county and year fixed effects, per capita income, and unemployment rate. Data available only through 1995.

* Statistically significant at the 5 percent level.
** Statistically significant at the 10 percent level.

interaction terms in the model, or accounting for serial correlation in the error structure. Several of these changes reduce the magnitude of the coefficient on the gun proxy somewhat from the base model but do not qualitatively change the findings. Using a model specification similar to that employed by Mark Duggan, in which the log burglary rate is regressed against the lagged and twice-lagged values of the log burglary and gun ownership variables, yields qualitatively similar findings (table 3A-1).[43]

In part because the gun-prevalence variable is lagged in these regressions, it seems unlikely that the results reflect the reverse-causal effect of burglary rates on the demand for gun ownership. To further explore this possibility, we regress gun prevalence on the lagged burglary rate; that is, equation 3 is reestimated with B and G interchanged. In this set-up the coefficient estimate for the lagged burglary rate ($\Delta B_{i,\,t-1}$) is typically quite close to zero. Only when region-period interaction terms are included in the model does the burglary coefficient become statistically significant, and even then the implied elasticity is on the order of

43. Duggan (2001).

+0.06 or +0.07, far smaller than the estimated effect of the lagged gun proxy on burglary rates. Thus it appears that gun prevalence drives burglary, but burglary does not drive gun prevalence.

Instrumental Variables Estimates. Another way to address the endogeneity issue is by finding an instrument for gun prevalence that is not plausibly correlated with the error term in the burglary regression. The ideal instrument must pass three tests: it must be highly correlated with gun prevalence, not affected by the current burglary rate, and uncorrelated with any influential omitted variables. The instrument that we use exploits the fact that the cross-section structure of gun ownership rates has been highly stable over time and is driven in large part by each area's local rural tradition.[44] The instrument is the fraction of a state's population that lived in a rural area in 1950. It passes the first two tests: it is highly predictive of each state's gun ownership rate in the 1980s or 1990s and is presumably not influenced by burglary rates occurring many years later. We have less confidence in how it does by the third test; "rural tradition" in a state may be correlated with other factors that influence burglary rates, not all of which are necessarily captured by the covariates in our specification (which in this case include a measure of current urbanicity). Subject to that warning, we find that gun prevalence, as instrumented, tends to have a positive association with burglary rates.

The "instrumental variables" estimates come from estimating equations 4 and 5 using two-stage least squares. Because our instrument is defined by a single year's data (1950), we are limited to a cross-sectional analysis of burglary. In the equations G_i represents state (i)'s gun ownership rate for the period 1987–96, B_i represents the state's average burglary rate over the period 1993 to 1995, X_i represents the average value of the state-level covariates described above for the 1993–95 period (including a measure of the fraction of the state's population currently living in a metropolitan statistical area), and R_i represents the fraction of state (i)'s population that lived in rural areas in 1950. The first-stage equation 4 yields a predicted value (Γ) for each state's gun ownership rate, which is then substituted for the actual gun proxy in the second-stage equation 5.

$$(4) \qquad G_i = \alpha_0 + \alpha_1 R_i + \alpha_2 X_i + v_i$$

$$(5) \qquad B_i = \theta_0 + \theta_1 \Gamma_i + \theta_2 X_i + e_i$$

44. Azrael, Cook, and Miller (2001).

Table 3-4. *Instrumental Variables Analysis of Effect of Guns on Burglary*

Stage	Results
State-level data, first-stage	
Effects of percent rural, 1950, on percent suicides with guns, 1987–96 (beta, se)	0.60 (.13)*
F statistic on instrument (df)	20.0 (1,47)*
Partial R^2 on instrument	.0296
State-level data, second-stage	
Effect of percent suicides with guns, 1987–96, on average burglary rate, 1993–95 (beta, se)	10.11 (10.99)
County-level data, first-stage	
Effects of percent rural, 1950, on percent suicides with guns, 1987–96 (beta, se)	0.34 (.06)*
F statistic on instrument (df)	35.7 (1,47)*
Partial R-squared on instrument	.0751
County-level data, second-stage	
Effect of percent suicides with guns, 1987–96, on average burglary rate, 1993–95 (beta, se)	9.02 (11.27)

Note: Regression model for state-level estimates includes covariates for state, age, and race distribution, region, prisoners per capita, unemployment rate, poverty rate, and percent living in metropolitan areas. Regression model for county-level data controls for region, county per capita income, and unemployment rate. All regressions estimated using state (county) population as weights.

* Statistically significant at the 5 percent level.

Table 3-4 shows that the instrument R has a very strong relationship with cross-sectional variation in gun ownership rates. Using state-level cross-section data (top panel, table 3-4) the F statistic for the significance of the instrument in the first-stage equation is equal to 20 ($p < .01$), while the partial R-squared is equal to 0.03. As seen in the bottom panel of table 3-4, the instrument has similarly strong predictive power when gun-ownership levels are measured at the county level (with standard errors adjusted for the fact that the instrument varies at the state rather than county level).

The second-stage estimates (table 3-4) are positive and thus consistent with a net inducement effect for both the state and county data. Although the point estimates are not statistically significant, the implied elasticities of burglary with respect to gun ownership are equal to +0.46 and +0.41, respectively, consistent with the panel-data results shown in table 3-3. Estimating the instrumental variables model using a different three-year cross-section from the mid-1980s through the late 1990s yields qualitatively similar results to those shown in table 3-4: the estimated effects of guns on burglary rates are positive or close to zero.

In interpreting the instrumental-variables estimates in table 3-4 reverse causation can be ruled out, but there remains the possibility that the influence on current burglary rates of "percent rural in 1950" is not only through gun prevalence but also through some other mechanism not otherwise accounted for. However, any bias that results from this problem is likely to exaggerate the deterrent effect of gun prevalence, because rural areas have on average lower burglary rates and higher gun ownership rates than urban areas even after conditioning on various local-area characteristics. (See appendix 3B for a formalization of this argument.) Because our instrumental-variables strategy arguably overstates the deterrent effect of gun prevalence yet still yields estimates suggesting a net inducement effect, more guns seem more likely to lead to more rather than fewer burglaries.[45]

NCVS Results

The National Crime Victimization Survey (NCVS) provides an alternative source of data on residential burglary that is superior to the UCR data in a number of ways, as discussed above (section IIIA). The UCR, unlike the NCVS, lump together residential burglaries with commercial burglaries, only include crimes that happen to be reported to the police, and classify some incidents that included a burglary as robberies or assaults. Further they are only available at an aggregate level. The geocoded version of the NCVS data allow a fine-grained analysis of geographic patterns in residential burglary. However, since we only have access to these data in geo-coded form for the period 1994–98, we cannot reproduce the analysis of intertemporal patterns reported in the previous section.

The Probability of Burglary Victimization. Table 3-5 reports the results of a cross-section regression analysis using almost 330,000 household survey responses taken from the 1994 through 1998 twice-annual waves of the NCVS. Only households in counties with a population of 100,000 or more are included. The dependent variable in each case is a 0–1 indicator of

---

45. We also experimented with a variety of other instrumental variables although with little success. The proportion of households headed by a female has mixed predictive power in first-stage equations. Since the second-stage point estimates are typically negative, equally consistent with either a net deterrent effect or the omitted variables bias that is likely to be in the direction of the deterrent effect, these results are not very informative. A variety of state sales and excise tax variables often had first-stage explanatory power but failed standard overidentification tests.

Table 3-5. *Determinants of Burglary-Victimization Probability*

Explanatory variable	Dependent variable (burglary in previous 6 months)		
	Model 1	*Model 2*	*Model 3*
Gun prevalence	.0137*	.0110**	.0126**
	(.0030)	(.0043)	(.0053)
Residential characteristics			
Type of building			
1 unit	. . .	. . .	. . .
2–4 units	−.1266	−.1388	−.1400
	(.1027)	(.1036)	(.1027)
5 or more units	−.7208*	−.7184*	−.7524*
	(.1034)	(.1033)	(.0992)
Mobile home	.3494***	.3330	.2505
	(.2032)	(.2057)	(.2064)
Other type	−.5303	−.5044	−.4290
	(.3330)	(.3350)	(.3272)
Location			
Urban area	. . .	. . .	. . .
Suburban area	−.5711*	−.4981*	−.5434*
	(.0754)	(.0763)	(.0749)
Rural area	−.6773*	−.6081*	−.4483**
	(.2020)	(.1901)	(.1951)
Household characteristics			
Male head	−.2144*	−.2115*	−.2016*
	(.0645)	(.0632)	(.0628)
Renter occupied	.3912*	.3816*	.3797*
	(.0863)	(.0862)	(.0850)
Children under 12			
None	. . .	. . .	. . .
1	.2570*	.2466**	.2418**
	(.0956)	(.0963)	(.0965)
2 or more	.5872*	.5705*	.5549*
	(.0938)	(.0945)	(.0939)
Children over 12			
None or 1	. . .	. . .	. . .
2	.1865**	.1807**	.1697**
	(.0839)	(.0833)	(.0835)
3 or more	.9443*	.9227*	.9116*
	(.0979)	(.0987)	(.0987)
Time at address			
More than 2 years	. . .	. . .	. . .
Two years or less	.1858**	.1884**	.1759**
	(.0779)	(.0779)	(.0787)
Unknown	1.3785*	1.3783*	1.3650*
	(.1139)	(.1136)	(.1136)

(continued)

Table 3-5. (*continued*)

Explanatory variable	Dependent variable (burglary in previous 6 months)		
	Model 1	Model 2	Model 3
Characteristics of household head			
Race			
White	. . .	. . .	. . .
Black	.4208*	.4292*	.4801*
	(.1267)	(.1296)	(.1241)
Other	−.2971***	−.3267**	−.4979*
	(.1653)	(.1563)	(.1721)
Age			
Under 25	. . .	. . .	. . .
25–34	−.9037*	−.9184*	−.9218*
	(.1898)	(.1889)	(.1879)
35–44	−.7549*	−.7684*	−.7774*
	(.1911)	(.1894)	(.1893)
45–54	−.9708*	−.9882*	−.9940*
	(.1991)	(.1976)	(.1975)
55–64	−1.3133*	−1.3331*	−1.3573*
	(.2134)	(.2118)	(.2127)
65 or older	−1.7764*	−1.7891*	−1.818*
	(.2405)	(.2399)	(.2415)
Marital status			
Married	. . .	. . .	. . .
Divorced	.9170*	.9169*	.8937*
	(.1221)	(.1217)	(.1217)
Separated	.8380*	.8320*	.8544*
	(.1945)	(.1940)	(.1936)
Widowed	.1745	.1813	.2011***
	(.1132)	(.1128)	(.1137)
Never married	.2498**	.2474**	.2492*
	(.1008)	(.1014)	(.1006)
Unknown	−.1969	−.2035	−.2355
	(.2677)	(.2677)	(.2668)
Education			
High school dropout	. . .	. . .	. . .
High school graduate	−.0559	−.0301	−.0473
	(.1103)	(.1138)	(.1147)
Some college	.0430	.0583	−.0042
	(.1234)	(.1263)	(.1299)
College graduate	−.2472**	−.2246****	−.2669**
	(.1124)	(.1151)	(.1163)
Unknown	−.3423***	−.3249*	−.3458***
	(.1993)	(.2003)	(.2006)

Table 3-5. (*continued*)

	Dependent variable (burglary in previous 6 months)		
Explanatory variable	Model 1	Model 2	Model 3
Work status			
Work past 7 days	−.2188**	−.2162***	−.1986*
	(.0857)	(.0861)	(.0859)
Unknown	−.4561**	−.4548**	−.4200*
	(.2171)	(.2176)	(.2136)
Away from home during evenings			
Every night	.3497*	.3536*	.3678*
	(.0884)	(.0877)	(.0869)
Once a week	.0308	.0358	.0393
	(.0663)	(.0662)	(.0657)
Less than once a week	. . .	. . .	. . .
Unknown	−1.1566*	−1.1542*	−1.1857
	(.2158)	(.2166)	(.2125)
County demographics			
Percent black		−.0046	
		(.0083)	
Percent Hispanic		.0057	
		(.0044)	
Percent in poverty		.0146	
		(.0173)	
Percent female labor force participation		.0167	
		(.0241)	
Density (1,000 persons per square kilometer)		−.0309**	
		(.0121)	
Intercept	3.0817*	2.7482*	3.200*
	(.3844)	(.5005)	(.4657)
State fixed effects?	No	No	Yes

Note: Table shows cross-section OLS regression results, National Crime Victimization Survey (NCVS) data, 1994–98, coefficients, and standard errors (×100). All regression specifications also included dummy variables for household income levels. Model 3 also included state fixed effects.

  * Significant at the 1 percent level.
  ** Significant at the 5 percent level.
  ***Significant at the 10 percent level.

whether or not the household reported being victimized by at least one illegal break-in or attempt during the preceding six months. The average for this variable is 2 percent.

The coefficients and standard errors are least-squares estimates and are to be interpreted as the change in the probability of burglary (in percentage terms) resulting from a one-unit increase in the independent variable. All our estimates are calculated using the survey's sampling weights, and Huber-White standard errors are calculated to adjust for the clustering of NCVS observations within counties.[46] Each regression controls for a variety of household characteristics, chosen in part on the basis of previous research.[47] The three models differ with respect to the inclusion of other controls; model 2 includes five county-level descriptors, while model 3 includes a complete set of state fixed effects.[48] As it turns out, most of the coefficient estimates on household characteristics are similar across the three models. Before commenting on the gun-prevalence estimates, we offer a few observations on the results for these household characteristics, which are not without interest in their own right.

The covariates can be classified as either socioeconomic-status (SES) variables or as variables that characterize the vulnerability of the household to burglary. The results for the SES variables are quite consistent: burglary risk falls as education, age, or income increases. It is lower for households headed by a married couple rather than an unmarried adult, and it is lower if the head is employed. Renter units are more likely to be burglarized than owner-occupied residences. Even accounting for those characteristics, blacks are more likely to be burglarized than whites or other ethnic groups. The results for the variables that characterize vulnerability are also quite sensible. Households are more likely to be burglarized if they are in an apartment building rather than in free-standing residences; if located in the city rather than in the suburbs and rural areas of these (predominantly urban) counties; if the head is away from home almost every night; and if it is new to the neighborhood, having moved there within the last two years. A bit mysterious is the finding that having children at home increases the risk of burglary victimization.

The estimated effects of county-population characteristics are also interesting. These might be expected to influence the effectiveness of law enforcement, as well as the supply of criminals. As it turns out, racial composition, poverty, and female labor-force participation have little apparent effect on the likelihood of burglary victimization. Population density has a negative effect.[49]

---

46. The choice of a linear-probability approach may be questioned: standard practice when there is a binary dependent variable is to estimate a nonlinear form, such as a probit or logit. As a test, we ran a probit regression of the basic burglary specification. The qualitative results were unchanged from the linear-probability model.

47. Smith and Jarjoura (1989); Shover (1991); Wright and Decker (1994).

48. The purpose for including state fixed effects was to control for regional culture and the relevant characteristics of the state criminal-justice system.

49. We also experimented with controlling for two county-level crime rates, motor-vehicle theft and larceny, either by themselves or in conjunction with the other county-level variables. These crime rates may be indicative of the supply of criminals in the county and of the effectiveness of the criminal justice system. Their inclusion had little effect on the results and are not reported here.

The key explanatory variable of interest in these models is the proxy for gun-ownership prevalence, the proportion of suicides in the respondent's county that involved firearms during the ten-year period from 1987 through 1996. As seen in table 3-5, the findings for this variable are strong and consistent with the findings from the UCR data. The probability of burglary victimization increases with gun prevalence in the county. In particular, an increase of 10 percentage points (from, say, 50 to 60) in the gun-prevalence indicator is associated with an increase in the probability of being burglarized by about 0.12 percent, for example, from 1.80 percent to 1.92 percent. These results imply an elasticity of burglary for the gun proxy equal to .36 at the mean value of 54.

Our preferred explanation for why higher gun prevalence would engender a higher burglary rate is in terms of the monetary payoff to burglary—guns are valuable loot because they are portable and are readily sold or fenced. The plausibility of this explanation is supported by a regression analysis of the likelihood that one or more guns are stolen in a burglary in the NCVS, using the same array of model specifications as in table 3-5. In every case the coefficient is positive and significantly different from zero, indicating the unsurprising result that higher gun prevalence is associated with more guns being stolen.

However, the implied effect of gun prevalence on the overall profitability of residential burglary is not great. The likelihood of a gun being stolen in a successful residential burglary included in this sample is just 5.1 percent overall; an increase of ten points in the gun-prevalence proxy would increase the probability of guns being part of the loot by 1 percentage point. On the basis of data from a special study of burglaries in Prince George's County, we estimate the expected market value of this "prize" as about $30.[50] NCVS data for 1994–98 suggest a somewhat higher value, perhaps as high as $70—equal to about 5 percent of the mean burglary ($1,505) and 20 percent of the median ($330).[51] The actual value to the burglar depends on the local black market. In most cities the value would be less than in the licit market.[52]

50. Data on successful burglaries in Prince George's County, Maryland, were provided by the police for the years 1998–2000. There were 10,592 reported to the police during that time, of which 4.2 percent had at least one gun stolen. On average 1.8 guns were stolen, valued at an average of $327.

51. Our estimate is based on the 4,809 burglary cases reported by respondents to the NCVS between 1994 and 1998 in which something was stolen. While the NCVS does not provide information on the value of the stolen guns, it does provide information on the total value of all items that were stolen as well as the types of goods that were stolen. The value of the stolen guns to the victim is inferred by regressing the total value of what was stolen against indicators for the types of items that were taken. The regression also controls for household income, whether the home is owner occupied, and the household head's educational attainment. The coefficient on the dummy variable indicating that guns were part of the loot equals $1,384. That may be biased if burglaries in which guns are stolen tend to involve households with greater portable wealth in ways that are not fully reflected in the covariates.

52. Cook, Molliconi, and Cole (1995).

This sort of expected-value calculation presumes that burglars encounter guns by chance. But in some burglaries the burglar has knowledge of the household and its possessions because he is a neighbor or former spouse or friend. In any event, it seems relevant that in 14 percent of the NCVS cases in which a gun was stolen, it was the *only* item stolen.[53]

Specification Checks. How credible is the causal interpretation of the positive coefficient on gun prevalence?[54] One concern is that gun prevalence may be correlated with an omitted variable that is an important determinant of burglary. The most familiar approach to dealing with this possibility is to utilize instrumental variables, as we did in the previous section for the UCR data. We did experiment with this approach for the NCVS data, and our results are reported in the next section. But first we present the results of a specification test in which other household-experience variables unlikely to be influenced by gun prevalence are substituted for burglary victimization in the regressions. This test is motivated by the intuitive notion that if gun prevalence is statistically associated with these other outcome variables, then there must be an influential omitted variable in those regressions. Such a finding would suggest that there may also be an influential omitted variable in the burglary regressions.

The choice of alternative outcome measures with which to conduct this "test" seems fairly arbitrary. Our intuition was that it would be most meaningful to look at other types of crime victimization. Among the possibilities included in the NCVS, the most attractive option was motor-vehicle theft, a household crime (like burglary) that is almost always a crime of stealth, for which household gun ownership would matter very little either as a deterrent or enticement. We also analyzed two quite different variables from the NCVS, namely, whether there was a telephone in the residence and whether the respondent used public transportation.

Table 3-6 reports the results of rerunning our basic set of regressions (from table 3-5) for these outcomes. The first column repeats the estimated coefficients on gun prevalence for the burglary regressions. The second column gives the estimated coefficients when the same regressions are run with motor-vehicle theft in place of burglary as the dependent variable. The coefficient estimates are reassuringly close to zero in all specifications. "Telephone in residence" (the third column) has a negative relationship to gun prevalence, but the estimated

---

53. In another 6 percent of cases in which guns were part of the loot, the only other item taken was cash.

54. Thanks to Bruce Sacerdote for suggesting this approach.

Table 3-6. *Specification Tests for Burglary Regressions*

Covariates in specification	Burglary	Motor-vehicle theft	Telephone in residence	Use public transportation
Simple	.0245*	.0010	−.0450*	−.733*
	(.0034)	(.0013)	(.0141)	(.103)
Household	.0137*	.0003	−.0255*	−.730*
characteristics	(.0030)	(.0014)	(.0100)	(.076)
Household	.0126**	−.0001	−.0277	−.937*
characteristics and	(.0053)	(.0029)	(.0175)	(.112)
state fixed effects				
Household	.0110**	.0003	.0040	−.550*
characteristics and	(.0043)	(.0019)	(.0130)	(.068)
county covariates				

Note: Table shows cross-section OLS regression results, NCVS data, 1994–98, coefficients, and standard errors. Each entry is the estimated coefficient and standard error on the gun-prevalence proxy from a regression with specification as indicated.

 * Significant at the 1 percent level.
 ** Significant at the 5 percent level.
 *** Significant at the 10 percent level.

coefficient shrinks to near zero when we introduce the county-level social and demographic covariates.[55]

The final column of table 3-6 reports the troubling results for the use of public transportation. The coefficient estimates are significantly negative in all specifications. Although it is possible that gun prevalence does have a negative effect on use of public transportation, it seems unlikely that this mechanism is what explains these strong results—more likely the explanation is omitted-variable bias. Perhaps, for example, the missing variable is trust and support for government. Prevalent distrust of government and a taste for self-reliance may lead to more guns and less investment in public transit. Whether that same omitted variable is also present in the burglary regressions is not clear; one test of these ideas proved inconclusive.[56]

55. Particularly important are the percentage of households that are headed by females (positively related to the prevalence to telephones) and the prevalence of poverty and of black households (both of which are negatively related).

56. One proxy for "trust in government" is voting Democratic in a presidential election. We computed the percentage of voters who chose Clinton over Dole in the 1996 presidential election for each of the counties included in our sample. Voters who chose a third candidate were dropped. When included in the "public transportation" regression, that variable proved to have a significant positive effect, but with little effect on the coefficient on gun prevalence. The same was true when we included this co-variate in the burglary equation.

Table 3-7. *Effects of Gun Prevalence on Probability of Burglary*

Covariates in specification	First stage (IV on gun prevalence)	Second stage (gun prevalence on burglary)
None	.5433*	.0199**
	(.0985)	(.0104)
Household characteristics	.5440*	.0098
	(.0591)	(.0083)
Household characteristics and	.3503*	.0108
county covariates	(.0642)	(.0130)

Note: Table shows two-stage least squares regression results, NCVS data, 1996–98, coefficients, and standard errors. Entries in the first-stage column are the estimated coefficients and asymptotic standard errors of the instrumental variable (percent rural in the state in 1950). Entries in the second stage are the estimated coefficients and asymptotic standard errors for gun prevalence proxy on the probability of burglary (N,192,286).

* Significant at the 1 percent level.
** Significant at the 10 percent level.

Results from Instrumental-Variable Regressions. Table 3-7 presents the results of two-stage least-squares regressions that rely on the same instrument as in the UCR results, namely, the percentage of the state population that lived in a rural area in 1950. This instrument performs very well in the first stage and is positively related to burglary in the second stage. The magnitudes of the coefficient estimates are very similar to the magnitudes in the ordinary-least-squares analysis but due to the inflated standard errors are no longer discernibly different from zero in a statistical sense.

We also ran these regressions with the other outcome variables, as in table 3-8, and with very similar results. Coefficient estimates for motor-vehicle theft and telephone are insignificant, but the use of public transportation remains strongly negatively related to gun prevalence.

Conclusions

Taken together, the results reported here provide suggestive evidence that increases in gun ownership may lead to more burglaries. Using a new geocoded version of the NCVS we estimate the elasticity of burglary-victimization probability with respect to our county-level gun proxy to be +0.3 to +0.4, an estimate that is fairly robust to different specifications. Panel-data estimates from the UCR imply an elasticity of +0.6 to +0.7. When we address the problem of reverse causation by instrumenting for current gun ownership rates using across-state variation in the proportion of the population living in rural areas in 1950 we obtain qualitatively similar results. While lagged urbanicity may well be correlated with unmeasured factors that affect burglary rates, the direction of bias runs in the opposite direction of our findings (toward overstating deterrence and understating inducement effects) and thus seems unlikely to explain away our findings described earlier. The causal mechanism by which higher gun prevalence would engender higher burglary rates could be through the effect on the value of loot.

Guns and Hot Burglaries

The empirical results just reported are for residential burglary of all kinds. But much of the public discussion about the possible deterrent value of guns has focused on hot burglaries of occupied dwellings. In what follows we use a simple model to demonstrate that an increase in gun prevalence has an ambiguous effect on the rate of hot burglary. Cross-section NCVS regressions indicate that in practice local gun prevalence has little effect on the share of burglaries that are hot.

Model

The previous section developed a simple utility-maximizing model for burglars, which highlighted the ambiguous effects of changes in gun prevalence on the overall burglary rate. The effect of guns on hot burglaries is highlighted by the aggregate burglary equation 6, in which G (as before) is the proportion of households that keep guns, $H[G]$ represents the rate of hot burglaries, $h[G]$ represents the proportion of burglaries that are hot, and $B[G]$ represents the overall burglary rate.

$$(6) \qquad H[G] = h[G] \times B[G]$$

$$(7) \qquad H' = h'B + hB'$$

In this setup an increase in gun ownership has an ambiguous net effect on the rate of hot burglaries, as suggested by equation 7. The sign of B' must be determined empirically, since more guns may in theory lead to either more or fewer burglaries. The empirical findings discussed earlier suggest that more guns may increase the burglary rate, in which case the second term on the right-hand side of equation 7, $B'h$, is positive. The sign of the first term on the right-hand side of (7) is negative ($h' < 0$) if higher gun prevalence diverts burglars away from

Table 3-8. *Effects of Gun Prevalence on Probability of Hot Burglary*

	Dependent variable (gun stolen in residential burglary)	
Covariates in specification	Burglary cases only (N = 6,929)	Complete sample (N = 329,101)
None	−.0837	.00587*
	(.0523)	(.00127)
Household characteristics	−.0495	.00348*
	(.0517)	(.00128)
Household characteristics and	−.0625	.00376**
state fixed effects	(.0909)	(.00228)
Household characteristics and	−.0226	.00339**
county covariates	(.0720)	(.00077)

Note: Table shows cross-section OLS regression results, NCVS data, 1994–98, coefficients, and standard errors. Each entry is the estimated coefficient and standard error on the gun-prevalence proxy from a regression with specification and data as indicated.

*Significant at the 1 percent level.

**Significant at the 10 percent level.

occupied homes through a deterrent effect and positive if the opportunity to steal a gun is worth enough so that higher gun prevalence encourages burglars to take a greater chance.

Even if more guns in circulation causes burglars to take extra care to avoid occupied homes, the effect on the parameter of greatest policy interest—the probability that an occupied home is burgled—is ambiguous because of the increase in the total number of burglaries.

NCVS Results

The results from a cross-sectional analysis of NCVS data in the period 1994–98 are presented in table 3-8. The first column of estimates are of the effect of gun prevalence on the likelihood that someone is at home when there is a burglary (22 percent on average). Although the coefficient estimates are negative in every case (suggesting a deterrent effect), they are not discernibly different from zero, and in all but the simple regression have t statistics less than one. While null findings may sometimes simply reflect a lack of statistical power, in this case the NCVS data support a quite precise estimate, with the standard errors all less than one-tenth of 1 percentage point.

If, as suggested by these results, more guns lead to more burglaries but do not change the proportion of burglaries that are hot, we would expect an increase in gun prevalence to be associated with higher rates of hot burglary. Consistent with this expectation, the estimates reported in the last column of table 3-8 show that an increase in gun prevalence increases the probability that a household is victimized by a hot burglary. A 10 percentage point increase in the gun proxy increases the rate of hot burglaries by .03 or .04 percent, roughly in proportion to the increase in the overall burglary rate.[57]

Discussion

This chapter is motivated by the plausible although untested claim that widespread gun ownership deters burglars and diverts them from occupied homes. Previous evidence on this point is indirect, anecdotal, or based on flawed data, and in any case provides no clear conclusion. The new results reported here suggest that if there is such a deterrent effect, it may well be swamped by other factors associated with gun prevalence—most likely, it seems to us, that guns are particularly attractive loot. Cross-section analysis of the NCVS and panel-data analysis of the UCR yield similar findings: a 10 percent increase in our measure of gun ownership increases burglary rates by 3 to 7 percent. These results do not seem likely to occur because of reverse causation: among other evidence on this matter is the findings from our instrumental-variable estimates, which are consistent with the OLS results. Most important, we find that gun prevalence has little effect on the fraction of residential burglaries in which someone is at home, and that the hot-burglary victimization rate tends to increase with gun prevalence. These results are robust to alternative specifications and data sets. We conclude that keeping a gun at home is unlikely to provide a positive externality in the form of burglary deterrence. If anything, residences in a neighborhood with high gun prevalence are at greater risk of being burglarized, hot and otherwise. There is an irony here: guns are often kept to protect the home, but the aggregate effect of individual decisions to keep guns at home may be an increase in the victimization rate.

---

57. We also repeated these OLS estimates for a sample restricted to a group that is unusually susceptible to hot burglary rates, female-headed households. The results are qualitatively similar, although with larger standard errors.

Appendix A

Table 3A-1. *Effects of Gun Prevalence on Burglary Rates*

Item	Burg$_{it}$	Log Burg$_{it}$	Log Burg$_{it}$
	Outcome measure		
G_{it}	14.6153**	0.0015**	
	(6.7823)	(0.0045)	
Log G_{it-1}			0.6977
			(0.2076)*
Log G_{it-2}			0.4682**
			(0.2665)
Log Burg$_{it-1}$			−0.3604
			(0.1660)*
Log Burg$_{it-2}$			−0.0246
			(0.1291)
State unemployment rate	7.6282**	0.0064	0.0014
	(3.8702)	(0.0031)*	(0.0032)
Per capita income	14.9466	−0.0239	−0.0089
(thousands of dollars)	(15.2464	(0.0150)	(0.0142)
Prisoners per capita	−0.4338*	-0.0003*	−0.0005*
	(0.1259)	(0.0001)	(0.0001)
Alcohol consumption per capita	15.8253	0.0318	0.0700
	(106.6787)	(0.0614)	(0.0705)
Percent poor	18.5883	0.0102	0.0103
	(11.7789)	(0.0070)	(0.0070)
Percent black	1.6348	0.0017	0.0025
	(2.9934)	(0.0022)	(0.0022)
Year effects included in model?	Yes	Yes	Yes
State fixed effects included in model?	Yes	Yes	Yes
N	253	253	202
R²	0.5863	0.6135	0.7102

Note: The table shows regression results from repeated thirty-six-month cross-sections, UCR state-level data, 1977–98, complete list of coefficients and standard errors. Missing values for covariates are set to zero with missing-data dummies included as additional controls (not shown). State population used as weights; robust standard errors presented in parentheses.

* Significant at the 5 percent level.
** Significant at the 10 percent level.

Appendix B: Assessing the Likely
Direction of Error in the Estimates

In this appendix we outline the argument for why any bias in our instrumental-variables (IV) estimates introduced by correlation between our instrument and the unobserved determinants of burglary rates is likely to lead us to overstate deterrence and understate inducement effects.

In equations B1 and B2 we reproduce the first- and second-stage equations that we use to derive our IV estimates for the state-level UCR data. $Burg_i$ represents state (i)'s burglary rate, G_i is the gun-prevalence proxy, e_i is a stochastic error term, and R_i represents the proportion of the state that lived in rural areas in 1950. We use two-stage least squares to estimate a predicted value of the gun index in the first-stage equation B1 as a function of the instrumental variable, the proportion of the state living in rural areas in 1950; the predicted value for the gun index from this first-stage equation is then substituted for the actual value in the second-stage equation B2. Note that the actual equations that we estimate also include a common set of exogenous control variables X_i and intercept terms. Because the inclusion of covariates does not change the analysis, we exclude covariates from the equations to simplify the discussion.[58] We also note that the county-level UCR analysis and household-level NCVS estimates are calculated using the same set of equations, with R_i measured at the state level, G_i measured at the county level, and the second-stage standard errors adjusted accordingly.

(B1) $$G_i = \alpha R_i + v_i$$

(B2) $$Burg_i = \theta \Gamma_i + e_i$$

John Bound, David Jaeger, and Regina Baker show that in this set-up the bias of the instrumental variables estimate for θ is given by equation B3, where σ_G^2 represents the variance of the gun index variable and $\sigma_{\Gamma,e}$ represents the covariance between the predicted value of the gun index from the first stage equation, $\Gamma = \hat{G}$ and the second-stage error term, e.[59]

(B3) $$\mathrm{plim}\ \theta_{IV} - \theta = \sigma_{\Gamma,e}/\sigma_G^2$$

Our argument that this bias is likely to overstate the deterrent effect of guns on burglaries stems from the fact that areas that were more rural in 1950 have higher gun ownership rates ($\alpha > 0$), as shown in table 3-4, and that areas that

58. Bound, Jaeger and Baker (1995).
59. Bound, Jaeger and Baker (1995).

are currently more rural have if anything lower burglary rates than urban communities. This second observation comes from cross-section analysis of the NCVS, which suggests that households outside of metropolitan statistical areas (MSAs) clearly have lower burglary rates than other respondents even after conditioning on the rich set of household characteristics described in the text. We similarly find in the UCR that states in which a larger proportion of residents currently live in MSAs have relatively higher burglary rates. These findings suggest that the covariance between the instrument and the second-stage error term, $\sigma_{R,e}$, is negative. If $\alpha > 0$ and $\sigma_{R,e} < 0$ then $\sigma_{\Gamma,e} < 0$ and, because $\sigma_G^2 > 0$, the IV estimate will be biased in the direction of overstating the deterrent effect from guns.

Note that while the equations presented in the tables include a set of exogenous control variables, X_i, we have replicated the empirical analysis *without* covariates and obtain qualitatively similar findings—a positive coefficient in the second stage for the effects of predicted gun prevalence on burglary. With the UCR, the second-stage estimate is equal to +1.9 with the state-level data ($p = .67$) and +14.2 with the county-level data ($p < .01$). With the NCVS (reported in the top row, table 3-9), the second-stage coefficient is equal to +.02 and statistically significant at the 10 percent level ($p = .06$).

COMMENT BY
Bruce Sacerdote

This chapter explores the critical policy question of whether the presence of guns in households deters household burglaries or induces them by providing valuable loot. The authors do an excellent job of tackling this question by using multiple data sets. In the final analysis, Philip J. Cook and Jens Ludwig show convincingly that there is no evidence in these data that increases in guns in households reduce burglaries on net. Instead the authors offer evidence to support the hypothesis that the presence of guns actually induces burglaries.

Ultimately the effect of guns on burglaries is an empirical question, and we do not have simple policy experiments in this area nor do we have good data on individual ownership of guns. For this reason the authors use a clever proxy for gun ownership and test for the proxy's effect on burglaries. They use the proportion of suicides in a state (or county in the results from the National Crime Victimization Survey [NCVS]) that involve firearms. This proxy turns out to be highly correlated with gun ownership rates across states, which makes it a useful measure. Given how quick and effective guns are as a method of suicide, it seems perfectly reasonable to think that the use of a gun in suicide would be strongly related to the presence of guns in the home.

The chapter has five separate tests of the inducement hypothesis. The first set of results comes from using state-level UCR data and regressing changes in burglaries for each state on changes in the lagged gun proxy. The great strength of this panel approach is that it allows the authors to control for state fixed effects (by taking changes) and state-specific time trends. One concern with this approach is that the gun proxy may only have limited useful time variation, and thus the first difference in the gun proxy could contain a great deal of noise. But the chapter acknowledges these concerns, and the panel estimators are robust to a wide variety of specifications. The authors carefully explore the possibility that changes in guns are responding to changes in burglaries, and they rule out this reverse causation story.

The next set of estimates uses "percent rural in 1950" to instrument for the gun measure. This is a clever idea and as reasonable as any other instrument the paper might try. This instrument, like most, is relatively weak. Hence any correlation between percent rural and burglaries that does not work through gun prevalence would cause a large amount of bias in the instrumental variables estimate. But the authors make the case that the instrument is biased toward finding a negative effect of guns on burglaries (appendix 3B). Despite the downward bias, the estimate still yields a positive effect of guns on burglaries, which supports the inducement hypothesis.

The authors, using microdata from the NCVS, provide a very nice set of cross-sectional results. The dependent variable is a dummy for being burglarized, and the key independent variable is the gun proxy. These estimates yield positive elasticities of the effect of gun prevalence on burglary, and these elasticities are similar to those from the UCR state-level analysis.

If guns provided large and obvious amounts of deterrence against burglaries, it is difficult to understand why the authors would keep finding a consistent, positive effect on burglaries using a variety of plausible estimators. (Certainly one might worry about the endogeneity of the level of guns, but as discussed, the authors make every effort to solve this issue.) This evidence overwhelms the weak evidence in favor of deterrence that is contained in some of the existing literature.

The next question is to what degree we buy the author's inducement hypothesis. The coefficients and standard errors support their argument. But is the loot from guns valuable enough for gun increases to cause large increases in burglaries? According to the chapter and to the NCVS, guns are a relatively small portion of total loot reported stolen. A 100 percent increase in guns is associated with a 36 percent increase in burglary but only a 5 percent increase in expected value of loot taken. In that light, the value of guns seems low, perhaps too low to affect overall levels of burglary. But the same 100 percent increase in guns yields a 20 percent increase in the value of the *median* robbery. And this large increase in value (at the median) very well could affect criminal behavior.

Finally, the authors look at the relationship between gun prevalence and the probability that a burglary is hot. Interestingly, gun prevalence seems to be uncorrelated with the "percent hot." This is the most extensive evidence assembled on the hot burglary question, and this analysis certainly provides little support for the deterrence hypothesis.

Another simple test of the deterrence hypothesis might count up the number of times per year that guns are actively used to deter household burglars. Unfortunately, there are conflicting data on this point, and the chapter does a nice job of presenting what data there are. The data from the NCVS suggest about 32,000 such defensive uses in burglaries each year. I agree with the authors that the NCVS numbers seem more credible than other, far higher, estimates because the NCVS uses a standardized survey method and generates crime rates that can be reconciled to other crime data. An ideal future use for the NCVS survey would be to use it to collect better data on gun ownership and defensive uses.

So what can we learn from this work that will inform policymaking? Most important there is no evidence that favors increasing gun ownership by households (from current levels) to deter burglaries. Furthermore, there is some evidence that the prevalence of guns may provide an inducement to burglars. The results indicate that policymakers should not be worried about a wave of burglaries being induced by legislation that mandates trigger locks, gun safes, or waiting periods to buy handguns. Since stolen guns are often used in future violent crimes, burgled guns are part of the cheap supply of weapons to criminals. So even if the guns are not the original motive for the burglary, few people would favor increasing the number of stolen guns. Overall this chapter does much to help us understand the relative costs and benefits of increases in gun holdings by households.

COMMENT BY
David B. Kopel

The Philip J. Cook-Jens Ludwig chapter is a valuable contribution to the social science of firearms, but its conclusion is somewhat overstated. Indeed, given the constraints of what was examined, the article could not possibly prove that,

I would like to thank Paul Blackman, Gary Kleck, Carlisle E. Moody, and Iain Murray for their helpful analysis.

overall, the burglary-inducing effect of guns in America exceeds the burglary-deterring effect.

International versus Local Effects

To begin with, the authors' new research examines only data from America. The authors rather brusquely dismiss the comparative international data. While they are certainly right that there is ample room for more detailed comparative research, they do not acknowledge the possibility that their findings are consistent with the comparative data suggesting that gun density is one important reason why the U.S. home invasion burglary rate is lower than in other countries.

To see why this is so, let us step back for a moment and consider two highly regarded books about firearms. In *Crime Is Not the Problem*, Franklin Zimring and Gordon Hawkins suggest that high rates of firearms ownership help explain why the U.S. homicide rate is higher than the rate in many other nations—principally because American assaults are more likely to turn into homicides, because Americans perpetrating an assault are more likely to have a firearm handy.[60] Of course the Zimring-Hawkins international comparison is subject to many of the same data-comparability objections that Cook and Ludwig raise about international burglary comparisons, but let us, for purposes of argument, accept that the Zimring-Hawkins thesis is true.

Now consider John Lott's famous *More Guns, Less Crime*. Like Cook and Ludwig, Lott looks mainly at county-level American data.[61] He finds that when adults who pass a background check and (in most states) a gun safety class are allowed to obtain permits to carry handguns for lawful protection, the violent crime rate, including homicide, falls. The more people who carry, the more the crime rate falls. Although Lott's work has been subjected to intensive and not always persuasive data torturing by people determined to disbelieve his conclusions, let us for the sake of argument assume that Lott's study is valid.

It is entirely possible that the Zimring-Hawkins international conclusion and the Lott county-level conclusion are both true. That is, as Zimring and Hawkins suggest, America's much higher rates of gun density do result in a much higher American homicide rate. (Perhaps in part because high gun density creates a large pool of stealable guns that are readily and casually obtained by thugs and other miscreants who go off half-cocked and all-crocked, starting fights with one another on street corners where drugs are sold or in the park-

---

60. Zimring and Hawkins (1997).
61. Lott (2000).

ing lots of bars after closing time. This population carries guns regardless of whether it is legal to do so.) At the same time, it is possible that allowing non-criminal adults to carry guns pursuant to a government permit might deter or thwart a certain amount of crime, an amount far larger than the tiny amount of crime that these permit holders would perpetrate.

Thus greater American gun density on the macro scale (Zimring and Hawkins, international) might cause more homicide, while greater gun carrying at the micro scale (Lott, county level) might reduce homicide. It would hardly be surprising that increased gun availability among criminals (people who perpetrate assaults) would increase unlawful homicide, while increased gun availability among the law-abiding (people who obtain government-issued permits) would reduce unlawful homicide. At least as a logical matter, there is no reason why both effects cannot be true.

Again, I am not necessarily arguing that Zimring and Hawkins or Lott are correct; Gary Kleck's much larger cross-national data set finds no statistically significant relation between gun availability and homicide, and Kleck argues that "shall-issue" concealed handgun laws result in too small an increase in actual gun carrying for Lott's crime-reduction results to be plausible.[62] Rather, my point is that as a logical matter, the Zimring-Hawkins findings and the Lott findings *could* both be true.

What Cook and Ludwig attempt to do is use county-level data to show that more guns lead to more burglary. It is entirely possible for this microlevel hypothesis to be true *and* for the Kopel and Kleck hypothesis that, on the international scale (macro), America's much higher gun density helps produce a lower burglary rate.[63] Indeed, it is easy to see how Cook and Ludwig, Kopel, and Kleck could be simultaneously true.

Compared with foreign burglars, a higher percentage of American burglars are apt to avoid occupied residences, for fear of getting shot, and this is why American home invasion burglaries are rarer than in other countries.[64] Nevertheless, an especially reckless or foolhardy cohort of American burglars are not deterred, and these burglars actually prefer to burglarize homes with guns, since guns are uniquely valuable loot; thus counties with more guns have relatively higher burglary rates according to Cook and Ludwig. Thus, at the most, the Cook-Ludwig chapter tells us about the relative effects of gun density in America, but the chapter does not disprove the evidence gained from data on burglary internationally.

62. Kleck (1997, pp. 253–54, 372).
63. Kopel (2001); Kleck (1997).
64. Kopel (2001); Kleck (1997).

What Cook and Ludwig Measured

A second reason why Cook and Ludwig's conclusion should not be so strongly stated is that the study itself looks at only a subset of counties. Low-population counties are excluded. The effect of this exclusion may not be neutral. Because low-population counties are especially likely to have a small, scattered population that is far away from law enforcement assistance, such counties may be precisely the places where people are most likely to rely on guns to resist burglars. Because of the relative impotence of sheriffs and police (owing to long distances) and because of the paucity of neighbors to report suspicious persons, the marginal burglary-deterrent effects of firearms in such counties might be especially high. Notably, smaller counties tend to be more rural and usually tend to have higher rates of gun ownership and lower rates of burglary than more heavily populated counties within a given state.

In short, Cook and Ludwig prove, at most, that within medium to large American counties, the burglary-inducing effects of marginal increases in gun density outweigh the burglary-deterring effects of marginal increases in gun density.

Even for the medium and large counties, the findings are not nearly as clear as Cook and Ludwig urge. The correlation coefficient is a tiny 0.01—meaning that different counties yielded extremely disparate results. If Cook and Ludwig included a scatter graph, we would not see points bunched in clusters. To the contrary, the points would more likely appear as a vague, dissipated cloud. To suggest that this cloud of weakly correlated results can be turned into a generally applicable principle of cause and effect is an overstatement.

Of course the study does not attempt to quantify the possible secondary costs and benefits of home firearms and burglary. For example, we know that about 98 percent of burglary alarm activations are "false positives" and that responding to false alarms wastes a great deal of police resources.[65] To the extent that gun owners are less likely to rely on alarm systems because of their confidence in their ability to protect their families and homes personally, gun ownership would create a positive social externality, by reducing the false alarm drain on police resources.

Treating Guns Like Cars

Even if, as Cook and Ludwig conclude, the collective decisions of many families to purchase firearms does, in the aggregate, very slightly raise the burglary rate, the families are not necessarily acting irrationally or antisocially. After all,

65. Blackstone and others (2002).

the collective decisions of many families to purchase automobiles (or to purchase second or third cars for the family) very likely does, in the aggregate, raise the automobile accident rate in a community (including accidents involving people who do not own cars; for example, cars may hit bicyclists or pedestrians). More cars, more driving. More driving, more accidents. Also, more autos, more auto theft—and thus more autos in criminal hands.

Yet before telling families not to buy cars, we would consider what the families gain in exchange for the increase in the incremental accident rate and the incremental increase in the supply of cars to criminals that is inflicted on the community. The family with the car gains mobility and independence, the option of coming and going according to the family's needs. Many people also derive pleasure from driving.

Similarly, whatever the effects of firearms on aggregate burglary rates, the family with firearms gains the opportunity to participate in shooting sports, as well as the ability to use a firearm to protect the family in various situations that might have nothing to do with home invasion burglary.

Prior Scholarship

In summarizing prior literature on the burglary and gun issue, Cook and Ludwig go overboard in their claims that evidence is conflicting and inconclusive. To the contrary, well-designed studies of prisoners, of active burglars, and of ordinary citizens consistently find that active armed defense against burglars by victims is frequent and is feared by most burglars.[66] Against this evidence, Cook and Ludwig merely cite studies that do *not* directly ask about use of firearms against burglars but simply allow for that information to be volunteered.[67]

Moreover, the brush-off of studies that do ask about armed defense is unnecessary for Cook and Ludwig's thesis. It is possible that armed home defense is frequent and widely feared by most burglars *and* that reckless and foolhardy burglars—attracted by guns as loot, or excited by the thought of a gun battle—commit extra burglaries when guns are thought likely to be in a victim's home. Thus Cook and Ludwig's conclusion does not depend on armed home defense being rare, and their chapter does nothing to disprove the research suggesting that armed home defense is common and widely feared by most but not all burglars.

But is the conclusion technically valid? Perhaps not. First, the article uses the percentage of suicides that are committed with guns (PSG) as a proxy for changes in gun ownership over time. However, the creator of the PSG proxy, Gary Kleck,

---

66. Wright and Rossi (1994); Wright and Decker (1994); Ikeda and others (1997).
67. Cook (1991); Kellermann and others (1995).

has demonstrated that the PSG is *not* a valid measure of gun ownership changes over time, although the PSG can measure differences between areas (or groups) at a common point in time.[68]

Indeed, the PSG correlates very well to surveys of household gun ownership— but this is simply correlation to another proxy, not correlation to the thing itself (actual gun ownership). Household surveys of American gun ownership rather consistently yield disparate results (as low as a third of homes, to as high as half of homes) which are well outside the margin of error—so we know that household surveys are not a particularly accurate reflection of reality.[69]

The accuracy of household gun surveys is seriously impaired by the "dark figure" created by gun owners who refuse to disclose their gun ownership to a pollster.[70] This fact becomes especially important in the burglary context. Cook and Ludwig plausibly suggest that in many cases for which stealing a gun was the sine qua non of the burglary, the burglary may be an inside job—perpetrated by an acquaintance who personally knows the victim and knows that the victim owns a gun. Obviously the kind of gun owner who is at greatest risk of such targeted burglary is the gun owner who freely tells people that he owns guns—in other words, the kind of gun owner who is likely to answer a household gun survey truthfully. Conversely, the secretive gun owner—who will not talk to a pollster— may be more likely to keep her gun ownership a secret from her acquaintances as well. Thus the secretive gun owner would be unlikely to be the victim of a targeted gun-seeking burglary.

Now since the PSG and the household surveys correlate so well, what Cook and Ludwig may have ended up measuring is not the actual availability of guns in various counties but the existence of loose-lipped gun owners. The proper conclusion might be changed from "Guns cause burglary" to "Talking about guns with the wrong people causes burglary."

Cook and Ludwig forthrightly acknowledge the problem of reverse causality: do guns cause burglary (by inducement), or does burglary cause guns (as a citizen response to rising crime)? One of Cook and Ludwig's approaches to the causality problem is to use an "instrumental variable," namely, the percentage of a state's population that was rural in 1950. This choice is based on the commonsense and explicitly stated assumption that rurality (or rural heritage) is correlated with participation in the American gun culture. The choice of rurality as an instrumental variable also requires the assumption that rurality does *not* affect participation in burglary. If this assumption is incorrect, then we have

68. Kleck (2002).
69. Kleck (1997).
70. Kleck (1997).

not escaped from the problem of reverse causality. Cook and Ludwig do not offer evidence that rurality does not affect burglary.

In the panel study, the causation problem recurs. Cook and Ludwig address this concern by lagging burglary rates and gun ownership; thus they account for someone who buys a gun in 1998 in response to burglary conditions in 1996. But what about people who buy guns in 1996 because of burglary conditions in 1996? The Cook and Ludwig model appears to assume that gun buying in response to burglary is always lagged by a year or more from actual burglary conditions. The model does not account for a current increase in the burglary rate causing a current increase in gun ownership.

Cook and Ludwig make a passing reference to a study by Mark Duggan in which the circulation of *Guns&Ammo* magazine was used as a proxy variable for gun ownership. As Carlisle E. Moody and Thomas B. Marvell detail, Duggan uses the coefficient from the proxy variable as if the proxy were the actual variable itself.[71] Moody and Marvell demonstrate how this error undermines Duggan's assertion that "guns cause crime" more than "crime causes guns." Moody and Marvell suggest that the same problematic use of the coefficient for the proxy variable affects the Cook and Ludwig study, undermining Cook and Ludwig's claim to have solved the causality problem. If the elasticity of the proxy (PSG) with respect to actual gun ownership is less than one, then Cook and Ludwig's causation conclusion would be reversed: burglary would cause guns to a much greater degree than guns would cause burglary.

Cook and Ludwig offer an additional attempt to address causality; they find a relationship between burglary victimization (as reported by NCVS respondents) and gun prevalence in the surrounding area (as measured by the PSG). But Cook and Ludwig fail to control for crime rates in the surrounding area. Their gun prevalence measure thus serves as a surrogate for rates of crime (and, therefore, the number of criminals) in the surrounding areas. Hence the coefficient for the gun prevalence variable at least partly represents a response to the presence of so many criminals in the respondent's neighborhood, rather than the burglary-inducing effect of gun availability. More criminals, more burglary. The data do show a relationship between burglary and gun prevalence, but not necessarily, as Cook and Ludwig argue, because guns induce burglary, rather than vice versa.

Even so, Cook and Ludwig have advanced the debate. At least in the scholarly world, the gun control discussion continues to evolve constructively, as scholars abandon arguments about whether guns, in general, are good or bad,

---

71. Duggan (2001); Moody and Marvell (2002).

and instead focus on the effect of firearms in particular situations. Cook and Ludwig provide an important contribution to the small but growing body of research on guns and burglary.

References

Australian Broadcasting Corporation. 2001. "Queensland Police Review Security After Guns Stolen from Circulation." (May).

Ayres, Ian, and Steven Levitt. 1998. "Measuring Positive Externalities from Unobservable Victim Precaution: An Empirical Analysis of Lojack." *Quarterly Journal of Economics* 113 (1): 43–77.

Azrael, Deborah, Philip J. Cook, and Matthew Miller. 2001. "State and Local Prevalence of Firearms Ownership: Measurement, Structure, and Trends." Working Paper 8570. Cambridge, Mass.: National Bureau of Economic Research.

Blackstone, Erwin A., Simon Hakim, and Uriel Spiegel. 2002. "Not Calling the Police (First)." *Regulation* 25 (Spring): 16–19.

Bound, John, David A. Jaeger, and Regina M. Baker. 1995. "Problems with Instrumental Variables Estimation When the Correlation between the Instruments and the Endogenous Explanatory Variable Is Weak." *Journal of the American Statistical Association* 90 (430): 443–50.

Bureau of Justice Statistics (BJS). 1997. *Criminal Victimization 1996: Changes 1995–96 with Trends 1993–1996. NCJ-165812.* U.S. Department of Justice.

Cook, Philip J. 1976. "A Strategic Choice Analysis of Robbery." In *Sample Surveys of Victims of Crime,* edited by Wesley Skogan, 173–87. Ballinger.

———. 1987. "Robbery Violence." *Journal of Criminal Law and Criminology* 70 (2): 357–76.

———. 1991. "The Technology of Personal Violence." In *Crime and Justice: An Annual Review of Research,* edited by Michael Tonry, 1–71. University of Chicago Press.

Cook, Philip J., and James A. Leitzel. 1996. " 'Perversity, Futility, Jeopardy': An Economic Analysis of the Attack on Gun Control." *Law and Contemporary Problems.* 59(1): 91–118.

Cook, Philip J., and Jens Ludwig. 1996. *Guns in America: Results of a Comprehensive Survey of Gun Ownership and Use.* Washington: Police Foundation.

———. 1998. "Defensive Gun Uses: New Evidence from a National Survey." *Journal of Quantitative Criminology.* 14(2): 111–31.

———. 2000. *Gun Violence: The Real Costs.* Oxford University Press.

———. 2001. "Litigation as Regulation: Firearms." In *Litigation as Regulation,* edited by W. Kip Viscusi, 67–105. Brookings.

Cook, Philip J., Jens Ludwig, and David Hemenway. 1997. "The Gun Debate's New Mythical Number: *How* Many Defensive Uses Per Year?" *Journal of Policy Analysis and Management.* 16 (3): 463–69.

Cook, Philip J., Stephanie Molliconi, and Thomas B. Cole. 1995. "Regulating Gun Markets." *Journal of Criminal Law and Criminology* 86 (1): 59–92.

Cutler, David M., Edward L. Glaeser, and Karen E. Norberg. 2001. "Explaining the Rise in Youth Suicide." In *Risky Behavior Among Youths: An Economic Analysis,* edited by Jonathan Gruber, 219–70. University of Chicago Press.

Duggan, Mark. 2001. "More Guns, More Crime." *Journal of Political Economy* 109 (October): 1086–1114.

Federal Bureau of Investigation. 1996. *Crime in the United States, 1995.* Government Printing Office.

———. 1999. *Crime in the United States, 1998.* Government Printing Office.

Glaeser, Edward L., and S. Glendon. 1998. "Who Owns Guns? Criminals, Victims, and the Culture of Violence." *American Economic Review* 88(2): 458–62.

Hemenway, David. 1997a. "The Myth of Millions of Self-Defense Gun Uses: An Explanation of Extreme Over-Estimates." *Chance* 10 (3): 6–10.

———. 1997b. "Survey Research and Self-Defense Gun Use: An Explanation of Extreme Over-Estimates." *Journal of Criminal Law and Criminology* 87 (2): 1430–45.

Home Office. 1999. "Burglary of Domestic Dwellings: Findings from the British Crime Survey." London: Home Office. Research, Development, and Statistics Directorate.

Ikeda, Robin M., Linda L. Dahlberg, Jeffrey J. Sacks, James A. Mercy, and Kenneth E. Powell. 1997. "Estimating Intruder-Related Firearm Retrievals in U.S. Households, 1994." *Violence and Victims* 12 (4): 363–72.

Kellermann, Arthur L., and Donald T. Reay. 1986. "Protection or Peril? An Analysis of Firearm-Related Deaths in the Home." *New England Journal of Medicine* 314 (June 12): 1557–60.

Kellermann, Arthur L., Lori Westphal, Laurie Fischer, and Beverly Harvard. 1995. "Weapon Involvement in Home Invasion Crimes." *Journal of the American Medical Association* 273 (22) (June 14): 1759–62.

Kleck, Gary. 1991. *Point Blank.* Aldine de Gruyter.

———. 1997. *Targeting Guns: Firearms and Their Control.* Aldine de Gruyter.

———. 1998. "Has the Gun Deterrence Hypothesis Been Discredited?" *Journal of Firearms & Public Policy* 10: 65.

———. 2002. "Measures of Gun Ownership Levels for Macro-Level Crime and Violence Research." Manuscript. Florida State University.

Kleck, Gary, and Marc Gertz. 1995. "Armed Resistance to Crime: The Prevalence and Nature of Self-Defense With a Gun." *Journal of Criminal Law and Criminology* 86 (1):150–87.

Kopel, David B. 2001. "Lawyers, Guns, and Burglars." *Arizona Law Review* 43 (Summer): 345–67.

Laub, John H. 1981. "Ecological Considerations in Victim Reporting to the Police." *Journal of Criminal Justice* 9: 419–30.

Lee, Roberta K., Richard J. Waxweiler, James G. Dobbins, and Terri Paschetag. 1991. "Incidence Rates of Firearm Injuries in Galveston, Texas, 1979–1981." *American Journal of Epidemiology* 134 (5): 511–21.

Levitt, Steven D. 1997. "Using Electoral Cycles in Police Hiring to Estimate the Effect of Police on Crime." *American Economic Review* 87(3): 270–90.

———. 1998a. "The Relationship between Crime Reporting and Police: Implications for the Use of Uniform Crime Reports." *Journal of Quantitative Criminology* 14 (February): 61–81.

———. 1998b. "Why Do Increased Arrest Rates Appear to Reduce Crime: Deterrence, Incapacitation, or Measurement Error?" *Economic Inquiry.* 36(3): 353–72.

Lott, John R. 2000. *More Guns, Less Crime,* 2d ed. University of Chicago Press.

Ludwig, Jens. 2000. "Gun Self-Defense and Deterrence." *Crime and Justice: A Review of Research, Volume 27,* edited by Michael Tonry, 363–417. University of Chicago Press.

Ludwig, Jens, and Philip J. Cook. 2000. "Homicide and Suicide Rates Associated with Implementation of the Brady Handgun Violence Prevention Act." *Journal of the American Medical Association.* 284 (5): 585–91.

———. 2001. "The Benefits of Reducing Gun Violence: Evidence from Contingent-Valuation Survey Data." *Journal of Risk and Uncertainty* 22 (3): 207–26.

Maltz, Michael D. 1999. *Bridging Gaps in Police Crime Data.* NCJ 176365. U.S. Department of Justice.

McDowall, David, Alan J. Lizotte, and Brian Wiersema. 1991. "General Deterrence through Civilian Gun Ownership." *Criminology* 29 (4): 541–59.

Miller, Matthew, Deborah Azrael, and David Hemenway. 2001. "Firearm Availability and Unintentional Firearm Deaths." *Accident Analysis and Prevention* 33: 477–84.

Miller, Matthew, and David Hemenway. 1999. "The Relationship between Firearms and Suicide: A Review of the Literature." *Aggression and Violent Behavior* 4(1): 59–75.

Moody, Carlisle E., and Thomas B. Marvell. 2002. "Pitfalls of Proxy Variables: Comment on Mark Duggan, 'More Guns, More Crime.' " Manuscript.

Perkins, Craig A., Patsy A. Klaus, Lisa D. Bastian, and Robyn L. Cohen. 1996. *Criminal Victimization in the United States, 1993: A National Crime Victimization Survey Report.* NCJ 151657. U.S. Department of Justice.

Rengert, George, and John Wasilchick. 1985. *Suburban Burglary: A Time and a Place for Everything.* Charles C. Thomas.

Shover, Neal. 1991. "Burglary." In *Crime and Justice: An Annual Review of Research, Volume 14,* edited by Michael Tonry, 73–113. University of Chicago Press.

Smith, Tom W. 1997. "A Call for Truce in the DGU War." *Journal of Law and Criminology* 87 (4): 1462–69.

———. 2000. *1999 National Gun Policy Survey of the National Opinion Research Center: Research Findings.* University of Chicago.

Smith, Douglas A., and G. Roger Jarjoura. 1989. "Household Characteristics, Neighborhood Composition and Victimization Risk." *Social Forces* 68 (2): 621–40.

Steyn, Mark. 2000. "In the Absence of Guns: In Britain, Defending Your Property Can Get You Life." *The American Spectator* (June): 46–48.

Tucker, William. 1996. "Maybe You Should Carry a Handgun." *Weekly Standard* 2(14), Dec. 16: 30.

United Nations. 1998. *United Nations International Study on Firearm Regulation.* New York.

U.S. Bureau of the Census. 1999. *Statistical Abstract of the United States.*

White, A. 1983. "Response Rate Calculation in RDD Telephone Health Surveys: Current Practices." In *Proceedings of the American Statistical Association, Section on Survey Research Methods,* 277–82. Washington: American Statistical Association.

Wintemute, Garen J., Carrie A. Parham, James Jay Beaumont, Mona Wright, and Christiana Drake. 1999. "Mortality among Recent Purchasers of Handguns." *New England Journal of Medicine* 341 (21): 1583–89.

Wright, James D., and Peter H. Rossi. 1994. *Armed and Considered Dangerous: A Survey of Felons and Their Firearms (expanded edition).* Aldine de Gruyter.

Wright, Richard T., and Scott H. Decker. 1994. *Burglars on the Job.* Northeastern University Press.

Zimring, Franklin E. 1968. "Is Gun Control Likely to Reduce Violent Killings?" *University of Chicago Law Review* 35: 721–37.

———. 1972. "The Medium is the Message: Firearm Calibre as a Determinant of Death from Assault." *Journal of Legal Studies* 1: 97–124.

Zimring, Franklin E., and Gordon Hawkins. 1997. *Crime Is Not the Problem: Lethal Violence in America.* Oxford University Press.

PART II

Regulating Ownership

PETER REUTER
JENNY MOUZOS

4 | Australia: A Massive Buyback of Low-Risk Guns

On April 28, 1996, in the historic Tasmanian penal colony of Port Arthur, a lone gunman killed thirty-five persons with a semiautomatic rifle. Following that incident, which was the largest of a series of mass homicides, the federal and state governments of Australia agreed on a broad plan of gun control, implemented over the following twelve months. The new controls included prohibitions on certain categories of firearms, to be supplemented by a large-scale buyback of those weapons and new licensing, registration, safe storage, and firearm training requirements.

Three features of this experience make it of potential interest to U.S. gun control scholars. First, in a federal system there was unanimous agreement by all the relevant governments to make changes that were consistent across states, rapidly implemented, and extremely far reaching. This offers an instance of gun control in a situation of high salience. The program had strong political support and competent execution. Second, the gun buyback program was vastly larger and better funded than comparable efforts in the United States. Third, the interventions had modest effects on the extent of suicide and violent crime. Suicide rates did not fall, though there was a shift toward less use of guns, continuing a very long-term decline. Homicides continued a modest decline; taking into account the one-time effect of the Port Arthur massacre itself, the share of mur-

We are grateful for assistance from Helen Begg.

121

ders committed with firearms declined sharply. Other violent crime, such as armed robbery, continued to increase, but again with fewer incidents that involved firearms. This relatively small effect is hardly surprising given that the type of firearms prohibited had not previously been used frequently in crime or suicide, as well as the low power of the potential tests, with less than five years of postban data. However, the principal goal of the intervention was ending the mass murders; in the five years since the buyback, there has been a modest reduction in the severity of these murders, and none have involved firearms, though the frequency of these events is so low that not much can be inferred from this occurrence.

Literature Review and Analytic Framework

The Australian response to the Port Arthur massacre was similar to the response of Britain to massacres in Hungerford in 1987 and Dunblane in 1996. Each British incident was followed by prohibitions on additional types of guns. In 1988 the newly prohibited guns were certain self-loading and pump-action rifles and shotguns; in 1997 handguns of .22 caliber or higher were prohibited.[1] Both times owners of these weapons were offered compensation for turning them in. According to the Home Office, the 1988 buyback resulted in the collection of approximately 3,500 self-loading rifles and carbines, with total compensation in the area of £600,000. The 1997 buyback resulted in the collection of more than 162,000 handguns and 700 tons of ammunition. Compensation payments totaled some £90 million (about $U.S. 130 million) plus administrative costs of £8 million including special grants to police forces.[2] Firearms covered by certificates (that is, legally owned) fell from 414,000 in 1996 to 305,000 one year later. These figures do not include the approximately 1.3 million shotguns for which certificates were also required.

There is no evidence that the new prohibitions and buybacks reduced violent crime in the United Kingdom. Recorded gun crimes fluctuated between

1. Self-loading and pump-action rifles and shotguns differ from other firearms in the number of shots they can fire with each pull of the trigger. Self-loading or semiautomatic firearms reload automatically after each shot, so the user does not have to insert a fresh round of ammunition after each bullet is fired. Each time the trigger is squeezed, a shot is fired. The size of the magazine will determine how many rounds can be fired in rapid succession. Some of these firearms can be equipped with trigger accelerators, a device that "pumps" the trigger repeatedly. The practical effect is that the firearm discharges multiple cartridges in quick succession without the shooter having to execute a complete pull of the trigger for each shot.

2. Wilkins and Addicot (1998) report that after passage of the 1997 act, 110,382 of large-caliber handguns were handed in, along with another 24,620 smaller-caliber handguns "in anticipation of further legislation."

4,900 and 6,900 over the period 1995 to 2000, with no clear trend. Homicides totaled 728 in 1999–2000, compared with 585 in 1996. Firearm homicides, always less than 10 percent of all homicides, did not fall. Firearm robberies as a share of all robberies continued a fall that had begun in 1993.[3] In a nation that already had strict gun control and low rates of firearm-related crime, these new restrictions could hardly be expected to make much difference in total violent crimes.

A number of foreign jurisdictions have implemented purer gun buyback programs. Following a civil war, some nations have tried to buy back the stockpile of combatants' guns. For example, it was recently reported that Japan is "considering accepting an informal United Nations request to provide $3 million in financial assistance to help finance the world body's small arms collection in Sierra Leone. . . . The U.N. has been paying $150 to each Sierra Leone militiaman who surrenders small arms."[4] Cambodia has also been the site of a Japanese-funded buyback program.

In the United States there has been a steady flow of initiatives at every level. For example, in 1998 President Bill Clinton set aside $15 million for the Department of Housing and Urban Development to buy guns from public housing residents. Cities or counties have also launched such programs on their own initiative; Baltimore, Boston, Seattle, St. Louis, and Washington, D.C., are just some of the more prominent. One of the attractions of gun buybacks is their promise of increasing popular participation in gun control and of raising the salience of the issue. Indeed, some have been launched by local nongovernmental organizations. For example, "Goods for Guns of Allegheny County" (in Pittsburgh) launched such a program in 1994 and reported in 2001 that the organization had collected 7,184 guns over an eight-year period, paying (with gift certificates) the equivalent of $50 for handguns and $25 for rifles and shotguns.[5]

Programs offer anonymity. Without that, those in possession of an illegal weapon, the programs' most highly valued targets, are less likely to participate. The programs are usually of limited duration (weeks or months), partly for incentive reasons and partly because of administrative costs. The returned weapon may be investigated to determine whether it was used in any criminal offense but is not used to pursue the individual who turned in the gun (for example, through fingerprints).

3. Home Office (2000).
4. H. Masaki, "Japan Funds Extension of Small Arms-Collection Program," *Japan Times,* January 18, 2002. In the context of Sierra Leone incomes, $150 is a very large sum, perhaps equivalent to three months' earnings.
5. "Goods for Guns of Alleghany County," press release, December 10, 2001.

The U.S. buyback efforts occur in the context of existing gun control laws and regulations. Their premise is that fewer guns will lead to lower levels of violence, since the availability of firearms is frequently asserted to be an important factor in explaining variation in violent crime rates; for example, research by Mark Duggan suggests a relationship between gun ownership and both homicide and suicide rates.[6] Arthur Kellermann and his colleagues found that possession of a gun in a household increased the risk of victimization.[7]

The literature on gun buybacks in the United States has strained to find any evidence of violence reduction.[8] Failure has often been ascribed to the small scale of the interventions; $100,000 for purchase of firearms, usually handguns, would produce a minimal reduction in the stock of firearms available in an American city.[9] For example, at $50 a weapon (a typical price), the program would produce only 2,000 guns. In a nation with 800 guns per 1,000 population (and roughly 280 handguns per 1,000) this will account for barely 1 percent of all guns in a city with 250,000 population.[10] If a large fraction of firearms handed in were weapons at high risk of use in criminal offenses there might still be a substantial effect on crime, but the characteristics of those handed in suggest quite the opposite. For example, David Kennedy, Anthony Braga, and Anne Piehl note that the type of pistols favored by youthful offenders are hardly represented among the guns turned in, and that "many guns were chambered in unusual and obsolete calibers, such as those used in older military style rifles."[11]

There are also more systematic threats to buyback effectiveness. It may be that buybacks increase the demand for guns, directly and indirectly. An offender contemplating acquisition of a weapon has in effect a price support program, a guaranteed minimum compensation, namely, the buyback price.[12] Though each program is of limited duration, its existence in any city suggests the possibility of a repeat. Just as amnesties undercut immigration controls, or compensation programs to coca growers for taking land out of production can promote coca growing, so buybacks lessen the risks of gun ownership. They can also provide an incentive for theft of guns. Though buyback programs set low prices, compared with sales through the illegal markets, transactions can be consummated more rapidly and safely in the buyback program.

6. See Duggan (2001) and his chapter 2 in this book.
7. Kellermann and others (1993).
8. See, for example, Rosenfeld (1996).
9. Kennedy, Braga and Piehl (1996).
10. Kleck (1996) estimates that the programs will remove no more than 2 percent of the total stock of guns.
11. Kennedy, Braga, and Piehl (1996), p. 158. See also Callahan, Rivara and Koepsell (1994).
12. Similar arguments are made by Mullin (2001).

The hypothesized link between buybacks and violent crime is straightforward. By making the most lethal weapons (firearms) less available, the number of violent crimes will fall and the average lethality of those crimes will also decline. There are many assumptions built into this chain of reasoning, and it has been subject to numerous attacks.[13] For example, buybacks may not reduce the stock of weapons available; a buyback may merely facilitate disposal of unwanted guns that the buyer will replace through purchase of other more desired guns. Even if the stock of active guns is reduced, offenders, by substituting less intimidating instruments of violence (such as knives), will have greater incentive to use the weapon rather than control the actions of victims merely through showing the gun; that may generate more violent crime, in particular homicides. However, the evidence suggests that substitution away from firearms does lead to fewer fatalities and serious injuries.

The theory of buybacks as a gun control measure rests on the guns purchased being at substantial risk of criminal use. Diminution of the stock of low-risk guns will do little to affect criminal options. Perhaps there is a complex substitution effect; with fewer of one class of gun available, the market price for the high-risk categories will rise as former owners attempt to maintain their stock of weapons, and that will lead to fewer being held by high-risk owners. That seems unlikely, but that is one proposition that the Australian program can test.

Australia is an attractive site for evaluation of a buyback because of its isolation. It is more difficult to import prohibited guns into Australia than into the United States or any western European country because there are no land borders. There is no domestic production for domestic sales. Unfortunately from a research point of view, the consistency of the approach taken by each state and territory government in Australia in the enactment of uniform firearm legislation, including buyback programs, together with the paucity of state-level data, has meant that an evaluation can only be conducted for the whole country and not for individual states or counties.[14]

Historical Background

Though Australia was initially settled as a penal colony at the end of the eighteenth century, it has not been characterized by high levels of gun violence. There was no frontier as Americans think of that, a region with a substantial settler population in which the power of the state was weak and the settlers resorted to guns to settle disputes, though Aborigines were subject to much brutality.

13. See Cook, Moore and Braga (2001).
14. For example, there are no data on total firearms holdings by state.

Australia, despite the prominence of the Outback in its international image, is overwhelmingly urban; 85 percent of its population lives in major metropolitan areas. Approximately one-quarter live in the Sydney metropolitan area and another quarter in Melbourne. The population was ethnically homogeneous until about 1950; the overwhelming majority was from the British Isles, though with a sharp social and political division between Irish (Catholic) and English (Protestant) populations. Since 1950 large-scale immigration has transformed the cities; Asians now account for more than 5 percent (and the share continues to rise), while among the European-origin population, the share from the British Isles, has fallen substantially. Australia now has much of the ethnic diversity of the United States. It too has an Indigenous population, which suffers much higher rates of violence, suicide, alcoholism, and unemployment. Indigenous persons (constituting about 2 percent of the total population) suffer from discrimination, despite large-scale government aid programs. One important difference from the United States is that there is no Australian counterpart to the large African American population, with a legacy of slavery and discrimination.

Crime rates generally have been close to the average of other wealthy Western nations. Comparing Australia to England/Wales, Canada, New Zealand, the United States, and Japan, Australia has neither the highest nor lowest rate for any of five major offense categories (homicide, robbery, assault, motor vehicle theft, larceny).[15] Australia does have an unusually large and rapidly growing heroin problem.[16] In 1998 the estimated prevalence of heroin addiction was about 690 per 100,000 persons 15 to 54 years old, very close to that for the United States. Moreover, whereas the heroin addiction rates in the United States and western Europe have generally been flat over the past ten years, rates have been rising rapidly in Australia, particularly in Sydney and Melbourne. Heroin addicts exhibit high rates of criminal offending, though the differences between them and any matched population are greater for property than violent crime.[17]

The Australian Bureau of Statistics maintains a historical series (based on Causes of Death data) on total homicides and firearm-related homicides starting in 1915. For total homicides the variation is between about 1 and 2.5 per 100,000; for firearm-related homicides, the lowest annual rate was 0.16 in 1950, and the highest was 0.78 in 1984. U.S. homicide rates per 100,000 in the mid-1990s were about 8.5 for all homicides and 6.5 for firearm-related homicides. In recent times, the homicide rate in the United States has decreased significantly but is still several times higher than other similar countries such as Canada, England and Wales, and Australia. However, a different picture emerges

15. See Barclay and Tavares (2000) for international comparisons of criminal justice statistics for the year 1998.

16. Bammer and others (2002).

17. EMCDDA (2001).

when firearm-related homicides are excluded from the homicide rates of these four countries. When firearm-related homicides are excluded from analysis, the homicide rates of these four countries not only converge over time, but the proportionate ratio between them decreases substantially.

Gun ownership rates in Australia are also in the middle of the range for Western nations. In 1994 the figure per 100,000 in Australia was 19,444, compared with 29,412 in New Zealand and 85,385 in the United States and 3,307 in Britain.[18]

Essentially all new guns in Australia are imports, perhaps facilitating control efforts.[19] Over the period 1988–97, total imports annually ranged between 40,000 and 70,000, approximately 1–2 percent of the estimated mid-1990s stockpile (table 4-1).[20] This figure included imports of handguns for use by police services, which accounted for a substantial fraction of total handgun imports.

Australia experienced thirteen mass killings (defined as four or more victims killed within a few hours) in the period 1989–90 to 1996–1997, an average of 1.3 incidents per annum.[21] Of these thirteen incidents, six involved a firearm; the others involved a knife (two), arson (two), or a blunt instrument (three). During the same period, the United States (with a population fifteen times as large) had approximately twenty-six such killings annually. James Fox and Jack Levin report an average of nineteen such incidents annually involving a firearm over the period 1976–95.[22] These constitute three-quarters of the mass homicides compared with about half in Australia. Though on a per capita basis the two nations are similar in mass homicides per 100,000 persons, mass killings account for a larger share of total homicide-related deaths in Australia than in the United States. Between 1989–90 and 2000–01, mass murders accounted for 3 percent of all homicides in Australia.

The share of homicides accounted for by firearms in the period before 1996 was 21 to 30 percent, much lower than for the United States (65 percent) and much higher than for England and Wales (8 percent). Knives and hands and feet accounted for more homicides than firearms.

18. Firearms Control Task Group (1995, table 1.1).

19. There is only one firearm manufacturer in Australia—Australian Defence Industries Limited, producing primarily Austeyr F88 military rifles. Of its roughly 110,000 production in the period 1988–96, only 159 were sold to Australian individuals. Most were sold to the Australian Defence Forces (John Fenton, personal communication, 2002).

20. Even if the average length of life for a firearm is fifty years, this import level would barely maintain the stockpile in the long run. Given annual population growth of about 1.5 percent, the stock of guns per capita is probably declining.

21. The definition excludes serial homicide, that is, incidents in which the same offender killed four or more victims but over a period of more than a few hours. See Mouzos (2000c, 2002a). The largest before Port Arthur included the death of seven victims and the suicide of the killer.

22. Fox and Levin (1998).

Table 4-1. *Imports of Firearms, by Type*

Year	Military style	Handguns	Shotguns	Rifles	Total
1988	1,920	6,596	11,319	20,594	40,429
1989	1,680	6,649	15,049	35,168	58,546
1990	4,548	6,065	20,497	45,687	76,797
1991	436	7,411	17,210	35,238	60,295
1992	7,888	7,829	7,510	18,798	42,016
1993	16,710	9,830	7,498	16,715	50,753
1994	15,267	9,994	10,004	21,629	56,894
1995	1,686	9,244	12,209	22,068	45,207
1996	357	9,795	21,356	37,864	69,372
1997	532	7,443	28,595	30,191	66,761
1998		12,484			
1999		10,047			
2000[a]		12,416			
Total, 1988–97					567,070

Source: Australian Bureau of Statistics (ABS) as reported by Gun Control Australia, Melbourne, 1998.
a. As of July 31, 2000.

Firearms have been involved in many more suicides than homicides; for example, in 1993 there were 435 suicides involving a firearm, compared with only 64 homicides.[23] The firearm-related suicide rate in Australia is much lower than the U.S. rate, about 1.25 compared with about 6 per 100,000 in the United States.[24] About 90 percent of firearm-related suicides in Australia in 1998 involved a long gun, either rifle or shotgun.[25]

Table 4-2 presents comparisons of the United States and Australia in various dimensions:

The firearm-related suicide rates had been declining for ten years before the Port Arthur incident; the two other series of interest (unintentional and homicide) were erratic over the same period.

The New Controls

Within two weeks of the Port Arthur massacre, the Commonwealth and state governments held a meeting (the Australasian Police Ministers' Council [APMC]), which produced a consensus report containing a series of new restrictions and pro-

23. See Mouzos (1999, table 1).
24. Cook and Ludwig (2000).
25. Mouzos (2000b).

Table 4-2. *Suicide and Homicide Rates, Australia and United States, 1998*[a]

Category	Australia	United States
Total homicide rate	1.80	6.80
Firearm-related homicide rate	0.30	4.40
Fraction of homicides committed with firearms	0.17	0.65
Total suicide rate	14.30	11.30
Firearm-related suicide rate	1.30	6.40
Fraction of suicides committed with firearms	0.09	0.55

Sources: Adapted from ABS, *Causes of Death* (1998); Centers for Disease Control (1998).
a. Total and firearm-related rates per 100,000 people.

grams (National Firearms Agreement [NFA]).[26] In order to own a firearm, an individual was required to show a legitimate purpose and fitness of character ("genuine reason and need for owning, possessing or using a firearm"), conform to stringent safe storage requirements, and undertake safety training if a new licensee.[27] This effectively introduced uniform licensing and registration of firearms in all eight states and territories in Australia, replacing a patchwork that included regimes of varying stringency. Moreover, certain classes of weapons (self-loading rifles, self-loading and pump-action shotguns) were prohibited, as was the importation of these weapons. To encourage compliance with the new prohibitions, the Commonwealth (federal) government financed a large-scale gun buyback program, conducted by the states.[28] The buyback initially covered only newly prohibited weapons, primarily long arms; later it was extended to include nonconventional weapons, such as submachine guns and heavy machine guns.[29] There was also an amnesty for handing in unlicensed firearms during that same period, but no payments were made for these weapons.

The focus on long guns was a consequence of two facts. First, semiautomatic weapons and rifles had been used in the most prominent of the mass killings. Second, handguns were already tightly regulated. The implication was that long guns were the appropriate target for any new legislative initiative.

By U.S. standards implementation was rapid and uniform. All states had passed legislation by May 1997, twelve months after the APMC meeting. The

26. Australasia includes New Zealand. The New Zealand government, despite its participation in the APMC, has not implemented the recommendations from the 1996 meeting.

27. APMC special firearms meeting, May 10, 1996.

28. Dealers were also eligible for compensation, indeed even for loss of value of stocks; payments to dealers totaled $A50 million. Australian National Audit Office (1997).

29. The most controversial purchase was of twenty-two World War II aircraft cannons, for which the Northern Territory government paid $440,000. Questions were raised about how much these purchases posed a threat to public safety.

buyback program had been completed by September 30, 1997. The differences among the states in regulation and statute were modest. The most serious was a technical aspect of the initial Queensland law that allowed for "inoperable" firearms to be deregistered. No other state had a similar provision. The Queensland provision was changed when a substantial number of guns were sold by two dealers in the "inoperable" version but then, lacking any registration information, reassembled in other states.[30]

Gun Buyback

The most novel feature of the National Firearms Agreement was the decision to support the new restrictions on gun types and ownership by attempting to buy back a substantial fraction of the stockpile.[31] An expert committee developed a price list, which would be used by all states so as to prevent any shopping around among states. Between 1996 and 1997, 643,726 prohibited firearms were handed in.[32] Prices were set to reflect "fair value" (market value). Individuals with permits could also turn in firearms that they had failed to register. Total public expenditures were about $A320 million ($U.S. 230 million[33]), approximately $A500 ($U.S. 359) per gun. The buyback program was financed by an additional 0.2 percent levy on national health insurance.

Estimates of the total stock of guns were few and drew on limited survey data. Estimates ranged as high as 11 million, but the high figures had no known provenance. Gun Control Australia cited a figure of about 4.25 million, building on the only academic estimate, then roughly twenty years old.[34] The most targeted population survey of gun ownership was conducted by Newspoll; the resulting estimate was approximately 2.5 million firearms in 1997, after the gun buyback. If that is approximately correct, it suggests that there were about 3.2 million firearms in 1996 and that the buyback led to the removal of approximately 20 percent of the total stock. In U.S. terms that would be equivalent to the removal of 40 million firearms.

---

30. Fitzgerald and others (2001).

31. Frank Zimring (conference discussion) observed that the Fourth Amendment on "takings" would probably require any new gun prohibition in the United States to be accompanied by an offer of compensation.

32. This was five times as many guns as were bought back in England and Wales in 1997. On a per capita basis, it was fifteen times as many. However, as a share of the stockpile it was probably smaller. Data on the numbers of unlicensed but nonprohibited guns handed in are not available for all states; in New South Wales, there were 37,000 of these compared with 155,000 prohibited weapons.

33. Exchange rate as of September 25, 1997.

34. Harding (1981).

There are no national published figures on the number of guns registered until 2001.[35] In Victoria, with about one-quarter of the Australian population, there were 750,000 registered weapons, of which 220,000 fell into the newly prohibited category in 1996. Approximately 210,000 prohibited guns were handed in, but 20 percent of these were unregistered, so that the success rate for registered prohibited firearms was about 70 percent.[36] It is possible that the firearms that were registered and technically "prohibited" were category C firearms, which are prohibited except for occupational purposes (that is, persons who are primary producers).

Nationally, estimates of the buyback penetration range between 40 percent and 80 percent, depending on differences in beliefs about the size of the stock of prohibited firearms in June 1996. The share probably varied by state. For Tasmania, the state in which the Port Arthur massacre occurred, the state police estimated that 90 percent of prohibited guns were handed in.[37] In New South Wales and Queensland, where the "shooters" lobby had been more politically prominent, the share may only have been 50 percent of the prohibited guns.[38]

The number of guns handed in per capita varied considerably, as shown in table 4-3. The low figure for the Australian Capital Territory, the capital city of Canberra, probably represents the high degree of urbanization, usually associated with fewer hunting weapons.[39] But there are no data that would allow systematic analyses of the correlates of gun turn-in. As of July 2001, there were 764,518 individual firearm license holders and 2,165,170 registered weapons in Australia. On a population basis approximately 5 percent of the total population (18 years and over) hold a current firearm license.[40]

Since the buyback there have been a series of "rolling amnesties." Firearm owners can hand over guns that are either prohibited or not registered, without penalty, during a fixed period. Substantial numbers of guns have been handed in. A four-month amnesty in New South Wales in 2001 resulted in 5,772 firearms being handed in and the registration of 72,000 firearms under the amnesty.[41] At the time of implementation of the NFA, 155,000 prohibited guns were handed in, along with 37,000 unregistered guns.

35. Mouzos (2002b)
36. Gun Control Australia, "Gun Buyback," press release, July 29, 1998, Melbourne.
37. Security Australia (1997).
38. Gun Control Australia, "Gun Buyback."
39. In a survey of electors in 1998, it was found that firearm ownership levels varied between urban and rural environments; only 4 percent of respondents living in inner metropolitan areas lived in a household with a gun present, compared with 24 percent of rural respondents. Makkai (2000).
40. Mouzos (2002b).
41. Helen Begg, personal communication, April 26, 2002. This amnesty did not have a financial component (that is, no compensation was paid for the surrendered weapons).

Table 4-3. *Gun Buyback, Totals and Expenditures, by Jurisdiction, August 2001*

Region	Number of firearms collected	Compensation paid to firearm owners (A$ thousands)	Population (100,000s, approximate)	Guns per 100,000
Victoria	207,409	101,823	48	4,300
New South Wales	155,774	83,535	65	2,400
Australian Capital Territory	5,246	2,803	3	1,800
Tasmania	34,584	19,650	5	6,400
Northern Territory	9,474	5,039	2	4,700
Western Australia	51,499	18,758	19	2,700
South Australia	64,811	25,369	15	4,300
Queensland	130,893	67,614	36	3,600
Total	659,940	359,600	193	3400

Source: Adapted from Commonwealth Attorney-General's Department (2002); ABS (2001).

Very little is known about the characteristics of the purchased guns beyond numbers in each state. Only for Victoria is a breakdown of gun types available. Nearly half were "Rimfires (Pea Rifle)"; almost all the remainder were shotguns (Victorian Firearms Licensing Branch). Only 204 automatics were handed in (fewer than the 247 machine guns), representing just one in a thousand of the guns received. There are no data from administrative records on who handed guns in during the buyback.

A survey found that, on the basis of self-reports, 573,000 persons claimed to have handed in a gun in the twelve months before July 1997, about 4.2 percent of those 16 and over.[42] At the time about 14 percent of households (and 10 percent of persons) reported owning at least one gun. More than half of households that owned firearms reported two or more guns; 16 percent had four or more. Consequently the fraction of households with firearms did not much decline with the buyback. The survey did estimate that three-quarters of those who had owned an illegal gun at the time of the new laws were no longer owners of any illegal guns.[43] Over 95 percent of the population knew of the new laws, and 56 percent strongly favored them. The published survey results included no demographic breakdowns.

The passage of the new statute led to a large increase in membership of firearm associations.[44] Membership enabled an applicant to meet the require-

42. Newspoll (1997).

43. Self-report of illegal gun ownership is particularly suspect at a time when disapproval was being so strongly, prominently, and frequently reported.

44. For example, membership of the Sporting Shooters Association of Australia (SSAA), the largest firearm association in Australia, increased from 42,000 in April 1996 to approximately 115,000 as of February 4, 2002.

ment of having a legitimate purpose for owning a firearm (long gun or hand-gun). The associations have been very critical of new training standards and the requirements for trainer eligibility. There have been corresponding complaints from the other side about laxity in regulation and enforcement.

Storage and Training Requirements

The specifics of these regulations need not concern us, but they were onerous. For example, most gun types had to be stored "in a locked receptacle constructed of either hard wood or steel with a thickness to ensure it is not easily penetrable. If the weight is less than 150 kilograms the receptacle shall be fixed to the frame of the floor or wall so as to prevent easy removal. The locks fitted to these receptacle shall be of sturdy construction." Firearm sales could be conducted only through licensed dealers. In turn, such dealers could mail only to other dealers. All other purchases had to be made in person.

Though requiring approximately eight hours of class time, training require-ments apparently were not onerous.[45] Of 15,000 persons who applied for a license to own a gun in Victoria in 2000, only ten failed to pass the test.[46]

Enforcement

Penalties for violations of firearms law were substantially enhanced. Possession of a prohibited firearm or handgun in New South Wales is punishable by a max-imum fourteen-year prison sentence; sale of such a weapon could earn a twenty-year sentence. New South Wales has a population of 6.5 million and in 1999, there were 24 firearm homicides and 737 firearm robberies. One study reports that 284 persons were convicted of possession of a firearm without a license (prin-cipal offense), where the maximum penalty is two-years' imprisonment.[47] Of these, only eleven received any prison time at all. A majority received only a fine (average value $A439).

New South Wales created a Firearms Trafficking Unit in September 1999, the first specialized unit to deal with illegal firearms.[48] In its first eighteen months of operation, which included undercover purchases, the unit seized 216 firearms and arrested twenty-eight people on firearm charges.[49] The arrest figure hardly

45. Australian Police Ministers' Council (2001).
46. Gun Control of Australia, "How Many Guns in Australia?" press release, June 29, 1998, Melbourne.
47. Fitzgerald and others (2001).
48. Helen Begg, personal communication, New South Wales Police Service, 2001.
49. See Fitzgerald and others (2001, p. 7). Recent figures indicate that the unit has seized almost 400 weapons. See *Daily Telegraph,* December 26, 2001.

suggests intense enforcement, but there is no means of measuring the base (number of sales of prohibited or unregistered firearms to persons without a license), a matter we return to at the end of this chapter.

Registration can be revoked, and there is some enforcement of those conditions. For example, if a Domestic Violence order is sworn out against an individual with a licensed gun, the gun will be seized by the police. Data on the frequency of such seizures were not obtainable.

Assessing the Results

A small number of indicators on the use of guns and crime levels are available and have been extensively analyzed by the Australian Institute of Criminology.[50] We examine seven indicators: homicides, homicides with a gun, suicides, suicides with a gun, other violent crime, prices for guns in illegal markets, and reported theft of firearms. We hypothesize that, given the characteristics of the guns purchased, effects will be found only in the share of these crimes that involve use of a firearm, but even these will be modest. Gun prices may also be only slightly affected, unless there is a substitution effect among firearm types.

— Number of homicides. The total homicide rate has been slowly declining throughout the 1990s (figure 4-1). In the five years post-NFA there has been no pronounced acceleration of that decline.

A study by Jenny Mouzos and colleagues examined the effect of the Port Arthur massacre on the incidence of subsequent homicides in Australia.[51] They found that the Port Arthur incident did not have a significant effect on the temporal behavior of total homicides but had a significant sudden effect on the temporal behavior of firearm homicides (there was an instantaneous increase in the average number of firearm homicides during the five days following the massacre). They also found that the daily rate of homicide, both total and firearm homicide, has declined since the Port Arthur incident. Overall, there has been a decline of 8.9 percent in the rate of total homicide and a 3.2 percent decline in the daily rate of firearm homicide. However, these observed declines in total homicide and firearm homicide continued a long-term trend rather than the effect of the Port Arthur incident.[52]

Between 1996–97 and 2000–01 there were four mass homicide incidents: two incidents involved four victims (knife and carbon monoxide gas), one incident had five victims (carbon monoxide gas), and another incident fifteen victims (arson/fire). All but the last mass murder occurred in a domestic situation.

50. Mouzos (1999, 2000a, 2000b, 2000c, 2001a, 2001b, 2002a, 2002b).
51. Carcach, Mouzos, and Grabosky (2002).
52. Mouzos (1999).

Figure 4-1. *Homicide Rate per 100,000 People, 1989–90 to 2000–01*

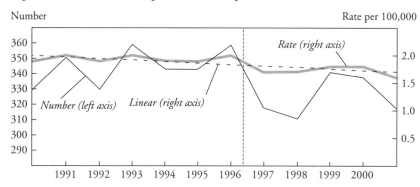

Source: Australian Institute of Criminology, National Homicide Monitoring Program, 1989–90 to 2000–01 (computer file). Figures 4-1 through 4-6 show statistics for Australia.
Note: Includes victims of Port Arthur. $y = -0.0273x + 2.0273$; $R^2 = 0.5598$.

There was at least one firearm mass murder in four of the six years before the Port Arthur incident (between 1989–90 and 1994–95); not including the year of the Port Arthur incident (1995–96). In the five years since the massacre, there have not been any firearm-mass murder incidents in Australia (between 1996–97 and 2000–01). Moreover, the average number of victims involved in these murders has been smaller than in the earlier mass murders.

— Homicides committed with a firearm. Firearm-related homicides declined between 1980 and 1995 and then fell sharply from 1996 to 1999 (figure 4-2). Jenny Mouzos reports that for the period 1989–1999 just under one quarter of all homicides were committed with a firearm.[53]

The share of firearm homicides that involved a handgun did increase sharply after the NFA, from less than one-sixth in 1992–93 to 50 percent in 2000–01.[54] This is consistent with a decrease in the availability of long guns. Between July 1, 1997 (after implementation of the NFA), and June 30, 1999, only 10 percent (11 out of 117) of firearm homicides involved use of a registered gun by a licensed owner; in five of the 117 deaths, the gun was owned by the victim.

New Zealand participated in the Australasian Police Ministers Council but chose not to implement the NAF. It is of some interest to compare changes in homicide and gun-related homicide rates in New Zealand with those in Australia. In New Zealand, there was no decline in the total number of homicides, but a significant decline occurred in the fraction committed with a firearm.[55]

53. We exclude 1996, since the Port Arthur massacre accounted for one third (35 of 111) of all firearm-related homicides that year. Mouzos (2000a).
54. Mouzos (2002a).
55. New Zealand Police National Headquarters, Homicide Statistics and Analysis.

Figure 4-2. *Proportion of Firearm Homicides, 1980–99*

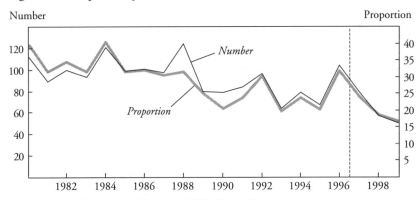

Source: Australian Bureau of Statistics (ABS), *Causes of Death.*
Note: Includes victims of Port Arthur.

— Suicides and suicides with a firearm. Substitution of weapon is as plausible for suicides as homicides, though the nature of the substitution is different.

Australian suicide rates have fluctuated around about 20 per 100,000 since the end of World War II. Suicide is just as sensitive to the age distribution of the population as is homicide; rates for suicide generally are much higher among the elderly. The age-adjusted rates for firearm-related suicides fell sharply over the entire period 1979–98; the NFA generated no noticeable break in the series.[56] Figure 4-3 shows age-standardized rates for suicide in total and suicide with firearms. A sharply increasing share of suicides is the result of hanging or suffocation, surely representing different dynamics from instrumentality.

In Australia, as elsewhere, men are much more likely than women to use a firearm for suicide. Despite this, figure 4-4 shows that the rate of firearms suicide declined as sharply in the 1990s for women as it did for men.

— Injuries with a firearm. Jenny Mouzos notes that accidental firearm injury rates declined over 1995–99.[57] The number of firearm-related hospitalizations has declined each year between 1994–95 and 1998–99.[58] Over that period, about half each year are classified as accidental. This decline in accidental injury is consistent with diminished stockpile and enhanced safety requirements, but the decline starts well before the NFA implementation and is no sharper following than in the two years before.

56. Harrison and Steenkamp (2000) report that age-adjusted rates for suicide showed similar fluctuations to the unadjusted rates.

57. Mouzos (2001b).

58. These are counts of "separations . . . the term used to refer to an episode of care, which can be a total hospital stay (from admission to discharge, transfer, or death) or a portion of a hospital stay ending in a change of type of care (for example, from acute to rehabilitation)." Mouzos (2001b, p. 1).

Figure 4-3. *Age-Standardized Suicide Rates Using Firearms versus Total Suicide Rates, 1979–98*

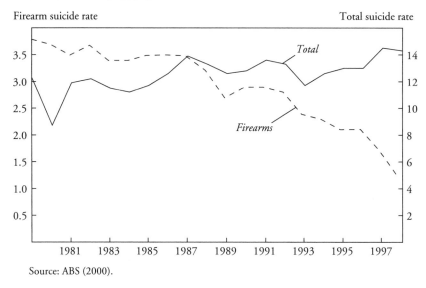

Source: ABS (2000).

Figure 4-4. *Suicide by Firearms, Males and Females, 1979–98*

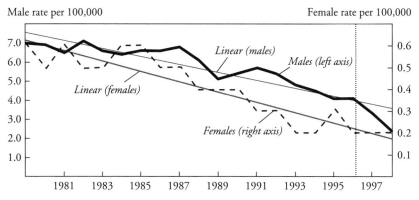

Source: ABS (2000). $R^2 = 0.8558$ for males; $R^2 = 0.8532$ for females.

Figure 4-5. *Proportion of Attempted Murders by Type of Weapon*

Percent

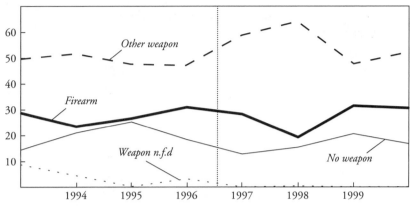

Source: ABS, *National Crime Statistics* (1994–96) and *Recorded Crime Australia* (1997–2001).

— Other violent crime. Limited data are available on the use of firearms in the commission of violent crime other than homicide. Official statistics on attempted murder indicate that the use of firearms has remained stable, fluctuating between 29 percent in 1993 and 31 percent in 2000 (figure 4-5). Although there has been an increase in the incidence of assault over the years, the use of firearms in the commission of assault is extremely rare. During 2000, Australia recorded 141,124 assaults, of which 786 involved the use of a firearm; that is, barely 0.5 percent of assaults were committed with a firearm.[59]

In contrast, the use of firearms in the commission of armed robbery has changed greatly over the years. Despite an overall increase in the number of armed robberies between 1993 and 2000, the proportion of armed robberies committed with a firearm has declined substantially.[60] For example, in 1993, 37 percent of armed robberies were committed with a firearm (1,983). Since then the proportion has declined to a low of 14 percent in 2000 (1,328) (figure 4-6). While the use of firearms to commit armed robbery has fallen, there has been a subsequent increase in the use of "other weapons" such as knives to commit armed robbery.[61]

— Gun prices. Prices of guns in illicit transactions are many times higher than the cost of the same gun in a legal retail purchase, suggesting tough enforce-

59. ABS (2001).

60. Mouzos and Carcach (2001). In 1993 Australia recorded 5,294 armed robberies compared with 9,474 in 2000. ABS (2001).

61. The use of "other weapons" in the commission of armed robbery increased from 3,068 in 1993 to 7,537 in 2000. ABS (2001).

Figure 4-6. *Proportion of Armed Robberies by Type of Weapon*

Percent

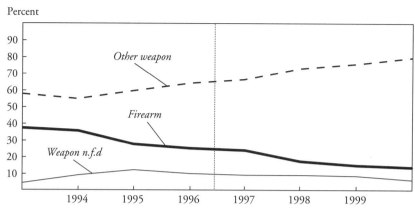

Source: ABS, *National Crime Statistics* (1994–96) and *Recorded Crime Australia* (1997–2001).

ment.[62] Data have been collected by a special firearm unit of the New South Wales Police Service on both retail and wholesale transactions involving four or more firearms. Data were available for five different guns. The only gun for which the illicit price is not at least four times that of the legitimate retail price is the Desert Eagle, a rare and high-end gun that may be perceived as having a relatively high risk of detection if used in a crime. No data were available on how prices had changed over time.

— Theft of firearms. A recently released report examining the theft of firearms in Australia between 1994–95 and 1999–2000 found that the majority of firearms reported stolen to police were rifles (51 percent), followed by shotguns (22 percent) and handguns (14 percent); most were stolen from a residential premise (81 percent).[63] Theft is a rare event; with a total stock of approximately 3 million firearms post-1997, only about one firearm in a thousand is reported stolen in the course of a year.

The number of firearms reported stolen declined sharply post-NFA. Data on the category of firearms stolen were available for South Australia only. Trend analysis for South Australia indicates that the number of category A firearms, that is, air rifles, rim-fire rifles, and single- and double-barreled shotguns, reported stolen increased after 1996–97 from about 266 in 1996–97 to 330 in 1999–00, whereas the number of category D firearms that are prohibited except for official purposes decreased from 280 in 1996–97 to less than 10 in 1998–99 and 1999–00.

62. Cook, Molliconi, and Cole (1995).
63. Mouzos (2002b).

The overall decline in the number of firearms reported stolen, and the specific decline in category D firearms, may reflect several factors: the effects of the NFA's increased storage requirements, the reduction in the number of newly prohibited category D firearms, and decreased willingness to report theft of these firearms precisely because they are prohibited. The third factor cannot be discounted as contributing to what otherwise appears to be one of the successful outcomes of the NFA.

Discussion

The NFA can be treated as a case study in the effects of tightening an already stringent gun control regime. It involved numerous changes, any of which could in theory have had a serious influence. The gun buyback in support of a new prohibition is the most distinctive but not necessarily the most important. The introduction of the uniform licensing and registration system across Australia has meant that persons who do not have a genuine reason and need to own a firearm will find it difficult to obtain a firearm *legally*. This consequently reduces the number of people who can obtain and have access to firearms legally; there is still, of course, access to firearms through the illegitimate firearm market.

There may have been a modest effect on homicides. The number declined continuing a preexisting trend. Given only five years of postban data, one could not reject the hypothesis that it had reduced homicides by 10 percent. The share of homicides committed with firearms fell sharply after the implementation of the NFA; among firearm homicides, an increasing share were with a handgun, whose ownership had been tightly restricted even before 1996. The fact that New Zealand, a similar nation in many respects, which did not introduce the new measures, saw no decline, provides a small piece of evidence in favor of an NFA effect.

Suicide did not decline, but again there was a sharp decrease in the share involving a firearm, continuing a long trend. Although there has been a significant decrease in the number of armed robberies committed with a firearm, the decline began before 1996; the decline was more pronounced post-NFA.[64]

All this is generally consistent with a story of substitution. Firearms were never the dominant means of homicide or suicide and reducing the availability of one form of firearm was not likely to have a large effect. The more stringent registration and licensing requirements (including a twenty-eight-day waiting period for

---

64. These conclusions are similar to those of Carcach, Mouzos, and Grabosky (2002).

purchasers) may have made a difference; not enough detail is yet available on the characteristics of licensed weapons to allow analysis of this possibility.

The buyback alone was an implausible candidate for reducing crime rates because the targeted gun type was one not much used in homicides or, presumably, other kinds of violent crime.[65] Even if half of long-gun homicides were eliminated, homicide rates would decline by only 5 percent, difficult to detect in a series as noisy as this one. The hypothesis that gun owners would try to maintain their total inventory of weapons and thus reduce offender holdings of higher-risk weapons, a hypothesis with low face plausibility, was not supported.

In important respects the NFA was similar to the U.S. ban on assault weapons and large capacity magazines, analyzed by Christopher Koper and Jeff Roth.[66] This again targeted a class of firearm that accounted for fewer than 8 percent of homicides before the 1994 ban, which also followed some highly publicized mass murders. Koper and Roth report very modest effects on homicide from that ban; their best estimate is a statistically insignificant 6.7 percent decline in the year immediately following the ban. Gary Kleck argues that even this figure is an overestimate and that the assault weapon ban could at most have led to a reduction of two homicides annually.[67]

The Australian evidence is slightly more promising when one looks at what the program targeted, namely, the occurrence of another "Port-Arthur" incident in Australia, which explained the choice of weapons prohibited and purchased. Five years post-NFA, no mass murders have been committed with a firearm in Australia. There have been three mass murders in five years, a statistically insignificantly lower rate than pre-1996, and two of the three incidents were lower salience and involved domestic disputes only. Given that mass murders cause so much community fear, it is appropriate to choose this as an evaluation outcome separate from homicide rates generally.

For those interested in gun buyback proposals as a means of reducing violent crime, the results provide little insight. The Australian buyback was certainly large scale. It acquired a substantial fraction of the prohibited firearms, perhaps three-quarters. Even as a share of all firearms, the buyback led to the removal of a noticeable fraction of holdings. However, it targeted a low-risk weapon, quite the opposite of U.S. gun buyback program targets. Whether a large-scale buyback with a more appropriate target can make a difference to violent crime rates remains to be tested.

65. Between July 1, 1992, and June 30, 1999, 16 percent of homicides were committed with firearms prohibited post-Port Arthur (10 percent if one excludes the Port Arthur incident) (Mouzos 2000a).
66. Koper and Roth (2001).
67. Kleck (2001).

Note on Sources

The gun control debate in Australia provokes rhetorical debate comparable to that found in the United States. The Sporting Shooters Association of Australia (SSAA) and the principal gun control advocacy group, Gun Control Australia Inc., occupy positions roughly comparable to those of the National Rifle Association and Handgun Control Inc. Their websites contain primarily materials supporting their views, though in 2002 they started to include more neutral papers.

The Australian Institute of Criminology (AIC) has a National Firearms Monitoring Program and a National Homicide Monitoring Program. The AIC provides objective statistical analysis of homicide trends and has published some analyses of the effects of various interventions. Other useful reports can be found on the site of the Bureau of Crime Statistics and Research of the New South Wales Attorney General's Department. Otherwise there are little data or published research.

COMMENT BY
Anne Morrison Piehl

It is often argued that a reduction in the ownership of guns through a buyback initiative will work to reduce gun violence. Programs to purchase guns from citizens have been implemented in many jurisdictions, with government or private sources providing the funding. Although the literature does not provide an optimistic view for their prospects, one could reasonably argue that past efforts were on a small enough scale or were so poorly implemented that the buyback idea has not been fully tested.[68] The buyback in Australia in the late 1990s analyzed by Peter Reuter and Jenny Mouzos is orders of magnitude larger than efforts undertaken in the United States and was, by all accounts, carefully and thoroughly implemented. Thus it seems a "fair test" of the prospects for gun buybacks.

The Australian Experience

In reaction to a mass killing of thirty-five people in Port Arthur in 1996, legislation was adopted by all Australian states implementing a (nearly) uniform sys-

---

68. See reviews in Reuter and Mouzos, chapter 4, in this volume; Sherman (2001); and Kennedy, Braga, and Piel (1996).

tem of licensing and registration of firearms. Weapons of the type used in the massacre (long guns) were newly prohibited (handguns were already heavily regulated), and a short-term buyback program was initiated for the newly prohibited firearms. By any measure, the buyback was massive and generous: more than 600,000 firearms turned in, more than $U.S. 350 paid out per gun. Since then, several amnesties have attracted even more weapons. Contemporaneous with these other changes, enforcement increased.

From a policy perspective, the Australian case is a clean example for evaluation. There is essentially no domestic supply of these weapons, imports were banned, and the buyback was well funded and had nationwide coverage. Yet, from a statistical perspective, evaluation is difficult. The reforms targeted the type of weapon used in one mass killing, and the legislation was supported by arguments that it would reduce future similar incidents. But mass killings are rare events; the authors report 1.3 a year in Australia, less than half of them involving firearms. So if one were to evaluate the effect of the reforms on mass killings, there would not be enough statistical power to establish conclusively even a large effect.[69]

The authors consider additional, broader outcomes of violent crime and suicide, presumably because of the infrequency of mass killings and because of an interest in the effect on these other outcomes regardless of the motivation for reform. Homicide and suicide are lower following the Port Arthur massacre and the subsequent gun control reform. However, these changes are not statistically different from longer-term downward trends. The number of armed robberies is up since the reform, but the proportion using a firearm is down. The trends complicate interpretation of the results. Without a well-developed understanding of the causes of these trends or without high-frequency variation across jurisdictions that experienced differential impact of the reform (owing to variation in preexisting regulation), strong conclusions are not possible.

What Does This Experience Tell Us about Buybacks?

Clearly, the change in regulatory environment analyzed by Reuter and Mouzos was much more extensive than a repurchase of existing weapons. What is less clear is what can be applied from the Australian experience to other environments and other proposals.

---

69. For example, Reuter and Mouzos (this volume) report that there were mass killings in four of six years before the reform (excluding the Port Arthur event) and no mass killings in the five years following. Assuming the probability of mass killing in a given year is 0.67, the binomial probability of observing zero events in five independent trials is 0.135. That is, there is a 13.5 percent chance that one would observe no mass killings in a five-year period even if the frequency were unchanged.

Even the authors indicate that it would not be reasonable to expect great impacts on crime from this intervention. They state that their findings for violent crime are "hardly surprising given that the type of firearms prohibited had not previously been much used in crime or suicide." It is common for buyback efforts to be overly broad, not targeting guns of high risk of being used in violence. In his review of the evidence, Lawrence W. Sherman declares, "Nothing in the structure of gun buyback programs attempts to focus the intervention on the risk." Furthermore, the characteristics of the guns collected reveal little overlap between crime guns and buy-back guns.[70] Yet Australia's effort was more highly specified than most efforts in the United States, suggesting that more targeted efforts are possible.

One also needs to sort out the role of the buyback in the larger reform effort, which included increased enforcement, prohibitions on certain weapons, and training and registration requirements. Perhaps it is not relevant to separate the gun bans from the buyback, as the former may not be feasible without the latter. But the results should be considered biased upward if applied to a buyback alone.

A related question is whether Australia's experience could inform policy discussion about comprehensive gun control legislation in the United States. As reported in table 4-2, the two countries have very different rates of firearm use in homicide and suicide. Although the homicide rate in the United States is nearly four times that in Australia, the firearm-related homicide rate is more than fourteen times higher. For suicides, the overall rate is higher in Australia, but the firearm-related suicide rate in the United States is five times Australia's rate. Equally important is the difference in the regulatory environment. Australia has much tighter regulation. For these two reasons, it is possible that similar nationwide legislation in the United States would have a much larger impact on violent outcomes.[71]

Should Policy Analysts Close the Book on the Buyback Idea?

From the literature on the effect of gun buybacks on violence, the answer to this question is probably yes. However, there are two qualifications. As mentioned, buybacks have not traditionally been tightly targeted to those weapons and own-

70. Sherman (2001, p. 19); Kennedy, Braga, and Piel (1996).
71. This is by no means a prediction of the impact of a tightening of the regulation of firearms in the United States. Many factors would need to be considered before making such a prediction (including modeling of enforcement actions, operation of the illegal market in firearms, impact of reform on extent and distribution of gun ownerships, and so on). An analysis of this sort is beyond the scope of this comment.

ers at highest risk for violence. Although a buyback will generally draw the least "risky" guns from any pool, defining the pool more narrowly (for example, not offering payment for old weapons or those not in working order) could cause the average repurchased weapon to have a higher likelihood of being involved in criminal violence. In light of recent evidence suggesting that marginal changes in gun availability might have substantial impacts on violent outcomes, crafting an initiative to repurchase guns that would have important local effects on violence may be possible.[72] More generally, gun buyback programs, or (perhaps equivalently) amnesty for those turning in guns, may be important aspects of more comprehensive efforts to reduce gun availability in certain locations. Finally, descriptions of buyback initiatives suggest that they are productive for community organizing, which may make them essential aspects of the larger law enforcement picture.[73]

COMMENT BY
Jim Leitzel

Australia's ban, buyback, and destruction of hundreds of thousands of guns within a few months in 1997 is one of the most massive government adjustments of a firearm regulatory regime in recent history. Indeed, the simultaneous licensing changes, new safe storage rules, and amnesty for unregistered guns would themselves constitute a major reform, even without the legislated disappearance of more than half a million guns. The Australian case is long overdue for analysis, and Peter Reuter and Jenny Mouzos have ably answered the call. My intention is to supplement their analysis by providing some additional context through a comparison with the contemporaneous British ban on handguns.

The post–Port Arthur Australian reforms involved a combination of a ban, a buyback, and other regulatory measures. The effects of the reforms, then, cannot be directly compared with the consequences of gun bans or buybacks implemented in isolation.[74] Note that the buyback portion of a combined ban-

---

72. See Duggan (2001) on gun availability and homicide, Duggan, chapter 2 in this volume, on gun availability and suicide, and Sherman and Rogan (1995) on gun seizures and gun violence.

73. Plotkin (1996).

74. The U.S. assault weapons ban, for instance, not only did not buy back the existing stock, but the ban itself only applied to future acquisitions; that is, the existing stock of assault weapons remained legally owned.

buyback might be a good idea even in the absence of any incremental reduction (that is, beyond the effects of the ban itself) in the social costs of firearm violence. Such "just compensation," which presumably would be required by the Fifth Amendment should a ban of existing weapons take place in the United States, would, among other things, help build public support for the reform. In other words, if a ban of some privately owned weapons is sound public policy, then a buyback might be a useful (or even required) measure to ease the path to the ban.[75]

Although the existing gun buyback literature is not directly relevant for Australia's combined ban and buyout, the British precedents are squarely on point. The British reforms were motivated by tragic mass murders, involved ban-buyback combinations and other measures such as amnesties for unregistered guns, and in the case of the 1988 reforms, even concerned the same class of firearms. Indeed, the post–Port Arthur firearm regulation regime in Australia moves it close to the circa 1996 British model: licensing of gun owners, based on having a legitimate reason to own a gun (primarily membership in a target shooting club) and fitness of character, and prohibition of self-loading and pump-action shotguns and rifles (which were the subject of the 1988 British ban-buyback.) At about the same time as the Australian reforms, Britain was moving toward its own new ban, this one on handguns, and my comments concentrate on the consequences of this measure. One important difference between the buybacks is that the long guns banned in 1988 in Britain and 1997 in Australia were not commonly used in firearm crimes before the bans—this is the sense in which Reuter and Mouzos refer to these guns as "low risk." But handguns, the object of the 1997 British ban, were involved in most British firearm crimes.[76]

Post-Dunblane Handgun Bans-Buybacks in Britain

In the wake of the murder of sixteen schoolchildren and a teacher in Dunblane, Scotland, in March 1996, Britain moved to ban handguns.[77] The policy reform took place in two stages: first, handguns above .22 caliber were banned, followed by a nearly total handgun prohibition a few months later. High-caliber

75. Buybacks also might be useful, even without direct impacts on reducing crime crime, by providing a convenient opportunity for those who have become ambivalent about their gun ownership to safely divest themselves of guns.

76. Most British gun crimes involve property damage caused by low-powered airguns. Such guns are not subject to the certificate control system, and crimes conducted with these guns are not included in the firearm crime statistics presented here. Handguns are involved in most firearm crimes when airgun crimes are not taken into account.

77. Squires (2000) is an excellent source for background into the post-Dunblane changes to British firearm regulations.

weapons had to be handed in by October 1, 1997, and the remaining hand-guns by March 1, 1998. Legal owners of newly prohibited firearms were en-titled to compensation for their guns, and for related equipment and ammuni-tion. As with the Australian buyback, weapons relinquished during the hand-in period were destroyed.

Analysis of the Australian reform package is challenging because the preva-lence of the newly banned guns before the buyback is not known with much precision. Because of the certification system that had long been in place, the number of legally owned handguns was somewhat less of a mystery in Britain. On the basis of the existing firearm certification system in Britain, the govern-ment originally estimated the legal handgun stock before the ban to consist of approximately 200,000 handguns. This figure turned out to be a significant overestimate, in part because of a discrepancy between the number of firearms that were authorized by certificates to be owned and the lesser number of those actually owned. Some of the "missing" guns had never been purchased, some had been destroyed, deactivated, sold abroad, or otherwise surrendered, and some long guns had been misclassified as handguns. (The 1997 acts that banned handguns also included provisions for informing police upon the "death" of a certified gun.) In the event, 162,353 guns were handed in, some 25,000 fewer than originally expected, though police forces generally felt that there was nearly universal compliance with the ban by licensed gun owners.[78]

Table 4-4 presents some information on trends in the prevalence of legally owned weapons in England and Wales. Between 1995 and 2000, the number of firearm certificates declined by 11.5 percent, while the number of firearms fell by more than 28 percent. As in Australia, most individuals who owned at least one firearm before the handgun ban continued to own a firearm. Nor does it seem that the handgun ban caused a resurgence in the popularity of shotguns. (The British certification system makes a distinction between shotguns and other types of guns. The system of control over shotguns has traditionally been less strict than that over "firearms." A long-standing upward trend in the num-ber of shotgun certificates was reversed following the 1988 ban-buyback of pump-action and self-loading shotguns.)

The years leading up to the Dunblane massacre witnessed a significant rise in British handgun crime, which peaked in 1993. In 1996, before the ban was in-troduced, there were 3,347 recorded handgun crimes—a number far higher than

78. "Home Office: Handgun Surrender and Compensation," HC 225 1998–99, National Audit Office Press Notice, London, February 26, 1999. The cost of the compensation (including that of the surrendered ammunition) was estimated as approximately 95 million pounds. The rough U.S. equivalent, circa 1998, to 95 million pounds was $150 million.

Table 4-4. *Legal Firearm Ownership, England and Wales*

Item	1995	1996	1997	1998	1999	2000
Firearm certificates	141,700	141,900	133,600	131,900	132,300	125,400
Authorized firearms	413,600	418,300	305,000	295,000	296,400	296,800
Shotgun certificates	653,800	638,000	623,100	627,600	625,700	600,700
Authorized shotguns	1,325,800	1,335,000	1,343,900	1,343,100	1,327,800	1,320,900
Firearm dealers	2,470	2,490	2,400	2,180	2,090	2,070

Source: Jenner and Gray (2001).

that recorded throughout the 1980s and previously surpassed only by the statistics for 1991–93.

What has happened to crime, and gun crime, in Britain following the handgun ban? Recently, there has been a major discrepancy in British crime figures. Although recorded crimes have seen major jumps since 1997, the British Crime Survey (which, as the equivalent to the National Crime Victimization Survey in the United States, includes unrecorded and even unreported crimes) has indicated steep declines, so that by 2001 the probability of being a crime victim in Britain reached a twenty-year low.[79] Table 4-5 provides some official statistics on recorded crime in England and Wales.

The immediate aftermath of Dunblane saw large reductions in handgun crime, overall firearm crime, and crime more generally. By the end of the 1990s, however, these gains were being eroded, and by 2001, gun crime had returned close to the record levels of 1993. Shotgun crime, however, remains low, at less than half the number of offenses recorded at the 1993 peak. The homicide rate in Britain has been rising since the mid-1990s, to 1.55 per 100,000 in 2000–01, though it remains extremely low by international standards, even in comparison to Australia. The percentage of homicides that involves guns is also low, at 8.8 percent.[80] There does not seem to be any trend since the mid-1990s in the percentage of homicides that involve guns or, more specifically, handguns: in 2000–01 England and Wales had a total of forty-seven handgun homicides and fourteen shotgun homicides. The fraction of suicides that involves guns is even lower than for homicides: 2.4 percent in 1998.[81]

Recent robbery statistics are a cause for concern: recorded robberies increased by 26.1 percent between 1998–99 and 1999–2000, and by a further 12.9 percent the following year. Gun robberies have seen a similar rise, though they still represent a small fraction (4.2 percent) of all robberies. For robberies, however, the discrepancies between recorded crime and statistics from the British Crime Survey are widest. Between 1999 and 2000, robberies increased by some 21 percent (in recorded statistics) or fell by 22 percent (according to the British Crime Survey)![82]

To the extent that the increase in recorded robberies is a real phenomenon and not a statistical anomaly, it is not the case that the additional robberies can be seen as motivated by further assurance for criminals that, following the hand-

---

79. Kershaw and others (2001).

80. There is considerable uncertainty in the gun crime figures, and especially in type-specific figures. Many crimes that are recorded as involving handguns may actually be carried out with unworkable imitation or replica weapons.

81. "Controls Over Firearms" (1999, para. 36).

82. Kershaw and others (2001).

Table 4-5. *Crime and Guns, England and Wales*

Item	1995	1996	1997	1997–98	1998–99ᵃ	1999–2000	2000–01
Recorded crime (thousands)	5,101.2	5,036.6	4,598.3	4,545.3	5,109.1	5,301.2	5,170.8
Recorded gun crime (excluding airguns)	5,866	6,063	4,904	4,903	5,209	6,843	7,362
Shotgun	984	933	580	565	642	693	607
Handgun	3,318	3,347	2,648	2,636	2,687	3,685	4,019
Homicide	663	585	612	612	655	693	818
Firearm homicide	70	49	59	54	49	62	72
Total homicide (percent)ᵇ	9.4	7.2	8.0	7.2	6.5	8.1	8.8
Robbery (thousands)	68.1	74.0	63.1	62.7	66.8	84.3	95.1
Firearm robbery	4,206	4,013	3,029	2,938	2,973	3,922	3,965
Total robbery (percent)	6.2	5.4	4.8	4.7	4.4	4.7	4.2
Handgun	2,647	2,575	1,854	1,811	1,814	2,561	2,700
Shotgun	544	484	299	266	331	355	297
Burglary (thousands)	1,239.5	1,164.6	1,015.1	988.4	953.2	906.5	836.0

Source: *Criminal Statistics* (2000).

a. New rules for offense coverage and counting came into effect on April 1, 1998. The changes had the effect of increasing the number of recorded crimes, though for firearm offenses, the extent of the inflation is unknown.

b. The percentage of homicides that involves firearms does not perfectly agree with the two previous rows for a variety of reasons: currently recorded homicides differ from originally recorded homicides, some gun homicides involve the use of the gun as a blunt instrument, and other reasons.

gun ban, potential victims would not be armed. For decades, firearms could not legally be carried (or even owned) for the purpose of personal protection, so the assurance that potential victims were unarmed was almost complete before the ban, too. Unlike robberies, however, burglaries may have seen a ban-induced change in the extent of deterrence. Nevertheless, the number of recorded burglaries has been falling in England and Wales since peaking in 1993. The use of a firearm in a burglary is a rare event: of approximately every 2,700 burglaries, only 1 is conducted with a firearm.

Although definitive conclusions are hard to come by, it seems that the handgun ban in Britain may have helped to sustain the mid-1990s reversal of the buildup to the relatively high handgun crime levels of a few years earlier. Crime and firearm crimes fell in the immediate aftermath of the ban, but that trend subsequently ended: according to statistics on recorded crimes, current rates are near pre-ban levels. It can be stated with more certainty that the handgun ban has not resulted in any sort of crime nightmare in Britain, as some had feared. First, the handgun ban did not lead to a perverse effect, where fewer guns in the hands of law-abiding citizens generated a huge crime spree by gun-toting criminals.[83] Second, the handgun ban did not lead to a noticeable substitution toward shotgun crime, though shotguns have long been by far the most commonly available type of gun, and fears of such a substitution are often voiced in discussion about proposed handgun controls in the United States.[84] Britain remains a nation with enviably low levels of homicide and firearm crime.

A Few Words but No Answers on Mass Gun Killings

The Australian and British ban-buybacks were motivated by horrific, high-profile mass murders. The perpetrators of these massacres were unmarried males, and they were unbalanced by any common reckoning—a profile that seems to extend to mass murderers more widely.[85] The British assailants were suicidal as well as homicidal, and they committed suicide at the end of their sprees. The suicidal intention of the Australian gunman was not as apparent, though he set fire to the house he was holed up in and emerged, surviving, with his clothes on fire.

---

83. Arguments based on such perverse effects are commonly arrayed in the United States against various proposals for stricter gun controls; see, for example, the discussion of the perversity argument in Cook and Leitzel (1996).

84. See, for example, Kleck (1984).

85. See, for instance, the discussion of the research by forensic psychologist Paul Mullen (*www.monash.edu.au/pubs/montage/Montage_97-02/killer.html.*). The motives of those who kill strangers more or less randomly apparently differ systematically from those murderers who target acquaintances and family members.

The suicidal tendencies of many mass murderers are important for control purposes, because they suggest that such potential killers will be hard to deter through threats of punishment. Preventive measures, therefore, take on increased importance with suicidal assailants. (Suicide bombers in the Middle East provide a similar instance: deterrence needs to be supplemented with ex ante controls.)

The perpetrators of the British and Australian massacres did not just happen to own guns; rather, they were all rather deeply immersed in the gun culture. Further, despite their unstable mental condition and the relatively strict gun laws that already prevailed in Britain and Australia, the assailants were legal gun owners. Somehow, the existing control systems failed to screen out these individuals. This fact helped to promote stricter controls following the massacres, even though it was understood that most gun crime was not committed by legal firearm owners.

It has been argued, on the basis of U.S. data, that liberalized laws governing concealed gun carrying are an effective means to combat mass firearm murders.[86] This is a reform for which there was essentially no public support in Britain or Australia, even though both countries contained vocal constituencies opposed to the ban-buybacks. In general, one would expect that the utility of having more guns in public settings would vary with such conditions as the existing prevalence of firearms and of firearm crimes. Further, the suicidal tendencies of many mass killers tend to undermine the deterrence value of an increasingly armed populace.[87] At any rate, in Britain and Australia, countries with a relatively low incidence of gun crime, liberalized carry rules (or other loosenings of gun controls) held little appeal as a means to lowering the social costs of firearm violence. Britain, like Australia, has not seen a similar large-scale mass shooting since the ban, but fortunately, as Peter Reuter and Jenny Mouzos note, these events were always sufficiently rare that the influence of the bans on mass firearm shootings is guaranteed to be hard or impossible to detect—though again, it is reassuring that nightmare "perversity" scenarios did not develop.

Although horrific mass murders motivated major firearm policy responses in Australia and Britain, the school shootings in Littleton, Colorado, and elsewhere, did not lead to similar changes in the United States. Why did the response differ so noticeably among these settings? Although I cannot pretend to put forward a complete answer to this question, some of the difference undoubtedly relates, again, to the preexisting firearm prevalence and crime. In Britain and Australia, law-abiding citizens can be significantly more assured that they will not face an assailant armed with a gun than can someone in the United States. As a result,

86. Lott and Landes (2000).
87. Lott and Landes (2000) argue that liberalized concealed-carry laws not only deter some mass public shootings but also reduce the number of victims in those shootings that nevertheless take place.

the perversity argument against gun controls—essentially, more guns, less crime—is not nearly as influential in Britain and Australia as it is in the United States.[88]

To conclude, in general it seems that both the Australian and the British ban-buybacks did not increase crime, and they may even have contributed to some short-term postban declines in criminal activity. This outcome is shared, even though the Australian ban-buyback applied to guns that were not frequently used in crime, while the British post-Dunblane ban-buyback involved the most common type of crime gun. But the real contribution of the ban in Britain (and Australia) may have little to do with such metrics as measured crime rates or the other indicators tracked by Reuter and Mouzos. For many British people, the fear of a widening gun culture and, as they saw it, the long-run potential for American levels of gun violence were the larger concern—a concern enhanced by the fact that the Hungerford and Dunblane perpetrators were legal gun own-ers.[89] A widening gun culture might set the stage for an arms race between crim-inals and the public: more gun prevalence would lead to more gun violence, which would lead to more gun prevalence for defensive purposes, and so on. This fear of an expanded gun culture is sufficiently widespread that even most police officers in Britain do not routinely carry firearms. The lower levels of legal gun prevalence following the ban-buybacks, from this perspective, represent a move in the right direction, irrespective of the marginal impact of the reforms on the short-run social costs of gun violence.

References

Australian Bureau of Statistics (ABS). Annual Issues. *Causes of Death.* Canberra.
———. Annual Issues. *National Crime Statistics.* cat. 4510. Canberra.
———. Annual Issues. *Recorded Crime Australia.* cat. 4510. Canberra.
———. 2000. *Suicides Australia 1921–1998.* cat. 3309.0. Canberra.
———. 2001. *Australian Demographic Statistics.* Canberra.
Australian National Audit Office. 1997. *The Gun Buy-Back Scheme.* Audit Report 25, 1997–98. Canberra.
Australian Police Ministers' Council. 2001. *Minimum National Standards for Firearms Safety Training in Australian States and Territories.* Commonwealth Attorney General's Depart-ment, Canberra
Bammer, Gabride, Wayne Hall, Margaret Hamilton, and Robert Ali. 2002. "Harm Mini-mization in a Prohibition Context—Australia." *Annals of the American Academy of Politi-cal and Social Sciences* 582: 20–32.
Barclay Gordon, and Cynthia Travares. 2000. *International Comparisons of Criminal Justice Statistics 1998.* Home Office, London.

88. See Leitzel (1998). *More Guns, Less Crime* is the title of Lott (1988).
89. See, for example, chaps. 4 and 6 in Squires (2000).

Callahan, C., F. Rivara, and T. Koepsell. 1994. "Money for Guns: Evaluation of the Seattle Gun Buy-Back Program." *Public Health Reports* 109 (4): 472–77.

Carcach, C., J. Mouzos, and P. Grabosky. 2002. "The Mass Murder as Quasi-Experiment: The Impact of the 1996 Port Arthur Massacre." *Homicide Studies* 6 (2): 107–27.

Centers for Disease Control. 1998. WISQARS Injury Mortality Data Reports (www.cdc.gov).

Commonwealth Attorney-General's Department. 2002. *The Australians Firearms Buyback: Tally for Number of Firearms Collected and Compensation Paid.* Canberra.

"Control Over Firearms." 1999. Select Committee on Home Affairs Second Report, House of Commons. London.

Cook, P. J., and J. Leitzel. 1996."Perversity, Futility, Jeopardy: An Economic Analysis of the Attack on Gun Control." *Law and Contemporary Problems* 59 (Winter): 91–118.

Cook, Philip J., and Jens Ludwig. 2000. *Gun Violence: The Real Costs.* Oxford University Press.

Cook, Philip J., Stephanie Molliconi, and Thomas B. Cole. 1995. "Regulating Gun Markets." *Journal of Criminal Law and Criminology* 86 (1): 59–92.

Criminal Statistics, England and Wales, 2000. Home Office. London: The Stationery Office, (December).

Cook, Philip J., Mark Moore, and Anthony Braga. 2001. "Gun Control." In *Crime: Public Policies for Crime Control,* edited by James Q. Wilson and Joan Petersilia. San Francisco: Institute for Contemporary Studies.

Duggan, Mark. 2001. "More Guns, More Crime." *Journal of Political Economy* 109 (October): 1086–1114.

European Monitoring Center on Drugs and Drug Abuse (EMCDDA). 2001. *Annual Report on the State of the Drug Problem in the EU.* Lisbon.

Firearms Control Task Group, Department of Justice Canada.1995. *A Review of Firearm Statistics and Regulations in Selected Countries* (March).

Fitzgerald, J., S. Briscoe, and D. Weatherburn. 2001. "Firearms and Violent Crime in New South Wales." *Contemporary Issues in Crime and Justice.* Bulletin 57. Bureau of Crime Statistics and Research. Sydney.

Fox, James Alan, and Jack Levin. 1998. "Multiple Homicide; Patterns of Serial and Mass Murders." In *Crime and Justice: An Annual Review of Research,* vol. 23, edited by Michael Tonry, 423–55. University of Chicago Press.

Harding, Richard. 1981. *Firearms and Violence in Australian Life.* University of Western Australia Press.

Harrison, J., and M. Steenkamp. 2000. "Suicide in Australia; Data and Trends in 1998." Australian *Injury Prevention Bulletin* 23. Adelaide.

Home Office. 2000. *Criminal Statistics, England and Wales, 1999.* London.

Jenner, John, and Alan Gray. 2001. *Firearm Certificates. England and Wales, 1999 and 2000.* www.homeoffice.gov.uk/rds/firearms1.html.

Kellermann, Arthur L., Frederick P. Rivara, N. B. Rushforth, J. G. Banton., D. T. Reay, J. T. Francisco, A. B. Locci, J. B. Prodzinski, B. B. Hackman, and G. P. Somes. 1993. "Gun Ownership as a Risk Factor for Homicide in the Home." *New England Journal of Medicine* 329 (15): 1084–91.

Kennedy, David, Anthony Braga, and Anne Morrison Piehl. 1996. "Gun Buy-Backs: Where Do We Stand and Where Do We Go?" In *Under Fire: Gun Buy-Backs, Exchanges and Amnesty Programs,* edited by Martha R. Plotkin, 141–74. Washington: Police Executive Research Forum.

Kershaw, C., N. Chivite-Matthews, C. Thomas, and R. Aust. 2001. "The 2001 British Crime Survey: First Results, England and Wales." Home Office Statistical Bulletin 18-01 (October 25).

Kleck, Gary. 1984. "Handgun-Only Gun Control: A Policy Disaster in the Making." In *Firearms and Violence: Issues of Public Policy,* edited by Don B. Kates. Ballinger.

———. 1996. "Gun Buy-Back Programs: Nothing Succeeds Like Failure." *In Under Fire: Gun Buy-Backs, Exchanges and Amnesty Programs,* edited by Martha R. Plotkin, 29–53. Washington: Police Executive Research Forum.

———. 2001. "Impossible Policy Evaluations and Impossible Conclusions—a comment on Koper and Roth." *Journal of Quantitative Criminology* 17 (1): 75–80.

Koper, Christopher, and Jeffrey Roth. 2001. "The Impact of the 1994 Federal Assault Weapon Ban on Gun Violence Outcomes: An Assessment of Multiple Outcome Measures and Some Lessons for Policy Evaluation." *Journal of Quantitative Criminology* 17 (1): 33–74.

Leitzel, James. 1998. "Evasion and Public Policy: US and British Firearm Regulation." *Policy Studies* 19 (June): 141–57.

Lott, John R. Jr. 1998. *More Guns, Less Crime: Understanding Crime and Gun Control Laws.* University of Chicago Press.

Lott, John R. Jr. and William M. Landes. 2000. "Multiple Victim Public Shootings." Working Paper (October).

Makkai, Toni. 2000. "Crime in Australia." In *Sociology of Australian Society,* edited by J. M. Nojmar and J. S. Western, 239–57. MacMillan Publishers.

Mouzos, Jenny D. 1999. *Firearm-Related Violence: The Impact of the Nationwide Agreement on Firearms.* Trends and Issues in Crime and Criminal Justice Series. No. 116. Canberra: Australian Institute of Criminology.

———. 2000a. *The Licensing and Registration Status of Firearms Used in Homicide.* Trends and Issues in Crime and Criminal Justice Series. No. 151. Canberra: Australian Institute of Criminology.

———. 2000b. *Firearm Related Deaths in Australia 1998.* Trends and Issues in Crime and Criminal Justice Series. No. 161. Canberra: Australian Institute of Criminology.

———. 2000c. *Homicidal Encounters: A Study of Homicide in Australia 1989–1999.* Research and Public Policy Series 28. Canberra: Australian Institute of Criminology.

———. 2001a. *Homicide in Australia 1999–2000.* Trends and Issues in Crime and Criminal Justice Series. No. 187. Canberra: Australian Institute of Criminology.

———. 2001b. *Firearm Related Morbidity in Australia, 1994–95 to 1998–99.* Trends and Issues in Crime and Criminal Justice Series. No. 198. Canberra: Australian Institute of Criminology.

———. 2002a. *Homicide in Australia: 2000–2001 National Homicide Monitoring Program (NHMP) Annual Report.* Research and Public Policy Series. No. 40. Canberra: Australian Institute of Criminology.

———. 2002b. *Firearms Theft in Australia.* Trends and Issues in Crime and Criminal Justice Series. No. 230. Canberra: Australian Institute of Criminology.

Mouzos, Jenny D., and C. Carcach. 2001. *Weapon Involvement in Armed Robbery.* Research and Public Policy Series. No. 38. Canberra: Australian Institute of Criminology.

Mullin, Wallace P. 2001. "Will Gun Buyback Programs Increase the Quantity of Guns?" *International Review of Law and Economics* 21(1): 87–102.

Newspoll Market Research. 1997. *Australian Firearms' Buyback Tracking Study-Phase Two Advertizing-June-July 1997.* Surry Hills, New South Wales, Australia.

Plotkin, Martha, ed. 1996. *Under Fire: Gun Buybacks, Exchanges and Amnesty Programs.* Police Executive Research Forum.

Sherman, Lawrence W. 2001. "Reducing Gun Violence: What Works, What Doesn't, What's Promising." *Criminal Justice* 1 (February): 11–25.

Sherman, Lawrence, and D. Rogan. 1995. "Effects of Gun Seizures on Gun Violence: Hot Spots Patrol in Kansas City. " *Justice Quarterly* 12: 673–93.

Squires, Peter. 2000. *Gun Culture or Gun Control? Firearms, Violence and Society.* London and New York: Routledge

Rosenfeld, Richard. 1996. "Gun Buy-Backs: Crime control or Community Mobilization." In *Under Fire: Gun Buy-Backs, Exchanges and Amnesty Programs,* edited by Martha R. Plotkin, 1–28. Washington: Police Executive Research Forum.

Security Australia. 1997. "Gun Buyback Reaps Slow Rewards." *Security Australia* 17 (7): 26.

Wilkins, G., and C. Addicot. 1998. *Firearm Certificate Statistics, England and Wales, 1997.* Home Office. London.

ELIZABETH RICHARDSON VIGDOR
JAMES A. MERCY

5 Disarming Batterers: The Impact of Domestic Violence Firearm Laws

Every day in the United States, an average of nearly four people are killed by intimate partners, and many others are injured. Approximately one in three female homicide victims and one in twenty male homicide victims are killed by current or former spouses or boyfriends each year; 60 percent of these homicides were committed using a firearm.[1] The social cost of intimate partner violence is substantial: in 1995 the total cost of intimate partner violence was more than $23 billion.[2] In recent years a number of laws have been enacted in an attempt to reduce the role of firearms in domestic violence. These laws were among the first to expand the categories of disqualification for purchasing or possessing a firearm beyond felony convictions to include persons with misdemeanor violations or restraining orders for violence against intimate partners. There is evidence of strong public support for these laws. In a recent national public opinion poll, 89 percent of adults and 80 percent of gun-owning adults favored prohibiting persons convicted of domestic violence misdemeanors from purchasing handguns.[3] To our knowledge,

We are grateful to Brian Jacob, Mark Kleiman, John Laub, Will Manning, Jacob Vigdor, Garen Wintemute, and participants in the Brookings Conference on Gun Violence for many helpful comments. We also thank Sneha Desai, Laura Lindsey, Julie Morse, and Althea Sircar for outstanding research assistance and Patricia Holmgreen for preparation of the data set used in our analysis. We take full responsibility for any errors.

1. Puzone and others (2000).
2. Centers for Disease Control and Prevention (forthcoming).
3. Teret and others (1998).

157

there have been no studies examining the impact of these laws on domestic violence outcomes.

We examine the impact of two types of state law on intimate partner homicides: laws preventing those individuals subject to a current restraining order from owning or purchasing a firearm; and laws that prevent individuals who have been convicted of domestic violence misdemeanors from owning or purchasing a firearm. We begin by constructing a logic model to help assess the potential impact of these laws in preventing assaults on intimate partners with firearms. Three key observations are derived from this model that help interpret these findings. First, it is much more common for perpetrators of intimate partner violence to have a restraining order taken out on them than be convicted of a misdemeanor. Second, states that have these laws in place seem to be much more advanced in their ability to use existing databases to identify persons with restraining orders than those with misdemeanor convictions. Consequently, we might expect to see a larger impact from laws prohibiting possession or purchase by those individuals subject to restraining orders than those with misdemeanor convictions. Third, even though some states impose time limits on firearm prohibitions stemming from domestic violence misdemeanors, the number of persons subject to these laws seems to be growing over time. This suggests that the impact of laws focused on misdemeanor convictions, rather than laws focusing on restraining orders that are often temporary, may increase over time.

We lack sufficient information to fully assess the potential impact of these laws. For example, we do not know what proportion of temporary restraining orders eventually become permanent, nor what proportion of firearm owners convicted of a domestic violence misdemeanor or subject to a restraining order surrender their firearms to authorities. Nor do we know the proportion of perpetrators who, denied the ability to purchase a firearm through a federal firearm licensee, may obtain one through other sources. Thus it is very difficult to even crudely quantify how many individuals in any given state could potentially be prevented from fatally assaulting their intimate partner because of these laws.

Despite our inability to quantify fully the potential impact of these laws, we attempt to ascertain their effectiveness by exploiting time variation in the passage of the state laws. We compare changes in intimate partner homicide rates over time in states that pass these laws versus states that do not adopt such laws. By looking at changes in homicide rates within states rather than absolute levels, we avoid the problems that arise from naively comparing states with time-invariant systematic differences. For example, some states have higher levels of crime than other states for reasons that are not fully explained by statistical analyses.

We find that states with a restraining order law in effect have significantly lower rates of intimate partner homicide, approximately 9 to 12 percent less than states that do not have these laws. We do not find any impact of domestic violence misdemeanor laws on intimate partner homicides. We also find that the restraining order laws are only effective in states that have the ability to check a database of those individuals under restraining orders against persons applying to purchase a firearm.

Background

Violence among intimate partners is a significant public health and social problem in the United States. Between 1981 and 1998, an estimated 45,513 homicides occurred among intimate partners.[4] Fatalities, however, are only a small fraction of this problem. As of 1996, an estimated 25 percent of adult women and 8 percent of adult men had been raped or physically assaulted by an intimate partner in their lifetime.[5] Intimate partner violence has significant medical, psychological, and social consequences for victims and places a substantial economic burden on society.[6] In 1995 the cost of intimate partner violence was approximately $23.5 billion.[7] This comprised approximately $18.5 billion in direct costs from the criminal justice system, $4 billion in expenditures on medical and mental health care, and nearly $1 billion in indirect costs from lost productivity.[8]

Intimate partner homicides represent the most lethal consequence of violence between spouses. Between 1981 and 1998 victims of intimate partner homicide were female in about 64 percent of cases, and female rates exceeded those for males for all groups except black. The rates were greatest for persons 20 to 39 years of age. Between 1981 and 1998, firearms were used in more than 60 percent of the homicides. Access to a firearm by the abusive partner significantly increases the risk of homicide for women in physically abusive relationships.[9] Not surprisingly, the type of weapon used in intimate partner violence is strongly associated

4. Paulozzi, Saltzman, and others (2001).
5. Tjaden and Thoennes (1998).
6. Crowell and Burgess (1996).
7. Centers for Disease Control and Prevention (forthcoming).
8. Direct costs were derived by combining domestic violence–related medical, mental health and criminal justice utilization reports from the National Violence Against Women Survey with health care utilization costs from the Medical Expenditure Panel Survey and criminal justice costs from the Metropolitan Dade County Department of Justice Assistance. Indirect costs were calculated by combining reported domestic violence–related days of lost pay from working and days of lost housekeeping from the National Violence Against Women Survey with estimates of the average daily value of work and household production from the Bureau of Labor Statistics and the U.S. Census Bureau; Centers for Disease Control and Prevention (forthcoming).
9. Campbell and others (forthcoming).

with the lethality of such violence. One study found that intimate partner assaults involving firearms were twelve times more likely to result in death than assaults involving knives or bodily force.[10]

Rates of intimate partner homicide declined by 47.2 percent in the United States between 1981 and 1998.[11] During this period victimization rates declined among white females by 23.0 percent, white males by 61.9 percent, black females by 47.6 percent, and black males by 76.4 percent. These long-term declines have been previously documented for the United States in aggregate and for large cities in the United States and extend back to at least 1976.[12] The trends for unmarried, white females appear to run counter to the downward trends observed in the rates of intimate partner homicide more generally. Several studies have found rates for this group have increased between 1976 and 1992, but since 1992 their rates have leveled off and may even have begun to decrease.[13]

Explanations for these declines include the changing nature of intimate partnerships in the United States, the improved economic status of women, and the increased availability of services for victims of domestic violence.[14] There has been a long-term increase in the age at first marriage and concomitant increases in the rates of couples living in nonmarital cohabiting relationships.[15] Consequently, because nonmarital cohabiting relationships are less durable than marriages, fewer people may be exposed to intimate partner violence during the period when they are at greatest risk of victimization (that is, young adulthood).

The economic status of women has improved substantially during the past several decades.[16] Such improvements have reduced the economic dependence of many women on men and thus potentially provide greater opportunity for them to leave violent relationships. The availability of services for intimate partner violence, including hotlines, shelters, counseling centers, and advocacy groups has also increased dramatically since the 1970s.[17] The increased availability of these services in recent years may offer greater opportunity for victims of intimate partner violence to leave violent relationships or reduce the level and severity of violence in those relationships. Efforts to test these explanations have

10. Saltzman and others (1992). See also Campbell and others (forthcoming).
11. Paulozzi and others (2001).
12. Browne and Williams (1993); Browne, Williams, and Dutton (1989); Dugan, Nagin, and Rosenfeld (1999); Greenfeld, Rand and others (1998); Mercy and Saltzman (1989); Puzone and others (2000).
13. Browne and Williams (1993); Browne, Williams, and Dutton (1999); Greenfeld and others (1998); and Puzone and others (2000).
14. Dugan, Nagin, and Rosenfeld (1999); Rosenfeld (1997); and Browne and Williams (1989).
15. Dugan, Nagin, and Rosenfeld (1999); Puzone and others (2000); and Rosenfeld (1997).
16. Dugan, Nagin, and Rosenfeld (1999).
17. Dugan, Nagin, and Rosenfeld (1999); Browne and Williams (1989).

found support for each of them, although support for the impact of declining rates of marriage appears to be the strongest.[18] Moreover, these explanations seem to exert their strongest effect on the rate at which women kill their male partners.

Underlying IPHs are incidents of nonfatal intimate partner violence that are far more common and often occur repetitively to victims. The frequency and severity of physical assaults by intimate partners are greater for women than men. In the National Violence Against Women Survey (NVAWS), 1.5 percent of women and 0.9 percent of men reported that they were raped or physically assaulted by an intimate partner in the previous twelve months.[19] Based on these numbers it is estimated that approximately 1.5 million women and 834,700 men experience violence at the hands of their intimate partners each year. Women who were raped averaged 4.5 rape victimizations at the hands of the same partner.[20] Women who were physically assaulted averaged 6.9 physical assaults by the same partner compared with 4.4 assaults for men. In physical assaults by intimates, women suffered injuries in 41.5 percent of incidents compared with 19.9 percent for men. Both injured male and female victims of assault required medical care in more than 70 percent of the incidents.

In this same survey, few victims of nonfatal intimate partner violence reported that an intimate partner used or threatened them with a gun.[21] Less then 1 percent of women (.7 percent) and only .1 percent of men reported being physically assaulted with a gun by their intimate partners. Pushing, grabbing, shoving, slapping, and hitting were the most common behaviors used to perpetrate nonfatal intimate partner violence. However, it is unknown whether the presence of a firearm serves as an implicit or explicit threat, making it more costly for the victim to leave the abusive relationship.

State and Federal Gun Laws

There is a great deal of legislation at the state and federal level aimed at reducing domestic violence. Some of this legislation has focused on firearms, making it more difficult for an abuser to gain access to a gun. We focus on two types of laws, those that prevent individuals subject to a current restraining order from owning or purchasing a firearm, and those that prevent individuals who have been convicted of domestic violence misdemeanors from owning or purchasing a firearm.

18. Dugan, Nagin, and Rosenfeld (1999); Browne and Williams (1989).
19. Tjaden and Thoennes (1998).
20. Tjaden and Thoennes (2000).
21. Centers for Disease Control and Prevention (forthcoming).

Federal Laws

At the federal level, there are two components of the federal Gun Control Act that pertain to domestic abuse and firearm possession or purchase. The first piece, added by Congress in September 1994 as part of the Violent Crime Control Act, makes it a federal offence to possess or receive a firearm while subject to a court order that restrains the individual from "harassing, stalking, or threatening an intimate partner of such person or child of such intimate partner or person, or engaging in other conduct that would place an intimate partner in reasonable fear of bodily injury to the partner or child."[22] This statute was enacted along with the Violence Against Women Act (VAWA), which created federal crimes of domestic violence such as interstate stalking and crossing state lines to violate a protective order. The law includes a due process provision that excludes temporary restraining orders; only those orders issued after a hearing at which the individual had an opportunity to participate invoke the federal firearm exclusion.

This component of the Gun Control Act was recently challenged in *United States* v. *Emerson*.[23] In this case, a man was indicted under the federal law in late 1998 when he threatened his estranged wife with a pistol after she had taken out a domestic violence restraining order on him. The U.S. District Court for the Northern District of Texas dismissed the indictment on the grounds that the federal law denying guns to those under restraining orders violates the Second Amendment constitutional right of these individuals to bear arms. In October 2001 the U.S. Court of Appeals for the Fifth Circuit reversed the decision. The Fifth Circuit ruling was notable because it concluded that the Second Amendment does protect an individual's right to own firearms, but the federal law prohibiting subjects of a restraining order from owning firearms was an acceptable limitation of that right. This marked the first time that a federal appellate court has suggested that the Second Amendment guarantees an individual's right to bear arms. Emerson appealed the case to the U.S. Supreme Court, which declined to hear it.

The second component of the Gun Control Act was passed as section 638 of Public Law 104-208, commonly known as the Lautenberg Amendment, in September 1996. This statute prohibits possession or receipt of a firearm by anyone who has ever been convicted of a misdemeanor crime of domestic violence.[24] This is defined as a crime that is a misdemeanor under state or federal law and

22. 18 U.S.C. § 921 (a)(32) defines intimate partner as a spouse, a former spouse, an individual with whom the person has a child in common, and an individual who cohabitates or has cohabited with the person. For quotation, see 18 U.S.C. § 922(g)(8).

23. *United States* v. *Emerson,* 46 F. Supp. 2d 598 (U.S. District Court for the Northern District of Texas 1999), reversed and remanded, No. 99-10331 (U.S. Court of Appeals for the Fifth Circuit).

24. 18 U.S.C. § 922(g)(9).

that contains the use or attempted use of physical force, or threatened use of a deadly weapon, against an intimate partner.[25] The latter means that the statute itself must contain this element. For example, violating a protection order may be a misdemeanor in a particular state, but unless by law violating a protection order requires the use of force, this will not be a qualifying misdemeanor *even if* the order is violated by the use of force.[26] In addition, certain due process requirements must be met: the individual must have been represented by counsel or knowingly waived such right and if the individual was entitled to a jury trial, he or she must have had such trial or knowingly waived the right.

The Lautenberg Amendment contains two particularly controversial elements. First, it is retroactive in the sense that any prior qualifying domestic violence misdemeanor invokes the law. Second, unlike the restraining order prohibition, it is not subject to the public interest exemption. This means that it is illegal for police officers and members of the armed forces who have a domestic violence conviction to possess weapons, even while on the job. The Lautenberg Amendment has been subjected to numerous legal challenges on various constitutional grounds, but to date the law has been upheld in every case.[27]

State Laws

In addition to the federal laws, many states have passed laws regarding firearms and domestic violence misdemeanors or restraining orders. There is tremendous variation in these laws, along dimensions such as the precise action prohibited (firearm purchase or possession), the definition of intimate partner, the level of due process required, and the timing of the exclusions (for example, a conviction in the past five years). Many of the state laws go well beyond the federal laws. Although it may seem redundant for a state to pass a firearm law relating to either restraining orders or domestic violence misdemeanors after the federal laws were enacted, there are a number of important differences between the state and federal laws that could extend the reach of a state law. Consequently, it is not surprising that many of these laws were passed subsequent to the federal legislation.

Eleven states have laws that prevent individuals with a domestic violence misdemeanor conviction from purchasing or possessing a firearm; in addition, one state (Colorado) had a law that was repealed in 1998 along with the state's instant background check legislation (table 5-1). The vast majority of these eleven states passed their laws before the federal legislation was enacted, although two states

25. 18 U.S.C. § 921 (a)(33).
26. Groban (1999).
27. See Nathan (2000) for a good discussion of the legal challenges.

Table 5-1. *States with Restrictions on Access to Firearms for Domestic Violence Misdemeanants*

State	Year passed	Type of firearm	Action prohibited
California	1994	All	Possession/sale to
Colorado[a]	1994	Handguns	Purchase
Delaware	1999	All	Possession/purchase
Florida	1995	All	Purchase
Hawaii	1988	All	Possession/purchase
Illinois	1996	All	Possession/purchase
Iowa	1987	Handguns	Purchase
		All	Carrying
Minnesota	1992	Handguns	Possession
	1994	All	
New York	1993	All	Possession
Pennsylvania	1995	All	Possession
Washington	1993	All	Possession
West Virginia	1996	All	Carrying
	2000		Possession

Source: See text for tables 5-1 through 5-10.
a. Repealed in 1998.

enacted their laws in early 1996. In every state but Colorado and Iowa all guns are covered under the law; Iowa restricts handgun purchase and carrying or transport of any firearm. Three states restrict purchasing or carrying but not possession.

Table 5-2 lists the states that have laws restricting access to guns by individuals under a court order. As of 2000, there were twenty-three states with such laws. Only three states exempt possession of firearms while disallowing purchase or receipt. In four states the law only refers to handguns. Approximately half of the states include temporary restraining orders along with those issued after a hearing. Unlike the domestic violence misdemeanor laws, most of the restraining order laws were passed after the federal law. Eight states, just over a third, passed their first law prior to the VAWA. However, only three of these states passed a law before 1994. There are several dimensions along which the state and federal laws may differ. The definition of who qualifies as a domestic abuser or intimate partner may be one of the differences between federal and state law. The federal law is fairly broadly defined, but one notable category that is excluded is former or current significant others with whom the victim has neither cohabitated nor had a child. Family members, other than intimate partners, for example, a brother-in-law or cousin, are excluded. Of the twelve states that passed domestic violence misdemeanor laws, seven include current boyfriends and girlfriends as possible offenders, and six include ex-boyfriends or girlfriends.

Table 5-2. *States with Restrictions on Access to Firearms for Persons under Restraining Orders*

State	Year passed	Type of firearm	Action prohibited	Includes temporary restraining orders?
Alaska	1996	All	Possession	No
California	1991	All	Purchase	Yes
	1995		Possession	Yes
Colorado[a]	1994	Handguns	Purchase	Yes
		All	Possession	Yes
Connecticut	1994	Handguns	Possession	No
Delaware	1994	All	Possession/purchase	No
Florida	1995	All	Purchase	No
	1998	All	Possession	No
Hawaii	1993	All	Possession/purchase	Yes
Illinois	1996	All	Possession	No
Indiana	1999	All	Possession	No
Maine	1997	All	Possession	No
Maryland	1996	Handguns	Possession/transfer to	No
Massachusetts	1994	All	Possession/purchase	Yes
Michigan	1996	Handguns	Possession/purchase	Yes
New Hampshire	1990	All	Possession	Yes
	2000	All	Purchase	Yes
New Jersey	1991	All	Possession/purchase	No
New York	1996	All	Possession	Yes
North Carolina	1995	All	Purchase	No
North Dakota	1997	All	Possession	Yes
Pennsylvania	1995	All	Possession	No
Texas	1996	Handguns	Transfer to	Yes
Virginia	1994	All	Purchase/transport	Yes
West Virginia	1996	All	Carrying	Yes
	2000		Possession	No
Wisconsin	1996	All	Possession	No

a. Purchase law repealed in 1998.

All twelve states also include certain people related by blood, and eleven include some related by marriage.

Another key difference between the state and federal laws is the set of misdemeanors that disqualify an individual. While a few states do specify that a conviction for a misdemeanor crime of domestic violence excludes individuals from purchasing or owning a firearm, most provide a specific list of crimes that happen to be misdemeanors. The crimes vary widely from state to state. For example, purchase of a firearm is prohibited in Iowa by anyone ever convicted of domestic abuse assault or stalking, in Florida by anyone arrested for an act of domestic violence, and in Illinois by anyone who has committed domestic battery with a firearm, violated a protective order, or committed a stalking crime. A related point is that many states have codified specific crimes of domestic violence, while others rely on general criminal offenses committed against family members or intimate partners. In the latter case it may be more difficult to identify individuals who are precluded from gun ownership or purchase as doing so relies heavily on adequate record-keeping and classification.

A final important component that distinguishes many state laws from the federal equivalent is the inclusion of temporary restraining orders. These are emergency restraining orders that grant an injunction against the respondent until a hearing is held. Of the twenty-two states that have laws restricting access to firearms by those under a court order, half include temporary orders. However, in most states the firearm restrictions are not automatic upon issuance of a court order (either temporary and permanent) but are left to the discretion of the court. We do not know the frequency with which a judge elects to prohibit purchase or possession of a firearm when a restraining order is issued.

For both the state and federal laws, almost nothing is known about the degree of enforcement, particularly for laws prohibiting possession of a firearm. Only two states—New Jersey and New Hampshire—permit the court to order a search and seizure order for weapons when issuing a restraining order.[28] The extent to which batterers voluntarily surrender their firearms once a restraining order has been issued against them is unknown. Anecdotal evidence suggests that the possession laws are not widely enforced, and that the system relies heavily on complaints by victims or subsequent criminal acts to identify noncompliers.[29]

Logic Model

A primary purpose of state and federal laws that prohibit persons convicted of domestic violence misdemeanors or stalking, or who are under restraining orders, from purchasing or possessing firearms is to protect the partners and children of these individuals from threats and potentially severe or lethal injury from a firearm. Individuals who are violent with members of their family are also more likely to engage in violence against acquaintances and strangers than persons who

28. Mecka (1998).
29. For example, see Jim Stingl, "Abuse Suspects Keeping Guns: Law In Domestic Violence Cases Mostly Ignored," *Milwaukee Journal Sentinel,* October 11, 1996, p. 1; Roy Malone, "Man Draws 41-Month Term for Firearms Violation; Little-Known Law Forbids Those Named in Protection Orders from Having Guns," *St. Louis Post-Dispatch,* January 29, 1998, p. B1; Josh Kovner, "A New State Law Backs Court Orders; Domestic-Violence Defendants Targeted," *Hartford Courant,* September 30, 1999 p. A3; *United States* v. *Emerson* (1999).

do not engage in such violence.[30] Consequently, these laws may also have an impact on other forms of violence involving firearms. The impact of these laws on threats or injuries from firearms in domestic situations or otherwise, however, depends on the occurrence of a series of actions involving law enforcement, the courts, and federal firearm licensees (FFL). Figure 5-1 displays a logic model that describes the process through which persons who batter their intimate partners or children may or may not be prevented from threatening or injuring others with a firearm. The manner in which the actions and processes described in this model are carried out differs from state to state. This model is helpful in estimating the potential impact of the laws but leaves aside whether or not they are effective in reducing firearm-related threats and injuries to intimate partners.

The first stage in this model involves whether or not a batterer or stalker gets arrested and convicted or becomes subject to a restraining order. Rape or physical assault of an intimate partner could result in a felony or misdemeanor conviction. If the individual is convicted of a felony, then he would be barred from possessing or engaging in the transfer of any firearm (that is, purchasing a firearm or obtaining a permit to purchase) based on the federal Gun Control Act. If instead he is convicted of a qualifying misdemeanor for domestic violence, he would be prohibited from purchasing or possessing a firearm in those states that included domestic violence misdemeanors among prohibiting factors before September 1996, and in all states after that time. If, however, he is under the authority of a restraining order, then he would also be prohibited from purchasing or possessing a firearm in those states that included permanent or temporary restraining orders among their prohibiting factors before September 1994, and in all states after that time. The federal Gun Control Act only pertains to permanent restraining orders, but as of 1998 eleven states have extended their laws to cover temporary restraining orders.

The potential impact of these laws will depend in part on the incidence of misdemeanor convictions and restraining orders. Within the universe of persons who rape, batter, or stalk their intimate partners, only a fraction are arrested and convicted. Estimates derived from the NVAWS indicate that 3 to 6 percent of self-reported rapes, physical assaults, and cases of stalking by intimate partners result in a conviction of the perpetrator (table 5-3).[31] Convictions, however, are probably more likely to take place in incidents involving the most severe injuries or circumstances.

In contrast to misdemeanor convictions, temporary restraining orders are much more common. Female victims of rape and physical assault obtain tem-

30. Fagan and Browne (1994).
31. Tjaden and Thoennes (2000).

Figure 5-1. *Logic Model*

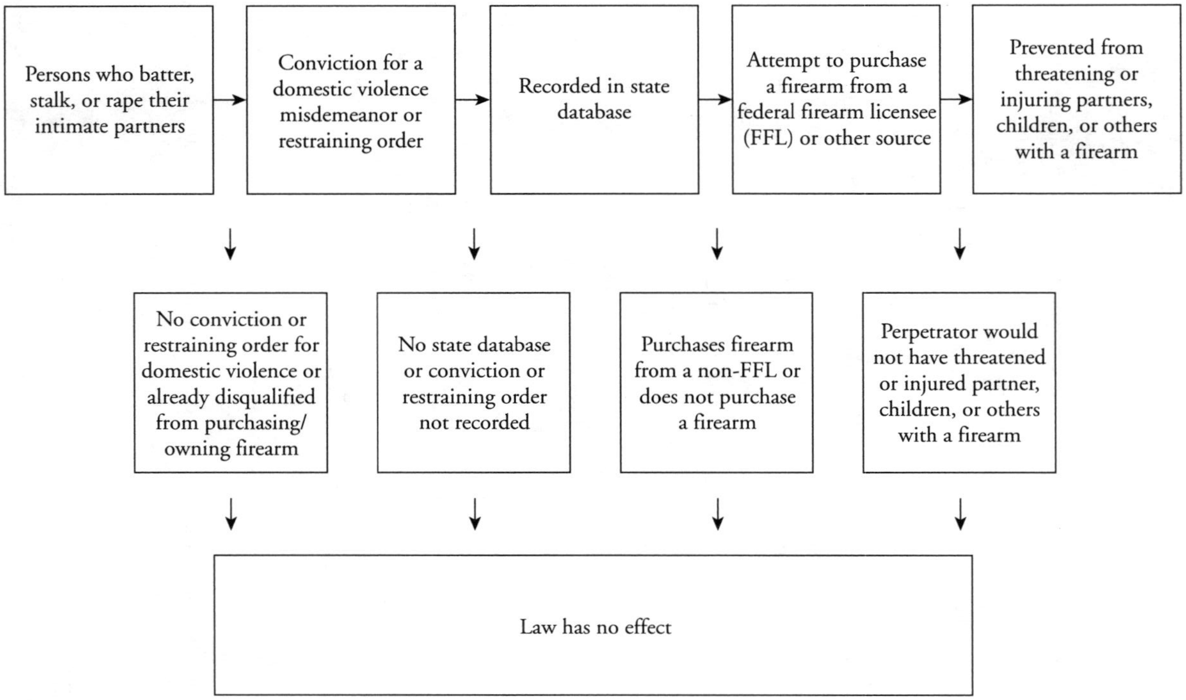

Persons who batter, stalk, or rape their intimate partners → Conviction for a domestic violence misdemeanor or restraining order → Recorded in state database → Attempt to purchase a firearm from a federal firearm licensee (FFL) or other source → Prevented from threatening or injuring partners, children, or others with a firearm

No conviction or restraining order for domestic violence or already disqualified from purchasing/owning firearm

No state database or conviction or restraining order not recorded

Purchases firearm from a non-FFL or does not purchase a firearm

Perpetrator would not have threatened or injured partner, children, or others with a firearm

Law has no effect

Table 5-3. *Distribution of Intimate Partner Rape, Physical Assault, and Stalking, by Criminal Justice Outcomes and Gender*
Percent

	Rape victims	Physical assault victims		Stalking Victims	
Criminal justice outcomes[a]	Women	Women	Men	Women	Men
Victimization reported to police	17.2	26.7	13.5	51.9	36.2
Attacker arrested or detained	8.2	9.7	1.7	14.9	...
Perpetrator was convicted	3.1	3.5	...	5.8	...
Victim obtained a temporary restraining order (TRO)	16.4	17.1	3.5	36.6	17.0
N	441	1,149	541	343	47

Source: National Violence Against Women Survey, 2000.
   a. Estimates are based on most recent intimate partner victimization since age 18 reported by persons who have reported a victimization at any time in their lives. Estimates not calculated for male rape victims because, when stratified by variables, there were fewer than five victims.

porary restraining orders in about one of every six incidents, while female victims of stalking obtain temporary restraining orders in about one of every three incidents. Male victims are less likely to obtain temporary restraining orders than female victims. We do not know, however, how many temporary restraining orders eventually become permanent restraining orders.

As convictions for domestic violence misdemeanors accumulate over time so does the potential impact of these laws. For example, the state of Illinois passed a law in 1996 prohibiting domestic violence misdemeanants from purchasing a firearm (this law was not retroactive). The number of people charged with domestic violence misdemeanors rose from 4,097 in 1996 to 6,717 in 1998 and then dropped down to 5,769 in 2000.[32] Between 1996 and 2000 more than 28,000 domestic violence convictions had accumulated. Consequently, about seven times as many people would be prohibited from purchasing firearms owing to domestic violence misdemeanors in 2000 as 1996 in Illinois.

If we make the assumption that estimates from the NVAWS provide an accurate indication of the incidence of rapes, physical assaults, and stalking by intimate partners and that these estimates are stable from year to year, then we can crudely estimate that each year about 45,000 people are convicted of domestic

32. Illinois State Police (2001).

violence misdemeanors, 30,000 are convicted of stalking misdemeanors, and 500,000 temporary restraining orders are issued for victimizations related to rape, physical assault, or stalking. Of the misdemeanor convictions, we do not know how many are first convictions. Given the repetitive nature of domestic abuse, it would seem likely that some of these misdemeanants are repeat offenders. Furthermore, some of these offenders may already be barred from owning a firearm because of a previous felony conviction. Many states have a time limit on firearm prohibitions stemming from a domestic violence misdemeanor, so a subset of abusers has their ability to own or purchase firearms restored each year. Therefore the number of excluded individuals will accumulate less rapidly than the number of domestic misdemeanor crimes.

The accuracy of the assumptions underlying these estimates is questionable, particularly as we go back further in time. These estimates, however, may be useful for providing a relative sense of the potential impact of laws that prohibit firearm possession and transfers by persons convicted of domestic violence misdemeanors versus restraining orders. Although we do not know how many permanent restraining orders are in place at a given time, nor do we know the rate at which the pool of individuals convicted of misdemeanors for domestic violence or stalking accumulates over time, we do know that in any given year temporary restraining orders are at least six times more commonly obtained then misdemeanor convictions. It seems likely, therefore, that in the first years after the implementation of the state-level laws we would expect to observe a larger effect from the state restraining order laws than from the domestic violence misdemeanor legislation.

The second stage of the logic model takes into consideration whether or not the misdemeanor conviction or restraining order is recorded in a state database that enables the appropriate authorities to conduct a background check for the existence of a misdemeanor conviction or restraining order in the criminal history of an applicant for purchase of a firearm. Despite the existence of federal and state laws, not all states maintain databases that would permit screening for domestic violence misdemeanors or restraining orders among firearm purchasers. In those states where misdemeanor convictions or restraining orders are not recorded in a state database, applicants for firearm purchases with these relevant convictions or restraining orders could easily violate federal or state laws regarding firearm purchases. In 1998 thirty-two states had the ability to conduct background checks for domestic violence misdemeanors and thirty-five states for restraining orders.[33] Other states either lacked databases to conduct background checks on these violations or had incomplete databases.

---

33. Regional Justice Information Center (2000).

In 1995 five of the seven states with state laws for domestic violence misdemeanors had the ability to conduct background checks on these misdemeanors.
This was the year before the federal Gun Control Act was amended to include
domestic violence misdemeanors. In contrast, thirty-one states had the ability
to conduct background checks for restraining orders in 1995. The federal Gun
Control Act had been amended in September of 1994 to exclude those with permanent restraining orders from purchasing firearms. The ability to check the
backgrounds of firearm purchasers for domestic violence misdemeanors has increased substantially since passage of the federal law in 1996, while the ability
to screen for restraining orders has been in effect in more states for a longer period. The existence and maintenance of these databases at the state level is an
essential ingredient in the enforcement of these laws and in assessing their
potential to reduce threats and injuries associated with firearms.

The third stage of the model involves the purchase or surrender of a firearm.
Firearm owners convicted of a domestic violence misdemeanor or under the authority of a restraining order are prohibited from possessing a firearm under federal and some state laws. Consequently, they are legally required to surrender
their firearms to authorities. It is unknown to what extent this provision of federal and state laws is enforced or otherwise adhered to. Furthermore, persons
with misdemeanor convictions and restraining orders may attempt to purchase
a firearm though an FFL or other means (for example, gun shows, acquaintances, straw purchases, and so on). If they attempt to purchase a firearm though
an FFL and are in a state that maintains a database of misdemeanants and restraining orders, then they are likely to be denied purchase. If they attempt to
purchase a firearm though other legal or illegal avenues (that is, unless their state
requires background checks at gun shows), they are unlikely to be denied their
purchase. The Bureau of Alcohol, Tobacco, and Firearms estimates that there
are more than 4,000 gun shows held annually in the United States and count-
less other flea markets and garage sales in which firearms are freely sold or
traded.[34] In most states firearms can be sold anonymously at these public markets and, consequently, even if a state maintains an adequate database, people
with domestic violence misdemeanors or under the authority of a restraining
order could potentially purchase firearms through these avenues. The frequency
with which persons with misdemeanant convictions or restraining orders attempt
to purchase firearms is unknown. Domestic violence misdemeanor convictions
and restraining orders often occur under emotionally turbulent circumstances
and, therefore, the acquisition of firearms by both perpetrators and victims may
not be uncommon.

34. Bureau of Alcohol, Tobacco and Firearms (1999).

From March 1994 to November 1998, the time before the permanent provisions of the Brady Act became effective, about 41,500 persons in the United States were denied purchase of a firearm or denied a permit to buy a firearm because of a disqualifying domestic violence conviction or restraining order.[35] This amounted to about 13.3 percent of the almost 312,000 applications rejected by state and local agencies or the FBI during the period. Almost three-quarters of the applications rejected for domestic violence misdemeanors or restraining orders were for misdemeanor convictions. It appears that the number of applications processed and the number of rejections has been increasing nationally from year to year, although it is unclear whether this is also true for rejections associated with misdemeanor convictions or restraining orders.[36] However, data from the state of Illinois indicate that the number of applicants for firearm purchases rejected in that state owing to domestic violence misdemeanors has increased steadily from 635 in 1997 to 1,314 in 2001.[37]

Interestingly, most domestic-violence-related purchase denials have been for misdemeanors rather than because of restraining orders. This may indicate that permanent restraining orders are rare relative to temporary orders (since only eleven states include temporary orders in their laws). It is also possible that many people subject to restraining orders are deterred from attempting to purchase firearms because of knowledge of the law.

The final stage of the model addresses the association between the ability to purchase a firearm and threats or injuries to intimate partners, children, or others. No data exist on how many persons convicted of domestic violence misdemeanors or under restraining orders, despite existing laws, will be able to purchase a firearm and go on to threaten or injure their partners or others with that firearm. We know that violence within intimate relationships is often repetitive, and these repeated incidents may escalate in severity.[38] We also know that access to a firearm may increase the likelihood that an incident of intimate partner violence could result in death.[39] We suspect that persons convicted of domestic violence misdemeanors and with restraining orders are more likely to seek access to firearms and are at higher risk of perpetrating violence within and outside of intimate relationships. The question remains, however, about whether laws to disqualify those convicted of domestic violence misdemeanors and with restraining orders from firearm purchases are effective despite the many factors that limit their potential impact.

35. Manson, Gilliard, and Lauver (1999).
36. Gifford and others (2000).
37. Illinois State Police (2001).
38. Tjaden and Thoennes (2000).
39. Saltzman and others (1992); Campbell and others (forthcoming).

Estimation and Data

We are interested in evaluating the impact of the state and federal laws restricting domestic abusers' access to firearms. Guns are not the weapon used in most domestic abuse incidents, and therefore we might not expect to find a large impact on domestic violence overall. However, firearms do contribute heavily to intimate partner homicides, and these laws are designed to reduce the ability of abusers to kill their partners. Therefore we can evaluate the effect of these laws by looking at changes in intimate partner homicides in states that have passed the laws compared with states that have not.

Since both the state and federal laws effectively increase the price of acquiring or possessing a firearm, we would expect these laws to lead to a reduction in gun-related domestic violence on the margin. However, we might also expect to find an effect on nonfirearm domestic violence. It is plausible that the mere presence of a gun in the household (or threat of acquiring one) aggravates the relationship between the abuser and the victim. For example, a woman may be more afraid to leave an abusive relationship if she fears her partner may come after her with a gun. Reducing access to firearms by abusers might shift the balance of power away from the abuser, allowing the victim to leave the relationship or otherwise seek help. However, we might also expect nonfatal domestic violence to increase if there is substitution into less lethal weapons by abusers.

Ideally we would like to examine the impact of these laws on intimate partner homicides, assaults, rapes, and other types of domestic abuse. Unfortunately, it is very difficult to obtain data on domestic violence. Statistics are not kept regularly on domestic violence outcomes, with the exception of homicide data. To evaluate the impact of state laws that were adopted at different times, we need annual, state-level data for our outcome measures. The National Crime Victimization Survey does ask questions about domestic abuse, but unfortunately the sample of domestic violence victims is too small to be reliable for analysis at the state level. Consequently, we focus on the one annual outcome measure that we were able to obtain, intimate partner homicides.

Estimation

The states that have laws limiting access to guns by abusers passed their legislation at different times. We exploit this time variation by effectively comparing IPH rates before and after passage of the law in states that have enacted these laws with those in states that did not pass such a law. Although we cannot be certain that we are isolating the impact of the laws, the time variation in the effective dates of the laws reduces the likelihood that we are capturing the effect of an omitted shock affecting all IPH rates.

Since intimate partner homicides are count data and there are a number of states that record no intimate partner homicides in a particular year, a Poisson or negative binomial model is most appropriate for our analysis. Goodness-of-fit tests rejected the Poisson model owing to overdispersion, so we use negative binomial regression for our estimation.[40] With the negative binomial model, the probability of a state having IPHs in a given year equal to h_{it} is given by:

$$\Pr\left(H_{it} = h_{it}\right) = \frac{\Gamma\left(y_{it} + \alpha^{-1}\right)}{\Gamma(y_{it} + 1)\Gamma\left(\alpha^{-1}\right)} \left[\frac{1}{1 + \alpha\mu_{it}}\right]^{\alpha^{-1}} \left[\frac{\mu_{it}}{\alpha^{-1} + \mu_{it}}\right]^{y_{it}}$$

where Γ is the Gamma function, $E(H_{it}) = \mu_{it}$ and $Var(H_{it}) = \mu_{it} + \alpha\mu_{it}^2$.

The mean number of IPHs, μ_{it}, is log-linearly related to the explanatory variables:

$$\ln\left(\mu_{it}\right) = \ln\left(POP_{it}\right) + \beta_1 RO_{it} + \beta_2 DVM_{it} + \beta_3 M_{it}$$
$$+ \beta_4 G_{it} + \beta_5 D_{it} + s_i + \tau_t + r$$

where POP_{it} is the population over age 10 in state i at year t (or the female population over age 10 in the regressions with female victims as the dependent variable). The coefficient on POP_{it} is constrained to 1, effectively modeling the incidence of IPHs as a function of the independent variables. RO_{it} is a dummy variable for whether a state had a restraining order law in effect that year, DVM_{it} is a dummy variable for whether a state had a domestic violence misdemeanor law in effect that year, M_{it} is stranger homicides per 100,000, G_{it} is a vector of other gun laws in effect that year and D_{it} is a vector of demographic and other variables. State fixed effects (s_i) are included to account for any unmeasured time-invariant state characteristics. Year dummies (τ_t) are also included to capture any nationwide trends, and regional time trends (r) capture any trends that vary within the country as a whole.[41] Note that the year dummies also pick up any constant effect of the two federal laws that took effect in all states simultaneously. Since we have included state fixed effects, we are identifying off within-state changes in the state laws over time.

---

40. Even though goodness-of-fit tests suggest that the Poisson model does not fit our data as well as the negative binomial, we obtain very similar results (both coefficients and standard errors) with both Poisson and negative binomial regression.

41. We also ran regressions including state-specific time trends (along with the state fixed effects). The incidence rate ratios in these regressions are virtually identical to those we present here (between .001–.01 different). The standard errors do go up but not enough to change our results qualitatively. Given this result, we believe that regional time trends capture trend variation within the United States adequately and more efficiently than state-specific time trends.

Although the year dummies capture any constant impact from the federal laws, they do not measure any differential impact of the federal laws by state. If states begin enforcing the federal laws at different rates and with varying effectiveness, the coefficients on the state law variables would be biased. The direction of the bias is not clear a priori: if states with their own laws in place already have the infrastructure to enforce the federal law and are therefore more effective in doing so, the coefficients will be biased toward showing a larger impact of the state laws. However, states with laws in place may already be screening out the prohibited parties and experience little or no impact from the federal laws. This would bias the coefficients toward showing a smaller effect of the state laws. To address this concern, we estimate one version of the model that simply measures the impact of any domestic violent misdemeanor law (state or federal) and any restraining order law.

Our dependent variable is the number of intimate partner homicides. We look at four categories: all intimate partner homicides, intimate partner firearm homicides, intimate partner homicides with female victims, and female intimate partner firearm homicides. Our unit of observation is a state-year. We have complete data from 1982 to 1998 for forty-six states. Four states and the District of Columbia are excluded because they did not report multiple years of homicide data.[42] Four states were only missing one year of homicide data. For these states, the homicide rates were imputed and a dummy variable included in the regression equal to one for the missing year for each of the four states. The coefficient on this dummy variable is not meaningful, but this allows us to use information from these states for the nonmissing years.

We also control for other firearm laws enacted by states over this time, including required private background checks, required dealer background checks, mandatory waiting periods, one-gun-a-month laws, Saturday Night Special bans, and requiring a permit to purchase a gun.[43] We determined that fourteen states also have laws that restrict access to firearms by people convicted of certain violent misdemeanors (apart from domestic-violence-related misdemeanors). It is very important to control for the passage of these laws as batterers may be prohibited from purchasing or owning guns even in states that do not explicitly have domestic violence provisions. Even in states that do have domestic-violence-related laws, these more general laws may cover violent misdemeanors that are not enumerated under the relevant domestic violence statutes. We include an indicator variable for each of these laws equal to 1 if the law was in effect for a particular state in a given year.

42. These states are Florida, Kansas, Maine, and Montana. These four states were missing at least two consecutive years of homicide data.

43. Vernick, Hepburn, and Schofield (2001).

Demographic variables included as controls in our regressions are percent of the population 20 to 34 years old, percent black, number of males per 1,000 population, percent of the population living in an urban area, the poverty rate, and the log of median income. Since the previous literature suggests that declining marriage rates and ease of divorce have contributed to the decline in intimate partner homicides, we also control for marriage rates and the presence of unilateral divorce laws.[44] Finally, we control for per capita ethanol consumption and the rate of homicide against strangers. Summary statistics for intimate partner homicide rates and the independent variables can be found in table 5-4.

Data Sources

We obtained counts of homicide data by state from the Federal Bureau of Investigation (FBI) Supplementary Homicide Report (SHR) files for the years 1982 through 1998. On a monthly basis, state and local law enforcement agencies voluntarily report homicides and other major crimes to the FBI through the Uniform Crime Reporting Program (UCR).[45] The term *homicide* refers to those offenses reported to the FBI as murder and nonnegligent manslaughter, that is, "the willful (non-negligent) killing of one human being by another."[46] The classification of this offense is based solely on police investigation rather than the determination of a court, medical examiner, coroner, jury, or other judicial body. The SHRs accompanying the UCR reports on murder and nonnegligent manslaughter include information on sex, age, race of victims and offenders, the victim-to-offender relationship, the circumstances under which the homicide occurred, the type of weapon used, and the geographic location of the homicide. In this study, all homicides that occurred in the United States for which we have data are included, and these homicides include both U.S. and non-U.S. residents.

In this analysis, we focus on IPHs. We confined our counts of IPHs to those where the victim was 10 years or older and the offender was an intimate partner. The SHR relationship categories that we used to classify intimate partner relationships included spouse, ex-spouse, common-law spouse, boyfriend, girlfriend, and homosexual relationships. The SHRs include no separate category for ex-boyfriend or ex-girlfriend, although such relationships can also be regarded as intimate.[47] In incidents involving more than two homicides, the SHRs

44. See Dugan, Nagin, and Rosenfeld (1999); Browne and Williams (1989); Stevenson and Wolfers (2000). Ideally we would like to control for age-specific marriage rates. However, these data are not available for all states nor for the entire time period we examine.

45. Federal Bureau of Investigation (1999).

46. Federal Bureau of Investigation (1999).

47. Saltzman and others (1999); Paulozzi and others (2001).

Table 5-4. *Summary Statistics*

Item	1998		All years (1982–98)	
Intimate partner homicides				
Intimate partner homicides per 100,000	0.68	(0.38)	0.90	(0.54)
Intimate partner firearm homicides per 100,000	0.39	(0.28)	0.57	(0.41)
Female intimate partner homicides per 100,000 women	0.92	(0.48)	1.13	(0.62)
Female intimate partner firearm homicides per 100,000 women	0.56	(0.40)	0.73	(0.49)
Proportion of states with laws:				
Prohibiting access to firearms if under a restraining order	0.43	(0.50)	0.10	(0.30)
Prohibiting access to firearms if convicted of domestic violence misdemeanor	0.22	(0.42)	0.07	(0.26)
Prohibiting access to firearms if convicted of violent misdemeanor	0.26	(0.44)	0.16	(0.36)
Prohibiting purchase of more than one gun a month	0.07	(0.25)	0.03	(0.17)
Requiring permit to purchase firearm	0.26	(0.44)	0.23	(0.42)
Requiring waiting period to purchase	0.63	(0.49)	0.48	(0.50)
Requiring background check in private transactions	0.37	(0.49)	0.26	(0.44)
Requiring dealer background check	0.63	(0.49)	0.40	(0.49)
Demographics and other characteristics				
Stranger homicides per 100,000	0.53	(0.45)	0.79	(0.60)
Population over age 10	4,649,812	(5,022,923)	4,305,856	(4,598,463)
Proportion age 20–34	0.21	(0.01)	0.24	(0.02)
Proportion black	0.11	(0.10)	0.10	(0.09)
Proportion male	0.49	(0.01)	0.49	(0.01)
Proportion urban population	0.69	(0.20)	0.66	(0.21)
Proportion under poverty line	0.12	(0.03)	0.14	(0.04)
Log median income	56,138	(7,558)	40,734	(10,120)
Marriages per 1,000	10.14	(11.21)	11.62	(13.71)
Proportion states with unilateral divorce law	0.89	(0.31)	0.88	(0.32)
Per capita ethanol consumption (gallons)	2.26	(0.48)	2.45	(0.61)
N	46		782	

Note: Standard deviations in parentheses.

are not explicit as to which homicide victim was the intimate partner of the offender.[48] Incidents in which more than two of the victims were 10 years or older are dropped from our homicide counts because the victim who was the intimate partner could not be identified with certainty. For incidents in which only one of the multiple victims was 10 years or older, we assumed that the victims less than 10 years old were not intimate partners of the offender and included the cases in our homicide counts.[49] The type of weapon used in homicides is not explicitly linked to victims or offenders in multiple-homicide and multiple-offender incidents in SHR data.[50] Therefore, counts of firearm-related homicides in this analysis are restricted to one-victim, one-perpetrator incidents. Such incidents, however, represent 97 percent of all intimate partner homicides.

The FBI-SHR files were used to create the dependent variables used in the analysis. Counts of the number of total and firearm-related homicides, intimate partner homicides and firearm-related intimate partner homicides, intimate partner homicides in which the victim was female, and firearm-related intimate partner homicides in which the victim was female were generated for each state for the years 1982 to 1998.

The explanatory variables of interest are whether a state had a law restricting firearm access by persons convicted of a domestic violence misdemeanor, and whether the state had a law restricting access to guns by individuals under a restraining order. To determine whether states had a particular law, we first checked several government publications of firearm laws.[51] We then used the legal databases Lexis-Nexis and Westlaw to locate additional laws. Many of the restraining order laws are codified under family law, and some are not referenced in the section of the state code that deals with firearms. Lexis-Nexis, Westlaw, and historical published versions of state code were used to ascertain the effective dates of the legislation.

As described above, there is tremendous heterogeneity in the scope and scale of the state laws. There are also unmeasured differences in the state laws, such as the degree to which they are enforced. However, our sample is not large enough to permit us to analyze the particular details of most of these laws. For this analysis, we generate indicator variables defined simply as whether a state had any type of law prohibiting access to firearms by domestic violence misdemeanants in effect that year; and whether a state had any type of law prohibiting access to firearms by persons subject to a restraining order in effect that

48. Paulozzi and others (2001).
49. Paulozzi and others (2001).
50. Paulozzi and others (2001).
51. Bureau of Alcohol, Tobacco and Firearms (2001); Regional Justice Information Center (1996, 1997, 1998, 2000, 2001).

year. After excluding states for the aforementioned reasons and the fact that our data only go through 1998, our analysis included ten states with domestic violence misdemeanor laws (excluding Florida), and twenty states with restraining order laws (excluding Florida and Maine). Carrying laws were included with possession; coding them as being no law did not have a significant effect on the results. A law was considered to be in effect for a given year if it was enacted in the first six months of the year.

Annual population data were obtained from Census Bureau population estimates. Annual poverty rate and median income data were obtained from the Current Population Survey. Marriage data were obtained from the Census Bureau's *Statistical Abstract of the United States;* information on unilateral divorce laws came from Friedberg.[52] The National Institute on Alcohol Abuse and Alcoholism provided the per capita ethanol consumption data.

Results

Figure 5-2 shows intimate partner homicide rates from 1982 to 1998. All types of intimate partner homicides declined over this period. Before 1990 there were greater fluctuations in the rates from year to year, with the highest rates occurring in the mid-1980s. Overall, however, all the IPH rates exhibit a general downward trend between 1982 and 1998. This is in contrast to rates of most other violent crimes, which tended to rise in the mid- to late 1980s, and then decrease throughout the 1990s. Throughout this period the IPH rates for women are higher than the overall IPH rate. The total IPH rate in 1998 was 0.7 homicides per 100,000 population, while for women the rate was 0.9 per 100,000 women. For firearm IPHs, the overall rate was 0.4 per 100,000 people and 0.6 per 100,000 women (table 5-4).

Who Passes Domestic-Violence-Related Firearm Laws?

Not all states have passed laws restricting domestic abusers' access to firearms. Only around 20 percent of states have their own laws about domestic violence misdemeanors and guns, while just under half have laws governing restraining orders and access to firearms. Table 5-5 illustrates the differences between states that pass these laws and those that do not. This table presents results from probit models comparing the characteristics of states that have these laws prior to the passage of the law with the characteristics of those that never passed such

52. Friedberg (1998).

Figure 5-2. *Intimate Partner Homicides, 1982–98*

Rate per 100,000

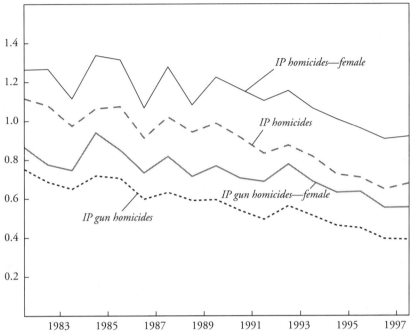

laws. The estimates shown in table 5-5 are the marginal effect of a one-unit increase on the probability that a state will pass one of these laws. State fixed effects are omitted, so that we can observe the state-specific characteristics that predict future passage of the laws.[53] The dependent variable in these models is whether a state has ever passed one of the two laws we are interested in. For states that do pass laws, only the years prior to the passage of each state's law are included in the analysis. Therefore we are comparing the characteristics of states that pass these laws in the period *before* the legislation is adopted with the characteristics of states that had not passed such laws by 1998.

States that pass either type of law are more white, male, and urban, and have more people living below the poverty rate. For example, increasing the rate of blacks per 1,000 by one at the mean (an increase of about 10 percent) decreases the probability of passing either law by 4 percentage points. The states also have lower marriage rates and are less likely to have unilateral divorce laws. They also

53. These probits were fitted using data from 1982–97. To control for potential confounding from the passage of the federal laws, the domestic violence misdemeanor law and restraining order law models were also fitted excluding the years after 1996 and 1994, respectively. The results are not significantly different from those presented here.

Table 5-5. *Factors Correlated with Passage of State Laws*

Item	Future domestic violence misdemeanor law	Future restraining order law
Crime rates		
Property crime per 1,000	−0.03***	−0.08***
	(0.01)	(0.01)
Violent crime per 1,000,	0.10***	0.14***
excluding murder	(0.03)	(0.03)
Stranger homicides per 100,000	−0.01	−0.29***
	(0.06)	(0.09)
Intimate partner homicides	−0.0001	0.11***
per 1,000,000	(0.01)	(0.03)
Demographics and behavioral characteristics		
Population over age 10 (100,000s)	0.0007	0.008***
	(0.0008)	(0.002)
People age 20–34 per 1,000	−0.003	0.19***
	(0.03)	(0.06)
Blacks per 1,000	−0.04***	−0.04***
	(0.007)	(0.01)
Males per 1,000	0.40***	0.58***
	(0.07)	(0.15)
Urban population per 1,000	0.02***	0.03***
	(0.004)	(0.01)
People below poverty rate per 1,000	0.04***	0.06***
	(0.01)	(0.02)
Median income (thousands of dollars)	−0.02**	0.06***
	(0.01)	(0.02)
Marriages per 1,000,000	−0.03	−0.20***
	(0.02)	(0.05)
Unilateral divorce law	−0.68***	−0.36***
	(0.12)	(0.07)
Per capita ethanol consumption	−0.01	0.10***
(tens of gallons)	(0.008)	(0.03)
Gun laws		
Some misdemeanants prohibited	−0.13**	0.24**
	(0.04)	(0.07)
Need permit to purchase	0.75***	0.68***
	(0.11)	(0.13)
Waiting period	0.28***	−0.25**
	(0.07)	(0.12)

(continued)

Table 5-5. (*continued*)

Item	Future domestic violence misdemeanor law	Future restraining order law
Background check required by dealers	−0.05	0.22
	(0.08)	(0.14)
Background check required in private transactions	−0.41***	−0.98***
	(0.09)	(0.02)
N	685	673

Note: Marginal effects on probability, evaluated at the mean, from state-year probit estimates for 1982–97. Each sample includes all years for states that do not pass the relevant law between 1982 and 1997, and years before passage of the relevant law for states that do enact a law between 1982 and 1997. Year fixed effects included. Standard errors in parentheses.

*p < .10.
**p < .05.
***p < .01.

have significantly lower levels of property crime rate and higher rates of violent crime other than homicide.

However, states that pass the two kinds of laws differ in their homicide rates. States that pass a domestic violence misdemeanor law do not have significantly different stranger or intimate partner homicide rates prior to the passage of the law than states that do not pass such a law. In contrast, states that pass restraining order laws have significantly lower stranger homicide rates and significantly higher intimate partner homicide rates. An additional stranger homicide per 100,000 (essentially doubling the rate at the mean) decreases the probability that a state will adopt a restraining order law by 30 percentage points. An additional IPH per million at the mean (from 6.5 to 7.5) increases the likelihood that a state will pass such a law by 11 percentage points.

This pattern of impact of historical homicide rates for the restraining order laws and lack of impact for the domestic violence misdemeanor laws is difficult to explain. It is not clear why there would be much difference in the characteristics of states passing one type of law as opposed to the other. Generally, we might expect states that pass these laws to have lower historical rates of homicide if the domestic violence firearm laws are just one component of legislation, social programs, and other factors representing an attempt to combat violence in the past. Or we might expect to see higher historical levels of homicide in states that pass these laws if the legislation is a response to a high prevalence of intimate partner homicide. It is not at all clear that either of these explanations should apply to restraining order laws and not to domestic violence misdemeanor laws.

There are several other differences between the states that pass the two types of laws. States with higher income levels are more likely to pass a restraining order law but less likely to pass a domestic violence misdemeanor law. States that consume more alcohol, are more populous, and have a higher percentage of young adults are significantly more likely to pass a restraining order law but not a domestic violence misdemeanor law. Another interesting difference is the effect of other gun law variables. One might expect that states with a history of passing other laws restricting access to firearms would be more inclined to adopt these domestic-violence-related laws. In fact the results are mixed: for example, requiring a permit to purchase significantly increases the likelihood that a state will adopt either of these domestic-violence-related laws, while requiring a private background check significantly decreases the chance that these laws will be passed. Interestingly, states that already have a law prohibiting misdemeanants from accessing firearms are significantly less likely to pass a domestic violence misdemeanor law in the future but significantly more likely to pass a restraining order law. Presumably states that already prohibit misdemeanants from acquiring or possessing firearms do not need a separate domestic violence misdemeanor law to achieve their aim of denying guns to abusers but might benefit from a restraining order law that would not be covered under a general misdemeanor exclusion.

The important thing to note from table 5-5 is that states that pass these types of laws are different from one another and from states that do not pass such legislation. Therefore it will be important to control for state characteristics, both those that do not change over time and those that do change over our sample period.

Effect of State Laws on Intimate Partner Homicide Rates

Table 5-6 shows the results from the regressions of various measures of intimate partner homicide rates on whether a law was in effect in a particular year. Columns 1 and 2 are all intimate partner homicides and only those committed with a firearm, respectively. The incidence rate ratio for the restraining order dummy variable is less than one and significant for both outcomes, although it is only significant at the 10 percent level for intimate partner firearm homicides. The magnitude is fairly large: at the mean, this implies a 9 percent reduction in both the overall intimate partner homicide rate and the rate of intimate partner homicides committed with a firearm. However, in absolute terms the numbers are small: in a year in which the law is in effect, a state has an average of 2.3 fewer intimate partner firearm homicides and 3.8 fewer total intimate partner homicides.

These results suggest that laws restricting access to firearms by abusers under a restraining order also lead to a reduction in nonfirearm homicides. There are

Table 5-6. *Effect of State Domestic Violence Gun Laws on Intimate Partner Homicides*
Incidence rate ratios

Item	All intimate partner homicides	Intimate partner firearm homicides	Female intimate partner homicides	Female intimate partner firearm homicides
Restraining order law	0.91**	0.91*	0.89***	0.88**
	(0.83, 0.99)	(0.81, 1.02)	(0.82, 0.97)	(0.78, 0.99)
Domestic violence misdemeanor law	1.06	0.96	1.03	0.95
	(0.97, 1.15)	(0.86, 1.08)	(0.94, 1.12)	(0.85, 1.07)
Stranger homicides per 100,000	1.10***	1.09***	1.06***	1.05**
	(1.05, 1.15)	(1.04, 1.14)	(1.02, 1.10)	(1.01, 1.10)
Percent age 20–34	77.85**	1,938.91***	103.8**	288.24*
	(1.00, 5,928)	(8.92, 421,629)	(1.00, 10,731)	(0.76, 109,926)
Percent black	177.89*	94.16	13.08	15.09
	(0.81, 34,959)	(0.096, 92,243)	(0.02, 8,122)	(0.004, 57,767)
Males per 1,000 population	0.98**	0.97**	0.99	0.98
	(0.96, 1.00)	(0.95, 1.00)	(0.97, 1.01)	(0.95, 1.01)
Percent urban population	1.49	1.05	1.78	1.56
	(0.53, 4.09)	(0.27, 4.09)	(0.61, 5.20)	(0.35, 6.87)
Poverty rate	1.26	1.50	0.92	1.00

	(1)	(2)	(3)	(4)
	(0.43, 3.62)	(0.42, 5.30)	(0.29, 2.98)	(0.24, 4.13)
Log median income	1.06	1.21	1.05	1.02
	(0.69, 1.63)	(0.72, 2.03)	(0.65, 1.70)	(0.55, 1.88)
Marriages per 10,000	1.00	1.00	1.00	0.99
	(0.99, 1.31)	(0.99, 1.01)	(0.98, 1.01)	(0.98, 1.01)
Unilateral divorce law	0.79**	0.84	0.73***	0.85
	(0.64, 0.98)	(0.68, 1.05)	(0.58, 0.90)	(0.63, 1.15)
Per capita ethanol consumption	1.23**	1.15	1.27**	1.21
	(1.02, 1.46)	(0.91, 1.45)	(1.03, 1.55)	(0.93, 1.57)
N	782	782	782	782

Note: State-year panel negative binomial regressions, 1982–98, with state and year fixed effects and region time trends. The incidence rate ratio (IRR) gives the relative rate for a one-unit increase in the explanatory variable, that is, a one-unit increase in the explanatory variable increases the intimate partner homicide rate by $(100*(IRR - 1))$ percent. 95 percent confidence intervals are in parentheses. Regressions also control for other gun laws in effect and whether homicide data were imputed that year.

*$p < .10$.

**$p < .05$.

***$p < .01$.

several reasons why this drop could occur. First, if an abuser does not have a firearm, his or her ability to credibly threaten the victim declines. If the abuser threatens to harm or kill the victim in violation of the restraining order, the victim may feel more secure about resisting knowing that the abuser does not have a gun. This removes the victim from a situation in which a potential homicide may occur. Second, the potential for losing one's firearms if the victim obtains a restraining order increases the cost of abuse. Suppose that some intimate partner homicides are a function of escalating abuse, occurring when the battering exceeds some threshold. If batterers respond to the higher price of violence by reducing the amount they "consume" in order to decrease the likelihood that the victim will obtain a restraining order, on the margin we would expect some homicides to be prevented. Finally, some intimate partner homicides are committed by victims in self-defense (either in response to an imminent threat or to end the abusive relationship). Since the abuser's ability to credibly threaten the victim decreases without a firearm, the victim may find it easier to leave the relationship or avoid situations in which she feels her life is in imminent danger, thereby reducing the perceived need to commit an intimate partner homicide.

Restricting the dependent variable to female victims (columns 3 and 4) yields similar results. As we would expect, the reduction in the incidence rate ratio increases as one moves across the table: the largest relative impact should be on women, since they are the group most at risk, and on firearm homicides. The incidence rate ratios for the restraining order variable are lower and more precisely estimated than for intimate partner homicides involving both genders. An 11 percent decline in the female intimate partner homicide rate and a 12 percent decline in the rate of such homicides committed with a firearm translates into an average of 2.9 fewer female homicides, 2.0 of which were committed using a firearm. Although not all domestic abuse victims are female, the slightly larger reduction of firearm deaths relative to overall homicides for female victims is consistent with the explanation that some of the reduction in nonfirearm intimate partner homicides stems from a reduction in "self-defense" homicides. However, this difference is small and almost certainly not statistically significant.

For all four dependent variables, we find no difference in intimate partner homicide rates when a state-level domestic violence law is in effect. The incidence rate ratios are less than one for firearm homicides and greater than one for intimate partner homicides with all weapons (both female and total), but none of the coefficients is significant. There are several reasons why we might expect the restraining order laws to be more effective than the domestic violence misdemeanor laws. First, many domestic violence misdemeanors may not be properly recorded. Most states do not have separately identified crimes of domestic violence, requiring that someone record the fact that a particular misdemeanor was committed against an intimate partner or family member.[54] Inadequate or insufficient record-keeping might prevent some of these individuals from being identified as prohibited persons, thereby enabling them to acquire or possess firearms without detection. This would diminish any impact of the laws on reducing intimate partner homicides.

Second, since the number of people excluded from owning or possessing a firearm under the state restraining order laws is likely to be quite a bit larger than the number excluded under state domestic violence misdemeanor laws over the period in our analysis, we would expect the impact of the latter to be much smaller.[55] Third, the vast majority of these laws were passed right around the time of the VAWA or subsequently. It is possible that the impact of these federal domestic violence laws, which are swept into the year dummies, dominates any small additional effect of the state misdemeanor laws. Finally, once the Lautenberg Amendment is passed, any difference between states that passed their own domestic violence misdemeanor laws will be reduced or eliminated, further obscuring any effect attributable to the state laws. Although it is true that many of the state laws are stricter than the Lautenberg Amendment, this difference is likely to be less pronounced than that of the restraining order laws and their federal counterparts since temporary restraining orders will be more prevalent than permanent orders.

Additional Impact of Federal Laws on Intimate Partner Homicide Rates

As mentioned above, one of the difficulties in evaluating the impact of the state laws is the passage of the federal laws, either subsequently or even before the state laws in some cases. The year dummies do not capture any differential impact of the federal laws by state, which could lead to bias in the state law coefficients. Furthermore, while there are numerous reasons why a state law might have an impact even in the presence of the federal law, it is possible that the incremental change is not large enough to be detected statistically. It would also be desirable to know what the impact of the federal laws was. The difficulty is that all states were affected at the same time. There is no obvious control group to remove any unmeasured factors that might have occurred simultaneously to the federal laws.

54. Even in those states that have codified specific domestic violence offenses, one could be convicted of a nondomestic violence offense (for example, harassment) committed against a family member or intimate partner. The same record-keeping issue would apply.

55. This is because most of the state laws were either not retroactive prior to the date of passage or subject to a time limit (for example, conviction in past three years).

To address some of the potential issues involved in just focusing on the state laws, we examine the impact of having a domestic violence misdemeanor or restraining order law at any level. Although it is impossible to isolate the effect of the federal laws from other contemporaneous effects, this is still a valuable exercise that will help us better understand the state results. To do this, we set our domestic violence misdemeanor and restraining order indicator variables to be one for all states after 1996 and 1994, respectively. We remove the year fixed effects but leave the region-specific time trends.[56]

Table 5-7 presents these results. They are similar to the state law-only results. As before, having a restraining order law in effect has a significant negative impact on all four outcome measures, while there is no effect of having a domestic violence misdemeanor law. With the exception of the overall intimate partner homicide rate, the incidence rate ratios on the restraining order variables are the same or slightly higher when the state and federal laws are combined. This suggests that the federal law did not have much of an impact relative to the state restraining order laws.[57] Interestingly, the incidence rate ratios for the domestic violence misdemeanor laws are now less than one for both total IPHs and female IPHs (and essentially the same for the firearm-only measures), although these ratios are still not significant.

Ability to Check Backgrounds

The effectiveness of these laws depends on several factors. One is the ability to identify individuals who are excluded from purchasing or possessing a firearm as a result of domestic violence. This is particularly true for purchases of new guns, as a court can always order the individual to relinquish any firearms currently in possession at the time of the disqualifying event. We would expect states that have a high ability to check for the relevant information to experience a greater reduction in domestic violence outcomes. To test this expectation, we categorize states as having either high or low ability to check for the appropriate background information.

56. Although we have no way to tell what the impact of this change is for these results, fitting the state-only regressions with a time trend instead of year dummies does not significantly change the results.

57. An alternative approach would be to follow Ludwig and Cook (2000) and classify states that already had laws before the passage of the federal laws as control states, comparing their outcomes to the states that are now subject to the laws for the first time. The problem with that approach in our case is that the timing of the state laws makes it difficult to assign a control group. For the restraining order laws, the majority of states passed their laws just after the VAWA, and several more enacted their legislation earlier in the same year. Many of the domestic violence misdemeanor laws also coincide with the passage of the VAWA.

Table 5-7. *Effect of State and Federal Domestic Violence Gun Laws on Intimate Partner Homicides*

Incidence rate ratios

Item	All intimate partner homicides	Intimate partner firearm homicides	Female intimate partner homicides	Female intimate partner firearm homicides
Restraining order law	0.89***	0.91**	0.89***	0.90**
	(0.83, 0.94)	(0.85, 0.99)	(0.84, 0.95)	(0.82, 0.98)
Domestic violence misdemeanor law	0.99	0.96	0.97	0.94
	(0.93, 1.05)	(0.89, 1.04)	(0.91, 1.03)	(0.87, 1.03)
N	782	782	782	782

Note: State-year panel negative binomial regressions, 1982–1998, with state fixed effects and region time trends. 95 percent confidence intervals are in parentheses. For interpretation of incidence rate ratios, see note in table 5-6. Regressions also include control variables shown in table 5-6, other gun laws in effect, and whether homicide data were imputed that year. Full results available from authors upon request.

* p < .10.
** p < .05.
*** p < .01.

The Bureau of Justice Statistics collects information on the ability of states to conduct background checks, including what criminal history data are available, whether these data are computerized and available on a statewide system, and who conducts the background checks for the states. We divided states into two groups: those with a high ability to ascertain the relevant information and those with a low ability to do so. The bureau's publications only provide information on whether states have access to domestic violence misdemeanor data or current restraining orders as far back as early 1996. For states that already had the ability to check for these exclusions by 1996 and had the relevant laws, we assume the ability to check existed prior to 1996 provided that the state conducted background checks. For example, suppose a state passed a law prohibiting domestic violence misdemeanants from purchasing a gun in 1992, started conducting background checks in 1994, and is listed as having statewide computerized domestic violence data by early 1996. We would classify that state as having low ability to check from 1992 until 1994 and high ability to check from 1994 onward.

States are considered to have low ability to check backgrounds if they do not have the relevant domestic violence data available to check, only have a small fraction of the data in the system, or only keep the data locally and do not have a computerized system. Of the ten states with domestic violence misdemeanor laws included in our analysis, six were classified as having high ability to check in 1998. The four that were classified as low ability to check did not have domestic violence data available for checking (Minnesota and Pennsylvania) or have only some of the data accessible (Washington and West Virginia). Of the twenty states in our analysis with restraining order laws, all but two (Hawaii and Pennsylvania) have a high ability to check backgrounds by 1998. When we consider all the states and their ability to put the federal law into operation, thirty-five states have high ability to check for current restraining orders, and twenty-two have high ability to check for domestic violence misdemeanor convictions.

These results are shown in table 5-8. Not surprisingly, there is no significant effect on any of the outcomes when a state is unable to screen for domestic violence misdemeanors or restraining orders. It seems that the combined results of having a restraining order law are driven entirely by states that can adequately check backgrounds. Removing the effect of the low-ability states produces coefficients on the high-ability variable that are somewhat larger in magnitude than those shown in table 5-7. Evaluated at the mean, this implies a 12 percent reduction in intimate partner homicides, including a 13 percent decrease in those committed with a firearm, and a 14 percent reduction in female intimate partner homicides, including 15 percent fewer firearm homicides. Once again the absolute decline is not large despite the large percentage decrease: on aver-

Table 5-8. *Effect of State and Federal Domestic Violence Gun Laws on Intimate Partner Homicides*

Incidence rate ratios

Item[a]	All intimate partner homicides	Intimate partner firearm homicides	Female intimate partner homicides	Female intimate partner firearm homicides
Restraining order law and high ability to check in database	0.88*** (0.81, 0.95)	0.87** (0.78, 0.97)	0.86*** (0.79, 0.94)	0.85*** (0.75, 0.95)
Restraining order law and low ability to check in database	0.85 (0.68, 1.07)	0.89 (0.66, 1.18)	0.88 (0.70, 1.11)	0.88 (0.65, 1.19)
Domestic violence misdemeanor law and high ability to check in database	0.99 (0.90, 1.09)	0.96 (0.85, 1.09)	0.96 (0.88, 1.06)	0.93 (0.81, 1.07)
Domestic violence misdemeanor law and low ability to check in database	1.11 (0.95, 1.30)	0.98 (0.81, 1.18)	1.06 (0.88, 1.28)	0.95 (0.77, 1.18)
N	782	782	782	782

Note: State-year panel negative binomial regressions, 1982–98, with state fixed effects and region time trends. 95 percent confidence intervals are in parentheses. For interpretation of incidence rate ratios, see note in table 5-6. Regressions also include control variables shown in table 5-6, other gun laws in effect, and whether homicide data were imputed that year. Full results available from authors on request.

* p < .10.
** p < .05.
*** p < .01.

a. State categorized by ability to check backgrounds.

age, these states would experience 4.8 fewer intimate partner homicides a year, of which 3.6 were females, and 3.2 fewer firearm intimate partner homicides, of which 2.4 were females.

The incidence rate ratio for the domestic violence misdemeanor laws is not significant for any of the outcomes. Even in states that have a high ability to check backgrounds, we are unable to detect an effect of these laws. Interestingly, coefficients on the domestic violence misdemeanor law variable in high ability to check states are in the predicted direction. With our data we are unable to determine whether these laws do not have an effect or whether we are simply unable to measure the effect with precision.

Robustness Checks

To interpret the results of our state law-only regressions as the actual impact of the particular law of interest on intimate partner homicide rates, we must assume that there are no omitted factors that are correlated with the passage of these laws and varying over time. Unfortunately it is not possible to rule out the existence of these factors with certainty, and it is extremely difficult to find instruments for this kind of legislation.

One possibility is that we are simply picking up secular trends in IPHs that vary at the state level and are not adequately captured by the region trend dummies. To test this, we ran the regressions in table 5-6 replacing the regional time trends with state-specific time trends (keeping the state fixed effects). The incidence rate ratios in these regressions were virtually identical to those we present here (between .001–.01 different). The standard errors do go up but not enough to change our results qualitatively. This suggests that the regional time trends are sufficiently capturing trend variation within the United States and our results are not an artifact of state-level secular trends.

Another way we can examine the robustness of our results is to trace out the effect of laws over time, both before and after passage. If we have adequately controlled for factors that also lead to a decline in IPHs over time, we should find no effect of the laws before passage and a significant effect after passage. A third way to examine the robustness of our results is to look at the relationship between our variables of interest and a variety of other outcome measures to see whether the pattern of results is credible.

Timing of State Laws

For this test, we use a series of dummy variables to trace out the timing of the laws. We include dummies for whether a restraining order or a domestic violence misdemeanor law was passed three or four years in the future, two years in the future, next year, in the current year or one year ago, two or three years ago, and four or more years ago. The omitted category is a law passed more than four years in the future. Table 5-9 shows the results from these regressions.

The first two lines of the first panel in table 5-9 indicate that states that pass restraining order laws do not experience significantly lower intimate partner homicide rates two to four years before the passage of the law. However, we observe a sharp drop in rates for all outcome measures in the year immediately preceding passage of the law. This seems to indicate some sort of anticipation effect of the laws. Initially it might seem odd to observe an anticipation effect for a law such as this; however, recall that more than half the states that pass restraining order laws do so after the federal law. One consequence of passing a state-level law might be an improved ability to enforce the federal law through better data collection, increased access to available data, and improved background check systems. If states start improving the ability to check backgrounds in anticipation of a new state law, we might observe an increase in the effectiveness of the federal legislation even before the state law takes effect.

These significantly lower rates persist after passage of the law, and decline further over time (though rather noisily). For firearm intimate partner homicides, incidence rates are quite a bit lower four or more years after passage, suggesting the presence of an implementation lag. For example, this could be a function of an increased ability to check backgrounds as the relevant data and systems are updated in the years following passage of a law. For intimate partner homicides with all weapons, the greatest decline in rates comes two to three years following passage of the laws. Some caution is warranted in interpreting these incidence rate ratios since the number of states that have had a restraining order law in effect for four or more years is relatively small. Nevertheless, the overall pattern of the effect of the restraining order laws shown in table 5-9 is reassuring.

The bottom panel of table 5-9 shows the analogous results for the domestic violence misdemeanor laws. Here we see no significant difference in IPH rates either before or after passage of the laws, nor is there any discernible pattern. This suggests that the domestic violence misdemeanor laws have not had any significant impact on IPH rates.

Other Crimes

Our second robustness check examines the relationship between the presence of a restraining order or domestic violence misdemeanor law and rates of crime other than intimate partner homicides. Table 5-10 shows the impact of state law-only indicator variables on stranger homicide rates, rapes, robberies, assaults, burglary, and motor vehicle theft. If the observed effect of the restrain-

Table 5-9. *Timing of Effect of State Domestic Violence Gun Laws on Intimate Partner Homicides*

Incidence rate ratios

Item	All intimate partner homicides	Intimate partner firearm homicides	Female intimate partner homicides	Female intimate partner firearm homicides
Restraining order law				
Passed 3 or 4 years in the future	0.95	0.97	0.96	0.98
	(0.89, 1.02)	(0.89, 1.06)	(0.90, 1.03)	(0.90, 1.07)
Passed 2 years in the future	0.95	0.96	1.00	1.01
	(0.87, 1.03)	(0.87, 1.07)	(0.92, 1.09)	(0.90, 1.13)
Passed 1 year in the future	0.88**	0.84***	0.89**	0.84**
	(0.80, 0.97)	(0.75, 0.95)	(0.81, 0.99)	(0.74, 0.96)
Passed 0 or 1 year ago	0.87**	0.85**	0.87**	0.83**
	(0.78, 0.97)	(0.74, 0.98)	(0.78, 0.98)	(0.72, 0.96)
Passed 2 or 3 years ago	0.82**	0.86*	0.82***	0.85*
	(0.73, 0.92)	(0.74, 1.00)	(0.72, 0.93)	(0.71, 1.01)
Passed 4+ years ago	0.82**	0.76**	0.82**	0.72***
	(0.69, 0.96)	(0.62, 0.94)	(0.68, 0.99)	(0.56, 0.92)

Domestic violence misdemeanor law

Passed 3 or 4 years in the future	0.99	1.01	1.01	0.98
	(0.90, 1.10)	(0.89, 1.14)	(0.91, 1.12)	(0.86, 1.13)
Passed 2 years in the future	0.98	0.99	0.99	0.96
	(0.86, 1.10)	(0.84, 1.16)	(0.88, 1.11)	(0.81, 1.15)
Passed 1 year in the future	1.03	1.04	1.08	1.06
	(0.90, 1.17)	(0.85, 1.26)	(0.97, 1.21)	(0.89, 1.27)
Passed 0 or 1 year ago	1.06	0.97	1.06	0.95
	(0.94, 1.20)	(0.83, 1.14)	(0.93, 1.21)	(0.81, 1.13)
Passed 2 or 3 years ago	1.12	1.05	1.09	1.07
	(0.97, 1.29)	(0.87, 1.26)	(0.94, 1.27)	(0.88, 1.29)
Passed 4+ years ago	0.91	0.85	0.89	0.85
	(0.76, 1.08)	(0.69, 1.05)	(0.74, 1.08)	(0.67, 1.09)
N	782	782	782	782

Note: State-year panel negative binomial regressions, 1982–98, with state and year fixed effects and region time trends. Omitted category is law passed 5+ years in the future. 95 percent confidence intervals are in parentheses. For interpretation of incidence rate ratios, see note in table 5-6. Regressions also include all control variables used in table 5-6.

  *p < .10.
 **p < .05.
***p < .01.

Table 5-10. *State Domestic Violence Gun Laws and Other Crimes*

Incidence rate ratios

Item	Stranger homicides	Rapes	Robberies	Assaults	Burglaries	Motor vehicle thefts
Restraining order law	0.96	0.97	.1.03	0.99	0.99	0.98
	(0.84, 1.09)	(0.92, 1.02)	(0.97, 1.08)	(0.94, 1.04)	(0.96, 1.02)	(0.93, 1.03)
Domestic violence misdemeanor law	0.84**	1.06**	0.91***	1.04	0.97*	0.90***
	(0.72, 0.98)	(1.01, 1.11)	(0.86, 0.96)	(0.98, 1.09)	(0.94, 1.00)	(0.85, 0.95)
N	782	782	782	782	782	782

Note: State-year panel negative binomial regressions, 1982–98, with state and year fixed effects and region time trends. 95 percent confidence intervals are in parentheses. For interpretation of incidence rate ratios, see note in table 5-6. Regressions also include control variables shown in table 5-6, other gun laws in effect, and whether homicide data were imputed that year. Full results available from authors on request.

* p < .10.
** p < .05.
*** p < .01.

ing order laws on intimate partner homicides were the result of an omitted measure of broad trends in crime, violence, or enforcement we would also expect to find some impact on crime rates other than intimate partner homicides. In fact, the restraining order law variable has no significant impact on any of these crimes.

The lack of a correlation between the presence of a restraining order law and the outcome measures in table 5-10 generally supports our findings regarding intimate partner homicides. We would not expect the restraining order laws to have an impact on property crime. Even if batterers are more likely to commit other criminal acts, there is no reason to expect a change in motor vehicle thefts or burglaries when access to firearms is reduced. However, it is not clear whether we would expect to observe a relationship between these laws and rates of violent crime. Since batterers are more likely to engage in violence against strangers and acquaintances than people who do not engage in domestic violence, we would expect these laws to lead to a reduction in crimes of violence on the margin. Without knowing what proportion of violent criminals are domestic abusers who would be subject to these laws, however, it is difficult to speculate on the expected magnitude of this effect. Notably, the incidence rate ratios for all the violent crimes except robbery are of the expected direction, so it is possible that we are simply unable to measure such a small effect with precision.

The domestic violence misdemeanor variable, however, is more difficult to interpret. Having such a law in place is associated with significantly lower rates of stranger homicide, robbery, and motor vehicle theft. It is weakly associated with fewer burglaries and is significantly and positively related to rapes. Even if one believes that the average individual prohibited from accessing firearms because of a domestic violence misdemeanor conviction is more likely to commit other crimes than the average person under a restraining order, it still seems implausible that these laws would lead to a 10 percent drop in motor vehicle thefts. Furthermore, a 16 percent drop in stranger homicides also seems rather large given that we find no effect on intimate partner homicides. These mixed results suggest that the domestic violence misdemeanor variable may be capturing the effect of an omitted variable that had a negative impact on certain types of crime and a positive or nil effect on others.

Conclusion

Our findings lead us to cautiously conclude that laws restricting access to firearms by abusers under restraining orders lead to reductions in intimate partner homicides. After a state passes such a law, those homicides are lower by

9 percent, or an average of 3.8 intimate partner homicides a year. The effect is even larger for women, around 11 percent fewer homicides each year (2.9 homicides). The effect is largest for women killed by a firearm, around 12 percent (2.0 homicides). In absolute terms, the effect on overall homicides is a little larger than that of firearm homicides, suggesting that guns may play an implicit role in domestic abuse even though they are not used by abusers nearly as frequently as other weapons. The effect of the restraining order laws is confined to states that have the ability to check a database of those under restraining orders against persons applying to purchase a firearm. We find no evidence of an effect from domestic violence misdemeanor laws.

Previous evaluations of the effect of laws restricting access to guns by certain individuals on violent outcomes have been mixed, although no other study that we know of has examined intimate partner homicides as an outcome, and no study has evaluated the impact of the domestic-violence-related firearm laws. One study of subsequent arrest rates for violent crime by felons showed that arrests were 19 percent lower than they would be had felons not been excluded from purchasing handguns.[58] A similar study for misdemeanants also found that the California violent misdemeanor conviction restriction significantly reduced subsequent violent crime arrests by 22 percent.[59] However, there is also evidence that people with a misdemeanor conviction are significantly more likely to commit a serious crime in the future.[60] A study evaluating the impact of the Brady Act found no statistically significant effect on homicides or suicides overall, but a significant reduction in suicides for persons 55 and older.[61] Our results are generally consistent with these previous results. Moreover, both the direction and magnitude of the effects are consistent with a policy that prevents a portion of abusers from gaining access to firearms in volatile domestic circumstances or deters abusers who already possess guns from using them abusively to avoid losing access to their guns.

Our findings on the domestic violence misdemeanor variable, however, cause us to be very cautious in drawing firm conclusions about the effectiveness of the restraining order laws. Specifically, the fact that domestic violence misdemeanor laws have an effect on several types of crimes (that is, robbery and motor vehicle theft) that we would not expect, as well as the finding that they have an effect on several types of violent crime but not on intimate partner homicides. This suggests that the domestic violence misdemeanor law is capturing the effect of some omitted variable and raises the concern that perhaps this omitted

58. Wright, Wintemute, and Rivara (1999).
59. Wintemute and others (2001).
60. Wintemute and others (1998).
61. Ludwig and Cook (2000).

factor is affecting the restraining order law as well. However, we are reassured by the fact that we find no relationship between the restraining order law and crimes other than intimate partner homicides.

It is possible that the effect we find for the restraining order laws is a result of some omitted or contemporaneous factor and not the result of the restraining order laws. However, since states passed these laws at different times, and since we control for year effects, any omitted factor would have to affect states differentially across time. Furthermore, such factor would have to produce a pattern of impact over time that is consistent with the timing of the restraining order laws. One change that did take place around the same time was the Brady Handgun Violence Prevention Act, which required background checks for firearm transfers from an FFL. However, it seems unlikely that any impact of the Brady Act explains our findings. All but three (Pennsylvania, Texas, and West Virginia) of the fifteen states that have restraining order laws in our sample were exempt from the Brady Act by the time their law was passed. We would not expect the Brady Act to have an impact in the Brady-exempt states; if anything, this should bias our results toward finding no effect. However, previous research suggests that the Brady Act may not have had a measurable impact on homicides, so the bias in this case is likely to be small.[62]

The restraining order laws could also be capturing the effect of other state legislation designed to reduce domestic violence. Perhaps states are passing comprehensive domestic violence legislation, making it impossible for us to distinguish between the effect of the firearm laws and other social programs or legal changes. Preliminary investigation suggests that this is not the case, but further research is needed to ascertain in detail what is transpiring at the state level. Laura Dugan, Daniel S. Nagin, and Richard Rosenfeld found that the availability of hotlines and legal services had "a statistically stable and negative impact on the rate at which wives murder their husbands" in the twenty-nine large cities they studied.[63] Unfortunately, we are unable to control for the availability of these types of services over time. However, even if we are measuring the overall impact of domestic violence legislation and not that of the restraining order laws, this legislation seems to have had a significant effect in reducing IPHs.

Another potential limitation of our study is that the FBI's SHR data are known to underreport intimate partner homicides for several reasons. First,

62. See Ludwig and Cook (2000). Furthermore, the Brady Act is unlikely to have an effect on possession of firearms. In results not presented here, we separate states into those whose laws restrict purchase and possession of firearms by abusers and those who only prohibit possession. We find a significant effect of both the purchase/possession restraining order laws and the possession-only restraining order laws on female intimate partner homicides. This suggests that our restraining order variable is not simply picking up the impact of the Brady Act.

63. Dugan, Nagin, and Rosenfeld (1999, p. 209).

some law enforcement agencies and even whole states fail to report homicide data to the FBI from time to time.[64] We minimize this problem by interpolating counts of intimate partner homicide for states missing one year of data and excluding states that are missing multiple years of data. Second, limitations in the way the SHR defines and categorizes the victim-offender relationships in homicides that are reported to them may also lead to underreporting. In Massachusetts, for example, researchers found that the FBI's SHR identified 71 percent of intimate partner victims.[65] Unfortunately there is no alternative source of data on intimate partner homicides that occur in the United States. Most important, however, we have no reason to suspect that underreporting is systematically associated with presence or passage of misdemeanor and restraining order laws restricting access to firearms by domestic violence offenders.

An important issue that cannot be fully explored in this chapter is the variability with which misdemeanor and restraining order laws are enforced at the state level. Controlling for general arrest rates had no impact on our results, but these rates are probably only crudely associated with the enforcement of these laws.[66] More specific measures of enforcement are unavailable. However, we were able to demonstrate that the positive benefits of these laws were restricted to those states that could identify individuals under the authority of a restraining order in state databases. This suggests that enforcement does indeed play an important role in the effectiveness of these laws. Future research should further explore the role of enforcement in the implementation and effectiveness of these laws.

We also a face a number of data limitations that prevent us from fully understanding the impact of these laws. For example, we are unable to determine the impact of the laws on domestic violence outcomes other than homicides. The small reduction in nonfirearm homicides suggests that the absence of a gun may also reduce nonfirearm violence, which would suggest that we are underestimating the impact of the laws on domestic violence as a whole. Furthermore, small sample sizes prevent us from further breaking down our analysis by different racial groups. Given that levels and patterns of intimate partner homicide rates vary substantially by race, this type of analysis is crucial for understanding the impact of domestic violence laws.[67] Additional studies are needed to assess the impact of these laws on outcomes other than intimate partner homicides and to further explore racial differences.

---

64. Williams and Flewelling (1987).

65. Langford, Isaac, and Kabat (1998).

66. The incidence rate ratios on the variables of interest changed by .001 or less with no meaningful changes in significance levels, and the arrest rate variable was not significant in any of the specifications.

67. Paulozzi and others (2001).

Finally, these findings only reflect the impact of these laws on intimate partner homicides at the state level. The effect of restraining order laws and domestic violence misdemeanor laws is of course much stronger on the individuals and families affected by the laws. These aggregate results are strongly affected by the ability and will of a state to enforce them to the extent that an effect is measurable. The fact that we found any effects in the face of these impediments is encouraging for the restraining order laws. The fact that we did not find an impact of the domestic violence misdemeanor laws certainly does not imply that there are not individuals and families who have benefited from these laws. Indeed, given the tremendous cost to society of domestic violence, even a small reduction in domestic abuse would generate large economic benefits. Further research should be conducted at the individual and aggregate level to confirm the findings of this research.

COMMENT BY
John H. Laub

Believing in the policy of full disclosure, I want to state at the outset that I approach this question as a criminologist who studies the causes of crime. I do not approach the study by Elizabeth Richardson Vigdor and James Mercy with a particular interest in domestic violence or firearm access statutes. In my current work, I am especially interested in what accounts for stability and change in criminal offending over the life course. In other words, what accounts for persistent criminal activity and what explains desistance from crime? Identifying changes in behavior in response to legal sanctions provides a potentially important window to better understand continuity and change in criminal trajectories over the life course.

Vigdor and Mercy assess the impact of laws restricting access to firearms by domestic violence offenders. Two kinds of law are examined: laws preventing individuals who have a restraining order from owning or purchasing a firearm and laws preventing individuals who have been convicted of domestic violence misdemeanors from owning or purchasing a firearm. The analysis centers on changes in intimate partner homicide in states that have passed these laws compared with states that have not. The main finding is that laws restricting access under restraining orders lead to reductions in such homicides. The effect is largest for females killed by a firearm. However, the effect of domestic misdemeanor laws is

I thank my friend and colleague Jeff Fagan for his insights, helpful comments, and wise advice. I also thank Djuna Perkins of the Suffolk County District Attorney's Office in Massachusetts for taking the time to talk with me. Finally, the research assistance of Melissa Reimer is gratefully acknowledged.

much more tenuous compared with the effects for restraining orders. A key point is that the effectiveness of the law is confined to states that have the ability to check a database of those individuals with a restraining order against persons applying to purchase a firearm. The ability of states to effectively implement laws and provide the necessary technology for background checks looms large.

The model underlying the chapter is consistent with the idea that removing guns from "places that have records of violent conflicts such as rowdy bars, homes where domestic violence often occurs, or other community 'hot spots' " will lead to less gun violence.[68] However, these strategies will only work if the population selected is truly at high risk. One troubling fact is that most gun crime is committed by people with minimal criminal records.[69]

Assessing the Chapter

My critique addresses three issues that I believe are crucial to establishing the authors' thesis.

The Declining Trend in Intimate Partner Homicide. As noted in the Vigdor and Mercy chapter, intimate partner homicide, especially spouse killings, has been declining since 1976. Moreover, the number of intimate murders with guns has declined. In a recent paper, Laura Dugan, Daniel S. Nagin, and Richard Rosenfeld find that the long-term decline in intimate partner homicide is owed to shifts in the rate of marriage and divorce, the improved economic status of women, and increased availability of domestic violence services.[70] In my view, these findings have serious implications for the chapter under discussion. Vigdor and Mercy note that any omitted factor in their models would have to affect states differentially across time. One such factor may be the availability of social services to victims of domestic violence. The analysis by Dugan, Nagin, and Rosenfeld shows for the twenty-nine large cities they studied "a statistically stable and negative impact of hotlines and legal services on the rate at which wives murder their husbands."[71] A key question is whether states that provide facilities and services to victims of domestic violence in conjunction with criminal justice responses like restraining orders have fewer intimate partner homicides compared with states that provide little or no service to victims of domestic violence.

68. Cook, Moore, and Braga (2002, p.328).
69. Sherman (2001, p.75) but compare with Wintemute and others (1998, 2001).
70. Dugan, Nagin, and Rosenfeld (1999).
71. Dugan, Nagin, and Rosenfeld (1999, p. 209).

The Variability in Enforcement. As background for this commentary, I spoke with a district attorney in Boston who works in the domestic violence unit about the restraining orders and misdemeanor laws. She told me that these laws are enforced on an "honor system." In other words, assuming a judge orders a defendant to turn over all firearms to the police, the enforcement of this order is not clear. If the victim gives specific information about a gun and its location, the police will find it. If not, compliance depends on the "honor system." This attorney also told me that she had no idea how many judges elect to prohibit purchase or possession of a firearm when issuing a restraining order, but she believes that most do so. She also said that gun enhancement statutes, with minimum mandatory sentences, have been an effective tool in plea bargaining with domestic violence defendants to "minimize their exposure."[72] Clearly she believed in incapacitation effects more than deterrence and said so in so many words. Finally, she added that the cases of domestic violence homicide handled by her office involved defendants with no previous record of domestic violence and sometimes no restraining order. This information suggests that intimate partner homicide may be impossible to predict and that individuals who engage in such behavior may not be particularly sensitive to either deterrence or treatment strategies.[73]

Along similar lines, Jeffrey Fagan has argued that neither misdemeanor laws nor restraining orders are particularly strong interventions, and both are implemented unevenly within and among states over time. Furthermore, there is so much variation in the conditions and remedies that different states offer for restraining orders that comparing states is very difficult.[74]

Thus a major gap in the Vigdor and Mercy chapter concerns the variability, implementation, and enforcement of restraining orders and misdemeanor laws at the state level. It would be helpful to have some measure of the number of restraining orders issued by states each year. Moreover, another measure of enforcement may be the misdemeanor arrest rate by state each year.

The Domestic Violent Offender. Criminological research has demonstrated time and time again that offenders are versatile in the types of offenses they commit.[75] Jeffrey Fagan and Angela Browne report that individuals who are violent with family intimates are also more likely to engage in violence against acquaintances and strangers than persons who do not engage in such violence.

72. Djuna Perkins, personal communication, January 17, 2002.
73. See Holtzworth-Munroe and others (2000); Browne (1987).
74. Jeffrey Fagan, personal communication, January 16, 2002.
75. See, for example, Gottfredson and Hirschi (1990).

The reverse is true as well. That is, individuals who engage in violence against acquaintances and strangers are more likely to be violent with members of their own family.[76] In light of the versatile offender, the findings from Vigdor and Mercy that show domestic violence misdemeanor laws (the better measure in my view) having significant effects on several types of crime (including stranger homicide, robbery, burglary, and motor vehicle theft) may not be so hard to explain. But the problem may be even more complex.

Within current criminological research there is considerable interest in identifying distinct pathways or groups of offenders. The implication of this research is that individual offending rates vary considerably in the shape and timing over a long period, and analytical strategies are needed that can take into account this variation. To a large extent, the heterogeneity of offending in domestic violence has not been adequately addressed and more research on domestic violence offenders is needed.[77] Moreover, research on the effects of legal sanctions, like research on treatment interventions, needs to recognize potentially important subgroup differences within the offending population.

Conclusion

Vigdor and Mercy have provided a careful and detailed analysis of a difficult issue. In a world of limited data, caution lights, and caveats, they have performed a masterly job. Nevertheless, I remain skeptical of their results. It is not clear whether the decline in intimate partner homicide they find is over and above the decline in intimate partner homicide witnessed during the past two decades. In their models, they do not consider the availability of victim services. Nor do they offer any measure of enforcement of restraining orders or misdemeanors. Moreover, the heterogeneity in the offending population, especially with respect to legal threats, needs to be recognized. Because of these shortcomings, the results in my view are suggestive but not conclusive.

COMMENT BY

Garen J. Wintemute

Elizabeth Richardson Vigdor and James Mercy have worked hard and carefully to evaluate laws that restrict access to guns by persons subject to domestic violence restraining orders or convicted of domestic violence misdemeanors. Their

76. See also Moffitt and others (2000).
77. See Holtzworth-Munroe and Stuart (1994); Holtzworth-Munroe and others (2000).

results are puzzling and seemingly self-contradictory. Restraining order laws were associated with an approximately 10 percent decrease in the incidence of intimate partner homicide, whether or not a gun was involved. Domestic violence misdemeanor laws had no effect on intimate partner homicides, and the authors' careful validity checks revealed paradoxical decreases in stranger homicide and robbery and an increase in rape.

Assuming for the moment that these results accurately reflect the impact of the laws on intimate partner homicide, can we account for them? Consider the discrepant findings for restraining order and misdemeanor laws. Prohibitions on purchase are partly unenforceable in most states, at least by any external mechanism. Perhaps 40 percent of all gun purchases are made from unlicensed—and unregulated—private party vendors.[78] Although licensed retailers must establish the identity of their customers and initiate criminal background checks, unlicensed vendors need not see identification and cannot initiate background checks. Persons denied the purchase of a gun on the basis of a domestic violence restraining order (and therefore, presumably, not convicted of a domestic violence misdemeanor) might be susceptible to the level of social control associated with the adoption of the statute alone. They would self-enforce and not purchase guns from unregulated parties. Misdemeanants, who plausibly are harder characters, might be less affected by this form of constraint. They might also be more likely to do violence with a gun having once acquired it. There is direct evidence for the second point: in a longitudinal study of persons who purchased handguns legally (before the adoption of prohibitions based on misdemeanor convictions), those with a prior conviction for a violent misdemeanor were 9.4 times as likely as those with no prior criminal record to be arrested later for homicide, aggravated assault, robbery, or forcible rape.[79]

A prohibition on continued possession, included in more than half the laws in the Vigdor and Mercy sample, is even more problematic. I suspect that by far the largest pool of prohibited persons with guns in the United States is made up of those who purchased guns legally and later become ineligible to possess them. Without aggressive and sustained enforcement, this prohibition requires affected persons to divest themselves of their guns not just voluntarily but on their own initiative.

I think it probable that the Vigdor and Mercy study does not accurately measure the impact of these laws on intimate partner homicide. The small effect estimates they present are well within the range of those that can be determined by factors not included in the analysis. Several of these missing factors are men-

78. Cook and Ludwig (1996).
79. Wintemute and others (1998).

tioned by the authors, and I would like to extend their remarks on perhaps the
most important one: enforcement.

Many steps separate a disqualifying event, such as a restraining order or criminal conviction, from a simple denial of gun purchase, let alone from the recov-
ery of guns already in the hands of a prohibited person. Are disqualifying events
reported? In Maryland in 1999, thousands of domestic violence restraining
orders—half of those in force—went unrecorded.[80] In 2002 only thirty-seven
states submitted restraining order records to the National Crime Information
Center's Protection Order File, used by the federal National Instant Criminal
Background Check System (NICS).[81]

Are background checks done at the time of purchase? In most states, the answer is no for the estimated 40 percent of gun transfers that do not involve a licensed retailer. Even when they are done, background checks are only as good
as the data they review, and serious problems with missing data are not limited
to domestic violence events. The Gun Control Act also prohibits the purchase
or possession of guns by addicts or unlawful users of controlled substances; in
2002 the NICS Prohibited Persons Index contained records for just 121 such
persons.[82]

If background checks are initiated, can they be completed quickly enough to
be of use? During 1998–2001, nearly 3,000 domestic abusers and more than
8,000 other prohibited persons acquired guns because background checks were
still under way when the three days allotted for them had passed.[83]

Are prohibited persons screened at any time to determine whether they are gun
owners? If so, what action follows? Maine's legislature recently defeated a bill
authorizing judges to order gun confiscations when they issue temporary domestic violence restraining orders.[84] The Fraternal Order of Police, whose members
carry guns in connection with their employment, opposed prohibiting domestic
violence misdemeanants from possessing guns and challenged the statute in court;
failures to enforce the prohibition on gun possession have been linked to fatalities in Maryland, Connecticut, and Texas.[85] My own informal survey suggests

---

80. Craig Whitlock, "Md. Fails to Log in Protective Orders: Domestic-Violence Suspects Are
Able to Purchase Guns," *Washington Post,* October 29, 1999, p. A1.

81. Bureau of Justice Statistics (2002).

82. Bureau of Justice Statistics (2002).

83. Dan Eggen, "Domestic Abusers Bought Guns: Background Checks for Thousands Not
Completed in '98-01'," *Washington Post,* June 26, 2002, p. A8.

84. Gregory Kesich "Legislators Vote Down Gun Measure," *Portland Press Herald,* May 17, 1991.

85. *Fraternal Order of Police* v. *United States,* 173 F.3d 898; certiorari denied 120 S. Ct. 324.
Annie Gowen and Craig Whitlock, "Warrant Unserved, Md. Man Kills Wife: Arrest Order in Court
Clerk's Office," *Washington Post,* January 4, 2000, p. A1; Dave Altimari, "Tragic Flaw in System,"
Hartford (CT) Courant, March 3, 2002, p. A1; "Take Their Guns Away," *American-Statesman,* edi-
torial, Austin (Tex.), October 24, 1999, p. H2.

that few if any law enforcement agencies routinely screen for gun ownership among prohibited persons with whom they come in contact, let alone recover their guns.

This study teaches us about the perils of seeking to measure changes in the incidence of rare events. In doing so, it calls to mind two other recent evaluations of gun violence prevention policies in the United States. In the first, Peter Cummings and colleagues sought to measure the effect of child gun access prevention laws on the incidence of unintentional shooting deaths of children.[86] As there are fewer than 1,000 such deaths each year, these investigators pooled data from all twelve adopting states and found a 23 percent decrease in deaths attributable to the laws. They noted that deaths decreased significantly only in the subset of three states, which they had again grouped for analysis, where a violation could be prosecuted as a felony. A subsequent examination revealed that the effect was due entirely to Florida's experience; there was no significant trend in any other state.[87]

Vigdor and Mercy appropriately discuss heterogeneity among states as an important unmeasured factor in their study. The laws varied widely, and data needed for adequate background checks were available only to a minority of states. They report that, as might be expected, a statistically significant decrease in homicides attributable to restraining order denials was limited to those states in which background checks could be conducted. But the point estimates of effect were essentially the same whether states were able to perform background checks or not; only the confidence intervals changed.

As the authors state, "It is very difficult to even crudely quantify how many individuals in any given state could potentially be prevented from fatally assaulting their intimate partner because of these laws." To be sure, but we are left with the real possibility that heterogeneity among states has compromised their findings.

The second instance involves denial of gun purchase based on other classes of criminal activity. An assessment of the Brady Handgun Violence Prevention Act's effect on homicide, which relied on trends in state-level data as Vigdor and Mercy have done, found that the law had no impact.[88] But the outcome of the study may have been determined by its design: so few persons were denied under Brady that, even if the denial (implausibly) reduced their risk of committing homicide to zero, no effect on state homicide rates would be detectable.[89] In contrast, a prospective study of identified individuals found that felony denial

86. Cummings and others (1997).
87. Webster and Starnes (2000).
88. Ludwig and Cook (2000).
89. Wintemute (2000).

was associated with a more than 20 percent decrease in the rate of significant new criminal activity.[90]

Given the rarity of denials based on domestic violence events, and the relative rarity of intimate partner homicides, it is entirely possible that the denials could have their intended effect on the persons directly affected and still produce no detectable change in intimate partner homicide rates. Again, there is direct evidence that this effect exists: a recent cohort study of violent misdemeanants who applied to purchase handguns demonstrated that denial is associated with a more than 20 percent decrease in risk for new crimes involving guns or violence, and no change in risk for crimes of other types.[91]

Taken in aggregate, these studies suggest—to me, at least—that denial laws are effective, and that we sometimes choose an insufficiently sensitive method to evaluate them. Sadly, the field of gun violence prevention is heavily populated by polemicists for whom no law's effect is too small if it comports with their views or sufficiently large if it does not. Studies that find no firm evidence of any effect, as here, are commonly and sometimes deliberately misconstrued as presenting firm evidence of no effect. The results of this study are likely to become ammunition in the battle to repeal restrictions on access to guns by persons who have committed, or are thought likely to commit, domestic violence.

COMMENT BY
Brian A. Jacob

Elizabeth Richardson Vigdor and James Mercy examine the impact of laws restricting access to firearms by domestic violence offenders. Considering that one-third of female homicide victims are killed by current or former spouses or boyfriends, this is clearly an important public policy issue. The authors examine the impact of two types of state laws on the occurrence of intimate partner homicides. The first type of law, referred to as restraining order laws, prevent individuals subject to current restraining orders from owning or purchasing a firearm. The second type of law, known as domestic violence misdemeanor laws, prevent individuals who have been convicted of domestic violence misdemeanors from owning or purchasing a firearm. To study the effect of these laws, the authors combine state-level data on the number of intimate partner homicides each year with information on whether (and, if so, when) a state passed restraining order

90. Wright, Wintemute, and Rivara (1999).
91. Wintemute and others (2001).

or domestic misdemeanor laws. They find that passage of a restraining law decreases intimate partner homicides by 9 percent, which is equivalent to a reduction of 3.8 intimate partner homicides a year. The effect is even larger for such homicides when the victim was a woman and a firearm was used. In these cases, passage of a restraining order law leads to a 12 percent reduction in intimate partner homicides. In contrast, they do not find any impact of domestic violence misdemeanor laws on intimate partner homicides.

This chapter makes a valuable contribution to our understanding of the relationship between domestic violence laws and intimate partner homicide. Indeed, the compilation of a comprehensive source of information on restraining order and domestic violence misdemeanor laws is in itself an important contribution. The data collected by the authors not only include information on whether a state passed such a law but also on what provisions were contained in the state law and the effective date of implementation. Although the results are not conclusive, the analysis presented by Vigdor and Mercy provides some interesting suggestive evidence.

The analysis conducted by the authors is careful and thorough, but it has several important limitations. To their credit, the authors acknowledge these shortcomings and make an effort to test the robustness of their findings. The three most significant limitations include the lack of information on other types of domestic violence, the lack of detailed and comprehensive information on the level and nature of enforcement within states, and the difficulty in disentangling the impact of the restraining order and domestic violence misdemeanor laws from the impact of other statewide policies, programs, or characteristics.

Although intimate partner homicides are clearly a serious concern, they are only one of many forms that domestic violence may take. Even though the laws were designed largely to address intimate partner homicide, it is important to understand how they might influence other types of domestic violence. On one hand, we might think that these laws would reduce domestic violence in general. On the other hand, it is possible that the laws will simply cause batterers to substitute other forms of violence, or perhaps by reducing the most dramatic forms of abuse, lead women to remain in dangerous relationships even longer.

A second limitation of the chapter involves the role of enforcement. This is clearly an important issue from a policy perspective. The authors' analysis focuses on a state's ability to conduct background checks on individuals, specifically whether the state had a computerized database of individuals with restraining orders. Given that even in states with sophisticated computer databases to conduct background checks individuals can still buy guns at gun shows, flea markets, garage sales, or informally from others, it is not clear that one should find an effect. The authors find that restraining order laws are only effective in states that have the ability to check a database of those individuals under restraining orders (table 5-8). Because the point estimates for low versus high enforcement states are virtually identical, however, the central finding is simply because the coefficients for the low-ability states are estimated quite imprecisely. This is not surprising considering that eighteen of the twenty states in the analysis with restraining order laws were categorized as having a high ability to check by 1998, and thirty-five states overall had a high ability to check for restraining orders. Because data on state ability to conduct background checks only go back to 1996, the authors are forced to impute values for earlier years, raising some concern about the enforcement indicator itself.

Perhaps the greatest limitation of the study involves its ability to isolate the causal impact of the laws. To the extent that there are differences across states over time that are systematically correlated with the passage of the restraining order and domestic violence misdemeanor legislation, it is difficult to attribute any changes in intimate partner homicide to the laws. In some cases, for example, these laws may have been passed as part of a larger statewide program to combat domestic violence. Similarly, there may have been secular trends in a state that coincide with the passage of the laws.

There are several reasons that one might be concerned about such things in this analysis. First, as we see in table 5-5, states that pass these laws seem different from other states. Most important, states with higher intimate partner homicide rates are more likely to pass restraining order laws, but intimate partner homicide rates do not have any significant relationship with the likelihood of passing domestic violence misdemeanor laws. This is particularly troubling since the analysis only finds a significant effect for restraining order laws. Second, the authors find that the effect of restraining order laws on all intimate partner homicides is roughly equal to the effect on only intimate partner homicides that involve a firearm. The authors provide several potential explanations for this result, but the fact that the magnitudes of the effects are virtually identical is still somewhat disturbing. Finally, as the authors show in table 5-9, state restraining order laws seem to have influenced intimate partner homicide in the year before passage. Since it is hard to imagine a traditional anticipation effect in this case, this result suggests that the measure of restraining order laws in the analysis may be picking up the effect of other statewide policies or programs designed to decrease domestic violence in general, or intimate partner homicide in particular.[92]

92. The authors note a number of the states passed their own RO laws following the passage of the federal RO law and, therefore, if states start improving the ability to check backgrounds in anticipation of a new state law, we might observe an increase in the effectiveness of the federal legislation even before the state law takes effect. This is a plausible hypothesis, but one that would require better data to test.

Given the limitations just described, what can we take away from the analysis conducted by Vigdor and Mercy? I believe that there are two important lessons. First, there is some preliminary evidence that restraining order laws help reduce domestic violence. The fact that the passage of state RO laws is not associated with stranger homicide, rape, robberies, assaults, burglaries or motor vehicle theft suggests that the laws were not simply proxies for other crime prevention measures (table 5-10). Combined with the findings from table 5-9, these results suggest that statewide efforts directed toward reducing domestic violence likely had some positive impacts on intimate partner homicide. Just as important, there does not seem to be any evidence that domestic violence misdemeanor laws affect intimate partner homicide. This suggests that states that are just beginning to address the issue of domestic violence would be well advised to focus their efforts on restraining order rather than domestic violence misdemeanor laws. At the same time, case study research that focuses on individual states and attempts to look in greater depth at the impact of restraining order and domestic violence misdemeanor laws would be useful.

Second, the analysis suggests that enforcement may be an important issue. Although the analysis sheds some light on this issue, there is much work to be done in describing existing enforcement efforts and their potential impact. For example, insofar as the restraining order and domestic violence misdemeanor laws make it more difficult for certain individuals to purchase firearms through a federal firearm licensee, one might expect to see a shift toward purchase at gun shows or other venues less affected by the background check requirements. In designing or refining policy, legislators and administrators ought to keep enforcement in mind.

References

Browne, Angela. 1987. *When Battered Women Kill.* Free Press.

Browne, Angela, and Kirk R. Williams. 1989. "Exploring the Effect of Resource Availability and the Likelihood of Female-Perpetrated Homicides." *Law and Society Review* 23 (1): 75–94.

———. 1993. "Gender, Intimacy, and Lethal Violence: Trends from 1976 Through 1987." *Gender and Society* 7 (1): 78–98.

Browne, Angela, Kirk R. Williams, and Donald G. Dutton. 1999. "Homicide between Intimate Partners." In *Homicide: A Sourcebook of Social Research,* edited by M. Dwayne Smith and Margaret A. Zahn, 149–64. Sage.

Bureau of Alcohol, Tobacco and Firearms. 1999. "Gun Shows: Brady Checks and Crime Gun Traces." U.S. Department of the Treasury.

———. 2001. "Published State Ordinances and Firearm Laws, 2000." U.S. Department of the Treasury.

Bureau of Justice Statistics. 2002. National Criminal History Improvement Program (NCHIP): *Improving Criminal History Records for Background Checks.* NCJ 192028. Bureau of Justice Statistics Highlights. U.S. Department of Justice.

Campbell, Jacquelyn C., and others. Forthcoming. "Risk Factors for Femicide in Abusive Relationships: Results from a Multi-Site Case Control Study." *American Journal of Public Health.*

Centers for Disease Control and Prevention. Forthcoming. "Cost of Intimate Partner Violence in the United States, 1995." Atlanta: U.S. Department of Health and Human Services, Centers for Disease Control and Prevention.

Cook Philip J., and Jens Ludwig. 1996. *Guns in America: Results of a Comprehensive National Survey on Firearms Ownership and Use.* Washington: Police Foundation.

Cook, Philip J., Mark H. Moore, and Anthony A. Braga. 2002. "Gun Control." In *Crime: Public Policies for Crime Control,* edited by James Q. Wilson and Joan Petersilia, 291–329. Oakland Institute for Contemporary Studies Press.

Crowell, Nancy A., and Ann W. Burgess, eds. 1996. *Understanding Violence against Women.* Washington: National Academy Press.

Cummings Peter, David C. Grossman, Frederick P. Rivara, and Thomas D. Koepsell. 1997. "State Gun Safe Storage Laws and Child Mortality Due to Firearms." *Journal of the American Medical Association* 278 (13): 1084–86.

Dugan, Laura, Daniel S. Nagin, and Richard Rosenfeld. 1999. "Explaining the Decline in Intimate Partner Homicide: The Effects of Changing Domesticity, Women's Status, and Domestic Violence Resources." *Homicide Studies* 3 (3): 187–214.

Fagan, Jeffrey, and Angela Browne. 1994. "Violence toward Spouses and Intimates: Physical Aggression between Men and Women in Intimate Relationships." In *Understanding and Preventing Violence: Social Influences,* vol.3, edited by Albert J. Reiss, Jr. and Jeffrey A. Roth, 115–92. Washington: National Academy Press.

Federal Bureau of Investigation. 1999. "Crime in the United States, 1998." Uniform Crime Reports. U.S. Department of Justice.

Friedberg, Leora. 1998. "Did Unilateral Divorce Raise Divorce Rates? Evidence from Panel Data." *American Economic Review* 88 (3): 608–27.

Gifford Lea S., and others. 2000. "Background Checks for Firearm Transfers, 1999." *Bureau of Justice Statistics Bulletin.* Publication NCJ 180882. U.S. Department of Justice.

Gottfredson, Michael, and Travis Hirschi. 1990. *A General Theory of Crime.* Stanford University Press.

Greenfeld, Lawrence A., Michael R. Rand, Diane Craven, Patsy A. Klaus, Craig A. Perkins, Cheryl Ringel, Greg Warchol, Cathy Maston and James Alan Fox. 1998. "Violence by Intimates: Bureau of Justice Statistics Factbook." Publication NCJ 167237. U.S. Department of Justice.

Groban, Margaret S. 1999. "The Federal Domestic Violence Laws and the Enforcement of those Laws." U.S. Department of Justice.

Holtzworth-Munroe, Amy, and Gregory L. Stuart. 1994. "Typologies of Male Batterers: Three Subtypes and the Differences among Them." *Psychological Bulletin* 116 (3): 476–97.

Holtzworth-Munroe, Amy, Jeffrey C. Meehan, Katherine Herron, Uzma Rehman, and Gregory L. Stuart. 2000. "Testing the Holtzworth-Munroe and Stuart (1994) Batterer Typology." *Journal of Clinical and Consulting Psychology* 68 (6):1000–19.

Illinois State Police. 2001. "Data on Persons Denied Purchase of Firearms Due to Domestic Violence Misdemeanor Convictions."

Langford, Linda, Nancy Isaac, and Stacey Kabat. 1998. "Homicides Related to Intimate Partner Violence in Massachusetts: Examining Case Ascertainment and Validity of the SHR." *Homicide Studies* 2 (4): 353–77.

Ludwig, Jens, and Philip J. Cook. 2000. "Homicide and Suicide Rates Associated with Implementation of the Brady Handgun Violence Prevention Act." *Journal of the American Medical Association* 284 (5): 585–91.

Manson, Donald, Darrell K. Gilliard, and Gene Lauver. 1999. "Presale Handgun Checks, the Brady Interim Period, 1994–98." *Bureau of Justice Statistics Bulletin.* Publication NCJ 175034. U.S. Department of Justice.

Mecka, Melanie L. 1998. "Seizing the Ammunition from Domestic Violence: Prohibiting the Ownership of Firearms by Abusers." *Rutgers Law Journal* 29 (607): 607–45.

Mercy, James A., and Linda E. Saltzman. 1989. "Fatal Violence among Spouses in the United States, 1976–1985." *American Journal of Public Health* 79 (5): 595–99.

Moffitt, Terrie E., Robert F. Krueger, Avshalom Caspi, and Jeff Fagan. 2000. "Partner Abuse and General Crime: How Are They the Same? How Are They Different?" *Criminology* 38 (1): 199–232.

Nathan, Alison J. 2000. "At the Intersection of Domestic Violence and Guns: The Public Interest Exception and the Lautenberg Amendment." *Cornell Law Review* 85: 822–58.

Paulozzi, Leonard J., Linda E. Saltzman, Martie P. Thompson, and Patricia Holmgreen. 2001. "Surveillance for Homicide Among Intimate Partners—United States, 1981–1998." *Morbidity and Mortality Weekly Report,* Surveillance Series 50 (SS03): 1–16.

Puzone, Carol A., Linda E. Saltzman, Marcie-Jo Kresnow, Martie P. Thompson, and James A. Mercy. 2000. "National Trends in Intimate Partner Homicide, United States 1976–1995." *Violence Against Women* 6 (4): 409–26.

Regional Justice Information Center. 1996. "Survey of State Procedures Related to Firearm Sales." Publication NCJ 160763. Bureau of Justice Statistics. U.S. Department of Justice.

———. 1997. "Survey of State Procedures Related to Firearm Sales, 1996." Publication NCJ 163918. Bureau of Justice Statistics. U.S. Department of Justice.

———. 1998. "Survey of State Procedures Related to Firearm Sales, 1997." Publication NCJ 173942. Bureau of Justice Statistics. U.S. Department of Justice.

———. 2000. "Survey of State Procedures Related to Firearm Sales, Midyear 1999." Publication NCJ 179022. Bureau of Justice Statistics. U.S. Department of Justice.

———. 2001. "Survey of State Procedures Related to Firearm Sales, Midyear 2000." Publication NCJ 186766. Bureau of Justice Statistics. U.S. Department of Justice.

Rosenfeld, Richard. 1997. "Changing Relationships between Men and Women." *Homicide Studies* 1 (1): 71–83.

Saltzman, Linda E., Janet L. Fanslow, Pamela M. McMahon, and Gene A. Shelley. 1999. "Intimate Partner Violence Surveillance: Uniform Definitions and Recommended Data Elements; Version 1.0." Atlanta: U.S. Department of Health and Human Services, Centers for Disease Control and Prevention.

Saltzman, Linda E., James A. Mercy, Patrick W. O'Carroll, Mark L. Rosenberg, and Philip H. Rhodes. 1992. "Weapon Involvement and Injury Outcomes in Family and Intimate Assaults." *Journal of the American Medical Association* 267 (22): 3043–47.

Sherman, Lawrence W. 2001. "Reducing Gun Violence: What Works, What Doesn't, What's Promising." Perspectives on Crime and Justice: 1999–2000 Lecture Series. Washington: National Institute of Justice.

Stevenson, Betsey, and Justin Wolfers. 2000. " 'Til Death Do Us Part': Effects of Divorce Laws on Suicide, Domestic Violence and Spousal Murder." Manuscript. Stanford Business School; Forrester Research.

Teret, Stephen P., Daniel W. Webster, Jon S. Vernick, Tom W. Smith, Deborah Leff, Garen J. Wintemute, Philip J. Cook, Darnell F. Hawkins, Arthur L. Kellermann, Susan B. Sorenson and Susan DeFrancesco. 1998. "Support for New Policies to Regulate Firearms." *New England Journal of Medicine* 339 (12): 813–18.

Tjaden, Patricia, and Nancy Thoennes. 1998. "Prevalence, Incidence, and Consequences of Violence against Women: Findings from the National Violence against Women Survey." Research in Brief. Publication NCJ 172837. Washington: National Institute of Justice and the Centers for Disease Control and Prevention.

———. 2000. "Extent, Nature, and Consequences of Intimate Partner Violence: Findings from the National Survey of Violence Against Women." Publication NCJ 181867. Washington: National Institute of Justice and the Centers for Disease Control and Prevention.

Vernick, Jon S., Lisa Hepburn, and Amy Schofield. 2001. "State and Federal Laws Affecting Firearm Manufacture, Sale, Possession and Use, with Effectiveness Dates, 1970–1999." Baltimore, Md.: Center for Gun Policy and Research.

Webster Daniel W., and Michael Starnes. 2000. "Reexamining the Association between Child Access Prevention Gun Laws and Unintentional Shooting Deaths of Children." *Pediatrics* 106 (6): 1466–69.

Williams, Kirk R., and Robert L. Flewelling. 1987. "Family, Acquaintance, and Stranger Homicide: Alternative Procedures for Rate Calculations." *Criminology* 25 (3): 543–60.

Wintemute, Garen, J. 2000. "Impact of the Brady Act on Homicide and Suicide Rates." *Journal of the American Medical Association* 284 (21): 2719–20 (Letter).

Wintemute, Garen J., Christiana Drake, James J. Beaumont, Mona A. Wright, and Carrie A. Parham. 1998. "Prior Misdemeanor Convictions as a Risk Factor for Later Violent and Firearm-Related Criminal Activity among Authorized Purchasers of Handguns." *Journal of the American Medical Association* 280 (24): 2083–87.

Wintemute, Garen J., Mona A. Wright, Christiana Drake, and James J. Beaumont. 2001. "Subsequent Criminal Activity among Violent Misdemeanants Who Seek to Purchase Handguns." *Journal of the American Medical Association* 285 (8): 1019–26.

Wright, Mona A., Garen Wintemute, and Frederick P. Rivara. 1999. "Effectiveness of Denial of Handgun Purchase to Persons Believed to Be at High Risk for Firearm Violence." *American Journal of Public Health* 89 (1): 88–90.

PART III

Restricting Gun Carrying

JACQUELINE COHEN
JENS LUDWIG

6 | *Policing Crime Guns*

etween 1985 and 1991 the homicide rate in the United
States increased by nearly 25 percent, from 7.9 to 9.8 per
100,000 residents. Almost all of this increase was accounted for by additional
gun homicides committed against and by young males.[1] Although the homicide
rate has declined substantially during the 1990s, homicide in the United States
is still dominated by young people and firearms and remains much more frequent than in other developed nations.[2] Policymakers who are concerned about
America's problem with lethal violence must ask: how can we prevent young
men from shooting one another?

One increasingly popular answer is to increase the risks of carrying guns illegally through stepped-up police enforcement. Under these "directed patrol"

The police enforcement efforts evaluated were undertaken by the Bureau of Police in Pittsburgh, Pa.
Both the implementation and evaluation were supported with funds from the Alfred P. Sloan Foundation. This project builds on earlier work funded by National Institute of Justice awards NIJ-95-IJ-CX-
0005 and NIJ 95-IJ-CX-0075. The authors thank the City of Pittsburgh Bureaus of Police and City Information Systems for their cooperation in this effort, especially the efforts of the Firearms Tracking Unit
in managing the police intervention. Invaluable data were provided with assistance from Deborah Fried-
man at the Allegheny County Injury Surveillance System (ACISS) and Wilpen Gorr of Carnegie Mellon
University. Thanks to Jeffrey Fagan, Lawrence Sherman, and participants in the Brookings conference on
gun policy for helpful comments.
    1. Cook and Laub (1998); Blumstein (2000).
    2. Blumstein and Wallman (2000).

217

programs, high-crime areas are targeted for additional police resources that focus on illegally carried firearms. The hope is that targeted patrols will deter high-risk people from carrying or misusing guns in public places, consistent with evidence that criminals seem to be deterred by the threat of punishment in other contexts.[3] Such patrols may also reduce illegal gun carrying through an "incapacitation effect" by taking illegal guns or those who carry them off the street. The aim of successful targeted policing programs is to reduce illegal gun carrying in public places, a proximate cause of many lethal and nonlethal gun assaults, while avoiding many of the practical and political difficulties of regulating private gun ownership.[4]

Whether targeted policing against illegal guns reduces gun violence in practice remains unclear. To date the evidence in support of such efforts comes largely from the widely cited Kansas City Gun Experiment, which assigned additional police resources to more vigorously pursue illegal guns in one high-crime neighborhood of the city but not in another. While the "treatment" neighborhood experienced a 65 percent increase in the number of guns seized by the police and a 49 percent reduction in gun crimes, neither outcome measure showed much change over this period in the "control" area.[5]

Although the findings from Kansas City are suggestive, the program is not an "experiment" as scientists use the term since there is no guarantee that the two neighborhoods *would have* had similar crime rates had the policing intervention *not* been launched. Some support for this concern comes from the fact that gun crimes were more common in the "control" neighborhood for extended periods even before the new policing program was initiated.[6]

Indianapolis implemented a similar targeted policing program in 1997. One area of the city was targeted for stepped-up vehicle stops for minor violations, while in another area police focused on stopping the most suspicious people within these communities. The results are somewhat puzzling: the number of gun seizures increased by around half with vehicle stops but changed very little with person stops, yet the latter area experienced a decline in gun crimes both in absolute terms and in comparison to other parts of the city.[7] Because of this discrepancy in impact, there is growing interest in the distinction between interventions targeted at "people" rather than simply "places," although it is also possible that the results in the targeted area are spurious. Despite the popular

3. Nagin (1998); Levitt (2001).
4. James Q. Wilson. "Just Take Away Their Guns," *New York Times Magazine,* March 20, 1994, sec. 6, p. 47; Sherman (2000).
5. Sherman and Rogan (1995); Sherman, Shaw and Rogan (1995).
6. Sherman, Shaw and Rogan (1995).
7. McGarrell and others (2001).

support for these police patrols and their increased use by urban police departments, reliable evidence on their effectiveness remains limited at best.[8]

In this chapter we present new evidence on the effects of police programs against illegal gun carrying that draws on data from Pittsburgh, Pennsylvania. As with all nonexperimental policy evaluations, identifying causal program effects is difficult. However, several features of Pittsburgh's 1998 policing program offer a unique opportunity to isolate the impact of the police patrols from the effects of other confounding factors that cause crime rates to vary across areas and over time.

The Pittsburgh police department stepped up police patrols in some areas but not others of the city, which enables us to compare trends in crime rates between the treatment and control areas before and after the police patrols were launched. Yet this type of across-area over-time comparisons is not without limitations: a standard concern is that crime rates in the treatment communities may simply follow a different trajectory over time from those of the control areas, and so differences in trends once the patrols are implemented in the target neighborhoods may not reflect the effects of the new policing intervention.

The unique aspect of Pittsburgh's program is that the police patrols were launched on some days of the week (Wednesday through Saturday, hereafter "on days") but not others (Sunday to Tuesday, "off days") within the treatment (or target) communities. We compare trends between the treatment and control neighborhoods in the periods before and after the policing program is launched, focusing on gun misuse during the on days. If the policing program has an effect, we would expect a greater decline during the on days of the week in the treatment than control communities, and this decline should be larger than the difference in trends across neighborhoods observed during the off days. To the extent that unmeasured confounding variables cause the treatment neighborhoods to have different trends from the control areas during every day of the week, this approach controls for these omitted factors by comparing across-area trends during on versus off days. This strategy thus isolates the causal effects of those factors unique to the target neighborhoods following the launch of the police patrols during the days when these patrols are active—factors such as the police patrols themselves.[9]

8. Survey data indicate that these targeted policing programs enjoyed widespread support from both black and white residents in Indianapolis and Kansas City. Shaw (1995); Chermak, McGarrell, and Weiss (2001); McGarrell, Chernak, and Weiss (1999).

Previous studies have also generated suggestive findings that community policing and focused problem-solving interventions may reduce gun crime. Dunworth (2000); Kennedy and others (2001), although these studies are susceptible to the same confounding problems as those with the Kansas City evaluation.

9. Gruber (1994); Joyce and Kaestner (1996); Ludwig (1998).

In our judgment the Pittsburgh program provides at least suggestive evidence that targeted patrols against illegally carried guns may reduce gun crime. Our analysis suggests the policing program may have reduced shots fired by perhaps as much as 34 percent, and hospital-treated assault gunshot injuries declined by 71 percent during on days in program-treated areas. These reductions are likely to occur because of deterred gun carrying or criminal behavior rather than incapacitation since the number of actual arrests and guns confiscated as a result of the patrols was fairly modest. There is also no evidence of spillover or displacement that affect gun crime levels in untreated areas or during off days.

Given the high costs that gun violence imposes on society—about $1 million per gunshot injury[10]—the fairly modest program cost of under $35,000 in overtime expenditures is small in comparison to the potential benefits to Pittsburgh residents, which may be as large as $25 million. Perhaps more important, the policing program in Pittsburgh was implemented in a way that was sensitive to concerns about individual liberty and police-community relations. No citizen complaints were filed against the police department as a result of the new program.

Policing in Pittsburgh

Pittsburgh shares many characteristics with other American cities that make the policing program evaluated in this chapter of national interest. While public attention has focused on the dramatic increase in gun violence starting in the mid-1980s in large cities such as New York, Los Angeles, and Chicago, similar increases were observed in the early 1990s in more modestly sized cities such as Pittsburgh.[11] The increase was driven largely by gun homicides committed against and by young African American males.[12] Given the substantial residential segregation by race in Pittsburgh and most other American cities, the concentration of criminal gun violence among young black males leads to geographic concentration of gun homicides as well.[13]

This concentration suggests the opportunity for an intervention that narrowly targets resources on an identifiable law enforcement target—illegal gun carrying by youth in high-risk neighborhoods. Like other "directed patrol" efforts, Pittsburgh's *firearm suppression patrol* (FSP) program assigned more police resources

---

10. Cook and Ludwig (2000); Ludwig and Cook (2001).
11. Blumstein (2000).
12. Cook and Laub (1998); Blumstein (2000).
13. Glaeser and Vigdor (2001).

to selected high-crime areas. These patrols were relieved from responding to citizen requests for service (911 calls) in order to work pro-actively to search for illegally carried guns.[14]

Police contacts were initiated mainly through traffic stops and "stop-and-talk" activities with pedestrians in public areas. Carrying open alcohol containers in public and traffic violations were frequent reasons for initiating contact. When warranted for reasons of officer safety (usually because of suspicious actions or demeanor), these stops sometimes moved to the types of pat-downs on the outside of clothing to check for weapons that are allowed under the Supreme Court's 1968 decision in *Terry* v. *Ohio*.[15] When there was reasonable suspicion of criminal activity, the contact might escalate to more intrusive searches inside pockets, under coats, and in waistbands as part of an arrest.

The Pittsburgh policing initiative was constructed with concerns about individual rights and police-community relations in mind. Not long before the intervention was fielded, the Pittsburgh police department entered into a consent decree with the Department of Justice in response to complaints about abuse of force, most notably several police shootings of civilian residents. As part of the consent decree, the police department issued new regulations governing police contacts with citizens. Included were explicit guidelines on when officers could engage in "*Terry*" pat-down safety frisks and specific reporting requirements of the circumstances that precipitated more intrusive searches of persons or vehicles and seizures of guns or other property. Notably, officers had to articulate the basis for their suspicion about criminal activity by the person(s) being searched. Participating officers were specially selected by police command staff based on their demonstrated capacities in pursuing a proactive style of law enforcement tempered by a professional attitude and demeanor in citizen encounters.

The goal of the Pittsburgh policing program was to focus resources on those neighborhoods most in need. In Pittsburgh, as in many other cities, youth homicides (victims 12 to 24 years old) and citizen reports to police about shots fired are highly concentrated in a relatively small number of neighborhoods; however, unlike other cities, these high-crime neighborhoods are not contiguous in Pittsburgh. The city of Pittsburgh includes three distinct areas separated by rivers. The highest-crime neighborhoods are in police administrative zone 1 on the

14. The Pittsburgh initiative was part of a larger effort funded by the Alfred P. Sloan Foundation that involved collaboration between university research teams and police in the cities of Pittsburgh, Pa., and Rochester, N.Y. Police in each city were encouraged to design their own strategies for addressing street-level gun violence. The results reported relate to the effort by police in Pittsburgh.

15. *Terry* v. *Ohio* (392 U.S. 1, 1968).

north side of the rivers and zone 5 in the eastern end of the city between the rivers. These two zones are the target areas for the FSPs.

Each of the target zones is a fairly large geographic area filled with neighborhoods that have different populations and problems with gun violence. The two zones each include about thirty-five census tracts and fifteen neighborhoods, spread out over nearly ten square miles each and home to 55,000 and 80,000 residents, respectively. In around a third of the tracts in zone 1 and a fifth of those in zone 5, fewer than 5 percent of the residents are African American. However, each zone also contains seven tracts in which more than half of all residents are black. Amid the high-crime neighborhoods in the target zones are many census tracts that experienced no youth homicides at all in the recent peak year, 1993.

Under the FSP program one additional patrol team was assigned to both zones 1 and 5, consisting of four officers and a sergeant (all in uniform) traveling in three vehicles—usually two marked patrol cars and one unmarked car. The teams in each zone worked four-hour shifts from 8 p.m. to midnight twice weekly for fourteen weeks from July 19 to October 24, 1998. These patrols were focused on the high-crime evenings of Wednesday through Saturday nights. Specific patrol days were designated to ensure a mix of different days covered in each zone. The most common pattern (found in half the weeks) was alternating days, either Wednesday and Friday or Thursday and Saturday, in individual zones. During this period, fifty-one special patrol details were fielded across the two zones involving nearly 1,000 officer-hours (including the sergeants' time).

With the assistance of maps and reports of recent shots-fired activity, patrol teams identified and targeted "high-risk places at high-risk times," looking for opportunities to initiate citizen contacts for the purpose of soliciting information and investigating suspicious activity associated with illegal carrying and use of guns.[16] The earlier Indianapolis program pursued a place-based strategy in one part of the city, which focused on maximizing the number of traffic stops, and a person-based strategy in another area, which focused on stopping only the most suspicious people within the target areas. Pittsburgh's program falls somewhere between these two models—the program used pedestrian and traffic stops and included some focus on suspicious people, but stops were not limited to this group.

Implementation of this strategy in Pittsburgh differed slightly between the two treatment areas. In zone 5 the three police vehicles typically traveled together as a unit, while in zone 1 the vehicles patrolled individually. Despite the greater dispersion of police patrols in zone 1, the number of police contacts recorded was

16. Sherman (2001).

greater in zone 5—perhaps because of this area's higher initial crime level. Compared with zone 1, table 6-1 shows that zone 5 experienced around twice as many vehicle stops (27 versus 12), person contacts (118 versus 57), arrests (12 versus 6), and confiscated guns (5 versus 2).

Given the size of these target zones the "dosage" of the intervention may seem low in absolute terms—just four-hour patrol details twice weekly in each targeted patrol zone, covering under 5 percent of all available hours weekly. However, the patrols covered more than 15 percent of high-risk times from 7 p.m. to 1 a.m. daily and 30 percent of high-risk times on high-risk days (Wednesday to Saturday) weekly. Moreover, the three-vehicle, five-officer teams represented a large increment to customary patrol resources in the target police zones. Police vehicles increased by 20 percent and patrol officers by 25 percent in target zone 5, the city's highest crime zone. The increases were even larger in the other target (zone 1), with a 35 percent increase in vehicles and a 50 percent increase in officers.

Data

Our goal is to focus on outcome measures that capture illegal gun carrying and criminal misuse in Pittsburgh. Gun homicides are an obvious choice, although such events are too rare to be useful given our research design. More frequent events such as gun robberies or assaults provide another possibility, although previous research suggests that standard police incident reports are often unreliable about whether a gun was involved in these types of criminal events.[17] As a result our emphasis is on measures of citizen reports to the police of shots fired and on gunshot injuries treated in hospital emergency departments.

Data on shots fired come from Pittsburgh's 911 Emergency Operations Center and include information about the date, time, and address of the reported incident. These data allow us to identify whether the events occurred in the treatment or control zones during the periods that the policing program was in effect, which we define as 8 p.m. to midnight on those days the firearm suppression patrols were deployed in target areas (Wednesday through Saturday evenings).

Because discharging a firearm within the city limits of Pittsburgh is against the law, our measure of shots fired captures an event that is itself technically a "gun crime." But more important, we expect shots fired to be strongly related to the prevalence with which guns are carried in public spaces by high-risk people who are willing to use them, even if only to show off.

17. McGarrell and others (2001).

Table 6-1. *Enforcement Activities during Firearm Suppression Patrols*

Activities	Zone 1	Zone 5	Total
Person contacts	57	118	175
With pat down/search	13	21	34
No pat down	44	97	141
Vehicle stops	12	27	39
Stolen vehicle recovered	1	3	4
Citations	4	21	25
Vehicle	3	11	14
Open container/alcohol	1	7	8
Disorderly/noise/nuisance	0	3	3
Warnings/other[a]	17	37	54
Search/seize	2	5	7
Gun and no other contraband	1	1	2
Gun and other contraband	1	0	1
Other contraband alone	0	4	4
Nothing found	11	17	28
Arrests	6	12	18
With gun	1	2	3
No gun	5	10	15
Guns confiscated	2	5	7
General activities with no contacts			
Pursuit—no contact[b]	17	24	41
Patrol—no contact[c]	171	46	217
Assist nonfirearm suppression unit	32	30	62
Nonfirearm suppression activities[d]	3	3	6
911 calls (total)	55	50	105
Person shot	0	2	2
Shots fired	13	21	34
Person(s) with gun[e]	16	8	24
Stolen gun	0	0	0

a. "Other" includes warnings without citations and requests that individuals "move along."

b. Combination "viewed only" and "pursuit—no contact" used for actors who fled or dispersed on police arrival.

c. "Patrol—no contact" also includes a few instances of stationary surveillance of an area and tactical foot patrols.

d. "Non-FSU activities" include supervision of officers and investigation of possible stolen car parked on street.

e. "Person(s) with gun" includes armed robbery calls.

One complication is that because shots fired can often be detected over a wide area, duplicate calls for the same incident may occur. We attempt to address this problem by eliminating duplicate calls that shared the same event number in the Emergency Operations Center system or calls that reported shots fired within five minutes and 2,000 feet of one another. We also eliminated reports that lacked information about the exact location of the event, since without this address information we would be unable to identify duplicate calls for the same event. Taken together these criteria eliminate 27 percent of the 9,884 original shots-fired reports in our sample.[18] Of course our procedure will not eliminate duplicate calls that are reported by residents who live more than 2,000 feet apart.

Another complication is the difficulty in pinpointing the exact location of shots-fired incidents, especially in urban neighborhoods where gunfire is common enough to make residents alert for similar sounds. Although we do not have any direct measure of this problem, gun suppression officers responding to shots-fired calls were unable to verify an actual incident in three out of four calls. In these cases witnesses or callers could not be located at or near the scene, and police could not locate physical evidence (such as shell casings or bullet holes) of shots being fired. The lack of verification does not mean that a gun was not fired, since witnesses or callers may not bother to meet with the police if they believe the danger has passed or if the police report to the scene with some delay. Finding shell casings on the street may be difficult if the event occurs at night and witnesses are lacking or uncertain about the exact location of the shooting, or even impossible when a revolver is used (since these guns do not automatically expel the shell casing after firing).

While there necessarily remains some uncertainty about the shots-fired data, we nevertheless believe that this measure is associated with gun carrying and misuse. Support comes from the fact that the frequency of shots-fired calls and youth homicides are highly correlated in both the cross section across Pittsburgh census tracts and over time for the city of Pittsburgh as a whole.

Gunshot injuries treated in hospitals serve as a complementary outcome measure, one that is not subject to the same potential reporting problems as shots fired and which provides a more direct indicator of gun violence. Data came

18. Of the 9,884 original shots-fired calls, 238 are eliminated because they are exact duplicate records (that is, they have the same event number, address, and time), 986 are eliminated because we do not have exact address information on the event, and 1,419 are eliminated because these reports are within five minutes in time and 2,000 feet in distance from another call, leaving us with a total of 7,241 shots-fired calls in our final analysis. There do not seem to be any substantial differences across Pittsburgh police zones in the fraction of the original shots-fired calls that are eliminated under these criteria.

from the injury surveillance system developed by the Allegheny County Health Department in cooperation with the Harvard Injury Control Research Center, which collects and analyzes data on gunshot injuries treated in four trauma centers at area hospitals. Together, data from these trauma centers capture more than 90 percent of gunshot injuries treated in hospitals in the Pittsburgh area.[19]

These data include information about the demographic attributes of the victims, the nature of the injury, and the circumstances of the event (assault, self-inflicted, or accidental). We focus on gunshot injuries from assaults since these events should be most sensitive to the policing intervention, although we also explore the sensitivity of our findings to different subsets of gunshot injuries. For privacy reasons the data do not include individual identifying information such as the victim's exact street address. However, we do have the victim's zip code of residence, which allows us to locate victims among the large police zones used in this project. Of the 1,125 gunshot injury reports in our sample, we lose only thirty-five cases because of missing information on the victim's zip code.

How well does zip code information on the victim's address capture criminal events that occur within the same police beat? Analysis of the 328 homicides that occurred in Pittsburgh from 1990 to 1995 suggests that the use of residence zip code data performs fairly well: in 81 percent of cases the victim lives within the same police zone in which the murder occurred. The offender lives within the same police zone in which the murder takes place in 69 percent of homicides.

Methods

In the absence of random assignment of Pittsburgh's policing program across neighborhoods, the challenge is to isolate the causal effects of the intervention from those of other factors that drive variation in crime rates across communities over time. As with any nonexperimental study there necessarily remains some question about whether this analysis has successfully identified the program's effects. Nevertheless, some unique features of Pittsburgh's policing program, including the fact that the gun patrols were implemented on some days of the week but not others within targeted neighborhoods, help us eliminate various competing explanations for the crime changes observed within the target areas.

Our research design, as well as some commonly used alternatives, can be illustrated by using table 6-2. Policymakers and reporters often judge the success

---

19. For more information about these data, see www.hsph.harvard.edu/hicrc/nviss. In principle, perpetrators who are shot by victims or police during the commission of a crime may avoid medical treatment for fear of being arrested, but we suspect that such cases are rare in practice. See Azrael and others, chapter 10, in this volume.

Table 6-2. *Research Design for Pittsburgh Policing Evaluation*

	Preperiod (6 weeks before)	Postperiod (14 weeks during)	Estimated differences
Part A: Comparing overall averages			
Target zones	A	B	(B − A)
Control zones	C	D	(D − C)
DD			(B − A) − (D − C)
Part B: Exploiting within-week variation in patrol activity			
Target zones			
Wednesday–Saturday	E	F	(F − E)
Sunday–Tuesday	G	H	(H − G)
DD_T			(F − E) − (H − G)
Control zones			
Wednesday–Saturday	I	J	(J − I)
Sunday–Tuesday	K	L	(L − K)
DD_C			(J − I) − (L − K)
$DDD = DD_T − DD_C$			[(F − E) − (H − G)] − [(J − I) − (L − K)]

Note: Estimates of program effects rely on various differences that compare outcomes in different subsets of the data. DD is a difference-in-differences, and DDD is a difference-in-difference-in-differences.

of programs such as the Pittsburgh FSPs by examining whether crime rates or other outcomes decline within the jurisdiction once the program is put into place. In terms of table 6-2, this type of estimate would come from comparing the average number of gunshot injuries or shots fired per day in the treatment zones (1 and 5) during the fourteen weeks of the program from July 19 to October 24, 1998, represented by the letter B in the top part of table 6-2, with what is observed during the six-week preprogram period from June 7 to July 18, given by letter A in table 6-2.[20] The obvious problem with this before-after approach is that crime rates change over time in a generally cyclical fashion at the local, state, and national levels—often dramatically—for reasons that remain poorly understood.[21]

An alternative approach with its own limitations comes from comparing the average number of gunshot injuries or shots fired in the treatment zones during the postprogram period (letter B in table 6-2) with the control zones over the same time frame (letter D in table 6-2). The primary limitation with this cross-sectional comparison is that the treatment zones have persistently higher crime

20. We initially define a six-week period as "pre-program" to keep this time frame within the high-crime summer months, although we also explore the sensitivity of our findings to different definitions.
21. Blumstein and Wallman (2000).

rates than the control zones, even before the Pittsburgh FSP program is enacted. Criminologists often try to address this problem by using multivariate regression to control for observable differences across areas in population and other local-area characteristics. But if, as seems likely, the zones systematically differ in ways that we cannot readily measure, we will inappropriately attribute differences in crime among them to the effects of the policing program rather than to the un-measured factors.

To address these "omitted-variables" problems, a third alternative is to focus on comparing how outcomes change in the treatment and control areas from the six-week "preprogram" period (June 7 to July 18, 1998) versus the fourteen-week postprogram period. This so-called difference-in-differences (DD) estimate comes from comparing the change (or difference) in outcomes in the treatment zones (given by B − A in the top panel of table 6-2) with the change in the con-trol zones (D − C). The estimate of program impact in this case [DD = (B − A) minus (D − C)] is unbiased if the unmeasured differences between the treatment and control zones in Pittsburgh remain fixed over the sample period.

However, if there are unmeasured variables that change over time in ways that would cause the treatment and control areas to experience different *trends* in shots fired or gunshot injuries, the DD estimate will yield biased estimates for the program's impact. For example, large and small cities follow different crime trajectories over time in the United States.[22] Attempts to evaluate the effects of big city interventions by comparing their crime trends with those in small cities are likely to confound the effects of the programs of interest with those of whatever other factors lead to divergent crime experiences over time by city size.

One important check on the reliability of the DD estimation approach is to examine whether treatment and control areas follow similar trends *before* the in-tervention is enacted.[23] In any case, while the DD estimate improves on both the standard before-after and cross-section research designs just discussed, the approach remains vulnerable to bias introduced by time-varying omitted vari-ables that affect crime trends as well as levels in the treatment and control neighborhoods.

In our evaluation we attempt to account for unmeasured, time-varying vari-ables that may cause treatment and control areas to have different trends by ex-ploiting the fact that the patrols are implemented on only selected days of the week (Wednesday through Saturday evenings). As a result observations for the off days (Sunday through Tuesdays) in the treatment areas can serve as an addi-

---

22. Blumstein (2000).
23. Bassi (1984); Heckman and Hotz (1989); Smith and Todd (forthcoming).

tional "control group" for measuring the program impact on gun crime in the on days. Put differently, to the extent that unmeasured variables cause the treatment and control areas to have different crime trends throughout the week, comparing on days with off days within the treatment areas should control for these confounding trends and help isolate the effects of the new police patrols.

This "*difference-in-difference-in-differences*" (DDD) estimate can be described more formally with the notation outlined in the bottom panel of table 6-2.[24] The difference (F − E) represents how shots fired or gunshot injuries change from the pre- to postprogram period on Wednesdays through Saturdays in the treatment zones of Pittsburgh. As already noted, our focus on changes in this analysis helps overcome the fact that some neighborhoods have persistently higher crime rates year after year compared with other areas. To account for the possibility that factors specific to the treatment zones may drive crime changes over time, we compare changes in the treatment areas during the on days (F − E) with changes on the off days (H − G), or $[DD_T = (F − E) − (H − G)]$.

Of course the high-crime evenings of Wednesday through Saturday may simply follow different crime trends than the lower-crime evenings of Sunday through Tuesday throughout the city of Pittsburgh as a whole. To account for this possibility, we compare the relative change over time in the treatment areas for Wednesday through Saturday versus Sunday through Tuesday $[DD_T = (F − E) − (H − G)]$, with the within-week change over the same period that is observed in the control areas $[DD_C = (J − I) − (L − K)]$. The DDD estimate in this case is given by $[(F − E) − (H − G)] − [(J − I) − (L − K)]$. This research design helps isolate the effects of those factors specific to the treatment zones during the on days of the postprogram period—factors such as the new FSPs introduced by the Pittsburgh police.

Our estimate for the effects of the Pittsburgh policing program can be derived from a simple regression framework as shown in equation 1. Let Y_{it} represent the number of either shots fired or gunshot injuries on day *(t)* within neighborhood *(i)* in Pittsburgh. The explanatory variables in the regression consist of a series of simple dichotomous indicators where $Treat_i$ is equal to one if the neighborhood is in the treatment zones (1 and 5) and equal to zero otherwise, $Post_t$ is equal to one if the day falls within the fourteen-week period that the policing program is in effect and equal to zero for the six-week preprogram period, and Day_t equals one if the observation is for a Wednesday, Thursday, Friday, or Saturday, the on days of the week when the police patrols may be operating.

---

24. This research design has also been applied to study the effects of Medicaid benefits for maternity and pediatric care on abortion (Joyce and Kaestner, 1996), mandated maternity benefits on child bearing (Gruber, 1994), permissive gun-carrying laws (Ludwig, 1998), and the Richmond, Virginia, Project Exile program. See Raphael and Ludwig, chapter 7 in this volume.

$$Y_{it} = b_0 + b_1 Treat_i + b_2 Post_t + b_3 Day_t + b_4 (Treat_i) \times (Post_t)$$

(1)
$$+ b_5 (Day_t) \times (Post_t) + b_6 (Treat_i) \times (Day_t)$$

$$+ b_7 (Treat_i) \times (Day_t) \times (Post_t) + e_{it}$$

The DDD estimate in this case is given by the coefficient b_7. In our analysis we present robust standard errors that are adjusted to account for heteroskedasticity as well as nonindependence of observations drawn from the same neighborhood.[25] Only omitted covariates that vary on a daily basis have potential for affecting model estimation. More enduring factors that are typically thought to affect crime, such as demographic and economic variables, will not influence program impacts estimated on a daily basis. Furthermore, the differencing strategy of the DDD research design should account for most of the potentially confounding factors that vary over time across neighborhoods.[26]

Results

Our central finding is that the Pittsburgh FSPs appear to substantially reduce citizen reports of shots fired and gunshot injuries in the target neighborhoods. While we find some evidence of a "phantom effect" for shots fired in 1997, the year before the police patrols are put into place, the findings for gunshot injuries generally hold up to a variety of specification checks.

Shots Fired

Table 6-3 shows our key findings for the average number of shots-fired reports per day in Pittsburgh neighborhoods. In the top panel of table 6-3 is the widely used difference-in-difference estimate, which compares the pre- to postprogram change in shots fired per day averaged across all days of the week in the treatment and control areas. These calculations show that the number of shots-fired reports declined in the treatment zones of the city by −.066 during the four-hour

---

25. Estimation uses STATA (version 7) software to perform OLS regressions with the "robust cluster" options to allow for an arbitrary variance-covariance error structure.

26. Consistent with this expectation, the results are unchanged when the estimating equation includes fixed effects for each of the police zones individually, measures of time and time squared to capture citywide crime trends, or indicators for weeks when school was in session or weekend nights (Friday and Saturday).

Table 6-3. *Impact Estimates for Shots Fired (daily averages per police zone)*

	Preperiod (6 weeks before)	Postperiod (14 weeks during)	Estimated differences
Part A: Standard difference-in-difference estimate			
Treatment zones	.750	.684	−.066
Control zones	.274	.327	.053
DD			−.119 (.152)
Part B: Exploiting within-week variation in patrol activity			
Treatment zones			
Wednesday–Saturday	.979	.670	−.310
Sunday–Tuesday	.444	.702	.258
DD_T			−.567 (.088)**
Control zones			
Wednesday–Saturday	.323	.281	−.042
Sunday–Tuesday	.208	.387	.179
DD_C			−.220 (.120)*
DDD			−.347 (.133)**

Note: Results come from estimating daily average shots fired during the four hours from 8 p.m. to midnight in each of Pittsburgh's six police zones. Standard errors in parentheses are adjusted to account for heteroskedasticity in the error variance across different zones, and nonindependence of observations drawn from the same police zone. Asterisks identify statistically significant reductions in one-tail z tests.

* Significant at 5 percent level.
** Significant at 1 percent level.

treatment window from 8 p.m. to midnight (hereafter "per day" for these shots-fired results), while this figure increased in the control areas by +.053. The DD difference in simple trends is thus equal to −.119, which implies a greater decline in the treatment than control neighborhoods, but one that is not statistically significant.

More compelling evidence of a program impact arises when we exploit variation across days of the week in the timing of the patrols, as seen in the bottom panel of table 6-3. Once the policing program was implemented, the number of shots fired declined by −.310 per day during the on days in the treatment zones. However, the number of shots fired increased by +.258 in the same treatment neighborhoods during the off days. The gap between the on and off days is a decline of $DD_T = -.567$ shots-fired calls. In the control neighborhoods that did not receive the policing program, the gap in shots fired between the high- and low-crime days of the week declined more modestly, $DD_C = -.220$. The difference-in-difference-in-differences estimate is thus DDD = −.567 − (−.220) = −.347, statistically significant at the 1 percent level using a one-tailed test for a reduction in shots fired. The estimate implies that the policing program has reduced shots fired during the on days in the treatment areas by around 34 percent.[27]

The bottom panel of table 6-3 also offers suggestive evidence that the control neighborhoods may provide a reasonable estimate for the counterfactual outcome of what would have happened in the target neighborhoods in the absence of the policing program. This can be seen by focusing on the changes over time in shots fired during the off days (Sunday–Tuesday), which are similar in the treatment and control neighborhoods (+.258 versus +.179). The similarity in shots-fired trends during the off days across areas also suggests that the policing program may reduce gun carrying and misuse primarily through a deterrent effect rather than an incapacitation effect arising from arrests that take high-risk people and guns off the street. The latter would presumably manifest itself by a reduction during the off days in target neighborhoods as well, but such a carry-over effect did not occur. The results are also consistent with the idea that any displacement of gun violence from on to off days within the target areas may be only modest.

As seen in the top panel of table 6-4 the results are broadly robust to variations in the choice of comparison groups. Increasing the length of the preprogram period from five to fourteen weeks does not materially change the results. Partitioning the postprogram period in half reveals stronger reductions in shots fired during the second half after the patrols were in effect for at least seven weeks. Finally, control zone 2 is distinctive. It comes closest to the target areas in initial crime rates and contains the downtown business district (characterized by a small residential population and little activity on most nights) as well as the city's oldest historically black neighborhood. Removing zone 2, with its unique population and structural characteristics, increases the magnitude of effects in the target zones.

One way to test for bias from omitted variables is to examine whether our procedure leads to statistically significant differences in trends between treatment and control neighborhoods in 1997, the year before the program is launched, and in 1999, the year after the program was in effect. That is, we calculate the DDD estimate using the same calendar days that define the pre- and postprogram periods and on and off days for nonprogram years. Since no gun-suppression patrols were actually launched in the treatment neighborhoods in the on days of

27. We define the proportional magnitude of the treatment effect by comparing our DDD estimate for the program's impact (−.347) with our estimate for the average number of shots fired each day that would have been observed during the "on" days in the treatment neighborhoods if the program were not in effect. This counterfactual outcome is equal to the rate that is observed during this period (.670) plus the estimated treatment effect (.347), so the proportional reduction equals .347/(.670 + .347) = 34 percent.

Table 6-4. *Robustness Checks for Estimated Program Effects on Shots Fired (daily averages per zone)*

| Estimating data | DDD (difference-in-difference-in-differences) | | | |
| | Target zone 1 | | Target zone 5 | |
	Beta	(se)	Beta	(se)
1998 program estimates				
6 weeks preprogram versus 14 weeks during program	−0.435**	(0.117)	−0.260**	(0.117)
14 weeks preprogram versus 14 weeks during program	−0.481**	(0.083)	−0.165**	(0.083)
6 weeks preprogram versus first 7 weeks during program	−0.329*	(0.213)	−0.172	(0.213)
6 weeks preprogram versus second 7 weeks during program	−0.540**	(0.080)	−0.348**	(0.080)
5 weeks preprogram versus 14 weeks during program	−0.378**	(0.090)	−0.034	(0.090)
Target zones versus control zones 3, 4, and 6	−0.504**	(0.132)	−0.329**	(0.132)
Nonprogram years				
1997 data, 6 weeks preprogram versus 14 weeks during program	−0.030	(0.102)	−1.117**	(0.102)
1997 data, 14 weeks preprogram versus 14 weeks during program	−0.266**	(0.107)	−0.915**	(0.107)
1999 data, 6 weeks preprogram versus 14 weeks during program	0.098	(0.180)	0.061	(0.180)
1999 data, 14 weeks preprogram versus 14 weeks during program	0.104	(0.103)	0.027	(0.103)

Note: Unless noted otherwise, all contrasts are between each target zone (1 or 5) and all control zones (2, 3, 4, and 6) in the six-week preprogram and fourteen-week postprogram periods. Estimates come from comparing changes over time in the daily average number of shots fired during the four hours from 8 p.m. to midnight in treatment versus control police zones (table 6-2). Standard errors in parentheses are adjusted to account for heteroskedasticity in the error variance across different zones and non-independence of observations drawn from the same police zone. Asterisks identify statistically significant reductions in one-tail z tests.

* Significant at 10 percent level.
** Significant at 5 percent level.

1997 and 1999, we expect no statistically significant differences to arise with the DDD approach. Of course the 1999 test is perhaps not as clean as that for 1997, given the possibility of "residual deterrence" of criminals even after the patrols have ended, but in any case evidence of a null effect in 1999 would provide useful evidence on the validity of our research design.

As seen in the bottom panel of table 6-4, while we find no statistically significant evidence of a phantom program "effect" in 1999 for either of the two treatment zones (1 and 5), we do find signs of a phantom effect in 1997, the year before the police patrols were launched. When we use a six-week preprogram period for 1997, the contrast between treatment zone 5 and the controls is statistically significant. Alternative definitions, ranging from five- to fourteen-week preprogram periods, yield statistically significant phantom effects in both zones 1 and 5. These findings make us cautious about interpreting the differences in shots fired between the treatment and control zones in 1998 as signs of the patrol program's effects. However, the results for gunshot injuries presented in the next section are more robust to our various specification checks.

Gunshot Injuries

The results for assault-related gunshot injuries show an even more pronounced program impact during the program year (1998) and little consistent evidence of statistically significant program effects during the years before and after the program is in effect. Gun assault injuries declined significantly in both of the target zones by roughly the same proportional amount, although the decline is only statistically significant over a variety of conditions in the higher-crime zone 5.

The top panel of table 6-5 shows that the standard difference-in-difference estimate that relies on average gunshot injuries per day (averaged across all days of the week) suggests that the program has reduced such injuries by $-.073$ per day. The bottom panel of table 6-5 shows that refining the simple difference-in-difference calculation to focus on the days on which the patrols were in operation (Wednesday through Saturday) increases the magnitude of program impact to $(-.161 - .007) = -.168$ fewer assault-related gunshot injuries on patrol days in the target zones.[28] The simple pre- and post-trends are much more similar during the off days (.103 and .050). While the difference in trends during the on days equals $-.168$, the difference in trends for the off days is only about one-third as large and represents an increase of $.053 = (.103 - .050)$. Exploiting this within-week variation in patrol implementation more formally yields a DDD estimate equal to $-.222$ (p<.10), a reduction in assault gunshot injuries

---

28. Daily rates refer to the average number of gunshot injuries during a full twenty-four-hour day.

Table 6-5. *Impact Estimates for Assault Gunshot Injuries*
(daily averages per police zone)

	Preperiod (6 weeks before)	Postperiod (14 weeks during)	Estimated differences
Part A: Standard difference-in-difference estimate			
Treatment zones	.155	.107	−.048
Control zones	.054	.079	.026
DD			−.073 (.022)**
Part B: Exploiting within-week variation in patrol activity			
Treatment zones			
Wednesday–Saturday	.250	.089	−.161
Sunday–Tuesday	.028	.131	.103
DD_T			−.264 (.208)*
Control zones			
Wednesday–Saturday	.073	.080	.007
Sunday–Tuesday	.028	.077	.050
DD_C			−.042 (.042)
$DDD = DD_T - DD_C$			−.222 (.165)*

Note: Results come from estimating daily average gunshot injuries from assaults in each of Pittsburgh's six police zones. Standard errors in parentheses are adjusted to account for heteroskedasticity in the error variance across different zones and nonindependence of observations drawn from the same police zone. Asterisks identify statistically significant reductions in one-tail z tests.

* Significant at 10 percent level.
** Significant at 5 percent level.

of 71 percent (.222/(.222 + .089)) from the expected level on patrol days in the target zones.

Table 6-6 shows that the results are generally not sensitive to how we define the pre- or postprogram periods. The estimated program impact on assault-related gunshot injuries in zone 5 is always statistically significant and of about the same magnitude when we partition the postprogram period in half, and whether we define the preprogram period using the five weeks before the patrols go into effect, the fourteen weeks before the patrols are launched, or any interval in between. The estimated impact in zone 1 is also statistically significant but only for longer preprogram periods (eleven weeks or more). Statistically significant proportional changes in assault gunshot injuries are approximately similar in magnitude across the two zones, ranging from 59 to 77 percent in zone 1 compared with 60 to 72 percent in zone 5.[29]

29. In shorter preprogram periods the proportional reductions are in the same range in zone 5 but are smaller in zone 1.

Table 6-6. *Robustness Checks for Estimated Program Effects on Assault Gunshot Injuries*

| | DDD (difference-in-difference-in-differences) | | | |
| | Target zone 1 | | Target zone 5 | |
Estimating data	Beta	(se)	Beta	(se)
1998 program estimates				
6 weeks preprogram versus 14 weeks during program	−0.015	(0.041)	−0.428**	(0.041)
14 weeks preprogram versus 14 weeks during program	−0.058**	(0.026)	−0.243**	(0.026)
All gunshot injuries (all causes)	−0.058	(0.052)	−0.542**	(0.052)
All gunshot injuries (youth only)	−0.061	(0.077)	−0.319**	(0.077)
Accidental gunshot injuries	−0.047**	(0.028)	−0.039*	(0.028)
6 weeks preprogram versus first 7 weeks postprogram	−0.036	(0.029)	−0.378**	(0.029)
6 weeks preprogram versus second 7 weeks postprogram	0.006	(0.065)	−0.479**	(0.065)
5 weeks preprogram versus 14 weeks postprogram	0.042	(0.032)	−0.348**	(0.032)
Target zone versus control zones 3, 4, and 6	−0.021	(0.055)	−0.434**	(0.055)
Nonprogram years				
1997 data, 6 weeks preprogram versus 14 weeks postprogram	−0.050	(0.051)	−0.052	(0.051)
1997 data, 14 weeks preprogram versus 14 weeks postprogram	0.028	(0.051)	−0.037	(0.051)
1999 data, 6 weeks preprogram versus 14 weeks postprogram	0.029	(0.016)	−0.118**	(0.016)
1999 data, 14 weeks preprogram versus 14 weeks postprogram	0.031	(0.010)	0.007	(0.010)

Note: Unless otherwise noted, all contrasts are between each target zone (1 or 5) and all control zones (2, 3, 4, and 6) in the six-week preprogram and fourteen-week postprogram periods. Estimates come from comparing changes over time in the daily average number of gunshot injuries in treatment versus control police zones (table 6-2). Standard errors in parentheses are adjusted to account for heteroskedasticity in the error variance across different zones and nonindependence of observations drawn from the same police zone. Asterisks identify statistically significant reductions in one-tail z tests.
*Significant at 10 percent level.
**Significant at 5 percent level.

The pattern of large and significant effects in zone 5 and insignificant effects in zone 1 persists when we vary the subset of gunshot injuries. Zone 5 experiences significant declines in accidental gunshot injuries, the combination of all gunshot injuries, and gunshot injuries involving youthful victims (under age 25). In zone 1, the effects are smaller in magnitude and only reach statistical significance for accidental gunshot injuries.[30]

The results are similar when we use a generalized least squares (GLS) approach that corrects for serial correlation in the error structure of our regression model, or when we use models that weight each observation by the zone's population.[31] We also obtain similar findings when we reduce some of the day-to-day variation in gunshot injuries by using a panel data set that averages gunshot injuries for each zone within a week over the on days and over the off days. In this case each zone contributes only two observations per week to the panel data (one each for the on and off sets of days), rather than seven daily observations per zone per week as in our baseline estimates.

There is also suggestive evidence that our estimates for gunshot injuries are not driven by unmeasured confounding factors, shown in table 6-6. We replicate the DDD calculation using the same calendar days, neighborhoods, and days of the week but now using assault gunshot-injury data for 1997, when the program was not in effect. As with our analysis of the program year of 1998, we examine the sensitivity of our estimates to how we define the preprogram period, ranging from five to fourteen weeks. For the twenty total DDD estimates that we calculate for the preprogram year of 1997 (each of the two treatment zones individually against the control areas, using ten possible definitions of the preprogram period for each comparison), two are statistically significant at the 10 percent level. We obtain a similar fraction of statistically significant comparisons for 1999. While each point estimate is of course not a truly independent trial, we are not alarmed that two of the twenty comparisons are significant at the 10 percent level in 1997 and 1999. By way of comparison, during the program year of 1998 fully fourteen of the twenty possible comparisons are statistically significant at the 5 percent level.

---

30. The declines in accidental gunshot injuries are not likely to result from the policing program since there is evidence of even larger declines in both target zones during 1997, and in zone 1 during 1999, which further motivates our focus on the assault-related gunshot injuries that better reflect the type of violent behavior targeted by the police patrols.

31. We estimate GLS models that assume that the error terms for periods $(t-1)$ and (t) are correlated but error terms more than one period apart are not (a first-order autoregressive process). The results are the same whether we assume that the serial correlation between error terms is the same or differs across police zones. In both cases the point estimate for the effect of the policing intervention increases in relation to the standard error and improves the significance level from .09 to .01.

Moreover, in 1998, after the fourteen-week patrol period is over, we observe a statistically significant increase in assault gunshot injuries in zone 5 equal to around one-quarter of the decline observed during the program period. This bounce back is consistent with what we might expect from the cessation of a program that has a causal effect on gun carrying or crime and generates some residual deterrence. The bounce back is observed soon after the patrol program terminates (within two weeks), which suggests that at least some subset of people at high risk of carrying and misusing guns is reasonably well informed about the local police environment. In any case, there is no similar bounce back over the same calendar period in the treatment areas in 1997 and 1999.

Discussion

Our estimates suggest that Pittsburgh's targeted policing program against illegal gun carrying may have reduced shots fired by 34 percent and gunshot injuries by as much as 71 percent in the targeted areas. Our evaluation pays careful attention to the problem of unmeasured, time-varying factors that may introduce bias into estimates of the policing program's impact. Although we cannot definitively rule out the possibility of omitted-variables bias with our analysis, the fact that the combined pattern of changes in gunshot injuries during the program period in 1998 is qualitatively different from what is observed in 1997 or 1999 is at least consistent with the idea that the FSPs had some effect on illegal gun carrying or misuse.

The relatively modest number of guns confiscated and arrests made as a result of Pittsburgh's directed patrols (table 6-1) suggest that incapacitation of illegal guns or their owners is unlikely to drive the large reductions that accompanied the policing program. Moreover, if the patrols reduce shots fired or assault gunshot injuries primarily through an incapacitation effect, by taking illegal guns and those who carry them off the street, we might expect the effects to carry over to the days of the week when the patrols were not in effect. This type of carryover does not appear to occur. Instead, the similarity in off-day trends between the treatment and control zones provides at least suggestive evidence of a deterrent effect that is specific to the treatment zones during the on days when the program is in effect and only reduces illegal gun carrying and misuse during those times. The absence of significant trends upward in the control areas during the program period also seems to rule out spatial displacement, where gun-carrying offenders shift their activities from the treatment to control neighborhoods.

Finally, one important policy question is whether the targeting of the police resources on illegal gun carrying in high-crime areas is an important part of the program's effects, or whether simply adding more resources to routine patrol activity would achieve similar ends. Unfortunately, the Pittsburgh data do not enable us to definitively rule out either possibility. Previous research by economist Steven Levitt suggests that a 10 percent increase in the number of police reduces violent crime by around 10 percent (that is, an elasticity of violent crime with respect to police officers of around −1.0), even if the additional police resources are deployed in standard ways.[32] Our findings suggest an elasticity of gunshot injuries with respect to additional targeted police officers on the order of −1.4.[33] However, given the standard errors around both sets of estimates we cannot confidently conclude that targeting the additional police resources in Pittsburgh to focus on illegal guns enhanced the overall impact of these expenditures on criminal behavior.

However, because the Pittsburgh program targets police resources on the most costly violent crimes—those that involve firearms—the targeting seems to enhance the cost effectiveness of the additional police resources.[34] Although blanket increases in police resources may yield from $1 to $5 in benefits to society for each extra dollar that is spent, the more targeted FSPs in Pittsburgh may generate even more substantial net benefits.[35] We estimate that the costs of the additional patrols in Pittsburgh are modest—something less than $35,000 in overtime expenditures during the fourteen-week program period. In contrast the costs of gun violence to society are substantial, about $1 million per gunshot injury.[36] If the estimates presented in this chapter are correct, then the investment of $35,000 or so in targeted antigun police patrols may yield benefits of as much as $25 million.[37] Equally important, Pittsburgh's experience suggests that targeted patrols against illegal guns can be implemented in a way that addresses community concerns about intrusive policing.

32. Levitt (1997).

33. This comes from comparing the 71 percent decline in assault-related gunshot injuries to the 50 percent increase in the number of police officers allocated to zone 5 during the "on days" of the Pittsburgh firearm suppression patrols.

34. Levitt (1997, p. 285) reports an average cost per violent crime of about $70,000 (in 1998 dollars), while the costs per assault-related gunshot injury are about $1 million. Cook and Ludwig (2000); Ludwig and Cook (2001). Of course this comparison is not perfect since the class of violent crimes includes those that do not involve injury to the victim, but the average cost per violent crime seems to be driven in large part by homicides that mostly involve firearms.

35. Levitt (1997).

36. Cook and Ludwig (2000); Ludwig and Cook (2001).

37. The estimates in table 6-4 imply a reduction in the average daily number of gunshot injuries per zone equal to 0.222, which, when multiplied by four patrol days a week over fourteen program weeks, implies a total decline of around twenty-five gunshot injuries.

COMMENT BY
Lawrence W. Sherman

The chapter by Jacqueline Cohen and Jens Ludwig is a valuable addition to an important literature. With this analysis, we now have eight published tests of a major hypothesis: that intensive police efforts to discourage illegal gun carrying in public places can reduce gun injury or death. All eight of those tests produce findings consistent with that hypothesis. Most impressive is the medical data on gunshot injury that Cohen and Ludwig contribute. With their data, all eight tests show that police efforts reduce either homicides or gunshot wounds. Not each result is statistically significant, but the likelihood of achieving all eight results in the same direction by chance alone grows lower with this study's contribution.

The focus on medically measured gunshot injury is a crucial decision for interpreting the sum total of available published research. The measures of gun crime in the literature have been mixed, given the failure of the FBI's Uniform Crime Reporting System to establish a separate category for crimes committed with guns, let alone for injuries occurring in crimes. As criminologists well know, FBI rules require counting all four of the following events as an "armed robbery":

— Someone pulls out a knife and threatens to stab a victim if he does not yield money;

— Someone points a gun and threatens to shoot a victim if he does not yield money;

— Someone shoots at, but does not hit, a victim, who then yields money; and

— Someone shoots at and wounds a victim and then takes the victim's money. Only when a victim dies as a result of a gunshot during a robbery do we obtain a clear measure of gun violence from the FBI's crime reporting system, followed by most urban police agencies in the United States. The robbery then becomes a murder but can be identified as a robbery murder by type of gun in the FBI's supplementary homicide reports.

The occurrence of death in a gun crime is the tip of an iceberg, as rare as 1 death per 250 commercial robberies. Most gun crimes do not cause death and probably do not even cause an injury. Police data on the percentage of incidents in which police fire at suspects and hit their human targets range from 43 percent in New York City in 1970–91 to 46 percent in Kansas City in 1972–91 to a possible high of 58 percent in Los Angeles in 1980–91.[38] Thus about half of incidents of shooting by police regularly trained in firearms cause no injury or death.

38. Geller and Scott (1992, pp. 516, 502, 519).

Of the shooting victims hit by shots fired by criminals in 4,177 Baltimore incidents in the mid-1990s, the monthly percentage who died from their injuries ranged from 11 percent to 20 percent, with an overall mean of 16 percent.[39] Applying that ratio to the roughly 50 percent of gunshot incidents with no wounds yields an estimate of some 8 percent of incidents in which shots are fired resulting in a death by gunshot wound, or 92 percent without medically treatable injury. The estimates of percentages of incidents in which guns are used without being discharged are controversial, but for commercial robberies alone they outnumber the cases in which guns are shot by 19 to 1 (95 percent), and for commercial robbery by 4 to 1 (22 percent).[40] In the case of commercial robbery, then, the tip of the iceberg of gun death is roughly 4 in 1,000 gun crimes.

In their attempts to measure gun crime more reliably, experimenters in police strategies against gun crimes have been driven to reading thousands of police incident reports to detect the use of a gun as described in the narrative of the incident.[41] A check on the reliability of Indianapolis police checking a box indicating "gun use" on crime incident reports found that 35 percent of crimes in which guns were used had no check on the relevant box in the report. James Shaw found drive-by gun crimes in Kansas City coded as "criminal damage to property" or "vandalism" when bullets fired had only hit buildings or cars.[42] These heroic efforts, however, give us little confidence that the measures of gun crimes are reliable over time or even well correlated with the more measurable tips of the iceberg. In the Indianapolis experiments, for example, homicides dropped in the east patrol area target beats from 4 to zero, while recorded aggravated assaults with guns rose from 19 to 30 and total gun crimes rose from 42 to 57. Since police disliked the mayor at that time, and since police controlled the decisions to report crimes, it is hard to put greater credence on the gun crime count than on the homicide count—the latter being less stable but less vulnerable to reporting discretion.

Cohen and Ludwig neatly sidestep these problems by turning to a measurement system that is devoid of police reporting biases. Hospital records on gunshot wounds by residence of the victim is an excellent approximation for the level of gun violence in the target beats. It raises from six to eight the number of published tests, to my knowledge, of the hypothesis that murder or wounding declines after the application of increased policing of gun carrying in a defined geographic area. Seven of those tests are based on a comparison to a control area,

39. Long-Onnen (2000, table 4).
40. See Cook (1983, p. 73).
41. Sherman and Rogan (1995); McGarrell and others (2001).
42. McGarrell and others (2001, p. 126); Sherman, Shaw, and Rogan (1995).

while one is an analysis of the entire United States over time without a control.[43] Those tests are as follows:

1992: Kansas City, Mo. Homicides and drive-by shootings (causing woundings) were significantly reduced in an on-off-on comparison of extra gun patrols in one area to no extra patrols in another area.

1993–94: Cali, Colombia. Homicides were 14 percent lower during eighty-nine police intervention days than nonintervention days, with bigger effects on paydays.

1995–97: Bogota, Colombia. Homicides were 13 percent lower on 67 intervention days than on nonintervention days, with bigger payday effects.

1997: Indianapolis east. Homicides declined from 4 to 0 in this beat while they rose 53 percent citywide and were unchanged in a comparison beat.

1997: Indianapolis north. Homicides declined from 7 to 1 in this beat while they rose 53 percent citywide and were unchanged in a comparison beat.

1998: Pittsburgh zone 1. Gunshot injuries declined significantly in this zone on intervention days, relative to both control zones and nonintervention days within target zones, for an overall reduction of 71 percent fewer injuries treated in target zones on intervention days.

1998: Pittsburgh zone 5. Same as in zone 1 above.

1984–98: U.S.A. Homicides rose from by 20 percent 1984 to 1993 as the ratio of homicides to weapons arrests remained unchanged; once that ratio rose by 50 percent and remained much higher each year, the homicide rate began a steady drop to over 20 percent below the 1984 figure.[44]

Explaining Consistent Results

These results are encouraging but not clearly explained. The question of causal mechanism is hard to answer by the seizure of more guns: three of the eight (Pittsburgh 1 and 5 and Indianapolis north) did not report any increase in guns seized, and one (Bogota) had no data on this point; the other four report increases in guns seized. Whether the police focused on high-risk places or people is somewhat easier to resolve; only the Indianapolis north experiment reportedly focused on people, rather than on anyone looking suspicious in gun crime hot spots. But the experiments all lack specificity on this point, and it would require new research with systematic observation of police conduct to resolve it.

---

43. Sherman (2000).

44. For 1992, Sherman and Rogan (1995); for 1993–94 and 1995–97, Villaveces and others (2000); for 1997, East, and 1997, North, McGarrell and others (2001); and for 1998, Pittsburgh, Zones 1 and 5, Cohen and Ludwig, chap. 6, in this volume; for 1984–98, U.S.A., Sherman (2000).

The most likely causal mechanism seems to be communication of a threat that police are looking for guns in certain places at certain times. That hypothesis is consistent with four of the eight tests (Pittsburgh and Colombia), which employed interventions that were limited to a few days at a time and then were turned off. How the threat was communicated, how widely it was received, and whether it would decay over time remain important and unanswered questions.

What Is An Experiment?

A final comment on the Cohen and Ludwig chapter is not a trivial point. They distinguish repeatedly between experimental and nonexperimental research. They imply that none of the eight tests we have, including their own, are "truly" experimental. This suggests that only a randomized experiment can be "true." As an ardent advocate of using randomized designs whenever possible, I appreciate the spirit in which their remarks are offered. But it does little good to reject the basic definition of an experiment as research on intentional changes in variables. All of these tests happened because someone decided to send police out to "get the guns off the street." That is a fundamentally different kind of test from a correlational analysis of "natural" differences in policing over time or across places.[45] We must recognize the Cohen and Ludwig chapter for being just as "experimental" as Boyle's tests or Newton's and not disparage the value of their careful methods. Our causal inference from experimental research is always limited, no matter how well bias is controlled. These tests collectively report effects whose sizes are large enough and consistent enough to draw substantial inferences even without random assignment.

COMMENT BY

Jeffrey Fagan

As crime rates in U.S. cities fell through much of the 1990s, "Do police matter" became a hotly contested question. On one side of this debate are researchers who suggest that police strategies directly and exclusively contributed to crime declines. These scholars claim that "but for" new police strategies, crime rates would have fallen neither as sharply nor as persistently as recent trends show.[46] On the other side are researchers who claim that crime has declined steeply

---

45. Cox (1958).
46. See, for example, Kelling and Sousa (2001); Silverman (1999); Heymann (2000).

across cities that applied quite different policing strategies, inviting explanations beyond policing to account for the steep declines in crime. Researchers looking across cities describe policing as one of many interacting social and economic forces that together produced downward pressures on crime.[47] Unfortunately, there is little hard evidence on either side of these claims.

Despite controversies in between-city comparisons, several studies *within* cities have shown that police practices can make a difference through small-scale, carefully targeted interventions. Many of these innovations have targeted guns, some with impressive results. These studies suggest that directed patrol practices and other selective and targeted strategies have produced declines in gun crimes that exceed the general regression in most cities. In Boston, police and other law enforcement agencies parsimoniously selected individuals for police surveillance and interdiction. In Indianapolis and Kansas City, police used directed patrols and proactive stops of citizens to reduce gun carrying and gun crimes in certain areas where gun violence rates were highest. Police in Chicago and San Diego engaged citizens in ongoing analysis of crime data to identify situations and locations with the highest crime rates and strategically focus interventions in those areas. Police in Jersey City targeted violence reduction strategies at specific problems within public housing projects to reduce violence.[48] The Cohen and Ludwig analysis of the *Firearms Suppression Program* (FSP) in Pittsburgh adds to this growing dossier of empirical evidence on the salutary effects of directed patrol and tightly focused proactive policing. The Pittsburgh Police Department launched an intervention in two of its six police districts that targeted guns via "gun suppression patrols." Cohen and Ludwig estimate the effects of these patrols on gun violence using two measures: gunshot injuries and gun shots fired. In the absence of an experimental design, Cohen and Ludwig use a "difference in difference in differences" (DDD) design to address three research challenges: heterogeneity of both crime problems and social structural factors in the six police districts, an intermittent application of the "treatment," and a relatively small number of observational units. Their expression of the DDD approach is well described in the chapter.

The structure of FSP creates a challenging identification problem and addressing it with this design is at once the strength and weakness of the chapter. The DDD model fits well with the quasiexperimental conditions. The third "D" is a time parameter to estimate the effects of the intermittent intervention by isolating the nonexperimental time intervals in the treatment sites. A fourth

47. Eck and Maguire (2000); Fagan, Zimring and Kim (1998); Bowling (1999); LaFree (1998).
48. Sherman (2000); Kennedy (1997); McGarrell and others (2001); Sherman and Rogan (1995); Skogan and Hartnett (1997); Greene (1999); Braga and others (1999).

"D" in this paper includes additional time periods to test for possible regression effects that predate the program. The method has been used productively by Jens Ludwig in his study of concealed firearm laws and in several studies of social welfare policy initiatives.[49] To avoid measurement problems associated with official statistics, Cohen and Ludwig use two independent measures of firearm activity in each of the two police zones where FSP was implemented. First, they use firearm injury surveillance data to estimate gunshot injuries. These public health records offer the comparative advantage of avoiding police "filtering" of reports. Second, they balance surveillance data with police reports of gun shots fired, carefully cleaned to reduce repeats and false reports. However, two facts suggest the possibility of reliability problems in shots-fired data: the elimination of 20 percent of these calls because of duplications and the inability of officers to validate actual incidents of shots fired in three of four calls. Nevertheless, the use of two alternate measures and data sources is first-rate measurement and design strategy.

The results were positive though internally contradictory and inconsistent. A significant and sizable reduction in shots fired was observed in both target districts. A significant and sizable reduction in gunshot injuries was observed in zone 1 but not in zone 5. For injuries, there were significant differences when zone 1 was included with zone 5, but there were no significant differences when zone 1 was analyzed separately. Moreover, there were no changes in gunshot injuries attributed to accidents, suggesting that perhaps the overall level of firearm possession remained the same but gun owners in zone 5 perhaps were less likely to carry their guns. Because of measurement problems in estimating gunshots fired, I put more stock in the injury data and hence the second analysis.

The accuracy of these estimates depends on assumptions in the modeling strategy that are provocative. First, the DDD model eschews statistical controls to estimate differences between observational units. This strategy fits well with state-level data to examine the effects of policy, where endogeneity of policy and structural variables may be less prominent in the adoption of policies to be tested. Besides, in the FSP study, measures for small areas such as census tracts were not available, a practical reason to use DDD models. Indeed, one of the strengths of DDD designs is their ability to remove endogeneity or heterogeneity as a confounding effect. DDD solutions assume that the between-unit differences in exogenous factors are accounted for in the initial differences among police zones in gun violence, and that changes over time in these differences are attributable solely to changes in the application of the intervention. The effects of the covariates can be "removed" because they are constant across time periods.

49. Ludwig (1998).

In other words, the factors that produce the initial differences—whether crime problems or social structure—are assumed irrelevant, because they are assumed to be invariant over the relatively short period in the study and hence remain stable among zones.

This is a Bayesian gamble, and the downside risk is not small. The covariates that are set aside in a DDD design are likely predictors of both crime problems *and* the decision to target the neighborhood.[50] Accordingly, there may be alternate contemporaneous effects that are not accounted for in the design. Put another way, crime problems and social structure may be endogenous to the selection of the areas to implement the intervention, a problem not easily addressed by the DDD design and its inherent treatment of covariates. Consider one example: since the two target zones were selected because of their high crime rates, general police practices may differ in these two places. If such contextual factors interact with the interventions, then they cannot be removed. This is a classic threat in quasi-experiments that may well confound the design.[51]

Nevertheless, there are some strategies to address these concerns. One method to account for differences in the intensity of policing among different areas is to use an instrument such as traffic stops or misdemeanor arrest rates. Cohen successfully used such a strategy in a study of city-level differences in deterrence. Since gun violence often reflects the dynamics of drug markets, a proxy for drug markets in local areas—for example, drug arrests, overdoses, or seizures—can be another hedge against selection.[52] Finally, as a specificity analysis, it would be conceptually helpful to include an instrument to account for other violent crime, such as (nongun) robbery, to sort out the unique effects of the gun suppression strategy on gun crimes versus general levels of violence versus crime generally. An instrument of robbery would help referee between competing measures and conflicting results (injuries versus gunshots) and resolve general crime reduction versus gun-specific effects.

Second, the DDD model itself is not without its controversies. There are potential biases in estimating the *standard error* around the estimates of treatment effects.[53] The estimation of standard errors in DDD models opens the door to potentially serious serial correlation problems, owing to the lengthy time periods (fourteen time points or more in this study), the general serial correlation in the dependent variables, and the relatively narrow range of the treatment variable. Marianne Bertrand and colleagues used "placebo laws" to test for these effects and

50. Fagan and Davies (2000); Sampson and Raudenbush (1999).
51. Cook and Campbell (1979).
52. Sampson and Cohen (1988); MacCoun and Reuter (2001).
53. Bertrand, Duflo and Mullainathan (2002).

showed a tendency toward overrejection of the null hypothesis across a range of studies using DD methods.[54] Using the third "D"—a diagnostic for preexisting effects, similar to Cohen and Ludwig—only slightly lowers the rejection rate. The problem persists, and the standard errors are underestimated. What Cohen and Ludwig could do, and I hope will in subsequent work, is to allow for a different covariance matrix that explicitly addresses the problem of repeated measurements over time. Comparison of these results with the DDD estimates in Cohen and Ludwig's chapter will provide a valuable benchmark for interpretation of DDD models and their applications to other experiments.

Finally, there are normative and constitutional questions about stops of citizens based on broad subjective notions of "suspicion" that animate police stops of citizens. There are many ways to police guns, some that promote strong citizen-police cooperation, and those that exact a high cost in citizen trust and cooperation with police.[55] The FSP was sparing and judicious in the extent of citizen contacts, compared with the directed patrol experiments in Kansas City or Indianapolis, or New York's policy of aggressive and widespread stops and frisks that most adversely affects predominantly African American communities. In cities that have adopted aggressive street-level enforcement, there have been explicit trade-offs of citizen rights and protections to obtain reductions in crime, reductions whose causal links to police efforts are contested. This ambivalence is strongest in the neighborhoods most affected by violence, the most heavily patrolled, and where social and economic disadvantage is most concentrated. Pittsburgh's recent history of police-citizen conflict suggests that the legitimacy of policing is a factor that should be a focal consideration in the assessment of programs like FSP.[56] If small gains are produced at high costs in due process and fair (procedural) treatment, citizens might withdraw their cooperation with police in the creation of security. If aggressive patrols have high social and legal costs, in the end they will be self-limiting.

References

Bassi, Laurie J. 1984. "Estimating the Effect of Training Programs with Non-Random Selection." *Review of Economics and Statistics* 66 (1): 36–43.

Bertrand, Marianne, Esther Duflo, and Sendhil Mullainathan. 2002. *How Much Should We Trust Differences-In-Differences Estimates?* Working Paper 8841. Cambridge, Mass.: National Bureau of Economic Research.

54. Bertrand, Duflo, and Mullainathan (2002).
55. Fagan (2002); Tyler and Huo (2003).
56. Fagan and Davies (2000); Harcourt (2001); Weitzer (2000); Livingston (1999).

Blumstein, Alfred. 2000. "Disaggregating the Violence Trends." In *The Crime Drop in America,* edited by Alfred Blumstein and Joel Wallman, 13–44. Cambridge University Press.

Blumstein, Alfred, and Joel Wallman. 2000. *The Crime Drop in America.* Cambridge University Press.

Bowling, Ben. 1999. "The Rise and Fall of New York Murder." *British Journal of Criminology* 39 (4): 531–54.

Braga, Anthony, and others. 1999. "Problem-Oriented Policing in Violent Crime Places: A Randomized Controlled Experiment." *Criminology* 37 (3): 541–80.

Chermak, Steven, Edmund F. McGarrell, and Alexander Weiss. 2001. "Citizen Perceptions of Aggressive Traffic Enforcement Strategies." *Justice Quarterly* 18: 365–91.

Cook, Philip J. 1983. "The Influence of Gun Availability on Violent Crime Patterns." In *Crime and Justice: An Annual Review of Research,* vol. 4, edited by Michael Tonry and Norval Morris, 49–90. University of Chicago Press.

Cook, Philip J., and John H. Laub. 1998. "The Unprecedented Epidemic in Youth Violence." In *Youth Violence. Crime and Justice: A Review of Research, Volume 24,* edited by Michael Tonry and Mark H. Moore, 27–64. University of Chicago Press.

Cook, Philip J., and Jens Ludwig. 2000. *Gun Violence: The Real Costs.* Oxford University Press.

Cook, Thomas D., and Donald T. Campbell. 1979. *Quasi-Experimentation: Design and Analysis Issues for Field Settings.* Houghton-Miflin.

Cox, David. 1958. (reprinted 1992). *Planning of Experiments.* Wiley.

Dunworth, Terence. 2000. *National Evaluation of the Youth Firearms Violence Initiative.* NCJ 184482. National Institute of Justice, U.S. Department of Justice.

Eck, John, and Edward Maguire. 2000. "Have Changes in Policing Reduced Violent Crime?" In *The Crime Drop in America,* edited by Alfred Blumstein and Joel Wallman, 207–65. Cambridge University Press.

Fagan, Jeffrey. 2002. "Policing Guns and Youth Violence." *Future of Children* 12 (2): 133–52.

Fagan, Jeffrey, and Garth Davies. 2000. "Street Stops and Broken Windows: Terry, Race, and Disorder in New York City." *Fordham Urban Law Journal* 28 (2): 457–504.

Fagan, J., F. E. Zimring, and J. Kim. 1998. "Declining Homicide in New York: A Tale of Two Trends." *Journal of Criminal Law and Criminology* 88 (4): 1277–1324.

Geller, William, and Michael Scott. 1992. *Deadly Force: What We Know.* Washington: Police Executive Research Forum.

Glaeser, Edward L., and Jacob L. Vigdor. 2001. "Racial Segregation in the 2000 Census: Promising News." Brookings Institution Center on Urban and Metropolitan Policy.

Greene, Judith. 1999. "Zero Tolerance: A Case Study of Police Policies and Practices in New York City." *Crime and Delinquency* 45 (2): 171–87.

Gruber, Jonathan. 1994. "The Incidence of Mandated Maternity Benefits." *American Economic Review* 84 (3): 622–41.

Harcourt, Bernard. 2001. *Illusion of Order: the False Promise of Broken Windows Policing.* Harvard University Press.

Heckman, James J., and V. Joseph Hotz. 1989. "Choosing among Alternative Nonexperimental Methods for Estimating the Impact of Social Programs: The Case of Manpower Training." *Journal of the American Statistical Association* 84 (408): 862–80.

Heymann, Philip. 2000. "The New Policing." *Fordham Urban Law Journal* 28 (2): 407–56.

Joyce, Ted, and Robert Kaestner. 1996. "The Effect of Expansions in Medicaid Income Eligibility on Abortion." *Demography* 33 (2): 181–92.

Kelling, George, and William Souza, Jr. 2001. "Do Police Matter? An Analysis of the Impact of New York City's Police Reforms." New York: The Manhattan Institute (December).

Kennedy, David M. 1997. "Guns and Violence: Pulling Levers: Chronic Offenders, High-Crime Settings, and a Theory of Prevention." *Valparaiso Law Review* 31 (2): 449–80.

Kennedy, David, Anthony A. Braga, Anne M. Piehl, and Elin J. Waring. 2001. *Reducing Gun Violence: The Boston Gun Project's Operation Ceasefire.* NCJ 18874. National Institute of Justice, U.S. Department of Justice.

LaFree, Gary. 1998. *Losing Legitimacy: Street Crime and the Decline of Social Institutions in America.* Westview Press.

Levitt, Steven D. 1997. "Using Electoral Cycles in Police Hiring to Estimate the Effect of Police on Crime." *American Economic Review* 87 (3): 270–90.

———. 2001. "Deterrence." In *Crime: Public Policies for Crime Control,* edited by James Q. Wilson and Joan Petersilia, 435–50. Oakland, Calif.: Institute for Contemporary Studies.

Livingston, Debra. 1999. "Police Reform and the Department of Justice: An Essay on Accountability." *Buffalo Criminal Law Review* 2 (2): 815–57.

Long-Onnen, Jamie Rene. 2000. "Measures of Lethality and Intent in The Geographic Concentration of Gun Homicides: An Exploratory Analysis." Ph.D. dissertation, University of Maryland at College Park.

Ludwig, Jens. 1998. "Concealed Gun-Carrying Laws and Violent Crime: Evidence from State Panel Data." *International Review of Law and Economics* 18: 239–54.

Ludwig, Jens, and Philip J. Cook. 2001. "The Benefits of Reducing Gun Violence: Evidence from Contingent-Valuation Survey Data." *Journal of Risk and Uncertainty* 22 (3): 207–26.

MacCoun, Robert, and Peter Reuter. 2001. *Drug War Heresies.* Cambridge University Press.

McGarrell, Edmund F., Steven Chermak, and Alexander Weiss. 1999. Reducing Firearms Violence through Directed Police Patrol: Final Report on the Evaluation of the Indianapolis Police Department's Directed Patrol Project. Report submitted to the National Institute of Justice, U.S. Department of Justice.

McGarrell, Edmund F., Steven Chermak, Alexander Weiss, and Jeremy Wilson. 2001. "Reducing Firearms Violence through Directed Police Patrol." *Criminology and Public Policy* 1 (1): 119–48.

Nagin, Daniel. 1998. "Criminal Deterrence Research: A Review of the Evidence and a Research Agenda for the Outset of the 21st Century." In *Crime and Justice: A Review of Research, Volume 23,* edited by Michael Tonry, 1–42. University of Chicago Press.

Sampson, Robert J., and Jacqueline Cohen. 1988. "Deterrent Effects of the Police on Crime: A Replication and Theoretical Extension." *Law and Society Review* 22 (1): 163–89.

Sampson, Robert J., and Stephen W. Raudenbush. 1999. "Systematic Social Observation of Public Spaces: A New Look at Disorder in Urban Neighborhoods." *American Journal of Sociology* 105 (3): 603–51.

Shaw, James W. 1995. "Community Policing against Guns: Public Opinion of the Kansas City Gun Experiment." *Justice Quarterly* 12 (4): 695–710.

Sherman, Lawrence W. 2000. "Gun Carrying and Homicide Prevention." *Journal of the American Medical Association* 283 (9): 1193–95.

———. 2001. "Reducing Gun Violence: What Works, What Doesn't, What's Promising." *Criminal Justice* 1 (1): 11–25.

Sherman, Lawrence W., and Dennis P. Rogan. 1995. "Effects of Handgun Seizures on Gun Violence: 'Hot Spots' Patrol in Kansas City." *Justice Quarterly* 12 (4): 673–93.

Sherman, Lawrence W., James W. Shaw, and Dennis P. Rogan. 1995. *The Kansas City Gun Experiment*. NCJ 150855. National Institute of Justice. U.S. Department of Justice.

Silverman, Eli. 1999. *The NYPD Battles Crime*. Northeastern University Press.

Skogan Wesley, and Susan M. Hartnett. 1997. *Community Policing, Chicago Style*. Westview Press.

Smith, Jeffrey, and Petra Todd. Forthcoming. "Does Matching Overcome Lalonde's Critique of Nonexperimental Estimators?" *Journal of Econometrics*.

Tyler, Tom R., and Yuen J. Huo. 2003. *Trust and the Rule of Law*. New York: Russell Sage Foundation Press.

Villaveces, Andres, Peter Cummings, Victoria E. Espitia, Thomas D. Koepsell, Barbara McKnight, and Arthur L. Kellerman. 2000. "Effect of a Ban on Carrying Firearms on Homicide Rates in 2 Colombian Cities." *Journal of the American Medical Association* 283: 1205–09.

Weitzer, Ronald. 2000. "Racialized Policing: Residents' Perceptions in Three Neighborhoods." *Law and Society Review* 34 (1): 129–55.

STEVEN RAPHAEL
JENS LUDWIG

7 | Prison Sentence Enhancements: The Case of Project Exile

Unlike gun control, enhanced prison penalties for gun crimes enjoy widespread support from all sides of the U.S. gun policy debate. Prison sentence enhancements have the potential to reduce gun violence by incapacitating individuals who have been convicted of gun crimes and deterring such crimes in the future. Moreover, such a policy does not affect the ability of law-abiding adults to keep guns for self-defense or recreation.

Given this conceptual and political appeal, the Bush administration has made enhanced prison penalties a centerpiece of its efforts to address gun violence. With a proposed budget of $550 million over two years, one important objective of the administration's Project Safe Neighborhoods is to enhance the penalties for gun crime by diverting those who have committed federal firearm offenses into federal court, where prison sentences are typically more severe than the ones found in most state systems.[1]

We wish to thank Jordan Leiter, Robyn Thiemann, and Eric Younger for assistance and Anthony Braga, Jeff Fagan, Peter Greenwood, Steve Levitt, Lois Mock, Lawrence Sherman, and seminar participants at the Brookings Institution and the University of Pennsylvania for valuable comments. This research was prepared with support from the Annie E. Casey and Smith Richardson foundations and the National Institute of Justice.

1. The two-year budget for Project Safe Neighborhoods includes $24.3 million to hire 207 new assistant U.S. attorneys devoted to prosecuting firearms cases, and $125 million in grants to local agencies to hire gun prosecutors (White House, press releases, 2001). See also "Bush Pitches $550 Million Fight Against Gun Crime," CNN, May 14, 2001; "Ashcroft Says Justice to Target Illegal Firearms," David Morgan, Reuters, August 27, 2001.

The Bush administration's proposal to prosecute more firearm cases in the federal system is based on Richmond, Virginia's, Project Exile, first announced on February 28, 1997. This program has since been declared a dramatic success by observers from across the political spectrum including the National Rifle Association, Handgun Control, and Virginians Against Gun Violence, as well as news outlets such as the *New York Times* and the *Washington Post* and even President George W. Bush.[2] These claims for Exile's success stem from the 40 percent reduction in gun homicides observed in Richmond from 1997 to 1998.

Despite this widespread acclaim, some skeptics have questioned the effectiveness of Project Exile, pointing out that homicides increased in Richmond in the last ten months of 1997 following the program's announcement. In fact, the Richmond homicide rate increased by 40 percent between 1996 and 1997. Despite these conflicting views of Project Exile's impact and the substantial policy interest in the program, surprisingly Project Exile has to date not been subject to a formal evaluation.

This chapter presents what we believe to be the first rigorous examination of the impact of Richmond's Project Exile on homicide and other crimes. We show that critiques of Exile focusing on the increase in homicide rates during the last ten months of 1997 may be misplaced, given that the number of federal gun convictions in Richmond did not show any appreciable change between 1996 and 1997. At the same time, claims that Exile was successful based on the reduction between 1997 and 1998 in Richmond are also misguided, since Richmond had an unusually high murder rate in 1997 and, more generally, crime declined throughout the United States over this period.

We argue that the reduction in Richmond's gun homicide rates surrounding the implementation of Project Exile was not unusual and that almost all of the observed decrease probably would have occurred even in the absence of the program. This conclusion is based on a very strong empirical regularity observed in city-level homicide rates: cities with the largest increases in homicide rates during the 1980s and early 1990s also experienced the largest decreases during the late 1990s. Richmond happened to be among the handful of cities that experienced unusually large increases in homicide rates during the 1980s. Consequently, nearly all of the reduction in murder rates experienced by Richmond following Project Exile may be attributed to this large increase in gun homicides occurring

---

2. See, for example, Elaine Shannon, "Have Gun? Will Travel," *Time Magazine,* August 16, 1999, p. 154; "Remarks by the President on Project Safe Neighborhoods," White House, Office of the Press Secretary, May 14, 2001; Michael Janofsky, "New Program in Richmond Is Credited for Getting Handguns Off Streets," *New York Times,* February 10, 1999.

before Exile's implementation. We also find nearly identical results for trends in other felony crimes.

In principle, comparisons of crime trends across cities may yield misleading inferences about Exile's effects if unmeasured factors specific to Richmond would have driven the city's rates up even further in the late 1990s in the absence of the program. We address this potential omitted-variables problem in part by examining how the gap between adult and juvenile homicide arrest rates change in Richmond over time compared with other cities. Typically only adults are eligible for the "felon-in-possession" prosecutions that form the heart of the Exile intervention. Juveniles typically do not have prior felony records and should be largely unaffected by the program, thereby serving as a within-city control group against which one would compare adult homicide arrest rates. Since both adults and juveniles should be exposed to many of the same city-specific factors that affect local crime rates, how much the decline in adult arrest rates exceeds the decline in juvenile arrest rates provides an alternative estimate of the impact of Project Exile.

In fact, we find that adult homicide arrest rates increase relative to juvenile arrest rates in Richmond during the period surrounding the program's implementation. In contrast, adult arrest rates decline on average in relation to juvenile rates in other cities. These findings taken together call into question the empirical evidence commonly offered as evidence of Exile's impact.

We also present a more general analysis of the relationship between federal prosecutions of gun cases and gun homicide. This approach uses data from the federal courts to identify the exact Exile "dose" experienced by Richmond and other cities that adopted Exile-like programs in each year. For the years 1994 through 1999, we matched information on the annual number of felon-in-possession and felony-gun-use cases prosecuted by each U.S. Attorney's office to the cities corresponding to each U.S. Attorney district. We then used standard panel data techniques that allowed us to control for unmeasured city fixed effects and test for contemporaneous and lagged effects of the number of felons prosecuted in the federal system on city-level gun homicide rates. Consistent with our findings for Richmond's Project Exile, this analysis yields little evidence of a reduced-form relationship between the number of federal firearm prosecutions and city-level murder rates.

Project Exile: Design and Objectives

The heart of the Project Exile program consists of the coordinated efforts of Richmond law enforcement and the regional U.S. Attorney's office to prosecute in federal courts all felon-in-possession-of-a-firearm (FIP) cases, drugs-gun cases, and domestic violence–gun cases, regardless of the number.[3] Exile also includes training for local law enforcement on federal statutes and search and seizure issues, a public relations campaign to increase community involvement in crime fighting, and a massive advertising campaign. The advertising campaign is intended to send the clear message of zero tolerance for gun offenses and to inform potential offenders of the swift and certain federal sentence.[4]

Project Exile is effectively a sentence enhancement program since the federal penalties for these firearm offenses are more severe than those in effect in Virginia at the time Exile was announced in 1997. The disparity between the federal and state systems may be particularly dramatic for FIP convictions, for which the federal penalty is five years with no chance of early release, and as we document below, most of the additional federal convictions under Exile appear to be FIP cases. Besides the differences in prison terms, gun offenders diverted into the federal system are denied bail at a higher rate than those handled in state courts and serve time in a federal penitentiary that is likely to be located out of state.[5] Both aspects of the program are thought to impose additional costs on offenders. In sum, the primary criminal-justice change introduced by Project Exile appears to be an increase in the prison penalties for carrying guns by those with prior felony convictions.

The potential public safety effects of programs such as Project Exile are suggested by previous empirical research on the incapacitation and deterrent effects of incarceration more generally. Incapacitation occurs when individuals who would engage in criminal activity were they free to roam the streets are prevented from doing so because they are incarcerated. The best available research suggests that incapacitation effects may be considerable for the current population of prisoners,[6] although the average effect may decline with expansions in the prison population if the rate of criminality declines for the marginal inmate.[7]

While disentangling the effects of deterrence from that of incapacitation is difficult, several studies suggest that the threat of punishment does seem to deter criminal behavior. For example, economists Ian Ayres and Steven Levitt find that areas where a larger fraction of cars are equipped with the antitheft radio

3. U.S. Code Title 18, 922(g) (1); U.S. Code Title 18, 924 (c). In principle the local U.S. Attorney for Richmond also has the option of prosecuting those who sell a handgun or ammunition to juveniles [U.S. Code Title 18, 924 (x)], although in practice federal prosecutors rarely take such cases, in part because the penalty for the first conviction of this offense is simply probation.

4. For a detailed description of Project Exile, see the summary statement available from the U.S. Attorney's Office for the Eastern District of Virginia.

5. Schiller (1998).

6. Levitt (1996).

7. Donohue and Siegelman (1998).

transmitter "Lojack" also experience lower rates of auto theft, consistent with a substantial deterrent effect on car thieves.[8] Additional support for the deterrence hypothesis comes from findings that areas with more police appear to experience lower rates of crime, and even by evidence that the presence of additional referees on the sporting field reduces the number of infractions.[9]

Despite evidence for incapacitation and deterrence effects from imprisonment in general, the available evidence on the effects of specific sentence enhancement laws is more mixed. David McDowall, Colin Loftin, and Brian Wiersema use before-after comparisons and find that areas enacting sentence enhancements for firearm offenses experience a decline in gun crime following implementation of these laws.[10] However, in the absence of information about how crime changed in comparison areas that did not enact sentence enhancements, one cannot be sure that the observed crime reductions are attributable to the new sentencing policy. Consistent with this concern, Thomas Marvell and Carl Moody find that crime trends in states that implement sentence enhancements do not decline relative to other states.[11]

The most compelling effort to date to isolate the causal effects of sentence enhancements comes from Daniel Kessler and Steven Levitt, who analyze the effects of the enhancements introduced by Proposition 8 in California.[12] The authors examine how the difference in crime rates between offenses that are covered by Proposition 8 versus those that are not changes over time before and after introduction of the new policy, and how this change over time compares to what was observed in the rest of the United States during this period. The analysis thus isolates the effect of those factors, specific to California when Proposition 8 was introduced, that affected only those crimes covered by the new law. The authors find a short-term reduction in crimes covered by the enhancements of around 4 percent (presumably the result of the law's deterrent effect on criminals). Crime rates continue to decline over time owing to the additional incapacitation effect that arises from incarcerating prisoners for a longer period.[13] However,

8. Ayres and Levitt (1998).

9. For studies on police presence and crime, see Marvell and Moody (1996); Levitt (1997); Corman and Mocan (2000). See also McCormick and Tollison (1984). For a more comprehensive review of the deterrence literature see Nagin (1998) and Levitt (2001).

10. McDowall, Loftin, and Wiersema (1992).

11. Marvell and Moody (1995).

12. Kessler and Levitt (1999).

13. Since those criminals whose sentences are enhanced by Proposition 8 would have been incarcerated in any case, the longer prison sentences caused by the new California sentencing system exert a deterrent but not an additional incapacitation effect on crime in the short run. The only incapacitation effects from the new law occur when those prisoners sentenced under Proposition 8 have served out the sentence that they would have received under the old regime and spend the additional years in prison as a result of the new sentencing system.

because the analysis by Kessler and Levitt does not focus on gun crimes, the implications for Project Exile are somewhat unclear.

Uncertainty about the effectiveness of sentence enhancements extends to whether such policies are cost effective. Philip Cook and Jens Ludwig show that if Project Exile yielded crime reductions of the same magnitude as California's Proposition 8—15 to 20 percent in the steady state—then the program would be enormously cost effective.[14] In this case the program's cost of $40 million through the first two years would yield a reduction in gun violence that is worth approximately $150 to $240 million to society. However, others have argued that the sentence enhancements generated by California's "three-strikes" law are no more cost effective than social programs that reduce crime.[15]

Whether Project Exile reduces crime in practice and whether any such crime reductions yield benefits in excess of the program's costs are empirical questions, to which we now turn.

Homicide in Richmond during the 1990s

Since the announcement of Project Exile in February 1997, several indicators of criminal activity in Richmond have improved substantially. For example, there has been a decrease in the number of guns seized by the police, a pattern often interpreted as a decreased propensity to carry guns among felons and those engaged in activities that can be prosecuted under Exile. The volume of crime tips from residents has also increased. But the outcome measure that has received the most attention, and also serves as the primary focus of this evaluation, is the city's homicide rate.

Gun Homicide in Richmond

Figure 7-1 presents the trends in annual homicides, gun homicides, and non-gun homicides that are the foundation for the perceived success of Project Exile in Richmond.[16] The numbers offered as evidence of Exile's effectiveness by the

14. Cook and Ludwig (2000, p. 128).
15. Greenwood and others (1994, 1996); Greenwood (2002).
16. We calculate homicide rates by weapon using the Combined Supplemental Homicide Reports (SHR) files covering the period from 1976 to 1999. To aggregate Federal Bureau of Investigation Organized Reporting Units up the level of individual cities, we use a special cross-walk file that maps the link between law enforcement districts and Federal Information Processing Standards geographic boundaries. To calculate homicide rates, we use place-level population data from the U.S. Census Bureau rather than the population data available in the SHR file, owing to some observed discrepancies for certain cities.

Figure 7-1. *All Homicides, Gun Homicides and Other Homicides per 100,000 Residents in Richmond, Virginia, 1990–99*

Rate per 100,000 residents

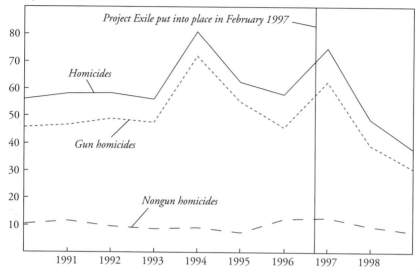

U.S. Attorney's Office for the Eastern District of Virginia and many others are calculated using the change in homicides occurring between 1997 and 1998. In this two-year period, the homicide rate declined by 35 percent while the gun homicide rate declined by nearly 40 percent, from 62 to 39 per 100,000.

However, offering this two-year period as evidence of the program's impact is problematic for several reasons. First, the program was (at least officially) in place for most of 1997, a year in which the homicide rate increased dramatically over the previous year. Hence, one could easily choose the two-year period from 1996 to 1997 to estimate the program's impact and conclude that Exile drastically increased homicide rates. Deciding which year should be counted as the first post-Exile period is crucial to any evaluation of the program's effects.

As seen in figure 7-2, the number of firearm prosecutions secured by the local U.S. Attorney's office for Richmond did not show any noticeable increase until 1998, when the number of such convictions more than tripled compared with the 1997 total (with most of the change accounted for by additional FIP convictions). In principle Exile may still have had some effect on crime in 1997 through an "announcement effect," in which the publicity surrounding the program changes the expectations that criminals have about the penalties for

Figure 7-2. *The Annual Number of Felon-in-Possession and Felony Gun-Use Convictions Prosecuted, Eastern District of Virginia, 1994–99*[a]

Number of convictions

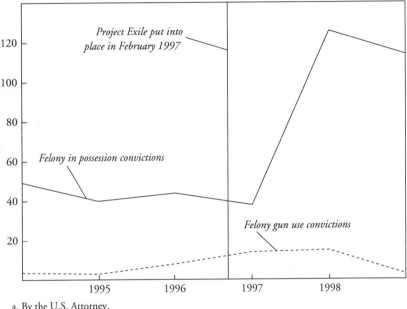

a. By the U.S. Attorney.

gun offenses. It is also possible that word about Project Exile spread among Richmond's criminal population following the initial wave of federal indictments (which may have occurred in 1997) rather than convictions (which seem to have started in 1998). However, we accept the argument that actual convictions under Exile are likely to be an important part of the program's deterrent effect and thus choose 1998 as the first year in which Exile is considered in full effect. The decision to count 1998 as the first post-Exile year has the effect of *increasing* the chances that we find a program effect.

Even with 1998 chosen as the first Exile year, whether the program has been successful is not obvious from figure 7-1. The large year-to-year changes in homicide rates observed in Richmond suggest that much of the increase observed in 1997 may reflect transitory factors that would have disappeared anyway. Using this unusual year as a base for calculating the change is bound to inflate the apparent impact of the program. Moreover, the patterns in figure 7-1 seem to indicate that, the year 1997 aside, homicide rates in Richmond were trending downward even before the launch of Project Exile. To the extent that the post-Exile declines simply reflect the continuation of trend, the

Table 7-1. *Change in the Gun Homicide Rate Compared with the Nongun Homicide Rate for Richmond during Project Exile*

Time and difference	Gun homicide rate	Nongun homicide rate	Gun minus nongun
1993–94	59.76	8.32	51.44
1995–96	50.55	9.19	41.36
1998–99	34.92	6.82	28.10
[1] Difference 1998–99 – 1995–96	−15.63	−2.36	−13.26
(percent change)	(−30.9)	(−25.7)	(−5.2)
[2] Difference: 1995–96 – 1993–94	−9.22	0.87	−10.09
(percent change)	(−15.4)	(10.5)	(−25.9)
[1] − [2] (difference in percent changes)	−6.41	−3.23	−3.17
	(−15.5)	(−36.2)	(20.7)

Source: Tabulations based on extractions from FBI (1976–99).

raw numbers offered in support of the program are likely to overstate Exile's impact.

To address these concerns, table 7-1 presents a number of calculations based on the homicide rates displayed in figure 7-1. Since Project Exile is designed to deter the use and illegal possession of firearms, the table and the following discussion focus primarily on gun homicide rates. Because of the possibility of substitution from gun to nongun violence, a reduction in gun homicide is a necessary but not sufficient condition for a program impact on the overall homicide rate. However, given that the large majority of homicides are committed with guns, we find similar findings when we focus on all homicides, gun and nongun together. To eliminate some of the year-to-year variation in gun homicides, the table presents the average annual firearm homicide rates for the three two-year periods 1993–94, 1995–96, and 1998–99. To avoid the problems associated with 1997, we omit this year. We derive our baseline estimate of the effect of Project Exile by calculating the change in average annual gun homicide rates from 1995–96 to 1998–99.

As seen in table 7-1, between 1995–96 and 1998–99 the gun homicide rate declined by 15.6 homicides per 100,000 residents. This is equivalent to a 31 percent decline in gun homicides (a figure somewhat smaller than the 40 percent decline between 1997 and 1998). However, table 7-1 also shows that gun homicides declined by 15 percent from 1993–94 to 1995–96, before Exile went into effect. If we assume that this trend in Richmond's homicide rate would have continued even in the absence of Exile, then a "difference-in-difference" calculation (last row, table 7-1) suggests that the decline attributable to Exile above and beyond the preexisting trend is approximately 6 gun homicides per 100,000 residents, or 15 percent.[17]

To be sure, it is impossible to assess whether the trend occurring earlier in the decade would have continued during the late 1990s in the absence of Project Exile. However, the following evidence suggests that the declines observed for Richmond around the time of Exile were not unusual, given the large increase in Richmond's homicide rates during the 1980s. For now, it is sufficient to say that more reasonable estimates of the potential impact of Project Exile on gun homicide rates range from around one-quarter to two-thirds of the program effects that have been claimed in the past and cited in popular press accounts (6 to 15 per 100,000 versus 23 per 100,000).

Richmond versus Other Cities

Although these calculations are smaller than the effects claimed by program proponents, the declines in Richmond are still large. Any program that can claim to reduce homicide rates by 15 to 30 percent is likely to be worth investing in and merits the attention of policymakers and researchers. Before concluding that the program has had such impacts, however, one should consider what happened to murder rates in other cities where Exile-type programs were not put into place. It is entirely possible that gun homicide rates declined uniformly across cities, which would indicate that the changes observed for Richmond are not unusual. Moreover, it may be that city-level variation in homicide rates is so great that changes in even two-year averages such as those depicted in table 7-1 are not uncommon.

Figures 7-3A and 7-3B begin to address these concerns by graphing the annual gun homicide rates in levels (figure 7-3A) and natural logs (figure 7-3B) for the period 1990 to 1999 for Richmond and for several groups of comparison cities. Besides gun homicide data for Richmond, each figure presents time series data for the ten cities with the highest average gun homicide rates during the 1990s, for other cities in Virginia and for cities located in those states that share a border with Virginia, for all cities in states on the eastern seaboard, and for cities from across the country that are about the same size as Richmond (defined as

17. In the U.S. Attorney's assessment of the percentage impact of Project Exile on murder rates it is stated that the program caused a nearly 40 percent decline in homicide rates. The averaged change between 1995–96 and 1998–99 shows a smaller change of approximately 30 percent. To calculate an estimate of the percentage change under the assumption that the 1993–94 to 1995–96 change reflects an underlying trend, we would need to calculate what the murder rate would have been in 1998–99 in the absence of Project Exile by subtracting the earlier change from the 1995–96 murder rate. Based on this assumption, the murder rate during 1998–99 would have been 41.33 in the absence of Project Exile. The estimated effect of a 6.4 per 100,000 decline in gun homicide rates constitutes 15.5 percent of this base. Hence, as with the absolute changes, the implicit percentage changes implied by the alternative estimates in table 7-1 are considerably more modest.

Figure 7-3A. *Gun Homicides per 100,000 Residents in Richmond and Other Regions*[a]

Rate per 100,000 residents

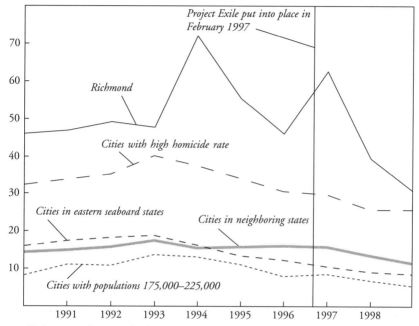

a. "Other regions" means other high-crime cities, cities in states surrounding Virginia, cities on the eastern seaboard, and cities with comparable populations.

those with residential populations between 175,000 and 225,000).[18] The gun homicide rate levels presented in figure 7-3A provide comparisons of the absolute change in gun homicide rates in Richmond versus the comparison groups. Changes in the natural log of homicide rates (graphed in figure 7-3B) are indicative of the relative percentage changes in gun homicide rates for each series.[19]

Figures 7-3A and 7-3B clearly highlight the unusually high homicide rates that Richmond has suffered throughout the 1990s. Figure 7-3A also indicates that the decline in homicide rates in Richmond around the time of Exile also occurred to some extent in other cities. On one hand, the absolute drop in Richmond homicide rates appears to exceed the drop experienced in the other high murder rate cities and those observed for the other comparison groups of cities. On the

18. Richmond is omitted from all comparison groups. Between 1990 and 1999, the population of Richmond varied between approximately 203,000 and 190,000 residents.

19. The change in the natural log of a variable is approximately equal to the percentage change in the variable.

Figure 7-3B. *The Natural Log of Gun Homicides per 100,000 Residents in Richmond and Other Regions*[a]

Rate per 100,000 residents

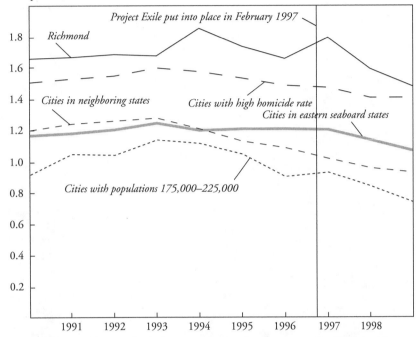

a. "Other regions" means other high-crime cities, cities in states surrounding Virginia, cities on the eastern seaboard, and cities with comparable populations.

other hand, figure 7-3B shows that year-to-year movements in the natural log of gun homicide rates around the time of Project Exile's introduction are comparable in Richmond and the comparison cities. Hence, while the absolute change in Richmond gun homicide rates surrounding the implementation of Project Exile is distinct, the relative (or percentage) change in gun homicide rates is comparable to those observed in the various comparison groups of cities.

This last point can be seen more clearly in table 7-2, which presents annual average gun homicide rates for Richmond and the four comparison groups of cities from figures 7-3A and 7-3B. The first two columns present the average annual gun homicide rate for the periods 1995–96 and 1998–99, the third column presents the absolute change in gun homicide rates, while the final column presents the percentage change in gun homicide rates. The absolute changes in the third column indicate that the change in gun homicide rates for Richmond omitting 1997 (−15.63) was considerably larger than the comparable changes

Table 7-2. *Change in Gun Homicides Rates in Richmond and Other Regions, 1995–96 to 1998–99*[a]

Group of cities	Gun homicide rate		Change	Percent change
	1995–96	*1998–99*		
Richmond	50.55	34.92	−15.63	−31
High homicide	32.50	25.88	−6.62	−20
Neighboring states	16.24	12.80	−3.44	−21
Eastern seaboard	12.92	8.85	−4.07	−32
Comparable populations	9.63	6.28	−3.35	−35

Source: Tabulations based on extractions from FBI (1976–99). The city groups correspond to those used in constructing figures 7-3A and 7-3B.

a. "Other regions" means other high-crime cities, cities in states surrounding Virginia, cities on the eastern seaboard, and cities with comparable populations, 1995–96 to 1998–99.

observed in all four comparison groups (ranging from −3.35 to −6.62). The relative changes in gun homicide rates, however, are comparable. Although gun homicides declined by 31 percent, the declines in the comparison groups of cities range from 20 to 35 percent.

When we expand the set of comparison cities to include all cities with populations of 100,000 or more with complete data, the findings are similar.[20] Figure 7-4A shows the number of cities (shown on the vertical axis) that experienced changes in gun homicide rates of various magnitudes from 1995–96 to 1998–99 (given on the horizontal axis), ranging from very large declines on the left to some modest increase in homicides over this period on the right. The graph shows that the change in gun homicide rates in Richmond around the time of Exile is larger in absolute value (that is, "more negative") than what was observed in most cities during this period.

However, as before, the story is somewhat different when we focus on changes in the natural log of gun homicide rates (again, approximately equal to the percentage change in gun homicide rates), as seen in figure 7-4B. Here, Richmond's decline is still larger than average but is less of an outlier when compared with the overall distribution of proportional changes. Put differently, the proportional change in Richmond's gun homicide rate is within the bounds of variation observed among other cities.

Taken at face value, the patterns discussed above are not inconsistent with a real effect of Project Exile on the number of homicides committed with firearms. Despite the comparable proportional declines in gun homicide rates displayed

20. Over this period, Richmond's population ranged between approximately 190,000 and 200,000. We dropped the city of Gary, Indiana, because the 1996 homicide total from the SHR was approximately one-half the number of homicides reported in published Uniform Crime Report, thus creating the false impression of a sharp increase in homicide rates during the late 1990s for this city.

Figure 7-4A. *Histogram of the City-Level Changes in Gun Homicide Rates, 1995–96 to 1998–99*

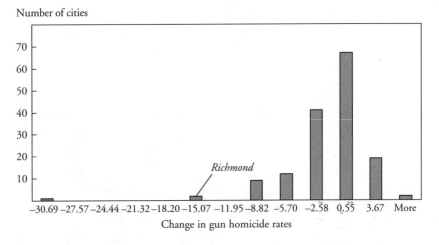

Figure 7-4B. *Histogram of the Change in the Natural Log of City-Level Gun Homicide Rates, 1995–96 to 1998–99*

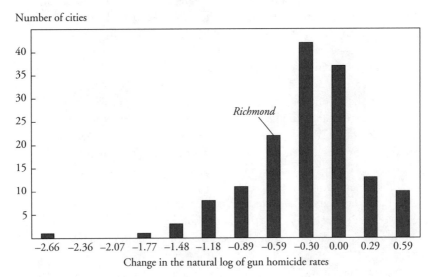

in figure 7-4B, the absolute reduction in gun homicides observed in Richmond was quite large and outside of the range of variation observed in other cities. However, we argue that the unusually large absolute declines observed in Richmond around the time of Exile are less "unusual" than the comparison in figure 7-4A seems to suggest.

Reassessing Exile: Accounting for Initial City Conditions

As already noted, two basic facts lend preliminary support for an effect of Project Exile on homicide rates. First, the pre-post absolute decline observed for Richmond was larger on average than the comparable changes for other cities. Second, the size of the decline was such that it exceeded the range of variation observed among other cities. While the same cannot be said for the proportional changes in gun homicide rates, the absolute changes provide a provocative comparison. However, these simple comparisons fail to account for the crucial role of Richmond's initial conditions in predicting future changes in city homicide rates.

Besides suffering among the highest urban homicide rates in the nation, Richmond also experienced unusually large *increases* in homicide rates during the decade or so preceding the implementation of Project Exile. These initial conditions carry important implications for our evaluation because those cities with the highest homicide levels during the early 1990s, and with the largest increases in homicide prior to this period, also experienced the largest decreases during the late 1990s. This suggests that the pre-post Exile change in homicides observed for Richmond may largely have been a function of the run-up in homicide rates during earlier periods.

The Relationship between Earlier and Later Changes in Homicide Rates

Why might we expect an inverse relationship between decreases in homicide rates during the late 1990s and increases occurring during the late 1980s and early 1990s? One possibility might be that the underlying factors causing the large increases in homicide rates during the 1980s such as the violence associated with the introduction of crack cocaine ran their course, and hence murder rates were bound to decline.[21] Another possibility might be that the incapacitation effects associated with the massive increase in incarceration rates may have disproportionately affected areas (or cities) with high crime rates.[22] A third source lies in the possibility that many homicide victims may themselves be

21. Blumstein (1995a).
22. Levitt (1996).

among the population of potential perpetrators.[23] To the extent that this is the case, a rash of homicides would be followed by a reduction in homicide rates, as the pool of likely offenders is reduced.

Regardless of the underlying causes, the implication of this empirical regularity for evaluating the impact of Project Exile is clear: to some degree the decline in homicide rates observed in Richmond was to be expected. Hence a careful evaluation of the program's impact requires taking into account earlier changes in the homicide rates.

Figures 7-5A and 7-5B provide more formal evidence of the relationship between later and earlier changes in city-level homicide rates during the 1980s and 1990s. Figure 7-5A plots each city's change in gun homicide rates from 1995–96 to 1998–99 (vertical axis) against the city's change over the prior decade, 1985–86 to 1995–96, on the horizontal axis. Figure 7-5B shows the comparable scatter plot for the same changes in the natural logarithm of gun homicide rates. Each figure includes fitted linear regression lines (along with the estimated equation) that summarize the overall relationships between the homicide changes across time periods. In addition, the Richmond data point is explicitly identified.

For Richmond, the figures also provide the standardized residual from each regression, defined as the fitted residual (the differences between the actual pre-post Exile change in homicide rates and the change predicted by the regression line) divided by the standard error of the regression (the summary measure of the amount of variation around the regression line observed for the sample). A negative residual for Richmond that is large (in absolute value) relative to the regression's standard error (for example, at least twice the standard error) would provide evidence of an effect of Project Exile.

Both scatter plots in figure 7-5 provide strong evidence of a negative relationship between earlier and later changes in homicide rates—that is, areas that experience larger increases in homicide rates initially go on to experience larger reductions thereafter. This relationship is expressed more formally by the fact that the regression coefficient relating previous homicide changes to later homicide changes is in both figures negative and highly statistically significant.[24]

In light of these findings, Richmond's experience during the 1990s does not appear to be unusual. As seen in figure 7-5A, based on the fitted regression line the increase of approximately 22 gun homicides per 100,000 residents experienced by Richmond during the late 1980s and early 1990s is predicted to cause

23. There seems to be considerable overlap between the populations of potential offenders and victims: the large majority of both groups have prior criminal records. See Kennedy, Piehl, and Braga (1996); McGonigal and others (1993); Schwab and others (1999); Kates and Polsby (2000).

24. The slope coefficient in figure 7-5A indicates that a one-unit increase in overall homicide rates between 1985–86 and 1995–96 is associated with a 0.48 decrease in gun homicide rates during the pre-post Exile period, while the comparable figure for gun homicide in figure 7-5B is 0.53.

Figure 7-5A. *Scatter Plot of the Pre-Post Exile Change in Gun Homicide Rates,*
Against the Change during the Prior Decade

Change in gun homicide rates, 1998–99 – 1995–96

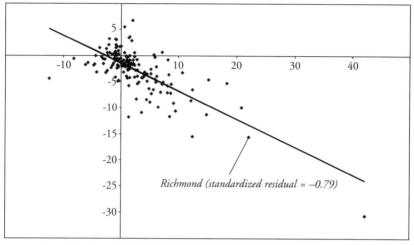

Change in gun homicide rates, 1995–96 – 1985–86

Note: Change (1998–99 – 1995–96) = − 1.48 − 0.3 * change (1995–96 – 1985–86);
$$(-5.76)\,(-13.15)$$

$R^2 = 0.53.$ *t* statistics in parentheses.

a decline in gun homicide rates following Project Exile of 13.3 per 100,000—
roughly 85 percent of the observed decline of 15.6. Moreover, the residual decline of 2.3 is less than the standard error of the regression (as is evidenced by
the small standardized residual).

Figure 7-5B shows that when we focus on the log of the gun homicide rate,
the proportional declines in gun homicide rates in Richmond following Exile
are fully explained by the large proportional increases that occurred before
Exile's implementation. In fact, the regression lines in figure 7-5B predict that
Richmond would have experienced an even *larger* proportional decline in homicide without Project Exile (as is evidenced by the fact that the Richmond data
point lies above the regression line). We obtain similar findings when we focus
on the overall homicide rate rather than restricting our attention to gun homicides only, or calculate the regression lines weighting each data point by the
city's mid-1990s population.

To summarize, the large increase in homicide rates occurring during the late
1980s in Richmond coupled with the inverse relationship between earlier and
later changes in homicide rates observed among other U.S. cities casts serious
doubt on the validity of previous claims about the effects of Project Exile. Ad-

Figure 7-5B. *Scatter Plot of the Pre-Post Exile Change in the Natural Log of Gun Homicide Rates, Against the Change during the Prior Decade*

Change in natural log of gun homicide rates, 1998–99 – 1995–96

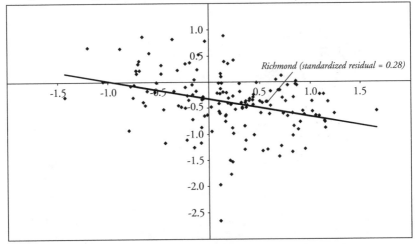

Change in natural log of gun homicide rates, 1995–96 – 1985–86

Note: Change (1998–99 – 1995–96) = –0.32 – 0.34 * change (1995–96 – 1985–86);
(–7.14) (–4.44)

$R^2 = 0.35$. *t* statistics in parentheses.

justing the decline in Richmond's homicide rates for the increase in murder rates during the 1980s leaves little residual decline in need of explanation.

Some Tests of Robustness

Perhaps the most obvious concern that one might raise in response to the results just presented is that we have included Richmond in the sample used to estimate the regression model. Since Richmond had a larger pre-Exile increase in homicide rates and experienced a large decline, perhaps the inclusion of this observation is causing us to overestimate the relationship between earlier and later changes in homicide rates and thus understate the effects of Exile. To assess whether this criticism is important, we reran the regressions for the changes in the level of gun homicides with Richmond omitted and then calculated a fitted residual for Richmond based on these alternative regression results. Again, nearly all of the decline observed for Richmond is explained by the prior increase in homicide rates. Moreover, the residual decline is small relative to the regression standard error, indicating no evidence of an impact of Project Exile.

For our analysis of the proportional changes in gun homicide rates (figure 7-5B), this criticism does not apply since the Richmond data point lies above the regression line. This indicates that omitting this observation would actually increase the slope coefficients (that is to say, make it more negative) and cause Project Exile to appear even less effective than it does in our figures.

A related criticism concerns the fact that in 1998 and 1999 several cities that are included in our sample implemented Exile-type programs. If these cities had unusually large increases in homicide rates before Exile's introduction that were then substantially reduced by the program, then part of the estimated relationship between earlier and later changes in homicide rates may reflect the impact of Exile programs. Again, this would lead us to attribute too much of the decline in Richmond to the prior increase in homicide rates and understate the impact of Project Exile.

To examine whether those cities that implemented an Exile-like program during our sample period experienced larger reductions in homicide than other cities, we re-estimated the regression models included in figure 7-5 with an additional dummy variable equal to one if the city has implemented a sentence enhancement program for gun crimes added to the model specification (results not shown).[25] In all cases the point estimate on the Exile variable is positive and not statistically significant, consistent with the idea that these programs have no measurable effect on homicide.[26]

Some might argue that despite the popular attention devoted to homicides as the outcome measure of choice for Project Exile, given the relative infrequency of homicides (even in a relatively violent city such as Richmond) it is more realistic to expect a program impact on other, more common types of crime. To address this concern, we replicated the analyses shown above using annual county-level crime and arrest data from the FBI's Uniform Crime Reports (UCR) system. Here, we restrict the sample of counties to those containing each of the cities in our sample analyzed above.[27] Because of the well-known problems associated with the UCR, including variation across areas and time in victim reporting to police

25. Cities that implemented Exile-type programs during our sample (besides Richmond) include Oakland, Buffalo, Norfolk, Rochester, Atlanta, Chicago, Philadelphia, Pittsburgh, and Kansas City. One complication with identifying the list of Exile-type cities is that many cities call their programs "Exile" although they do not follow the same practice as in Richmond of diverting gun offenders from state to federal courts. At the same time some cities that do substantially increase the number of diversions may have different names for their programs that we may have missed. We address this problem in the next section by using data from local U.S. Attorney offices on the number of gun convictions per year to identify the Exile "dose" that each city experiences.

26. Another way to test this hypothesis is to calculate the ratio of each city's fitted residual to the city's actual or imputed error standard deviation; ratios that are negative and larger than two in absolute value are consistent with an effect of Exile to reduce homicide. None of the cities that we identify as having Exile-type programs had such residuals.

27. Since there are several instances in our city sample where more than one city is in a single county, this county-level data set has fewer observations (131 to be exact) than our city-level data set. The city of Richmond is separately identifiable in the county data.

Table 7-3. *Pre-Post Project Exile Changes in FBI Index of Crimes Compared with Changes in All Other Cities*[a]

Crime	Richmond residual[b]	Regression standard error[c]	Standardized residual[d]
Murder	−1.85	2.48	−0.75
Rape	−9.49	8.81	−1.08
Robbery	−67.51	80.47	−0.84
Assault	−104.04	104.34	−0.99
Burglary	−258.51	159.02	−1.62
Larceny	−259.79	417.27	−0.62
Auto theft	234.46	177.99	1.32
Arson	17.83	27.52	0.65

Source: Data come from county-level tabulations of FBI (1976–99).

a. Adjusted for pre–Project Exile changes in crime rates.

b. These figures are the fitted residuals for Richmond from a regression of the 1998–99 − 1995–96 change in the rate of the given crime on the 1995–96 − 1985–86 change.

c. These figures are the estimates of the regression standard error from regressions of the 1998–99 − 1995–96 change in the rate of the given crime on the 1995–96 − 1985–86 change.

d. The standardized residual is calculated by dividing the fitted residual for Richmond by the regression standard error.

and police reporting of crime data to the FBI, our UCR findings are far from definitive. Nevertheless, investigating the potential impact on other UCR "index" crimes provides a good robustness check to our analysis of murder rates.

Table 7-3 presents our analysis using the UCR crime data. The table presents three columns of information for each of the eight UCR index crimes. The first column presents the fitted residual from Richmond from a regression of the change in the crime rate from 1995–96 to 1998–99 (before and after Exile) on the change in crime rates from 1985–86 to 1995–96. The second column provides the regression standard error for each model while the third column presents the fitted residual for Richmond divided by the regression standard error (which we refer to as the standardized residual). For all crimes, the observed residual is small relative to the standard error of the regression. Hence there is little evidence in table 7-3 of an impact of Project Exile on any of the "part I" (serious) felonies recorded by the FBI.

The most important concern with our analysis is whether we are able to distinguish the effects of Project Exile from those of other unmeasured factors that drive crime trends over time at the local level. Our comparison of Richmond homicide trends to those of other cities is intended to address this concern. However, such comparisons may be invalid because of unobserved differences among cities in policing, age structure, and other factors likely to influence homicide rates.

Table 7-4. *Change in Homicide Arrests, Richmond and Other Large Counties, by Age, from 1995–96 to 1998*

Item	Change in all murder arrests	Change in adult murder arrest	Juvenile murder arrests	Adult change – juvenile change
All counties	−0.83	−0.74	−0.14	−0.60
Richmond	10.53	9.77	0.25	9.52
All counties less Richmond	−0.83	−0.74	−0.14	−0.60

Source: Data come from county-level tabulations of FBI (1976–99).

An alternative way to identify the effects of unmeasured factors would be to define a control group of offenders within the city of Richmond who are not subjected to the stipulations of Project Exile. With such a control group, one could compare offense rates (measured, for example, by homicide arrests) for this within-Richmond control group to offense rates for criminals who are subject to Exile's provisions. We pursue this strategy by comparing changes in juvenile homicide arrests (pre-post Exile) to changes in adult homicide arrests using county-level arrest data. The logic behind this comparison is based on the observation that juveniles will in general be ineligible for federal prosecution under Project Exile, since very few juveniles have been convicted of a felony in the adult criminal justice system. In other words, illegal gun possession by teens will not be eligible for federal prosecution under the "felon in possession" statute that seems to account for the large majority of Richmond's federal gun convictions (figure 7-2).

Table 7-4 presents the results of these calculations.[28] Tabulations of changes in homicide arrests per 100,000 residents are presented for all counties with population exceeding 100,000, Richmond, and all large counties excluding Richmond. The first column presents changes in all murder arrests. The second and third column present changes in adult murder arrests and juvenile murder arrests, respectively. Finally, the last column presents the difference between the change in adult murder arrests and the change in juvenile murder arrests.

The disaggregated arrest data from the UCR indicate that adult homicide arrests actually increased relative to juvenile homicide arrests in Richmond, pre-post Project Exile. Moreover, adult homicide arrests declined on average during the late 1990s for adults relative to juveniles for other counties with populations

28. In this instance, we use the change in arrests 1995–96 to 1998 as the key dependent variable rather than the change from 1995–96 to 1998–99 because arrest data by age are not yet available for 1999.

of 100,000 or more. Taken together these findings are not consistent with the idea that some intervention specific to Richmond—such as Project Exile—reduced crime rates among adults relative to juveniles.

Testing for an Impact of Federal Prosecutions Using Panel Data

Although the program implemented in Richmond entailed a host of efforts ranging from community outreach to new officer training, the main provision of Project Exile is the unlimited prosecution of those found to be in violation of federal gun laws by the regional U.S. Attorney's office. An alternative way to test the impact of this intervention is to directly examine the effects on homicide from increases in the number of federal firearm convictions secured by the local U.S. Attorney's office.

Relating federal gun convictions to homicide rates directly has several advantages. First, this strategy recognizes that the Exile "dose" that Richmond experiences is not the same during every year of the program's existence. The most notable example is the similarity of federal gun convictions between 1997 and 1996 in Richmond, even though Project Exile was officially announced in February 1997.

A second advantage of defining federal gun cases as the "treatment" of interest is that we can directly control for the fact that other cities may have copied Richmond and implemented Exile-style programs during the late 1990s; to the extent that these cities replicated Richmond's Project Exile faithfully, they will also experience an increase in federal firearm convictions. More generally, Project Exile is not the only or even the first concerted effort by law enforcement to use federal prosecutions of gun cases. In the early 1990s, the federal program Project Triggerlock was introduced to systematically prosecute in federal courts violent offenders that use firearms during drug offenses and certain violent offenses. The number of federal prosecutions under this program was curtailed somewhat by a 1995 Supreme Court decision ruling that defendants in drug-gun cases must have actively used the firearm in committing the offense to be charged in a federal court.[29] Nonetheless, a certain amount of activity of this sort is observed in all regional U.S. Attorney's offices.

To implement this analysis we assembled information on the number and type of convictions secured for each of the local U.S. Attorney's offices throughout the country for each year from 1994 to 1999. We focus initially on measuring changes in the number of felon-in-possession-of-a-firearm (FIP) convictions, since many

29. The case *Bailey* v. *the United States* along with a discussion of trends in federal firearm prosecutions is discussed in Scalia (2000).

Table 7-5. *Panel Data Regression Models of the Percent Change in Gun Murder Rates Caused by a Percent Change in the Number of Felon-in-Possession Cases*

Item	(1)	(2)	(3)	(4)
Change, in possession	−0.013	−0.012	. . .	. . .
	(0.021)	(0.021)		
Change, uses a firearm	−0.029	0.005	. . .	. . .
	(0.063)	(0.064)		
Change, in possession lagged	. . .	. . .	0.007	0.003
			(0.023)	(0.023)
Change, used a firearm lagged	. . .	. . .	−0.058	−0.093
			(0.060)	(0.067)
Year dummies	No	Yes	No	Yes

Note: The dependent variable is the year-to-year change in the gun homicide rate. All models include a constant term. In each model, the assumed error structure is a variance-components model with random effects for each district. The "in possession" variable is the number of cases per 100,000 city residents in which one of the primary offenses of the felon charged in the regional office is possession of a firearm. The "used a firearm" variable is the number of cases per 100,000 in which one of the primary offenses involves the use of a firearm. Changes in these variables and the dependent variable refer to one-year single differences. Lagged variables refer to one-period lagged explanatory variables. Our data set refers to cases handled by regional federal attorneys and covers the period from 1994 to 1999. For specifications 1 and 2, the year 1994 is omitted by necessity. For the specifications 3 and 4, the sample is restricted to observations between 1995 and 1999. Standard errors are in parentheses.

observers believe that increases in the penalty for this offense is the real innovation of Richmond's Project Exile. However, we also replicate our analysis with cases in which the defendant was convicted of any federal firearm charge. For each of the cities in the analytic sample used in the previous section we identify the local U.S. Attorney's office responsible for prosecuting federal cases in that area.

Table 7-5 presents the results of regressing the year-to-year change in the number of gun homicides per 100,000 residents against the year-to-year change in the number of FIP convictions per 100,000 city residents (or their first difference).[30] Our focus on changes in gun homicides helps account for the influence of unmeasured city fixed effects that cause some areas to have persistently higher or lower gun homicide rates year after year. The first two columns regress the change in the gun homicide rate on the contemporaneous change in the number of convictions, while the last two regressions relate changes in gun homicides to last year's change in convictions. Regression results are presented with and without year dummies. Since the FIP and gun-use conviction rates are the same for cities located within the same U.S. Attorney jurisdiction, the assumed

30. We also estimated these models taking the log of dependent and explanatory variables. The results are similar to those presented in table 7-5.

error structure for all models includes district-level variance components. This ensures that we do not underestimate the standard errors of the slope coefficients owing to within-district correlation of the regression error terms.

Table 7-5 shows that these regression models provide little support for the idea that additional federal FIP convictions, or gun convictions more generally, have a statistically significant negative relationship to city homicide rates. This finding is robust to whether we regress the change in gun homicide rates against the contemporaneous or lagged change in FIP or other gun convictions, and to whether we control for period effects by including year dummies in the model.

As a further check we reestimate the model where the dependent variable is the change in the two-year averages of gun homicide rate four years apart—that is, 1999–98 minus 1994–95—and the explanatory variables are the comparable changes in the FIP and gun use conviction rates. Using these longer time periods provides a good robustness check for several reasons. First, there is greater variation in the FIP and gun-use conviction rates over the longer period, a fact that increases the likelihood of identifying an effect. Second, looking at changes over a longer time period will yield an estimate of the relationship that should be less sensitive to the lag specification.[31]

This alternative approach yields qualitatively similar results to those presented in table 7-5. Again, the relationship between FIP or other gun convictions and homicides is near zero and not statistically significant.

The results presented now and in the previous section taken together do not provide support for the idea that Project Exile had any detectable effect on homicide rates in Richmond or in the larger set of cities that began to divert eligible gun offenders from state to federal courts.

Conclusion

The widespread enthusiasm for Richmond's Project Exile (and other programs designed to enhance prison terms for gun crime) is understandable: the program enjoys political support from all sides in America's contentious debate about gun control, and a superficial examination of the data suggests that Exile may have had a dramatic impact on gun homicides. Setting aside the troublesome data from 1997 in Richmond, when Exile was ostensibly in effect even though there was no increase in federal gun convictions, the declines from 1995–96 to 1998–99 in gun homicide rates in Richmond are larger than those observed

31. Over a longer period, whether the proper lag is one, two, or three periods (and so on) is less relevant, since the impact of the trend in the explanatory variable should have ample time to exert an impact on the dependent variable.

in most other cities of comparable size (although the proportional decline in Richmond is less remarkable by comparison).

However, the impressive declines in gun homicide rates in Richmond around the time of Project Exile can be almost entirely explained by the fact that the city had unusually large increases in gun homicides through the mid-1990s, and that cities with larger-than-average increases in gun homicide rates subsequently experience unusually large declines. This finding is robust to a variety of ways to analyze the available data, including decisions about whether to measure changes in homicide rates in actual or proportional terms or to define the treatment as the existence of an Exile-type program or instead as the actual number of federal firearm convictions secured.

Our results also hold when we define the outcome measure of interest as the difference in homicide or other arrest rates between adults and juveniles. Since Exile's design makes the program applicable primarily to adult offenders, program impacts should be concentrated among adults. On the other hand, other unmeasured local factors may affect both adult and juvenile arrest rates, and so focusing on the difference between adult and juvenile trends in Richmond versus other cities helps isolate Exile's effects from those of other confounding variables.

One potential qualification to our empirical methodology concerns the possibility that the mean-reversion observed in city-level homicide trends may in and of itself be driven by efficacious local policy responses. Specifically, if localities implement creative and effective policies to reduce homicide only when homicide levels cross some unacceptable threshold, then the larger reductions in homicide observed among high-homicide cities may be the result of the policy responses of those cities. Hence the large drop observed for Richmond may be attributable to the aggressive federal prosecution of FIPs, while the declines observed for cities like Boston or New York may be attributable to alternative policy responses, such as community policing programs or crack downs on "quality-of-life" infractions. If this were the case, the effective policies of other localities would serve to empirically mask the effectiveness of Project Exile in Richmond.

However, if this were true, one would still expect to see an impact of FIP convictions on homicide rates among cities that implemented a variety of other crime-fighting programs. For example, an increase in FIP prosecutions in federal courts in New York City should yield additional crime reductions above and beyond those produced by the city's changes in policing practices. We were unable to find such an effect in our panel data analysis. Moreover, we have argued that the Exile intervention in Richmond focuses largely on adult offenders. Presumably whatever criminal justice or other interventions that are implemented in other jurisdictions around 1997 are not so narrowly targeted. In this case we would expect to observe a greater decline in adult offenses compared to juveniles over time in Richmond than in other cities; however, the best available data are not consistent with this expectation.

Possibly, however, the effect of Richmond's Project Exile is partially obscured by increased prison penalties for gun carrying and other offenses that are being imposed through state courts across the country. What we can say at the very least, however, is that federal prosecutions of such crimes does not appear to be substantially more effective than state prosecutions during this time period.

To be sure, our finding that Project Exile did not drive the decline in Richmond gun homicides following the program's launch begs the question of what exactly was responsible for the observed decline. One natural starting point for any explanation of the decline in criminal violence during the 1990s rests with the cause of the substantial increase in homicides starting in the mid-1980s, most of which was driven by gun homicides committed against and by young minority males.[32] The leading explanation for the crime surge of the 1980s is the growing involvement in crack distribution by young minority youth, who increasingly turned to firearms to enforce property rights in drug-market transactions.[33] Support for this explanation comes in part from the similarities in timing between the introduction of crack in cities and increases in youth homicides.[34]

The crack hypothesis would lead us to predict a substantial increase in homicides starting in the mid- or late 1980s for Richmond, since more than half of the city's population is African American, which is consistent with the homicide patterns presented here.[35] And Richmond's experience does not look very different from that of the rest of the country when we focus on homicides to young black males. From 1985–86 to 1995–96 the gun homicide rate for African American males between the ages of 15 and 34 increased by 72 percent (from 87 to 150 per 100,000), compared with an increase of 50 percent for the same group in the United States as a whole (35 to 53 per 100,000). The subsequent decline from 1995–96 to 1998–99 is smaller in proportional terms in Richmond compared with the United States as a whole (16 versus 25 percent).[36] Some change in the involvement of youth and guns in crack markets is thus an obvious candidate to explain the decline in gun homicide during the 1990s in Richmond

32. Cook and Laub (1998).
33. Blumstein (1995a).
34. Cork (1999); Grogger and Willis (2000).
35. U.S. Bureau of the Census (1998, p. 49).
36. It should be noted, however, that the decline from 1995–96 to 1998–99 among all other population groups excluding African American males 15 to 34 years old were larger in Richmond than in the rest of the country (40 versus 25 percent), perhaps partly because the homicide rate among this population increased by 39 percent from 1985–86 to 1995–96 in Richmond, while the rate declined by 5 percent in the rest of the country.

and elsewhere, although a complete explanation must account for the fact that nongun homicides also declined substantially over this period.[37]

One larger lesson from our analysis of Richmond's Project Exile is the apparent tendency of the public to judge any criminal justice intervention implemented during a period of increasing crime as a failure, while judging those efforts launched during the peak or downside of a crime cycle as a success. This heuristic device is particularly unfortunate in the case of government interventions directed at crime and gun violence, problems that impose enormous costs on society. Of course, it may be worthwhile to implement interventions that have quite modest effects on gun violence. While our analysis confidently rules out the possibility that Project Exile achieved the dramatic reductions in gun violence that have been claimed in the past, more modest (and perhaps more realistic) program effects are unlikely to be detected by the methods used here. Moreover, such modest effects are equally unlikely to be noticed by the policymakers, news reporters, and voters who focus on simple and dramatic changes over time as the benchmark of a program's success.

COMMENT BY
Steven D. Levitt

In this excellent chapter, Steven Raphael and Jens Ludwig analyze the effects of an innovative antigun criminal justice intervention known as Project Exile. Initiated in Richmond, Virginia, in 1997, the program's centerpiece is stepped-up prosecution of felon-in-possession-of-a firearm (FIP) cases. The program also included an advertising campaign stressing zero tolerance toward gun offenses. Proponents cite a 40 percent reduction in gun homicides in Richmond as evidence of its success. Based on this initial success, the budget of the program (under the new name Project Safe Neighborhoods) has been expanded tenfold.

In light of this apparent success, it is perhaps surprising that Raphael and Ludwig come to the conclusion that Project Exile, in reality, seemed to have no impact on crime in Richmond. The arguments they present are simple. First, the 40 percent decline in gun homicides between 1997 and 1998 is greatly exaggerated because the 1997 gun homicide rate was itself an aberration—up 30 percent from 1996 even though the trend in Richmond and elsewhere has been persistently downward. The blip up in 1997 is particularly problematic for proponents of Project Exile given that the program went into effect in February

37. Cook and Laub (2001).

1997, and thus this spike in gun homicides occurred postprogram implementation. Second, crime rates were falling everywhere and falling more steeply in high-crime places. Thus, when Richmond is compared with other cities that did not have Project Exile, Richmond does not seem to be an outlier in the crime reductions it experienced. Subject to the inherent limitations of this sort of case study approach, I find the arguments presented in the Raphael and Ludwig chapter convincing. Furthermore, the authors were kind enough to make their data available to me. I found their results remarkably robust to a wide range of alternative specifications.

In this discussion, I focus on two primary issues. First, I offer further context as to why one might expect Project Exile to represent a very sensible approach to criminal justice. Second, I provide some rough calculations of how large the impact of Project Exile on crime might have been expected to be based on existing estimates of the relationship between crime and punishment. The answer, it appears, is that even if Project Exile were far more effective than the standard criminal justice approaches, its expected impact on crime would be small enough to be undetectable with the methods employed in this chapter.

The form that Project Exile takes reflects the collision of two of the defining elements of the U.S. criminal justice experience in the past three decades: the incarceration boom and the explosion of gun violence by youth in the early 1990s. Since the early 1970s, an explosion in incarceration has occurred in the United States. The number of Americans behind bars today is seven times as high as three decades earlier. Gun violence—especially by youth—soared in the late 1980s and early 1990s. The homicide rate for young black males tripled between 1985 and 1992, for instance. All of this increase was concentrated in gun homicides.

In light of those two features—large increases in incarceration and gun homicides—the premise of Project Exile appears sound. Although there is strong evidence that this increase in incarceration has reduced crime, the cost has been substantial, with annual government expenditures on courts and corrections currently running more than $50 billion annually.[38] Furthermore, it seems reasonable to assume that as the prison system expands, the marginal benefit to society of locking up one more criminal is declining. If the criminal justice system is at all good at doing its job, the millionth criminal locked up should pose a threat to society that is a lot smaller than the first criminal. That being the case, a general expansion of the prison population does not seem desirable from a cost-benefit perspective, even to people like me who believe prisons work. Instead, selectively targeting resources toward hard-core, gun-toting violent of-

38. Marvell and Moody (1994); Levitt (1996).

fenders who impose the greatest costs on society might plausibly represent a more sensible plan of attack, and this is precisely the logic underlying Project Exile. There is some scholarly work suggesting that such targeted programs might work, based on sentence enhancements in California and a youth anti-crime initiative in Boston.[39]

Although I am convinced by the authors' analysis that Richmond's crime experience was not out of the ordinary, one might question whether Project Exile, even if successful, would be expected to affect crime sufficiently to be detected in aggregate crime statistics. The centerpiece of Project Exile was an increase in federal FIP convictions. After the program was initiated, there were roughly eighty additional FIP convictions a year. Those convicted on these charges might well have been convicted on other charges in absence of Project Exile. Thus the eighty convictions do not imply an extra eighty offenders off the streets each year in the period analyzed. As the evidence suggests in the analysis of California sentence enhancements, only a small fraction of the total impact of the laws is felt in the first few years (the only period for which Raphael and Ludwig have data).

Even putting aside that issue, is the increase in punishment implied by an extra eighty convictions enough that one would predict an observable change in the crime rate? In my own past research I find some of the largest estimated impact of incarceration on crime.[40] Each additional prisoner is associated with a reduction of .004 homicides annually (this effect captures deterrence and incapacitation). Thus, if the eighty convictions through Project Exile were of typical criminals, the predicted decline in homicide would be .32! Even if those targeted by Project Exile were ten times more likely to commit murder than the marginal prisoner, we would only expect a reduction of three homicides—a decline that would simply be lost in the noise of the estimation.

Another way of determining the expected impact of Project Exile on crime is to calculate the increase in expected punishment implied by the extra prosecutions. There are roughly 3,000 violent crimes and 15,000 property crimes reported each year in Richmond. The average clearance rate in large cities is 45 percent for violent crime and 15 percent for property crime. If these averages hold in Richmond, there are roughly 3,500 arrests for violent and property crimes a year in that city. On average in the United States, about 25 percent of violent arrests lead to imprisonment. For property crime arrests the corresponding figure is 10 percent. Thus about 500 Richmond residents are sentenced to prison each year for these crimes. If one includes drug-related and

39. Kessler and Levitt (1999); Braga and others (2001).
40. Levitt (1996).

other offenses, I estimate the number imprisoned as about 850 each year. If on average these individuals expect to serve about 2.5 years each in prison, this translates into a total punishment of roughly 2,100 person-years of time behind bars handed out each year in Richmond. If the eighty Project Exile convictions represent new punishments (as opposed to substituting for other punishment), and each Project Exile conviction represents an increase of three years in prison, then Project Exile accounts for 240 extra person-years of imprisonment, or roughly a 10 percent increase in the total punishment in Richmond. A reasonable estimate of the elasticity of crime with respect to expected punishment is −.25.[41] Thus one might expect a 2.5 percent reduction in crime in Richmond as a result of Project Exile.

That would translate into a reduction of two to three homicides a year, about 70 violent crimes and 350 property crimes. Given the inherent volatility in city crime rates, such small changes would be imperceptible in the data.

COMMENT BY
Peter Greenwood

Steven Raphael and Jens Ludwig have demonstrated fairly conclusively that one of the more popular strategies developed during the past decade to reduce firearm violence is a bust. It has no impact. It does not work.

The authors have restrained themselves admirably from poking holes in the theoretical underpinnings of the basic model. They concede that the evidence is not entirely negative on deterrence effects and yes, of course, they agree that there is surely a significant incapacitation effect when former felons who are found carrying a gun are locked up. They make Project Exile sound like a plausible and well-thought-out concept and help the reader understand several ways in which it might work. Well done on the objectivity scale.

But the numbers tell the tale. That which climbs the highest is going to eventually fall down the most as well—regression to the mean. There is no evidence of impacts on adults compared with impact on juveniles, who, theoretically, are not affected by the program.

What do you think is going to happen now that these findings are out? Is the president going to withdraw his endorsement of the program? Is Attorney General John Ashcroft going to tell his assistants to take or hold back all that extra funding ($550 million) his agency has set aside to replicate the program in

41. See Levitt (1996, 1997).

other jurisdictions? Will they shut down or redesign the program in Richmond? I think not.

Project Exile was developed by the U.S. Attorney's Office in Richmond, Virginia, as its contribution to local efforts to reduce gun violence. The primary focus of the program is a coordinated effort by Richmond law enforcement agencies and the U.S. Attorney's Office to prosecute, in federal court, all felon-in-possession-of-a-firearm (FIP) cases, drug-gun cases, and domestic violence with gun cases, where federal sentencing guidelines call for longer sentence terms than local laws. For felons-in-possession-of-a-firearm federal sentencing means an effective sentence enhancement of about five years, with no chance of early parole and less likelihood of making bail. Project Exile proponents and supporters argue that the much tougher sentences handed out by the federal system for simple felon-in-possession cases should deter some ex-felons from carrying firearms, and thus the likelihood that they will engage in gun violence.

Would that it were so. The 40 percent drop in gun homicides in the year following Project Exile's actual, as opposed to official, implementation certainly suggests that it may be so. The U.S. Attorney, the National Rifle Association, HandGun Control, Inc., the Bush administration, and Virginians Against Gun Violence all claim that it is so. Raphael and Ludwig have some bad news for them.

After comparing trends in Richmond's homicide rate with those in other similar cities, they find that the decline experienced in Richmond is no greater than what would have been expected without any intervention. They also find that juvenile and adult gun homicide rates declined at about the same rate, not showing any effects from Exile, which only applies to adults. Replicating Project Exile seems to be a waste of money.

Now wait a minute. What are the characteristics of felons who have been prosecuted by the federal government as part of this project? Are they really "bad news" characters who obviously need to be taken off the street, or are they only marginal offenders whose primary characteristic is being dumb? As the body of criminal career research has shown, there are lots of the latter type around. It would have been nice to have the social history and prior records on those individuals selected for federal prosecution, compared with those who were not. In fact it would be extremely useful to see a breakdown of the prior records of all those individuals arrested for gun homicide in Richmond during the years under study. The fraction of homicides committed by gun-wielding parolees would seem to set an upper limit on the number of homicides that Project Exile could prevent and is the kind of analysis engaged in by the Boston Gun Project before deciding what the intervention should be. Remember, it's ready, aim, fire—not ready, fire, aim.

The authors do not give us this information. It might help some people better understand why the project did not appear to have any effect. Then again, crime control strategies that primarily involve tough sentencing enhancements for some designated group of offenders believed to represent a high-risk to society seldom deliver their promised punch. A situation the mandatory sentencing crowd finds hard to stomach.

What Happens Next

If one believes the results of the Raphael and Ludwig study it is time to "call off the dogs," "call in the sheep," and find some other program for the Justice Department to franchise this year.

Unfortunately, not everyone who needs to get this word will do so. Many who do will choose to ignore it. Other U.S. Attorneys will be encouraged and influenced by Department of Justice grants to implement similar programs. Many local law enforcement officials will lobby their U.S. Attorneys to mount similar efforts, and numerous legislators will propose state laws that provide the same outcome—much longer sentences for any felon found in possession of a gun.

The saga of Project Exile reads amazingly like the prison baseball game being played in California—three strikes and you're out. Many people's first reaction to any type of crime threat is to propose longer sentences for those who seem to represent the highest risk. In California, it was violent crimes by repeat offenders (remember Richard Allen Davis—the killer of little Polly Klaas?), hence three strikes.[42] In Richmond, it was gun homicides, hence Project Exile. In neither instance did the proponents do much homework to see if the proposed program was appropriately targeted and could be expected to work.

Both programs were implemented in response to rising crime rates, and both benefited from the nationwide decline in crime rates that followed. None of the proponents had any question about whether their program would work. Both sets of proponents claimed success at the first sign of any positive results and continued to claim success even after the statisticians announced there were no impacts to cheer. The end result is that millions of hard-to-come-by crime prevention dollars are being squandered on correctional facilities that seem to have minimal effects, and thousands of defendants are serving unusually long terms because somebody came up with a theory and a good bumper sticker title that captured the public's fancy.

42. Richard Allen Davis, a repeat offender, was convicted of the 1993 kidnapping and murder of 12-year-old Polly Klaas and was sentenced to death by the Santa Clara County Superior Court.

Why is this so? How can it happen? Why does scientific evidence carry so little weight in this field? A perfectly conducted study can usually be demolished by the opinion of one ill-informed police officer or prosecutor.

In California, very few legislators have been willing to speak out against three strikes in the seven years since it was passed. This in spite of numerous media stories about cookie thieves and pizza bandits getting life terms. Finally, this past November, the Ninth Circuit struck down a third strike sentence of fifty-years-to-life for stealing $140 worth of videotapes as cruel and unusual punishment.

Police officials continue to be in favor of the law. It has been the prosecutors, those traditional defenders of the bastions of liberalism, who have stepped forward to say enough is enough. The current incumbent, Steve Cooley, defeated Gil Garcetti for the office of Los Angeles District Attorney on a platform of only filing third-strike enhancements for serious and violent offenses. Many other California district attorneys have adopted similar policies. Here at last we find individuals with the wisdom, integrity, and political clout to face down the slogan mongers and demagogues.

The value of a Project Exile approach may depend on the quality of the selectivity with which it is applied. If they use it only against felons scoring high on some objective risk prediction scale, then it might be worthwhile. But as a normal response to every single ex-con found in possession—it will cost a great deal of money that could be better spent on early prevention, delinquency programs, and drug treatment, with a much greater payoff in reduced crime. In fact governmental investments in appropriate early childhood and delinquency prevention programs have been shown to produce future savings that exceed their costs.[43]

One of the questions that needs to be asked about Project Exile is whether it made any sense as a pilot project back in 1996 or whenever people started kicking around the idea of finding creative ways of increasing the penalties for illegal gun possession. The selective use of federal prosecution for "felon-in-possession" is one of the key levers in the "pulling levers" strategy of the nationally acclaimed Boston Gun project. The Boston Gun project was also developed in 1996.[44]

What was our state of knowledge in 1996 when Exile was developed? The first place to look is the University of Maryland Preventing Crime Report, which was produced in the fall of 1996. Surprisingly, the topic of increasing penalties for offenders is not even mentioned. In Doris MacKenzie's chapter we learn that

43. Karoly and others (1998); Karoly and others (1998); Aos and others (2001).
44. Kennedy and others (2001).

incapacitation of chronic offenders does work, but the chapter emphasized that specific deterrence (shock probation, scared straight) does not. Neither do boot camps.[45]

Another source would be *Crime,* published in 1994, in which Al Blumstein wrote the chapter on prisons. "While the threat of a lengthy prison sentence is undoubtedly very effective at deterring white collar crimes that tend to be committed by middle class individuals, they are probably far less effective in deterring the crimes committed by underclass individuals, who are the primary occupants of prisons, and for whom the increment of pain associated with prison time may be far less severe than it would be for those ensconced in a comfortable job."[46]

Raphael and Ludwig address an important policy issue, using the best methodology available. They have achieved clear and unambiguous results. Let's hope their study gets the attention it deserves.

References

Aos, Steve, Polly Phipps, Robert Barnoski, Roxanne Lieb. 2001. *The Comparative Costs and Benefits of Programs to Reduce Crime. (Version 4.0).* Washington State Policy Institute.

Ayres, Ian, and Steven D. Levitt. 1998. "Measuring the Positive Externalities from Unobservable Victim Precaution: An Empirical Analysis of Lojack." *Quarterly Journal of Economics* 113 (1): 43–77.

Blumstein, Alfred. 1995a. "Youth Gun Violence, Guns, and the Illicit Drug Industry." *Journal of Criminal Law and Criminology* 86(1): 10–36.

———. 1995b. "Prisons." In *Crime,* edited by James Q. Wilson and Joan Petersilia. Institute for Contemporary Studies Press.

Braga, Anthony, David M. Kennedy, Elin J. Waring, and Anne M. Piehl. 2001. "Problem-Oriented Policing, Youth Violence, and Deterrence: An Evaluation of Boston's Operation Ceasefire." *Journal of Research in Crime and Delinquency* 38 (3):195–255.

Cook, Philip J., and John H. Laub. 1998. "The Unprecedented Epidemic in Youth Violence." In *Youth Violence. Crime and Justice: A Review of Research, Volume 24,* edited by Michael Tonry and Mark H. Moore, 27–64. University of Chicago Press.

———. 2001. "After the Epidemic: Recent Trends in Youth Violence in the United States." Terry Sanford Institute of Public Policy Working Paper Series, SAN01-22. Sanford Institute for Policy Studies, Duke University.

Cook, Philip J., and Jens Ludwig. 2000. *Gun Violence: The Real Costs.* Oxford University Press.

Cork, Daniel. 1999. "Examining Space-Time Interaction in City-Level Homicide Data: Crack Markets and the Diffusion of Guns among Youth." *Journal of Quantitative Criminology* 15 (4): 379–406.

45. Sherman and others (1997, chap. 9, pp. 1–75).
46. Blumstein (1995b, p. 417).

Corman, Hope, and Naci Mocan. 2000. "A Time-Series Analysis of Crime and Drug Use in New York City." *American Economic Review* 90 (3): 584–604.

Donohue, John J., and Peter Siegelman. 1998. "Allocating Resources among Prisons and Social Programs in the Battle against Crime." *Journal of Legal Studies* 27 (1): 1–43.

Federal Bureau of Investigation (FBI). 1976–99. *Uniform Crime Reports, Supplementary Homicide Reports.* Washington.

Greenwood, Peter W. 2002. "Juvenile Crime and Juvenile Justice." In *Crime: Public Policies for Crime Control,* edited by James Q. Wilson and Joan Petersilia, 75–108. Oakland: Institute for Contemporary Studies Press.

Greenwood, Peter W., K. E. Model, C. P. Rydell, and J. Chiesa. 1994. *Three Strikes and You're Out: Estimated Costs and Benefits of California's Mandatory-Sentencing Law.* Santa Monica: Rand Corporation.

———. 1996. *Diverting Children from a Life of Crime: Measuring Costs and Benefits.* Santa Monica: Rand Corporation.

Grogger, Jeffrey, and Michael Willis. 2000. "The Emergence of Crack Cocaine and the Rise of Urban Crime Rates." *Review of Economics and Statistics* 82 (4): 519–29.

Karoly, Lynn A., Peter W. Greenwood, Susan M. Sohler Everingham, Jill Hoube, M. Rebecca Kilburn, C. Peter Rydell, Matthew R. Sanders, and James R. Chiesa. 1998. *Investing in Our Children: What We Know and Don't Know About The Costs and Benefits of Early Childhood Interventions.* MR-898-TCWF. Santa Monica: Rand Corporation.

Kates, Don B., and Daniel D. Polsby. 2000. "The Myth of the 'Virgin Killer': Law-Abiding Persons Who Kill in a Fit of Rage." Paper presented at the American Society of Criminology annual meetings.

Kennedy, David M., Anne M. Piehl, and Anthony A. Braga. 1996. "Youth Violence in Boston: Gun Markets, Serious Youth Offenders, and a Use-Reduction Strategy." *Law and Contemporary Problems* 59 (1): 147–83.

Kennedy, David M., Anthony A. Braga, and Anne Morrison Piehl. 2001. *Developing and Implementing Operation Ceasefire in Reducing Gun Violence: The Boston Gun Project's Operation Ceasefire.* National Institute of Justice.

Kessler, Daniel P., and Steven D. Levitt. 1999. "Using Sentence Enhancements to Distinguish between Deterrence and Incapacitation." *Journal of Law and Economics* 42 (April): 343–63.

Levitt, Steven D. 1996. "The Effect of Prison Population Size on Crime Rates: Evidence from Prison Overcrowding Litigation." *Quarterly Journal of Economics* 111 (2): 319–51.

———. 1997. "Using Electoral Cycles in Police Hiring to Estimate the Effect of Police on Crime." *American Economic Review* 87 (3): 270–90.

———. 2001. "Deterrence." In *Crime: Public Policies for Crime Control,* edited by James Q. Wilson and Joan Petersilia, 435–50. Oakland: Institute for Contemporary Studies Press.

Marvell, Thomas, and Carlisle Moody. 1994. "Prison Population Growth and Crime Reduction." *Journal of Quantitative Criminology* 10 (1): 109–40.

———. 1995. "The Impact of Enhanced Prison Terms for Felonies Committed with Guns." *Criminology* 33(2): 247–81.

———. 1996. "Specification Problems, Police Levels, and Crime Rates." *Criminology* 34 (4): 609–46.

McCormick, Robert, and Robert Tollison. 1984. "Crime on the Court." *Journal of Political Economy* 92: 223–35.

McDowall, David, Colin Loftin, and Brian Wiersema. 1992. "A Comparative Study of the Representative Effect of Mandatory Sentencing Laws for Gun Crimes." *Journal of Criminal Law and Criminology* 83 (2): 378–94.

McGonigal, Michael D., John Cole, C. William Schwab, Donald R. Kauder, Michael F. Rotondo, and Peter B. Angood. 1993. "Urban Firearm Deaths: A Five-Year Perspective." *Journal of Trauma* 35 (4): 532–36.

Nagin, Daniel. 1998. "Criminal Deterrence Research: A Review of the Evidence and a Research Agenda for the Outset of the 21st Century." In *Crime and Justice: A Review of Research*, vol. 23, edited by Michael Tonry, 1–42. University of Chicago Press.

Scalia, John. 2000. "Federal Firearm Offenders, 1992–98." NCJ 180795. Bureau of Justice Statistics Special Report. U.S. Department of Justice.

Schiller, David. 1998. "Project Exile." *www.vahv.org/Exile/intro.htm* [November 15, 2001].

Schwab, C. William, and others. 1999. "Urban Firearm Deaths: Trends Over a Decade." Working Paper. University of Pennsylvania School of Medicine.

Sherman, Lawrence W., Denise Gottfredson, Doris MacKenzie, John Eck, Peter Reuter, and Shawn Bushway. 1997. *Preventing Crime: What Works, What Doesn't, What's Promising.* A Report to the U.S. Congress in collaboration with the University of Maryland Department of Criminology and Criminal Justice. NCJ-165366. U.S. Department of Justice.

U.S. Bureau of the Census. 1998. *Statistical Abstract of the United States: 1998.* Washington.

JOHN J. DONOHUE

8 The Impact of Concealed-Carry Laws

Thirty-three states have "shall-issue" laws that require law-enforcement authorities to issue permits to carry concealed weapons to any qualified applicant who requests one—that is, to adults with no documented record of significant criminality or mental illness. A spirited academic debate has emerged over whether these laws are helpful or harmful. While it is fairly easy to list the possible consequences of the passage of these laws, it has not been easy to come to agreement about which effects dominate in practice. Many scholars fear that these laws will stimulate more ownership and carrying of guns, leading to adverse effects such as an increase in spur-of-the-moment shootings in the wake of arguments or opportunistic criminal acts, increased carrying and quicker use of guns by criminals, more opportunities for theft of guns, thereby moving more legally owned guns into the hands of criminals, and more accidental killings and gun suicides. However, a pathbreaking article by John Lott and David Mustard in 1997 and a subsequent book by Lott have made the case that opportunistic crime should fall for everyone as criminals ponder whether

This chapter draws freely on the work done in Ayres and Donohue (1999) and (forthcoming) and has profited from the outstanding research assistance of Matt Spiegelman, Emily Ryo, Melissa Ohsfeldt, Jennifer Chang, David Powell, and Nasser Zakariya. I am grateful for comments from John Lott, David Mustard, Willard Manning, and other participants in the Brookings Conference on Gun Violence.

I thank Christopher M. Cornwell, John R. Lott Jr., and the participants in the Brookings Conference on Gun Violence for their helpful comments.

they will be shot or otherwise thwarted by a potential victim or bystander carrying a concealed weapon.[1]

Scholars have lined up on both sides of this debate. For example, Frank Zimring, Gordon Hawkins, Jens Ludwig, Dan Nagin, Mark Duggan, and others have been highly critical of the evidence marshaled by Lott and Mustard.

At the same time, criminologist James Q. Wilson calls Lott's book "the most scientific study ever done of these matters, using facts from 1977 through 1996 and controlling for just about every conceivable factor that might affect the criminal use of guns."[2] Wilson gives a ringing endorsement to Lott's thesis:

> Lott's work convinces me that the decrease in murder and robbery in states with shall-issue laws, even after controlling statistically for every other cause of crime reduction, is real and significant. Of the many scholars who were given Lott's data and did their own analyses, most agree with his conclusions. States that passed these laws experienced sharp drops in murder, rape, robbery, and assault, even after allowing for the effects of poverty, unemployment, police arrest rates, and the like. States that did not pass these laws did not show comparable declines. And these declines were not trivial—he is writing about as many as 1,000 fewer murders and rapes and 10,000 fewer robberies. Carrying concealed guns reduces—it does not increase—the rate of serious crime, and that reduction is vastly greater than the generally trivial effect of gun-carrying on accidental shootings.[3]

Sorting out who is right in this debate is important for social science and for public policy. Indeed, the resolution of this academic controversy may also influence the current dispute over the meaning of the Second Amendment, which states that "a well regulated Militia, being necessary to the security of a free State, the right of the people to keep and bear Arms, shall not be infringed." As Erwin Griswold, Nixon's solicitor general and former dean of Harvard Law School, noted a decade ago: "Never in history has a federal court invalidated a law regulating the private ownership of firearms on Second Amendment grounds. Indeed, that the Second Amendment poses no barrier to strong gun laws is perhaps the most well settled proposition in American constitutional law."[4] Not

---

1. Lott and Mustard (1997). Note the importance of the requirement that the weapon be concealed, thereby creating a possible protective shield for those not carrying weapons. Guns that are carried openly do not create this protective shield in that they may simply cause criminals to shift their attack to the unarmed. Thus concealed guns may protect unarmed citizens, while openly carried guns put unarmed citizens at greater risk (unless criminals believe the open carriers will frequently come to the aid of unarmed crime victims).

2. Wilson (2000).

3. Wilson (2000).

4. Erwin N. Griswold, "Phantom Second Amendment 'Rights,' " *Washington Post,* November 4, 1990, p. C7.

any more. Buoyed by the new research claiming a substantial life-saving benefit from laws enabling citizens to carry concealed handguns and some revisionist
literature on the intent of the founders, the Fifth Circuit Court of Appeals has
recently contradicted Griswold's interpretation of the Second Amendment.[5]
The National Rifle Association and its supporters argue that the way is now
paved to make the right to carry concealed handguns a constitutional mandate
governing the fifty states rather than just a legislative initiative in thirty-three
predominantly small or southern and western states. But are Lott and Mustard
correct that laws facilitating the carrying of concealed handguns reduce crime?
With the benefit of more complete data than were available initially to Lott and
Mustard, I conclude that the best statistical evidence does not support the claim
that shall-issue laws reduce crime.

Although the discussion of the approach used by and problems with the work
of Lott and Mustard can get technical, the points can be summarized in a more
intuitive fashion. First, their initial analysis compares the changes in crime in ten
states that passed shall-issue laws between 1985 and 1991, including states like
Maine, West Virginia, Idaho, and Montana, with states that did not, such as New
York, California, Illinois, and New Jersey. However, I suspect the changes in crime
in the late 1980s were quite different in these two groups for reasons that had
nothing to do with the shall-issue laws, but rather with the criminogenic influence
of the new crack cocaine trade in more urban, poor inner city areas (most commonly found in states that did not adopt shall-issue laws). If this suspicion is true,
then the relatively smaller crime increases in adopting states over this period
would be incorrectly attributed to the law when wholly separate forces were really
the explanation.

Second, because the adoption of shall-issue laws does not occur randomly
across states and over time, it is harder to discern the impact of the law (just as
a randomized medical experiment to determine the effectiveness of a drug will
provide better guidance than merely observing who chooses to take the drug and
what happens to those who do and do not). Since there is evidence of a "treatment effect" even before the laws are adopted, one needs to be cautious in drawing conclusions about the actual effect of the shall-issue laws. This concern is
heightened by fears that spikes in crime encourage the adoption of shall-issue
laws, and then the accompanying drops in crime (representing a return to more
normal times or "regression to the mean") will be inaccurately attributed to the
passage of the law. When the Lott and Mustard statistical model is run for the period in the 1990s when the spikes in crime reversed themselves, suddenly shall-

5. *U.S.* vs. *Emerson*, 281 F.3d 1281 (Fifth Circuit 2001).

issue laws are associated with uniform *increases* in crime. Thus, with the benefit of five more years of data, during which time thirteen states and the city of Philadelphia adopted shall-issue laws, one sees very different patterns than what Lott and Mustard observed in their initial study on ten adopting states with dates ending in 1992.

With the expanded data set, there is much evidence that could be amassed to support the view that shall-issue laws tend to increase crime, at least in most states. But the third set of factors that undermines the more-guns, less-crime hypothesis probably weakens that conclusion too: the results tend to be sensitive to whether one uses county or state data, which time period one looks at, and what statistical method one employs. While scholars may be able to sort out some of the disputes about coding adoption dates for shall-issue laws, which when corrected tend to modestly weaken the Lott and Mustard results, there are still uncertainties about data quality and model specification that may not easily be resolved with the current aggregated crime data. In the end, the most that can be said is that when adopted in the states that have so far adopted them, shall-issue laws may not increase crime as much as many feared. But these laws still may create social unease if citizens are apprehensive that even greater numbers of individuals walking through shopping malls, schools, and churches and sitting in movie theatres are carrying lethal weapons.

Lott and Mustard emphasize that few holders of gun permits are found to have committed murder, but they fail to recognize that the number of murders can rise from the passage of shall-issue laws, even if no permit holder ever commits a crime. First, knowing that members of the public are armed may encourage criminals to carry guns and use them more quickly, resulting in more felony murders. Second, as already mentioned, the massive theft of guns each year means that anything that increases the number of guns in America will likely increase the flow of guns into the hands of criminals, who may use them to commit murders. Notably, the typical gun permit holder is a middle-aged Republican white male, which is a group at relatively low risk of violent criminal victimization with or without gun ownership, so it is not clear whether substantial crime reduction benefits are likely to occur by arming this group further.

The Basic Methodology of Lott and Mustard

Lott and Mustard follow the basic contours of the current gold standard of microeconometric evaluation—a panel data model with fixed effects. That is, Lott and Mustard collect data over 1977–92 for individual states and counties across the United States, and then use panel data regression techniques to estimate the effect of the adoption of shall-issue laws, controlling for an array of social, economic, and demographic factors.[6] Essentially this approach determines for the ten states that adopted the shall-issue laws over this period how crime looks different after passage than it was before passage. In a study of this magnitude, the researcher must make many choices about data issues, model specification, and control variables, each of which has the potential to influence the outcome of the analysis in ways that are not often predictable.[7]

The Use of County Data

Lott relies most heavily on county crime data rather than state crime data (although he presents some state data results), noting that the far greater number of counties than states can add precision to the estimates and that county fixed effects will explain a great deal of the fixed cross-sectional variation in crime across the country. The use of these county fixed effects diminishes the inevitable problem of omitting some appropriate, but possibly unavailable, time-invariant explanatory variables. The county data have some disadvantages, though: Mark Duggan notes the concern that using county data to assess the impact of a (generally) statewide intervention may artificially elevate statistical significance by exaggerating the amount of independent data available to the researcher.[8] Furthermore, county data on the arrest rate (the ratio of arrests to crime in a county) are often unavailable because they are missing or because the county experienced no crime in a particular category in a particular year (leaving the rate undefined owing to the zero denominator). Since Lott uses the arrest rate as an explanatory variable, many counties are thrown out of the Lott analysis by virtue of the realization of the dependent variable (if it is zero in a given year, that county is dropped from the analysis), which can potentially bias the results of the regression estimation. Finally, Michael Maltz and Joseph Targonski raise some serious questions about the quality of UCR county-level data (at least for data before 1994).[9]

---

6. The "fixed effect" is a dummy variable that is included for each county or state that is designed to reflect any unvarying trait that influences crime in that county or state yet is not captured by any of the other explanatory variables. Lott and Mustard (1997).

7. As noted, the initial paper on this topic was by Lott and Mustard and the subsequent book (Lott [2000]) (now in its second edition) is by Lott. For ease of reference I henceforth refer to Lott as a shorthand for both Lott's work and that of Lott and Mustard.

8. One exception is Pennsylvania, which initially excluded Philadelphia from its 1989 shall-issue law. In 1995 the law was extended to include Philadelphia. Duggan (2001, p. 1109, note 20).

9. Maltz and Targonski (2001).

Model Specification

Lott basically uses two models to test the impact of a shall-issue law, but there are advantages in employing a third—hybrid—model discussed in the following paragraphs.[10]

— The dummy variable model: After controlling for all of the included explanatory variables, this model essentially tests whether on-average crime in the prepassage period is different in a statistically significant way from crime in the postpassage era. Since the dependent variable is the natural log of the crime rate, the coefficient on the postpassage dummy variable can be interpreted as the percentage change in crime associated with the adoption of the law.

— The Lott spline model: Rather than simply measuring the average pre- and postpassage effect (net of the controls), this model attempts to measure whether the trend in crime is altered by the adoption of a shall-issue law. Lott stresses this model may be needed to capture a reversal in trend that a simple dummy variable model might miss (because the law reverses an upward trend, but the symmetry of a rise in the prepassage crime rate and a fall in the postpassage crime rate leaves the average pre- and postcrime level the same).

— The hybrid or main effect plus trend model: Ayres and Donohue have argued that the at times conflicting results of the two previous models suggest that a third more general model may be needed. This hybrid model allows a postpassage dummy to capture the main effect of the law but also allows the law to change the linear trend in crime for adopting states. This model could be important if an announcement effect initially scares some criminals into fearing possible victim or bystander retaliation, but the ultimate effect is that more guns lead to more serious criminal acts—perhaps as fistfights end with someone dead or seriously injured instead of with a bloodied nose. Under this scenario, one might even see an initial drop in crime followed by a subsequent turnaround as the number of concealed guns being carried and crime increase in tandem. Although Lott does not employ this model (except in a modified model in a paper by Stephen Bronars and John R. Lott discussed below), it can be used to test whether one or both of the first two models is appropriate.[11]

---

10. Ayres and Donohue (forthcoming).

11. Ayres and Donohue (forthcoming); Bronars and Lott (1998). If the estimated coefficient on the postpassage dummy were virtually zero, one would reject the first model, and if the estimated coefficient on the time trend were virtually zero, one would reject the second model. If they were both virtually zero, one would conclude that the law had no effect on crime.

Note that the third model will generate two estimated effects that could be reinforcing (both the dummy and trend have the same sign) or in conflict in that one effect is positive and the other is negative. It is theoretically difficult to tell a story in which the main effect of the law would be pernicious while the trend effect is benign, so if we were to see such a pattern, it would probably be suggestive of some model mis-specification rather than evidence that the law actually generated this pattern.[12]

Lott and Mustard's Data

Lott begins his analysis by examining county-level data over 1977–92. Line 1 of table 8-1 shows the predicted effect on nine crime categories using the dummy variable model and his data (which he has generously supplied to numerous scholars interested in examining his work). A quick examination of the line 1 results reveals four of the five categories of violent crime (the exception is robbery) have negative and statistically significant coefficients, suggesting that shall-issue laws reduce these types of violent crime by 4 to 7 percent; and all four property crimes have positive and statistically significant coefficients, suggesting that the laws increase property crime by 2 to 9 percent. Lott accepts the regression results at face value and concludes that the passage of these laws causes criminals to shift from committing violent crime to committing property crime, where, he argues, they are less likely to be shot since the victim is frequently not present when the crime occurs. Thus we see violent crime decreasing by 3.5 percent and murders falling by more than twice that percentage, while property crime rises by more than 5 percent. As Ayres and Donohue stressed, however, the fact that robbery is not dampened by the adoption of a shall-issue law constitutes a major theoretical problem for Lott's interpretation of the results of the dummy variable model.[13] If there is to be the type of substitution away from violent crime that Lott predicts, one would expect that the new law would induce potential robbers to avoid confronting victims and shift to more stealthy property crime; yet in the first row of table 8-1, we see no evidence of any dampening

12. Lott does suggest a way in which a pernicious main effect could be followed by a benign long-term trend effect, but this argument is unconvincing. In discussing his findings that public shootings increase for a few years after passage of nondiscretionary handgun laws, Lott suggests that people planning such shootings might "do them sooner than they otherwise would have, before too many citizens acquire concealed-handgun permits." Lott (2000, p. 102). This Procrustean explanation seems designed to make contrary evidence appear supportive of a preferred theory.

13. Ayres and Donohue (1999).

Table 8-1. *The Estimated Impact of Shall-Issue Laws on Crime, County Data*
Percent

Item	Violent crime	Murder	Rape	Aggravated assault	Robbery	Property crime	Auto theft	Burglary	Larceny
Lott's time period (1977–92)									
1. Dummy variable model	**-3.5**	**-7.3**	**-4.8**	**-5.3**	-0.1	**5.2**	**8.9**	**2.3**	**5.9**
Robust std. error	(1.2)	(2.5)	(1.5)	(1.6)	(1.9)	(1.1)	(2.0)	(1.1)	(1.9)
2. Lott-Spline model	-0.4	**-4.7**	**-1.7**	0.5	**-1.9**	0.1	0.1	-0.4	0.8
Robust std. error	(0.5)	(1.1)	(0.6)	(0.7)	(0.8)	(0.7)	(0.9)	(0.5)	(1.4)
3. Hybrid model									
Postpassage dummy	**6.7**	2.9	**6.5**	**9.6**	-2.9	0.2	0.3	-2.5	0.3
Robust std. error	(2.3)	(4.9)	(2.9)	(3.0)	(3.2)	(1.8)	(2.9)	(1.9)	(3.0)
Trend effect	**-2.0**	**-5.4**	**-3.2**	**-1.7**	-1.2	0.0	0.0	0.2	0.8
Robust std. error	(0.8)	(1.5)	(0.9)	(1.0)	(1.1)	(0.6)	(1.2)	(0.6)	(1.2)
Entire period (1977–97)									
4. Dummy variable model	0.2	**-7.8**	**-2.9**	-0.1	-0.4	**7.6**	**10.8**	**1.5**	**9.6**
Robust std. error	(1.1)	(1.7)	(1.1)	(1.3)	(1.3)	(0.8)	(1.5)	(0.9)	(1.2)
5. Lott-Spline model	**-1.6**	**-2.7**	**-2.7**	**-2.7**	**-3.6**	**-0.4**	**-0.8**	**-2.6**	**-1.1**
Robust std. error	(0.2)	(0.5)	(0.4)	(0.4)	(0.4)	(0.2)	(0.4)	(0.3)	(0.4)
6. Hybrid model									
Postpassage dummy	0.2	**6.8**	**6.1**	**6.1**	3.5	-0.7	**8.9**	**4.2**	**5.4**
Robust std. error	(1.4)	(2.9)	(2.1)	(2.3)	(2.3)	(1.1)	(2.4)	(1.7)	(2.1)
Trend effect	**-1.6**	**-3.5**	**-3.4**	**-3.4**	**-4.0**	-0.3	**-1.8**	**-3.0**	**-1.7**
Robust std. error	(0.3)	(0.7)	(0.5)	(0.6)	(0.6)	(0.2)	(0.6)	(0.4)	(0.5)

Note: The dependent variable is the natural log of the crime rate named at the top of each column. The data set is composed of annual county-level observations (including the District of Columbia). The top panel uses data from the time period that Lott analyzes, 1977–92. The bottom panel uses the same data set but with appended entries for the years 1993–97. County- and year-fixed effects are included in all specifications. All regressions are weighted by county population. Standard errors (in parentheses) are computed using the Huber-White robust estimate of variance. Coefficients that are significant at the .10 level are underlined. Coefficients that are significant at the .05 level are displayed in bold. Coefficients that are significant at the .01 level are both underlined and displayed in bold.

effect on robbery. Hence the dummy variable model undermines a key prediction that Lott offers to explain the line 1 regression results for the period 1977–92.[14]

Lott presents his version of the line 1 regression evidence in the first regression table in his book. Interestingly, this table shows that robbery reduces crime by 2.2 percent, which is statistically significant at the .10 level (considered marginally significant). But Ayres and Donohue reveal that this −2.2 percent figure is an error that results from a miscoding of the effective date of the shall-issue laws.[15] The problem was that, instead of following his own strategy of assuming that the effect of the law would emerge in the first year after passage, Lott coded the shall-issue law in that fashion only for Florida and Georgia, with all other states being coded so that the effect of the law begins in the year of passage. Correcting this error to adhere consistently to the articulated Lott protocol wipes out the size and significance of the estimated effect on robbery.[16] These same incorrect results appeared in 2000 in the second edition of the book. Thus both editions incorrectly suggest that the dummy variable model shows that shall-issue laws reduce the number of robberies.

14. Lott and Mustard respond that the implications of the passage of a shall-issue law are uncertain since, for example, banks and businesses have always been protected by gun-toting personnel. Therefore, they contend, there may be substitution from highway robberies to robberies of banks and convenience stores, with uncertain implications for the overall number of robberies. I am not persuaded by this point. In 1999, 64.1 percent of robberies were either highway robberies (48.3 percent of the total) or robberies that occurred in churches, schools, trains, etc. (15.8 percent of the total)—the remainder being robberies in commercial firms including banks or in residences. FBI (1999, table 2.20). Thus the substantial majority of robberies are exactly the sort of crimes that Lott and Mustard argue should be deterred. In fact, the proportion of robberies that occur in public places is greater than the proportion of aggravated assaults occurring in public places. In 1999 aggravated assaults occurring in public places constituted 58.6 percent of the total. Bureau of Justice Statistics (1999, table 61). Moreover, even in the 8.2 percent of robberies that occur in convenience stores or gas stations, the armed citizenry are supposed to be protecting against crime (indeed, Mustard argues they even protect armed police officers! See Mustard (2001)).

15. Lott (2000, table 4-1); Ayres and Donohue (1999).

16. Ayres and Donohue (1999) replicate Lott precisely with the coding error and then show how the correction eliminates the robbery effect. The line 1 results in table 8-1 of this chapter are identical to the results in Lott's table 4-1 with three exceptions, which are maintained in all the regressions presented here: the coding error is corrected; standard errors are corrected to adjust for heterogeneity; and one explanatory variable—a measure of the real per capita income maintenance, SSI and other, for those over 65—was dropped. One can compare the results in table 1 of Ayres and Donohue (1999) with those of table 8-1 here to see that the only change that influences the basic story is the correction for the coding error. The explanatory variable of real per capita income maintenance for the elderly was omitted because, in expanding the data set to include the period 1993–97, we were unable to match the series for this variable with Lott's series through 1992. Since the omission had little impact on the pre-1993 results, and the theoretical argument for inclusion is not strong, we simply dropped the variable completely.

Lott's Spline Model

The only numbers that Lott reports in his book concerning his trend analysis are found in a single row of figures representing the difference between the before-passage linear trend and after-passage linear trend for the states that passed shall-issue laws.[17] Lott's regressions include year effect dummies, so the pre- and post-passage trend coefficients would capture linear movements in crime in the ten passing states, apart from the general movements in crime for the nation as a whole (which would be captured by the general year dummies). Lott's message is that a trend analysis shows that shall-issue laws lower all crime categories—both violent and property—and in all cases but one (larceny) the reduction is statistically significant. But Lott's regressions incorrectly identify the passage date of four jurisdictions that adopted shall-issue laws, which make the laws look more effective than they are.[18] The corrected numbers are presented in line 2 of table 8-1, which shows that the shall-issue laws reduce crime in a statistically significant way in only three of the nine categories (murder, rape, and robbery).

Note that the story in line 2 is changed in several respects from that of line 1 (the dummy variable model). Instead of all violent crime (but robbery) falling and property crime rising, line 2 suggests that shall-issue laws have no effect on property crime (or overall violent crime and aggravated assault) but dampen murder, rape, and the heretofore unaffected robbery. Consequently, Lott's discussion of the impact of shall-issue laws causing criminals to shift from committing violent to committing property crime is no longer central if the Lott spline analysis (regression 2 in table 8-1) is the appropriate estimation approach.

The Hybrid Model Testing for Main and Trend Effects

The Lott spline results predict that shall-issue laws decrease murder, rape, and robbery, thereby eliminating the problem for Lott's theory posed by the dummy variable model's failure to show a dampening of robbery. To sort out the conflicts between the dummy and trend models, Ayres and Donohue suggest using the hybrid regression 3 in table 8-1, which is the generalized model of regressions 1 and 2.[19] Regression 3 confirms the prediction of regression 2 and contradicts that of regression 1 that the shall-issue laws have virtually no effect on property crime. Once again, robbery largely drops out of the picture (although

17. Lott (2000, table 4-8).
18. Lott coded the enactment dates in Oregon, Pennsylvania, Virginia, and Philadelphia earlier than was proper. In his dummy variable analysis, Lott similarly miscoded these three states (and five others, but he correctly coded Philadelphia), as noted in Ayres and Donohue (1999, p. 449, note 21).
19. Ayres and Donohue (forthcoming).

it is negative in sign), thus reviving the theoretical problem that the shall-issue law does not reduce the one crime for which one would most expect a reduction if the Lott hypothesis were correct. For the other four violent crime categories, we see a pattern that is the exact opposite of what one might expect—the main effect of the shall-issue laws is positive, but over time this effect gets overwhelmed as the linear trend turns crime down. In other words, according to the hybrid model, in the year after passage the main effect of the shall-issue law is a 6.7 percent increase in violent crime, which is dampened by the 2 percent drop associated with the negative trend variable, for a net effect of 4.7 percent higher crime. After 3.5 years the conflicting effects cancel out, at which point crime begins to fall. This particular result of a positive main effect and a negative trend effect is inconsistent with any plausible theoretical prediction of the impact of a shall-issue law, since it is not clear why the law should initially accelerate crime and then dampen it.[20] The anomalous results suggest that even the most general form of the three crime models is still misspecified and hence that its results are unreliable.

Extending the County Data through 1997

Lott's initial analysis using 1977–92 data captured the period in which only ten states newly adopted shall-issue laws, and therefore Lott's regression results should be taken as the predicted effect of the adoption of the law in these ten states. Since 1992, however, thirteen more states and the city of Philadelphia have adopted the law, and therefore one might hope to gain more accurate results by extending the period over which the effect of the law is estimated. Before doing so, however, it is worth noting that Ayres and Donohue ran the precise table 8-1 and table 8-2 models on the period from 1991–97 during which fourteen jurisdictions adopted a shall-issue law. In both the county and state data and for all three models (dummy, spline, hybrid), shall-issue laws were uniformly associated with crime *increases*.[21] This sharply different finding from Lott's 1977–92 results

20. As noted above, if the results had been flipped with the main effect dampening crime and the time trend suggesting a longer term increase, one could interpret those results in a straightforward manner: the announcement of the law scared potential criminals, thereby dampening crime initially, but as more guns got out on the street or as the fear subsided, crime ultimately turned up (or returned to its previous level).

21. Ayres and Donohue (forthcoming). For the county data, virtually all the dummy model estimates were statistically significant, as were many of the estimates in the spline model. For the state data, the individual coefficients were frequently statistically significant for the dummy model, while generally not for the spline model. In both data sets, the results tended to be jointly statistically significant for the hybrid models.

should be kept in mind during my discussion of the aggregated results over the entire period 1977–97.

Regressions 4 through 6 in table 8-1 simply repeat the models of regressions 1 through 3, but now estimate them over the longer period 1977–97 (and thus measure the effect of adoption of the law in twenty-four states). Comparing lines 1 and 4 (the dummy variable model), we see that adding more years of data weakens Lott's story, which should not be surprising given the strong "more guns, more crime" finding for the 1991–97 period that was just discussed. Importantly, violent crime is no longer negative, so the basic story that the prospect of meeting armed resistance shifts criminals from violent crime to property crime is undermined. Lott might respond that murders fall by nearly 8 percent and rape by almost 3 percent, as murderers and rapists shift over to committing property crime, thereby raising its prevalence by 8 percent. But the suggestion that this pattern could be explained by the changed behavior of would-be murderers and rapists is not compelling.[22] Indeed, the idea that a thwarted rapist would decide to switch to property crime because rape had become more dangerous (to the perpetrator) seems rather fanciful. Again, the possibility of model misspecification seems to be a serious concern.

Interestingly, while the added five years of data weaken Lott's story based on the dummy variable model (line 1 versus line 4), the added data appear to strengthen the story using Lott's spline analysis (compare lines 2 and 5 in table 8–1). For the spline model in line 5, all the estimated coefficients are negative, and all are significant at the .05 level (except property, which is significant at the .10 level). Unlike in both dummy variable models, the Lott spline estimated effect for robbery for both time periods is negative and significant—an almost indispensable finding if the Lott deterrence story is true.

Finally, for the hybrid model, the added five years of data again repeats the unexpected conflicting effects of a positive main effect and a negative trend effect that was observed for the 1977–92 period for violent crime (line 3 of table 8-1) and extends it to property crime, as seen in line 6 of table 8-1. While this regression purports to show declines in overall violent crime and robbery, it suggests that crime initially rises before falling for murder, rape, aggravated assault, auto theft, larceny, and burglary. The absence of a plausible explanation for why a shall-issue law would first increase and then reduce crime again provides

22. Consider Florida—one of the states that is most conducive to the Lott story in that murders fell after the passage of a shall-issue law in 1987. If the law caused the predicted drop in murders and rape and accompanying rise in property crime from the 1987 level, then one would expect to see 106 fewer murders and 176 fewer rapes in the state and an increase in property crime of 68,590. It seems unlikely that the shall-issue law could explain an increase in property crime of this magnitude, by virtue of declining murders and rapes.

a clear indication of model misspecification. Although I have previously criticized Lott's suggestion that the passage of the laws may cause violent criminals to speed up their attacks to successfully complete them before the effect of shall-issue laws can kick in, this argument becomes even more untenable because of the property crime effects seen in line 6 of table 8-1. Why would auto theft, burglary, and larceny be rising then falling because of the passage of a shall-issue law, apparently mimicking the effect on violent crime? The entire argument of substitutability from violent to property crime, which has ostensible support in lines 1 and 4 of table 8-1 (the dummy variable model), breaks down completely either because there is no effect on property crime (lines 2 and 3) or because the effect is virtually identical to that estimated for violent crime (lines 5 and 6). The instability in these models to changes in the five extra years of data or the inclusion of both a dummy variable and a time trend effect is striking in the table.

A State Data Analysis

As already noted, strong criticism has been leveled at the use of countywide data. Thus it is useful to explore whether the estimated effects of the passage of the shall-issue law hold up when the analysis uses statewide data for the three different models and the two different time periods.

Again, the striking finding is how sensitive the results are in the six different regressions presented. The state data results in table 8-2 are clearly stronger for the Lott argument than the county data results in table 8-1, but again there are anomalies. First, the strongest story one could probably find to support the Lott thesis would be to find violent crime dropping and no effect on property crime (since the latter will frequently not entail contact with the victim, unless by chance in the home, where guns are already prevalent without shall-issue laws). The dummy variable models (lines 1 and 4 of table 8-2) show this pattern and would thus be strongly corroborative of Lott's thesis but for one obstacle: the two hybrid models reject that specification because the postpassage dummy is virtually never significant.

Second, the spline and hybrid models for the full period (lines 5 and 6 of table 8-2) seem to suggest that crime fell for all categories by roughly 2 percent, which again raises the question of why property crime should be falling in just the same way that violent crime is falling. The supporters of shall-issue laws will probably be glad to jettison the previous argument that the laws cause shifts from violent to property crime, but the lack of any theory for the crime drop in property crime may well suggest that the regression is simply picking up unrelated trends in crime and incorrectly attributing them to the shall-issue law.

Table 8-2. *The Estimated Impact of Shall-Issue Laws on Crime, State Data*

Percent

Item	Violent crime	Murder	Rape	Aggravated assault	Robbery	Property crime	Auto theft	Burglary	Larceny
Lott's time period (1977–92)									
1. Dummy variable model	**-8.3**	**-9.4**	-4.1	**-9.3**	**-11.4**	-2.2	-0.6	**-6.0**	-1.1
Robust std. error	(2.6)	(3.5)	(2.8)	(3.2)	(3.9)	(1.9)	(3.9)	(2.4)	(1.9)
2. Lott-Spline model	-1.6	**-5.4**	-0.8	-1.9	**-6.1**	-0.8	**-3.3**	**-2.0**	0.0
Robust std. error	(1.0)	(1.4)	(1.0)	(1.2)	(1.7)	(0.8)	(1.4)	(1.1)	(0.8)
3. Hybrid model									
Postpassage dummy	**6.4**	7.5	-2.6	7.6	0.7	1.4	**13.4**	1.6	-0.3
Robust std. error	(3.7)	(5.6)	(4.4)	(4.8)	(5.6)	(2.7)	(5.0)	(3.3)	(2.7)
Trend effect	**-3.2**	**-7.3**	-0.2	**-3.8**	**-6.2**	-1.2	**-6.7**	**-2.4**	0.1
Robust std. error	(1.3)	(2.0)	(1.5)	(1.6)	(1.8)	(0.9)	(1.8)	(1.3)	(0.9)
Entire period (1977–97)									
4. Dummy variable model	**-7.0**	-4.5	**-4.7**	**-5.9**	**-7.3**	0.3	**5.8**	**-4.2**	0.7
Robust std. error	(2.4)	(2.9)	(2.3)	(2.5)	(3.1)	(1.6)	(3.1)	(2.0)	(1.5)
5. Lott-Spline model	**-2.3**	**-2.3**	**-1.8**	**-1.9**	**-3.0**	**-1.1**	**-1.7**	**-2.3**	**-0.9**
Robust std. error	(0.6)	(0.8)	(0.6)	(0.6)	(0.8)	(0.4)	(0.6)	(0.5)	(0.4)
6. Hybrid model									
Postpassage dummy	-2.5	-0.7	-0.6	-2.4	0.0	1.8	**8.9**	0.5	1.5
Robust std. error	(2.7)	(3.8)	(2.9)	(3.2)	(3.7)	(1.7)	(3.6)	(2.3)	(1.6)
Trend effect	**-2.0**	**-2.2**	**-1.8**	-1.6	**-3.0**	**-1.3**	**-2.7**	**-2.3**	**-1.0**
Robust std. error	(0.7)	(0.9)	(0.7)	(0.8)	(0.9)	(0.4)	(0.7)	(0.5)	(0.4)

Note: The dependent variable is the natural log of the crime rate named at the top of each column. The data set is composed of annual state-level observations (including the District of Columbia). The top panel uses data from the time period that Lott analyzes, 1977–92. The bottom panel uses the same data set but with appended entries for the years 1993–97. State- and year-fixed effects are included in all specifications. All regressions are weighted by state population. Standard errors (in parentheses) are computed using the Huber-White robust estimate of variance. Coefficients that are significant at the .10 level are underlined. Coefficients that are both underlined and displayed in bold. Coefficients that are significant at the .01 level are both underlined and displayed in bold.

County and State Data Results from Tables 8-1 and 8-2

The foundation of the Lott thesis essentially is captured in regressions 1 and 2 in tables 8-1 and 8-2, with the greatest prominence in Lott's book going to the dummy variable model of table 8-1 but with greater emphasis now placed on the spline model of the same table. Although these results are not the same as those presented in Lott's book, these are the ones to look at because some coding errors have been corrected. The results are not as stable as one might like, but if one were to examine only those four regressions, the evidence would tend to support Lott's thesis. Obviously, the analyst's task would be easiest if the regressions generated by three different models (dummy, spline, hybrid), for three different time periods (1977–92, 1991–97, and 1977–97), on two different data sets (county and state) all conveyed essentially the same picture. Unfortunately, they do not. For the county data, we see that the hybrid model essentially rejects the dummy variable and trend analyses but yields only flawed results itself. The hybrid model's prediction of initial jumps in crime followed by subsequent declines in response to the adoption of a shall-issue law seems to conflict with any plausible story of how the laws might influence criminal conduct. This pattern again suggests the likelihood of model misspecification, perhaps resulting from some other omitted variable that is generating a drop in crime, which is being spuriously attributed to the shall-issue law. Accordingly, the county data set results of table 8-1 do not provide compelling support for Lott's thesis.

Perhaps surprisingly, though, the state results—which Lott has tended to argue against—seem generally more supportive (table 8-2). First, robbery is always negative in table 8-2, as are most of the violent crime categories—although not always significantly. Second, the strange results of the county data set in the hybrid model is not repeated, as we generally do not see uniform large and positive main effects offset by negative trend effects for the full time period. While in table 8-1 the hybrid model rejected both the county dummy variable and spline models, the table 8-2 hybrid model, if anything, seems to reject the dummy variable model and support the spline model, particularly in the full data set. The inconsistency in the hybrid model across time periods (regressions 3 versus 6) is somewhat unsettling. Still, if one took regressions 5 and 6 in table 8-2 as perhaps the "best" regressions from these two tables, one might argue that shall-issue laws seem to be associated with drops of roughly 2 percent across all crime categories. Although this is perhaps a weaker story than Lott initially ventured, it has the virtue of not having the theoretically problematic result of no effect on robbery, even though it does stumble on two other anomalies: first, the peculiar finding that the estimated effects are virtually identical for both violent and property crime, and second, the problem that shall-issue laws are associated with *higher* crime in the regressions (both county and state) run over the 1991–97 period. The anomalies suggest that further exploration is needed before any conclusions on the impact of shall-issue laws can be drawn.

Robustness and Endogeneity

The basic Lott regression using panel data with fixed state and year effects essentially acknowledged that the included explanatory variables do not fully capture all of the differences in crime across states or the changes in crime over time within states. Using fixed state and year effects corrects for a certain amount of omitted variable bias, and if the remaining excluded effects are random, then we should be able to determine the impact of shall-issue laws if we have the correct model.[23] If there are county or state trends in crime that are persistent and not explained by the included independent variables, though, the models of tables 8-1 and 8-2 can give misleading results. To address this issue we added state fixed trends to the regressions presented in tables 8-1 and 8-2. These new regressions, presented in tables 8-3 and 8-4, allow each state to have its own time trend and see whether shall-issue laws cause departures from these state trends.

Table 8-3 (county data) reveals the familiar but unsettling pattern of strong positive main effects and strong negative time trend results in regressions 2 and 4. This finding essentially rejects the appropriateness of the Lott spline model in this case, so those regressions are not presented (nor were they run). Once again, the county data results of table 8-3 seem as flawed and inconclusive as those of table 8-1.

While I suggested earlier that the table 8-2 state results were probably the strongest in favor of Lott's thesis, these results are largely undermined by the inclusion of state fixed trends in table 8-4. In other words, what might look to have been caused by the shall-issue law may have only been a trend over time that got improperly attributed to the shall-issue law. Adding fixed state trends may not always be appropriate, however, especially if it causes the standard errors on the estimated coefficient to rise sharply. But since that is not a problem in this case (compare tables 8-2 and 8-4), it would appear that the earlier results that might have tentatively supported the Lott thesis are greatly weakened with the inclusion of state fixed trends.

---

23. The fixed county or state effects essentially imply that crime rates are always higher by a fixed percentage in New York than in, say, Vermont unless some included explanatory variable explains the difference. Similarly, the fixed year effects imply that there are national influences that will operate proportionally on all states or counties.

Table 8-3. *The Estimated Impact of Shall-Issue Laws on Crime Controlling for State Trends in Crime, County Data*

Percent

Item	Violent crime	Murder	Rape	Aggravated assault	Robbery	Property crime	Auto theft	Burglary	Larceny
Lott's time period (1977–92)									
1. Dummy variable model	0.1	**-8.7**	-1.5	**3.4**	**-7.5**	-1.4	-1.2	**-3.6**	0.6
Robust std. error	(1.6)	(3.4)	(2.1)	(2.0)	(2.2)	(2.1)	(2.2)	(1.4)	(4.5)
2. Hybrid model									
Postpassage dummy	**6.9**	5.8	**5.5**	**6.0**	**6.3**	-0.1	**5.2**	1.1	-3.1
Robust std. error	(2.3)	(5.3)	(3.1)	(3.0)	(3.4)	(1.9)	(2.9)	(2.0)	(3.0)
Trend effect	**-3.2**	**-6.6**	**-3.2**	-1.2	**-6.3**	-0.6	**-3.0**	**-2.2**	1.7
Robust std. error	(0.8)	(1.8)	(1.1)	(1.0)	(1.3)	(1.1)	(1.2)	(0.8)	(2.5)
Entire period (1977–97)									
3. Dummy variable model	1.7	0.0	2.7	**7.3**	0.3	-0.6	**4.1**	0.4	**4.1**
Robust std. error	(1.4)	(2.3)	(1.6)	(1.8)	(1.9)	(1.3)	(2.0)	(1.3)	(2.2)
4. Hybrid model									
Postpassage dummy	0.9	**5.8**	**6.7**	**6.7**	**5.5**	-1.4	**7.1**	**4.3**	**4.6**
Robust std. error	(1.5)	(2.7)	(2.0)	(2.2)	(2.2)	(1.2)	(2.3)	(1.7)	(2.1)
Trend effect	0.5	**-3.9**	**-2.7**	0.4	**-3.5**	0.5	**-2.1**	**-2.7**	-0.3
Robust std. error	(0.4)	(0.8)	(0.6)	(0.6)	(0.7)	(0.4)	(0.7)	(0.5)	(0.7)

Note: The dependent variable is the natural log of the crime rate named at the top of each column. The data set is composed of annual county-level observations (including the District of Columbia). The top panel uses data from the time period that Lott analyzes, 1977–92. The bottom panel uses the same data set but with appended entries for the years 1993–97. County- and year-fixed effects are included in all specifications. All regressions are weighted by county population. Standard errors (in parentheses) are computed using the Huber-White robust estimate of variance. Coefficients that are significant at the .10 level are underlined. Coefficients that are significant at the .05 level are significant at the .01 level are both underlined and displayed in bold. Coefficients that are significant at the .01 level are both underlined and displayed in bold.

Table 8-4. *The Estimated Impact of Shall-Issue Laws on Crime Controlling for State Trends in Crime, State Data*

Percent

Item	Violent crime	Murder	Rape	Aggravated assault	Robbery	Property crime	Auto theft	Burglary	Larceny
Lott's time period (1977–92)									
1. Dummy variable model	0.2	<u>−6.7</u>	−3.2	−0.9	−7.1	−0.9	5.4	−2.8	−0.4
Robust std. error	(3.4)	(4.0)	(2.8)	(3.2)	(5.2)	(2.5)	(4.9)	(2.8)	(2.6)
2. Hybrid model									
Postpassage dummy	4.8	7.7	−3.0	1.9	7.9	1.1	**16.6**	3.5	−1.1
Robust std. error	(4.5)	(5.7)	(4.4)	(3.9)	(7.7)	(3.0)	(6.7)	(3.7)	(3.0)
Trend effect	−2.3	**<u>−7.1</u>**	−0.1	−1.4	**−7.4**	−1.0	**−5.5**	**−3.1**	0.4
Robust std. error	(1.6)	(2.1)	(1.6)	(1.5)	(3.1)	(1.0)	(2.4)	(1.5)	(1.1)
Entire period (1977–97)									
3. Dummy variable model	0.0	−1.9	−1.2	0.1	−0.7	1.9	4.6	0.7	2.0
Robust std. error	(2.6)	(3.0)	(2.2)	(2.8)	(3.2)	(1.7)	(3.0)	(2.1)	(1.7)
4. Hybrid model									
Postpassage dummy	0.2	2.7	1.2	−1.0	**6.2**	**3.4**	**<u>10.1</u>**	3.1	<u>2.8</u>
Robust std. error	(2.9)	(2.9)	(2.5)	(3.3)	(3.1)	(1.7)	(2.8)	(2.2)	(1.7)
Trend effect	−0.2	**<u>−3.5</u>**	**−1.8**	0.9	**<u>−5.3</u>**	**−1.2**	**<u>−4.3</u>**	**<u>−1.9</u>**	−0.6
Robust std. error	(0.8)	(1.0)	(0.7)	(1.0)	(1.2)	(0.6)	(0.9)	(0.7)	(0.6)

Note: The dependent variable is the natural log of the crime rate named at the top of each column. The data set is composed of annual state-level observations (including the District of Columbia). The top panel uses data from the time period that Lott analyzes, 1977–92. The bottom panel uses the same data set but with appended entries for the years 1993–97. State- and year-fixed effects are included in all specifications. All regressions are weighted by state population. Standard errors (in parentheses) are computed using the Huber-White robust estimate of variance. Coefficients that are significant at the .10 level are underlined. Coefficients that are significant at the .05 level are displayed in bold. Coefficients that are significant at the .01 level are both underlined and displayed in bold.

Dropping the Arrest Rate and Including the Incarceration Rate

Donohue and Steven Levitt did not use the arrest rate (that is, arrests divided by crimes) in estimating crime equations to test the impact of interventions unrelated to shall-issue laws.[24] Instead, they relied on state incarceration data because of the bias of having the crime rate on both the left-hand and right-hand side of the regression equation when the arrest rate is used as an explanatory variable.[25] As noted, the problems with the arrest rate are compounded when county data are used because a number of counties will be excluded from the analysis because of missing arrest rate data or the fact that when no observations of a crime are reported in a certain county in a certain year, the arrest rate for that county is undefined, which will disproportionately exclude low-crime areas from the analysis.[26] As Ayres and Donohue emphasized, the incarceration rate may be a useful proxy in its place, and I have repeated the analysis of tables 8-1 through 8-4 by replacing the arrest rate with the state incarceration rate as a control variable.[27] The bottom line is that in most ways the analysis changes little from this alteration, although if anything the Lott story is weaker still using the incarceration rate.

At the Brookings Conference on Gun Violence, Willard Manning suggested that it might be preferable simply to eliminate the arrest rate and incarceration rate since they are not truly exogenous variables but will be in part caused by the crime rate (which is the dependent variable in the various regressions). William Alan Bartley and Mark A. Cohen report that generally simply dropping the arrest rate tends to marginally weaken the Lott story across the board. Since both changes (replacing the arrest rate with the incarceration rate or simply dropping the arrest rate) tend to modestly hurt the more-guns, less-crime hypothesis, I will continue to present regressions with the arrest rate in order to be conservative and to promote greater comparability with the Lott results.[28]

24. Donohue and Levitt (2001).

25. Measurement error in the crime variable will cause spurious negative correlation between the crime rate and the arrest rate (arrests/crime).

26. Excluding data by virtue of the realization of the value on the dependent variable is generally problematic. In the dummy variable model for violent crime for the 1977–92 period, the regression had 46,052 county-year observations when the incarceration rate was the explanatory variable but only 43,451 when the arrest rate data were used. Thus using the incarceration rate rather than the arrest rate increases the sample size by 6 percent.

27. Note the state incarceration rate is not perfect for the two county data analysis tables since we do not have incarceration rates by county.

28. Bartley and Cohen (1998). When I ran the hybrid model on a disaggregated basis for the county data set for 1977–97, the results overwhelmingly showed that more jurisdictions experienced increases than decreases in crime from shall-issue laws. Dropping arrest rates from this regression reduces (but not to one) the ratio of jurisdictions experiencing crime increases to those experiencing crime decreases.

Introducing Lead and Lag Dummies

The dummy, spline, and hybrid models used in tables 8-1 through 8-4 to estimate the effect of the adoption of a shall-issue law imposed a great deal of structure by limiting the response to an upward or downward shift in crime or a
changed linear time trend. Obviously, more complex responses are possible, and
by including a series of postpassage dummies, we can allow the data to reveal the
pattern in crime change (if any) that follows the adoption of the shall-issue laws,
rather than constraining the estimates to fit a prespecified structure.

Panel data analyses of the type that we have shown thus far implicitly assume
that the passage of the shall-issue law is an exogenous event. This assumption is
necessary if, for example, the estimated coefficient on a postpassage dummy is
to be interpreted as an unbiased measure of the impact of the law. Including
a series of prepassage dummies can tell us whether crime is changing in unexpected ways before the shall-issue laws are passed.

As David Autor, John Donohue and Stewart Schwab have indicated in analyzing the impact of state laws involving exceptions to employment at will: "Ideally, from the perspective of getting a clean estimate of the impact of the [rele-
vant state laws], the lead dummies would be close to zero and statistically
insignificant."[29] Conversely, if the coefficients on the lead dummies are statistically significant, then this reveals the presence of systematic differences between
adopting and nonadopting states that are not captured by the statistical model
and that are present even before the laws are implemented. Since the statistical
model cannot explain the differences between the two sets of states before passage, there is less reason for confidence that the model is able to explain the differences between the two sets of states after passage. In other words, significant
lead dummies can be taken as another indicator of model misspecification.

Indeed, it is not hard to envision how such problems could exist in the shall-
issue law context. For example, Douglas Bice and David Hemley find that the
demand for handguns is sensitive to the lagged violent crime rate, which may
suggest the following causal sequence: increases in crime lead to increased demand for guns, which in turn leads to increased pressure on legislatures to adopt
laws allowing citizens to carry concealed handguns.[30] In this event, crime would
be elevated from some extraneous event, the shall-issue law would be adopted,
and when crime returned to normal levels the regressions shown in tables 8-1
through 8-4 would erroneously attribute the crime drop to the shall-issue law.

---

29. Autor, Donohue, and Schwab (2001).

30. Bice and Hemley (2001). We have recent evidence that one consequence of the terrorist attacks of September 11 is that gun sales rose sharply.

This phenomenon would then bias our estimates of the effect of shall-issue laws by making them seem to reduce crime even if they did not.

To explore the possibility of this endogeneity or other model misspecification, we estimated the impact of shall-issue laws while introducing three lead dummies, one estimating the crime rate five to six years before adoption, the second estimating the crime rate three to four years before adoption, and the third estimating the situation one to two years before adoption. Other time dummies are included to estimate the crime situation in the year of and after adoption, two to three years after adoption, four to five years after adoption, six to seven years after adoption, and eight or more years after adoption. Tables 8-5 and 8-6 show the results of this estimation of lead and lag dummies for the initial Lott and expanded time periods for both the county and state data sets.[31]

Table 8-5 tells a story that is about as far as possible from the ideal. Rather than the lead dummies being close to zero and statistically insignificant, they are often quite large and highly significant. For example, for the entire 1977–97 period, table 8-5 (estimated on county data) reveals that for every crime category except murder there are very large positive and statistically significant coefficients in the three dummies before passage occurred. This implies that in the years *before* adoption, crime was higher than average in the adopting states, controlling for national effects occurring each year, the average rate of crime in each county overall, and an array of explanatory variables. Of course, no one would make the mistake of attributing the large positive prepassage coefficients to a *subsequently* adopted shall-issue law, but their presence suggests that one must be very careful in attributing the negative coefficients in the postpassage period to the shall-issue law. At the very least, one must acknowledge the possibility that high crime levels induce passage of shall-issue laws, and that the subsequent return to more normal crime levels is now being incorrectly attributed to the laws.

How are the lead and lag results to be interpreted? Look at the table 8-5 results for 1977–97. A good place to start is to compare the estimated effects for one or two years before passage with the effects for two or three years after. This comparison has two advantages: all twenty-four states enter into the estimate of this prepassage period, and twenty-one of the twenty-four enter into this postpassage dummy.[32] (For the next two dummies, only the ten original states that Lott evaluated for the 1977–92 period are included in the estimation; and it

31. In both tables 8-5 and 8-6, the dummies were chosen to reflect the information available as of 1992. Thus, even though we know, for example, that four states (Alaska, Arizona, Tennessee, and Wyoming) adopted shall-issue laws in 1994, these states do not appear in the lead dummies for three to six years before adoption.

32. The reason is that states that pass the law in 1996, say, will contribute data to the "year of or year after" dummy in both 1996 and 1997 but will never contribute to the successive dummies.

Table 8-5. *The Estimated Impact of Shall-Issue Laws on Crime—Leads and Lags to Adoption, County Data*

Percent

Item	Violent crime	Murder	Rape	Aggravated assault	Robbery	Property crime	Auto theft	Burglary	Larceny
Lott's time period (1977–92)									
5 or 6 years prior	-1.9	2.3	1.0	-2.4	0.5	2.3	2.5	1.6	2.6
Robust std. error	(1.5)	(3.3)	(1.9)	(2.2)	(2.8)	(1.3)	(2.4)	(1.5)	(1.6)
3 or 4 years prior	**-7.0**	5.2	-2.0	**-10.0**	0.8	**2.7**	3.6	0.4	2.6
Robust std. error	(1.6)	(3.2)	(1.9)	(2.0)	(2.4)	(1.3)	(2.5)	(1.3)	(2.3)
1 or 2 years prior	**-2.8**	3.0	-2.2	**-9.7**	**8.9**	**6.5**	**10.1**	**4.8**	**7.7**
Robust std. error	(1.5)	(3.0)	(1.9)	(1.8)	(2.2)	(1.5)	(2.3)	(1.3)	(2.5)
Year of or year after	**-3.2**	2.1	-1.2	**-9.3**	**6.9**	6.2	**14.3**	**5.9**	2.6
Robust std. error	(1.6)	(3.1)	(2.1)	(1.9)	(2.4)	(2.5)	(2.3)	(1.5)	(6.0)
2 or 3 years after	**-3.8**	-0.1	**-5.8**	**-8.5**	5.4	**9.8**	**14.0**	**6.0**	**10.1**
Robust std. error	(1.8)	(3.3)	(2.3)	(2.0)	(2.6)	(1.4)	(2.8)	(1.6)	(1.7)
4 or 5 years after	**-10.5**	**-17.3**	**-15.0**	**-15.4**	1.8	**7.1**	**17.5**	2.6	**8.9**
Robust std. error	(2.5)	(4.3)	(3.0)	(2.9)	(3.8)	(1.7)	(4.8)	(1.9)	(3.0)
6 or 7 years after	**-47.2**	-26.8	7.1	**-64.0**	-22.3	**9.7**	-8.5	**14.3**	**9.2**
Robust std. error	(4.9)	(15.7)	(6.3)	(6.9)	(8.7)	(2.7)	(5.0)	(2.9)	(3.2)

Entire period (1977–97)

5 or 6 years prior	3.7	0.4	1.3	3.9	5.6	6.4	3.9	6.7	7.9
Robust std. error	(1.1)	(1.7)	(1.3)	(1.2)	(1.5)	(1.1)	(1.7)	(1.0)	(1.9)
3 or 4 years prior	4.3	1.0	1.6	4.7	9.1	7.2	8.1	5.6	9.6
Robust std. error	(1.2)	(2.0)	(1.3)	(1.5)	(1.6)	(1.1)	(1.8)	(1.0)	(1.9)
1 or 2 years prior	6.5	-2.9	3.7	6.7	13.2	10.3	11.0	6.5	13.9
Robust std. error	(1.7)	(2.2)	(1.5)	(1.7)	(1.9)	(1.2)	(1.9)	(1.2)	(2.0)
Year of or year after	8.3	-2.0	5.7	9.1	14.0	12.8	17.8	9.6	14.5
Robust std. error	(1.9)	(2.5)	(1.6)	(1.9)	(2.1)	(1.6)	(2.3)	(1.3)	(3.3)
2 or 3 years after	6.1	-4.2	2.6	6.3	10.7	13.3	17.7	9.0	17.4
Robust std. error	(2.0)	(2.8)	(1.8)	(2.1)	(2.4)	(1.4)	(2.6)	(1.5)	(2.1)
4 or 5 years after	1.6	-11.2	-8.1	2.4	7.8	16.0	20.6	6.2	22.0
Robust std. error	(2.1)	(3.2)	(2.1)	(2.3)	(2.5)	(1.4)	(2.6)	(1.6)	(2.1)
6 or 7 years after	2.6	-14.4	-3.0	6.2	6.1	19.0	25.6	8.8	26.9
Robust std. error	(2.1)	(3.2)	(2.3)	(2.3)	(2.7)	(1.5)	(3.1)	(1.8)	(2.2)
8 or more years after	2.6	-34.1	-18.1	-15.5	-10.6	17.8	6.3	-11.3	6.9
Robust std. error	(2.6)	(5.8)	(5.0)	(5.0)	(5.1)	(1.8)	(5.2)	(4.1)	(4.6)

Note: The dependent variable is the natural log of the crime rate named at the top of each column. The data set is composed of annual county-level observations (including the District of Columbia). The top panel uses data from the time period that Lott analyzes, 1977–92. The bottom panel uses the same data set but with appended entries for the years 1993–97. County- and year-fixed effects are included in all specifications. All regressions are weighted by county population. Standard errors (in parentheses) are computed using the Huber-White robust estimate of variance. Coefficients that are significant at the .10 level are underlined. Coefficients that are significant at the .05 level are displayed in bold. Coefficients that are significant at the .01 level are both underlined and displayed in bold.

Table 8-6. *The Estimated Impact of Shall-Issue Laws on Crime—Leads and Lags to Adoption, State Data*

Percent

Item	Violent crime	Murder	Rape	Aggravated assault	Robbery	Property crime	Auto theft	Burglary	Larceny
Lott's time period (1977–92)									
5 or 6 years prior	-3.4	0.1	1.1	0.5	8.8	-0.7	-2.6	-0.9	-0.6
Robust std. error	(2.7)	(4.6)	(2.7)	(2.7)	(5.4)	(1.9)	(4.6)	(2.2)	(1.8)
3 or 4 years prior	-12.7	2.5	-1.6	-11.7	0.2	-4.2	-6.0	-6.5	-3.6
Robust std. error	(2.8)	(4.1)	(2.5)	(2.9)	(4.9)	(1.9)	(4.0)	(2.3)	(2.0)
1 or 2 years prior	-14.3	-0.9	-1.1	-15.6	-1.7	-3.2	-0.3	-5.6	-3.4
Robust std. error	(3.0)	(3.8)	(3.2)	(3.5)	(5.7)	(2.5)	(4.8)	(2.8)	(2.7)
Year of or year after	-16.5	-1.0	-3.8	-17.8	-4.0	-3.4	5.5	-5.7	-4.8
Robust std. error	(3.8)	(4.9)	(4.1)	(4.5)	(5.9)	(2.8)	(5.1)	(3.3)	(2.9)
2 or 3 years after	-20.2	-6.3	-7.6	-21.4	-10.2	-3.8	0.8	-10.1	-2.9
Robust std. error	(3.8)	(4.8)	(4.8)	(3.9)	(5.9)	(2.7)	(6.2)	(3.4)	(2.7)
4 or 5 years after	-31.5	-25.2	-3.3	-34.6	-25.3	-10.0	-18.0	-19.9	-6.0
Robust std. error	(6.0)	(9.4)	(5.5)	(6.0)	(8.6)	(3.8)	(7.8)	(5.1)	(3.6)
6 or 7 years after	-53.7	-62.2	-11.7	-65.9	-43.0	-9.0	-13.2	-9.0	-10.2
Robust std. error	(7.1)	(13.7)	(8.7)	(9.2)	(11.5)	(6.1)	(9.5)	(7.2)	(6.1)

Entire period (1977–97)

5 or 6 years prior	**3.4**	3.9	1.3	**4.2**	3.4	1.8	4.4	2.0	2.3
Robust std. error	(1.7)	(2.7)	(1.9)	(2.0)	(3.1)	(1.7)	(3.0)	(2.1)	(1.8)
3 or 4 years prior	0.8	**6.8**	-0.9	2.6	0.7	0.8	3.5	-0.8	1.7
Robust std. error	(2.3)	(3.1)	(2.2)	(2.6)	(3.3)	(1.8)	(3.1)	(2.5)	(1.8)
1 or 2 years prior	-2.0	<u>5.6</u>	-0.4	-1.5	2.4	1.2	<u>**9.5**</u>	-0.5	1.5
Robust std. error	(2.7)	(3.0)	(2.5)	(3.2)	(3.5)	(1.9)	(3.6)	(2.3)	(2.0)
Year of or year after	-4.1	**7.8**	-1.6	-3.6	1.1	2.7	<u>**16.9**</u>	0.3	2.0
Robust std. error	(3.4)	(3.8)	(3.0)	(4.1)	(4.0)	(2.2)	(4.2)	(2.7)	(2.1)
2 or 3 years after	-6.3	5.7	-4.2	-4.6	-2.8	3.4	<u>**17.4**</u>	-1.7	3.8
Robust std. error	(4.2)	(4.6)	(3.9)	(4.5)	(5.0)	(2.4)	(5.2)	(3.2)	(2.4)
4 or 5 years after	<u>**-15.9**</u>	-4.4	<u>-11.7</u>	<u>**-13.1**</u>	<u>**-14.9**</u>	-1.6	**12.0**	<u>-11.1</u>	0.1
Robust std. error	(4.6)	(5.7)	(4.9)	(4.8)	(5.5)	(2.8)	(5.8)	(3.8)	(2.8)
6 or 7 years after	<u>-14.7</u>	-1.9	<u>-12.8</u>	-12.0	-14.8	-0.8	11.7	<u>-12.6</u>	0.8
Robust std. error	(5.5)	(5.8)	(5.0)	(5.7)	(6.7)	(3.2)	(5.1)	(4.3)	(3.3)
8 or more years after	-17.1	-2.8	<u>-12.4</u>	-11.8	-20.5	-3.8	4.3	<u>-13.8</u>	-2.4
Robust std. error	(7.9)	(9.2)	(7.3)	(8.9)	(8.0)	(4.1)	(5.3)	(5.0)	(4.5)

Note: The dependent variable is the natural log of the crime rate named at the top of each column. The data set is composed of annual state-level observations (including the District of Columbia). The top panel uses data from the time period that Lott analyzes, 1977–92. The bottom panel uses the same data set but with appended entries for the years 1993–97. State- and year-fixed effects are included in all specifications. All regressions are weighted by state population. Standard errors (in parentheses) are computed using the Huber-White robust estimate of variance. Coefficients that are significant at the .10 level are underlined. Coefficients that are significant at the .05 level are displayed in bold. Coefficients that are significant at the .01 level are both underlined and displayed in bold.

seems plausible that any effect of the law should show up by two or three years after passage.)

For the 1977–97 period, the effect for the "two or three years after" dummy is seen to be highly positive and statistically significant in seven of the nine categories. The other two categories are insignificant, with one negative (murder) and one positive (rape). Importantly, in all cases the dummy just before passage has virtually the same size and sign as the dummy after passage. Certainly, there is no evidence of any statistically significant decline in the value of the estimated effect across these two periods, which is not what one would expect if shall-issue laws reduced crime. Lott mentions one danger in this particular pre- and post-passage comparison—it may fail to capture a beneficial impact of the law if crime is peaking at the time of passage and then the law reverses the upward trend—the so-called inverted V hypothesis. Although there might be some hint of this for violent crime, rape, aggravated assault, and robbery, the effects are not statistically significant (and, even if real, could reflect a regression to the mean effect as opposed to a benign influence of the shall-issue law).

The comparable lead-lag regressions on the state data are shown in table 8-6. The first difference to note in comparing the 1977–97 results for tables 8-5 and 8-6 is that while the lead dummies in table 8-5 were all positive (suggesting crime was higher than expected just before passage), the lead dummies in table 8-6 are only positive and significant for murder and auto theft. Thus, if we believe the county data, it seems that shall-issue laws are adopted during unusually high crime periods, but the state data results suggest this is not true for all crimes (but may be true for murder and auto theft). The pre- and postpassage comparison with table 8-6 leads to a similar conclusion to that of table 8-5: there is no evidence of a statistically significant drop in crime from the passage of the shall-issue law, and the inverted V story does not appear to be a factor (the only hint of the story is for murder, but again the effect is not statistically significant).[33]

Although the county and state results have some discrepancies, the general pattern is that any result that is statistically significant for the "two and three years after" dummy was similarly signed and significant in the period before adoption, suggesting that the "effect" (the change in crime) preceded the alleged cause (the shall-issue law). A supporter of the Lott thesis might note that the dummies for the periods more than three years after passage tend to become negative and sta-

33. The analysis was also repeated by adding state time trends to the county and state analyses shown in tables 8-5 and 8-6. The county results again showed that crime was significantly higher during the prepassage period and if anything tended to rise (though not significantly) in the second and third year after the shall-issue law was adopted. The state pre- and postpassage comparisons show a tendency for crime to fall after passage (except for aggravated assault), but none of the changes is statistically significant.

tistically significant, but in my opinion the coefficient estimates for the dummies lagged beyond three years tend to weaken Lott's case rather than buttress it. First, drops in crime of 50 to 60 percent, which can be seen for certain crimes in the 1977–92 period in both the county and state data are simply too large to be believed. Second, the ostensibly growing effect on crime—see the increasingly larger negative numbers after passage in table 8-5—are taken by Lott as evidence that shall-issue laws become more beneficial over time, but something very different is at work. The observed pattern again shows that numerous states experiencing *increases* in crime after passage drop out of the analysis because these states' laws were adopted too close to 1997 to be included in the estimate for beyond three years. (Indeed, none of the fourteen shall-issue laws that were adopted after the period for inclusion in Lott's original work affect the estimates of these "after three years" dummies). Presumably, more complete data that would allow those states to remain in the estimation would weaken the observed negative effect for the period after three years, for as already noted, if one runs the dummy variable or Lott spline model for the period 1991–97, the results are striking: in every case the shall-issue law is associated with more crime, and these increases are always statistically significant for the dummy variable model and statistically significant at least at the .10 level for every crime but murder.

One comes away from the lead-lag discussion with a concern that endogeneity may be undermining the previous panel data estimates of the effect of shall-issue laws. Lott is aware of this problem and indeed confirms it in his book in noting that shall-issue laws "have so far been adopted by relatively low-crime states in which the crime rate is rising."[34] To his credit, he tries to use the appropriate two-state least squares (2SLS) technique to address the problem of endogenous adoption of shall-issue laws. However, it is well known that finding a suitable instrument that is correlated with the presence of a shall-issue law but uncorrelated with crime (except through the influence of the shall-issue law on crime) is notoriously difficult. Lott creates his instrumental variable by regressing the presence of a shall-issue law on rates for violent and property crime and the change in those rates; percent of state population in the National Rifle Association, percent of state population voting for Republican presidential candidate, percent of blacks and whites in state population, total state population; dummies for the South, Northeast, and Midwest; and year dummies.[35]

The effort is commendable, but the results prove unreliable. My immediate thought on seeing this list of instruments is that one should not be including the crime rates since they are not exogenous influences. The percent of the state

34. Lott (2000, p. 120).
35. Lott (2000, p. 118).

population in the National Rifle Association might be a good instrument, but I do not have that information (and have been unable to get it), so I am unable to conduct my own 2SLS estimation. As Dan A. Black and Daniel S. Nagin and Jens Ludwig have stressed, Lott's 2SLS regressions yield such implausibly high estimates for the crime reduction generated by a shall-issue law—reductions in homicides of 67 percent, in rapes of 65 percent, and in assaults of 73 percent—that one is forced to conclude that Lott's instruments, and hence his 2SLS estimates, are not valid.[36]

Disaggregating the Results by State

On the surface, the initial tables 8-1 and 8-2 created the impression that the panel data regressions establish a prima facie case that shall-issue laws reduce crime (or, at least in the dummy variable county model, reduce violent crime while increasing property crime). The analysis done so far has always estimated an aggregated effect for the laws across all adopting states. Since the previous discussion of the estimates on the 1991–97 period indicates that the later-passing states experienced statistically significant *increases* in crime, there is reason for concern that the aggregated estimates may be creating a misleading picture of the effect of the shall-issue laws. This effect is buttressed by the fact that the county-level data suggest a problem of endogeneity in the lead-lag analysis, and the most focused inquiry on the comparison of pre- and postpassage effects when most states are included in the analysis suggests that the aggregated analyses are misleadingly affected by the changing composition of the states included in the postpassage period beyond three years.

One way to explore the factors that drive the overall results in these aggregated analyses is to change the specification in both models to predict a state-specific effect from the passage of the law. This approach—that is, having a separate post-passage dummy in the dummy variable model for each adopting state and a separate postpassage trend in the linear model for each adopting state—can reveal whether the patterns estimated in the aggregated regressions hold up in the more disaggregated analysis.

Disaggregating the Dummy Variable Model

Figures 8-1 through 8-4 use a modified dummy variable model to depict the estimated effects on violent crime, murder, robbery, and property crime from passing a shall-issue law for each of the twenty-four states (or more precisely, twenty-

36. Black and Nagin (1998, p. 211); Ludwig (1998, p. 242).

Figure 8-1. *Estimated Effect of Shall-Issue Laws on Violent Crime, Dummy Variable Model*

Shall-issue violent crime effect (percent)

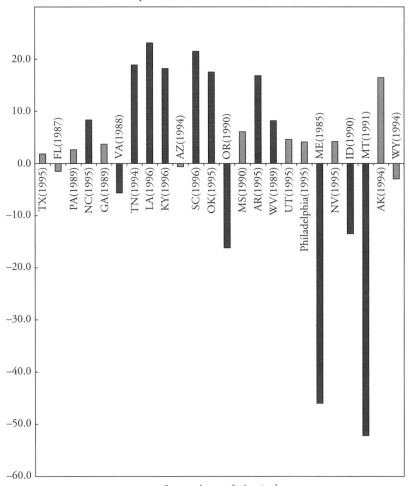

State and year of adoption[a]
Estimated effect for all jursidictions: .21% (t value: .19)

a. The dark shade means statistically significant.

three states and one city) that adopted such statutes between 1977 and 1996. These figures array the twenty-four jurisdictions in declining order of population size and indicate the year in which the shall-issue law was adopted, the estimated effect by state, and the estimated effect across all jurisdictions. Beginning with violent crime, one again sees that the aggregated effect (shown at the bottom of the

Figure 8-2. *Estimated Effect of Shall-Issue Laws on Murder, Dummy Variable Model*

Shall-issue murder effect (percent)

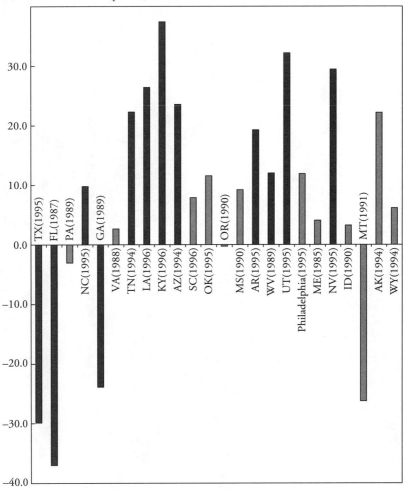

State and year of adoption[a]
Estimated effect for all jursidictions: –7.77% (t value: –4.57)

a. The dark shade means statistically significant.

Figure 8-3. *Estimated Effect of Shall-Issue Laws on Robbery, Dummy Variable Model*

Shall-issue robbery effect (percent)

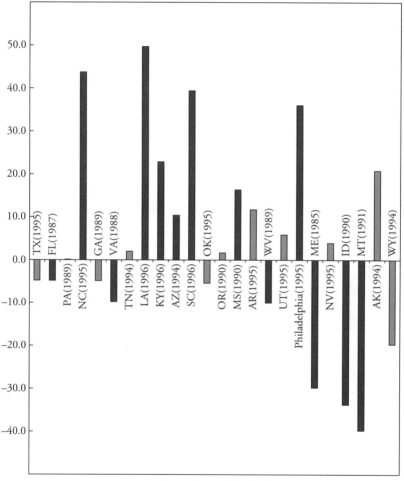

State and year of adoption[a]
Estimated effect for all jursidictions: −.38% (t value: −.29)

a. The dark shade means statistically significant.

Figure 8-4. *Estimated Effect of Shall-Issue Laws on Property Crime, Dummy Variable Model*

Shall-issue property effect (percent)

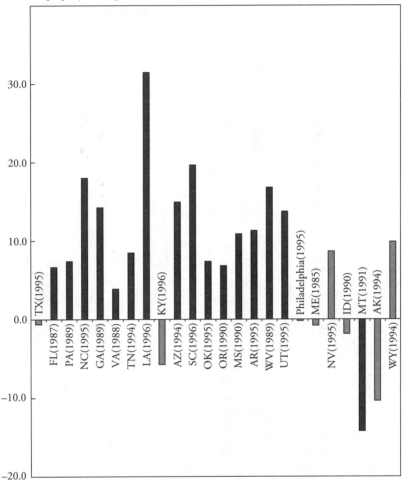

State and year of adoption[a]

Estimated effect for all jurisdictions: 7.6% (t value: 9.3)

a. The dark shade means statistically significant.

table) is small and statistically insignificant once Lott's data set is expanded to add the years 1993–97 (figure 8-1).[37] While the extension of the data set destroys Lott's claim that shall-issue laws reduce overall violent crime (that is, the move from regression 1 to regression 4 in table 8-1 eliminates the estimated negative effect for violent crime), and the aggregated results for robbery have never been sizable or statistically significant in the county dummy variable model (regressions 1 and 4 of table 8-1), the aggregated murder results remain large and statistically significant in support of Lott's claim that shall-issue laws lower crime (regressions 1 and 4 of table 8-1). But when we look at the disaggregated individual state results for murder in figure 8-2, we see a pattern that is contrary to what the Lott aggregated regression suggested. Instead of shall-issue laws broadly reducing murder in adopting states, we find that the estimated postpassage effect is negative in only six of the twenty-four jurisdictions, of which only four are sizable, and only three are statistically significant. Conversely, eighteen jurisdictions have an estimated increase in murders after passage, and nine of these are statistically significant and sizable. Thus, while the overall aggregated estimate from the dummy variable model suggests that shall-issue laws lower murder rates dramatically, the picture looks remarkably different in the disaggregated analysis—there are three times as many statistically significant increases in murder as decreases.

The reason for this apparent anomaly is worth exploring. First, note that weighting by population gives far greater influence in the regression to large states: Texas and Florida (the two largest states) and Georgia (the fifth largest) were the three states with large and statistically significant estimated drops in murder after they passed shall-issue laws. As figure 8-2 indicates, the estimated aggregated effect on murder in the dummy variable model is a drop in crime of 7.8 percent. Running the aggregated regression without weighting by population lowers the estimated effect on murder from −7.8 percent to −5.1 percent. Hence, weighting clearly increases the apparent murder-reducing capacity of shall-issue laws in the aggregated dummy variable model, but it is not the entire story.

Second, as already noted, the fact that a state adopts a shall-issue law earlier means that it will have a greater impact in the estimation of any postpassage dummy in the aggregated analysis. Thus imagine a scenario under which only two states (with equal populations) adopt shall-issue laws—one in 1987 and another in 1996. Assume the effect in the two states is exactly opposite. In the early adopter crime drops by 10 percent in the first year after passage and stays at that lower level through 1997, while in the late adopter crime increases by 10 percent and will stay that way for ten years. In the disaggregated analysis, one will see equal and opposite impacts, suggesting no overall net effect on crime. This is

---

37. The aggregated estimate comes from table 8-1, regression 4.

what the aggregated dummy variable analysis would show if the laws had been adopted at the same time. But because one state has adopted the shall-issue law nine years later, the aggregated analysis will generate a very different result than the disaggregated analysis of the type shown in figures 8-1 through 8-3. The later adoption in the second state means that its impact will be diminished when the aggregated dummy variable model is estimated. Indeed, the aggregated effect in this hypothetical will be a drop in crime of roughly 8 percent because the ten years of a crime drop of 10 percent will be averaged with the one year of the crime increase of 10 percent. Since we have seen that the fourteen late adopters had an aggregate effect of *increasing* crime, while Lott found a dampening effect for the previous ten adopters, we can see that the aggregated analysis will give much greater weight to the earlier adopters. This explains how a few early adopters can alter the analysis to show an aggregated predicted crime drop even though most individual states are showing crime increases when their laws are adopted.

What should be concluded from this analysis? If one accepts the regression output at face value, it suggests that the clear majority of states experience *increases* in violent crime, murder, and robbery when shall-issue laws are adopted. It is only the happenstance that some of the early adopters experienced crime drops, which are disproportionately weighted in the aggregated analysis, that has generated the impression of uniform crime reductions. Figure 8-4 shows the results of this disaggregated analysis for property crime. Since virtually every adopting state experiences an increase in property crime (fifteen statistically significant crime increases, one statistically significant crime drop), the disaggregated results conform to the aggregated prediction of substantial property crime increases. This result is stronger than any crime-reducing result associated with a shall-issue law that has been presented anywhere. Thus, if one accepts the panel data results, the strongest possible conclusion about the effect of shall-issue laws is that they increase property crime. But the only theory that would explain that result is the Lott substitution hypothesis from violent crime to property crime, which is not borne out in the disaggregated analysis of figures 8-1 through 8-3. Most of the states for which we see statistically significant increases in property crime do *not* experience any drops in violent crime. If the Lott substitution story were true, it would have to be the case that the states that experienced the property crime increases also experienced a violent crime drop, and this we do not see.[38] Reading the regression results at face value, shall-issue laws increase prop-

---

38. For the seventeen states that experienced an *increase* in property crime shown in figure 8-4, eleven experienced an *increase* in robbery shown in figure 8-3 (of which five were statistically significant increases). The other six states conformed to the Lott story of increased property crime coupled with decreased robbery, but only three of these were statistically significant drops in robbery.

erty crime, yet without a theoretical reason to believe this effect that has any empirical backing, one may be inclined to say the regression is not working properly (perhaps because of problems of misspecification or omitted variable bias).

Disaggregating the Linear Trend Model

The patterns revealed in figures 8-1 through 8-4 for the disaggregated analysis of the dummy variable model also emerge in the comparable figures based on the linear trend model (available from the author). Recall that in table 8-1, line 5, we saw that when the linear trend model was estimated on an aggregated basis, it showed that robbery fell by a statistically significant 3.6 percent and property crime remained virtually unchanged. Although the apparent drop in robbery might be taken as support for the more guns, less crime story for the 1977–97 county data, the story collapses if one disaggregates by state. In the disaggregated analysis, robberies increased in eighteen of the twenty-four jurisdictions (nine of them were significant). In the six jurisdictions where robberies fell, in only one case (Oregon) was there a statistically significant increase in property crime. Moreover, for the seventeen (of twenty-four) states that experienced an *increase* in property crime, fifteen also experienced an *increase* in violent crime, and ten of them were statistically significant increases in violent crime. Of the remaining two states, which experienced an increase in property crime but a decrease in violent crime, in only one was the decrease statistically significant. Indeed, for the clear majority of states for all four crimes in the disaggregated analysis, shall-issue laws are associated with increases in crime, which are generally statistically significant. Although the story of murder or robbery dropping can be found in the aggregated analysis with the linear trend model, it is purely an artifact of the happenstance of early adoption that weights a few large states most heavily.

Summary

Lott and Mustard have clearly launched an enormous amount of scholarly work on the effect of laws enabling citizens to carry concealed handguns. It is not hard to see why they and others may have believed that these laws reduce crime, because simple panel data regression models for the 1977–92 data period that they first analyzed provided support for the view that some or most violent crime rates fell for the ten states that adopted shall-issue laws over that period. Indeed, some superficially supportive work—for example, a paper by Bronars and Lott (1998) arguing that the passage of a shall-issue law pushed criminals across the border into non-shall-issue states[39] and a paper by Lott and William M. Landes indicating the multiple victim homicides fell when shall-issue laws were adopted—might have been thought to buttress the more-guns, less-crime hypothesis.[40] Moreover, if the statistical evidence backed up the more-guns, less-crime hypothesis, the anecdotal evidence of cases in which guns were used defensively to thwart attacks and the overall estimates of the number of incidents of defensive gun might seem to provide some plausibility to the initial Lott and Mustard findings.[41]

Right from the start, though, there have been concerns. Several analysts showed that disaggregating the 1977–92 data to estimate effects on ten individual states led to a more mixed picture with some states showing increases and others showing decreases in crime.[42] Others expressed concern that the Lott and Mustard result was vulnerable because the panel data model may not adequately control for "unobserved or difficult-to-measure factors that influence local crime rates but change over time."[43] Indeed, Ludwig noted that because all shall-issue laws have minimum age requirements, any deterrent effect related to these laws should be concentrated among adults, yet the evidence did not support this prediction.

39. The Bronars and Lott piece seemed at first to be important buttressing evidence since it purported to show that for a given metropolitan area, crime fell on the side of the border that adopted the shall-issue law but rose on the other side of the border. Unfortunately, the disaggregated results depicted in figures 8-1 through 8-4 give every reason to be suspicious of the highly aggregated Bronars and Lott result. In essence, all that Bronars and Lott showed was that a highly aggregated dummy variable for nonpassing jurisdictions bordering the ten adopting states seemed to show crime increases while crime was falling for the ten adopting states. But as shown, the disaggregated results typically reveal that crime rises for most jurisdictions, which almost certainly undermines the claimed substitution effect across state lines. Unless Bronars and Lott can show that the substitution across state lines is actually occurring by linking drops in crime to passing state X with increases in crime in neighboring nonpassing state Y (which I doubt will be the case), then the Bronars and Lott article really illustrates the unreliability of the aggregated analysis that is uniformly used in the papers endorsing the more-guns, less-crime hypothesis.

40. In the wake of a recent school shooting in Germany that killed fourteen, Lott summarized his finding from the Lott and Landes study: "multiple-victim public shootings fell on average by 78 percent in states that passed [right-to-carry] laws." John Lott, "Gun Control Misfires in Europe," *Wall Street Journal*, April 30, 2002, p. A16. Although the results may at first seem persuasive, there is a major problem with the Lott and Landes data. Lott and Landes (2001). The FBI Supplementary Homicide Report (SHR) reveals more than 800 such multiple-victim deaths a year, while Lott and Landes use a Lexis search that generates only about 20. FBI (2000). While it may be that not all 800 should be included (for example, Lott and Landes would eliminate some of the murders in the FBI data because they are not committed in public places), the true number of cases is vastly greater than the number that Lott and Landes employ. Indeed, Lott and Landes have now found that when they use the SHR data, their results "were rarely statistically significant." Consequently, if their story doesn't emerge when they use the best data, why should we believe their results using much less accurate data?

41. Ludwig (1998 provides an illuminating discussion of the prevalence of defensive gun use, and that paper and Duggan (2001) provide evidence that at least raises doubts about how much the actual carrying of guns increases in the wake of the adoption of shall-issue laws.

42. Black and Nagin (1998); Dezhbakhsh and Rubin (1998); and Plassmann and Tideman (2000).

43. Ludwig (1998, p. 244); Ayres and Donohue (1999); Zimring and Hawkins (1997).

Using a difference-in-difference-in-differences model, Ludwig showed that the evidence refuted the view that shall-issue laws resulted in relative decreases in adult homicide rates.[44]

All of this work speculated that factors such as the enormous, but geographically nonuniform, stimulus to crime caused by the crack cocaine trade in the late 1980s and early 1990s could well be generating spurious results. Ayres and Donohue noted some coding errors that, when corrected, tended to weaken some Lott results, and Duggan offered interesting evidence that more guns generate more murders and that Lott's results were eliminated with proper adjustments to the standard errors.[45]

At the same time, Bartley and Cohen showed that a hybrid model (admittedly with the Lott data set and its coding errors and in the aggregated model that Ayres and Donohue have questioned) could withstand an extreme bounds analysis to reveal drops in murder and robbery after a shall-issue law was passed for the 1997–92 full and large-county data sets.[46] Using the 1977–92 data and aggregated dummy variable and spline models, David E. Olson and Michael D. Maltz presented some generally supportive findings that shall-issue laws reduced homicides, but their finding that firearm homicides fell by 20 percent while nonfirearm homicides rose by 10 percent did not seem to fit well with a story that shall-issue laws had a deterrent impact on crime. Again, the inconsistencies were troubling, but for some these problems and the array of skeptical voices were largely ignored, especially with other studies expressing apparent approval of the Lott findings.[47] Those studies, however, were based solely on analyses of the now discredited or superseded aggregated dummy variable models that use the 1977–92 data with coding errors identified by Ayres and Donohue.[48]

But whatever the number of articles embracing or rejecting the initial Lott and Mustard results—and it is not clear to me that more articles supported Lott and Mustard or that counting the number of articles is the best measure of resolving

44. Ludwig (1998).
45. Ayres and Donohue (1999); Duggan (2001).
46. Bartley and Cohen (1998). The extreme bounds analysis simply estimates the effect of the law using all combinations of the Lott and Mustard explanatory variables and documents whether the resulting estimates are always nonzero. When the dummy variable model was used, Bartley and Cohen found that only violent crime and assault fell consistently (although perhaps the Lott inverted V story can explain some of this discrepancy). Moody (1999) also provides an extended inquiry into the Lott aggregated dummy variable model for the county data set (with the coding errors) for the period 1977–92 and finds that the shall-issue laws are associated with lower violent crime in various permutations of this aggregated dummy variable model over the early time period.
47. Moody (1999); Benson and Mast (2001); and Plassman and Tideman (2000).
48. Ayres and Donohue (1999).

the debate—there is now much more evidence on the issue than was available to almost any of the researchers who have previously examined the more-guns, less-crime hypothesis. Ayres and Donohue have shown how important the extension of the Lott and Mustard data set is to an assessment of the validity of the earlier Lott and Mustard work, and none of the researchers just discussed were aware of the Ayres and Donohue finding that running the Lott and Mustard models for the period 1991–97 generates uniform estimates of *increased* crime associated with shall-issue laws.[49] The very sharply different results between regressions run for early and late legalizers show that aggregated regression models will be misspecified.

Indeed, the lead and lag analysis discussed earlier shows that, particularly for the county data set, there is evidence of a serious problem of endogeneity or omitted variable bias, since the prepassage dummies are frequently large, positive, and statistically significant. Moreover, pre- and postpassage comparisons based on the lead and lag analysis did not provide support for any story that shall-issue laws reduced crime.

The evidence from the disaggregated state-specific estimates for the 1977–97 data should put to rest any notion that shall-issue laws can be expected to lower crime.[50] The overwhelming story that leaps out from the eight figures (looking at four crimes with both the dummy variable and the spline models) is that most states experienced *increases* in crime from the passage of shall-issue laws. In other words, if one simply runs a disaggregated state-specific version of the Lott and Mustard models on the full 1977–97 data set, a few states will be shown to have decreases in crime, but most will not, and the statistically significant estimates of increased crime will far outweigh the significant estimates of crime decreases.

If one had previously been inclined to believe the Lott and Mustard results, one might now conclude that the statistical evidence that crime will rise when a shall-issue law is passed is at least as compelling as the prior evidence that was amassed to show it would fall. However, there are still enough anomalies in the data that warrant caution. Admittedly, the updated disaggregated data push toward a more-guns, more-crime conclusion, but that model still does not address the endogeneity or omitted variable problems that seem to be lurking in the results shown in tables 8-5 and 8-6. Moreover, the figure 8-4 dummy variable disaggregated model shows that widespread increases in property crime follow the adoption of shall-issue laws, but there is no internally consistent theory that would explain this effect.[51] When a regression predicts both a potentially plau-

    49. Ayres and Donohue (forthcoming).
    50. Ayres and Donohue (forthcoming).
    51. In the linear trend disaggregated model (not shown), shall-issue laws are still associated with property crime increases, although they are less pronounced than for the dummy variable model.

sible finding (that shall-issue laws increase violent crime) and an implausible one (that the same laws also increase property crime), my confidence in the regression is weakened.

The overall evidence suggests to me that broad (and conflicting) crime swings that occurred in the late 1980s and 1990s happened to correlate with the passage of shall-issue laws, and the panel data model seems unable to separate out the contribution of the relatively minor influence of the shall-issue law from the major impacts of these broad swings. With data problems making it unclear whether the county or state data are more reliable, with the lack of good instruments available to directly address the problems of endogeneity and the lack of good controls available to capture the criminogenic influence of crack, it is hard to make strong claims about the likely impact of passing a shall-issue law. The tidal swings in crime rates during the late 1980s and the 1990s have both helped stimulate passage of shall-issue laws as a fearful population searches for relief from anxiety and obscured what the true effect of these laws on crime has been.

COMMENT BY

David B. Mustard

More than seven years ago John Lott and I decided to examine the impact of shall-issue laws on crime and accidental deaths. As someone who passionately disliked firearms and who fully accepted the conventional wisdom that increasing the gun ownership rate would necessarily raise violent crime and accidental deaths, I thought it obvious that passing these laws would cause a host of problems. It is now almost six years since I became convinced otherwise, and John Lott and David Mustard concluded that shall-issue laws reduce violent crime and have no impact on accidental deaths.[52] Since then we have distributed the data to about seventy groups of scholars and policymakers, thus facilitating an extensive research agenda concerning the efficacy of right-to-carry laws. John Donohue's chapter first evaluates the basic Lott-Mustard arguments and the subsequent research, and second, provides some new empirical work.

Lott-Mustard and Subsequent Research

An overview of the right-to-carry scholarly research in the past six years is a good start. One fundamentally important point is how much the terms of the debate

52. Lott and Mustard (1997).

have been significantly altered. Before this explosion of research, many presumed that shall-issue laws would increase crime. However, since Lott-Mustard no empirical research has made a case for shall-issue laws increasing crime. Instead, the literature has disputed the magnitude of the decrease and whether the estimated decreases are statistically significant. This work is notable in the broader gun literature because right-to-carry laws are the first gun law to produce an empirically verifiable reduction in criminal activity. The empirical work in refereed scholarly journals presents a much stronger case for the efficacy of shall-issue laws to reduce crime than any other gun control law. From a public policy perspective, if one believes there is insufficient evidence to endorse concealed-carry laws, then to be logically consistent one must also oppose the implementation of waiting periods, safe-storage laws, and other gun laws even more adamantly.

Given the sizable empirical research devoted to this issue and the hundreds of thousands of regressions that have been run, the small number of positive and statistically significant estimates is absolutely striking. Even if one uncritically accepts the most negative reviews of Lott-Mustard at face value, there is still more evidence that shall-issue laws reduce, rather than raise, crime. For example, Mark Duggan, widely recognized as producing one of the most critical papers, reports thirty regressions of the impact of right-to-carry laws on violent crime. Only one of the thirty coefficient estimates is positive and statistically significant (robbery in one specification). In contrast, fourteen of the thirty have negative and statistically significant coefficient estimates, and most of the rest are negative and statistically insignificant.[53] Similarly Daniel A. Black and Daniel S. Nagin obtain a positive and significant coefficient in one specification for assaults but only while using the problematic quadratic estimation procedure. However, this same table reports thirteen negative and statistically significant coefficient estimates, and the remaining estimates are disproportionately negative and statistically insignificant.[54]

Donohue's chapter starts by discussing the basic model and methodology of Lott-Mustard. Unfortunately, many of the criticisms have already been addressed extensively in the literature.[55] Some criticisms were even discussed in the original Lott-Mustard article. Because space constraints limit the number and depth of the issues that I can address, I encourage you to investigate these additional sources more thoroughly in evaluating Donohue's chapter.

53. Duggan (2001). Although only twelve are designated as statistically significant in the table, rape and assault in specification 2 are also statistically significant given the reported estimates of the coefficients and standard errors.

54. Black and Nagin (1998).

55. Bronars and Lott (1998); Lott (2000); Lott and Whitley (2001); articles in "Guns, Crime, and Safety" issue of *Journal of Law and Economics* 44 (2, pt. 2) (October 2001).

Like many critics, Donohue contends that different results for the impact of shall-issue laws on property crime undermine the Lott-Mustard work. He dramatically states, "Lott might respond that . . . murderers and rapists shifted over to committing property crime" and that the initial argument asserted, "that Shall-Issue laws induced massive shifts by thwarted murderers and rapists toward property crime." Regrettably, these misrepresentations of the original work continue to be made even though Lott and I have repeatedly asserted, "No one believes that hard-core rapists who are committing their crimes only for sexual gratification will turn into auto thieves."[56] Results of differing signs in no way indict our work. In the original paper we maintained that the deterrent effect should be larger on violent crime than on property crime, so the total effect on violent crime should be more negative than on property crime. Because financial gain is an important motive in some violent crimes there may be some substitution to property crime. However, to the extent that offenders reduce their involvement in all illegal activity as a result of the laws, property offenses may also decrease. Therefore, the theoretical prediction is ambiguous. In some specifications in the original paper property crimes increase, in others there is no effect, and in some there is a decrease. In writing the cost-benefit portion of the paper, we emphasized the results showing the effect of the law on property crime was positive (which also showed the smallest drops in violent crime), because we sought a lower bound on the total benefit and biased the findings *against* our conclusion that the laws provide net social benefits. Consequently, if shall-issue laws have no impact or actually reduce crime, the benefits of the law are even larger than we estimated.

Similarly, Donohue highlights another frequently repeated, yet incorrect, statement about how the relatively small decline in robbery as a result of shall-issue laws, "constitutes a major theoretical problem for Lott's interpretation." These comments about robbery neither acknowledge our initial arguments about how robbery should be affected, nor respond to Lott's subsequent arguments.[57] To briefly reiterate, the theoretical effect of shall-issue on robbery is ambiguous, because the offense category is composed of seven types of robberies. Only one of these categories involves the robbery of one person of another in a public place, which is the most likely type of robbery to be deterred by concealed carry. Clearly, the theory predicts that this type of crime should decrease. However, the theoretical prediction about the entire classification of robbery is not so clear. The other types of robbery could increase if as a result of right-to-carry laws offenders substitute from street robbery to other forms of robbery. Consequently, the effect of the law on the total category is ambiguous.

56. Lott (2000, p. 134).
57. Lott and Mustard (1997, note 26).

One last example is that utilizing the arrest rate as a control variable in the crime rate regressions is problematic. However, Donohue does not mention that Lott and Mustard include extensive explanations of these problems, that the original article tested the robustness of the results to the inclusion of the arrest rate in a number of ways, or that Lott further tests the sensitivity of the results to different arrest rate specifications.[58] These papers show that the qualitative results were robust to omitting arrest rates from the regression, using moving averages of arrest rates, using predicted values of arrest rates, and examining large counties that had well-defined arrest rates. Furthermore, Donohue's discussion of the arrest rate misses an important point. Omitting arrest rates may generate a truncation problem because many counties with zero crime rates will be included in the regression. By construction it is impossible for a shall-issue law to reduce crime in a county that has no crime, no matter how effective the law is.[59]

Post-1992 Analysis

Donohue's second principal objective is to examine the results when the data are extended to 1997. Of all the empirical papers that examine the impact of right-to-carry laws, Donohue's chapter is unique, because it is the first to argue that the laws may increase crime. Tables 8-1 through 8-6 in his chapter present this evidence by portraying the coefficient estimates and standard errors of a series of leads and lags before and after the law passes. He contends that adding subsequent years of data demonstrates that there are differential effects between the early and late adopters of laws. I outline three central concerns about this analysis.

First, Donohue neither discusses nor controls for very important changes in right-to-carry laws. There are at least four trends that have made it more costly for law-abiding citizens to protect themselves. One, fees have increased substantially. For example, the average fee for states that implemented laws since 1994 was about 2.5 times greater than the states that adopted right-to-carry laws from 1985 to 1992. Two, the training requirements for obtaining permits have increased significantly. Of the eight states that adopted their laws before 1960, only one state had any training requirement. Of the laws adopted between 1985 and 1992, only half the states required training, which on average was relatively short. In sharp contrast, most of the states that passed laws since 1994 require training periods, and the average length of those periods is relatively long. Three, there are fewer places in which licensed individuals are legally permitted to carry. Other than the areas prohibited by federal laws, early states had few, if any, excluded

58. Lott and Mustard (1997); Lott (2000).
59. Plassman and Tideman (2001).

areas. While many states that adopted their laws between 1985 and 1992 have few restrictions, the states since 1994 typically have extensive lists of excluded areas. Pennsylvania, which passed its law in 1989, excludes only courthouses and some government buildings, while Texas, which passed its law six years later, lists forty-eight places where carrying a concealed weapon is forbidden. Fourth, states that passed their laws later generally have more punitive penalties for carrying in unauthorized places. By raising the cost that law-abiding citizens bear in carrying a concealed weapon for self-protection, these four trends decrease the number of law-abiding citizens who can carry and the opportunities each license holder has to use a weapon for self-defense. Consequently, there are strong theoretical reasons for expecting the later laws to have different effects than earlier laws. Future empirical research should control for these changes and test the degree to which such provisions affect the carrying and crime rates. To the extent that these more restrictive laws reduce the carrying rate and the opportunities for self-defense, laws implemented later may be less efficacious.

A second concern about the new empirical work is that although it is important to know whether the coefficient estimates in the postlaw years are positive or negative, it is also important to understand how they compare to the prelaw estimates. For example, if the prelaw coefficient estimate is 8.5, and the postlaw estimate 5.5, the law may have lowered the crime rate in shall-issue states relative to the other states. To show these intertemporal effects more clearly, figure 8-5 plots the coefficient estimates from Donohue's table 8-5 county-level regression covering the 1977 to 1997 period. This figure clearly shows that all four violent crime rates plunge precipitously after the law is adopted. During the prelaw period, the murder rates are the same in shall-issue and non-shall-issue counties. After the law goes into effect, the murder rate for shall-issue counties drops dramatically. Crime rates for the other three offenses (rape, robbery, and assault) increase in the right-to-carry states before the law and plummet after the law. These drops are not simply reversions to the mean as some have suggested, because the postlaw rates for all three offenses are markedly lower than any of the prelaw rates.

Lott addressed this prelaw increase in crime in various ways in his many papers. Some methods include dropping the years immediately before and after the passage of the law, estimating regressions with instrumental variables and two-stage least squares, including nonlinear time trends, and showing that the postlaw crime rates drop far below the prelaw trend. Stephen Bronars and Lott used another strategy when they showed that when a given state passed a right-to-carry law, the crime rates in surrounding states increase.[60] There is no theoretical reason why the adoption of a law in one state should be a function of neighboring

60. Bronars and Lott (1998).

Figure 8-5. *"Entire Period" Coefficient Estimates*

Percent change

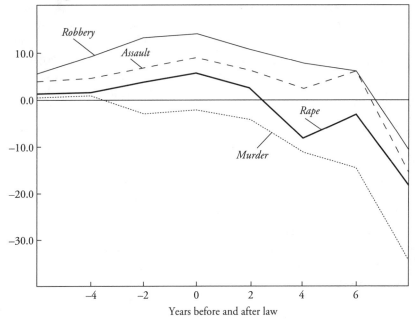

Years before and after law

Source: John Donohue, chapter 8, in this volume.

crime rates. Last, if gun laws are adopted in response to random periods of high crime, other gun laws should exhibit similar drops in postlaw crime. However, shall-issue laws are unique among gun laws in that they are the only ones that show these large decreases in postlaw crime.

My last concern about Donohue's allegation that allowing law-abiding citizens to protect themselves increases crime rates is his lack of articulating and documenting a clear mechanism through which such an increase would occur. The most frequently articulated claim is that permit holders will use their guns to commit crimes instead of using their guns for self-defense. However, many years of evidence across different states and time periods overwhelmingly rejects such claims. In Multnomah County, Oregon, only 1 of 11,140 permit holders was arrested for a crime during a four-year period—an annual rate of only 0.2 incidents for every 10,000 holders.[61] The annual rate in Florida over a seven-year period was even lower at 0.1. In Virginia as of the beginning of 1997, not a

---

61. Lott and Mustard (1997).

single concealed-carry permit holder had committed a violent crime. In North Carolina through 1997, permit-holding gun owners had not had a single permit revoked as a result of use of a gun in a crime. In South Carolina through 1997, only one permit holder had been indicted for a felony, a charge that was later dropped. Mustard showed that even those who vehemently opposed shall-issue laws have been forced to acknowledge that license holders are extremely law abiding and pose little threat.[62] Glenn White, president of the Dallas Police Association, twice lobbied against the proposed right-to-carry law, but after it finally passed he acknowledged, "I'm a convert." The president and the executive director of the Florida Chiefs of Police and the head of the Florida Sheriff's Association admitted that despite their best efforts to document problems arising from the law, they were unable to do so. Speaking on behalf of the Kentucky Chiefs of Police Association, Lt. Col. Bill Dorsey stated, "We haven't seen any cases where a [concealed-carry] permit holder has committed an offense with a firearm."[63] Many who believed that concealed-carry permit holders would threaten society actively tried to document that danger. However, they were compelled to change their minds as they observed law-abiding citizens who have no mental health histories, pay fees, and give authorities personal information do not use their weapons for inappropriate purposes. Much of the debate about concealed carry has involved detailed comments about empirical specifications and statistical estimation procedures, which has often left the average person confused. However, sometimes the most straightforward evidence, namely, the lack of criminality among law- abiding citizens who carry concealed weapons, is the most convincing and easy to understand.

COMMENT BY
Willard Manning

John J. Donohue's chapter examines the sensitivity of the results in earlier work by John Lott and his colleagues on the impact of laws granting a right to carry

---

62. Mustard (2001).

63. Scott Parks, "Charges against Texans with Gun Permits Rise. Law's Supporters, Foes Disagree on Figures' Meaning," *Dallas Morning News,* December 23, 1997, p. A1; Steve Patterson, "Concealed-Weapons Law Opponents Still Searching for Ammunition," *Florida Times-Union,* May 9, 1998, pp. A1, A3; Terry Flynn, "Gun-Toting Kentuckians Hold Their Fire," *Cincinnati Enquirer,* June 16, 1997, p. A1. Kentucky state police trooper Jan Wuchner is also quoted as saying that he has "heard nothing around the state related to crime with a gun committed by permit holders. There has been nothing like that I've been informed of."

a concealed weapon on several different measures of criminal activity.[64] His primary concern is with the sensitivity of the results to a series of specification and analytical issues, especially with how time trends are modeled, with special attention given to allowing for state-specific time trends. Much of the earlier work assumes an additive effect of the law against the backdrop of a time trend common to states that already had a right-to-carry law, enacted such a law during the period, or did not have one during the period. He also raises other concerns about data quality and the inclusion of an additional endogenous explanatory variable. His results indicate that some of the conclusions in the seminal paper by Lott and Mustard and other publications by Lott are not robust to specification changes.

Instead of only critiquing Donohue's chapter, in this comment I examine a set of issues common to the original work and to Donohue's chapter in this volume.[65] My focus is on econometric or statistical issues that can lead to biases in the estimates of the coefficients, the standard errors and inference statistics for the models, or both. I consider four areas:

— Correlated errors—going beyond fixed effects;
— Multiple comparisons;
— Endogeneity of the right-to-carry laws; and
— General concerns about estimation and interpretation of log models.[66]

The first two are serious because both Donohue and Lott seem to have a false sense of confidence in their results. The results are not as statistically significant as they indicate and may not be significantly different from zero at all. The third and fourth raise the prospect that the estimates themselves are biased. Some of the following remarks are based on my own analysis of the state-level version of the data that Lott provided to me earlier.[67]

Correlated Errors

The data employed here and in earlier work separately by Donohue and Lott involve sixteen or more years of data for states, standard metropolitan statistical

---

64. Lott (2000); Lott and Mustard (1997).

65. Lott and Mustard (1997); Lott (2000).

66. My original comments also included a concern about the endogeneity of the incarceration variable as an explanatory variable. Apparently, excluding the variable does not alter the results appreciably.

67. I have used these data in an applied regression course offered to students at the University of Chicago because the dataset exhibits a number of estimation problems. By using the state-level data, I do not have to deal with problems of zeroes at the county level. That is even more complicated than the ones dealt with here.

areas (SMSAs), or counties within states. This panel characteristic raises the prospect that the error terms for a state (or a county) are correlated over time if some unobserved factors are stable over time within a cluster (for example, state) or changing slowly. Both sets of authors have addressed this problem by employing a standard panel data solution with state (or county) fixed effects but no other correction for autocorrelated error terms within state. They also employ fixed effects for year to deal with the complex time trends in crime rates. There has been some exploration of state-specific time trends.

Over short periods, fixed or random effects may provide a good approximation to the variance-covariance matrix for the error term within a state. For a short period, slow-moving changes in unobservables in the error term will not change much. However, over longer periods of time, the approximation may be poor. I examined the autocorrelation function for the residuals from the fixed effects models for the two summary measures—violent crime and nonviolent crime per capita. The results indicate that the error structure within a state has a more complex form of autocorrelation than that indicated by a simple fixed-effects-only model. Moreover, it does not appear to fit a fixed effect combined with an autoregressive (AR) error model, such as an AR(1).

This raises the prospect that the standard errors and inference statistics for these models are biased because no further correction beyond the inclusion of fixed effects was made for autocorrelated errors.[68] Leaving out such a correction can have a pronounced effect on the efficiency of the estimates and bias in the standard errors and other inference statistics, especially if the key variables are time trended. Bias in the inference statistics can go either way depending on whether the remaining correlation in the residuals after adding the fixed effects for states and time has the same sign as the time trend in covariates (the x's) net of fixed effects. The direction and magnitude depend on the specific data.

There are several alternatives available to correct the inference statistics. Two options are relatively easy to implement. The first is to conduct a bootstrap of the analysis, bootstrapping all of the observations for each state as a cluster, rather than bootstrapping individual state-year observations. The second alternative is to use general estimating equations (GEE) after determining the form of the autocorrelation after a fixed effect for each state has been included.[69]

---

68. The various papers report either weighted least squares results under a fixed-effect specification or weighted with robust standard errors (corrected for heteroscedasticity using the sandwich estimator or Eicker-Huber-White correction).

69. Diggle and others (1994).

My analysis of the state-level data on violent crimes indicates that the reported standard errors from the fixed effects models for the right to carry a concealed weapon are biased toward zero, and the reported t statistics are biased away from zero by about 30 percent.[70]

Multiple Comparisons

One of the most common practices in applied work is that the authors make multiple comparisons in a paper (with all of the comparisons having the same nominal significance level), without any further correction for having made multiple comparisons. This is a problem in both the Donohue chapter and the Lott and Mustard papers, and in the Lott book. The problems may be severe because there are two summary measures (violent and property crime separately) and seven alternative, less aggregated measures that are reported.

Failure to correct for multiple comparisons causes the true significance level to be much less than the nominal level would suggest. If there are seven comparisons, then a nominal 5 percent standard applied to each is actually more like a 30 percent standard. The former is usually considered statistically significant if it is met, while the latter is considered statistically insignificant, and not noteworthy unless one is looking for a null finding.

There are two alternative solutions to the multiple comparison problem. One is to use a Bonferroni bound, dividing the nominal α level of 5 percent by seven to achieve a true nominal 5 percent combined over all seven comparisons. This is equivalent to using a 0.7 percent nominal level for each of the comparisons. This implies that the t statistics have to exceed 2.69 rather than 1.96 to achieve an overall significance level of 5 percent. This approach tends to overcorrect if the errors across the equations are not independent. No correction is needed if the error terms are perfectly correlated. The correlations of the errors across equations are on the order of 0.4 or less for the disaggregated measures and 0.6 for the aggregated measures.

The second alternative is to use Zellner's seemingly unrelated regression approach.[71] In this case, one can use an F test to determine the statistical significance of the right-to-carry variables jointly across all equations.

70. I have not determined the magnitude of the correction for the county-level analysis. There it seems very unlikely that a county-specific fixed effect will be sufficient to correct for both temporal and spatial correlation within state at a point in time or over time. To capture both for the county-level data, one would probably have to bootstrap clusters of all of the observations in the counties in a state as a group to correct the standard errors and other inference statistics.

Given the positive intrastate correlation within a state, I would expect the full correction for the county-level data to be even larger than the correlation for the state-level data.

71. Greene (2000, sec. 15.4).

If we combine the corrections for multiple comparisons and a more complicated form of autocorrelation, then the results should have t statistics that are about 50–60 percent of their reported value.[72] With such a correction, the results at the top of tables 8-2 and 8-4 appear to be statistically significantly different from zero about as often as one would expect if they had occurred at random.

Endogeneity

Both the chapter by Donohue and the prior work by Lott and by Lott and Mustard include endogenous explanatory variables.[73] The primary variable of interest is endogenous—the right to carry a concealed weapon.[74] Given the primary research interest, inclusion of the laws is unavoidable.

Is there a simultaneous equation bias caused by the endogeneity of enacting the right-to-carry laws? The use of fixed effects for state and year and of specific state slopes for time is not enough to capture why the right-to-carry law was enacted. It is the change in the law that is of interest, given that the fixed effects approach only relies on within-state variation in the laws to estimate the effect of the rightto-carry laws. Lott and Mustard recognize this issue and use instrumental variable, two-stage least squares (IV/2SLS) solutions to eliminate the simultaneous equations bias. The difficulty is that their instruments are questionable. The papers do not provide compelling evidence or arguments to indicate whether the instruments meet the econometric criteria for proper instruments.[75] For instrumental variables, the burden of proof is on the proponent of the specific model.

Lott and Mustard should provide solid evidence and arguments for the statistical merits of their instruments. With data with this much autocorrelation in the dependent and independent variables, one cannot use leads and lags to meet the IV/2SLS criteria. If suitable instruments cannot be found, then the authors

---

72. Given the concerns discussed in note 4, the corrections for the county-level data reported in table 8-3 would be even larger.

73. Lott (2000); Lott and Mustard (1997).

74. In addition, Lott and his colleagues include a measure based on arrests and Donohue includes incarcerations as covariates; the main results are largely insensitive to the inclusion of the additional endogenous variables.

75. The major requirements for the instrumental variables in the linear model to yield consistent estimates of the effect of the endogenous explanatory variable on the outcome of interest are the instruments correlated with the endogenous explanatory variable(s); the instruments do not conceptually belong in the equation of interest nor are they proxies for variables which should be in the equation of interest but are omitted from the specification; the instrument is uncorrelated with the error term in the equation of interest; and the instruments are not weak in the sense of Staiger and Stock (1997) or Bound and others (1995). See Angrist, Imbens, and Rubin (1996) for a fuller exposition of the requirements.

and their critics should consider using the bounding approach of Charles Manski to deal with the simultaneous equations bias in their estimates.[76]

TNSTAAFL . . . There's No Such Thing as a Free . . .

In this case, the econometric equivalent of the free lunch is a free log transformation of the dependent measure. Several authors, including Donohue, Lott and Mustard, and Lott, have used models with logged dependent variables to deal with skewness in the dependent measures or to obtain estimates of proportional effects of the right-to-carry laws on the outcomes (crime rates). Although such transformation is widespread in applied econometrics, its use in conjunction with ordinary least squares (OLS) or other least squares estimators can generate biased inferences about the effect of various covariates (x's) on the ultimate outcome of interest, the underlying dependent variable y, as distinct from inferences on $\ln(y)$. In general, OLS with $\ln(y)$ is estimating the geometric mean function (conditional on x), rather than the arithmetic mean function. Ultimately, the public and public figures are concerned about E(crime per capita $|$x), not the response of the log crime rate. Mathematically, the problem is that: $E(\log(y)|x) \neq \log (E(y|x))$. If we exponentiate both sides, we may have two quite different results. One econometric problem that can lead to this discrepancy is heteroscedasticity in the error term ε from the log scale regression model: $\ln(y) = x\beta + \varepsilon$, where the variance of ε is some function of the covariates x.

People are used to dealing with heteroscedasticity as a problem that biases standard errors and other inference statistics. Correcting such statistics via the sandwich estimator is commonplace.[77] However, such a correction does not deal with the bias of going from the OLS on $\ln(y|x)$ to statements about $E(y|x)$. Consider the following example, where the underlying error term ε is normally distributed with a variance: $\sigma^2(x)$, which is not a constant. In general, the expected value of y given x is:

$$E(y) = e^{x\beta}E(e^{\varepsilon})$$
$$\neq e^{x\beta}$$

---

76. Manski (1990).
77. The sandwich estimator is also known as the Eicker-Huber-White correction, or some combination of the three.

unless $\sigma^2 = 0$. If the error term is normally distributed, then the expected value of y given x is:

$$E(y) = e^{x\beta + 0.5\sigma^2(x)}$$
$$> e^{x\beta}$$

The former is the arithmetic mean, while the latter is the geometric mean.

If the covariate x is a continuous measure then the marginal effect of x on $E(y|x)$ is:

$$\frac{\partial(y|x)}{\partial x_i} = \left[e^{\left(x\beta + 0.5\,\sigma^2(x)\right)} \right] \left(\beta_i + 0.5\frac{\partial\sigma^2(x)}{\partial x_i} \right)$$

The second term is the one that has to be added to make the retransformation from the log scale to the raw scale give the correct, unbiased estimate of the incremental effect.

If there are two treatment groups or we are interested in the effect of an indicator variable, the formulation is slightly different. If there are two groups, A and B, where $\ln(y)_G \sim N(\mu_G, \sigma_G^2)$, with $G = A$ or B, then the contrast between the two groups is:

$$\frac{E(y_A)}{E(y_B)} = e^{(\mu_a - \mu_B) + 0.5\left(\sigma_A^2 - \sigma_B^2\right)}$$

Under homoscedasticity ($\sigma^2 =$ a constant)

$$\frac{E(y_A)}{E(y_B)} = e^{(\mu_a - \mu_B)}$$

The second of these is the usual way of doing comparisons in log OLS models. However it is unbiased if and only if the two groups have (the same) error variance. The extension to multiple covariates does not alter the concern that heteroscedasticity can lead to bias when the results are retransformed unless a suitable correction is made.[78]

In the case of the Donohue and Lott formulations applied to the state-level data, the error is not heteroscedastic in the right-to-carry law variables themselves. However, the errors are heteroscedastic in year and some of the other vari-

78. Manning (1998).

ables; the specific variables vary depending on whether we are dealing with violent or property crimes. This could influence both the detrending of the data for secular change and some of the secondary hypotheses.

There are two alternatives that can be employed. The first is to find the functional form for the expectation of e^ε as a function of x to apply as a correction factor[79] or to employ a suitable variation of Duan's smearing estimator.[80] The second is to employ one of the generalized linear models with a log link,[81] which would provide estimates directly of log $(E(y|x))$. These GLM estimates can be exponentiated to obtain $\ln(E(y|x))$ with all the usual interpretations of log model results, but without the complications caused by using least squares on log (y).

My examination suggests that the correct family for these data from the set of available GLMs suggests an overdispersed Poisson model. Further, it also appears that the log is not the correct link function if the concern is skewness in the error, because the residuals from their models are significantly skewed left. The log transformation overcorrects for skewness. A better power transformation could be the square root.

Conclusions

Donohue indicates that the earlier results by Lott and Mustard and by Lott may not be robust to a variety of specification and data issues.[82] The sensitivity of the findings could have major implications for the policy debate on right-to-carry concealed weapons. I share some of his concerns. For example, Donohue indicates that there are important differences in time trends before the right-to-carry laws were enacted. My own estimates also suggest differences pre- and postenactment by states that enacted during the sixteen-year interval.

But I find that both the critique and the original work suffer from several problems that could bias the coefficient estimates and the inference statistics. There are three major areas of concern. First, there may be a major simultaneous equations bias in the earlier estimates, as well as in Donohue's chapter on the effect of enacting right-to-carry laws.[83] Second, the precision of the findings (t, F, and p values) in the earlier work by Lott and by Lott and Mustard and in Donohue's chapter are substantially overstated because of failure to capture the full

79. Manning (1998).
80. Duan (1983).
81. McCullagh and Nelder (1986); Mullahy (1998); Blough and others (1999).
82. Lott and Mustard (1997); Lott (2000).
83. Donohue also discusses the instrumental variable analysis reported by Lott and Mustard (1997).

autocorrelation structure and making multiple comparisons without suitable adjustment. Correcting for both of these may be sufficient to cause the results from the original analysis and those in the critique to be statistically insignificant. Thus, if I can paraphrase Gertrude Stein, "there may be no there there."

Finally, Donohue's and my results indicate that there is a need to check whether the model estimated "fit" the data. Seemingly innocuous specification choices or decisions about how to deal with autocorrelated errors seem to substantially influence the findings in terms of both the estimates themselves and their statistical significance.

References

Angrist, Joshua D., Guido W. Imbens, and Donald B. Rubin. 1996. "Identification of Causal Effects Using Instrumental Variables." *Journal of the American Statistical Association* 91 (June): 444–55.

Autor, David, John Donohue, and Stewart Schwab. 2001. "The Costs of Wrongful Discharge Laws." Paper presented at the Labor Studies Workshop of the National Bureau of Economic Research. Cambridge, Mass.

Ayres, Ian, and John Donohue. 1999. "Nondiscretionary Concealed Weapons Law: A Case Study of Statistics, Standards of Proof, and Public Policy." *American Law and Economics Review* 1 (1): 436–70.

———. Forthcoming. "Shooting Down the More Guns, Less Crime Hypothesis." *Stanford Law Review* 55.

Bartley, William Alan, and Mark A. Cohen. 1998. "The Effect of Concealed Weapons Laws: An Extreme Bound Analysis." *Economic Inquiry* 36 (2): 258–65.

Benson, Bruce, and Brent Mast. 2001. "Privately Produced General Deterrence." *Journal of Law and Economics* 44 (2): 1–22.

Bice, Douglas, and David Hemley. 2001. "The Market for New Handguns: An Empirical Investigation." Working Paper. Eastern New Mexico University. Abstract available from the Social Science Research Network Electronic Library.

Black, Dan A., and Daniel S. Nagin. 1998. "Do Right-To-Carry Laws Deter Violent Crime?" *Journal of Legal Studies* 27 (1): 209–19.

Blough, David K., Carolyn W. Madden, and Mark C. Hornbrook. 1999. "Modeling Risk Using Generalized Linear Models." *Journal of Health Economics* 18 (2): 153–71.

Bound, John, David A. Jaeger, and Regina M. Baker. 1995. "Problems with Instrumental Variables Estimation When the Correlation between the Instruments and the Endogenous Explanatory Variable Is Weak." *Journal of the American Statistical Association* 90 (June): 443–50.

Bronars, Stephen, and John R. Lott, Jr. 1998. "Criminal Deterrence, Geographic Spillovers, and the Right to Carry Concealed Handguns." *American Economic Review* 88 (2): 475–79.

Bureau of Justice Statistics. 1999. *Criminal Victimization in the United States, 1999 Statistical Tables.* U.S. Department of Justice.

Dezhbakhsh, Hashem, and Paul H. Rubin. 1998. "Lives Saved or Lives Lost? The Effects of Concealed-Handgun Laws on Crime." *American Economic Review* 88 (2): 468–74.

Diggle, Peter J., K. Y. Liang, and Scott L. Zeger, 1994. *"Analysis of Longitudinal Data."* Oxford: Oxford Clarendon Press.

Donohue, John, and Steven Levitt. 2001. "The Impact of Legalized Abortion on Crime." *Quarterly Journal of Economics* 116 (2): 379–420.

Duan, Naihua. 1983. "Smearing Estimates: A Non-Parametric Retransformation Method." *Journal of the American Statistical Association* 78 (September): 605–10.

Duggan, Mark. 2001. "More Guns, More Crime." *Journal of Political Economy* 109 (5): 1086–1114.

Federal Bureau of Investigation. 1999. *Crime in the United States.* Washington.

———. 2000. *Uniform Crime Reports. Supplementary Homicide Reports.* Washington.

Greene, William H. 2000. *Econometric Analysis.* 4th ed. Prentice Hall.

Lott, John R. Jr., 2000. *More Guns, Less Crime: Understanding Crime and Gun-control Laws.* 2d. ed. University of Chicago Press.

Lott, John R. Jr., and William M. Landes. 2001. "Multiple Victim Public Shootings." Working Paper. American Enterprise Institute and University of Chicago Law School. Available from the Social Science Research Network Electronic Library.

Lott, John R. Jr., and David B. Mustard. 1997. "Crime, Deterrence, and Right-to-Carry Concealed Handguns." *Journal of Legal Studies* 26 (1): 1–68.

Lott, John R., Jr., and John E. Whitley. 2001. "Safe-Storage Gun Laws: Accidental Deaths, Suicides and Crime." *Journal of Law and Economics* 44 (2, pt. 2): 659–90.

Ludwig, Jens. 1998. "Concealed-Gun-Carrying Laws and Violent Crime: Evidence from State Panel Data." *International Review of Law and Economics* 18 (3): 239–54.

Maltz, Michael, and Joseph Targonski. 2001. "A Note on the Use of County-Level UCR Data." Working Paper. Available from the University of Illinois at Chicago.

Manning, Willard G. 1998. "The Logged Dependent Variable, Heteroscedasticity, and the Retransformation Problem." *Journal of Health Economics* 17 (June): 283–95.

Manski, Charles F. 1990. "Nonparametric Bounds on Treatment Effects." *American Economic Review* 80 (July): 319–23.

McCullagh, Peter, and J. A. Nelder. 1989. *Generalized Linear Models,* 2d ed. London: Chapman and Hall.

Moody, Carlisle E. 1999. "Testing for the Effects of Concealed Weapons Laws: Specification Errors and Robustness." Paper presented at the Conference on Guns, Crime, and Safety at the American Enterprise Institute.

Mullahy, John. 1998. "Much Ado about Two: Reconsidering Retransformation and the Two-Part Model in Health Econometrics." *Journal of Health Economics* 17 (June): 247–81.

Mustard, David. 2001. "The Impact of Gun Laws on Police Deaths." Working Paper. Available from the Terry College of Business at the University of Georgia.

Olson, David E., and Michael D. Maltz. 2001. "Right-to-Carry Concealed Weapon Laws and Homicide in Large U.S. Counties: The Effect on Weapon Types, Victim Characteristics, and Victim-Offender Relationships." *Journal of Law and Economics* 44 (2): 1–23.

Plassmann, Florenz, and T. Nicholas Tideman. 2000. "Does the Right to Carry Concealed Handguns Deter Countable Crimes? Only a Count Analysis Can Say." Paper presented at the Economics Brownbag Seminar of the University of South Carolina. Available from the University of South Carolina.

Staiger, Douglas and John H. Stock. 1997. "Instrumental Variables Regression with Weak Instruments." *Econometrica* 65 (3): 557–86.

Wilson, James Q. 2000. "Guns and Bush." *Slate Politics. http://slate.msn.com/?id=91132.* (October 13).

Zimring, Franklin, and Gordon Hawkins. 1997. "Concealed Handguns: The Counterfeit Deterrent." *Responsive Community* 7 (2): 46–60.

PART IV

Facilitating Research

JON S. VERNICK
LISA M. HEPBURN

9 | State and Federal Gun Laws: Trends for 1970–99

In the field of public health, crafting interventions to reduce the incidence of death and disability involves a multistep process. Epidemiology assesses the magnitude of the problem and identifies possible risk factors. Next, interventions are designed and implemented to address those risk factors. The disciplines of political science, the behavioral sciences, law, medicine, economics, and other fields may contribute to a proposed intervention. Finally, the impact and effectiveness of those interventions are evaluated, potentially relying on quantitative and qualitative data collection. This process is not unique to public health. Many social science disciplines, such as economics or criminology, may also use this general approach.

One goal of this approach is to permit public policy, including legislation, to be informed by evidence. In theory, scholars can evaluate the effectiveness of laws, and only those that are judged (on balance) beneficial will be retained or replicated. In practice, legislative interventions are rarely designed, implemented, and evaluated in such a systematic fashion.

We are especially grateful for the expert assistance of Amy Schofield in the collection and organization of the statutory material. We also thank Shannon Frattaroli, Stephen Teret, and Daniel Webster for insightful comments regarding the discussion of the data; Sharon Wakefield for expert assistance with tables and formatting; Franklin Zimring and Mark Kleiman for their comments at a recent Brookings Institution meeting; and Sayre Weaver of the Legal Community Against Violence for her work examining state preemption laws. Support from the Annie E. Casey Foundation for the legal research component of this chapter is gratefully acknowledged.

345

The disjunction between this form of evidence-based decisionmaking and actual policymaking may be even more pronounced in highly politicized and controversial areas like the prevention of firearm-related injuries.[1] Researchers and advocates on both sides of the gun control debate are sometimes frustrated by the perceived inability of research to influence policy.

But there may be another reason why gun violence research has not exerted a greater influence on public policy—the absence of a critical mass of high-quality published studies evaluating the effectiveness of specific gun laws. There are several possible reasons for this comparative scarcity of research. Researchers may be intimidated by political pressures, lack adequate funding, or feel inadequately trained. One other possible reason, however, may be the absence of certain kinds of data.[2] In particular, a comprehensive data set of state and federal gun laws, with precise effectiveness dates for each law, has generally not been available.

This chapter reports on the preparation of just such a data set, covering the period from 1970 to 1999 for all fifty states and the federal system. By making it possible to easily identify which laws were (and were not) in effect in each state during a given time, we hope this data set will facilitate new evaluation research. By providing not just the year of enactment, but in most cases the precise date of effectiveness, researchers can more accurately determine whether any outcome of interest occurred before or after a given law took effect. The data set will also allow researchers to better isolate the effects of specific laws by more accurately controlling for the presence of other relevant gun laws. The data set was provided to prospective authors of other chapters in this volume. Besides evaluating the effects of specific laws, the longitudinal data set created for this project provides an interesting opportunity to examine how gun control laws have evolved at the state level during the past thirty years.

Methods

Our primary source of information about federal and state firearm laws was the compiled statutes of each state and the United States Code. These were reviewed at various law libraries and on-line via electronic legal research services such as Lexis and WestLaw.

We also referred to several secondary compilations of firearms laws. These included "State Laws and Published Ordinances—Firearms," compiled by the

1. Spitzer (1998).
2. Teret, Wintemute, and Beilenson (1992).

Bureau of Alcohol, Tobacco, and Firearms; "Gun Control in the United States: A Comparative Survey of State Firearm Laws," prepared by the Open Society Institute; "Survey of State Procedures Related to Firearm Sales, Midyear 2000," compiled by the Bureau of Justice Statistics; and websites of national organizations such as the National Rifle Association, and Handgun Control, Inc. (now known as the Brady Campaign to Prevent Gun Violence).[3] These compilations often conflict with one another; our final resort was always the state or federal code itself. Sometimes conflicts among the compilations are attributable to differences in how certain kinds of laws are defined. When there might be confusion, we have provided our definitions of the laws (later in this chapter and in the appendix tables in this chapter).

None of the compilations routinely provides the date of effectiveness for state gun laws. Once the relevant state code section is identified, determining the effectiveness date for that section usually requires locating the original state bills that were enacted to create that code section. These are called state session laws and, especially for older laws, are generally only available on microfiche in law libraries. Occasionally, the state code will have renumbered or recodified the relevant law. In these cases it was sometimes also necessary to refer to older, superseded state codes to identify the appropriate state session laws. Once the session laws are obtained, the effectiveness date is derived from one of three sources, in order of preference: specific language in the enacted bill indicating its effectiveness date; a separate provision of the state code or constitution establishing effectiveness dates for laws where none are otherwise provided in the bill; or the date of the bill's enactment.

For some older laws we were unable to obtain the relevant state session law. Using superseded state codes, we were nevertheless able to confirm that these laws had been part of the state's code since at least 1970. Therefore, for some laws, rather than a specific date, the tables in the appendix to this chapter will specify "pre-1970" as the effectiveness date. We chose 1970 as our cut-off in part for convenience and in part because most recent time-series analyses of the effects of state gun laws have not included outcome measures before 1970.

We have made every effort to ensure the accuracy of the information in the tables, cross-checking our data with those of other organizations when possible. However, with almost twenty gun laws (and variations) in fifty states over thirty years, the number of possible state-law-years is approximately 30,000. We acknowledge, therefore, that some errors remain possible.

3. Bureau of Alcohol, Tobacco and Firearms (2000, 1998, 1994, 1988); Open Society Institute, Soros Foundation (2000); www.nra.org. (December 20, 2001); www.bradycampaign.org. (December 20, 2001); Bureau of Justice Statistics (2000).

Laws Included

We did not obtain information about every possible state-level gun law. In general, we chose to focus on what we consider the most important and pervasive laws intended to affect the manufacture, design, sale, and purchase of firearms. We also include certain laws limiting who may own firearms, how they must be stored, and when they may be carried concealed. Although we generally exclude most purely punitive laws, we include two types of firearm sentencing laws: those requiring a mandatory minimum sentence for certain firearm crimes, and those that include a required additional sentence for certain offenses if a firearm is also used (sometimes called minimum add-ons). These two laws are included because they are among the most common of all gun laws and because prior evaluation attention has been focused on them.[4]

Obviously, some of our choices were subjective. Among the state laws we did *not* capture were firearm immunity laws insulating manufacturers from municipal or individual lawsuits[5]; statutes, court cases, or attorneys general opinions that preempt municipalities from enacting some or all kinds of local gun laws (though some cross-sectional information about these laws is included in the next section); certain variations in categories of persons prohibited from owning a gun under state law, such as restrictions on gun ownership by misdemeanants or domestic abusers; and most criminal prohibitions on the use of guns, such as illegally brandishing a gun or armed robbery—unlike mandatory minimums or minimum add-ons these laws do not provide *extra* punishment for use of a gun.

We recognize that the laws we do not include may also be potentially important.[6] We hope that as researchers focus on their areas of interest, this data set can be expanded and updated over time with information provided by others. And, in fact, other authors in this volume have already begun to provide new state gun law information in some of these areas.[7]

Local Laws

We have not attempted to identify local (that is, city and county) firearm laws in the same way as state and federal laws. Many local laws are not available online or in out-of-state law libraries and so are notoriously difficult to collect. Therefore, it is extraordinarily labor intensive to determine the effectiveness dates for a large group of local laws, scattered throughout the country.

4. McDowall, Loftin, and Wiersema (1992); Marvell and Moody (1995).
5. Vernick and Teret (1999).
6. Wintemute (1999).
7. See Vigdor and Mercy, chapter 5, in this volume.

To provide some information for researchers, however, we have first identi-fied the sixty-seven U.S. cities with a population of at least 250,000 people as of the 2000 census. For city population purposes, we use the census definition for a "place," not a metropolitan statistical area (MSA). Using the "place" defi-nition helps to identify the number of people who would actually be affected by the lawmaking authority of the jurisdiction, rather than also including people living in a neighboring suburb.

Next, we refer to the Bureau of Alcohol, Tobacco and Firearms compilation of "State Laws and Published Ordinances—Firearms," published in 2000. The ATF compilation provides information about the existence, but not the effec-tiveness date, for some kinds of local laws.

Complicating any effort to collect local laws is the existence of statewide laws preempting all or some types of local firearm laws. Preemption may be derived from state statutory law, judicial rulings, attorney general interpretations, or some combination of all of these. Based on research conducted by the Firearms Law Center of the Legal Community Against Violence,[8] as of early 2002, forty-one states preempted some or all local gun control laws; in nine states localities retain authority to regulate guns, though the full scope of that authority has not always been tested.[9] In some states, all or certain preexisting local laws were "grand-fathered" after a subsequent preemption law was enacted and so remain in force.

Even in the forty-one states with full or partial preemption, however, the pa-rameters of that preemption vary considerably. In four of these states, certain well-defined areas of firearm regulation are preempted, but otherwise localities in these states retain broad home rule powers.[10] In seventeen others, express pre-emption language is much broader, yet the preemption laws carve out certain, fairly substantial exceptions—for example, local laws pertaining to children or concealed weapon carrying might be permitted.[11] Finally, in twenty of the forty-one states, the preemption provision permits no or relatively limited local reg-ulation.[12] In some of these states, for example, localities may retain the authority to enact zoning or taxation laws related to gun dealers, or laws pertaining to the unlawful discharge of weapons.

---

8. Firearms Law Center (2002).

9. The nine states without express preemption of local gun laws are Connecticut, Hawaii, Illi-nois, Kansas, New Hampshire, New Jersey, New York, Massachusetts, and Ohio.

10. These four states are Alaska, California, Colorado, and Nebraska.

11. These seventeen states with express preemption but reasonably substantial exceptions are Arizona, Florida, Idaho, Indiana, Kentucky, Louisiana, Maryland, Minnesota, Mississippi, Missouri, Montana, North Carolina, Oregon, Texas, Washington, West Virginia, and Wisconsin.

12. These twenty states are Alabama, Arkansas, Delaware, Georgia, Iowa, Maine, Michigan, Nevada, New Mexico, North Dakota, Oklahoma, Pennsylvania, Rhode Island, South Carolina, South Dakota, Tennessee, Utah, Vermont, Virginia, and Wyoming.

Implementation and Enforcement

Our legal research can determine whether a certain law is included among the statutes of a given state. However, we do not have information about how or whether the law is, in practice, implemented or enforced. When there might be some doubt about whether a specific state has a given law, our final resort is always to the language of the statute itself.

Description of the Federal, State, and Local Laws

This section describes the federal, state, and local laws and how they vary within a given category of law.

Federal Laws

Table 9A-1, in the appendix to this chapter, includes a brief description of the major federal gun laws enacted since 1934 that still affect gun policy today. Precise implementation dates are provided for major federal laws since 1968.

The first important federal gun control law in the United States, remaining largely in force today, was the National Firearms Act of 1934.[13] The National Firearms Act was passed, in part, as a response to a perceived increase in the misuse of firearms associated with organized crime.[14] As a result, the law focused primarily on only a few specific firearms such as sawed-off shotguns and machine guns, requiring these guns to be registered and a transfer tax to be paid upon their sale.

In many ways the Gun Control Act of 1968 is the bedrock federal gun control legislation in the United States. Among its numerous initial provisions, the Gun Control Act requires firearm dealers and manufacturers to be licensed;[15] prohibits gun purchase or possession by certain categories of persons such as convicted felons or fugitives from justice;[16] prohibits the sale of handguns by licensed dealers to persons under age 21 (18 for rifles and shotguns);[17] and limits the importation of certain firearms deemed not suitable for "sporting purposes."[18] Most subsequent federal gun laws are codified as amendments to the Gun Control Act.

---

13. 26 U.S.C. § 5801 *et seq.*
14. Zimring and Hawkins (1992).
15. 18 U.S.C. § 923 (a).
16. 18 U.S.C. § 922 (g).
17. 18 U.S.C. § 922 (b)(1).
18. 18 U.S.C. § 925 (d)(3).

In 1986, during the presidency of Ronald Reagan, the Firearm Owners Protection Act (FOPA) was enacted. As its name suggests, the FOPA was introduced at the behest of firearm owners' groups, particularly the National Rifle Association, and eased certain restrictions on firearm owners and dealers. For example, the FOPA forbids the federal government from establishing a national firearm registration system[19] and limits the ability of the Bureau of Alcohol, Tobacco, and Firearms (ATF) to inspect the premises and records of licensed dealers.[20] The FOPA also included a section that effectively banned the possession or transfer of machine guns that were not lawfully owned before May 19, 1986.[21]

In 1991 the Gun Free School Zones Act became effective. That law forbids, with certain exceptions, the possession of a gun on or within 1,000 feet of a school. The law was declared unconstitutional by the U.S. Supreme Court in 1995 but was reenacted in 1996 in similar form to address the constitutional infirmity.[22]

The process of purchasing a gun from a licensed dealer was overhauled by the Brady Handgun Violence Prevention Act, effective February 28, 1994.[23] The Brady Act applied primarily to states without their own qualifying background check law. In those states, licensed gun dealers were required to process background checks (through a chief law enforcement officer) of prospective handgun purchasers. A maximum five-day waiting period was instituted to allow time for the background check to be completed. On June 27, 1997, the U.S. Supreme Court declared the background check portion of the Brady Act unconstitutional.[24] Most states, however, continued to conduct the checks on a voluntary basis.[25] By the terms of the Brady Act itself, as of November 30, 1998, its waiting period provisions were replaced with a national instant background check system. The new system was applicable to handguns and, for the first time, long guns (for example, rifles and shotguns).

Also in 1994, the Violent Crime Control and Law Enforcement Act became effective. It included several different provisions applicable to firearm manufacture, purchase, and possession and established a minimum age of 18, with limited exceptions, for the purchase or possession of handguns or ammunition suitable for handguns only.[26] Unlike the Gun Control Act, the new minimum

19. 18 U.S.C. § 926 (a)(3).
20. 18 U.S.C. § 923 (g).
21. 18 U.S.C. § 922 (o).
22. 18 U.S.C. § 922 (q); *United States* v. *Lopez,* 514 U.S. 549 (1995).
23. 18 U.S.C. § 922 (s)-(u).
24. *Printz* v. *United States,* 521 U.S. 898 (1997).
25. Ludwig and Cook (2000).
26. 18 U.S.C. § 922 (x).

age applied to *all* handgun purchase or possession, not just those acquired from a licensed dealer. The law also banned manufacture, transfer, or possession of certain semiautomatic assault weapons that were not lawfully owned before September 13, 1994.[27] It defined an assault weapon by reference to a list of banned guns, or by whether the gun contained a combination of certain design features. Ownership of newly made, large-capacity feeding devices capable of holding more than ten rounds of ammunition was similarly outlawed.[28]

Finally, effective September 30, 1996, a new category of persons proscribed from purchasing or possessing guns was created. The so-called Lautenberg Amendment added a "misdemeanor crime of domestic violence" to the list of criteria, originally established by the Gun Control Act, disqualifying lawful gun ownership.[29]

Relationship between Federal Laws and State Laws

In general, federal gun laws do not preempt state laws on the same topic "unless there is a direct and positive conflict between the [federal law] and the law of the State so that the two cannot be reconciled or consistently stand together."[30] However, federal law does provide a minimum standard applicable in all states. For example, as described in the preceding section, a 1994 federal law provided that, with limited exceptions, no person under 18 could purchase or possess a handgun. Before 1994, some states had enacted their own laws establishing various minimum ages for the purchase and/or possession of a firearm (see next section, tables 9A-4 and 9A-5). Beginning in 1994, the federal minimum applies in all states. State laws mandating a higher minimum age (for example age 21) remain, of course, in effect.

As just described, the initial provisions of the federal Brady Act were a special case that might be deemed "reverse preemption." Congress decided that the background check portions of the Brady Act would only apply to states without their own qualifying background check law. For states with such background check laws (including those that were part of permit-to-purchase systems), the Brady Act's background check and maximum five-day waiting period did not apply in that state. This was the case even if the state (Virginia, for example) had a background check but did not have a separate waiting period.

27. 18 U.S.C. § 922 (v).
28. 18 U.S.C. § 922 (w).
29. 18 U.S.C. §§ 922 (d)(9), (s)(3)(B)(1).
30. 18 U.S.C. § 927. This antipreemption section technically applies only to federal gun laws that are codified in 18 U.S.C. §§ 921–930. However, nearly all federal gun laws are codified in these sections, as part of the Gun Control Act of 1968, or as amendments to it.

State Laws

We collected information about approximately eighteen different state gun laws from 1970 to 1999. Because some categories of laws have several possible variations, we provide data for more than eighteen separate types of gun laws.

The state laws are organized into four categories: laws banning certain firearms (table 9A-2); sales and purchase restrictions (tables 9A-3 and 9A-4); possession, carrying, and storage laws (table 9A-5); and sentence enhancement laws for the use of a firearm in a crime (table 9A-6). Other ways of organizing the material are certainly possible.[31,32] Our goal was not to provide a new conceptual framework. Given the laws we chose to collect, we hope that our organizational strategy will foster ease of use of the data set.

Placing state laws into discrete categories is necessary to make the task of producing a panel data set a manageable one. However, this arrangement may also obscure potentially important differences among state laws. When relevant, our definitional choices are explained. Some issues for evaluators to consider, related to lumping (rather than splitting) certain state laws into one category, are discussed later in this chapter. Except as noted, all counts of state laws are current as of the end of calendar year 1999.

Laws Banning Certain Firearms (table 9A-2). We report on laws banning three different types of firearms: all handguns, Saturday night specials, and assault weapons. Just one jurisdiction included in our sample bans most handgun possession—the District of Columbia. Private handgun possession is generally forbidden in Washington, D.C., unless the gun was owned and registered before 1969 and then reregistered in 1976. The District is omitted from most of the other tables—its handgun ban places the District in a very different category. The only other major U.S. city with a virtual ban on handgun possession is Chicago (since 1982), although New York City also makes it difficult for most residents to own firearms.

As of 1999, five states ban the manufacture, purchase, or possession of Saturday night special handguns, sometimes also referred to as "junk guns." In general, these guns have been described as small, low-caliber, cheaply constructed, relatively inaccurate, and inexpensive.[33] States have chosen to define a Saturday night special handgun in several different ways. For example, some states focus primarily on the melting point of the cheap metals used in most such guns;

---

31. Zimring (1991).
32. Teret and Wintemute (1993).
33. Sherril (1973).

others rely on expert boards to identify guns to be permitted or banned.[34] Two other states, California and Massachusetts, have adopted Saturday night special bans that went into effect after 1999.

Six states ban the manufacture, ownership, or transfer of newly made assault weapons.[35] Again, definitions of affected guns vary. Like the federal law, these guns are often defined by reference to a list of specifically banned gun models or other design criteria such as the presence of certain quasi-military features like a flash suppressor.

Sales and Purchase Restrictions (tables 9A-3 and 9A-4). Sales and purchase restrictions constitute the bulk of state laws focusing on the gun itself. The sales and purchase restrictions we collected were permit-to-purchase licensing; registration; background checks for gun sales from licensed firearm dealers; background checks for gun sales from nondealers; minimum waiting periods, usually associated with background checks; maximum waiting periods, usually associated with permit-to-purchase systems; one-gun-per-month laws; laws establishing a minimum purchase age; dealer licensing laws; and mandatory dealer inspection laws.

Permit-to-purchase licensing refers to a system in which prospective gun purchasers must first obtain a license or permit, typically issued by the state police, before purchasing a firearm. These laws are different from rules requiring a background check at the point of sale, though a background check is generally required for the permit to be issued. There is great variation in the other substantive and procedural preconditions that states apply before issuing a permit. Some of this variation is identified in table 9A-3, including whether the law applies to handguns or all guns, and the duration of any applicable waiting period. However, there are also other differences among state laws (not included in the table), such as the requirement for fingerprints, the expiration period of the permit, whether an additional state background check is required for each separate gun purchase, and the amount of discretion that law enforcement may have to deny licenses to those without a "good reason" for gun ownership.[36]

We define a registration law as one in which a permanent record of each gun sale is kept in a central location: just eight states meet our criteria.[37] This may

34. See Hawaii, Illinois, Minnesota, and South Carolina, in table 9-2. Maryland law establishes a handgun roster board to create a list of handguns that may be sold within a state. Vernick, Webster, and Hepburn (1999).

35. See California, Connecticut, Hawaii, Maryland, Massachusetts, and New Jersey, in table 9-2.

36. Webster, Vernick, and Hepburn (2001).

37. See California, Connecticut, Hawaii, Maryland, Massachusetts, Michigan, New Jersey, and New York, in table 9-3.

be a more restrictive definition than others have employed. It excludes states where records of sale are kept by local law enforcement or for a limited time only. Within states mandating gun registration, some apply to handguns only, and most do not require the registration of previously acquired guns brought into the state by new residents.

Since 1994 federal law has required a background check for handguns purchased from federally licensed dealers (expanded to include long guns in 1998). Thirty states also require a background check under state law; many of these laws predate the federal law. We include background checks conducted as part of a permit-to-purchase application, and those initiated by gun dealers at the time of sale. Table 9A-3 shows which of these state laws apply to all guns and which apply to handguns only. The table does not specify variations in state law regarding the criteria for disqualifying a handgun purchase. These rules generally include felony convictions but may also include certain misdemeanors, a history of substance abuse, mental illness, or certain restraining orders. As a result, there is also variation among states in the kinds of record systems (and their completeness) that are consulted to determine if a buyer is disqualified. As is also the case under federal law, persons holding a gun dealer's license are usually exempted from state background check rules when they buy guns.

Unlike federal law, sixteen states also require background checks for guns purchased from nondealers, sometimes called private sales.[38] Again, these are conducted under varying exclusionary criteria and may apply to all guns or to handguns only. Efforts to close the so-called gun show loophole would require background checks for all gun sales occurring at gun shows, even from nondealers. These are essentially a subset of private sale background check laws, which apply to all gun transactions whether or not they occur at a gun show. We have not recorded information about state laws that apply special background check provisions to gun show sales only.

We record two kinds of state waiting periods for the purchase of firearms—minimum waits generally associated with background checks at the time of sale, and maximum waits generally associated with permit-to-purchase licensing systems. Table 9A-3 indicates the duration of the minimum waiting period (in parentheses); how that duration has changed, if at all, over time; whether the waiting period applies to handguns or all guns; and whether a maximum waiting period is applicable (see footnotes to table 9A-3). We also indicate whether a state has adopted an instant background check system without a waiting period. One state, Florida, has both an instant background check system and a minimum three-day waiting period.

38. Cook, Molliconi, and Cole (1995); Jacobs and Potter (1995).

Through 1999, just three states—Maryland, South Carolina, and Virginia—had adopted laws that, with certain exceptions, limit the purchase of handguns to a maximum of one per person per month. These so-called one-gun-per-month laws are designed to make it more difficult for gun traffickers to purchase a large number of guns at one time for later resale to proscribed purchasers such as juveniles or felons.[39] California has recently enacted such a law that became effective after 1999.

Several states have enacted laws establishing a minimum age for the purchase of a firearm. Most of these laws are written to forbid sellers from transferring firearms to those below a threshold age. Among the states, the minimum age has varied over time from 15 to 21 (table 9A-4). Table 9A-4 also records changes to the minimum age within a state and whether the law is applicable to handguns or all guns. Some state laws indicate that sale to minors is forbidden but do not define a "minor." For these states, we assume a minimum age of 18 but provide a footnote so that researchers can make their own choices.

Federal law requires persons who "engage in the business" of selling firearms to obtain a dealers license issued by the ATF.[40] Eighteen states require gun dealers to also obtain a state license. Just two states, Massachusetts and Rhode Island, require the inspection of a dealer's business records or premises at regular intervals. Of course, many other states permit such inspections (but do not require them). Actual practice in these states in the frequency or scope of inspections is likely to vary.

Possession, Carrying, and Storage Laws (table 9A-5). Three major possession, carrying, and storage laws are included in our data set: minimum possession age laws; concealed weapon carrying (CCW) laws; and child access prevention (CAP) laws.

State minimum possession age laws establish ages varying from 15 to 19 years old for handgun ownership. Many of these laws were enacted before the federal minimum was established in 1994. Some states with permit-to-purchase laws establish higher minimum ages for obtaining the permit, which may act as a de facto possession or purchase age limit (table 9A-5).

Laws establishing criteria for obtaining a permit to carry a concealed weapon have been among the most controversial of all recent gun legislation.[41] In fact, even the appropriate way to categorize some states has been a matter of dis-

---

39. Weil and Knox (1996).
40. 18 U.S.C. § 923(a).
41. Lott and Mustard (1997); Ludwig (1998); Black and Nagin (1998); Zimring and Hawkins (1997).

agreement among researchers and advocates.[42] Table 9A-5 divides these laws into three categories: shall issue, may issue, and states where concealed carrying is generally prohibited. "Shall issue" refers to states where applicants who meet certain objective criteria *shall* be issued a concealed-carry permit. As of 1999 we categorized twenty-nine states as having a "shall-issue" system. This includes Vermont, where concealed weapon carrying is allowed even without a permit.

In the fourteen "may-issue" states, the issuing authority retains some discretion to deny permits. In these states, applicants must often demonstrate that they have some good reason for the permit and that they are not unfit for the privilege. Based on the language of their respective statutes, we categorize Alabama and Connecticut as may-issue states. Others differ here (see notes to table 9A-5), and actual practice in these states was not determined. Finally, in the "prohibited" category are seven states that make it very difficult or impossible for most private citizens to obtain a concealed-carry permit.

In the 1990s, child access prevention (CAP) laws became popular, culminating in sixteen state laws by the end of the decade. The CAP laws provide criminal penalties for adults who store a firearm in a manner so that a child can gain easy access. In some states, a child must gain access to the gun and harm himself or another as an element of the crime. The crime is a misdemeanor in some states, a felony in others.[43] The age of the child to be protected also varies.

Sentence Enhancement Laws for Use of a Firearm (table 9A-6). Two kinds of sentence enhancement laws are considered: laws establishing a mandatory minimum term for crimes committed with firearms and those providing a minimum additional sentence (an add-on to the basic sentence) for such crimes. In the construction of table 9A-6, we rely heavily on a prior work by Thomas Marvell and Carlisle Moody.[44] Our table 9A-6 updates the earlier work but allows the reader to identify changes in the law since Marvell and Moody produced their table.[45]

Local Laws (table 9A-7)

Table 9A-7 displays our cross-sectional information about the existence of certain local firearm laws in the sixty-seven U.S. cities with a population of at least 250,000 persons. The firearm law categories in the table reflect the local law

42. Webster, Vernick, Ludwig, and Lester (1997).
43. Cummings, Grossman, Rivara, and Koepsell (1997).
44. Marvell and Moody (1995).
45. Readers who wish to better understand the many variations in state laws in this complex area should carefully examine the notes to table 9A-6.

information provided by the Bureau of Alcohol, Tobacco and Firearms in its 2000 compilation of laws. Because this information has not been independently verified, we cannot be sure that it reflects all of the relevant local laws. Furthermore, in some localities a given law may remain on the books (unenforced), even though it has been subsequently preempted by the state legislature. Finally, we are unable to provide precise dates of effectiveness for these laws.

Nevertheless, table 9A-7 suggests the wide range of local firearm laws. Many cities have few or no local laws, while others have enacted a comprehensive regulatory scheme. This table gives researchers who are focusing on a given jurisdiction or type of law a starting place for further investigation.

State Gun Laws over Time

For the purposes of analyzing the geographic and temporal distribution of state gun laws, we use the total of eighteen different laws described earlier. The analyses exclude the introduction of shall-issue CCW laws. This allows an examination of trends in the enactment of restrictive, rather than permissive, gun laws. For all figures, changes in the type of gun affected (handguns versus long guns), or in the duration of waiting periods, are not counted as a separate law. We count a state as having a particular law in a given year if that law became effective at any time during the year. During our study period (1970–99), eleven different laws were repealed in their respective states. Similarly, these laws were subtracted from our state counts as of the beginning of the year in which they were repealed. Washington, D.C., is generally excluded from these analyses. Its 1976 law banning most handgun ownership, and its unusual status as a federal district, make it too different from the states in our analyses.

Changes

As of 1970, there were 105 different restrictive state gun laws that met our inclusion criteria described earlier (figure 9-1). By 1999, there were more than 275. The number of laws per state ranged from 1 to 13. Among the most common of the state laws in 1999 were mandatory minimum sentencing laws (38); dealer background check laws (30); dealer licensing (18); and CAP laws (16). Much less common were handgun bans (0 when Washington, D.C., is excluded); dealer inspection (2); and assault weapons bans (6).

Figure 9-1 suggests that the middle-to-late 1970s, and also the early-to-mid 1990s, saw a faster increase in the rate of new state gun laws than in other time periods, particularly by comparison with the 1980s. Figure 9-2 makes these

Figure 9-1. *Cumulative Number of Gun Laws Each Year, 1970–99*

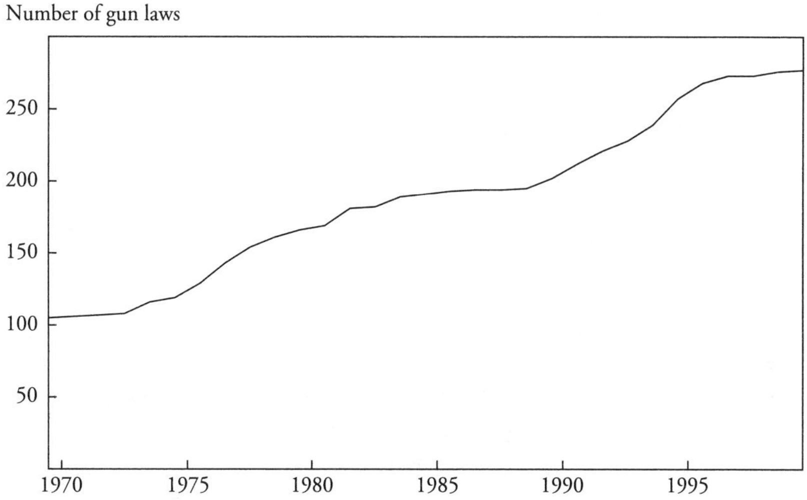

Number of gun laws

Figure 9-2. *Number of New Gun Laws by Year, 1970–99*

Number of new gun laws

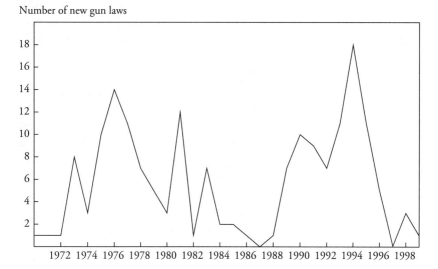

differences easier to perceive by displaying just the number of *new* state gun laws by year. Clearly, the 1980s were a less fertile period for state gun laws than were the late 1970s and most of the 1990s.

There are several possible explanations for these observed differences. The late 1970s and most of the 1990s were periods when Democratic administrations occupied the White House (Presidents Jimmy Carter and Bill Clinton). Although we do not include federal gun laws in our analysis, a Democratic administration may encourage a national environment and dialogue more conducive to the enactment of state gun control laws. By comparison, Ronald Reagan, a Republican and NRA member, served as president from 1981 through 1988. During his term, the federal Firearm Owners Protection Act was enacted. Of course, the political party of the president in power may also be a proxy for many other political, social, or economic factors likely to influence the enactment of state and federal gun laws.

Another possible explanation for trends in the enactment of state gun laws relates to rates of homicide and other violent crime in the United States. Gun homicide rates increased sharply in the late 1980s to early 1990s, just as they had done from the late 1960s to early 1970s.[46] As any social problem grows more acute—and gains more media attention—states are more likely to seek legislative solutions. However, it is reasonable to expect that there will be some lag time in the enactment of new laws, as politicians recognize the trend, propose new laws, and then those laws gradually gather the necessary support.

Of course, the specific kind of legislative solution popular with state legislatures may be quite different in the 1990s compared with the 1970s. For example, figure 9-3 shows that all but one CAP law became effective in the 1990s. By comparison, many permit-to-purchase licensing laws were enacted before 1970, with a modest flurry of activity in the late 1970s.

Other state laws, not displayed in this figure, have also been associated with specific time periods. Remarkably, thirty of the thirty-eight mandatory minimum sentencing laws became effective between 1975 and 1982. In the past fifteen years, the NRA has been particularly successful in advocating for shall-issue CCW laws. Eighteen of the twenty-nine shall-issue CCW laws in our study period went into effect after Florida adopted its law in 1987.

A social contagion effect may also explain why certain laws are enacted at certain times and places. This social contagion may be facilitated by several factors. National organizations that advocate for gun laws (often coupled with local affiliates) may choose a particular kind of law as the focus of their efforts at any given time and may also decide to concentrate on one or two states, be-

---

46. Centers for Disease Control and Prevention (2001); Ikeda and others (1997).

Figure 9-3. *Cumulative Number of Child Access Prevention (CAP) and Licensing Laws, 1970–99*

Number of laws

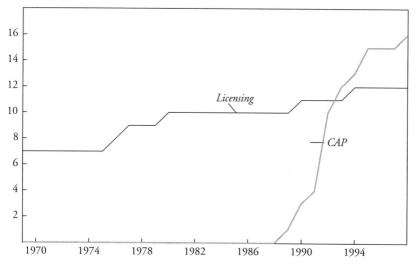

fore moving on to other targets. After a law is enacted in a sentinel state, other politically "susceptible" states may quickly enact the law. Eventually that kind of law is adopted in all or most of the states where it can be easily enacted. The trend will then slow and stop as more politically challenging target states are considered.

Cultural and political factors in a state and region may also contribute to a contagion effect. Thus states within the same region (more likely to share a similar cultural or political environment) may be more likely to adopt similar laws at similar times than more distant states.

"20,000 Gun Laws"

The belief that there are approximately 20,000 gun laws in the United States has become received wisdom. A search of an electronic news database for "20,000 gun laws" or "20,000 gun control laws" yielded more than 200 uses of these phrases in the past five years.

By itself, the exact number of gun laws in the United States should be of almost no interest. However, the 20,000 figure is often quoted by opponents of gun regulation. Their argument is that the United States already has so many gun laws that more are not needed—better enforcement of existing laws is the real solution to gun violence.[47] So, it may be instructive to explore this claim a bit further.

The precise provenance of the 20,000 figure is difficult to determine. The earliest reference that we located appears in testimony provided in 1965 by Representative John Dingell (D-Mich.) before a Senate Judiciary Subcommittee pursuant to proposed new federal gun legislation. Near the beginning of his testimony, Dingell states:

> Consider the fact that we now have on the lawbooks of this Nation over 20,000 laws governing the sale, distribution, and use of firearms. Contrary to what some of the more zealous antifirearms editorial writers would have us believe, the situation in the United States is certainly not one of unrestricted and unregulated firearm sale and usage. . . . Yet, despite 20,000-odd laws which, one way or another, are directed toward the same purpose, a rising national crime rate gives alarming evidence that the criminal element does not want for weapons with which to wage war against our law-abiding citizenry.[48]

No additional references to the 20,000 figure appear in Dingell's testimony, and no source for the estimate is given. George Newton and Franklin Zimring cite Dingell's use of the figure in their seminal 1969 work, *Firearms and Violence in American Life,* but they also note that "the basis of this estimate is not provided."[49]

Despite the apparent lack of a scientific basis, the 20,000 figure has become influential and widely cited. In 1981, just eleven weeks after surviving an attempt on his life, President Ronald Reagan rejected a call for additional legislation, arguing at a press conference that "there are today more than 20,000 gun control laws in effect—Federal, state and local—in the United States."[50] The figure also appears in prominent books by advocates and scholars.[51]

Given the 20,000 figure's rhetorical importance, we can also use the information in our data set to consider its likely accuracy. We identify approximately 300 different state laws as of 1999. Of course, as already described, some laws have multiple subparts or components, and we have not included every possible state gun law. Even a very liberal interpretation of what should count as a separate (or new) law, however, would leave the total well short of 20,000.

47. Among numerous examples, see National Rifle Association. *Fact Sheet: Firearm Facts 2001;* www.nra.org; (December 10, 2001); "More Gun Laws Not the Solution," editorial, *Atlanta Journal and Constitution,* March 7, 2001, p A12; "Clinton Urges Legislation to Reject Gun Lobby Tactics," *Washington Post,* March 5, 2000, p. A7.

48. Dingell (1965, pp. 374–90).

49. Newton and Zimring (1969; p. 87).

50. " 'I Have Recovered,' President Declares," *New York Times,* June 17, 1981, p. A17.

51. Shields (1981, pp. 80, 125); Wright, Rossi, and Daly (1983, p. 244).

But when people refer to 20,000 gun laws, they are clearly including federal and local laws as well. Inclusion of the relatively few federal gun laws, even if most also have several subparts, would not substantially increase the total count. The key to the 20,000 calculation, therefore, would appear to be the contribution of local laws to the total. Since the early 1980s, though, the NRA has mounted a very successful campaign to encourage state governments to enact "preemption" laws, forbidding local governments to enact their own gun laws.[52] Today, more than forty states preempt all or most local gun laws. But clearly there remain some local laws that are not within the scope of statewide preemption laws. Our cross-sectional examination of local laws (table 9A-7) in cities with a population of at least 250,000 suggests approximately an additional ninety laws. Of course this does not include the numerous smaller cities and towns in the United States that may also have relevant laws.

Another problem with this estimate, as others have also noted, is the lack of a precise definition of a "gun law."[53] For example, many local laws prohibit carrying or firing guns in public places. Inclusion of such laws would certainly inflate national estimates of the number of gun laws. But if one thinks of laws that control the manufacture, design, sale, purchase, or possession of guns—the cluster of laws many probably imagine as constituting gun *control* laws—the number of local laws will be much smaller.

However the 20,000 figure was initially derived, the almost overwhelming trend toward preemption of local laws is likely to have greatly reduced the total. And in our view, that there may be as few as 300 major statewide laws that fit our inclusion categories, with some states having only one or two such laws, is the far more relevant figure for public policy today. Better enforcement of gun laws is clearly a laudable goal. But at least in some states, there are only a very limited number of statewide gun control laws to enforce at all.

Issues for Researchers

Preparation of the data set also highlights several other issues relevant for researchers and policymakers. State gun laws were not enacted as carefully integrated regulatory schemes. Instead, as the effectiveness dates in the tables in the appendix to this chapter reveal, gun laws are usually enacted one or two at a time as political will or opportunity allow. The result is a within- and across-state patchwork of laws with some evidence of both consistency and inconsistency. An

52. Teret, DeFrancesco, and Bailey (1993).
53. Vizzard (2000).

example of inconsistency: of the sixteen states with a CAP law, five do not have a minimum possession age law. And of consistency: of the twelve states with restrictive permit-to-purchase licensing, only one also has a permissive shall-issue concealed weapon carrying law. This patchwork can create important challenges for researchers.

Implementation and Enforcement of Gun Laws

Implementation and enforcement are critical issues for evaluators examining the effectiveness of gun laws. Implementation refers to the administrative and other processes that must be put in place for the law to function. Closely related to implementation, enforcement refers to the practice by which violators of the law are identified, apprehended, and punished.

Laws that are imperfectly implemented are unlikely to have the desired or expected effects. Worse still, researchers may conclude that a particular gun law is ineffective when, in reality, it is simply not being enforced. As we explained earlier, we do not attempt to assess how or if the gun laws in our data set are implemented or enforced. Nevertheless, some observations are possible by combining information from our data set with findings from other sources.

There are reasons to believe that, at least for some laws in some states, implementation or enforcement of those laws is very different than a simple reading of the statute would suggest. For example, laws requiring a background check for guns bought from nondealers—so-called private sale background check laws—have been adopted by sixteen states. Of those states, however, just eight also have a registration system. To enforce a private sale background check law, the state must have a record of the last lawful owner of the gun. Then, if that owner fails to conduct a background check when the gun is sold, he or she can be identified by the police if the gun is ultimately misused. Without some form of registration system, it becomes very difficult to properly enforce a private sale background check law.

Simply having a registration system, though, is not enough. The state or local police must have the will and resources to use the system to enforce the background check law. For example, Maryland has a registration system and a background check law applicable to private sales. Yet research by Shannon Frattaroli has demonstrated that background checks for private sales are seldom conducted, and that the police have rarely used Maryland's registration system to prosecute violators of the law.[54]

54. Frattaroli (1999).

Another example is provided by concealed-weapon-carrying (CCW) laws. As already noted, since 1987 a number of states have changed their CCW laws from may issue to shall issue. Yet even within these two categories, the ease of obtaining a permit may vary considerably as a result of judicial or police enforcement. For example, Clayton Cramer and David Kopel report that in California and Virginia, local officials have sometimes enforced their own rules, simply refusing to issue or reissue permits despite the language of the statewide law.[55]

Issues of enforcement may also arise when federal and state laws substantially overlap. Examples include state minimum age laws, assault weapons bans, or dealer licensing requirements. Most researchers would probably choose to assume that, before the effective date of the relevant federal law, only those states with the law should be credited with having the policy in place; but after the date of the federal law, essentially all states could be assumed to have such a law. This is certainly a rational approach. Yet it is also possible that those states retaining a separate state law, even after the federal law becomes effective, may be able to do a better job of enforcing that law. It may be easier for state and local police officials to enforce a state law than it might be, in some circumstances, to enlist the assistance of federal authorities in investigating and prosecuting a federal offense. This might enhance the effectiveness of a state law, even when an identical federal law exists. So perhaps all states should not be treated equally by researchers after a federal law is enacted.

Many commentators have noted the problem of enforcing state or local laws when neighboring states have less restrictive laws. Other research suggests that interstate trafficking is indeed a problem for many states.[56] Therefore, in some circumstances federal laws may be far easier to enforce than isolated state laws— they prevent traffickers from using the weaker laws of one state to circumvent the tougher laws of its neighbor.

Without a federal law, there may also be a threshold effect for some state laws to be effective. Only when some (unknown) national or regional threshold in the number of such laws is reached might interstate trafficking be controllable and enforcement feasible.

For researchers, the benefits of assessing if (or how well) a law is implemented or enforced as part of the evaluation process suggest many possible approaches. Ideally, a careful analysis of the implementation process, perhaps including qualitative interviews with local officials, would precede a more quantitative evaluation. Another approach is to consider intermediate outcome measures that

---

55. Cramer and Kopel (1995).
56. Bureau of Alcohol, Tobacco and Firearms (2000).

should theoretically be affected by a well-implemented gun law, before considering more distal outcomes. For example, in an evaluation of Maryland's ban on Saturday night special handguns, the researchers first examined the law's effects on the type of guns used by criminals, before analyzing the effect on homicides.[57] The choice of other intermediate outcomes, useful as proxy measures for enforcement or implementation, will depend on the law being considered. Philip Cook developed and analyzed a widely used proxy measure of gun prevalence within a jurisdiction, the proportion of suicides committed with a firearm.[58] If a given law might be expected to reduce gun ownership, before affecting other outcomes like homicide, examination of Cook's (or other) proxy measures can provide insight into the success of implementation. Policymakers can help researchers to consider implementation and enforcement issues by supporting the collection of relevant data as part of ongoing demographic and health behavior surveys.

Variation Among Similar Laws

To evaluate the effectiveness of certain kinds of state laws, researchers will usually choose to place all relatively similar laws into one category. This permits the effects of the laws to be aggregated and potentially increases the generalizability and robustness of the research design. But as demonstrated earlier, seemingly similar laws are rarely identical from state to state. Sometimes these differences are trivial; other times the differences may be more important. For the most part, though, we do not know what effect these differences may have, if any.

But recent analysis of the effects of child access prevention (CAP) laws suggests that the differences among similar laws can sometimes make a difference. In 1997 Peter Cummings and colleagues reported a statistically significant 23 percent reduction in unintentional shooting deaths among children age 15 or younger in the twelve states with a CAP law.[59] Writing in 2000, Daniel Webster and Marc Starnes reanalyzed the data and disaggregated the state laws. They reported that the three states where CAP law violations were prosecuted as felonies had experienced a 31 percent decline in unintentional shooting deaths among children, largely attributable to a dramatic change in Florida. But in the remaining misdemeanor states, the CAP laws had no discernible effect.[60]

Most other variations within a category of gun laws have yet to be examined in detail. For example, the definition of certain banned guns—like Saturday night

57. Vernick, Webster, and Hepburn (1999); Webster, Vernick, and Hepburn (2002).
58. Cook (1979).
59. Cummings, Grossman, Rivara, and Koepsell (1997).
60. Webster and Starnes (2000).

specials (SNS) or assault weapons—varies from state to state. Some states with SNS bans produce a list of prohibited guns, others a list of approved guns, and most have no list at all.[61] With assault weapons, some states use the same definition as federal law, others rely primarily on lists of banned guns, and some attempt more generic definitions.

The limited information available for local laws further complicates efforts to classify states into broad categories. For example, Ohio has relatively few of the gun laws in our data set. Yet some major cities within that state—notably Cincinnati, Columbus, and Toledo—have much more restrictive regimes.

There is no simple solution to these problems. Our data set will allow researchers to examine the possible effects of different categorization schemes for some laws. But we believe that researchers must be genuinely sensitive to the perils of overgeneralizing conclusions about the effects of potentially dissimilar laws.

Conclusion

Carefully designed and executed research—if it is used by legislators, advocates, and others—can allow for better public policy decisionmaking. We hope that this data set will contribute to that goal.

But we also hope that researchers will take our caveats about enforcement and state law variation seriously. As Zimring has noted, it is "difficult to measure variations in firearm control by reading statutes."[62] We agree, although we would add that reading statutes is a necessary first step. But the next steps are also important, though daunting. Understanding enforcement and implementation may require qualitative research methods and will certainly increase the complexity and cost of research.

Evaluators must carefully consider the pros and cons of studies that include summary data for many or all states, versus the in-depth analysis that focusing on fewer states can allow. Multiple state studies have certain methodological advantages, but our research suggests that they may also risk missing potentially important differences among state laws. They also make accounting for the possible effects of local laws much more difficult.

What is really needed are multiple analyses of the same law, with differing (though complementary) methodologies. But for now, with relatively few careful evaluations of gun laws at all, the political impact of just one prominent study—whatever its findings—can be great. This makes the choice of methodology all the more important to social scientists and to policymakers.

61. Fennel (1992).
62. Zimring (1993, p. 117).

Table 9A-1. *Major Federal Firearm Laws (still in effect), 1934–99*

Title	Code section	Effective date	Summary
National Firearms Act	26 U.S.C. § 5801 et seq.	1934	Among other provisions, requires certain weapons, such as sawed-off shotguns and machine guns, to be registered and a transfer tax to be paid upon sale.
Gun Control Act of 1968	18 U.S.C. § 921 et seq.	October 22, 1968, and December 16, 1968	Basic gun control law in the United States. Among its many initial provisions, the Gun Control Act: 1) requires a license for gun dealers, manufacturers, and importers; 2) prohibits gun purchase or possession by certain persons, such as convicted felons; 3) prohibits handgun sale by licensed dealers to persons under age 21; 4) prohibits long-gun sale by licensed dealers to persons under age 18. Most of the other federal gun laws are codified as amendments to the Gun Control Act.
Firearm Owners Protection Act	18 U.S.C. § 921 et seq. (scattered sections)	November 15, 1986	Among its several provisions: 1) forbids the federal government from establishing any "system of registration of firearms, firearm owners, or firearms transactions or distributions . . ." (18 U.S.C. § 926(a)(3)); 2) places certain limits on the ability of the ATF to inspect the premises and records of licensed dealers (18 U.S.C. § 923(g)); 3) bans the possession or transfer of a machine gun that was not lawfully owned prior to May 19, 1986 (18 U.S.C. § 922 (o)).
Gun-Free School Zones Act of 1990	18 U.S.C. § 922 (q)	January 30, 1991 (initial version)	1) Forbids, with exceptions, possession of a firearm in a school zone. 2) Declared unconstitutional by U.S. Supreme Court on 4/26/95 (*U.S. v. Lopez*, 514 U.S. 549). 3) Reenacted in a substantially similar form but with a new requirement related to interstate commerce, effective September 30, 1996.

Act	Citation	Date	Provisions
Brady Handgun Violence Prevention Act	18 U.S.C. §§ 922 (s)–(u)	February 28, 1994 November 30, 1998	1) Required states to conduct background checks for handgun purchases if state law did not already provide for a background check. 2) Maximum 5-day waiting period in those states was instituted to allow time for the check. 3) Increased the cost of obtaining a federal firearms license. 4) Background check provision declared unconstitutional by U.S. Supreme Court on 6/27/97 (*Prinz* v. *U.S.*, 521 U.S. 898). Most states continued background checks voluntarily. 5) Waiting period replaced by national instant background check system instituted for both handguns and long guns on November 30, 1998.
Violent Crime Control and Law Enforcement Act of 1994	18 U.S.C. § 922 (scattered sections)	September 19, 1994	1) Must be 18 years old to purchase or possess handguns or ammunition for handguns only, subject to limited exceptions (18 U.S.C. § 922 (x)). 2) Semi-automatic assault weapons may not be manufactured, transferred, or possessed—applies only to those firearms that meet the definition of an assault weapon and that were not lawfully possessed prior to 9/13/94 (18 U.S.C. § 922 (v)). 3) Large capacity ammunition feeding devices may not be transferred or possessed unless lawfully owned prior to 9/13/94 (18 U.S.C. § 922 (w)). 4) Persons subject to certain domestic violence restraining orders may not purchase or possess firearms (18 U.S.C. § 922 (g)(8)).
Gun ban for individuals convicted of a misdemeanor crime of domestic violence: Lautenberg amendment	18 U.S.C. §§ 922(d)(9), (g)(9), (s)(3)(B)(1)	September 30, 1996	Adds a "misdemeanor crime of domestic violence" to the list of categories of persons proscribed from gun purchase or possession.

Table 9A-2. *State Laws Banning Certain Firearms, 1970–99*

State	Handgun ban	Saturday night special ban	Assault weapon ban
Alabama	No	No	No
Alaska	No	No	No
Arizona	No	No	No
Arkansas	No	No	No
California	No	No[1]	Cal. Penal Code § 12275 June 1, 1989[2]
Colorado	No	No	No
Connecticut	No	No	Conn. Gen. Stat. Ann. § 53-202a Oct. 1, 1993[3]
Delaware	No	No	No
District of Columbia	D.C. Code Ann. § 6-2301 Sep. 24, 1976[4]	No	No
Florida	No	No	No
Georgia	No	No	No
Hawaii	No	Haw. Rev. Stat. § 134-15 May 27, 1975	Haw. Rev. Stat. § 134-4(e) July 1, 1992[5]
Idaho	No	No	No
Illinois	No[6]	Ill. Rev. Stat. ch.5, para. 24-3(h) Feb. 21, 1974	No
Indiana	No	No	No
Iowa	No	No	No
Kansas	No	No	No
Kentucky	No	No	No
Louisiana	No	No	No
Maine	No	No	No
Maryland	No	Md. Ann. Code art. 27, § 36 Jan. 1, 1990	Md. Ann. Code art. 27, § 36H June 1, 1994[7]
Massachusetts	No	No[8]	Mass Ann. Laws, ch 140, § 131M Oct. 21, 1998
Michigan	No	No	No
Minnesota	No	Minn. Stat. § 624.712(4) June 4, 1975	No
Mississippi	No	No	No
Missouri	No	No	No
Montana	No	No	No

(*continued*)

Table 9A-2. (*continued*)

State	Handgun ban	Saturday night special ban	Assault weapon ban
Nebraska	No	No	No
Nevada	No	No	No
New Hampshire	No	No	No
New Jersey	No	No	N.J. Stat. § 2C:39-5[9] May 30, 1990
New Mexico	No	No	No
New York	No[10]	No	No
North Carolina	No	No	No
North Dakota	No	No	No
Ohio	No	No	No
Oklahoma	No	No	No
Oregon	No	No	No
Pennsylvania	No	No	No
Rhode Island	No	No	No
South Carolina	No	S.C. Code Ann. § 23-31-180 July 9, 1973	No
South Dakota	No	No	No
Tennessee	No	No	No
Texas	No	No	No
Utah	No	No	No
Vermont	No	No	No
Virginia	No	No	No
Washington	No	No	No
West Virginia	No	No	No
Wisconsin	No	No	No
Wyoming	No	No	No

1. California's statewide SNS ban law took effect after 1999. A number of California communities, however, had banned the sale of these weapons before 1999.

2. To be lawful in California, an assault weapon must have been lawfully owned prior to June 1, 1989, and then registered by January 1, 1991, or within ninety days of a specific weapon being added to the list of proscribed firearms.

3. To be lawful in Connecticut, an assault weapon must have been lawfully owned prior to October 1, 1993. The owner must then have applied for a permit by October 1, 1994.

4. Enforcement of Washington, D.C.'s, law was briefly interrupted by a court decision and then became effective again on February 21, 1977.

5. Hawaii's assault weapons ban applies to assault pistols only.

6. The city of Chicago has had a virtual handgun ban since 1982; only handguns both lawfully owned and registered prior to 1982 can be possessed.

7. Maryland's assault weapon ban applies to assault pistols only. Such weapons lawfully possessed prior to June 1, 1994, must also have been registered by August 1, 1994.

8. Massachusetts's SNS ban law took effect after 1999.

9. New Jersey's ban of assault weapons does not apply to those who obtain a special license. See N.J. Ann. § 2C:58-5.

10. The city of New York has had a very restrictive permit-to-possess system for handguns since before 1970.

Table 9A-3. *Sales and Purchase Restrictions 1970–99 (1)*

State	Permit to purchase[1]	Registration[2]	Background checks for sales from dealers[3]	Background checks for private sales	Waiting period[4]
Alabama	No	No	No	No	Ala. Code § 13A-11-77 H Eff pre-1970 (2)
Alaska	No	No	No	No	No
Arizona	No	No	Ariz. Rev. Stat. Ann. § 13-3114 H Eff. Apr. 19, 1994 R Eff. Nov. 30, 1998	No	No
Arkansas	No	No	No	No	No
California	No	Cal. Penal Code § 12076(b), § 12077 H Eff. Sep. 9, 1953 R Eff. Jan. 1, 1991	Cal. Penal Code § 12076(c) H Eff. Aug. 31, 1969 R Eff. Jan. 1, 1991	Cal. Penal Code § 12072(d) H Eff. Jan. 1, 1991 R Eff Jan. 1, 1991	Cal. Penal Code § 12072 (c) H Eff. Jan. 1, 1966 (5) Jan. 1, 1976 (15) April 1, 1997 (10)
Colorado	No	No	Colo. Rev. Stat. Ann. § 12-26.5-103(2) H Eff. Feb. 28, 1994–Feb. 28, 1999[5]	No	Colo. Rev. Stat. Ann. § 12-26.5-104 Instant H Eff. Feb. 28, 1994–Feb. 28, 1999
Connecticut	Conn. Gen. Stat. Ann. § 29-36(g) H Eff. Oct. 1, 1995	Conn. Gen. Stat. Ann. § 29-33 H Eff. pre-1970 Conn. Gen. Stat. Ann. § 29-37a	Conn. Gen. Stat. Ann. § 29-33 H Eff. Oct. 1, 1995[6] Conn. Gen. Stat. Ann. § 29-37a	Conn. Gen. Stat. Ann. § 29-33(e) H Eff. Oct. 1, 1995	Conn. Gen. Stat. Ann. § 29-33 H Eff. Oct 1, 1965 (7) Oct. 1, 1975 (14) Minimum wait ends on Oct. 1, 1995

	No	R Eff. Oct. 1, 1990	R Eff. Oct. 1, 1999	No[8]	Conn. Gen. Stat. Ann. § 29-369G Permit maximum wait (60) Oct. 1, 1995[7]
Delaware	No	No	Del. Code Ann. tit. 11 § 1448A H Eff. July 20, 1990	n.a.	Del. Code Ann. tit. 11 § 1448A Instant H Eff. July 20, 1990
District of Columbia	n.a.	D.C. Code Ann. § 6-2301 Sept. 24, 1976 (see handgun ban)	n.a.	No	n.a.
Florida	No	No	Fla. Stat. Ann. § 790.065(1)(c)[9] H Eff. Oct. 1, 1990 R Eff. Oct. 1, 1990	No	Fla. Stat. Ann. § 790.0655 H Eff. Oct. 1, 1991 (3)
Georgia	No	No	Ga. Code Ann. § 16-11-170 H Eff. Jan. 1, 1996	No	Ga. Code Ann. § 16-11-170 Instant H Eff. Jan. 1, 1996
Hawaii	Haw. Rev. Stat. Ann. § 134-2 H Eff. pre-1970 R Eff. June 9, 1988	Haw. Rev. Stat. Ann. § 134-2 H. Eff. pre-1970 R Eff. pre-1970	Haw. Rev. Stat. Ann. § 134-2 H Eff. pre-1970 R. Eff. June 9, 1988	Haw. Rev. Stat. Ann. § 134-2 H Eff. pre-1970 R. Eff. June 9, 1988	Haw. Rev. Stat. Ann. § 134-2[10] H Eff. June 9, 1988 (10) June 29, 1992 (14)
Idaho	No	No	Idaho Code § 19-5403 H Eff. Apr. 7, 1994	No	Idaho Code § 19-5403 Instant H Eff. Apr. 7, 1994

(continued)

Table 9A-3. (continued)

State	Permit to purchase[1]	Registration[2]	Background checks for sales from dealers[3]	Background checks for private sales	Waiting period[4]
Illinois	430 Ill. Comp. Stat. Ann. § 65/2 H Eff. July 1, 1968	No	430 Ill. Comp. Stat. Ann. §§ 65/3, 65/8 H Eff. July 1, 1968 R Eff. July 1, 1968	430 Ill. Comp. Stat. Ann. §§ 65/3, 65/8 H Eff. July 1, 1968	720 Ill. Comp. Stat. Ann. § 5/24-39(g) H Eff. Aug. 1, 1967 (3)[11]
Indiana	No	No	Ind. Code Ann. § 35-47-2-8 H Eff. April 22, 1983	Ind. Code Ann. § 35-47-2-8 H Eff Nov. 30, 1998	Ind. Code Ann. § 35-47-2-8(c) H Eff. April 22, 1983– Nov. 30, 1998 (7)[12]
Iowa	Iowa Code Ann. § 724.15 H Eff. Jan. 1, 1978	No	Iowa Code Ann. § 724.17 H Eff. Apr. 5, 1990	Iowa Code Ann. § 724.17 H Eff. Apr. 5, 1990	Iowa Code Ann. § 724.20
Kansas	No	No	No	No	No
Kentucky	No	No	No	No	No
Louisiana	No	No	No	No	No
Maine	No	No	No	No	No
Maryland	No	Md. Ann. Code art. 27, § 442(e) H Eff. June 1, 1966	Md. Ann. Code art. 27, § 442(h) H Eff. June 1, 1966	Md. Ann. Code art. 27, § 442(d) H Eff. Oct. 1, 1996	Md. Ann. Code art. 27, § 442(c) H Eff. June 1, 1966 (7)
Massachusetts	Mass. Gen. Laws Ann. ch. 140, § 131A H Eff. Aug. 21, 1957 R Eff. May 25, 1972	Mass. Gen. Laws Ann. ch. 140, §§ 128B, 129C H Eff. pre-1970 R Eff. pre-1970	Mass. Gen. Laws Ann. ch. 140, §§ 129B, 129C H Eff. pre-1970 R Eff. pre 1970	Mass. Gen. Laws Ann. ch. 140, §§ 129B, 129C H Eff. pre-1970	Mass. Gen. Laws Ann. ch. 140, § 131A H Eff. pre-1970 (30)[14]

State					
Michigan	Mich. Comp. Laws § 28.422 H Eff. Sept. 5, 1927	Mich. Comp. Laws § 28.422 H Eff. Sept. 5, 1927	Mich. Comp. Laws § 28.422 H Eff. Sept. 5, 1927	Mich. Comp. Laws § 28.422 H Eff. Sept. 5, 1927	No[15]
Minnesota	Minn. Stat. Ann. § 624.7132 H Eff. May 27, 1977[16]	No[17]	Minn. Stat. Ann. § 624.7132(1)-(2) H Eff. May 27, 1977	No	Minn. Stat. Ann. § 624.7132 H Eff. May 27, 1977 (7)[18]
Mississippi	No	No	No	No	No
Missouri	Mo. Stat. Ann. § 571.090 Eff. Sept. 28, 1981	No[19]	Mo. Stat. Ann. § 571.090(3)[20] H Eff. Sept. 28, 1981	Mo. Stat. Ann. § 571.090(3) H Eff. Sept. 28, 1981	Mo. Stat. Ann. § 571.090 H Eff. Sept. 28, 1981(7)[21]
Montana	No	No	No	No	No
Nebraska	Neb. Rev. Stat. Ann. § 69-2404 H Eff. June 7, 1991	No	Neb. Rev. Stat. Ann. § 69-2404 H Eff. Sept. 5, 1991	Neb. Rev. Stat. Ann. § 69-2404 H Eff. Sept. 5 1991	Neb. Rev. Stat. Ann. § 69-2404 H Eff. June 7, 1991 (2)[22]
Nevada	No	No	No	No[23]	No
New Hampshire	No	No[24]	N.H. Rev. Stat. Ann. § 159-C:1 H Eff. Jan. 1, 1995	No	N.H. Rev. Stat. Ann. § 159-C:1 Instant H Eff. Jan. 1, 1995
New Jersey	N.J. Stat. Ann. § 2C:58-3 H Eff. pre-1970 R Eff. pre-1970	N.J. Stat. Ann. § 2C:58-3 H Eff. pre-1970	N.J. Stat. Ann. § 2C:58-3(a)-(b) H Eff. Mar. 30, 1927 R Eff. Aug. 5, 1966	N.J. Stat. Ann. § 2C:58-3 H Eff. Mar. 30, 1927	N.J. Stat. Ann. § 2C:58-3 H Eff. pre-1970 (7)[25]
New Mexico	No	No	No	No	No
New York	N.Y. Penal Law § 400.00 H Eff. July 1, 1934	N.Y. Penal Law § 400.00 H Eff. July 1, 1934	N.Y. Penal Law § 400.00 H Eff. July 1, 1934	N.Y. Penal Law § 400.00 H Eff. July 1, 1934	N.Y. Penal Law § 400.00 H Eff. pre-1970 (180)[26]

(continued)

Table 9A-3. *(continued)*

State	Permit to purchase[1]	Registration[2]	Background checks for sales from dealers[3]	Background checks for private sales	Waiting period[4]
North Carolina	N.C. Gen. Stat. Ann. § 14-402 H Eff. April 1, 1919	No[27]	N.C. Gen. Stat. Ann. § 14-404 H Eff. Dec. 1, 1995	N.C. Gen. Stat. Ann. § 14-404 H Eff. Dec. 1, 1995	N.C. Gen. Stat. Ann. § 14-402 H Eff. Dec. 1, 1995 (7)[28]
North Dakota	No	No	No	No	No
Ohio	No	No	No	No	No
Oklahoma	No	No	No	No	No
Oregon	No	No[29]	Or. Rev. Stat. § 166.412(2) H Eff. Jan. 1, 1990	No	Or. Rev. Stat. § 166.420 H Eff. Jan. 1, 1990 (15) Instant H Eff. July 1, 1996[30]
Pennsylvania	No	No[31]	Pa. Stat. Ann. tit. 18, § 6111(b) H Eff. Oct. 11, 1995 R Eff. Oct. 11, 1995	Pa. Stat. Ann. tit. 18, § 6111(c) H Eff. Oct. 11, 1995	Pa. Stat. Ann. tit. 18, § 6111(a) H Eff. June 6, 1973 (2) Instant H Eff Nov. 30, 1998
Rhode Island	No	No	R.I. Gen. Laws § 11-47-35(a)(2) H Eff. Jan. 26, 1959 R.I. Gen. Laws § 11-47-35.2(b) R Eff. July 1, 1990	R.I. Gen. Laws § 11-47-35(a)(2) H Eff. Jan. 26, 1959	R.I. Gen. Laws § 11-47-35 H Eff. Jan. 1, 1930 (7) January 26, 1959 (3) June 18, 1990 (7)
South Carolina	No	No[32]	No	No	No

State					
South Dakota	No	No	No[33]	No	S.D. Codified Laws § 23-7-9 H Eff. Mar. 14, 1935(2)
Tennessee	No	No	Tenn. Code Ann. § 39-17-1316(c) H Eff. Mar. 19, 1959 R Eff. Nov. 1, 1998	Tenn. Code Ann. § 39-17-1316(d) H Eff. Mar. 19, 1959– Nov. 1, 1998[34]	Tenn. Code Ann. § 39-17-1316(b) H Eff. Mar. 19, 1959 (3) Apr. 1, 1961 (15) Instant[35] H Eff. Nov. 1, 1998
Texas	No	No	No	No	No
Utah	No	No	Utah Code Ann. § 76-10-526(5) H Eff. Feb. 28, 1994 R Eff. Nov. 30, 1998[36]	No	Utah Code Ann. § 76-10-526 Instant H Eff. Feb. 28, 1994
Vermont	No	No	No	No	No
Virginia	No	No	Va. Code Ann. § 18.2-308.2:2 H Eff. Nov. 1, 1989 R Eff. Apr. 3, 1991	No	Va. Code Ann. § 18.2-308.2:2 Instant H Eff. Nov. 1, 1989
Washington	No	No	Wash. Rev. Code Ann. § 9.41.090(2)(a) H Eff. Aug. 11, 1969	No	Wash. Rev. Code Ann. § 9.41.090 H Eff. Aug. 11, 1969 (3) May 17, 1983 (5)[37]
West Virginia	No	No	No	No	No
Wisconsin	No	No	Wisc. Stat. Ann. § 175.35(2) H Eff. Dec. 1, 1991	No	Wisc. Stat. Ann. § 175.35 H Eff. Mar. 16, 1976 (2)
Wyoming	No	No	No	No	No

(continued)

Table 9A-3. (continued)

1. H Eff: Effective date of law as applied to handguns; R Eff: Effective date of law as applied to long guns (rifles and shotguns).

2. Registration is defined as when a permanent record of the firearm sale is kept at a central location. Some states require records of sales to be kept by local officials and/or man-date that these records be kept for a limited time only. We have noted many of these states with a separate footnote.

3. Background checks for sales from dealers includes permit-to-purchase systems requiring a background check for a permit, even if not conducted at the point of sale.

4. Waiting periods apply to handgun sales from dealers. In some states, they may also apply to private sales or to long guns as well. Parenthetical numbers denote minimum waiting periods in days, unless otherwise indicated.

5. Colo. Rev. Stat. Ann. § 12-26.5-109 repealed the state criminal background check requirement as of February 28, 1999.

6. In Connecticut before enactment of its permit-to-purchase system, state law provided no explicit requirement for a background check. However, beginning October 1, 1965, state law did require that relevant authorities receive information about the purchaser (see registration provision) and that "any such municipal authority or said commissioner hav-ing knowledge of the conviction of such applicant of a felony, shall forthwith notify the person, firm or corporation to whom such application was made and no pistol or revolver shall be by him or it sold or delivered to such applicant." See 1965 Feb. Sp. Sess. P.A. 36 §1.

7. In Connecticut the maximum sixty-day wait to receive a permit starts after FBI background check is complete.

8. In Delaware as of July 8, 1994, private sellers had the option of conducting background checks through licensed dealers. See Del. Ann. Code. tit. 24 § 904A.

9. Fla. Stat. Ann. § 790.065(14) provided that the state background check provision was to be repealed, effective June 1, 2000. However, Fla. Stat. Ann. § 790.065(14) (2000 and Supp. 2001) provides that the state background check requirement shall remain in effect until June 1, 2002.

10. Hawaii's waiting period law applies to first-time applicants for a permit to purchase.

11. In Illinois there is a thirty-day maximum wait to receive a Firearm Owner Identification Card (Permit). Then, when applying to purchase a gun there is a mandatory three-day waiting period before the handgun may be delivered to the purchaser.

12. Indiana's seven-day waiting period was repealed by P.L. 17-1997, § 9, effective November 30, 1998.

13. Iowa has no maximum wait to receive a permit to purchase a handgun. There is a three-day minimum wait after a person receives a permit and applies to purchase a handgun.

14. Massachusetts has a thirty-day maximum waiting period to acquire a permit to purchase a firearm.

15. In Michigan the issuing authority "shall with due speed and diligence issue licenses to purchase." No specific time period for issuing the permit is provided.

16. Minnesota's permit-to-purchase law is not mandatory. If a person applies for and receives a permit then the maximum wait to receive a permit is seven days, and a person may purchase an unlimited number of handguns without undergoing additional background checks. If a person wants to purchase a handgun without a permit, there is a manda-tory seven-day waiting period before the handgun may be transferred, and he or she must undergo a background check for each additional purchase.

17. In Minnesota records of sale are kept that do not meet our definition of a registration system.

18. See note 16 regarding Minnesota's permit-to-purchase system.

19. In Missouri records of sale are kept that do not meet our definition of a registration system.

20. Missouri's background check law requires only that the local sheriff conduct "inquiries as he deems necessary."

21. Missouri state law provides for a maximum waiting period. Firearms may be delivered before the maximum waiting period has expired, provided all requirements for the transfer are met.

22. Nebraska's two-day waiting period is a maximum waiting period to receive a permit to purchase a handgun.

23. While Nev. Rev. Stat. Ann. § 202.254 authorizes a private person to obtain a background check on a transferee, that section is permissive only and does not require private parties to obtain background checks prior to transferring firearms.

24. N.H. Rev. Stat. Ann. § 159:9, which required local police departments to maintain records of dealer sales, was repealed by 1996, 116:1, I, effective July 14, 1996. However, New Hampshire law actually prohibited recordkeeping of firearm sales by police departments as early as January 1, 1995, when N.H. Rev. Stat. Ann. § 159-C:3(IV) became effective.

25. New Jersey has a seven-day minimum wait for the transfer of a handgun and a maximum thirty-day wait to receive a permit to purchase.

26. New York has a maximum of six months (180 days) to issue a permit to purchase.

27. In North Carolina records of sale are kept that do not meet our definition of a registration system.

28. North Carolina has a seven-day maximum wait to receive a permit.

29. In Oregon records of sale are kept that do not meet our definition of a registration system.

30. For the effective date of Oregon's instant check, see 1995 Or. Laws ch. 729, § 11.

31. In Pennsylvania records of sale are kept that do not meet our definition of a registration system.

32. In South Carolina records of sale are kept that do not meet our definition of a registration system.

33. In South Dakota information regarding all prospective buyers must be sent to the police, but there is no legal requirement for a background check. See S.D. Codified Laws Ann. § 23-7-10.

34. Tenn. Code Ann. § 39-17-1316(m)(3), effective November 1, 1998, repeals the requirement of background checks in private sales.

35. Tenn. Code Ann. § 39-17-1316(d) abolishes the waiting period and provides for instant background check and firearm delivery.

36. Utah Code Ann. § 76-10-526(1), effective May 4, 1998, provides that the state background check requirement will become applicable to rifles upon the date federal law so requires.

37. In Washington the waiting period was changed from a minimum to a maximum term.

Table 9A-4. *Sales and Purchase Restrictions 1970–99 (2)*

State	Minimum purchase and sale age for handguns to youth	One-gun-per-month law	Dealer license[1] and inspection[2]
Alabama	Ala. Code § 13A-11-57/76* Since 1951 (18)	No	Ala. Code § 13A-11-78 Sep.11, 1951
Alaska	No	No	No
Arizona	Ariz. Rev. Stat. Ann. § 13-3109** April 1, 1953 (18)	No	No
Arkansas	Ark. Stat. Ann. § 5-73-109* Jan. 1, 1976 (18)	No	No
California	Cal. Penal Code § 12072 July 9, 1963 (16)** Aug. 22, 1967 (18)** Jan. 1, 1989 (18)*	No[3]	Cal. Penal Code § 12070(a) Sep. 9, 1953
Colorado	Colo. Rev. Stat. Ann. § 18-12-108.7* Sep. 13, 1993 (18)	No	No
Connecticut	Conn. Gen. Stat. Ann. § 29-34* Sale: Since 1949 (18) Permit: Oct. 1, 1995 (21)*	No	Conn. Gen. Stat. Ann. § 29-28 June 30, 1959
Delaware	Del. Code Ann. § 11/1445** Pre-1970 (16) July 8, 1994 (18)	No	Del. Code Ann. tit. 24, § 901 Pre-1970
Florida	Fla. Stat. Ann. § 790.17** July 1, 1965 (18)	No	No

State			
Georgia	Ga. Code Ann. § 16-11-101.1* July 1, 1969 (21) April 11, 1994 (18)	No	Ga. Code Ann. § 43-16-2 July 1, 1963
Hawaii	Haw. Rev. Stat. Ann. § 134-2 (d) Permit: Pre-1970 (20)[4] April 28, 1972 (18)[4] July 1, 1994 (21)[4]	No	Haw. Rev. Stat. Ann. § 134-31 March 14, 1921
Idaho	Idaho Code § 18-3308** April 5, 1990 (16) April 7, 1994 (18)	No	No
Illinois	430 Ill. Comp. Stat. Ann. § 65/2 Permit: July 1, 1968 (21)[4,5]	No	No
Indiana	Ind. Code Ann. § 35-47-2-7* April 22, 1983 (18)	No	Ind. Code Ann. § 35-47-2-15 April 22, 1983
Iowa	Iowa Code Ann. § 724.22* [6] Jan. 1, 1978 (18) Jan. 1. 1979 (21)	No	No
Kansas	Kan. Stat. § 21-4203* July 1, 1970 (18)	No	No
Kentucky	Ky. Rev. Stat. Ann. § 527.110* July 15, 1994 (18)	No	No
Louisiana	La. Rev. Stat. Ann. § 14.91** Since 1921 (21) July 12, 1972 (18)	No	No
Maine	Maine Rev. Stat. § 17A-554** May 1, 1976 (16)	No	No

(continued)

Table 9A-4. (continued)

State	Minimum purchase and sale age for handguns to youth	One-gun-per-month law	Dealer license[1] and inspection[2]
Maryland	Md. Ann. Code art. 27, §§ 406, 445(c)** Since 1966 (21)	Md. Ann. Code art. 27, § 442 (a) October 1, 1996	Md. Ann. Code art. 27, § 443(a) June 1, 1966
Massachusetts	Mass. Gen. Laws Ann. ch. 140, § 130** March 15, 1945 (15) June 7, 1951 (18)	No	Mass. Gen. Laws Ann. ch. 140, § 122[7] May 27, 1911
Michigan	Mich. Comp. Laws § 750.223* Sale: April 20, 1970 (18) Permit: Sept. 5, 1927 (18)[4] July 15, 1968 (21)[4] Feb. 19, 1972 (18)[4]	No	No[8]
Minnesota	Minn. Stat. Ann. Permit: May 27, 1977 (18)[4]	No	No
Mississippi	Miss. Code Ann. § 97-37-13** Since 1942 (18)	No	No
Missouri	Mo. Ann. Stat. § 571.06** Sale: Sep. 28, 1981 (18) Permit: Sep. 28, 1981 (21)* [4]	No	No
Montana	No	No	No
Nebraska	Neb. Rev. Stat. Ann. § 28-1204.01* Sale: April 15, 1994 (18) Permit: June 7, 1991 (21)[4]	No	No

State				
Nevada	Nev. Rev. Stat. Ann. § 202.31* March 22, 1955 (18)	No		No
New Hampshire	N.H. Rev. Stat. Ann. § 159.12* May 4, 1923 (21) June 3, 1973 (18)	No	N.H. Rev. Stat. Ann. § 159:8 May 4, 1923	No
New Jersey	N.J. Stat. Ann. § 2C-39-10** Since 1969 (18)	No	N.J. Stat. Ann. § 2C:58-2(a) March 30, 1927	No
New Mexico	No	No	No	No
New York	No separate sale law. NY has a permit-to-purchase system with no defined age criteria.	No	N.Y. Penal Law § 400.00(1) July 1, 1963	No
North Carolina	N.C. Gen. Stat. Ann. § 14-269.7* April 6, 1893 (18)[9]	No	N.C. Gen Stat. Ann. § 105-80[10] March 24, 1939; repealed July 1, 1997	No
North Dakota	N.D. Cent. Code § 62.1-03-02* April 15, 1985 (18)	No	No	No
Ohio	Ohio Rev. Code Ann. § 2923.21** Oct. 1, 1953 (17) Nov. 9, 1995 (21)*	No	No	No
Oklahoma	Okla. Stat. Ann. § 21-1273* Since 1910 (18)[9]	No	No	No
Oregon	Or. Rev. Stat. § 166.47* Since at least 1970 (18)	No	No	No
Pennsylvania	Pa. Stat. Ann. § 6110* June 6, 1973 (18)	No	18 Pa. Cons. Stat. Ann. § 6112 June 24, 1939	No
Rhode Island	R.I. Gen. Laws § 11-47-30* Since 1956 (21)	No	R.I. Gen. Laws § 11-47-38[11] May 18, 1959	No

(continued)

Table 9A-4. (continued)

State	Minimum purchase and sale age for handguns to youth	One-gun-per-month law	Dealer license[1] and inspection[2]
South Carolina	S.C. Code Ann. § 16-23-30* Since 1966 (21)	S.C. Code Ann. § 23-31-140 June 17, 1975	S.C. Code Ann. § 23-31-130 May 27, 1965
South Dakota	No	No	No
Tennessee	Tenn. Code Ann. § 39-17-1303** Nov. 1, 1989 (18)	No	Tenn. Code Ann. § 39-17-1316(e)(1) March 14, 1961
Texas	Texas Penal Code § 46.06** Jan. 1, 1974 (18)	No	No
Utah	Utah Code Ann. § 76-10-509.9* Oct. 21, 1993 (18)	No	No
Vermont	Vt. Stat. Ann. tit. 13, § 4007** Since 1948 (16)	No	No
Virginia	Va. Code Ann. § 18.2-309* July 1, 1960 (18)	Va. Code Ann. § 18.2-308.2 July 1, 1993	Va. Code Ann. § 15.2-1208 March 29, 1944
Washington	Wash. Rev. Code § 9.41.080** April 23, 1935 (21)	No	Wash. Rev. Code Ann. § 9.41.100 July 1, 1935
West Virginia	W.Va. Code Ann. § 61-7-10** July 1, 1994 (18)	No	No
Wisconsin	Wisc. Stat. Ann. § 948.6* July 8, 1989 (18)	No	No
Wyoming	Wisc. Stat. Ann. (18)[9] Since 1955 (18)[9] No	No	No

Note: Minimum purchase/sale age laws may apply to dealer sales, private sales, or both. Some of the states have changed their age requirements over time. These multiple implementation dates are reflected in the table. Minimum ages are noted in parentheses following the date. In general, even states with a relevant law still allow the transfer of a firearm to or possession by underage youth if they are under supervision of their parent or guardian.

*Minimum age law applies to handguns only; **law applies to all firearms (handguns and long guns).

1. Indicates that state law requires a separate state license for those engaged in the business of selling firearms. Those states that refer to licensed dealers exclusively by reference to federally licensed dealers under the Gun Control Act of 1968 do not have a separate state licensing requirement. Local zoning or other rules applicable to firearm dealers, not captured by this table, may also be in effect in some states.

2. Indicates that state law requires mandatory periodic inspection of firearm dealers. Although many states require that licensed dealers maintain a record of their sales that must be open to inspection by state authorities, just two states (Massachusetts and Rhode Island) require periodic inspection of dealer records. See individual notes.

3. California's one-gun-per-month law took effect after 1999.

4. These states have permit-to-purchase laws that designate the legal age to acquire a permit to purchase a handgun or firearm, often in addition to a minimum age purchase law. In certain states there are no separate purchase laws. The age of eligibility to apply for a permit and the implementation date of the permit-to-purchase law are indicated in this table.

5. In Illinois a person may receive a permit to purchase a handgun if he or she is under 21 years of age and has written permission of a parent.

6. Iowa also has a separate permit-to-purchase law, which follows the same age restrictions and dates of effectiveness.

7. Massachusetts also requires annual inspections of firearm dealers, effective July 23, 1998.

8. Michigan does require certain safety and security rules for federally licensed dealers. See Mich. Comp. Laws § 9.41.135.

9. Law states that sales and possession are forbidden by minors. No definition of minor was found in the law, and therefore under age 18 is assumed to be the definition of a minor. See North Carolina, Oklahoma, Wisconsin.

10. North Carolina repealed its law requiring a state dealer's license, effective July 1, 1997.

11. Rhode Island also requires monthly inspections of firearm dealers, effective May 21, 1975.

Table 9A-5. Possession, Carrying, and Storage Laws, 1970–99

State	Minimum age for youth possession of handguns	Concealed weapon carrying (CCW):[1] shall issue, may issue, or prohibited,[2] with effective date for change to shall issue (if applicable)[3]	Child access prevention (CAP) law
Alabama	No	May Issue[4] Ala. Code § 13A-11-75	No
Alaska	Alaska Stat. § 1.61.220** Jan. 1, 1980 (16)	Shall Issue Alaska Stat. § 18.65.700 Oct. 1, 1994	No
Arizona	Ariz. Rev. Stat. Ann. § 13-3111** April 22, 1993 (18)	Shall Issue Ariz. Rev. Stat. Ann. § 13-3112 April 14, 1994	No
Arkansas	Ark. Stat. Ann. § 5-73-119* March 17, 1989 (18)	Shall Issue Ark. Stat. Ann. § 5-73 Feb. 23, 1995	No
California	Cal. Penal Code § 12101* July 14, 1965 (16) August 22, 1967 (18)	May Issue Cal. Penal Code § 12050	Cal. Penal Code § 12035 Jan. 1, 1992
Colorado	Colo. Rev. Stat. Ann. § 18-12-105.1* Sep. 13, 1993 (18)	May Issue Colo. Rev. Stat. Ann. § 18-12-105.1	No
Connecticut	No	May Issue[5] Conn. Gen. Stat. Ann. § 29-28	Conn. Gen. Stat. Ann. § 29-37(i) Oct. 1, 1990
Delaware	Del. Code Ann. § 11/1448* July 8, 1994 (18)	May Issue Del. Code Ann. Tit. 11 § 1441	Del. Code Ann. tit.11 § 1456 July 12, 1994
Florida	Fla. Stat. Ann. § 790.22* Jan. 1, 1994 (18)	Shall Issue Fla. Stat. Ann. § 790.06 Oct. 1, 1987	Fla. Stat. Ann. § 784.05 Oct. 1, 1989

State			
Georgia	Ga. Code Ann. § 16-11-101.1* April 11, 1994 (18)	*Shall Issue* Ga. Code Ann. § 43-38-10 Aug. 25, 1989	No
Hawaii	No	*May Issue* Haw. Rev. Stat. Ann. § 134-9	Haw. Rev. Stat. § 134-10.5 June 29, 1992 No
Idaho	Idaho Code § 18-3302F* April 7, 1994 (18)	*Shall Issue* Idaho Code § 18-3302 April 5, 1990	No
Illinois	No	*Prohibited* 720 Ill. Comp. Stat. Ann. § 5/24-1	Ill. Rev. Stat. ch. 5, para 24-9 Jan. 1, 2000 No
Indiana	Ind. Code Ann. § 35-47-10-5* July 1, 1994 (18)	*Shall Issue* Ind. Code Ann. § 35-47-2-3 April 23, 1973	
Iowa	No	*May Issue* Iowa Code Ann. § 724.10	Iowa Code Ann. § 724.22 April 5, 1990 No
Kansas	No	*Prohibited* Kan. Stat. § 21-4201	No
Kentucky	Ky. Rev. Stat. Ann. § 527.100* July 15, 1994 (18)	*Shall Issue* Ky. Rev. Stat. Ann. § 527-020 Oct. 1, 1996	No
Louisiana	No	*Shall Issue* La. Rev. Stat. § 40:1379.1 July 16, 1991	No
Maine	No	*Shall Issue* Maine Rev. Stat. tit. 25, § 2003 Sep. 18, 1981[6]	No
Maryland	Md. Ann. Code Art. 27 § 445(c)* Oct. 1, 1996 (21)	*May Issue* Md. Ann. Code Art. 27, § 36E	MD Ann. Code art. 27, § 36K Oct. 1, 1992

(*continued*)

Table 9A-5. (*continued*)

State	Minimum age for youth possession of handguns	Concealed weapon carrying (CCW):[1] shall issue, may issue, or prohibited,[2] with effective date for change to shall issue (if applicable)[3]	Child access prevention (CAP) law
Massachusetts	No	*May Issue* Mass. Gen. Laws Ann. ch. 140, § 131	Mass. Ann. Laws ch. 140, § 131L Oct. 21, 1998
Michigan	No	*May Issue*[7] Mich. Comp. Laws Ann. § 28.92	No
Minnesota	Minn. Stat. Ann. § 624.713* June 4, 1975 (18)	*May Issue* Minn. Stat. Ann. § 624.714	Minn. Stat. § 609.666 Aug. 1, 1993
Mississippi	Miss. Code Ann. § 97.37-15* July 1, 1994 (18)***	*Shall Issue* Miss. Code Ann. § 45-9-101 July 1, 1990	No
Missouri	No	*Prohibited* Mo. Stat. Ann. § 571.030	No
Montana	No	*Shall Issue* Mont. Code Ann. § 45-8-321 May 16, 1991	No
Nebraska	Neb. Rev. Stat. Ann. § 28-1204* June 1, 1977 (18)	*Prohibited* Neb. Rev. Stat. Ann. § 28-1202	No
Nevada	Nev. Rev. Stat. Ann. § 202.3** Since 1963 (18)***	*Shall Issue* Nev. Rev. Stat. Ann. § 202.366 July 7, 1995	Nev. Rev. Stat. Ann. § 902.300 Oct. 1, 1991
New Hampshire	No	*Shall Issue* N.H. Rev. Stat. Ann. § 159.6 Pre-1970	No

State			
New Jersey	N.J. Stat. Ann. § 2C-58-6.1** Since 1969 (18)	*May Issue* N.J. Stat. Ann. § 2C:85-4	N.J. Stat. Ann. § 2C:58-15 Jan. 17, 1992 No
New Mexico	N.M Stat. § 17-2-33* July 1, 1994 (19)	*Prohibited*[8] N.M. Stat. Ann. § 30-7-2	No
New York	N.Y. Penal Law § 265.05* July 20, 1965 (16)	*May Issue* N.Y. Penal Law § 400.00	No
North Carolina	N.C. Gen. Stat. Ann. § 14-269.7* Sep. 1, 1993 (18)	*Shall Issue* N.C. Gen. Stat. Ann. § 14-415.10 July 10, 1995	N.C. Gen. Stat. Ann § 14-315.1 Dec. 1, 1993
North Dakota	N.D. Cent. Code § 61.1-02-01* April 15, 1985 (18)	*Shall Issue* N.D. Cent. Code § 62.1-04 April 15, 1985	No
Ohio	No	*Prohibited* Ohio Rev. Code Ann. § 2923.12	No
Oklahoma	Okla. Stat. Ann. § 21-1273* July 1, 1994 (18)	*Shall Issue* Ok. Stat. Ann. Tit. 21 § 1290.9 Sep. 1, 1995	No
Oregon	Or. Rev. Stat. § 166.25* Since at least 1970 (18)	*Shall Issue* Or. Rev. Stat. § 166.291 January 1, 1990	No
Pennsylvania	No	*Shall Issue*[9] Pa. Stat. Ann. tit 18, § 6109 June 21, 1989	No
Rhode Island	R.I. Gen. Laws § 11-47-33** Since 1959 (15)	*May Issue* R.I. Gen. Laws § 11-47-11	R.I. Gen. Laws § 11-47-60.1 June 19, 1995
South Carolina	No	*Shall Issue* S.C. Code Ann. § 40-17-120 Aug. 23, 1996	No

(continued)

Table 9A-5. (continued)

State	Minimum age for youth possession of handguns	Concealed weapon carrying (CCW):[1] shall issue, may issue, or prohibited,[2] with effective date for change to shall issue (if applicable)[3]	Child access prevention (CAP) law
South Dakota	S.D. Code § 23-7-44* March 5, 1994 (18)	Shall Issue S.D. Code § 23-7-7.1 March 13, 1985	No
Tennessee	No	Shall Issue Tenn. Code Ann. § 39-17-1315 Oct. 1, 1994	No
Texas	No	Shall Issue Texas Gov't Code § 411.177 Jan. 1, 1996	Tex. Penal Code § 46.13 Sep. 1, 1995
Utah	Utah Code Ann. § 76-10-509.4** July 1, 1973 (18)	Shall Issue Utah Code Ann. § 53-5-704 April 28, 1986	No
Vermont	Vt. Stat. Ann. tit. 13, § 4008* Since 1948 (16)	No permit required to carry a concealed weapon.	No
Virginia	Va. Code Ann. § 18.2-308.7* April 23, 1993 (18)	Shall Issue Va. Code Ann. § 18.2-308 July 1, 1995	Va. Code Ann. § 18.2-56.2 July 1, 1992
Washington	Wash. Rev. Code § 9.41.040** July 1, 1994 (18)	Shall Issue Wash. Rev. Code § 9.47.070 Pre-1970	No

West Virginia	W.Va. Code Ann. § 61-7-8**	July 8, 1989 (18)	Shall Issue	W.Va. Code § 61-7-4	Aug. 8, 1989	No
Wisconsin	Wisc. Stat. Ann. § 948.6*	Since 1955 (18)***	Prohibited	Wisc. Stat. Ann. § 941.23	Wisc. Stat. Ann. § 948.55	April 16, 1992
Wyoming	No		Shall Issue	Wyo. Stat. Ann. § 6-8-104	Oct. 1, 1994	No

Note: In general, even states with a relevant minimum possession age law still allow the possession of a firearm by underage youths if they are under supervision of a parent or guardian or are in their home. Some of the states have changed their age requirements over time. These multiple implementation dates are reflected in the table. Minimum ages are noted in parentheses following the date.

* Minimum age law applies to handguns only; **law applies to all firearms (handguns and long guns); ***law states that sale or possession is forbidden by minor; no definition of minor was found in the law, and therefore (under the age of 18) was assumed to be the definition.

1. As with all of the tables, this information is based on the statutory language within each state. For CCW laws in particular, implementation within a specific state may vary from the statutory language and may not be uniform throughout the state. See also notes for Alabama and Connecticut.

2. The "prohibited" category indicates states where licenses to carry concealed weapons are generally not available. It is often the case in these states, however, that certain special categories of persons, such as private detectives, may remain eligible for a concealed carry license.

3. Effective dates are for state changes to a shall-issue system. We are not aware of any state that changed its law from shall issue to may issue or prohibited from 1970 to 1999.

4. Alabama's statutory language uses the word "may." The National Rifle Association characterizes Alabama as a shall-issue state. The Brady Campaign to Prevent Gun Violence characterizes Alabama as a may-issue state.

5. Connecticut's statutory language uses the word "may." The National Rifle Association characterizes Connecticut as a shall-issue state. The Brady Campaign to Prevent Gun Violence characterizes Connecticut as a may-issue state.

6. Maine has made a number of changes to its CCW law over a period of several years.

7. Michigan has changed its law to shall issue, effective after 1999.

8. New Mexico has changed its law to shall issue, effective after 1999.

9. Pennsylvania adopted a shall-issue law for all parts of the state except Philadelphia.

Table 9A-6. *Sentence Enhancement Laws for Possession or Use of a Firearm: Mandatory Minimum and Minimum Add-On, 1970–99*

State	Mandatory minimum	Term	Minimum add-on	Term
Alabama	Ala. Code § 13A-5-6 Eff. May 27, 1981	10 yrs.[a,e]	No	
Alaska	Alaska Stat. § 12.55.125(c)(2)(A)[a,b] Eff. Jan. 1, 1980	7 yrs.[a,b]	No	
Arizona	Ariz. Rev. Stat. Ann. § 13-604[a,b] Eff. Aug. 9, 1974	2/3 sent.[a,b]	Ariz. Rev. Stat. Ann. § 13-604[a,b] Eff. Aug. 9, 1974	Other[d,1]
Arkansas	Ark. Code Ann. § 16-90-121 Eff. June 16, 1981	10 yrs.[c]	**Ark. Code Ann. § 16-90-120** Eff. June 16, 1981	Other[d]
California	Cal. Penal Code § 1203(e) Eff. Jan. 1, 1976	NS[c]	**Cal. Penal Code § 12022** **Eff. Sep. 9, 1953–June 29, 1977** **Cal. Penal Code § 12022(a)(1)** **Eff. June 29, 1977**[2]	**5–10 yrs.** **n.a.**[g]
Colorado	Col. Rev. Stat. Ann. § 16-11-309(1)(a) Eff. July 1, 1976	NS[c,e]	Col. Rev. Stat. Ann. § 16-11-309(8)(a) Eff. July 1, 1976	Other[d,3]
Connecticut	Conn. Gen. Stat. Ann. § 53a-216 Eff. Oct. 1, 1981	5 yrs.	**Conn. Gen. Stat. Ann. § 53-202k** **Eff. Oct. 1, 1993**	**5 yrs.**
Delaware	Del. Code Ann. tit. 11, § 1447 Eff. July 1, 1973	3 yrs.[b]	Del. Code Ann. tit. 11, § 1447(c) Eff. July 1, 1973	3–30 yrs.
District of Columbia	No		No	
Florida	Fla. Stat. Ann. § 775.087 Eff. Oct. 1, 1975	3 yrs.	**Fla. Stat. Ann. § 775.087(1)** **Eff. July 1, 1975**	**n.a.**[g]
Georgia	No		Ga. Code Ann. § 16-11-106(b) Eff. July 1, 1976	5 yrs.[4]
Hawaii	Haw. Rev. Stat. Ann. § 706-660.1(a) Eff. June 7, 1976	3 yrs.[c,5]	No	

Idaho	No		Idaho Code § 19-2520 Eff. July 1, 1977	15 yrs.
Illinois	730 Ill. Comp. Stat. Ann. 5/5-5-1[6] Eff. Feb. 1, 1978	6 yrs.[f]	No	
Indiana	Ind. Code Ann. § 35-50-2-(b)(4) Eff. before 1970	NS[b,c]	No	
Iowa	Iowa Code Ann. § 902.7 Eff. Jan. 1, 1978	5 yrs.[e]	No	
Kansas	Kan. Stat. Ann. § 21-4618(a) Eff. July 1, 1976	NS[c,e]	No	
Kentucky	Ky. Rev. Stat. Ann. § 533.060(1) Eff. June 19, 1976	NS[c]	No	
Louisiana	La. Code Crim. Proc. Ann. art. 893.3 Eff. Sep. 11, 1981	5 yrs.[e]	No	
Maine	Me. Rev. Stat. Ann. tit. 17-A, § 1252(5) Eff. Sep. 23, 1971	1 yr.[a,b,e]	No	
Maryland	Md. Ann. Code art. 27, § 36B(d)(1)(i) Eff. June 1, 1972	5 yrs.[7]	Md. Ann. Code art. 27, § 36B(d)(1)(i) Eff. June 1, 1972	5–20 yrs.[4]
Massachusetts	Mass. Gen. Laws Ann. ch. 265, § 18B Eff. April 1, 1975	2 yrs.[8]	Mass. Gen. Laws Ann. ch. 265, § 18B Eff. April 1, 1975	2–5 yrs.
Michigan	Mich. Comp. Laws Ann. § 750.227b(3) Eff. Jan. 1, 1977	2 yrs.	Mich. Comp. Laws Ann. § 750.227b(1)-(2) Eff. Jan. 1, 1977	2 yrs.[4]
Minnesota	Minn. Stat. Ann. § 609.11 Eff. Aug.1, 1979	1 yr.[a]	No	
Mississippi	No		No	

(continued)

Table 9A-6. (*continued*)

State	Mandatory minimum	Term	Minimum add-on	Term
Missouri	Mo. Ann. Stat. § 571.015(1) Eff. Aug. 13, 1976	3 yrs.	Mo. Ann. Stat. § 571.015(1) Eff. Aug. 13, 1976	3 yrs.[b]
Montana	Mont. Code Ann. § 46-18-221(1) Eff. Jan. 1, 1978	2 yrs.[c]	Mont. Code Ann. § 46-18-221(1) Eff. Jan. 1, 1978	2–10 yrs.[4]
Nebraska	No		Neb. Rev. Stat. Ann. § 28-1205 Eff. before 1970	1–25 yrs.[b]
Nevada	Nev. Rev. Stat. Ann. § 193.165 Eff. July 1, 1979	NS[c,f]	**Nev. Rev. Stat. Ann. § 193.165** **Eff. May 3, 1973**	**n.a.[g]**
New Hampshire	N.H. Rev. Stat. Ann. § 651:2(II-b) Eff. Sept. 3, 1977	1 yr.	N.H. Rev. Stat. Ann. § 651:2(II-b) Eff. Sept. 3, 1977	1 yr.[4]
New Jersey	N.J. Stat. Ann. § 2c:43-6(c) Eff. Feb. 12, 1981	3 yrs.	No	
New Mexico	N.M. Stat. Ann. § 31-18-16 Eff. before 1970	1 yr.	N.M. Stat. Ann. § 31-18-16 Eff. before 1970	1 yr.[4]
New York	No		**N.Y. Penal Law § 265.09** **Eff. Nov. 1, 1996**	**5 yrs.[e,f]**
North Carolina	**No[9,10]**	2 yrs.[a]	**N.C. Gen. Stat. § 14-2.2** **Eff. March 26, 1994**	**n.a.[g]**
North Dakota	N.D. Cent. Code § 12.1-32-02.1 Eff. July 1, 1977	3 yrs.[f]	No	
Ohio	**Ohio Rev. Code Ann.** **§ 2929.14(D)(1)(a)(i)[11]** Eff. Jan. 5, 1983		**Ohio Rev. Code Ann.** **§ 2929.14(D)(1)(a)(I)** Eff. Jan. 5 1983	3 yrs.[a]
Oklahoma	No		Okla. Stat. Ann. Tit. 21, § 1287[12] Eff. before 1970	2–10 yrs.[4]

Oregon	Ore. Rev. Stat. § 161.610 Eff. Oct. 2, 1979	5 yrs.[c,4,13]	No	
Pennsylvania	42. Penn. Con. Stat. Ann. § 9712(a) Eff. June 6, 1982	5 yrs.[f]	No	
Rhode Island	No		R.I. Gen. Laws § 11-47-3 Eff. before 1970	n.a.[g,14]
South Carolina	S.C. Code Ann. § 16-23-490 Eff. June 3, 1986	5 yrs.	No	
South Dakota	**No[15]**	5 yrs.	S.D. Codified Laws § 22-14-12 Eff. April 3, 1985	n.a.[g,16]
Tennessee	Tenn. Code Ann. § 39-6-1710 **Eff. July 1, 1976–Nov. 11, 1989[17]**	5 yrs.	Tenn. Code Ann. § 39-6-1710 **Eff. July 1, 1976–Nov. 11, 1989[18]**	5 yrs.
Texas	Tex. Crim. P. Code Ann. § 42.12(3f)(a)(2) Eff. Aug. 29, 1977	NS[c,e]	No	
Utah	No	No	**Utah Code Ann. § 76-3-203[19]** Eff. May 1, 1976	1–5 yrs.[20]
Vermont	No	No	Vt. Stat. Ann. tit. 13, § 4005 Eff. before 1970	n.a.[g]
Virginia	Va. Code Ann. § 18.2-53.1 Eff. Oct. 1, 1975	2 yrs.	Va. Code Ann. § 18.2-53.1 Eff. Oct. 1, 1975	2 yrs.
Washington	Wash. Rev. Code Ann. § 9.94A.310(3)(c), (e) Eff. July 1, 1984	1 yrs.[e]	Wash. Rev. Code Ann. § 9.94A.310(3)(c), (e) Eff. July 1, 1984	1 yr.[a]
West Virginia	W. Va. Code Ann. § 62-12-2(b) Eff. June 8, 1979	NS[c]	No	
Wisconsin	Wisc. Stat. Ann. § 939.63(2) Eff. March 1, 1980	3 yrs.[c,4]	No	
Wyoming	No	No	Wyo. Stat. Ann. § 6-8-101 Eff. May 25, 1979	n.a.[b,g]

(continued)

Table 9A-6. (continued)

Note: The information in this table is largely drawn from Marvell and Moody (1995, table 3, pp. 247, 259). We are grateful for their excellent work and have sought to update their table's contents. Bold entries indicate information contrary or in addition to that provided by Marvell and Moody. Footnotes a–g are taken from Marvell and Moody's table 3 and reproduced in full below. Numbered footnotes are provided by the present authors. Bold entries indicate a change from Marvell and Moody's original table.

Mandatory minimum sentences: Per Marvell and Moody's methods, only sentencing enhancement laws that require the judge to impose a mandatory term of imprisonment for commission of a crime while armed qualify as mandatory minimum sentences. There are, however, several important exceptions to this general rule. First, we include laws where the judge has the limited discretion to disregard the mandatory minimum sentence in cases where justice so requires. Second, we include laws that apply mandatory minimums only to the commission of especially serious, enumerated, underlying offenses.

Minimum add-on sentences: Minimum add-on sentences must be mandatory, additional sentences that run consecutively to the sentence for the underlying offense. Per Marvell and Moody's methods, we exclude minimum add-on laws that exempt felonies for which arming was an element of the underlying offense (for example, armed robbery). Also, per Marvell and Moody, we include minimum add-on laws that provide the judge with discretion to impose an add-on sentence greater than or equal to ten years. Finally, we include laws where the judge has the limited discretion to disregard the mandatory minimum sentence in cases where justice so requires.

With the increasing popularity of sentencing guidelines, several states have enacted laws that shift the permissible sentence range for a given offense upward when the offense was committed while armed. We include laws of this type as minimum add-on sentences only when the sentence ranges with and without possession of a firearm are nonoverlapping. This decision results from the requirement that the possible sentence for an underlying offense must increase when that offense is committed with a firearm. Overlapping ranges allow for the possibility that, as a result of judicial discretion, a defendant would receive the same punishment whether or not he or she committed the offense while armed.

It should also be noted that the term lengths of both the mandatory minimum and minimum add-on sentence enhancements provided in the table are those provided in the enacting law. The table does not reflect subsequent increases or decreases in term length by state legislatures. We assumed the term lengths provided by Marvell and Moody were also the enacting terms, and we did not update their data to reflect current term lengths.

a. Also, higher minimums or enhancement for some important crimes. Minnesota has a three-year minimum for firearm use.

b. Earlier laws differed. Alaska, six years for firearms until 1982; Arizona, 120 days to five years until 1978; Delaware, five years until 1981. Code sections changed in Arizona, Indiana, Maine, Missouri, Nebraska, and Wyoming. See also note e.

c. There can be no suspension (NS) of the minimum sentence.

d. Arizona, up to three times sentence (this is no longer applicable because of changes in Arizona's sentencing laws); Arkansas, up to fifteen years; Colorado, up to double maximum.

e. The court has discretion not to apply the minimum. In Alabama and Arkansas the court can suspend sentence except in major crimes. In Texas the jury, but not the judge, can suspend in special circumstances. Otherwise, the judge can suspend sentence for special reasons given in writing (Iowa since 1985, Kansas since 1989, Louisiana since 1988, Maine since 1989; in Colorado the judge cannot suspend the first 120 days).

f. Limited to violent crimes and does not include burglary. In North Carolina applies to robbery (sec. 14–87) and to second conviction of crime with deadly weapons.

g. These laws are not true FSE laws. They create an extra crime for felonies with weapons, but the laws are weak because the additional sentence is not mandatory or is not applied when weapon use is an element of the underlying crime.

1. Ariz. Rev. Stat. Ann. § 13-604 (Supp. 2000) shifts the entire sentencing range upward whenever a defendant is in possession of a firearm during the commission of a felony. However, the sentencing range for felonies committed without a firearm overlaps that for felonies committed with a firearm. Therefore, it is possible that a defendant could receive the same sentence for a felony committed with a firearm as for a felony committed without a firearm. Consequently, sentencing range shifts that overlap are not true add-on provisions. Instead, sentencing range shifts that overlap but differ in the minimum sentence required will be treated as mandatory minimum laws. This treatment is appropriate because such shifts require a unique mandatory minimum sentence for felonies committed while in possession of a firearm.

2. Cal. Penal Code § 12022 provided for a five- to ten-year minimum add-on from September 9, 1953, to June 29, 1977. Effective June 29, 1977, the five- to ten-year minimum add-on was repealed and replaced by Cal. Penal Code § 12022(a)(1), which provided for a one-year add-on. However, this one-year add-on does not apply when possession of a firearm is an element of the underlying offense.

3. Add-on only applies when silencer, machine gun, short rifle, short shotgun, or semi-automatic assault weapon is used in the commission of the underlying offense.

4. Penalties increase for repeat offenders.

5. Penalties increase according to the severity of the underlying offense.

6. Marvel and Moody cite this provision for the proposition that Illinois law requires a mandatory minimum of six years when the defendant commits a felony while in possession of a firearm. However, the current section does not provide for this minimum and the appropriate section cannot be located.

7. Mandatory minimum only applies to possession of concealable firearm during the commission of the underlying offense.

8. Penalties increase for possession of semi-automatic and automatic weapons.

9. N.C. Gen. Stat. Ann. § 14-2.2 became effective April 15, 1981, not January 1, 1981.

10. N.C. Gen. Stat. Ann. § 14-2.2, cited by Marvel and Moody, was repealed in 1974 and replaced with a new N.C. Gen. Stat. Ann. § 14-2.2, effective March 26, 1994, which does not provide for a mandatory minimum.

11. Ohio Rev. Code Ann. § 2929.71, cited by Marvel and Moody, was repealed in 1995 and analogous provisions were recodified as Ohio Rev. Code Ann. § 2929.14.

(continued)

Table 9A-6. (continued)

12. Marvel and Moody call this Oklahoma provision not applicable on the grounds of note g above. However, the Oklahoma statute requires a minimum add-on of two years even if possession of a firearm is an element of the underlying offense, and the court is required to impose the minimum additional sentence. Oklahoma's provision is, therefore, a true minimum add-on law according to Marvel and Moody's methods and note g is inapplicable.

13. Mandatory minimum only applies if the defendant is convicted of a felony having as an element the defendant's use or threatened use of a firearm during the commission of the offense.

14. R.I. Gen. Laws Ann. § 11-47-3 (2000) creates a separate offense for carrying a dangerous weapon during the commission of a crime of violence. This offense is punishable by not less than three years and not more than ten years in prison. Because the Rhode Island statute creates a separate offense for carrying a firearm, it is not a true mandatory minimum provision. However, the Rhode Island statute does not require that this additional term be served consecutively and, therefore, is not a true minimum add-on either. Marvel and Moody cite this provision not applicable on the grounds of note g above, although the three-year sentence for this offense is mandatory and applies even when use of a firearm is an element of the underlying offense. This Marvel and Moody notation suggests that the creation of a separate offense for use of a firearm during the commission of a felony is alone sufficient to warrant note g.

15. Marvel and Moody cite S.D. Codified Laws § 22-14-12 as providing for a mandatory minimum of five years. However, S.D. Codified Laws § 22-14-12 as originally enacted and still in existence provides for an additional, consecutive sentence of five years to be imposed. Thus S.D. Codified Laws § 22-14-12 is a minimum add-on provision rather than a mandatory minimum provision.

16. Marvel and Moody cite S.D. Codified Laws § 22-14-12 as providing a minimum add-on sentence of five years. However, S.D. Codified Laws § 22-14-14 provides that the minimum add-on provided for in S.D. Codified Laws § 22-14-12 does not apply when the use of a dangerous weapon is a necessary element of the underlying felony. Therefore, in accord with Marvel and Moody's methods, S.D. Codified Laws § 22-14-12 is more appropriately designated n.a.g.

17. Tenn. Code Ann. § 39-6-1710 was repealed by Acts 1989, ch. 591, § 1, effective November 11, 1989, and was not replaced by an equivalent mandatory minimum provision. The five-year mandatory minimum and five-year minimum add-on were only in effect from July 1, 1976, to November 11, 1989.

18. Tenn. Code Ann. § 39-6-1710 was repealed by Acts 1989, ch. 591, § 1, and was not replaced by an equivalent minimum add-on provision. The five-year minimum add-on was only in effect from July 1, 1976, to November 11, 1989.

19. Marvel and Moody cite to Utah Code Ann. § 16-3-203 as the minimum add-on provision. However, the current minimum add-on provision is codified at Utah Code Ann. § 76-3-203, although its contents are unchanged.

20. The court has discretion not to apply the minimum add-on for lesser felonies.

Table 9A-7. *Selected Local Laws for U.S. Cities*

City, State	Population in 2000 Census (thousands)	Age limit for purchase or possession	Prohibits ownership by certain persons	Dealer's license required	Child access prevention (CAP) law	Regulates a specific class of firearms	Permit to purchase or own	Other (see note below)
Albuquerque, NM	449	X	X					
Anaheim, CA	328			X				
Anchorage, AK	260	X						
Arlington, TX	333							
Atlanta, GA	416							
Aurora, CO	276	X	X			X		
Austin, TX	657							
Baltimore, MD	651				X			
Boston, MA	589	X				X		X
Buffalo, NY	293							
Charlotte, NC	541							
Chicago, IL	2,896	X				X		
Cincinnati, OH	331	X		X	X	X	X	X
Cleveland, OH	478					X		
Colorado Springs, CO	361							
Columbus, OH	711	X				X	X	
Corpus Christi, TX	277							
Dallas, TX	1,189							
Denver, CO	555	X	X			X		X
Detroit, MI	951							
El Paso, TX	564							

(continued)

Table 9A-7. (continued)

City, State	Population in 2000 Census (thousands)	Age limit for purchase or possession	Prohibits ownership by certain persons	Dealer's license required	Child access prevention (CAP) law	Regulates a specific class of firearms	Permit to purchase or own	Other (see note below)
Fort Worth, TX	535							
Fresno, CA	428	X						
Honolulu, HI	372							
Houston, TX	1,954							
Indianapolis, IN	782		X		X			
Jacksonville, FL	736							
Kansas City, MO	442							X
Las Vegas, NV	478	X	X	X				
Long Beach, CA	462	X		X				X
Los Angeles, CA	3,695					X		
Louisville, KY	256							
Memphis, TN	650							
Mesa, AZ	396							
Miami, FL	362							
Milwaukee, WI	597							
Minneapolis, MN	383							
Nashville, TN	546							
New Orleans, LA	485			X			X	
New York, NY	8,008					X	X	X

Newark, NJ	274						
Oakland, CA	399	X		X	X	X	X
Oklahoma City, OK	506	X		X		X	
Omaha, NE	390						
Philadelphia, PA	1,518						
Phoenix, AZ	1,321						
Pittsburgh, PA	335						
Portland, OR	529						
Raleigh, NC	276						
Sacramento, CA	407			X		X	X
San Antonio, TX	1,145			X		X	
San Diego, CA	1,223			X	X	X	X
San Francisco, CA	777	X	X	X		X	
San Jose, CA	895	X	X		X	X	
Santa Ana, CA	338	X	X	X		X	
Seattle, WA	563						
St. Louis, MO	348						
St. Paul, MN	287						
Tampa, FL	303						
Toledo, OH	314	X	X	X	X	X	X
Tucson, AZ	487					X	
Tulsa, OK	393						
Virginia Beach, VA	425		X	X			
Washington, DC	572	X	X	X		X	X
Wichita, KS	344	X			X		X

(continued)

Table 9A-7. (continued)

Note: Cities have populations of 250,000 or more. Local laws for this table are derived from descriptions contained in Bureau of Alcohol, Tobacco, and Firearms (2000). The existence of these local laws has not been independently verified; some may remain on the books of the city despite having been preempted or overturned by a court. The table does not include local laws associated with discharge of weapons. Local laws may affect some or all classes of firearms (for example, handguns only). City populations are based on 2000 census figures for "places"; these do not include suburbs or other areas that are outside of the jurisdictional boundary of the city.

"Other" gun laws are as follows:

Boston: limits the sale of high-capacity ammunition magazines.

Cincinnati: conducts a background check with a waiting period; limits the sale of high-capacity ammunition magazines.

Columbus: limits the sale of high-capacity ammunition magazines.

Los Angeles: has a one-gun-per-month law and limits the sale of high-capacity ammunition magazines.

Las Vegas: has a waiting period.

New York: requires trigger locks to be sold with guns; limits the sale of high-capacity ammunition magazines.

Oakland: imposes additional restrictions on gun dealers, including requiring liability insurance; requires ammunition sales to be registered.

Sacramento: imposes additional restrictions on gun dealers.

San Diego: requires trigger locks to be sold with guns.

San Francisco: imposes additional restrictions on gun dealers; limits the sale of certain ammunition.

San Jose: requires trigger locks to be sold with guns.

Wichita: has a waiting period.

COMMENT BY
Franklin E. Zimring

The survey reported by Jon S. Vernick and Lisa M. Hepburn is intended to help observers understand firearm control in the United States in two ways. First, the categorization and discussion of different types of laws can provide information on what types of regulation were considered important at different levels of government in the United States and when and where such laws were adopted. While the legislation analyzed at the state level was limited, there are enough data on state-level gun control to suggest some conclusions about the legislative process. Particular forms of firearm control seem to follow fashion cycles—at the state level, recent cycles have involved shall-issue permit-to-carry laws in states with low political support for gun control and what have been called "safe storage" or "cap" laws for states with larger regulatory enthusiasm. The most significant trend that the chapter reports at the state level of government is preemption laws that limit the ability of cities to pass their own forms of transfer and access regulations. Because large cities are more inclined to regulate gun ownership, the net impact of state preemption is to reduce the intensity of governmental regulation.

A second use of the data reported would be to test whether broad categories of regulation (permits-to-purchase, shall-issue carry laws, child access protection laws, and so on) are associated with different levels of firearm violence. With this study providing effective dates and the cross-sectional inventories of laws at the state level, it is a straightforward matter to see whether differences in regulatory statutes are associated with differences in firearm violence.

There are, however, problems galore in generating reliable data on the impact of gun law enforcement in this fashion, and many of these are acknowledged in the Vernick and Hepburn analysis. In the first place, the presence or absence of a law on the statute books says nothing about the extent of its enforcement. In the second place, the categories used in this analysis contain wide variations in the designed intensity of the regulatory system and the strategic approach aimed at reducing gun violence.

Both California and New York administer handgun permit-to-purchase systems in the Vernick and Hepburn framework. The California system, typical of "permissive licensing" strategies, grants permits to all those persons who are not disqualified by age, criminal record, or other disability. There is no attempt to reduce the number of handguns in circulation, so any reduction in gun misuse would probably be the result of the limited access to defined high-risk users. The New York system, particularly in New York City, grants permits to less than

1 percent of citizens and attempts to reduce violence with handguns by making handguns scarce. But these two distinct strategies are aggregated into a single type of regulation, permit-to-purchase, which can produce misleading results.

I believe careful study of individual instances of legal change that document the strategies and intensities of enforcement before searching through crime data for evidence of regulatory impact is a better approach to testing legal impact than aggregate cross-sectional comparisons. So the tool kit provided by Vernick and Hepburn should be used with qualified enthusiasm.

One of the passive but important virtues of this current analysis is its clear understanding that counting up a jurisdiction's firearm regulatory statutes is a poor measure of the intensity of firearm regulation and the plausibility of a state's regulatory strategy. When gun legislation is aggregated into point totals that are used as a scorecard judgment of the quality of gun control, the enterprise probably creates more problems than it solves.[63] The evident caution and specificity of the current study are signs of progress.

COMMENT BY
Mark A. R. Kleiman

The chapter by Jon S. Vernick and Lisa M. Hepburn is a catalogue, by state, of laws concerning firearms. As such, the work is a great boon to those who want to explore the relationships between gun laws and various outcomes, and to those who need information about particular states. The chapter also serves as a useful corrective to the claim about "20,000 gun laws" so often used to deflect attention from the question of whether a proposal does, or does not, make sense.

Inevitably, design choices create limitations. The authors look at state laws, not local ones; they put aside laws about civil liability; they look at categories of prohibited behavior, rather than penalties (other than penalty enhancements) or enforcement mechanisms; and, curiously, when the authors begin to count legal provisions, they count only what might be called "antigun" laws, as opposed to, for example, shall-issue or preemption statutes. The count of statutory provisions seems, in effect, to be an attempt to construct a measure of how antigun each state's laws are. All of this, say the authors, is in the service of a public health inquiry.

The chapter's approach seems, to an outsider, to reflect the polarized nature of the debate over gun policy. That polarization echoes, though with the cultural

---

63. See Open Society Institute (2000).

poles reversed, the debate over drug policy, where the division is between those committed to stamping out "the drug culture" and those concerned with drug use only insofar as it causes observable damage.[64]

As Abraham Lincoln summed up the even older debate over alcohol, the question is whether we're dealing with the use of a bad thing or the misuse of an otherwise good thing.[65]

This commentary suggests a different line of inquiry, one with roots in policy analysis rather than public health, and one that might (or, admittedly, might not) lead to a less polarized approach.

Firearms are used by some people to damage themselves and to threaten or damage others. Otherwise, there would be no such topic as firearm policy. Firearms are also used for recreation and, more urgently, for self-defense. Otherwise, firearm policy would be easy.

From a policy analyst's perspective, the basic question is how firearm policies (including not just statutes but enforcement and other administrative practices) influence, and how they could influence, the frequency of injuries and threats of various kinds, and with what benefits and side effects, including, of course, the forgone benefits of whatever nonharmful gun uses the laws prevent.

This is not precisely the same as the public health inquiry that looks only at morbidity and mortality and how to prevent them, ignoring nonhealth costs and eliding the distinctions among criminal violence, intentional self-injury, and accident. In most public health analysis, each death incurred or prevented (or at least each quality-adjusted life year lost or saved) is treated as equally important, and, by omission, every value but health is treated as of no importance at all. These simplifications may sometimes be serviceable, but they are simplifications, and as such must be judged by Einstein's maxim that our theories should be as simple as possible but no simpler.

There is more at stake in firearm policy than changing the body count. Intentional injury to self (suicide, suicide attempt, or suicide gesture), intentional injury to others (assault), and unintentional injury (what we used to call accident) are different kinds of events for purposes of policymaking, even if they look the same to the trauma surgeon. As Justice Oliver Wendell Holmes remarked, even a dog knows the difference between being tripped over and being kicked.[66] Nor is physical injury the only thing worth considering; being robbed, or threatened with a gun, or hearing gunshots outside one's window, can do damage even if no physical injury is sustained.

---

64. Kaplan (1979). Kaplan's paper anticipates much of the argument of the present essay.
65. Basler (1953).
66. Holmes (1881, chap. 3).

JON S. VERNICK AND LISA M. HEPBURN

Even if the losses to victims were identical, there are moral and benefit-cost arguments for privileging crimes (or, on the other side of the equation, crimes prevented by self-defense) over self-inflicted and unintentional injuries.

Morally, the role of public authority in defending us from one another seems more obvious and is certainly more widely agreed to than its role in defending us from ourselves and can often be done at less cost to personal liberty and autonomy.

In terms of benefits and costs, crime causes fear and induces costly avoidance efforts in those who may never become its victims in any direct sense. No one ever moved out of a neighborhood because the suicide rate had gotten out of hand. That is not to say that preventing impulsive suicides and other deliberate or accidental self-woundings is not a legitimate public concern, only that preventing firearm assault deserves a higher priority than its sheer relative frequency would justify.

Speaking crudely, there are three approaches to reducing crimes committed with guns, which might be called broad acquisition policies, tailored acquisition policies, and use policies.

Broad acquisition policies aim at reducing the number of weapons in circulation and the number of persons who have ready access to weapons.

Tailored acquisition policies aim at reducing access to weapons by those whose personal characteristics and histories suggest a higher-than-average risk of misuse, or reducing access (broadly) to narrowly tailored classes of weapons. It is widely agreed that criminals, children, and the dangerously insane should not be allowed to have guns; the controversy surrounds just how to define those categories and just what rules are required to effectively reduce the access of gun-ineligible persons to firearms. Bans on the private ownership of machine guns, sawed-off shotguns, hand grenades, and weapons of mass destruction are relatively uncontroversial examples of tailoring by weapon class; controversial examples include "assault weapons" (however defined), high-caliber weapons, armor-piercing bullets, and weapons that pass through metal detectors. (Bans on cheap handguns, variously called junk guns or Saturday night specials, are probably better thought of as attempts to reduce the number of those with access to weapons by raising the minimum price of being armed. Attempts to disguise them as safety measures are unconvincing.)

Use-oriented policies aim at deterring those who do have access to weapons, legally or illegally, from carrying them, brandishing them, pointing them, firing them, or wounding with them. Use deterrence can be broad or narrow with respect to its target populations and can operate at the individual level or at the level of the poly-crime-committing group, such as a street gang.[67]

---

67. Kennedy and Braga (1998); Kennedy, Braga, and Piehl (1997).

Reducing the number of guns and gun holders—the broad acquisition approach—seems the obvious strategy: if the problem is guns, the solution must be fewer guns. Franklin E. Zimring has argued strongly that the link between the prevalence of guns and the prevalence of gun crimes will not be easily broken.[68]

But that obvious strategy has two equally obvious problems attached: there are lots of guns out there, and some of their owners are powerfully attached to them. Even those who would be perfectly willing—or even eager—to pry the gun from the dead, cold fingers of the last guns-rights advocate confront the problem of belling the cat.

To this political problem there corresponds the policy-analytic argument that guns do good as well as evil, especially if one is prepared to count as a benefit— in keeping with the usual practice in measuring economic welfare—someone's willingness to pay for whatever psychic benefits gun possession may confer as well as its practical benefits in self-defense or crime deterrence.

Thus narrow acquisition strategies and narrow use strategies have both operational and political advantages over broad acquisition and use strategies. To the extent that the benefits sought from broad acquisition strategies could be obtained instead with a set of gun control measures that allowed the apparently nondangerous majority to buy, keep, and even carry firearms with only minimal regulatory inconvenience, the political obstacles to reducing firearm violence, and the social costs of doing so, would be markedly reduced.

The Brady law is a primary example of a law intended to implement a narrow acquisition strategy. So far, its impact on crime, as measured by Jens Ludwig and Philip J. Cook, has been unspectacular.[69]

That poses a research question: "How much of the remaining gun crime reflects the inadequacy of that law on paper—either the conceptual failure of the narrow acquisition approach or excessive narrowness in the list of those forbidden to buy guns—and how much reflects failures to enforce its provisions?"

In operational terms, that question could be phrased: "Of current gun crimes, how many are committed by those eligible to buy and own guns under the Brady law? And of that group, how many could be covered by relatively narrow extensions of the Brady restrictions to include, for example, persons convicted of (perhaps more than one instance of) misdemeanor assault, driving under the influence, possession of drugs, violent crimes committed as a juvenile?"

68. Zimring (1968); Zimring (1991).
69. Ludwig and Cook (2000).

If the answer turns out to be that currently or potentially Brady-ineligible persons commit almost all gun crime, the argument for broad acquisition strategies and broad use strategies would be greatly weakened, unless the problem of leakage from Brady-eligible to Brady-ineligible persons, by means of voluntary illicit transfer or theft, were somehow shown to be intractable. That massive leakage is inevitable is a plausible, but by no means self-evident, proposition. The sheer number of firearms in circulation may be less important than their geographic and social location, since information flows less smoothly in illicit markets than in licit ones. Much may depend on the skill and vigor of enforcement against illicit gun trafficking.

But finding that most gun criminals are already, or potentially, Brady-ineligible would leave intact, and might even strengthen, the argument for changes to make the Brady law more enforceable: tougher measures against gun traffickers, swifter crackdowns on scofflaw gun dealers, a background check requirement for private gun sales, and increased capacity to trace a gun (or, ideally, even a bullet or shell casing) used in a crime back to its last legal transfer.

It would also strengthen the case for narrow use-oriented strategies, such as those embodied in Boston's Operation Ceasefire and its progeny.[70]

The research strategy proposed here is very different from the econometric approach embodied in most of the chapters in this volume. Measuring crimes prevented means measuring things that did not happen, and econometrics is uniquely the science of the counterfactual. Starting implicitly with counterfactual assumptions ("If states that passed shall-issue laws had instead not passed them . . ."), it has proved capable, in skilled hands, of reaching counterfactual conclusions as well. It is thus superbly equipped for the difficult task of measuring what is not there.

By contrast, what *is* there, actual rather than hypothetical events such as the number of crimes committed by holders of concealed-carry permits, can be measured with a somewhat older and less assumption-driven technique: counting. The ability to count how many of today's gun homicides (though not other gun crimes) are committed by people already forbidden to possess guns might flow from the proposed National Violent Death Surveillance System, though that system's currently proposed design conspicuously focuses on the decedent and the circumstances of death, omitting such items as the killer's criminal history. However, there is no need to wait for the construction of such a system; a sample of a few thousand gun assaults with known assailants would suffice to answer the question adequately for most purposes. Counting incidents might then turn out to be more useful than counting laws.

70. Braga and others (2001).

References

Basler, Roy P., ed. 1953. "Temperance Address." Springfield, Ill., February 22, 1942. In *The Collected Works of Abraham Lincoln*, vol. 1, 271–79. Rutgers University Press.

Black, Dan A., and Daniel S. Nagin. 1998. "Do Right-to-carry Laws Deter Violent Crime?" *Journal of Legal Studies* 27 (January): 209–19.

Braga, Anthony A., David M. Kennedy, Anne M. Piehl, and Elin J. Waring. 2001. *Reducing Gun Violence: The Boston Gun Project's Operation Ceasefire*. Washington: National Institute of Justice Research Report (September).

Bureau of Alcohol, Tobacco, and Firearms. 2000, 1998, 1994, 1988. "State Laws and Published Ordinances—Firearms." U.S. Department of the Treasury.

————. 2000. "Crime Gun Trace Reports (1999)—The Youth Crime Gun Interdiction Initiative." U.S. Department of the Treasury.

Bureau of Justice Statistics. 2000. "Survey of State Procedures Related to Firearm Sales, Midyear 2000." U.S. Department of Justice.

Centers for Disease Control and Prevention (CDC). 2001. "Surveillance For Fatal and Non-fatal Firearm-related Injuries—United States, 1993–1998." *Morbidity and Mortality Weekly Report* 50 (No. SS-2): 1–36.

Cook, Philip J. 1979. "The Effect of Gun Availability on Robbery and Robbery Murder." In *Policy Studies Review Annual*, edited by Robert H. Haveman and B. Bruce Zellner. Sage Press.

Cook, Philip J, Stephanie Molliconi, and Thomas B. Cole. 1995. "Regulating Gun Markets." *Journal of Criminal Law and Criminology* 86 (1): 59–92.

Cramer, Clayton E., and David B. Kopel. 1995. " 'Shall Issue': The New Wave of Concealed Handgun Permit Laws." *Tennessee Law Review* 62 (3): 679–757.

Cummings, Peter, David G. Grossman, Frederick P. Rivara, and Thomas D. Koepsell. 1997. "State Gun Safe Storage Laws and Child Mortality Due to Firearms." *Journal of the American Medical Association* 278 (13): 1084–86.

Dingell, John D. 1965. Hearings before the Senate Subcommittee to Investigate Juvenile Delinquency of the Committee on the Judiciary. 89 Cong. 1 sess. Government Printing Office.

Firearms Law Center of the Legal Community Against Violence. 2002. "Local Authority to Regulate Firearms in the Fifty States and the District of Columbia." Unpublished study (on file with authors).

Fennel, Monica. 1992. "Missing the Mark in Maryland: How Poor Drafting and Implementation Vitiated a Model State Gun Control Law." *Hamline Journal of Public Law and Policy* 13: 37–71.

Frattaroli, Shannon. 1999. "The Implementation of the 1996 Maryland Gun Violence Prevention Act." Unpublished Doctor of Philosophy dissertation (on file with authors). Johns Hopkins University, School of Public Health.

Holmes, Oliver Wendell. 1881. *The Common Law*.

Ikeda, Robin M., Rachel Gorwitz, Stephen P. James, Kenneth E. Powell, and James A. Mercy. 1997. "Fatal Firearm Injuries in the United States, 1962–1994." Violence Surveillance Summary Series. No. 3. Atlanta: National Center for Injury Prevention and Control.

Jacobs, James B., and Kimberly A. Potter. 1995. "Keeping Guns Out of the 'Wrong' Hands: The Brady Law and the Limits of Regulation." *Journal of Criminal Law and Criminology* 86 (1): 93–120.

Kaplan, John. 1979. "Controlling Firearms." *Cleveland State Law Review* 28 (1): 1–28.

Kennedy, David M., and Anthony A. Braga. 1998. "Homicide in Minneapolis: Research for Problem Solving." *Homicide Studies* 2 (August): 263–90.

Kennedy, David M., Anthony A. Braga, and Anne M. Piehl. 1997. "The (Un)Known Universe: Mapping Gangs and Gang Violence in Boston." In *Crime Mapping and Crime Prevention,* edited by David Weisburd and J. Thomas McEwen, 219–62. New York: Criminal Justice Press.

Lott, John R., and David Mustard. 1997. "Crime, Deterrence and Right-to-Carry Concealed Handguns." *Journal of Legal Studies* 26 (January): 1–68.

Ludwig, Jens. 1998. "Concealed-Gun-Carrying Laws and Violent Crime—Evidence from State Panel Data." *International Review of Law and Economics* 18: 239–54.

Ludwig, Jens, and Philip J. Cook. 2000. "Homicide and Suicide Rates Associated with Implementation of the Brady Handgun Violence Prevention Act." *Journal of the American Medical Association* 284 (5): 585–91.

Marvell, Thomas B., and Carlisle E. Moody. 1995. "The Impact of Enhanced Prison Terms For Felonies Committed with Guns." *Criminology* 33 (2): 247–81.

McDowall, David, Colin Loftin, and Brian Wiersema. 1992. "A Comparative Study of the Preventive Effects of Mandatory Sentencing Laws for Gun Crimes." *Journal of Criminal Law and Criminology* 83 (2): 378–94.

Newton, George D., and Franklin E. Zimring. 1969. "Firearms and Violence in American Life." Staff Report of the National Commission on the Causes and Prevention of Violence. Washington.

Open Society Institute. 2000. "Gun Control in the United States: A Comparative Survey of State Firearm Laws." New York: Soros Foundation.

Sherrill, Robert. 1973. *The Saturday Night Special.* Charterhouse.

Shields, Pete. 1981. *Guns Don't Die—People Do.* Arbor House.

Spitzer, Robert J. 1998. *The Politics of Gun Control.* Chatham House Publishers.

Teret, Stephen P., Garen J. Wintemute, and Peter Beilenson. 1992. "The Firearm Fatality Reporting System—A Proposal." *Journal of the American Medical Association* 267 (22): 3073–74.

Teret, Stephen P., and Garen J. Wintemute. 1993. "Policies to Prevent Firearm Injuries." *Health Affairs* 12 (4): 96–108.

Teret, Stephen P., Susan DeFrancesco, and Linda A. Bailey. 1993. "Gun Deaths and Home Rule: A Case for Local Regulation of a Local Public Health Problem." *American Journal of Preventive Medicine* 9 (3 Suppl): 44–46.

Vernick, Jon S., Daniel W. Webster, and Lisa M. Hepburn. 1999. "Effects of Maryland's Law Banning Saturday Night Special Handguns on Crime Guns." *Injury Prevention* 5 (4): 259–63.

Vernick, Jon S., and Stephen P. Teret. 1999. "New Courtroom Strategies Regarding Firearms: Tort Litigation against Firearm Manufacturers and Constitutional Challenges to Gun Laws." *Houston Law Review* 36 (5): 1713–54.

Vizzard, William J. 2000. *Shots in the Dark: The Policy, Politics, and Symbolism of Gun Control.* Rowan and Littlefield Publishers.

Webster, Daniel W., Jon S. Vernick, Jens Ludwig, and Kathleen J. Lester. 1997. "Flawed Gun Policy Research Could Endanger Public Safety." *American Journal of Public Health* 87 (6): 918–21.

Webster, Daniel W., and Marc Starnes. 2000. "Reexamining the Association between Child Access Prevention Gun Laws and Unintentional Shooting Deaths of Children." *Pediatrics* 106 (5): 1466–69.

Webster, Daniel W., Jon S. Vernick, and Lisa M. Hepburn. 2001. "Relationship between Licensing, Registration and Other Gun Sales Laws and the Source State of Crime Guns." *Injury Prevention* 7 (3): 184–89.

———. 2002. "Effects of Maryland's Law Banning 'Saturday Night Special' Handguns on Homicides." *American Journal of Epidemiology* 155 (5): 406–12.

Weil, Douglas S., and Rebecca C. Knox. 1996. "Effects of Limiting Handgun Purchases on Interstate Transfer of Firearms." *Journal of the American Medical Association* 275 (22): 1759–61.

Wintemute, Garen J. 1999. "The Future of Firearm Violence Prevention: Building on Success." *Journal of the American Medical Association* 282 (5): 475–78.

Wright, James D., Peter H. Rossi, and Kathleen Daly. 1983. *Under the Gun*. Aldine Publishing Company.

Zimring, Franklin E. 1968. "Is Gun Control Likely to Reduce Violent Killings?" *University of Chicago Law Review* 35 (4): 721–37

———. 1991. "Firearms, Violence, and Public Policy." *Scientific American* 265 (5): 48–54.

———. 1993. "Policy Research on Firearms and Violence." *Health Affairs* 12 (4): 109–22.

Zimring, Franklin E., and Gordon Hawkins. 1992. *The Citizens Guide to Gun Control*. MacMillan Publishing Company.

———. 1997. "Concealed Handguns: The Counterfeit Deterrent." *Responsive Community* (Spring): 46–60.

DEBORAH AZRAEL
CATHERINE BARBER
DAVID HEMENWAY
MATTHEW MILLER

10 | *Data on Violent Injury*

The nation's public policy response to the burden of firearm injury—which accounts for 30,000 lives lost each year—and to the problems of suicide and homicide more broadly, have been hindered by lack of data to describe and monitor the problem.[1] National data should provide empirical answers to questions like the following, none of which can be answered today:

— Did the number of people shot with assault weapons rise, fall, or stay level following passage of the 1994 federal assault weapons ban?

— How many people are killed with so-called junk guns every year? Has the number been increasing or decreasing over time? Are teenaged homicide perpetrators more likely to use these weapons than are others?

— What are the three most common circumstances leading to unintentional gun deaths? Are more of these deaths self-inflicted or inflicted by others? Are handguns or long guns more frequently involved? Are certain makes or models overrepresented?

— Where do youths who shoot themselves or others obtain their guns?

— How often do mass public shootings occur?

— In what proportion of intimate partner homicides does the offender also take his or her own life or the lives of the victim's children or protectors?

---

1. Centers for Disease Control and Prevention (CDC) (2001e).

412

— What circumstances (such as depression, terminal illness, relationship breakup) are most commonly associated with suicide, whether by firearm or other means?

Answers to these questions and others like them are vital to formulating and evaluating interventions aimed at reducing suicide, homicide, and unintentional firearm deaths. We lack answers not because violent deaths are not closely investigated and documented—they are—but because our nation currently lacks a comprehensive surveillance system to join the findings from death investigations into a uniform, usable database.

This chapter introduces the reader to surveillance systems as a fundamental tool of rational public policy. We begin by defining surveillance and introducing examples of its use and importance in various fields including economics, criminal justice, and public health. We outline the shortcomings of existing national data systems with respect to firearm and violent deaths and discuss a new effort by the Centers for Disease Control and Prevention (CDC) to establish a National Violent Death Reporting System (NVDRS) that would do much to fill the current information gap.[2] Because that system has not yet been implemented, we describe the pilot version of the system tested in a multiagency pilot test since 2000.

Surveillance Systems

Public health surveillance is defined as "the ongoing, systematic collection, analysis, interpretation, and dissemination of data regarding a health-related event for use in public health action to reduce morbidity and mortality and to improve health."[3] Unlike short-term data collection efforts, surveillance systems are ongoing institutions that collect data on an identifiable population using variables that are standardized over time and across jurisdictions. Surveillance data are therefore well suited to characterizing types of events, measuring trends, formulating interventions, evaluating the impact of policies, and generating and testing hypotheses.

National surveillance systems have existed for decades in the realms of economics, criminal justice, and public health, among others. Their contributions to stabilizing economies, understanding crime, fighting medical illness, and, in injury prevention, reducing traffic deaths, have been widely recognized.

2. In December 2001, CDC received a 1.5 million dollar appropriation to begin implementing NVDRS. Monies from this appropriation will be used to fund, among other things, six NVDRS sites in late 2002.

3. CDC (2001d, p. 2).

Economics

Before the 1930s, policymakers tried to determine appropriate economic policy using limited and fragmentary information about the state of the economy. Presidents Herbert Hoover and Franklin D. Roosevelt, for example, attempted to design policies to combat the Great Depression on the basis of such sketchy data as stock price indexes and freight car loadings. In the 1930s, the National Bureau of Economic Research (NBER) was commissioned by the Department of Commerce to develop a set of national economic accounts. The timely, comprehensive, and accurate data on the economy provided by the national accounts have been credited with reducing the severity of business cycles and with bolstering a postwar era of strong economic growth. According to James Tobin, Nobel Laureate in economics, the combination of the national income accounts and modern macroeconomic theory "deserve much credit for the improved performance of the economy in the second half of the century."[4] Indeed, as the twentieth century drew to a close, the Department of Commerce named the development of the national income accounts "its achievement of the century." Others have echoed this assessment, calling the creation of gross domestic product and the rest of the national income accounts "truly among the great inventions of the twentieth century."[5]

Criminal Justice

Although the phrase "surveillance system" is not used in the criminal justice field (surveillance instead referring to the undercover observation of suspected criminals), the benefits of ongoing data collection have long been recognized by criminologists. Two major data collection programs sponsored by the federal government, the FBI's Uniform Crime Reports (UCR) program—a census of offenses known to police—and the National Crime Victimization Survey (NCVS) by the Bureau of Justice Statistics—a survey measuring the incidence of reported and unreported crime in the U.S. population—are long-term, established systems.[6] These sources have been used, for example, to better describe the problem of intimate partner violence and to track changes in patterns of intimate partner violence over time.[7] Data from the UCR and NCVS are presented annually by the Bureau of Justice Statistics in the *Sourcebook,* a massive

---

4. *Survey of Current Business,* January 2000 (*www.bea.gov/bea/aw/0100/0d/maintext.htm* [July 2002]).

5. Samuelson and Nordhaus (2000).

6. FBI (1984); Bureau of Justice Statistics (1994).

7. Rennison and Welchans (2000); CDC (2001b).

compendium of over 600 tables, which serves as a testament to the federal government's commitment to tracking crime trends.[8]

The benefits of systematized data collection as an effective tool in crime fighting have been embraced more recently by local law enforcement agencies. For example, the sharp downturn in violent crime in New York City in the mid-1990s has been credited in part to the availability of precise, neighborhood-specific, real-time crime data that enabled police officers to deploy their forces more effectively.[9] Boston's much-heralded youth gun violence initiative was associated with equally impressive declines in violent crime. That successful effort highlighted the importance of data collection in pinpointing individuals and neighborhoods for intensive crime enforcement and helping police understand the forces that drive youth gun violence.[10]

Public Health

In 1999 the Centers for Disease Control and Prevention listed its candidates for the ten major public health achievements of the twentieth century. These included the establishment of schools of public health, the creation of city and county health departments, the development of periodic standardized health surveys (for example, the Behavioral Risk Factor Surveillance System and the Youth Risk Behavior Survey), and the institution of morbidity and mortality surveillance.[11]

In the last quarter of the nineteenth century, morbidity reports were collected on cholera, smallpox, plague, and yellow fever for use in quarantine. By 1928 all states were participating in the national reporting of twenty-nine diseases. By midcentury, the focus had changed from the tracking of persons with disease to tracking trends in disease occurrence. Early benefits of the morbidity surveillance system included the information it provided on malaria and hepatitis. For example, the surveillance system showed, to the surprise of many, that malaria—deeply entrenched in the South in the 1930s–40s—had almost disappeared in a single decade, largely through natural processes, weakening the case for indoor DDT spraying.[12] In 1947, under the auspices of the newly created Centers for Disease Control, the first fully national disease surveillance system was established. Eight years later, in 1955, surveillance data helped to determine the cause of poliomyelitis among children recently vaccinated with an inactivated vaccine.[13]

8. Maguire and Pastore (2001).
9. Walsh (2001).
10. Kennedy and others (2001).
11. CDC (1999).
12. Langmuir (1963).
13. CDC (1999).

Trends in disease incidence that would have been difficult to identify at the local or state level are often identified with surveillance data aggregated to the multistate and national level. For example, the U.S. Foodborne Illness Active Surveillance Network provided data that permitted a quick response to multistate outbreaks, identifying listeria in hot dogs, Salmonella in toasted oat cereal, and E-coli in alfalfa sprouts.[14] In 1999 an increase in total cases of salmonellosis was identified and traced to new sources such as unpasteurized orange juice, imported mangos, and raw sprouts.[15]

In 1984 the Centers for Disease Control and Prevention developed an annual survey to monitor the state-level prevalence of behavioral risks associated with premature morbidity and mortality. The Behavioral Risk Factor Surveillance System (BRFSS) provides data that have been critical in planning, implementing, monitoring, and evaluating public health–related programs and legislation. These BRFSS data have provided support for legislation restricting indoor smoking and mandating seat belt use (in Alabama), for restricting the availability of cigarette vending machines to minors (in Hawaii), and for monitoring the impact of tobacco control legislation (in California and Maine). In Illinois, BRFSS data helped support legislative initiatives requiring the inclusion of mammography screening in all health insurance coverage, and in Massachusetts the data were used to monitor the effect of adult immunization and teen pregnancy prevention programs. In Connecticut, information provided by the BRFSS was important in monitoring the effect of bicycle helmet legislation, and in Vermont it helped to pass improved driving while under the influence (DUI) legislation.[16]

At least as important as the contribution that the BRFSS has made to state-level programs and legislation has been its usefulness in comparing conditions across states over time. For example, information from the BRFSS has been used to assess the association between firearm ownership and violent death among children and to track the percentage of women who have never received a screening mammogram.[17]

Fatality Analysis Reporting System

The National Highway Safety Administration's Fatality Analysis Reporting System (FARS), which became operational in 1975, is the largest and most comprehensive national surveillance system for *injuries* in the United States. The system, which collects information on approximately 37,000 crashes and

14. U.S. Department of Health and Human Services (2000).
15. Public Health Foundation (2001).
16. CDC (2001a).
17. Miller, Azrael, and Hemenway (2002); CDC (2001c).

40,000 fatalities annually, is federally funded. Data are gathered at the state level from each state's own source documents (for example, police accident reports, state vehicle registration files, state driver's license files, vital statistics data) and are coded into standard FARS forms.[18] More than one hundred variables are documented on each incident, including information on vehicles (for example, make, model, safety features, inspection status), crash features (for example, points of impact, speed), environment (for example, type of roadway, weather conditions, visibility, time of day), people (for example, seating, extent of injuries, use of restraints and helmets), and drivers (for example, impairment, alcohol use, license status, previous infractions). This specificity enables researchers to study the impact of various interventions with precision.

The FARS data system is available to researchers at no charge and has been used extensively. For example, data routinely collected by FARS have allowed researchers to evaluate the impact of lowering the minimum legal drinking age and legal blood alcohol limits for young drivers, the efficacy of motorcycle helmet-wearing laws, and the effect of revising speed limits on mortality.[19]

The FARS has never been formally evaluated, but its benefits seem to far outweigh costs (estimated at approximately $7 million annually). Take, as one example, the Institute of Medicine's assessment of the critical role that FARS played in evaluating and revising minimum legal drinking age laws. The report credits FARS surveillance data as being "essential for the enactment and assessment of legislation establishing the minimum age for the purchase of alcoholic beverages."[20] In the early 1970s about half of the states lowered the minimum age for alcohol purchase. Beginning in 1976 states reversed course and began to raise the minimum age, a trend that continued into the early 1980s. Multistate research based on FARS and vital statistics data showed the beneficial effects of this reversal.[21] The research findings were instrumental in leading to federal legislation that influenced states to establish 21 as the minimum age for purchase. This policy is in effect in all states and is credited with having saved more than 20,000 lives from 1975 through 2000.[22] The policy also appears to have reduced youth suicide.[23]

The FARS data are not ideal—for example, direct measurement of the blood alcohol content of drivers is obtained only sporadically—but data quality and completeness have improved greatly since the first few years, when the system

18. Fatality Analysis Reporting System (*www.bts.gov/ntda/farsdb* [September 2001]).
19. For example, for drinking age and blood alcohol, see Hingson, Heeren, and Winter (1994); Williams and others (1983); Smith and others (1984); Hingson and others (1983). For motorcycle helmets, see McSwain and Belles (1990); for speed limits, see Garber and Graham (1990).
20. Bonnie, Fulco, and Liverman (1999, pp. 117–18).
21. Cook and Tauchen (1984).
22. National Highway Traffic Safety Administration (2001).
23. Birckmayer and Hemenway (1999).

was sometimes ruefully dubbed the FARCE system. The system has also been modified over time to capture changes in automotive technology (for example, it now includes a variable for airbag deployments).

Existing National Surveillance Data on Violent Deaths

Among the leading causes of death in the United States, dedicated surveillance systems exist for communicable and noncommunicable medical illness and for motor vehicle fatalities, but not for violent deaths. Consequently, data for violent death have been largely inadequate even though homicide and suicide are the second and third leading cause of death among people 1–34 years of age and annually account for more than 45,000 deaths among people of all ages.

Two systems of data on violent deaths exist at the national level: the FBI's *Supplementary Homicide Reports (SHR)*, which are voluntarily submitted by police departments as a supplement to the Uniform Crime Reporting program, and the National Center for Health Statistics' National Vital Statistics System, which is based on death certificate information. Both systems provide critical information on aspects of the violent death problem. Vital Statistics supplies demographic information about the victim, and SHRs give basic information about both victims and offenders (age, race, sex, ethnicity), victim/offender relationship, and precipitating circumstances. Unfortunately, the two systems currently cannot be accurately linked (except for infrequent types of homicide like child victims or unintentional homicides) because death certificates and SHRs collect so few personally identifying variables in common.

Both systems have marked limitations. Vital Statistics provides no information on suspected offenders or circumstances leading to homicides, and SHRs give no information on suicides. In addition, the SHR system is limited in its ability to characterize multiple-victim events and assigns only one circumstance per case. While the National Incident-Based Reporting System format (NIBRS, an enhanced version of UCR reporting)[24] would address those shortcomings, police departments in most major metropolitan areas (where most homicides occur) continue to report under the standard SHR format, not NIBRS. Furthermore, neither Vital Statistics nor SHR data provide information about the specific type and model of the gun involved in firearm deaths or about the circumstances contributing to suicides or self-inflicted gun accidents.

The paucity of data on violent deaths has led many to call for a reporting system for firearm and other violence-related deaths modeled after FARS. Proposals

24. FBI (1996).

for a firearm fatality reporting system first appeared in the CDC's *Cost of Injury* report to Congress in 1989 and subsequently in the *Journal of the American Medical Association* and the *American Journal of Public Health*.[25] In 1999 the Institute of Medicine called for a national data system for homicides and suicides to provide objective data with which to monitor trends and evaluate the effectiveness of prevention programs and policies. In 2001 the Surgeon General set as a national suicide prevention objective "[implementation of] a national violent death reporting system that includes suicides and collects information not currently available from death certificates."[26]

Establishing a Surveillance System for Violent Deaths

In 1999 the Harvard Injury Control Research Center (HICRC) began collaborating with the Medical College of Wisconsin and ten other universities, health departments, and medical centers around the country to design and pilot a reporting system for violent deaths. Six foundations (the Center on Crime, Communities and Culture of the Open Society Institute; the Joyce Foundation; the John D. and Catherine T. MacArthur Foundation; the David and Lucile Packard Foundation; the Annie E. Casey Foundation; and Atlantic Philanthropies) supported the HICRC effort, viewing it as a means of jump starting a federally funded, national system. The collaborators (called the National Violent Injury Statistics System [NVISS] Workgroup) jointly developed uniform data elements, software, reporting protocols, and training manuals for the reporting system. Each site piloted the system in its state or county, starting with firearm-related deaths in 2000 and expanding to all violent deaths in 2001. Violence-related deaths were defined as those for which the "underlying cause of death" code on the death certificate fell under the broad category of homicide, suicide, legal intervention, terrorism war operations, or late effects of any of the preceding. Also included were unintentional firearm-related deaths and firearm deaths of unknown intent.[27]

The pilot system closely mirrors FARS in its incident-based, relational database structure, the detail it gathers, and the methods by which data are abstracted. Abstractors from the collaborating sites identify cases initially from death certificate or coroner and medical examiner (C/ME) data. For each case they request the C/ME's narrative report on the case, autopsy results, and toxi-

25. Rice and others (1989); Teret, Wintemute, and Beilenson (1992); Teret (1996); Barber and others (2000).
26. U.S. Department of Health and Human Services (2001).
27. Azrael, Barber, and Mercy (2001).

cology test results. Data on victims who died in the same incident are recorded in the same incident record.

The narrative reports are often a rich source of information on the circumstances of the deaths, especially suicides and unintentional shooting deaths. Abstractors link the C/ME information on a case with data from the death certificate and, for homicides, with data from the Supplementary Homicide Report. Most sites also review police records for more in-depth information on homicides. For cases involving firearms, sites also collect information on the weapon's type, make, model, and caliber from (in descending order of authority) police crime lab reports, police homicide investigation records, or C/ME reports. Box 10-1 lists variables captured by the reporting system. If a variable cannot be filled in based on a review of records, it is marked as unknown. Pilot sites do not conduct active surveillance (such as survivor interviews) to fill in missing data. Once data collection is complete at the local level, records are stripped of personal identifiers and forwarded to the multisite database at Harvard.

To demonstrate the advantages of the pilot reporting system, we present the following two case examples and illustrate their coding under the current national data systems and under the pilot.

Case Examples

Case 1. The decedent was a 34-year-old white man who returned to his exgirlfriend's house in violation of a restraining order and shot her and her two children before shooting himself in the right temple with a Smith and Wesson .38 Special. The victim was despondent over their breakup and a recent job loss. He had a history of depression, a blood alcohol level of .09, and a current prescription for sertraline (Zoloft).

— Death certificate. The death certificate captures this as a firearm suicide, most likely without distinguishing it as a handgun suicide. The International Classification of Disease coding system used in death certificates differentiates handgun from long gun deaths, but more than two-thirds of gun deaths fall into an unspecified category.[28] Valuable information about the decedent's age, race, sex, place of birth, years of education, veteran status, and marital status are captured. However, the fact that this death was part of a murder-suicide is not reflected, and there is no way to link this death with that of the woman and two children. Similarly, the information that the victim was intoxicated, being treated with an antidepressant, and had relationship and job problems is not available, nor is the specific information on the weapon.

28. CDC (1998).

Box 10-1. *Variables Collected in the Pilot for the National Violent Death Reporting System*

Incident information Incident ID Version Incident narrative Investigating police agency Death investigation source Number of nonfatal victims	*Supplementary homicide report variables (homicides only)* SHR homicide type and situation SHR victim/offender relationship SHR circumstance SHR justifiable shooting circumstance
Person (victim and suspect) information Person ID Person type Age Sex Race Ethnicity Incident at person's residence? At work Intoxication suspected?	*Victim demographics* Residential address Homeless status Marital status Veteran status Birthplace Pregnant Education Employment status Usual occupation Usual industry
Suspect characteristics Attempted suicide?	*Victim injury information and substance use* Place of death Number of wounds and wound location
Victim information Weapon type Incident type Medical examiner/coroner manner of death Death certificate underlying cause of death Victim/suspect relationship—abstracted Abuse Date and time of injury Date and time of death Incident location type Address of incident	Death certificate multiple condition codes Autopsy performed Alcohol presence Blood alcohol level Drug presence Date and time body specimen collected
Victim circumstance Violence circumstances Accident/unintentional circumstances Suicide—mental health Suicide intent Suicide circumstances	*Firearm information* Firearm ID Type of firearm physical evidence Firearm type Firearm make Firearm model Firearm caliber/gauge Firearm victim table Stolen Youth access to firearms

— SHR. The SHR records the murder of the woman and children but not the suicide. The age, race, ethnicity, and sex of the victims and the offender are recorded. If the exgirlfriend is the first victim listed, her relationship to the offender is captured but is likely to be coded as "acquaintance" as there is no SHR code for exgirlfriend. The case is therefore lost as a domestic violence case. The SHR database captures only the relationship of the first victim to the offender, so the children's relationship to the offender is not characterized. The SHR data for 1998 indicate that 24 percent of child homicide victims 14 years old and under are killed in multiple-victim incidents, indicating information on children's killers is lost in a sizable proportion of cases. The weapon is coded as a handgun, and the circumstance is coded as "argument."

— Pilot reporting system. In the NVISS reporting system all four deaths are linked in one incident record. The murder-suicide is recorded, as is the relationship of each victim to the suspect. The woman is coded as "ex-lover" and the children as "child of suspect's lover/exlover." Variables indicating whether the suspect was a caretaker of the victim (useful in identifying child abuse and elder abuse) and whether there is evidence of ongoing abuse of the victim by the suspect (as there would be in this case for the woman) are recorded. All available demographic variables on each person involved in the incident are captured. In addition, the gunman's blood alcohol level, history of depression, mental health treatment status, job problem and relationship problem are coded. The gun is recorded as a revolver, and its make, model, and caliber are coded

Case 2. The decedent was an 11-year-old boy who was playing with a 13-year-old friend. The two boys discovered a gun belonging to the 13-year-old's father. The gun, a 9 mm Glock, was stored in a bedside table drawer. The magazine was removed from the gun, and the boys believed it was unloaded. The 13-year-old boy pulled the trigger, not realizing a bullet remained in the firing chamber, and shot his friend once in the heart.

— Death certificate. The death certificate is likely to code this case as a gun homicide, not a gun accident. We examined all Supplementary Homicide Reports on negligent (unintentional) gun manslaughters in 1997 and linked the cases to their matching death certificate. Seventy-five percent were coded as homicides on the death certificate.[29] The death certificate carries no information about the relationship of the victim to the shooter, what type of gun was involved, and what circumstances led to the child's death.

— SHR. If SHR reports the case at all (reporting of negligent manslaughters became a nonrequired component of the SHR in 1984 and compliance is believed to be low), it may be coded appropriately as a negligent manslaughter. A precipitating circumstance of "child playing with gun" will be assigned the case. However, the specific circumstance and gun type will not be recorded.

— Pilot reporting system. This case is recorded as an unintentional firearm injury inflicted by the boy's friend. The specific circumstances, "children playing with gun" and "thought gun was unloaded—magazine disengaged," are coded, as is the gun type, make, model, and caliber. Because the shooter is a youth, information about who owned the gun (for example, self, parent), whether the gun

29. Barber and others (2002).

was stored locked or loaded, and whether the child had authorized access to the gun are also coded.

As can be seen from these cases, a tracking system that links data from existing systems while accessing previously untapped data resources has substantial advantages—more, better, and more specific information is collected. For example, with a system such as NVISS it will be possible for the first time to track the occurrence of murder-suicides (domestic and otherwise) and to differentiate among accidental shootings that may be preventable by design changes (for example, devices that prevent a pistol from firing when the magazine is disengaged), safer storage practices, or more responsible handling.

The two examples show the system's promise as an aid to policy formulation. For example, preliminary data from the NVISS pilot indicates that in 57 percent of the cases in which a woman is killed by an intimate partner, the suspect also takes his own life, as occurred in case 1. This finding suggests that laws requiring the removal of guns from persons named as perpetrators in domestic violence restraining orders may have a measurable effect in preventing suicides by perpetrators. Similarly, case 2 indicates the ability of the system to identify whether many, few, or no unintentional firearm deaths might be prevented with a "magazine disconnect" (a device that prevents a pistol from firing when the magazine is disengaged).

Limitations of the System

The pilot is not without its limitations. As a system that links data from various sources, it is subject to the limitations of each data source. Coroner and medical examiner reports, for instance, vary across jurisdictions in the level of detail they provide. One coroner may regularly document whether suicide victims were known to have any mental health disorders or to be in mental health treatment, while another may not. Some jurisdictions regularly test for the presence of drugs and alcohol in the victim's blood, while others test only when substances are suspected of contributing to the death. However, as was true with the FARS system, there is reason to expect that data consistency and quality will improve over time as data providers become aware of which variables are being abstracted from their reports and when they see that the data are put to use. Improvement in data provider participation and data quality is a priority of both NVISS and NVDRS. NVISS sites have been able to increase data provider buy-in by ensuring that system data are available to them in a timely and useful fashion (for example, some NVISS sites provide geocoded data back to medical examiners) and have met regularly with data providers to explain the system and rationale for collecting specific variables.

The nature of many violent deaths also leads to incomplete data. Many homicides are unsolved, and no information may be available on the suspect, precipitating circumstances, and weapon involved in these cases. Some suicide victims leave little clue as to the precipitants leading them to take their lives. During the first year of data collection under the pilot, for all fatal firearm incidents, involving more than 900 victims, information on precipitating circumstances was unavailable for 4 percent of the suicide victims and 23 percent of the homicide victims.

Utility of the System

Information collected under the proposed NVDRS would improve on available violent injury data. The fact that the data are collected in an incident-based format will allow for more accurate characterization of complex events, the specificity of the data will allow more useful descriptions of rare events, and the data's uniformity across sites and over time, combined with the application of uniform and policy-relevant definitions, will allow monitoring of trends and comparison across jurisdictions. All of these improvements will contribute to the data's relevance and likely utility for developing or repealing legislative and programmatic interventions, as well as in evaluating the effectiveness and cost effectiveness of those interventions.

To illustrate the benefits of such detailed, multisource data, we describe ways in which the NVDRS will improve our capacity to monitor trends among subtypes of violent deaths, evaluate the impact of legislative and programmatic prevention strategies, and assess the impact of firearm design modifications.

Monitoring Trends. Routinely collected data in the United States are currently inadequate to monitor important trends, such as in school-based violence, intimate partner violence, drug-related violence, youth suicide, or workplace violence.

— School-based violence. To begin to characterize school-based violent events, the CDC and the U.S. Departments of Education and Justice undertook a special study of school-associated violent death.[30] Because no existing data source could identify school-related events reliably, or identify important characteristics of the incidents, cases were identified through a systematic search of two computerized newspaper and broadcast media databases, reports from a newspaper clipping service, voluntary reports from state and local education agencies, and interviews with principals and police in jurisdictions with school

30. Anderson and others (2001).

deaths. Major findings included a statistically significant shift between 1994 and 1999 from single-victim to multiple-victim school-related homicides, a concentration of violent events before school, at lunch and after school, and a large proportion of incidents preceded by a note, threat, or other action indicating the risk for violence. In their conclusion, the authors call for ongoing, routine assessment of school-related shootings. The incident-based NVDRS, designed to capture school-based events and to record multiple victim-offender relationships, is precisely the type of system required for such monitoring.

— Intimate partner violence. Intimate partner homicides cannot be tracked by using death certificates because death certificates do not routinely record the victim's relationship to the perpetrator. Supplementary Homicide Reports (SHRs) are far from ideal, as they do not report all homicides, do not tie all victims (for example, children) to an intimate partner event,[31] and do not always properly characterize intimate-partner-related events (for example, exboyfriends and exgirlfriends are often not coded as intimate partners, see case 1 above). A recent report used the SHRs to summarize information on intimate partner homicides that occurred in the United States during 1981–98.[32] Data from the SHR file were weighted by comparison with homicide data from death certificates to compensate for underreporting. Limitations of the study that would be readily ameliorated by data provided by NVDRS include the narrowness of the SHR's definition of "intimate partner," the need for weighting, the absence of even crude socioeconomic information (such as is available on the death certificate and which would be collected as part of NVDRS) and, for firearm-related deaths, information about the firearm.

Policy Evaluation. Evaluation of firearm policies, at the national, state, and local levels, is currently hindered by lack of data on outcomes specific enough to allow testing of hypotheses regarding the mechanisms by which policies are expected to act and the distribution of the effects of policies across time, space, or subgroups of the population.

— *Firearm Design Assessment.* During the past five years there has been an increase in the number of policies aimed at increasing the safety of firearms, such as local laws requiring purchase of a trigger lock at point of sale or mandating design changes to new firearms. Unfortunately, these laws have been enacted in the absence of empirical data supporting their efficacy and with little promise of sensible evaluation. Currently, we do not even know whether safety devices or firearm storage practices prevent unintentional firearm deaths, let alone

31. Langford, Isaac, and Kabat (1999, 1998).
32. CDC (2001b).

which devices or storage practices are most effective and for whom. Some safety devices may themselves be associated with unintended firearm deaths (for example, a jammed or malfunctioning loaded chamber indicator may mislead a gun user into thinking that a loaded gun is unloaded), and it is unclear how the potential benefits and potential harms of particular safety devices are distributed among different groups. Analogous to the actual roadway experience with air bags, it is possible that different groups may benefit (or be harmed) by different safety devices. A trigger lock may protect children but not adults; a drop safety device may protect all groups but have little net effect if dropped guns represent a small fraction of unintentional firearm deaths; adults, but not young children, may be misled and harmed by a jammed chamber indicator; a magazine disconnect, which prevents a gun from firing when the magazine is removed, may protect children and nongun owners but few experienced gun owners.

Since unintentional firearm deaths are rare, only a system that tracks deaths across states and over several years can hope to have the power to detect any effect of technological modifications such as magazine disconnects. For example, fewer than 900 unintentional firearm deaths were recorded in the United States in 1998, 53 of which occurred in very young children (ten years of age and younger). If magazine disconnects are present in 20 percent of households with guns in the general population and if magazine disconnects actually prevent 50 percent of all unintentional firearm deaths in this age group, it would take three years of data collection across all fifty states to have at least an 80 percent probability of detecting (as statistically significant) this large effect. A case control study of the effect of a highly effective safety device to prevent unintentional firearm deaths among children would take decades to amass a sufficient number of cases if the study were conducted in a single state and would be subject to various biases from which uniformly collected surveillance data are more immune.

— *Child Access Protection Laws.* Child access prevention (CAP) laws (that is, laws that make a gun owner criminally liable if his gun is not stored safely and a child uses it to injure himself or others) have been evaluated twice.[33] Fifteen states have CAP laws, and in 2000 Daniel W. Webster and Marc Starnes found that they were associated with a 17 percent decline in unintentional firearm death rates among children. However, Florida's CAP law was associated with a 51 percent decline, and there were no statistically significant effects in the other fourteen states.[34]

The three limitations acknowledged by the authors illustrate the contributions NVDRS can make to firearm policy evaluation. First, longitudinal data on gun storage practices among owners of guns used in fatal events by children, the

33. Cummings and others (1997); Webster and Starnes (2000).
34. Webster and Starnes (2000).

behavior targeted by the law, were not available to researchers but are the kind of data NVDRS will collect. Second, some medical examiners code deaths in which someone shoots another person as homicides, regardless of the shooter's intention to harm the victim.[35] When an individual apparently does not realize a gun is loaded and shoots himself or someone else, these deaths are coded as suicides or homicides by some medical examiners and as unintentional firearm deaths by others. The NVDRS will apply uniform definitions, reducing the measurement error introduced by inconsistent death certificate coding. Third, available data on mortality from unintentional shootings do not include data about the person who pulled the trigger, such as the shooter's age, the relationship to the decedent, and other potentially relevant data such as where the death occurred and from whom the youth obtained the gun. The NVDRS would supply this information.

If CAP laws are actually responsible for the decline in unintentional firearm deaths among children, this effect should be concentrated among children who obtained their firearm from an adult (for example, parent) who, under CAP laws, is responsible for the illegal and injurious use of the firearm (category A). For the sake of illustration, assume that category A constitutes 70 percent of all such incidents. For simplicity, assume that the remaining 30 percent of unintended deaths (category B) occurred among children who obtained the gun from nonresponsible parties (for example, the firearm belonged to the child). Consequently, in this simplified instance, the 17 percent decline in unintentional firearm deaths in children overall should be concentrated in category A. If the effect of CAP laws is not concentrated in this way, it is more likely that important unobserved variables are responsible for the findings.

— *Concealed-Carry Laws.* Another example of how NVDRS can assist evaluations of firearm policies is illustrated by the sensitivity analyses the surveillance system would make possible in evaluating concealed-carry laws (CCWs). These laws ease restrictions on who can carry a concealed firearm. Such laws should have little effect on homicides inside the carrier's home but may affect the risk of homicide outside the home. If CCWs have their intended effect, a decrease in the homicide rate should, all other things equal, be accompanied by a decrease in the proportion of all homicides that occur outside the victim's home. Information available today (from the death certificate) about the location of homicides specifies only whether a homicide occurred inside or outside a "home," but not whether the incident occurred at the victim's own home. The NVDRS specifies whether the incident occurred at the home of the victim or the suspect. Using NVDRS data, therefore, it will be possible to assess whether homicides outside the home of the *suspect* are disproportionately influenced by passage of concealed-carry laws. Using this better specification of "home"

---

35. Webster and Starnes (2000).

increases the power the evaluator has to detect an effect (if there is one) and allows an assessment of whether an observed drop in homicide rates associated with the passage of a CCW law is consistent with the purported mechanism through which CCWs are thought to benefit the public.

Conclusion

A coalition of medical societies, public health organizations, suicide prevention groups, and child welfare organizations was formed in 2000 to advocate that a reporting system based on the NVISS model be adopted nationally. Congress responded by appropriating $1.5 million for the CDC to begin implementing a National Violent Death Reporting System in fiscal year 2002. The CDC is committed to the system and assigned responsibility for its implementation to the agency's National Center for Injury Prevention and Control (NCIPC) with the assistance of the National Center for Health Statistics and in partnership with other federal criminal justice and mental health agencies. Figure 10-1 is a schematic design by NCIPC to indicate how the system will operate. The agency plans to enter into cooperative agreements with state public health departments to conduct the system, with the CDC providing the software, training, and funding for the system, and the state agencies (or their subcontractors) hiring the abstractors to conduct the data collection. When fully implemented in all fifty states, it is estimated that the system will cost up to $20 million a year.

In the United States, dedicated surveillance systems exist for communicable and noncommunicable medical illnesses and for motor vehicle fatalities, but not for violent deaths, even though violent deaths are the second leading cause of death among children and account for more than 45,000 fatalities annually. This omission has led to calls for the creation of a National Violent Death Reporting System (NVDRS) modeled on the reporting system for motor-vehicle-related deaths. The new system will link data already collected, but not always readily available, from medical examiners, police, death certificates, and crime laboratories.

The reporting system will provide many benefits, including a capacity to identify and quantify rare events in a way that allows focused interventions and evaluations. At an annual cost of $20 million, even interventions that are narrowly targeted may save enough lives to justify implementing the system. If a life is worth some $2.5–5 million, saving more than eight lives annually (a reduction in violent deaths of 0.02 percent) would make the system cost effective.

Figure 10-1. *Flow Chart of Information for the Proposed National Violent Death Reporting System*

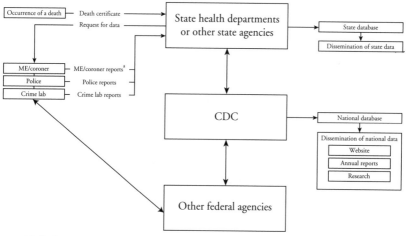

a. Medical examiner (ME).

The reporting system will never provide all the information that could prove helpful in devising and evaluating violence prevention policies. For example, a system that can accurately track nonfatal injuries would also enhance our capacity to understand the impact of policies. The interpretability of the data collected by NVDRS would also be improved by the systematic collection of population-based information about people who do not die violent deaths. For example, having information about firearm storage practices among households with children would provide information necessary to calculate the unintentional firearm death rate among children in households where guns are stored unlocked. Special studies will continue to be needed to deepen our understanding of violence and to more fully characterize the implementation and effects of policies.

Calls to develop a surveillance system for firearm injury—and violent injury more generally—have been heard for more than a decade. The recent drive to create NVDRS has been the work of large numbers of people and institutions—foundations, the federal government, state health departments, academic institutions, medical associations, and so on. The NVDRS represents the most well-developed and realistic opportunity for such a system that the United States has ever had. Progress against social problems, as Daniel Patrick Moynihan has noted, can only begin once it becomes possible to measure them.[36] By providing

36. Cook and Ludwig (2000).

more comprehensive, uniform, and accurate data about violent death, NVDRS will help move us toward reducing the problem of lethal violence in America.

COMMENT BY
Alfred Blumstein

The chapter by Deborah Azrael, Catherine Barber, David Hemenway, and Matthew Miller makes a strong argument for the value and even the necessity for the nation to institute efforts to establish a surveillance system on violent deaths. The National Violent Death Reporting System (NVDRS) would provide a rich variety of information that could enhance understanding of the factors that contribute to violent deaths in the United States. The authors make a strong case for the necessity of such a system and provide the initial features of the system. Indeed, the initial work they have already undertaken represents the pilot project that should be analyzed and be a basis for scaling up to a national system.

As always, there are several issues that still need to be addressed as we move toward the national surveillance system they propose. They build their case on the traffic fatality system already in place, which has contributed significantly to the reduction in traffic fatalities. It would certainly be desirable to see similar contributions in the violent-death reporting system. However, factors that could contribute to a traffic fatality are far more limited than those that contribute to violent deaths, whether they are classified as homicides or suicides. The violent deaths cover many interpersonal interactions and circumstances that are of a higher dimensionality than what has to be considered in traffic fatalities. This additional complexity will call for a much more elaborate data structure—or it might make it much simpler because there is no way any surveillance system can address all the complexity needed.

This introduces the concern over the data elements that should be included in the initial implementation of the system. One could easily swamp any reporting system by asking for so much that cooperation becomes problematic. This indeed happened with the National Incident-Based Reporting System (NIBRS), which was designed as an incident-level reporting system for police reporting of criminal events. The hope was that this would replace the Uniform Crime Reports (UCR), which is a compilation by the FBI of tabulations provided by individual police agencies of the monthly counts of incidents of crimes reported to the police and of arrests by crime type and demographic group for the arrests. The hope was that the NIBRS would permit analysis of variables not included in the UCR and offer the opportunity to correlate variables associated with individual incidents.

The effort to design NIBRS was initiated jointly by the Bureau of Justice Statistics (BJS) and the FBI in 1982 with the inspired goal of facilitating incident-level analysis. This would ease the preparation of UCR counts that could be done automatically by aggregating the incident-level counts; it could also incorporate the various kinds of crimes that occur in a single incident, since the current hierarchical rule limits the count to only the most serious crime. More important, it would provide a platform for much richer understanding of crime by enabling analysis of common factors in each incident. Currently, that is done only in the Supplementary Homicide Reports (SHR), which is one of the precursors of the NVDRS, and even there in much too limited a way.

For a good number of years, there were virtually no takers of the NIBRS because the rich data structure initially proposed was sufficiently daunting to the potential users that they simply avoided it. A few years ago a major effort was made to reduce that data structure appreciably and incorporate it into software that permitted the individual department to drop a large fraction of the data elements. Even with this accommodation, in only thirteen states are NIBRS reports filed by agencies that represent more than 20 percent of the population. The total NIBRS usage comes from agencies that cover only 16 percent of the U.S. population. This is in the face of six-figure awards to the states to facilitate the collection of the NIBRS data.[37]

This experience is certainly of relevance to the design and implementation of the NVDRS. It highlights the importance of giving full consideration to how best to achieve cooperation from the reporting agencies. Some pilot testing of the concepts is crucial to identify which variables are of greatest value, which are easily recorded, and which are recorded only infrequently. Thus, since it will inherently be important to limit the size of the recording instrument, one should be able to carry out an elementary cost-benefit analysis for each variable in the instrument. The variables listed in box 10-1 represent a reasonable start, but it would be valuable to draw on the experience of the pilot project to make some of those assessments.

The implementation of the reporting system is an important challenge that requires the cooperation of multiple agencies with very different data-collection traditions: medical examiners, hospitals, and police. It is one thing to pick some trial jurisdictions that are committed to the effort and quite another to move that to a representative sample of jurisdictions. Certainly the trial effort currently under way should have identified where the complexities will arise, but these places are undoubtedly the most cooperative ones.

The foundation-supported pilot project looking only at firearm injuries that has been carried out by the Harvard Injury Control Research Center (HICRC)

37. Based on information from www.ojp.usdoj.gov/bjs/nibrsawd.htm.

is an important first step. The participating agencies in that effort should be in a good position to assess at least the cost side of the variable list included. They, as well as other operational and research users, will supply important insights into the benefits. This could give rise to a partitioning of the variable list into the essentials, the desirables, and the nice-to-haves.

Tastes of some potential users should be called on to indicate what variables they would like to have that are not currently included. My own experience with the SHR leads me to want some of its more salient shortcomings corrected. The most serious concern relates to its permitting only one "circumstance." In its collection of data on homicide incidents, the National Consortium on Violence Research (NCOVR) has dichotomized (coded as present or absent) each of the basic circumstance categories (for example, drug-related, gang-related, argument), thereby permitting a richer assessment of the circumstances surrounding the homicide. I would also like to know more about location; besides the victim's address, I would like to add the addresses of the suspect and of the incident, thereby providing richer information about the suspect and victim and how the homicide came about. Since I have earlier emphasized the necessity for trade-offs on the variables included in the data structure, I would be prepared to forego some of the details on the gun involved in the pilot project, which was oriented at firearms.

I doubt that anyone concerned with violent deaths has any doubts about the importance of moving forward with the NVDRS. It would be a major new opportunity to understand and thereby lessen the prevalence of violent deaths. But any such effort must countenance the many political forces in the United States that see any research that might potentially examine the role of firearms in violent deaths as the start of a slippery slope that might lead to increased gun control. It is not surprising, for example, that the HICRC pilot project had to be sponsored by foundations rather than the CDC, which certainly represents a strong government interest in the issue. I wish I had some great wisdom on how to overcome the political obstacles likely to be imposed. Perhaps we will have to look once again to the private sector to initiate the next stage of implementation.

COMMENT BY

David McDowall

The surveillance system that Deborah Azrael, Catherine Barber, David Hemenway, and Matthew Miller describe will greatly expand opportunities to study homicides, suicides, and fatal gun accidents. The inadequacies of available data are currently a major obstacle to research on firearm violence. Existing studies are confined to small amounts of information distilled from the separate national data systems or to local data that do not easily generalize to other areas. Much of the literature reflects a creative adaptation of research questions to fit the meager resources available to answer them. As a result, many studies of firearm policies only indirectly address the issues in which they are most interested, spawning endless, tiresome debates about their findings.

As the authors of this chapter show through a variety of interesting and well-chosen examples, the National Violent Death Reporting System (NVDRS) will give researchers new insights into presently murky topics. Although their work concentrates on firearm deaths, the NVDRS should also be valuable for research on homicides and suicides more generally. As the data accumulate, the reporting system will allow trend analysis, further increasing its utility. When it is fully operational, the system may be as large a breakthrough for the study of fatal violence as were the other surveillance efforts that the chapter describes.

Perhaps the most notable feature of the reporting system is its reliance on existing information sources. While developing the infrastructure for a new data collection program would be extremely expensive, linking records that public agencies already gather can enhance their value at very modest cost. A central insight is that the problems of current data are less because of their availability than because of their fragmentary nature. Piecing together these previously isolated indicators will open new possibilities for evaluation and basic research. The quality of the system's individual sources should improve as the personnel involved address the system's inconsistencies and omissions.

The NVDRS rests on extensive pilot studies that carefully evaluate the feasibility of its procedures. The Centers for Disease Control and Prevention supported early work, and privately funded demonstration versions are operational at eleven sites. This careful attention to testing and development increases the likelihood that the system will operate successfully on a national scale.

The system's data will unquestionably raise the quality of firearm policy research and research on fatal violence more broadly. Yet any large-scale data collection effort, even one with the many strong points of the NVDRS, will confront problems that can at least modestly limit its success.

Completeness and Consistency of the Data

The system is extremely ambitious in its goals, and not all of its data elements are now available in all (or even many) areas. When these elements do exist, they vary in quality and completeness. Erratic reporting and inconsistent quality may then reduce the ability of the system to answer the type of questions that Azrael and her coauthors use for illustration.

Some NVDRS data elements are currently not collected in most jurisdictions. These include, for example, data from firearm ownership traces. Few agencies routinely trace all guns used in fatal violence, especially weapons involved in suicides and accidents. No surveillance system can claim complete coverage, and a strength of the NVDRS is that its personnel may help to reduce the gaps. Still, missing items complicate data analyses by raising the possibility of selection bias. If areas that report information differ systematically from those that do not, one may make incorrect inferences from the available cases. Partial data are better than no data, but the answers that partial data can provide are equivocal.

Omissions owing to incomplete reporting can, in theory, be eliminated. Yet killings in which the police do not apprehend an offender will always create problems for homicide surveillance. The percentage of homicides in which investigators could not learn the relationship between the victim and offender has generally increased during the past twenty years. This in turn has led to uncertainty about trends in victim-offender relationships, especially killings by strangers.[38] By its nature, homicide places limits on the completeness of a recording system. As Azrael and coauthors point out, suicide surveillance faces similar problems in determining a victim's motivations.

Some of the most interesting details on violence mortality also depend on judgments that are not easily standardized. Studies of Supplementary Homicide Report (SHR) data on homicide circumstances, for example, find large differences in coding within and across agencies.[39] While a reporting system might reduce inconsistencies through additional training and tighter definitions, the ambiguities inherent in some decisions imply that variations will continue to exist.

Many NVDRS data elements will come from organizations not highly interested in reporting and without strong incentives for accuracy. Police agencies often do not completely fill out SHR forms (or other crime reports), and the information that they provide is sometimes of questionable validity.[40] The NVDRS's multiple data sources will help project personnel resolve inconsistencies and track down missing items. Still, the quality of the data will depend on the diligence of sometimes unenthusiastic external agencies.

Personnel

The preceding issues emphasize the importance of thoroughly trained and highly motivated personnel. Difficult coding decisions and incomplete data elements

---

38. Riedel (1998).
39. Loftin (1986); Maxfield (1989).
40. Maltz (1999).

will require careful attention and good judgment from the individual recorders. In addition, data sources will inevitably conflict with one another about some cases, and the recorders must understand the system and its purposes well enough to resolve disagreements.

The NVDRS pilot sites depend on academic researchers to staff the projects. This ensures near-optimal conditions for gathering data, and it greatly reduces the problems posed by training and supervision. In contrast, police crime reporting personnel (who compile SHR and other major data series) often receive little training and are under heavy time pressures.[41] The operational version of the NVDRS will rely on state health departments to hire abstractors. Whether the departments can afford well-trained abstractors, or instead must follow the model of police reporting agencies, will greatly influence the value of the data that the system produces.

Conclusions

Any system for recording violent deaths has limitations. Yet this does not question the wisdom of increased surveillance efforts generally or of the NVDRS in particular. Current studies of fatal violence are forced to draw large conclusions from very limited information. The weaknesses of the data encourage doubts even about basic issues, and much research amounts to arguments over how best to interpret a few shaky numbers.

Enhanced surveillance systems can generate new possibilities for studying violence and provide the empirical basis necessary to support or refute factual claims. The NVDRS is an exceptionally well thought-out program, and it promises to be the most complete and accurate source of violence data available. The system would have been invaluable to the authors of many of the chapters in this volume. When the system is expanded to cover the entire nation, it should be an unparalleled resource for gun policy research.

References

Anderson Marc, Joanne Kaufman, Thomas R. Simon, and others. 2001. "School-Associated Violent Deaths in the United States, 1994–1999." *Journal of the American Medical Association* 286 (21): 2695–02.
Azrael, Deborah, Catherine Barber, and James Mercy. 2001. "Linking Data to Save Lives: Recent Progress in Establishing a National Violent Death Reporting System." *Harvard Health Policy Review* 2 (2): 38–42.

41. See, for example, Braga, Piehl, and Kennedy (1999); Brownstein (1996).

Barber, Catherine, David Hemenway, Stephen Hargarten, Arthur Kellermann, Deborah Azrael, and Susan Wilt. 2000. "A 'Call to Arms' for a National Reporting System on Firearm Injuries." *American Journal of Public Health* 90 (8): 1191–93.

Barber, Catherine, David Hemenway, Jenny Hochstadt, and Deborah Azrael. 2002. "Underestimates of Unintentional Firearm Fatalities: Comparing Supplementary Homicide Reports with Vital Statistics." *Injury Prevention* 8 (3): 252–56.

Birckmayer, Johanna, and David Hemenway. 1999. "Minimum-Age Drinking Laws and Youth Suicide, 1970–90." *American Journal of Public Health* 89 (9): 1365–68.

Bonnie, Richard J., Carolyn E. Fulco, and Catharyn T. Liverman, eds. 1999. *Reducing the Burden of Injury: Advancing Prevention and Treatment.* National Academy Press.

Braga, Anthony A., Anne M. Piehl, and David M. Kennedy. 1999. "Youth Homicide in Boston: An Assessment of Supplementary Homicide Report Data." *Homicide Studies* 3 (4): 277–99.

Brownstein, Henry H. 1996. *The Rise and Fall of a Violent Crime Wave: Crack Cocaine and the Social Construction of a Crime Problem.* Criminal Justice Press.

Bureau of Justice Statistics. 1994. "Bureau of Justice Statistics Bulletin: Technical Background on the Redesigned National Crime Victimization Survey." NCJ-151172. U.S. Department of Justice (October).

Centers for Disease Control and Prevention (CDC). 1998. WONDER Mortality Data (*wonder.cdc.gov/mortsql.shtml* [December 2001]).

———. 1999. "Achievements in Public Health, 1900–1999: Changes in the Public Health System." *Morbidity and Mortality Weekly Report* 48: 1141–47.

———. 2001a. "BRFSS in Action: A State-by-State Listing of How Data Are Used."

———. 2001b. "Surveillance for Homicide among Intimate Partners—United States, 1981–1998." *Morbidity and Mortality Weekly Report* 50 (SS-3): 1–15.

———. 2001c. "Tracking Major Health Risks Among Americans: The Behavioral Risk Factor Surveillance System."

———. 2001d. "Updated Guidelines for Evaluating Public Health Surveillance Systems: Recommendations from the Guidelines Working Group." 50 (RR-13): 1–35.

———. 2001e. "Web-Based Injury Statistics Querying and Reporting System."

Cook, Philip J., and Jens Ludwig. 2000. *Gun Violence: The Real Costs.* Oxford University Press.

Cook, Philip J., and George Tauchen. 1984. "The Effect of Minimum Drinking Age Legislation on Youthful Auto Fatalities." *Journal of Legal Studies* 13 (1): 169–90.

Cummings, Peter, David C. Grossman, Frederick P. Rivara, and Thomas D. Koepsell. 1997. "State Gun Safe Storage Laws and Child Mortality Due to Firearms." *Journal of the American Medical Association* 278 (13): 1084–86.

Federal Bureau of Investigation (FBI). 1984. *Uniform Crime Reporting Handbook.* Washington.

———. 1996. *Uniform Crime Reporting: National Incident-Based Reporting System, Volume 1.* Washington.

Garber, Steven, and John D. Graham. 1990. "The Effects of the New 65 Mile-per-Hour Speed Limit on Rural Highway Fatalities: A State-by-State Analysis." *Accident Analysis and Prevention* 22 (2): 137–49.

Hingson, Ralph W., Norman Scotch, Tom Mangione, and others. 1983. "Impact of Legislation Raising the Legal Drinking Age in Massachusetts from 18 to 20." *American Journal of Public Health* 73 (2): 163–70.

Hingson, Ralph W., Timothy Heeren, and Michael Winter. 1994. "Lower Legal Blood Alcohol Limits for Young Drivers." *Public Health Reports* 109 (6): 738–44.

Kennedy, David M., Anthony A. Braga, Anne M. Piehl, and Elin J. Waring. 2001. "Reducing Gun Violence: The Boston Gun Project's Operation Ceasefire." NCJ-188741. U.S. Department of Justice, National Institute of Justice (September).

Langford, Linda, Nancy E. Isaac, and Stacey Kabat. 1998. "Homicides Related to Intimate Partner Violence in Massachusetts." *Homicide Studies* 2 (4): 353–77.

———. 1999. "Homicides Related to Intimate Partner Violence in Massachusetts, 1991–1995." Boston: Peace at Home.

Langmuir, Alexander D. 1963. "The Surveillance of Communicable Diseases of National Importance." *New England Journal of Medicine* 268: 182–92.

Loftin, Colin. 1986. "The Validity of Robbery Murder Classifications in Baltimore." *Violence and Victims* 1 (3): 259–71.

Maguire Kathleen, and Ann L. Pastore, eds. 2001. *Sourcebook of Criminal Justice Statistics.* (*www.albany.edu/sourcebook/* [April 2002]).

Maltz, Michael. 1999. *Bridging Gaps in Police Crime Data.* U.S. Department of Justice.

Maxfield, Michael G. 1989. "Circumstances in Supplementary Homicide Reports: Variety and Validity." *Criminology* 27 (4): 671–95.

McSwain, Norman E. Jr., and Anita Belles. 1990. "Motorcycle Helmets–Medical Costs and the Law." *Journal of Trauma* 30 (10): 1189–97.

Miller, Matthew, Deborah Azrael, and David Hemenway. 2002. "Firearm Availability and Unintentional Firearm Deaths, Suicide and Homicide Among 5–14 Year Olds." *Journal of Trauma* 52 (2): 267–75.

National Highway Traffic Safety Administration (NHTSA). 2001. "Traffic Safety Facts 2000: Alcohol." DOT HS 809 323. U.S. Department of Transportation.

Public Health Foundation. 2001. "Return on Investment of Nationwide Health Tracking." Washington. (*health-track.org/reports/phf0809/* [September 2001])

Riedel, Marc. 1998. "Counting Stranger Homicides: A Case Study of Statistical Prestidigitation." *Homicide Studies* 2 (2): 206–19.

Rennison, Callie M., and Sarah Welchans. 2000. "Bureau of Justice Statistics Special Report: Intimate Partner Violence." NCJ 178247. U.S. Department of Justice, Bureau of Justice Statistics (May).

Rice, Dorothy, Ellen Mackenzie, and others. 1989. "Cost of Injury in the United States: A Report to Congress." Institute for Health and Aging, University of California and the Johns Hopkins University Injury Prevention Center.

Samuelson, Paul A., and William D. Nordhaus. 2000. *Economics.* 17th ed. Mc-Graw-Hill.

Smith Robert A., Ralph W. Hingson, Suzette Morelock, and others. 1984. "Legislation Raising the Legal Drinking Age in Massachusetts from 18 to 20: Effect on 16 and 17 Year-Olds." *Journal of Studies on Alcohol* 45 (6): 534–39.

Teret, Stephen P. 1996. "The Firearm Injury Reporting System Revisited." *Journal of the American Medical Association* 275 (1): 70.

Teret, Stephen P., Garen J. Wintemute, and Peter L. Beilenson. 1992. "The Firearm Fatality Reporting System: A Proposal." *Journal of the American Medical Association* 267 (22): 3073–74.

U.S. Department of Health and Human Services (HHS). 2000. "HHS Initiatives to Reduce Foodborne Illness." HHS Fact Sheet (March).

————. 2001. *National Strategy for Suicide Prevention: Goals and Objectives for Action.* Rockville, Md.

Walsh, William F. 2001. "Compstat: An Analysis of an Emerging Police Managerial Paradigm." *Policing* 24 (3): 347–62.

Webster, Daniel W., and Marc Starnes. 2000. "Reexamining the Association between Child Access Prevention Gun Laws and Unintentional Shooting Deaths of Children." *Pediatrics* 106 (6): 1466–69.

Williams, Allan F., Paul L. Zador, Sandra S. Harris, and Ronald S. Karpf. 1983. "The Effect of Raising the Legal Minimum Drinking Age on Involvement in Fatal Crashes." *Journal of Legal Studies* 12 (1): 169–80.

PART V

The Policy Process

FRANKLIN E. ZIMRING

11 | *Continuity and Change in the American Gun Debate*

My license to survey the gun control debate is a tribute not to wisdom but to accumulated seniority: I have been associated with the study of firearms and violence for more than three decades, and the hope was that experience of that length might generate perspectives useful in a debate not known for its awareness of history or sense of proportion. What has changed over thirty-five years in debates about firearms and violence? What is constant? Are there long-range trends so far or just cyclical fluctuation? Is the great American gun policy debate heading toward any clear destination or dancing in circles?

The Gun Debate in the 1960s

Before the late 1960s, guns and gun control had not been a major issue at any level of American government for a generation. State and local control efforts in the urban northeast were a product of the early decades of the twentieth century, most famously with New York's Sullivan law in 1911. Serious federal control proposals first appear in the early years of the Roosevelt administration and produce two federal laws within five years, a 1934 act that all but banned automatic weapons and sawed-off shotguns, and 1938 legislation that created a thin layer of regulation over firearm dealers and the sale of more popular firearms as well as prohibitions against minors, felons, and other disqualified classes of citizens acquiring weapons.[1] What happened after 1938 in the United States on the legal regulation of firearms was practically nothing. World War II effectively ended federal anticrime concerns until 1965. Rates of criminal homicide, after peaking in 1933, fell during the Great Depression and war years and drifted downward thereafter until the early 1960s. Two New England senators, John F. Kennedy in the 1950s and Thomas Dodd in the 1960s held hearings on the dangers of cheap foreign guns, but the threats that inspired this warning were as much to the domestic firearm industry as to the public health.

The mid-1960s witnessed a series of events that created concern about guns, beginning with the assassination of President John F. Kennedy and the increases in urban violent crime reported from 1964 onward. Blue ribbon commissions were appointed first on crime and then on riots and on violence. Gun legislation proposals were taken much more seriously after 1965, and crime was, by 1967, an issue that attracted sustained national attention. Then came the watershed year of 1968. Whatever the slow progress toward federal firearm legislation from earlier events, a new dynamic emerged from the Martin Luther King Jr. and Robert Kennedy assassinations, the urban riots, and public anxiety about violent crime. The Congress that had passed no federal firearm legislation in thirty years passed two major acts in one year and created the new federal enforcement presence that the Bureau of Alcohol, Tobacco and Firearms was to become. The year 1968 also witnessed the birth of the symbolic politics of gun control, and the basic regulatory framework upon which the incremental politics of gun control would play out for the remainder of the twentieth century.

My concern is more with the nature of the debate about guns that was generated in the late 1960s than with the details of the 1968 act.[2] The firearm control issue had taken the nation and Congress by surprise. No agency of government had the responsibility for information about guns other than the Commerce Department's census of manufacturers. There were no academic experts on firearms and violence in criminology in the United States or anywhere else in research universities. Before mid-1968, there were no published studies on the relationship between gun use and the death rate from assault. No credible estimate of the number and kind of firearms in the United States had been published. No taxonomy of firearm control laws had been attempted. No studies of the impact of various regulations of gun ownership and use had been attempted.

The politics of gun control was predictable and symbolic. Big city liberals were procontrol and rural and small town conservatives were anticontrol—the specific

1. Zimring (1975, part I).
2. See Zimring (1975) for the legislative details.

nature of the control proposal did not matter much to the support and opposition elements. The only special firearm interest in Washington was the National Rifle Association.

Violent death was the central concern of those who worried about guns and supported gun control, but there was no clear hierarchy of problems or choice of control tactics. In the first installment of the Gun Control Act of 1968, long guns and handguns were regulated equally, while in the second installment the handgun was the subject of special regulatory attention. As the focus shifted from political assassination to crime, and as data on firearms and violence were published, a priority concern with handguns settled in for a long run as the most serious of American's gun problems.

Constant Elements

There are five consistent elements of the gun debate over the generation since 1970 that I wish to nominate as significant influences on how policy has been selected: symbolic dominance, generality of preferences, the free lunch syndrome, the gender gulch, and the centrality of handguns as the subject and object of the controversy.

The first three constant elements are interrelated and, jointly, quite influential on how gun policy is debated in the United States. I will address them together. Although the specific content of proposals to regulate firearms varies over time and cross sectionally, most citizens have a set of general attitudes about firearms and laws to regulate them that are stable over time. I believe the debate about gun policy is one in which these general sentiments are dominant in predicting citizens' preferences on certain issues and predicting the reasons citizens give for support or opposition to policies. This is the condition I call *symbolic dominance*.

A substantial majority of the public holds pretty strong sentiments for or against gun control as a whole. Because the symbolic aspects dominate orientation toward specific policy proposals, the details of a program have little to do with the level of support or opposition to it. If most opponents of gun control are dominated by general attitudes, the type of control and the type of gun will not explain or predict much opposition. Similarly, if most citizens who favor controls are motivated from a general sentiment, they will be disposed toward support of a wide variety of approaches.

One evidence of this is that a wide variety of proposals have similar levels of support and opposition, what Tom Smith called "the 75 percent solution."[3] This means that the same core constituencies of pros and antis will debate waiting

3. Smith (1980).

periods for handgun sales, the requirement of licensing for sales at gun shows, and punitive damages against gun manufacturers and distributors. Further, because most of the values to be vindicated are symbolic, the intensity of support for large and small proposals will be nearly equal. Small changes in policy can be urged and opposed with the same vigor as large changes. The heavy emphasis in 1999 and 2000 by both procontrol and anticontrol groups on what is called the gun show loophole in the Gun Control Act of 1968 is a clear illustration that intensity of commitment is not closely linked to operational importance in debates about gun control.

The tendency for citizens to be for or against almost any gun control proposals has some limits. More substantial interventions that carry larger cost and restrict gun owners generate much lower levels of public support. The primary example in the 1980s and 1990s was proposals to "ban" handguns. And measures without any visible cost to most citizens—such as increased prison sentences for firearm criminals—can generate greater than 75 percent support. That there is some discrimination between control proposals is good news for the development of a more sophisticated public response to gun control. But if only the perceived costs of control proposals influence public support, then support will cluster around proposals without regard to the potential benefits of the intervention.

This leads to a phenomenon of *generality of preferences.* People who favor "gun control" are positively disposed toward a general idea and will follow that general preference to support many different proposals. It is the major premise—support in general—rather than the particular program that is the center of citizen concern. And anticontrol partisans seem willing to oppose any type of control, a general tendency that procontrol forces like to exploit by proposing bans on ammunition that is labeled "cop killer bullets," which nonetheless produces opposition from many gun owner groups, even at the price of great political embarrassment.

The Free Lunch Syndrome. Since many of the central values that are in play are symbolic, and since almost any specific proposal can carry the symbolic colors of firearm control in congressional debate, there is a tendency for procontrol forces to pick on small and fairly uncontroversial control proposals but to invest these programs with the suggestion that their passage will have a large impact on rates of lethal violence. Pass a ban on cop killer bullets or a five-day waiting period on handgun sales, and the rhetorical suggestion is that serious progress will be made on the totality of firearm violence.

This tendency to push small policy increments as if they were major programs is what I call the *free lunch syndrome,* a tendency to couple small operational changes with the full weight of firearm control symbolism. Free lunch rhetoric is good politics without question, but it removes realistic analysis of the impacts of specific control strategies from public discussion. There is nothing wrong with an incremental politics of gun control, but expecting large benefits from small investments is unreasonable.

The Gender Gulch. "Forty-four percent of motorcycle owners are women. Forty-eight percent of truck owners are women. We even know a few who can wipe that stupid smirk off your face!"[4]

The generation after 1965 witnessed dramatic changes in the social, cultural, and economic status of women in the United States. In the wake of these shifts, activities and tastes formerly associated with men have become more evenly distributed by gender. That is the background to the surprising statistical claims of a recent ad about truck and motorcycle ownership in the preceding paragraph.

All the more remarkable, then, that the very great gender differences in gun ownership continue to be the major dividing line between United States adults; gender is more important for predicting handgun ownership than region, politics, income, and usually than all those elements put together. When ownership rates by gender were first publicly disclosed in the mid-1960s, about 7 percent of U.S. gun owners were identified as women in the crude manufacturers mail survey research we reviewed at the National Violence Commission. A precise ownership estimate could not be made from these data, but the female ownership was obviously low. Thirty years later, Tom Smith and Robert J. Smith report an analysis of fifteen years of National Opinion Research Center General Social Survey with no evidence of any expansion in female ownership of handguns or firearms generally during the period 1980–94 while so much else was changing in the United States.[5]

Although just under half of all males own a firearm, the "any gun" ownership rate for females is 1 in 8, and four times as many men as women report handgun ownership.[6] The authors conclude, "The ownership of firearms among women is not increasing, the gender gap is not closing, and the level of ownership is much lower than commonly stated, with about 11 percent to 12 percent of women owning a gun and 4.5 to 8 percent owning a handgun."[7]

Speculation that female ownership and attitudes might change has been recurrent since 1970. Milestones in the anticipated increase in female demand include an advertising campaign for self-defense handgun ownership that was

4. Oxygen advertisement, *New Yorker,* October 16, 2000, p. 87.
5. Smith and Smith (1995).
6. Smith and Smith (1995, table 3, p. 147).
7. Smith and Smith (1995, p. 145).

targeted on women (for the notorious "Lady Smith") in the 1980s by Smith and Wesson. Books and articles about gun women and media coverage of women seeking self-defense handgun training have become a staple of National Rifle Association public relations and local television slow-news-week feature stories. But the ownership gap persists even as the number of female-headed households has sharply expanded, multiplying the instances in which a woman's ownership decision determines the presence or absence of a gun in the house.

The huge gap in ownership is accompanied by two more subtle gender differences. Women are more likely to support legal restrictions on firearms, and when men and women in the same household disagree about the wisdom of having a handgun, it is the woman who is more often antigun.

The gender differences in self-defense handgun ownership are important in the struggle for the moral high ground in the self-defense debate. If women, after all the traditional weaker sex, were aggressive in wanting and using handguns, the political pressure to allow and approve such usage would be substantial. But the refusal of most women to acknowledge the need for self-defense handguns undercuts male claims that the weapons are necessary. In this connection, Smith and Smith show very low rates of handgun ownership among single women (1.4 percent for the never married, 6.4 percent for the not currently married). In these head-of-household settings, the gender gap is greater than the overall 4-to-1 figure. Female need is, in such circumstances, a story that continues to be told mainly by male gun owners.

The Handgun Focus

One further consistent strain in the gun policy debate of the last generation is the focus on handguns and special handgun regulation as the greatest priority in new policy. With the exception of short periods when semiautomatic firearms that could be either handguns or long guns attracted attention (the "assault weapon" issue), the handgun has held center stage in the American gun control debate for thirty years.

The case for special regulation of handguns is not a matter of firepower—shotguns and rifles often have more destructive force, and long guns are also easier to use accurately from medium and long range. But the handgun, easy to conceal and transport, is nine times as likely as a long gun to be used in a homicide and even more dominant than that in robbery with firearms. As the chief concern about firearm violence shifted from assassination to violent crime, the handgun became the focus of procontrol efforts by the early 1970s. While gun owning organizations prefer not to distinguish between types of firearms, their general opposition to all control proposals is most often manifest in opposition to proposed handgun regulation. And the focus of procontrol advocates on handguns has become a defining element of special interests organized to support firearm regulation. It is neither an accident nor a trivial detail that the major gun control lobby in the United States was named "Handgun Control."

Special attention to handguns is a common characteristic of legal systems throughout the developed world. Even nations with high rates of long gun usage, such as Switzerland and Israel, have low ownership and usually special restrictions on handguns. So the consistent emphasis on handguns is by no means an American invention. Nor is the debate about the special status of handguns an American exclusive. The tendency for anticontrol groups in all nations is to urge opposition to handgun controls because they threaten long guns as well. But this effort to make common cause of all gun owners has been more successful in the United States than elsewhere.

What Changed?

There are four important changes in the character of public debate about government and firearms. What used to be an issue that was only cyclically important has become a priority concern on a continuing basis. What used to be an undocumented dispute with little data and no specialist experts has become a debate between special interests that are well informed but often heavily biased by anti- or procontrol orientations. What used to be a debate in which the Second Amendment to the U.S. Constitution had no importance is now a debate in which the Second Amendment's implications are ambiguous. What used to be a debate about firearms and crime has been reframed, in expert and political areas, as a concern with firearm and violence.

From Episodic to Consistent Public Priority

In the first two decades after the Gun Control Act of 1968, public and political concern with the firearm control was episodic. At the federal level, there was no further strong interest in firearm control until about 1975, and after no laws passed in the mid-1970s, it was not until after the shooting of President Ronald Reagan in 1981 that serious attention was paid to a debate about further federal laws. Things were even quieter at the state and local level in most places. Concern with crime was a constant, but the firearm issue was cyclical.

The long gaps between high-visibility debates on guns was not a product of fickle public attitudes about the wisdom of gun control. Public support of most mainstream gun regulation was consistent over time, but the gun issue was not very important to most citizens most of the time. It was the salience of gun control rather than attitudes about appropriate government action that varied over time.

If the late 1990s are a sign of the new order, long gaps between high-visibility debates about guns will soon be regarded as a historical curiosity. In the late 1960s, the passage of a gun law like the Gun Control Act of 1968 was a signal for Congress to ignore the field for a decade or so. In the aftermath of the Brady bill in 1993, however, there has not been any sustained period of time off from high-visibility gun policy debates. In 1998, 1999, and 2000, gun policy disputes at the federal level were the single most important crime policy issue. At the state level, legislative proposals and legislation, running the gamut from easing restrictions on permits to carry concealed weapons to assault weapon and Saturday Night Special legislation make gun proposals an annual event in big states. At the city level tactics from municipal gun regulations to lawsuits against gun producers framed on the tobacco company litigation are a hardy perennial. The gun question does not take time off from being a salient concern in the media, the political process, and public consciousness.

This chapter cannot fully explore the reasons for this shift from cyclical to consistent public priority. In part, the vociferous energies of single-issue special interests on both sides of the gun debate fan the flames. In part, the usefulness to both political parties of guns as a wedge issue for different segments of the electorate keeps the pot boiling. Partisan tactics guarantee that gun politics will be spread among all levels of government. The National Rifle Association finds solace in state governments, particularly when rural and town representation is strong. Big cities are the home team for almost all forms of handgun restrictions. This has tended to make the gun issue into a levels-of-government version of a three-ring circus throughout the past decade. Consistent public and media attention, parallel markets for control and anticontrol new ideas in states and cities, and a longer public attention span for gun issues are markers of a brand new era in the politics of gun control in the United States.

But how long will this era of intense interest continue? Two further elements of the 1990s contributed to the consistent priority of gun control at the federal level. One was the high level of public concern about life-threatening violence. At the beginning of the decade, public worries were linked to high rates of criminal homicide. By the end of the decade, the worry was school shootings.

A second element that maintained the public focus on gun control after 1992 was a two-term president who pushed firearm control proposals throughout his eight years in office. How much presidential leadership and public concern about particular violence problems has contributed to the public interest in gun control may soon be known. The current president of the United States has no strong interest in firearm control, and rates of lethal violence are at the lowest levels in thirty years. If consistent public interest continues, it will indicate that the issue of gun control has "legs" even when the political environment is unfavorable. In that sense, the George W. Bush presidency can be seen as a natural experiment.

Information: From Ignorance to Special Pleading

The growth of information about firearms and their effects has been impressive but uneven during the past three decades. Any growth rate from a zero base will seem high, and guns are no exception. Official data on firearm manufacture, gun use in crime and violence, and patterns of regulation of firearms in the United States is far superior to the statistical base of thirty years ago. The number of university-based researchers who specialize more than half time in firearms probably exceeds fifty in the United States. There were none as recently as 1972.

The available data on firearms, violence, and firearms control are both abundant and spotty. Death statistics and some crime statistics are good. Production and import data are reliable, but the total stock of usable guns cannot be reliably estimated. The federal Bureau of Alcohol, Tobacco, and Firearms does a vast number of traces to first retail purchase of guns but little research on the flow of guns from that point on. Nobody knows the average use-life of a handgun in the United States.

The information available on the effects of gun control policies on firearms deaths and injury are spotty, in part because the legal changes to study in recent years have been of the modest "free lunch" variety.

Many of the full-time researchers on the topic are organized into sectarian groups. Public health professionals put heavy emphasis on the impact of gun use in raising the death rate from assault and robbery and support most control efforts. Sociologists are split into "contra" factions (for example, James Wright, Gary Kleck) and a larger number of procontrol partisans. In this contentious atmosphere, the margins for disagreement are not slight: Are guns used in 100,000 self-defense episodes each year or twenty times that many?[8] Do safe storage laws have little impact on violence or cost the citizens of the fifteen states that passed them 250,000 extra violent crimes in five years?[9]

The known facts should produce a clean split in factional morale. The evidence that guns increase the death from violence is firm—this is the strong suit of the procontrol forces. The evidence that modest changes in legal regulation can make a dent in the gun violence toll is weak. This is the strong suit of the anticontrol partisans and skeptics.

8. Cook, Ludwig, and Hemenway (1997); Kleck and Gertz (1995).
9. Lott and Whitley (2000).

The Second Amendment: From Irrelevance to Ambiguity

The Second Amendment's language describing a "right of the people to bear arms" has always played an important symbolic role in the rhetoric of opposition to gun controls, but the Second Amendment has been considered a dead letter as a potential obstacle to state and federal gun control laws. *United States* v. *Miller,* decided in 1939, was neither a closely reasoned nor prominently publicized case, but it was widely considered a conclusive rejection of an individual right to bear arms as a limit on the power of any level of government to regulate guns.[10] Outside of gun owner groups, the federal constitution's Second Amendment was not regarded as an important part of American legal culture or history.

In recent years, academic interest in a personal right to bear arms has been growing from a variety of different points of origin. There are, of course, the gun interests who have supported and publicized historical arguments about an expansive reading of the Second Amendment. There has also been at least one study of the English origins of the Second Amendment that is consistent with individual claims against governmental regulation and legal theory of personal right based on personal rights to oppose tyranny.[11] What this work has done so far is put the possibility of a personal right to bear arms in play in academic settings where it had received neither attention nor mention previously in constitutional scholarship. The increased salience of the issue has in turn produced antipersonal right historical scholarship and legal argument.[12]

One Fifth Circuit panel has expressly endorsed a "personal right" theory of the Second Amendment but nonetheless rejected a criminal defendant's attempt to challenge an indictment under one section of the federal Gun Control Act.[13] In an era when judicial activism from the right has already significantly reshaped constitutional law relating to federal-state relations, the judicial recognition of a personal right in the Second Amendment is by no means far-fetched.

But the effect any personal right to bear arms would have on restricting regulation of guns is difficult to predict. The key questions are, first, whether particular weapons (for example, handguns, automatic firearms, and so on) would be covered and, second, what sort of balance between personal and governmental interests would animate decisions. The discussion of such questions has not been substantial to date, and because the entire constitutional calculus would have to be created without any background in prior case reasoning, the

10. *United States* v. *Miller,* 307 U.S. 174 (1939).
11. Malcolm (1994); Levinson (1989).
12. Bogus (1998).
13. *U.S.* v. *Emerson* 270 F. 3d 203 (2001).

impact of a personal legal right on the field of choice for gun regulation is still a wide open question.

From Crime to Violence

One further shift in American sentiment occurred in the 1990s as a result of several concurrent developments. While the public anxieties most closely associated with the gun debate had traditionally been thought of as about crime and criminals, the problem of lethal violence emerged by the turn of the century as discrete from general concerns about crime and its control.

The last eight years of the 1990s witnessed the broadest and most sustained drop in crime rates that America had experienced in half a century. But just as the criminal stranger was seen as a smaller threat, the boy next door became a potential menace: a cluster of school shootings in the late 1990s culminated in the killing of twelve students and a teacher by two high school students in Littleton, Colorado. The Columbine High School shootings of 1999 provoked a shift in focus for American anxieties. The "Trench Coat Mafia" of Littleton differed from Willie Horton not in degree but in kind. No longer was the threat associated with a distinct criminal class, nor could it be blamed on avarice. Columbine High was an inside job, not the work of aliens.

The justifying ideology of free availability of firearms in the United States is that lethal violence is the threat of a criminal class, a discrete and insular minority. When the children of good people are the enemy we fear, it is more than difficult to pretend that the millions of guns tolerated as home furnishings are not connected to the guns that kill schoolgirls in Jonesboro and Paducah and Littleton. The boundaries between legitimate and illegitimate arms were blurred in the minds of many when good people's guns went to school. And the violent outbursts of adolescent assassins seemed closer to suicide than to mercenary crime, far less comprehensible in terms of rational choice or pecuniary motivation than the criminal classes of previous public imagination. As the great cartoon character Pogo had prophesied a generation before, "We have met the enemy and he is us." This clear focus on violence without a differentiating criminal identity is one of the primary causes of sustained attention to guns and gun control in the United States at the turn of a new century.

Conclusion

It turns out to be much easier to predict the volume of debate about changes in gun policy than the magnitude or direction of policy changes in the United States in the next decade. High levels of activity at the federal, state, and municipal government are a safe bet. But whether the sum of the changes will amount to a shift in substantive direction for gun policy, particularly handgun policy, is not at all clear. The symbolic politics of guns will play a prominent role in politics at all levels of government.

One reason the shape and net impact of new gun policies are difficult to predict is that there are no clear priorities among the new control activists. Citizens are still for or against gun control as a general sentiment, never mind the details. And most of the new academic experts on guns have done little to push the gun control debate toward specifics and priorities.

Yet there are a huge number of different types of gun regulations being debated in the contentious American present. There are gun show permit requirements, "gun-free school zones," sharp restrictions on handgun ownership, mandatory minimum penalties for firearm crimes, tort suits against handgun manufacturers, buy-back schemes, and waiting periods. It would be an amazing coincidence if all these approaches were equally promising or futile. Just because gun use elevates the death rate from assaults does not mean that any law that concerns guns will save lives.

Indeed, when the symbolic politics of the issue produce chestnuts like the gun-free school law, the academic expert with sympathy for government efforts to control firearm violence should be the first to note the unlikely prospect that putting signs up by schoolyards will save the lives of children.

For similar reasons, the sweeping generalities of opponents of gun regulations are symptoms of analytic immaturity. The only reason gun regulations as a class could be excluded as a harm reduction technique would be if gun use did not influence the harms produced by violent assaults. Does any serious researcher believe this?

What will improve the gun debate at the top end of the policy community is careful attention to the differences between types and intensities of firearm regulation. If experts start avoiding the silly overgeneralizations that come from assuming that all gun regulations were created equal, there is some hope that a more specific and pragmatic approach to reducing the harms of gun violence might trickle down the intellectual food chain to the powerful and powerfully confused citizenry who will shape gun policy in the fast-approaching future.

References

Bogus, Carl T. 1998. "The Hidden History of the Second Amendment." *University of California Davis Law Review* 31: 309–408.

Cook, Philip, Ludwig, Jens, and Hemenway, David. 1997. "The Gun Debate's New Mythical Number: How Many Defensive Uses per Year?" *Journal of Policy Analysis and Management* 16 (3): 463–69.

Kleck, Gary, and Marc Gertz. 1995. "Armed Resistance to Crime: The Prevalence and Nature of Self-Defense with a Gun." *Journal of Criminal Law and Criminology* 86: 150–87.

Levinson, Sanford. 1989. "The Embarrassing Second Amendment." *Yale Law Journal* 99: 637–59.

Lott, John R., and John E. Whitley. 2000. "Safe Storage Gun Laws: Accidental Deaths, Suicides and Crime." Working Paper 237. Yale Law School, Program for Studies in Law, Economics, and Public Policy.

Malcolm, Joyce Lee. 1994. *To Keep and Bear Arms: The Origins of an Anglo-American Right.* Harvard University Press.

Smith, Tom W. 1980. "The 75% Solution: An Analysis of the Structure of Attitudes on Gun Control, 1959–1977." *Journal of Criminal Law and Criminology* 71: 300–16.

Smith, Tom W., and Robert J. Smith. 1995. "Changes in Firearms Ownership among Women, 1980–1994." *Journal of Criminal Law and Criminology* 86: 133–49.

Zimring, Franklin E. 1975. "Firearms and the Federal Law: The Gun Control Act of 1968." *Journal of Legal Studies* 4: 133–98.

Contributors

Deborah Azrael
Harvard School of Public Health

Catherine Barber
Harvard School of Public Health

Alfred Blumstein
Carnegie Mellon University

Jacqueline Cohen
Carnegie Mellon University

Philip J. Cook
Duke University

John J. Donohue
Stanford Law School

Mark Duggan
University of Chicago

Jeffrey Fagan
Columbia University

Peter Greenwood
Greenwood and Associates

David Hemenway
Harvard School of Public Health

Lisa M. Hepburn
Harvard School of Public Health

Brian A. Jacob
*John F. Kennedy School of Government,
Harvard University*

Mark A. R. Kleiman
University of California, Los Angeles

David B. Kopel
Independence Institute

455

John H. Laub
University of Maryland

Jim Leitzel
University of Chicago

Steven D. Levitt
University of Chicago

Jens Ludwig
Georgetown University

Willard Manning
University of Chicago

David McDowall
University at Albany, State University of New York

James A. Mercy
Centers for Disease Control and Prevention

Matthew Miller
Harvard School of Public Health

Jenny Mouzos
Australian Institute of Criminology

John Mullahy
University of Wisconsin-Madison

David B. Mustard
University of Georgia

Karen Norberg
Boston University

Anne Morrison Piehl
John F. Kennedy School of Government, Harvard University

Steven Raphael
University of California, Berkeley

Peter Reuter
University of Maryland

Bruce Sacerdote
Dartmouth College

Lawrence W. Sherman
University of Pennsylvania

Jon S. Vernick
Johns Hopkins University

Elizabeth Richardson Vigdor
Duke University

Garen J. Wintemute
University of California, Davis

Franklin E. Zimring
University of California, Berkeley

Index

gun association membership,
132–33; historical background,
125–28; and homicide rates, 121,
126, 134–35, 140; isolation of Australia as factor in evaluation of, 125;
literature review, 122–25; National
Firearms Agreement (NFA) program,
129–30; Port Arthur massacre as cat-
alyst for, 121, 134, 142–43; registration and licensing of guns, 129, 134,
140; storage and training requirements, 133; and suicide rates, 121,
128, 136, 140; theft of guns, 139–40;
variations in laws among states,
129–30; waiting period for gun purchases, 140. *See also* Australian buyback program
Australian Institute of Criminology (AIC),
134, 142
Autor, David, 306
Availability of guns: and suicide, 13–14,
42, 51, 53; and violent crime, 11–13.
See also Ownership of guns
Ayres, Ian, 254, 293, 295, 296, 297, 323,
324
Azrael, Deborah, 67

Background checks on gun purchasers, 52;
Brady Act, 9, 20–22, 199, 351;
domestic violence misdemeanors or
restraining orders, 170–71, 188–92;
failure of states to submit domestic
violence restraining orders for, 206;
gun shows, 171; state laws, 354, 355;
timeliness of, 206
Baker, Regina, 106
Baltimore gun crimes and number of
injuries, 15, 241
Bartley-Fox Amendment (Massachusetts),
27
Bartley, William Alan, 305, 323
BCS. *See* British Crime Survey
Behavioral Risk Factor Surveillance System
(BRFSS), 416
Bice, Douglas, 306
Black, Daniel A., 326
Blumstein, Al, 284

Bogota, Columbia, and reduction of gun
crimes after targeted police activity,
242
Boor, Myron, 56
Boston Gun Project's Operation Ceasefire,
31, 281, 283, 408
Bound, John, 106
Brady Campaign to Prevent Gun Violence,
347
Brady Handgun Violence Prevention Act,
20–22, 351; applicability to states,
352; background checks required, 9,
199; enforcement of, 407–08; and
homicide rate, 207; impact of, 21,
24, 407; and suicide rate, 52, 198
Braga, Anthony, 124
Britain. *See* Great Britain
British Crime Survey (BCS): decline in
crime rates after handgun ban, 149;
hot burglary rates, 80–81
Bronars, Stephen, 292, 321, 329
Browne, Angela, 203
Burglary, 16–17, 74–118; case studies,
81–83; comments on study, 107–16;
crime rates correlated with gun
prevalence, 74, 83–86; flaws in study,
112; Great Britain after handgun
ban, 151; gun as sole item stolen, 99;
"hot" burglaries, 17, 75, 76, 79–81,
102–04; household gun prevalence
and burglary rates, 75, 86–101;
increases in gun ownership correlated
to increases in burglary, 101–02,
104, 107; inducement created by
guns as loot, 75, 78–79, 98, 104,
108–09; international comparisons
on household guns as deterrence,
79–81; interviews with burglars on
guns as deterrence and inducement,
78–79; Kennesaw, Georgia, case
study, 81, 83; likely direction of error
in study estimates, 106–07; literature
review, 76–83, 113–16; low-
population counties and guns as
deterrence to burglaries, 112;
National Crime Victimization Survey
data, 16, 75, 76, 85, 93, 103–04;

ences, 445–46; international comparisons, 51, 74, 110, 127; measuring of,
54–56, 85–86; positive aspects, 113;
proxies used for, in research, 54–56,
66–67, 68, 85–86; statistics, 74; and
suicide rates, 50, 56–65; typical
owner, 4

Parasuicidal persons and choice of method,
71
Pennsylvania: background checks of gun
purchasers, 190; domestic violence
misdemeanor conviction and gun
purchase/ownership, 164; restraining
orders and gun purchase/ownership,
165, 199
Personalized guns, 8
Piehl, Anne, 124
Pittsburgh firearm suppression patrol
(FSP), 26, 220–47; background,
220–23; comments on study,
240–47; comparison of crime rates
before and after, 219; costs of additional patrols, 26, 239; data, 223–26;
effectiveness, 220, 238–39; "experimental" nature of study, 218, 219,
226, 243; gunshot injury data,
225–26, 234–38, 240, 241–42;
methods and limitations, 226–30,
243–47; reduction of gun crimes
after, 242; results, 230–38; "shots
fired" data, 223, 225, 230–34; zip
code data of victim, 226
Planned suicide and choice of method,
71–72
Police officers: and domestic violence convictions, 163, 206; targeting illegal
firearms, 25–26, 217–50
Police stops: due process issues, 247; Pittsburgh firearm suppression patrol
(FSP) using, 221
Policy debate on gun control, 441–52;
constant elements of debate, 443–47;
crime issue transition to violence
issue, 447, 451; episodic to consistent
public priority, 447–49; gender differences in attitudes, 445–46; and

generality of preferences, 444; gun
show loophole, 444; handgun bans,
444, 446–47; improved availability of
information, 449; 1960s, 441–43;
Second Amendment issues, 447, 450;
small policy proposals producing
modest results, 24, 444–45; symbolic
dominance, 443. See also Legislation
on gun control; Research needs
Port Arthur massacre (Australia), 121, 134,
142–43
Preemption: of local gun control laws,
349, 363; of state gun control laws,
352
Price of guns: Australia, 138–39; secondary market prices, 19–20
Printz v. United States (1997), 351
Prison sentence enhancements, 27–28,
251–86; state laws, 25, 357, 392–98.
See also Project Exile (Richmond,
Virginia)
Private sales and background checks, 355,
364. See also Gun show loophole
Project Exile (Richmond, Virginia),
27–28, 251–86; accounting for initial
city conditions, 265–72; comments
on study, 277–84; comparison of
Richmond's and other cities' homicide rates, 260–65, 275; costs, 256;
design and objectives, 253–56; effectiveness in reducing homicide and
crime rates, 2, 252, 267–68, 275–77;
federal prosecutions' effectiveness,
253, 272–74; felon-in-possession-of-
a-firearm (FIP) convictions statistics,
272–74, 279; gun homicide rates in
Richmond, 256–60; and incarceration rates, 278; philosophy of,
278–79; public willingness to view as
success, 277; relationship between
earlier and later changes in homicide
rates, 265–68; robustness of analysis,
268–72; undetectable impact, 28,
278–80; value of approach in ongoing efforts, 282–84
Project Safe Neighborhoods, 251
Project Triggerlock, 272